TRAVELLERS AND THE SETTLED COMMUNITY

A Shared Future

Edited by
John Heneghan,
Mary (Warde) Moriarty
and Micheál Ó hAodha

The Liffey Press

Published by
The Liffey Press Ltd
Raheny Shopping Centre, Second Floor
Raheny, Dublin 5, Ireland
www.theliffeypress.com

© 2012 John Heneghan, Mary Moriarty and Micheál Ó hAodha

A catalogue record of this book is
available from the British Library.

ISBN 978-1-908308-04-7

The views and opinions expressed in this volume are those of the authors
of the essays and do not necessarily state or reflect the views of the editors
of this volume or of the University of Limerick.

Printed in Ireland by Sprint Print.

Contents

PART 3 – TRAVELLER ISSUES AND CHALLENGES

On the occasion of the CAMPUS Engage Conference 2009, 'The ACCESS Bridge' by John Heneghan, University of Limerick

The ACCESS Bridge

John Heneghan

I
You stood before me and said
'Education is no burden'
Our halting site, a near place.
Alert, the quizzical gaped.

II
You stood before me and said
'Some values I declare as core'
Our hinterland, a shared space.
Tuned-in, the tell-me-more clapped.

III
You do not know each other
Yet you both grasped Vitruvius.
Barricades stiffen defence
But pillars declare the bridge.

Dedicated to all of the Travellers who engaged with the Traveller Initiative at the University of Limerick, the agencies of the Limerick County Steering Group and the staff at UL who make the campus such a welcoming place.

Foreword

It would sound almost predictable to describe this collection of essays and articles as giving voice to the experiences of Travellers. The writers here, Travellers and non-Travellers have produced works that have been hugely influenced by the experience of engagement. The former in their writings evoke a confidence and a stridency that anticipates and expects a meaningful interaction with the world while the latter group, benefitting from engagement with the Traveller community, are assertive in articulating ideas and frameworks that have been tested and applied. Having made these observations it became evident that the words in the title – a Shared Future – were appropriate.

The University of Limerick recognises its role in the community and declares its commitment to its hinterland in the University's Strategic Plan. Many of the Travellers who have participated in programmes at UL have taken up leadership positions in various local and national committees. All have enriched the teaching experience of the lecturers they have met.

We can expect that future writings will emerge from the Traveller community as confidence and encouragement converge through the educational process. We hope that readers will be informed, even inspired, by the writings here.

My sincere thanks to my co-editors of this book, Dr. Micheál Ó hAodha and Mary Warde, both of whom were unrelenting in seeing this through to the end.

John Heneghan,
Lecturer, Kemmy Business school
Coordinator, HEA ACCESS
University of Limerick

Part One

TRAVELLER REPRESENTATIONS AND REALITIES

1.

Travellers as an Ethnic Group

Martin Collins

The question of recognising Traveller's as an ethnic minority has gained prominence in public discourse, in recent years. This issue has generated an interesting and energetic debate between successive governments, Traveller organisation, academics and legal practitioners and probably more importantly than all, it is an issue that is being increasingly discussed among Traveller activists/leaders, which in itself is a sign of our growth, development and politicisation.

This departure is an important step, we as a community need to take more ownership and further progress on this important debate. As Traveller activists/leaders, we also have an important responsibility to reach out and include other Travellers who are not politically involved in the movement. Not only is this important from an ownership point of view but not to do so could result in it becoming elitist and the preserve of a few.

There is a policy context that cannot be ignored as it directly relates to and impacts on Travellers being recognised as an ethnic group. A key component of this policy is the 1963 Commission on Itinerancy Report. This was the first explicit government policy response to Travellers. There are a number of substantive points that I would like to make in this regard:

There was no Traveller voice at the table when this report was being complied, which raises the following issues:

- Is this because there were no Travellers interested in what the government and the state institutions had to say about us?

- Was it assumed by others that Travellers wouldn't be interested?

- Or was it that it was felt that we lacked the basic skills to engage in the work of the commission?

Another concern was the use of the term itinerant which was not and is not used by us when speaking about each other, and indeed for many of us it is a pejorative term as it is very often associated with vagrancy and deviancy.

One also has to be alarmed at the terminology used by this commission especially in its terms of reference: 'The commission sets out to enquire into the problem arising from the presence in the country of itinerants in considerable numbers; to examine the economic, educational, health and social problems inherent in their way of life.'

It is clear from this, that us as people were defined as a problem and as a consequence there was no acknowledgement of the discrimination and the human rights violations experienced by our people. The commission recommended a policy of assimilation and absorption, in other words ridding society of Travellers. I would like to point out that it is my belief that the people on the commission were well intentioned and set out to do the right thing to alleviate the hardship being experienced by Travellers as they saw it. However, ultimately their analysis was misguided, offensive and damaging.

The second policy response from the government was published in 1983, entitled 'Travelling People Review Body Report'. This report had the advantage of twenty years of experience since the earlier publication of the Commission on Itinerancy. This report also coincided with the emergence of new groups advocating a new analysis on Travellers. This analysis revolved around Traveller issues being seen as human rights issues, Travellers having a voice and the right to shape policies that affect our lives and also having the right to one's own cultural identity. The groups in question were: The Committee on the Rights of Travellers, Mincéir Misli and DTEDG (Dublin Travellers Education Development Group – subsequently to become Pavee Point). As a consequence of this, it must be acknowledged that this report is an improvement on the earlier report, 'The Commission on Itinerancy', but not a progressive as one would like it to be. The most obvious things to note from this report is that the word 'Traveller' was used in the title of the report and also that there was Traveller involvement on the committee that oversaw the report.

The review body report also set out to look at the needs of Travellers who wanted to continue in a nomadic way of life which was a welcome development. Also, concepts such as assimilation, absorption and settlement did not feature in the report, at least not explicitly. Some critics of the report have argued that while the rhetoric and terminology had changed compared to that of the Commission of Itinerancy, the subtext remained the same, i.e. the assimilation and settlement of Travellers.

The fundamental problem with both reports as I see it is that there is no understanding or acknowledgement of Travellers distinct cultural identity and how this identity might be validated and supported. Also, there was no analysis and articulation of Traveller issues being located within the human rights framework and the need for laws and policies to vindicate the rights of Travellers, i.e. the right not to be discriminated against, having a legal right to adequate culturally appropriate accommodation and having legal enforceable rights in relation to the other areas such as education, healthcare and employment etc.

Pavee Point is widely accredited with offering a distinct analysis on Travellers and Traveller issues and how these issues should be responded to. Our innovative and unique analysis was at times not well received and it could be argued that some in fact felt threatened by it. I recollect one situation where Anco, now FÁS, were anonymously contacted to say they shouldn't fund our training programmes. Essentially our focus was on consciousness raising and politicising Travellers. Effectively this meant creating the conditions whereby Travellers could reflect, analyse and develop strategies to affect social change. This process enabled us to recognise that our situation was a result of oppression and racism inflicted on us by others and was not God's will as some would have us believe.

The racism experienced by Travellers is clearly manifested in poor educational attainment, high unemployment, poor living conditions and high mortality rates. Pavee Point also pioneered a community development approach to the work with Travellers as this was recognised as the most effective tool in addressing Traveller issues. The associated principles with this approach include Traveller participation, collective action, dealing with root causes rather than symptoms and to effect structural change. There is no doubt in my mind that as a result of this approach that we Travellers are in a much better place than where we were in the 1980s.

Another key focus of our work has been and continues to be on cultural identity and cultural rights. We were the first organisation to suggest that Travellers should be recognised as an ethnic minority. In the 25 years I have been involved in the struggle, I still recognise that there is a lot more work that needs to be done in this area. When you consider that we as people have experienced and endured oppression and racism over a long period of time and as part of this experience there has been a particular dynamic at play which we now understand to be internalised oppression. This is to have us believe that we as people are primitive and inferior to non-Travellers and to have us feel ashamed of who we are and that we must aspire to become settled. This dynamic is not unique to Ireland or the Traveller/settled relationship; this is something that takes place right across the globe in terms of majority/minority relations. It might be more apt to suggest power relations and how it gets played out.

When one considers that this dynamic has been at play for decades if not centuries, it is therefore not surprising that some Travellers lack pride in their Traveller identity and some even actively conceal who they are in the vain hope that they can both survive and thrive. In fact I am aware of a number of situations where individuals in our community with very recognisable Traveller surnames have decided to change their name by de-pole, what can be sadder than this. This is not to be interpreted as a reflection on the Traveller who makes a decision to change his or her name but rather it should be seen as an indictment on society. It is akin to what is going on in the United States where the black slaves were forced to take on the name of their so-called master.

In spite of all of this, I am both surprised and delighted to say that as a community we have survived which demonstrates a huge depth of resilience and adaptability which does suggest that for most Travellers there is a great sense of pride and dignity in who we are and this is reflected in *'Our Geels': The All Ireland Traveller Health Study*, launched September 2010. This study asked Travellers how important are these for you: membership of the Traveller community, 71 per cent and nomadism, 54 per cent, Traveller culture, 73 per cent and Traveller identity, 74 per cent. These findings are very encouraging and give me great optimism for the future of our people.

The third policy response to Travellers and without a doubt the most significant was the publication of the Task Force Report in 1995. At this time, Traveller organisations such as Pavee Point, the Irish Travellers Movement and others had become well established and advocated from a clear perspective of human rights violations experienced by Travellers. This of course in turn challenged the old and failed approach which defined us as an impoverished undereducated group in need of charity and hand-outs. The Task Force Report and its recommendations were very significant. The report unlike its two predecessors recognised that Travellers experience discrimination and the need for legislation to protect Travellers and offer redress where they did experience discrimination.

The report also acknowledged the role played by Traveller organisations and the need for Traveller participation in the decision making processes. It also makes many other important recommendations in relation to Traveller women, the Traveller economy, education etc. I would suggest that the most significant and symbolic recommendation in the report is the recognition of Travellers distinct cultural identity. Suffice to say this issue when it was being discussed was highly contentious and there was resistance to it from representatives of government and government departments but I think it is a testament to the tenacity and conviction of the Traveller organisations that we succeeded in getting this recommendation through.

As part of the dialogue that took place in the compiling of the Task Force Report the recognition of Travellers as an ethnic group was raised and discussed, even though a number of politicians have now denied this, which I think is highly disingenuous of them. The fact is no agreement could be reached on this issue, which was a great source of disappointment to the Traveller representatives. Many of us viewed the recommendation that Travellers cultural identity should be recognised as a stepping stone and at some stage in the future we would secure the full and unequivocal recognition of our ethnicity. In the intervening years Traveller organisations have gained the support of very prominent and credible human rights organisations both domestically and internationally in calling for Travellers to be recognised as an ethnic minority, for example the Human Rights Commission, the Equality Authority and at an international level the Convention on the Elimination of All Forms of Racial Discrimination, in fact this committee have now twice challenged the Irish Government on its stance on this issue. We also have the Framework Convention on the Protection of National Minorities expressing its concern at the government's premature and definitive stance on this issue. All of these organisations have said that the Traveller community meet all of the legal criteria and definitions of what constitutes as an ethnic group. One such definition is seen in the 1983 case, referred to as the *Mandla v Dowell Lee* whereby the judge noted that:

> For a group to constitute as an ethnic group in the sense of the Act of 1976, it must, in my opinion, regard itself, and be regarded by others, as a distinct community by virtue of certain characteristics. Some of these characteristics are essential; others are not essential but one or more of them will commonly be found and will help to distinguish the group from the surrounding community. The conditions which appear to me to be essential are these:
> - A long shared history, of which the group is conscious as distinguishing it from other groups, and the memory of which it keeps alive;
> - A cultural tradition of its own, including family and social customs and manners,
> - Often but not necessarily associated with religious observance.

In the summer of 2000, in the case of *O'Leary & Others v. Allied Domecq & Others*, unreported 29 August 2000, the Central London County Court was dealing with a claim by a number of Irish Travellers that they had been refused service in 5 public houses in

Northwest London. The court had to consider whether this constituted discrimination on the grounds of ethnic origin for the purposes of the Race Relations Act. It was not contented that the reason why the Plaintiffs had been discriminated against was because they were Irish since one of the offending pubs catered for an almost exclusively Irish clientele.

It was agreed that the court should decide as a preliminary issue where Travellers constituted a 'separate ethnic group' for the purposed of the 1976 Act. Judge Goldstein and two assessors sat for six days listening to expert evidence and then applied the *Mandla v. Dowell Lee* criteria. They held that the Travellers met the two essential conditions laid down in that case:

- Possessing a long shared history which distinguished them from other groups (the court held that a history that could be traced back to at least the middle of the nineteenth century was sufficient to fulfil the Mandla test)

- Having a distinct cultural tradition of their own.

Having heard evidence both for and against the recognition of Travellers as an ethnic group and having applied the Mandla criteria the court summed up its findings:

> Our conclusions therefore are that of the two essential characteristics, namely the long shared history and the cultural tradition, we are satisfied that both these criteria have been sufficiently satisfied. Of the other, the common geographical origin or descent from a small number of ancestors – clearly that is satisfied; they all come originally from Ireland. The common language we have dealt with, the literature we have dealt with and the religious and minority aspects we have dealt with. It follows therefore, that our conclusions clearly are that we are satisfied that the Mandla criteria are satisfied in this case, and therefore Irish Travellers may be properly identified as an ethnic minority, so we answer the preliminary question in the affirmative.

The 1997 Northern Ireland Race Relations Order Act also gives explicit recognition to Travellers as an ethnic group. This definition says that 'Traveller Community' means the community of people who are commonly called Travellers and who are identified (both by themselves and others) as people with a shared history, culture and traditions including, nomadic way of life on the island of Ireland. This very same definition is read across into our own Equal Status Act in the Republic of Ireland. It is both interesting and bizarre that the same definition in one part of the island grants ethnic status to our people and in another part of the island it does not. I believe that this is also in breach of the Good Friday Agreement of 1998, which promotes an equivalence of rights across the island.

We have a compelling case as to why Travellers should be recognised as an ethnic group. We have the support of international human rights bodies and case law is on our side as earlier cited. We also have the support of imminent human rights bodies in Ireland e.g. IHRC and Equality Authority and yet to spite this, the government have steadfastly refused to recognise our ethnicity. Not only this, but they have also failed to offer any rationale as to why they won't.

I believe the recognition of our ethnicity would have both symbolic and practical benefits. I think symbolically it would be a confidence building measure for our people and would boost our morale and self-esteem. Recognising Traveller ethnicity is not to be interpreted as some have sought to do, that we are less Irish. There is no conflict between nationality and ethnicity, they both can and should mutually co-exist. I'm very proud of my Irishness but I'm equally as proud of my Traveller identity.

I think some of the practical benefits would be reflected in policy decisions, for example, nomadism would be recognised as a valid way of life and would be supported by the state, Traveller history and language would be researched and recorded, we could look to the educational curriculum and how it might be inclusive of Traveller identity, history etc. I am not suggesting for one moment that recognising Traveller ethnicity would be a panacea but I think it would give us a very useful platform from which to demand our entitlements and rights as people who have been living on the island since the 5th century.

In conclusion, I'll finish with a quote from a leading Traveller activist:

If they don't recognise us as an ethnic minority then they could assume that we are failed settled people who with the right support could fit in again. This is assimilation and was the Government's policy from the 1960s to the 1980s. It failed to address Traveller issues as it failed to tackle discrimination, it failed to acknowledge and validate our culture. This is racism in action and it must be properly addressed.

2.

Reflections on Traveller Identity

Helen O'Sullivan

Mary first asked me to write this piece almost twelve months ago. Procrastination is one of my vices but rarely, if ever, has it taken me so long to put pen to paper. Why am I finding it so difficult to write a piece on the people, it has been my pleasure and privilege to have worked with for the past sixteen years? The answer is now quite simple really: it is impossible to write anything about people that generalises them. Everything I wrote, and scrapped, seemed condescending, unfair or downright incorrect. So for starters, my very first statement is: I cannot write a reflection on Travellers that will accurately cover all angles and possibilities. Not all Travellers are the same.

Travellers, like the general population, come in all shapes and sizes, the good, the not so good and the indifferent. Just like the rest of us. That is my starting point. There are Travellers who are traditional and who want to maintain that way of life, there are those who want to retain their Traveller identity but who want to complete their schooling and fully participate in the workforce, there are those who wish to move away from the Traveller ways and hide their identity. There are also those who do not fit into any of these categories. It is impossible and wrong to generalise and categorise.

There are a number of areas that I am clear on however:

- Travellers generally are subject to discrimination in their everyday lives.

- The State has done a disservice to the Travelling people by its policies, practices and procedures; there is a dependency culture amongst many Travellers which I believe the State created.

- There are no easy answers to the problems and difficulties faced by many Travellers: poor housing, discrimination, unemployment, early school leaving, ill health, inter-family feuding, dependency and addictions.

- To begin to sort these issues more Travellers need to become actively involved in the decision making processes at all levels – local, regional, national and international.

- Resources are needed which will enable Travellers to live a life in which they are equal citizens. Education is the key.

Discrimination

It has been well documented that relations between Travellers and settled people have been fraught with difficulties and that the prejudice and discrimination has ensured that the boundaries between both groups are rarely crossed (Fanning, 2002; Hellenier, 1997, 2000; Lenit and McVeigh, 2006; MacGréil, 1996, 2001, 2010; Ó hAodha, 2007; Tovey and Share, 2003; Hourigan and Campbell, 2010). In my experience many Travellers are discriminated against purely on the basis of their Traveller identity. They are denied access to venues and services based on identity. There is no quick fix solution.

A number of service providers, whilst sympathetic to Travellers, have refused access to Travellers based on prior experiences of violence and aggression for some members of the Community. Violence and aggression are unacceptable, so also is discrimination.

Laws must be enforced which protect the rights of individuals and groups. It is unacceptable to refuse a service to anyone, purely on the basis of their identity.

State agencies must lead the way in creating a more equal society. Individual Travellers and Traveller organisations must also lead the way in breaking down barriers and in condemning violence and anti-social behaviour. Those who speak out deserve to be supported. State agencies must support Traveller groups who are seeking solutions and a more just and tolerant society.

The Role of the State

The role of the State, in terms of its policies to the Traveller community has also been well documented (Ní Shúinéir, 1998; Helleiner, 2000; Fanning, 2002; Norris and Winston, 2005). In practice, these policies have not served the Travellers or the general population well. One of the unintended results of the State's welfare policy is to create welfare and poverty traps and to ensure that many Travellers remain in the 'Black Economy'. Many Travellers I know would not take paid employment as they were financially better off with welfare payments. This situation applies to many, not just members of the Travelling community. The State must change these policies, whilst supporting those in need but in ensuring the dignity of work and helping people to help themselves.

Schools must become more flexible in dealing with children who come from diverse backgrounds. They need to be resourced to do this.

Negotiating the welfare system and state agencies is very difficult for most people; it is particularly difficult and cumbersome for people with literacy difficulties. Access to services must be made easier.

Conclusions

I believe that nomadism is a valid way of life and should be facilitated and resourced. Many Travellers still wish to travel and it should not be impossible to provide a necklace of managed nomadic sites countrywide.

These are very challenging and difficult economic times. Unemployment is soaring. Long-term unemployment and welfare dependency are a blight amongst Travellers. I believe that this unemployment and dependency play a large role in the feuding, ill health and addictions which are inflicting many in the community. Feuding and violence are not acceptable in any society. It is no coincidence that in areas where there is high unemployment there are also high incidences of anti-social behaviour. Finding solutions to these complex and multi-layered problems is not easy. Surely a starting point must be a quality education for all – children and adults.

The Equality Authority (2007) reported that the second largest number of cases on its files dealt with Travellers' access to education. Since then, funding for Traveller education has taken a high cut.

Education funding which has been withdrawn for Travellers must be reinstated and ring-fenced for Travellers. Traveller children have the same right to an education as every other child in the country. These children need to be supported until they achieve equality of access, participation and outcomes. Adults, who missed out on first chance education, should also be supported in returning to education.

Many Traveller parents are actively involved in their children's education, many are not. All parents who do not send their children to school should be reprimanded, there has to be a mechanism whereby each child in the country gets a quality education. Parents must get more involved.

Traveller specific adult education services are in the process of being dismantled. It is not enough to state that the closure of the Senior Traveller Training Centres (STTCs) will mean that adult Travellers will access other services. In some parts of the country, where there is a high level of integration, this will happen. Many Travellers I know, will not willingly access a service in which there are no other Travellers or where Travellers are in a minority.

There is also the question of training allowances. For years, the State has paid allowances for Travellers to return to education. There are arguments for and against this policy. When it was first introduced it was the right thing to do. It should have been a short term measure. It continued for over thirty years. The payment of a training allowance will be a thing of the past within the next twelve months. Many Travellers associate education with payment and work. This mind set will not be easily changed. I believe that an interim measure is needed which will support Traveller transition to mainstream adult education until such time as education sake is of an intrinsic value to Travellers.

Reflecting on my many years working with the Travelling community I have many fond memories and I like to think I have made lifelong friendships. I have been shown great warmth, love and re-spect. I have seen many successes but also many areas where the suc-cess has been very limited. I would like to see far more Travellers become involved in decision making roles. It is happening but not fast enough. Our education system, in its entirety, need to empower individuals and groups to reach their potential and to effect change. Individual

Travellers themselves must come forward and become more in-volved in finding solutions and in creating a more just society.

3.

The Story of a Traveller Support Group: A Local Resident's View

Seán Ó Riain

I am neither a sociologist nor a philosopher nor a historian. My contribution to this book will be a simple one. I am what is known in discussions about the Traveller issue as a 'local resident'. However, that term usually refers to settled people who oppose Travellers and their just demands for suitable accommodation. I hope that I am a different kind of local resident.

As far back as I can remember my family in Cork city were sympathetic to Travellers. I think we called them 'tinkers', I do not know what they called themselves, perhaps *mincéirí*. I don't think that what they were called caused any friction or discussion at that time.

The first Travellers I knew lived on the side of the road. In Cork in the 1950s many Traveller families lived on the Black Ash Road. The O'Driscolls and the Carmodys were well known. Old Mrs Carmody was a regular visitor to our house. While she came in the hope of getting food or money, I believe the relationship between my mother and Mrs Carmody was more mutually beneficial, much richer and more complex than the simple relationship of donor and beggar. The two women would discuss the ways of Travellers and settled people for an hour or more as they sat drinking tea at the kitchen table. Looking back now, I think that my mother gave the most valuable thing she had, her time and respect, to Mrs Carmody. My mother

17

and Mrs Carmody were not unique, in the 1950s there were many such friendships. I fear that is not so anymore and that is one of the major changes for the worse in Traveller/settled relationships.

By 1984 I had spent almost ten years as a part-time voluntary worker in the Dublin Simon Community. That was a mind opening experience. I had never seen or imagined such deprivation, such sadness. I worked on the soup run, in the emergency night shelter and especially in the residential house in Lower Seán McDermott Street in the heart of the (in)famous Monto district. I came to value and love the people in that house. I think they also loved me and that must be the most amazing experience I have ever had.

Soon the work became a great source of happiness. I sometimes tell of the day I met a homeless person whom I knew well in O'Connell Street. 'Come here to me,' John shouted, his long arms out-stretched, a great smile on his face. The pedestrians were now giving us a wide berth. 'It's ages since I saw you,' and he gave me a marvellous tight hug. Going home later that day was the first time in ages that I remembered the Bible story about the man who was filled with joy when he greeted the lepers he met on the road. And generally that is the story I tell when people ask me to explain why I associated with homeless people and with Travellers. Other times I reply 'I have no choice' and let people figure that out for themselves.

I sometimes think that working with the Simon Community or similar groups could become quite comfortable. Was I doing it for myself, to feel good? It could be easy and 'cool' to slum it for a few hours 'down among the dead men'. Easy to do my shift and then go home to my snug semi-detached house in the suburbs. But I knew in my heart that the real challenge, the really difficult situation, the frightening challenge which would demand an answer would arrive one day at my front door.

* * *

That day arrived in the summer of 1984. A group of Travellers desperate for somewhere legal to park their caravans had eventually moved into a field beside my parish church in Foxrock in affluent south county Dublin. It was rumoured that a property developer who wished to build houses on the field but whose plans were being thwarted by local objections, had either invited the Travellers to occupy the field or had paid them to move in or had turned a blind eye when they did move in. Feelings were very high. There were neither rubbish collections nor sanitation facilities on the site. There were rumours of Travellers harassing local residents. The matter went to the courts and one day the Sheriff arrived to remove the Travellers from the field.

That eviction was a very frightening and traumatic experience for the Travellers and their supporters. None of the priests of the parish offered support. One priest, Fr Kevin Rice, who had been away on holidays at the time of the eviction, thought that if he had been at home he might not have had the courage to face the protestors or to support the Travellers. At least he was honest.

Most of the Travellers' supporters were women. There had always been a group of philanthropic women in Dublin who became involved in various social causes on behalf of the less well off. They were upper class women and some had the accent to prove it. Yet they fought for playgrounds for inner city children long before the need was widely recognised. They drove the buses that brought Traveller children to school. A few who were nuns from a 'posh' Order lived on a Traveller site in west Dublin. Another nun from the same Order, Sr Colette Dwyer, became a spokesperson for Travellers and along with Victor Bewley and Fr Tom Fehily worked to help Travellers realise their full potential. Are people like this who worked on the ground at the dirty coal face around any more?

Back in Foxrock in 1984 the question was where were all the men of goodwill? Some, I suppose, were at work. Some, I suspected, thought that their jobs and their status were too important for them to be seen to be supporting this raggle-taggle group. Others who like myself were probably suffering from cowardice, stayed away. The vast majority of those who objected to the Travellers were men, there was no loss of status involved in that.

Nevertheless, down through the years other people in Foxrock parish had made it their Christian business to get to know the Travellers who lived in the area. They had befriended and respected them. But gradually these support groups had faded away.

Shortly after the 1984 eviction a group of those brave women who had stood by the Travellers and who had literally embraced them, called a public meeting in Dún Laoghaire to see what practical support could be given to Travellers in the area. At that crowded meeting the South Dublin Travellers' Support Group (SDTSG) – later the Southside Travellers' Action Group (STAG) – was formed. I joined the group after its formation. From the start Travellers and settled people (known to Travellers as 'buffers' or 'country people') were equal members of the group.

One of the early criticisms thrown at us was that we were too pro-Traveller and that we should put more pressure on Travellers to live up to their responsibilities. While one might sympathise with that viewpoint, I felt at the time that we already made plenty of demands on Travellers. We demanded that Travellers live in deplorable conditions on dangerous roadsides and in muddy fields without water or toilets or refuse collections. We demanded that Travellers tolerate an infant mortality rate that was over three times the mortality rate of infants in the settled population. Travellers had a much shorter life than the rest of us. Only 5 per cent of Travellers were aged fifty years or over and less than 1 per cent were aged seventy years or more – compared to 25 per cent and 7 per cent respectively of the settled population.

We had many crowded, noisy and often hilarious meetings in smoky halls long before the smoking ban. Priests and nuns came and politicians from all parties. We were well aware that we were ignorant of Traveller ways and that our first task was to help ourselves and the Travellers to get to know each other. We went to the roadside camps and introduced ourselves. We visited the group housing schemes. We discovered that Travellers also lived in standard housing. Back then there were no halting sites in the area. We insisted that Travellers call us by our first names, I didn't want to be called 'sir'.

And right or wrong, we gave material help, food and money, to those who needed it. Were we merely making Travellers more dependent? Maybe so but it was one very effective way of getting to know Travellers. Everywhere we were welcomed kindly and with that graciousness that I have very often found among Travellers.

As a bonding exercise and as a way of completing one definite project, on bitter winter days in 1984 on a derelict site by the sea we built a wooden shelter for a Traveller family who were alcoholic and destitute. The response took us by surprise. Some passers-by gave us materials, others stopped to help us and give us their strength and good advice (building wasn't our strong point!). Most surprising of all neither An Garda Síochána nor the local authority hindered our work in any way - would we get away with it now? I think not. Not even for an hour.

When Spring softened the frost we felt we had made a difference. And that winter we realised that all Travellers have the same need for love and acceptance as the rest of us, they have the same fears and aspirations as the rest of us, they have the same capacity for love as the rest of us.

We joined the National Council for Travelling People (NCTP) and received advice and encouragement from its chief executive, Betty Neville. She was one of the new activists who tried to empower rather than patronise Travellers but I do not think that she ever believed, as some other activists seemed to believe, that empowering and 'helping' were mutually exclusive actions or that 'help' was always patronising.

We took part in a solidarity march through Dublin organised by Mincéir Mislí, a Traveller movement which grew into the Dublin Travellers' Education and Development Group and which still exists today under the name Pavee Point.

Our core group – down in numbers from the heady early days – began to lobby politicians to take a more active role in the provision of Traveller accommodation. We discovered that all politicians are not alike, some are brave and committed, some are not. One I remember well was tall, powerful. He mixed up the names of the four persons on our deputation and announced that whatever we thought about it, he was going to smoke whether we liked it or not. What ignorance. I also remember the plush offices. We lobbied leaders of churches and asked that they speak about the plight of Travellers and the duties of churchgoers towards them.

In 1986 Dublin County Council published a plan which would give each electoral area two sites for Travellers. This led to very heated debates. We leafleted local residents and collected hundreds of signatures in support of the plan. We wrote letters to the newspapers and during this campaign we had a high profile, much higher, I believe, than that of the larger Traveller groups. Some of us were even threatened – 'we will be down to burn you out tonight'.

In 1989 the Archbishop of Dublin, Desmond Connell, in a letter to Catholics placed the official church as an institution on the side of Travellers. We were very happy, this was what we had asked for but in general the response of the clergy to the Archbishop's letter was a far cry from the aspirations of the outspoken 1985 report The Travelling People, drawn up by the Council for Social Welfare (CSW), a committee of the Catholic Bishops' Conference. The report said that the church was in a unique position to influence public attitudes towards Travellers. 'In the current situation, this will require more than preaching of a general nature; it will mean clearly defining what the obligations of parishioners are in any given community. It will require also that bishops and clergy be prepared to face, and continually oppose, not only the indifference, but the outright hostility of many of their congregations – particularly in relation to specific proposals for the provision of accommodation.' Today both the Archbishop's letter and the CSW report are forgotten and Catholic congregations do not seem to be aware of or exercised by Travellers' need for accommodation.

We continued our efforts to promote the involvement of Travelling People in their own destiny. We continued to enlighten politicians about the facts of Travellers' lives. We continued to fight evictions, sometimes in High Court cases which were financed by the NCTP. We made it difficult for the local authority and others to evict Travellers. I believe we made a difference.

On 3 July 1989 five Traveller families moved into a beautiful new halting site at Burton Hall on the Leopardstown Road. Early on the morning of 4 July, Independence Day, Bridget Connors was rushed to hospital where her daughter, Mary, the sixth child of Bridget and Willie, was born. She was like a ray of hope. There had been prolonged and fierce opposition to the Burton Hall site. We had resisted and absorbed that opposition. Here too I believe we made a difference. I am still friends with that group of Travellers.

The events described above are just a fraction of the work the South Dublin Traveller Support Group undertook. A comprehensive account is given in my book *Solidarity with Travellers – A Story of Settled People Making a Stand for Travellers* (Roadside Books, 2000). Now out of print the book is available through all public libraries.

The important thing about our work was that it was carried out by a small core of voluntary workers. Apart from funding for court cases, our only source of income was the collection of £1 per person at our meetings.

* * *

Gradually times changed and so our group – with a new name STAG Southside Travellers' Action Group – became a funded group at a time when money was plentiful. I didn't feel fully at ease with the new approach but to be critical would be unfair to the hard-working people who stayed with the group and who are still there today.

Probably my last action as a (almost lapsed) member of the group was to seek funding to try to stop the eviction of a Traveller family. I was extremely disappointed when I was told that the group no longer got involved in eviction cases – they were too costly and time consuming. That was a horrible decision given the history and origin of our group.

I secured funding from Crosscare, an agency of the Dublin Catholic Archdiocese. We went to court and won! It was moving to hear the judge say that the family was entitled to accommodation and that the children were entitled to education and that they could have recourse to the High Court if any further attempts were made to jeopardise those rights. I felt that the group would have liked to take some of the credit for that victory. After that I no longer felt quite the same about the group.

* * *

Today there are 113 Traveller families in the Dún Laoghaire Rathdown County Council (DLR CC) area, that is, a tiny group of about 400 Travellers in a population of over 194,000 (2006 census). These families live in standard local authority houses, group housing schemes, halting sites, private rented accommodation; a small number of families are sharing accommodation, often with parents. Eight families are in the homeless/emergency category and live in hostels or B&Bs.

The DLR CC area has fewer Travellers than it had in 1984 and has far fewer Traveller families than other Dublin local authority areas. County councillors have told this writer that the settled community is not as exercised as heretofore about Travellers and that Travellers are not a huge issue for the councillors either. But they warn that this could change!

Councillors may stress the calmness of the present situation and may imply, perhaps, that there seems to be no great demand/need for Traveller specific accommodation in the DLR CC area. However, the Traveller accommodation unit in DLR CC shows the real situation. The 'Traveller Accommodation Programme 2009 – 2013' of DLR CC details the council's programme with regard to the construction programme and the management and maintenance of Traveller sites. Details of the plan are on www.dlrcoco.ie and show a projected requirement for 26 halting site bays, 12 grouped houses and 21 standard houses during the period of the Programme.

Here are some comments on Traveller accommodation from local councillors:

> There is a legal requirement to draw up an accommodation plan every five years but no obligation to implement it ... sites are better minded, most of the budget is spent on maintenance, making sure the issue doesn't become an issue ... there has been no allocation of capital funds over the past few years, this will continue into the future given the recession ... the FG/Lab majority aren't bringing Traveller issues to the table ... by and large the accommodation programme has come to a standstill ... councillors are generally, with a few honourable exceptions, appalling when it comes to Traveller accommodation ... the Traveller unit of the county council (staff, caretakers, outreach worker) is working well with the Travellers ...

That last comment is a far cry from the antagonism that existed between some DLR CC staff and Travellers. In 1994 DLR CC was formed from DLR borough council and the old Dublin County Council. We missed the very good working relationship we had had with officials of the old county council.

DLR CC informed me that they have nobody working long enough in the Traveller Accommodation Unit to be able to give me an overview of the work of the unit since 1984. I think that is a great pity. The committed local authority official who has an understanding and a knowledge of Travellers over a long time is a very valuable person. Over the years local authority Traveller units seem to have been places where officials toiled for a time before they qualified for promotion to another unit. A purgatory?

However, one thing has changed for the better. The office of DLR CC Traveller Unit suggested I contact STAG, 'as they have a number of wonderful programmes'. This most welcome positive approach can only be applauded.

* * *

Colin Thomson of the Dublin Parish of the Travelling People works on social inclusion issues at community and parish level. He points to the Travellers whose quality of accommodation is still very poor but admits that there has been some progress. A lot of Travellers don't feel there has been much progress and that maybe things were better in the old days. A case of rose tinted spectacles? Nowadays it is harder to travel and even though accommodation may be better 'there is still something not right and that is reflected in the high level of suicide among young Travellers' countrywide.

According to a seven-year study, *Suicide among the Irish Traveller Community, 2000–2006*, Travellers are three times as likely to die by suicide as members of the general population. The rate of suicide among the Traveller community rose to five times the national average in 2006. The actual number of Traveller suicides in seven years was 74. The report finds suicide is even more starkly a male issue in the Traveller population than in the settled population. While it is four times more prevalent among settled men as settled women, among Travellers the male rate is nine times the female rate.

The author of the report, Mary Rose Walker, social worker with Wicklow County Council and a member of the National Office for

Suicide Prevention, says the Traveller community clearly has a 'serious problem' with suicide. According to Walker a significant factor was a sense of the progressive loss of Traveller identity and culture, and the loss of a lot of their own traditions, such as horse-keeping and travelling. At the same time they are discriminated against in many areas of life, 'most of them cope and adapt but a number of them are vulnerable. If life seems to have little purpose, it takes little to convince them to end it.'

Thomson says that drugs are causing havoc and are an 'added curse' that Travellers have to deal with. Drink has always been part of Traveller life. But Thomson refers to the important All-Ireland Traveller Health Status survey which shows that Travellers drink less than binge drinkers in general society. There is a higher percentage of Travellers who don't drink than there are of settled people who don't drink.

Men's health has not improved, they are dying younger, they don't seem to have made the same progress as women. Men's groups are slower to take off. Men are harder to reach, Travellers say that you must be a man's man and take care of your family ... but that can lead to problems.

But Thomson insists on the positive aspect. (I myself often say to people that for every criticism you make of Travellers, I can give you a contrary happy and positive example). There are Traveller men who are great role models and it's great to be able to point to them (psychotherapist, barrister, actor, writer, boxers, Garda, speaker at a UN conference, singer in New York's Carnegie Hall). There is a generation coming up who are expanding their options. 'That is a slow process. I think we are emerging from the notion that Travellers are a subculture of poverty.'

The all-Traveller group, Mincéirs Whiden, is helping all Travellers and especially men to talk to each other, to reflect more on what it means to be a Traveller and to explore their own sense of self (www. minceirswhiden.org)

Thomson admits there is still a lot of community disintegration - drugs, community tensions, violence - and that can be aggravated by lack of mobility because Travellers often coped by putting distance between themselves and the source of conflict.

* * *

In the third volume of his trilogy, *Pluralism and Diversity in Ireland: Prejudice and Related Issues in Early 21st Century Ireland* (2011), Micheál Mac Gréil, SJ, says that Travellers, along with drug addicts and alcoholics, remain the most unaccepted people in Irish society, and young people are the most prejudiced against them.

Will this disturbing finding in Mac Gréil's study awaken any worry in our schools and churches? Do Travellers and settled people meet in any social occasions? I believe Travellers are more isolated now than they were forty years ago. Go to a Traveller funeral to see their isolation. Count the number of settled people at the funeral – it won't take long.

In 1990 the break-up of the National Council for Travelling People was brought about by activists who thought that the Traveller movement should be controlled by Travellers and that there was no role for the prominent settled people who had led the movement until then. I found the bitterness and anger that accompanied the break-up excessive and very upsetting and unfair to the settled people who according to their principles had worked so hard.

Nowadays there is almost no opportunity for a well-disposed settled person to take part in the Traveller struggle. That is a change from thirty or forty years ago. Since then the funded groups have taken over, as they have in many of the local community groups in the settled population. Since STAG came to prominence not one voluntary Traveller support group was founded in the DLR CC area. How can Traveller and settled people meet and become friends? A crucial question.

Funded groups are falling on hard times. Cutbacks in funding mean cut backs in services. Already one community group in an inner-city estate in Dublin are looking back to the 1970s and 1980s when all their work was done on a voluntary basis. They remember those years as a time of idealism and hope. They remember them too as a time when priests and nuns were active in social ministries and as a time when religious returned from Central America with inspiring tales of the courage of people who had to fight for their rights.

What have we to learn from those times? Maybe those times will come again?

Prior to the 2011 general election STAG invited all candidates to meet Travellers. Just two took up the invitation, Ivana Bacik and Aidan Culhane, both from the Labour Party. So much for politicians' commitment. Is the Traveller vote too small to be important? Culhane told me that the Traveller movement is well equipped and articulate but he wondered if the movement was connecting with the people, especially men, who were in most need. 'Those who become involved in Traveller support and advocacy groups, community associations etc, are by definition those Travellers who are most connected to state networks and who are most motivated to change things for themselves.' Culhane ventures the opinion that those most in need and most marginalised are not those who are to be found in the support networks.

Culhane also said that he was somewhat 'shocked' at the pre-election meeting when a teenage Traveller boy had no idea about the bigotry against Travellers and thought that the opposition to Traveller accommodation was because of money issues.

I myself noticed that in the past year or so a few Traveller teenage boys from a very small number of families seem to be starting the habit of door-to-door begging in the DLR CC area.

It is clear from the above references to men and from Colin Thomson's comments earlier that Traveller groups still have much work to do with male Travellers.

* * *

Today the Southside Travellers' Action Group (STAG) operates from its resource centre in Sandyford, County Dublin. The group website (www.southsidetravellers.com) gives a very good overview of its wide programme of work. Employing 39 people of whom 28 are local Travellers, STAG has grown rapidly as a community development organisation funded by ten statutory agencies.

Its core programme of work involves promoting awareness of Traveller culture and traditions; advocacy and accommodation; community health; developing the potential of Traveller children and young people; adult education; training and employment. STAG is also an active partner in the local development/social inclusion infra-structure in the DLR CC area. The Foxrock field seems to belong to a different world.

In its mission statement STAG envisages an Ireland where the human and civil rights, dignity, hopes and distinct cultural identity of Travellers are acknowledged and respected.

> Operating within the context of community development principles and practice, we seek to realise our vision through the design, development and implementation of a series of integrated programmes which respond – proactively – to the needs of Travellers in the Dun Laoghaire/Rathdown area.

I find it very disappointing that STAG's mission statement makes no mention of the settled population. There is no indication that it aims to get to know that population and draw near them in mutual understanding. That is another difference from the Foxrock field.

* * *

Nowadays my connection with Travellers is confined to friendship with individual Travellers. Just a very few people still call looking for help, I cannot turn them from the door, I don't demean them if I give them help. I welcome them as friends and they bring me news of other Traveller families.

While I was writing this article James (a young Traveller in his twenties) and his girlfriend, Ann, called. James had spent time in gaol. They were sleeping in a car and trying to secure accommodation so that they could get their children out of care. They were doing parenting courses, they had social workers and a key worker. They were doing their level best but when they had left I thought to myself, 'What they need is an ordinary friend, a true friend.'

In the study mentioned earlier Micheál Mac Gréil wrote:

> There is evidence of a level of desired avoidance which per-petuated ostracisation of Travellers in Irish society ... Travel-lers need the intercultural solidarity of their neighbours in the settled community ... they are too small a minority to survive in a meaningful manner without ongoing and supportive per-

sonal contact with their fellow citizens in the settled community.

And that brings me back to where I began – to Mrs Carmody and my mother.

* * *

Thanks to Ciara Maguire (Dún Laoghaire Rathdown County Council), Colm O'Brien, Colin Thomson, Mary Rose Walker (Wicklow County Council), Dún Laoghaire Rathdown Councillors Gerry Horkan and Denis O'Callaghan and former councillor, Aidan Culhane, now special advisor to the Minister for Housing and Planning, Frances O'Rourke (STAG). BUÍOCHAS.

4.

'Telling It As It Is' – A Point of View from the Galway Traveller Movement

Margaret Ó Riada

Recognition is essential to secure the rights of minority groups in a state. Lack of recognition can lead to instability and conflict. The legal recognition of minorities and the subsequent respect of their rights contribute to peaceful co-existence. Since non recognition hinders the enjoyment of internationally recognised rights, it leads to the violation of the economic, social and cultural rights of minorities, and to their ultimate marginalisation in society.[1]

The Traveller women and men who work with the Galway Traveller Movement are one of the most resilient group who work day after day challenging the discrimination experienced by them. They work as activists to challenge injustice in the areas of health, accommodation, education, employment, poverty, administration of justice and the whole area of realising rights. They are committed to working from community work approaches and often times are frustrated by the slow progress. They have against the odds used education as a means to reclaim some of the power taken from them and are very active in representing the needs of the Traveller community in Galway city and county and at a regional and national level. They are members of the Irish Traveller Movement who proactively campaign and challenge policies makers to improve the living conditions of the community. They in conjunction with the Irish Travel-ler Movement, National Traveller Women's Forum, Pavee Point and Minceir Whiding (Traveller Only Space) are campaigning for gov-ernment recognition of their ethnic status which to date is still being denied even though the Committee on the elimination of all racial discrimination has called for this recognition to be granted and legis-lated for. At a local level they work to raise awareness of their culture and distinct identity through partnership arrangements with the lo-cal service providers and the educational institutions for example the Western Health Service Executive and National University Galway Education Department and Community Technology Initiative. They believe and they promote that they are a distinct ethnic group and use the definition currently being used in both the Equal Status and Employment Equality Legislation.[2]

> The community of people who are commonly called Travel-lers and who are identified(both by themselves and others) as people with a shared history, culture and traditions including, historically, a nomadic way of life on the island of Ireland. (Equal Status Act 2000)

Irish Travellers are a small indigenous group who can trace their origins to the twelfth century. There is no doubt the Traveller com-munity are one of the most marginalised groups in Irish society. (Task Force on the Travelling community 2005).[3] Community work ap-proaches and Human Rights Based approaches offer an opportunity to challenge the injustice experienced by the Traveller community.

> Travellers' separateness, partly by choice, enables them to re-tain their identity as an ethnic group in the face of much op-position and pressure to conform to sedentary society. Their experience of low social status and exclusion – which prevents them from participating as equals in society-is mostly due to the widespread hostility of settled people towards them. This hostility is based on prejudice, which in turn gives rise to dis-crimination and affects Travellers in all aspects of their lives. (Fay, R., 2001: 99)[4]

Development, in particular community development, calls for change in the status quo. Where inequality is evident it needs to be challenged. However a difference worth noting here is that the call for change is coming from the people experiencing the humiliation and or inequality. Community development works to empower the local communities to articulate their perspectives and proactively works to identify the injustice and hold people to account for the inequality. To date at a local and national level it has proved difficult to find anyone to take responsibility for example in relation to addressing the discrimination and racism experienced by the Traveller Community in Ireland.

> Travellers are widely acknowledged as one of the most marginalised and disadvantaged groups in Irish Society. Travellers fair poorly on every indicator used to measure disadvantage: unemployment, poverty, social exclusion ,health status, infant mortality life expectancy, illiteracy education and training levels, access to decision making and political representation, gender, access to credit Accommodation and living conditions (O' Connell, J.: 19)[5]

There has been a body of national policies developed in relation to the Traveller community since the early 1960s. Much of the policy framework up to the 1990s was one of denial that the Traveller community were a distinct group and as a result the aim was to assimilate Travellers into mainstream society. 'The thinking at the time was that Travellers were more in need of charity as opposed to rights.'[6] By the mid-1990s there was a shift in the way that Travellers were identified by policy makers. This was highlighted in the reporting of the 'Task Force on the Travelling Community' which was published in 1995. This document pioneered a new approach to the Traveller community and gave recognition to the discrimination experienced by Travellers. It even went so far as to make the link between discrimination and racism in the main body of the report' Academic debate and various international fora focus attention on the link between racism and cultural difference, particularly in scenarios of unequal power relationships. The forms of prejudice and discrimination experienced by the Traveller community equate with racism in the international context' (Task Force on the Travelling Community, 1995)

The fight for this recognition was pursued at the time by key Traveller support groups who lobbied and campaigned policy makers to initiate this policy change. The Traveller groups at the time had adopted a community work approach as a means to articulating the real issues that were having a negative impact on the lives of the Traveller community. It was also around this time that the activists at a local level began to frame the local issues as a denial of Traveller rights. This began the international focus on the plight of the Traveller community which in turn brought pressure to bear on the Irish Government. There are many theorists working in this area of trying to make sense of how local issues can influence the human rights debate and visa versa.

The Traveller Support groups in essence have taken international ideas and adapted them to suit the Traveller community in an Irish context. The issue of racism and addressing racism against the Traveller community has been one such area. Due to the level of discrimination experienced by the Traveller community and the lack of recognition of the Traveller Community as an ethnic group there was a planned programme agreed by the three National Traveller Organisations. The Irish Traveller Movement, Pavee Point and the National Traveller Women's forum in conjunction with the Traveller projects working at a local level to proactively campaign for the recognition of Traveller as an ethnic group and for their protection against racism. The strengths of this campaign to date have been:

- Participation in and development of the Task Force on the Traveller Community 1995.

- The inclusion of Travellers as a group to be protected in the Employment Equality Act 1998 and the Equal Status Act 2000 and 2004.

- Peer-led primary health care programmes.

- The Traveller community named in housing legislation.

- The campaign calling for the Irish Government to ratify the UN convention on the elimination of all forms of racial discrimination. This was ratified in the year 2000.

- The National Traveller Health Strategy naming Travellers as a distinct ethnic group and a commitment of resources to begin to address the inequalities in health.

- The profiling of the Traveller community at an international level through the development of Shadow reports and the representation of the Traveller community at the Third UN Conference Against Racism in Durban 2001.

- Active membership of the European Network against Racism – Ireland.

- Working to develop and implement Planning for Diversity – National Action Plan against Racism 2005–2008. Once again Travellers are named as a group that experience racism.

- Shadow reporting by Pavee Point, Irish Traveller Movement and the National Traveller Women's Forum to the International and regional Human Rights Treaties. The standard of the reporting and representation has been acknowledged at an international level.

- Traveller Leadership and the development of 'Minceir Whiden', a Traveller-only space.

- Traveller innovation in enterprise development. The social enterprise project in Galway city and county.

- The insulation project has a Traveller Manager and seven Traveller men making up the team. They have 600 houses insulated to date with a 100 per cent quality rating.

This has been a very strong campaign orchestrated by Traveller non government organisations to keep the issue of racism against Travellers on the States agenda. Community work was the basis for this action but in a rights based framework. The UN mechanisms were used to influence the national agenda. There is a belief that the NGOs need to be much more systematic in demanding rights for the Traveller community and part of this work will be to identify the violations, identify the duty bearer and hold them to account.

There are opportunities as part of community development approaches to build solidarity with other marginalised groups in an effort to realize rights. Economic social and cultural rights need to be given a much greater attention in a way that places them at the* centre of concerns for human dignity and development. The Traveller community have shown huge resolve to continue their fight for recognition and live in the hope that there will be structural change that will bring about equality for their community.

Conclusion

> Democracy and human rights have at their foundations a fundamental concern for the well being of individuals and society. When democracy and human rights are understood in minimalist terms the participatory nature of the concepts is lost as they no longer provide support for empowerment and a substantive concern for human dignity (Richard Burchill).

The Traveller community are a very resilient group even in the face of a denial of their ethnicity. They have lobbied and campaigned for culturally appropriate service delivery and have watched while successive programmes have failed to deliver. This has not deterred their resolve to continue to campaign with other non governmental organisations for recognition. They have also worked in solidarity with the Irish Human Rights Commission and the Equality Authority to have their issues heard through the courts. They have been instrumental in supporting the work of Community and Specialist Law Centres to build a legal rights movement and the development of a legal system to work for justice and fairness for Travellers before the law. The need for all this work to be done within a human rights framework is essential and will demand' a specific focus on economic, social and cultural rights. We need to keep the high moral ground and demand human rights for all individuals. Collective action to bring about change.

Endnotes

1. Panayote Elias Dimitras, 'Recognition of Minorities in Europe: Protecting rights and Dignity' (Briefing) (April 2004) Minority Rights Group International, ISBN 1 904584 18 7.

2. The Equality Authority, (2006) *Traveller Ethnicity: An Equality Authority Report.*

3. *Task Force on the Traveller Community*, 1995, Government Publications.

4. Fay, R. 'Health and Racism: A Traveller Perspective' in Farreil, F. and Watt, P. (2001) *Responding to Racism in Ireland*, Veritas Publications, pp. 99-114.

5. O'Connell, J. 'Travellers in Ireland: An examination of discrimination and racism' in Lentin, R. and McVeigh, R. (2002) *Racism and Anti-Racism in Ireland*, Beyond the Pale Publications Ltd, Belfast.

6. Ibid.

5.

An 'Other' Perspective: Emancipation in Alterity?

Majella Breen

Introduction

The local newspaper usually publishes a photo of the Traveller women who have attended our back to education and training programme. On each occasion there are a number of women who do not wish to be included in the photo, for very plausible reasons. For example, in a previous year one of the participants progressed on to a Community Employment scheme. She specifically requested that her new colleagues would not be informed that she was a member of the Traveller community. When I asked her why, she said that she was afraid that she would be treated differently in a negative way.

It is not surprising that individual Travellers fear negative treatment. This article will look at the bases of those fears, and explore where the negativity comes from. I will outline the stereotyping that is perpetuated in the media in general, and how education has a central role in challenging these myths and stereotypes. My positioning to discuss this issue is located in my own experience as 'The Other' (de Beauvoir, 1949). In the article, I will explore the concept of otherness or alterity and discuss the potentiality of the concept in challenging stereotypical norms and the ways in which this positioning provides me with a singular vantage point. I will look at examples of

38

educational approaches, from our own programme underpinned by adult education principles derived from Freire (1972) and Noddings, (1984) and the University of Limerick Initiative, on the integrated framework. I will consider the possibilities of otherness, and finally, on my own experience of alterity, which has enabled me to reflect on why I do what I do and how the notion of embracing otherness has been a personal motivation.

Otherness

The old adage 'no news is good news' is particularly true of the portrayal of Travellers in the media in general. As Hayes (2006) points out they are portrayed as 'Other', different from the norm, leading to their subaltern status in Irish society. In her ground-breaking work *The Second Sex* (1949) Simone de Beauvoir outlines how a patriarchal and male-dominated society defines women as 'Other', i.e. other than the male perceived as the norm.

The quality of otherness is relevant to the status of Travellers. For example, when a member of the Traveller community becomes seriously ill, their extended community rallies round. This has been known to cause alarm among health professionals when a large number of Travellers flood a waiting room in a hospital. That a group of individuals who are trying to be supportive can be perceived as a threat can be explained in the context of 'othering'.

In his book *Irish Travellers: Representations and Realities* (2006, p. 113), Michael Hayes examines the social construction of the Irish Traveller as 'Other':

> A visitor to Ireland today who chanced to pick up a newspaper would see little in the non-Traveller's depiction of Travellers that would differ from the common and historical portrayals of the Traveller community as 'Other'. At its simplest and worst, present-day perceptions of Travellers continue to build on a collection of primarily negative constructs – e.g. disorder, nomadism, laziness, dishonesty, backwardness, dependency, etc.

It is not uncommon for those who have been identified as 'Other', e.g. women, Travellers, people with disabilities, gay people and all marginalised people to suffer from internalised oppression. As Mason (1990, p. 27) puts it:

> Internalized oppression is not the cause of our mistreatment, it is the result of our mistreatment. It would not exist without the real external oppression that forms the social climate in which we exist.
>
> Once oppression has been internalized, little force is needed to keep us submissive. We harbour inside ourselves the pain and the memories, the fears and the confusions, the negative self-images and the low expectations, turning them into weapons with which to re-injure ourselves, every day of our lives.

Internalised oppression is based on real fear. As I said in the introduction, some of our participants hide their identities outside of the programme environment because of the fear that negative perceptions in the world of work will turn into those very weapons of re-injury and negative self-image. Part of the work of education is to nurture confidence and pride among Travellers, and to facilitate them to challenge negative media constructions. The next section will discuss the role of the media in creating those negative constructions.

The Role of the Media in Social Construction

The media 're-present' images and stories back to society and play an active part in constructing meaning in the world in which we live. Creedon (1989, p. 18) suggests that not only do the media contribute to the construction of reality but also to a dominant consensus view of what reality is:

> Mass communications theorists who take a cultural approach to communication also argue that reality is nothing more than – and nothing less than – a 'collective hunch'. They suggest that when countless personal and interpersonal interpretations are communicated via mass channels meaning tends to become homogenised and consensus values prevail.

Touchman argues that even a non-fictional genre such as news is not just an objective reporting of the facts but is a construction of reality. News is '… a depletable consumer product that must be made fresh daily' (1978, p. 149). Thus, the constant renewal of the 're-presentation' reinforces the homogenised consensus around stereo-types, almost without question. Further, Habermas defines the public sphere as a realm of social life in which public opinion is formed. Of the role of the media Habermas says: 'today newspapers and magazines, radio and television are the media of the public sphere' (1984, p. 49). He is highly critical of what he calls the 'refudalization' of the public sphere, whereby public opinion is manipulated by the mass media. This is particularly relevant to the portrayal of Travellers, where the norm creates the otherness where Travellers are concerned. For example, *My Big Fat Gypsy Wedding* portrays some Travellers in a voyeuristic, mocking manner, on Channel 4. This is buttressed further by new media, e.g. 'tackyweddings.com' that is devoted to sneering at the kinds of wedding dresses that Travellers wear at their marriage ceremonies. And there are more explicitly racist sites. These are the fundamental issues that education, and in particular, adult education, needs to address, which I will discuss in the next section.

Challenging the Myths through Education

Until recent times Travellers themselves have had very little say in how they have been portrayed. Hayes (2006) has tracked their depic-tion in the early Irish state as a regressive group, out of kilter with the emerging modern nation. Further, they have been considered as a counter-cultural group: 'a society within a society' (Ó hAodha, 2007, p. 9). Thus, with this negative stereotyping, it is not surprising to find people wanting to hide who they really are as oppression becomes internalised. An aspect of hiding, or disguising the self, is interest-ing in the context of Cant, Gammon (or Shelta as it is referred to in academic circles) the Traveller language. It is obvious that many of the words are an inverted form of Irish. St John O Donnobhain (2007, pp. 97-8) explores the aspect of Cant as a secret language and a means of protection against the dominant society:

> … the repeated testimony of Travellers such as Pecker Dunne, that Shelta functions to help keep Travellers' lives private and for secrecy, can leave us in very little doubt that disguising is

(and has been for some time) a very important part of Shelta use in the course of daily life.

However, he then goes on to examine how Cant can function as a binding agent, creating a sense of belonging to a specific group amongst those who speak it.

This resonates with my experience in adult education. For example, near the beginning of our previous programme, I was approached by a couple of younger participants who were bemoaning their loss of knowledge of Cant. I recall the exact words of one young woman 'We don't know our own language'. Furthermore, they requested if there was any way that we could teach it to them. With the approval of the whole group, in consultation with Dr. Micheál Ó hAodha of the University of Limerick (I will discuss this connection later in the article) and with the unstinting help of an enthusiastic tutor we devised a course outline in Cant. Following negotiations with the CEF of County Wicklow VEC and FETAC it was agreed that an exploration of the language could be included in the Living in a Diverse Society module. That is, the private and binding language was re-introduced through the basic principle of adult and community education, starting with participants's own starting point (Freire, 1972), enabling learners to identify their needs, and meeting those needs through a learning programme. This is the fundamental tenet in challenging the norms that create otherness. This underpinned another innovative programme around creating narrative.

In December 2008, Bray Travellers Community Development Group published 'Beoirs' Stories, a collection of narratives written and recorded by the women on the training programme. 'Beoirs' is the Cant word for women, and the booklet was a collection of factual and fictional stories documenting some of the heritage and traditions unique to Traveller women culture. Heneghan (2007) discusses the relevance of publications relating to Traveller culture, to Travellers who are in education:

> To the Traveller community, these books, particularly the two
> biographies, are recognised as 'one of our own' and it is to be
> hoped that all such publications will feature in schools in the

years to come to enhance a greater understanding of Traveller culture and history (2007, p. 66).

With the assistance of talented and caring tutors, the Beoirs programme attempted to address some of the needs of Traveller women, outlined above, by running a module in Personal Development and providing an opportunity for participants to explore their own culture through, for example, the Living in a Diverse Society module. Again, the role of education is central to building the capacity of the participants to deepen their own knowledge through their own story or narrative (Freire, 1972) in addition to providing resources for their wider community.

However, the ability to stay focused on the positive requires confidence. In my experience, once again because of internalised oppression Travellers sometimes suffer from their own negative thinking. Cognitive distortion and strategies to overcome it as outlined by Ellis (1962) have some relevance in this regard.

> The task of the helper who seeks to change the beliefs and appraisals of the person in need is to modify the thinking and belief system of the person. This is done by disputing the beliefs... (Murgatroyd, 1985, p. 78)

Noddings' (1984) ethics of caring underpin the approach that we take in our programme. She argues that moral decisions, in addition to logic and values should also include reciprocity and relationships with others. Reciprocity includes a willingness on behalf of tutors/teachers to learn about another culture and language. Training needs to be based on a model of education that views the participants as adults with knowledge, skills and life experience. Additionally, tutors need to acknowledge the expertise of the participants in the subject area of their own identity and culture and act as facilitators to build on and strengthen existing capacity. As educators, we take on a role similar to Murgatroyd's helper. We encourage the participants to develop a knowledge of and pride in their own culture and an understanding of their sense of alienation and consequently we can strive to counteract their feelings of negativity and shame.

Making Connections

Our own learning and development was also relevant in this context. In 2009 we learned that there was a specific seminar room and collection Library in UL devoted to Traveller culture. A number of our participants and a couple of tutors travelled to Limerick to see it and to meet Dr. Micheál Ó hAodha and John Heneghan, Co-ordinator of the Traveller access programme. John Heneghan was so struck by the potential for leadership within this group that he later contacted me. At a subsequent meeting, he outlined the framework model (Heneghan, 2010) for Traveller inclusion that he has developed (see figure below) and we discussed possible modes of dialogue and interaction as relating to our group.

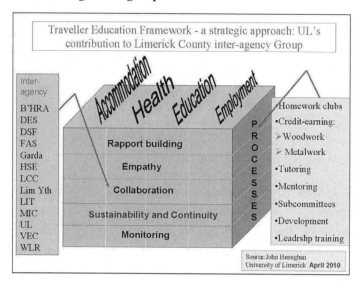

As Heneghan (2007, p. 68) puts it:

> ... it has been the growth in the number of participants, partners and advisors from the Traveller community itself that really strengthens the project.

In simple enough terms, this 'Limerick County Traveller Inter-Agency Framework' created by John Heneghan at the University of Limerick is based on a number of principles. First is that dialogue, mutual dialogue, is absolutely essential – conversations and discussions over time with local Travellers, and all institutions involved in

Traveller affairs, are a prerequisite to starting off real 'action' in the area of educational access; education, in turn, links to issues related to accommodation, health, and meaningful work/business/employment. Most central here is dialogue with Travellers themselves, creating some rapport which over time builds mutual trust, without which one is simply wasting one's time; without empathy and trust, substantive communicative action on the key pillars of the framework cannot emerge, nor will they be sustained over time. It addresses the cultural barrier of Travellers perceived as a 'society within a society' as referred to above.

In the meantime, some of those participants have moved on and with Traveller community development workers have been trained as Diversity Trainers in Traveller Culture. This action is supported by the County Wicklow Traveller Interagency and aims to provide training to Travellers enabling them to, in turn, provide awareness training about their own culture and traditions. It also aims to promote an understanding of Traveller culture among school-goers and the wider community. The Traveller Access Initiative at UL generously provided transport and tuition in leadership skills to those involved. Once again, a talented and enthusiastic tutor greatly assisted in the process of encouraging and supporting the Travellers involved in speaking about their own culture with pride.

Reflections

I have become a fan of YouTube. I rarely watch the items with the most hits but I look up the music videos of favourite artists and sometimes I come across speakers with interesting ideas. One such idea is from a man called Simon Sinek (2010) who argues convincingly that inspiration is derived from why we do things rather than what we do. Reflecting on why I do what I do has caused me to examine my views at a deeper level and to consider the importance of why I felt inspired to work with Travellers.

In the now famous Stanford Commencement Address (2005) by the late Steve Jobs, he exhorts his audience to be passionate about what they do. I believe that when we hide even a part of ourselves, there is a resulting guardedness that restricts spontaneity and limits our ability to be truly passionate. Barthes discusses passion and hiding:

> To hide a passion totally (or even to hide, more simply, its excess) is inconceivable: not because the human subject is too weak, but because passion is in essence made to be seen: the hiding must be seen: I want you to know that I am hiding something from you, that is the active paradox I must resolve: at one and the same time it must be known and not known: I want you to know that I don't want to show my feelings: that is the message I address to the other (1977, p. 42).

Through personal experience, I have become passionate about the celebration of otherness but I am acutely aware of the negativity and even shame that many Travellers have to overcome in order to be able to celebrate their difference.

Two Examples of the Positivity of Having 'Other' Perspectives

Since I was a child I have had an abiding interest in astronomy. I watched a programme, part of a series called *Beautiful Minds* on BBC Four, transmitted on 12 April 2010, which was about the Irish astrophysicist Jocelyn Bell Burnell. In December 1967 as a postgraduate student she discovered Pulsar stars, though it was some time before the news filtered out partly due to the fear of ridicule (in the form of little green men) on behalf her male academic supervisors. Ironically, and reflecting the misogyny of the times, it was they and not she who were awarded the Nobel Prize for the discovery in 1974.

In the programme, when questioned closely about why she specifically had made this discovery, Jocelyn Bell Burnell made a couple of points that I found intriguing. One was that as a student she did not have a reputation to lose and therefore was not constrained by that fear. What really struck me, however, was when she said that as a woman she felt that she had brought a different way of looking at things to the proceedings. Is it just possible that not 'being an absolute human type' (de Beauvoir, 1949) was an advantage?

The second example of alterity is the Ron Davis' story. The interviewer asked him why he had named his book the *Gift of Dys-*

lexia (2010). Born with a form of autism he explained how, in middle age he realised that the talents that allowed him to be creative and view things from different perspectives were what caused his disorientation regarding the written word. He overcame his dyslexia by formulating mental pictures of words. He co-founded the Reading Research Council in 1982 and helped to develop methods that are now of assistance to people suffering from Dyslexia worldwide. Davis and Braun explain the phenomenon:

> The talents which create the vulnerability for confusing symbolic information are assets in other ways. For example, individuals who 'see' the dimensional attributes in our world understand intuitively how things work...Tasks which require the ability to visualise something in a creative or different way are often simple for individuals with these talents (2010, p. xii).

Conclusion

Involvement with the Traveller community has been a huge learning experience for me. Furthermore, it has given me the opportunity to reflect on how my practice sits on a theoretical framework and reflects my beliefs. Having initially struggled with my own alterity as a lesbian, I have been fortunate to realise for a long time that being different can give one another perspective. For example, concepts such as dominant discourse were easy for me to grasp as I grew up in a world where the heterosexual voice was virtually all pervasive. Involvement with gay politics taught me that minorities need to raise their own voices and can offer equally valid perspectives. The ability to look at things another way can be an enormous resource and I believe that it is only when we embrace our difference that we can fully exploit the potential that lies within it. If I am to start with why, then this is why and I believe this passionately.

In the course of running some parenting skills classes, a tutor came to me to complain that a sister of one of the participants was interfering in the relationship between a mother and child. I tried to explain to her that extended family bonds are much stronger in Traveller society. While the tutor in question perceived this as a negative influence, it is possible to look at this from another angle. Many Traveller mothers derive a great deal of support from their sisters, mothers and female relations in general in terms of childminding, advice and exchange of information. This is not at the expense of children as the extended Traveller family appears to be very child-centred.

If we focus on the positive we can see that Travellers demonstrate a strong sense of community and extended family bonds when they rally around a sick relative. In this way they demonstrate their 'ethics of caring'. If we can begin to appreciate what Travellers have to offer us through their rich cultural diversity then perhaps we can begin to give them the support and encouragement necessary for them to share their unique perspectives. If we can encourage them to focus on the positive aspects of their culture, perhaps we can help them to counteract the negative ways in which they are perceived. As one of the participants on the Beoirs training programme put it, Education should be based on respect.

Note

This article is reproduced with the kind permission of AONTAS, the national adult learning organisation and publisher of The Adult Learner Journal where it was published at the end of August, 2012.

Endnote

1. The 'Beoirs' back to education and training programme was run by Bray Travellers Community Development Group and sponsored by FAS, County Wicklow VEC and the Bray Area Partnership and Pobal.

References

Barthes, R. (1977) *A Lover's Discourse: Fragments* (trans. Richard Howard 1978). New York: Hill & Wang

Bell Burnell, J. (2010) (www.bbc.co.uk/iplayer/.../Beautiful_Minds_Jocelyn_Bell_Burnell/)

'Beoirs' Stories, (2008) Bray Travellers Community Development Group, National Library of Ireland Reference: 6327

Creedon, P. (ed.) (1989) *Women in Mass Communication*. London: Sage

Davis, R. with Braun, E. (2010 revised and updated) *The Gift of Dyslexia*. London: Souvenir

de Beauvoir, S. (1949) *The Second Sex* (trans. H.M. Parshley 1972.). New York: Penguin

Ellis, A. (1962) *Reason and Emotion in Psychotherapy*. New Jersey: Lyle Stuart

Freire, P., (1972) *The Pedagogy of the Oppressed,* Penguin, Harmondsworth.

Habermas, J. (1984) *The Theory of Communicative Action*, Vol. 1. Boston: Beacon Press

Hayes, M. (2006) *Irish Travellers: Representations and Realities*, Dublin: The Liffey Press

Heneghan, J. (2007) 'Travellers and access: the 'Empathy and Mechanisms' Model at the University of Limerick' in Ó hAodha, M. et al. (eds) *The Stranger in Ourselves: Ireland's Others*. Dublin: A & A Farmer

Heneghan, J, (2010) The Traveller Education Framework at the University of Limerick, Education as a Catalyst for Regeneration conference, June 2nd

Jobs, S. (2005) Stanford Commencement Address, (http://www.youtube.com/results?search_query=steve+jobs+stanford+commencement+speech+2005&aq=1)

Mason M. (1990) *Disability Equality in Education*, in Reiser, R. and Mason, M. (eds) London: ILEA

Murgatroyd, S. (1985) *Counselling and Helping*. London: British Psychological Association & Methuen

Noddings, N. (1984) *Caring: A Feminine Approach in Ethics and Moral Education*. Berkeley, C.A.: University of California Press

Ó hAodha, M. (2007) 'A counter-cultural group: some past representations of the Irish Traveller Community' in Ó hAodha, M. et al (eds) *The Stranger in Ourselves: Ireland's Others*. Dublin: A & A Farmer

O'Donnabhain, St John (2007) 'Shelta and Verlan: Outsiders Talking Back 'in Ó hAodha, M. et al (eds) *The Stranger in Ourselves: Ireland's Others*. Dublin: A & A Farmer

Sinek, S. (2010) Start with Why (http://www.youtube.com/watch?v=u4ZoJKF_VuA)

Touchman, G. (1978) *Making News: A Study in the Construction of Reality*, New York: Free Press

6.

Roma and Self-Representation: Some Aspects of a Roma Activist's Experience

Ana Oprişan

In this essay, Ana Oprişan, who was born into a part-Roma/part-Romanian family in Romania, describes the process whereby she came to an understanding of her own particular part-Roma ethnic identity in adulthood. She also describes her work as a Roma activist in Turkey and gives some insights into the situation of various Roma communities in the Middle East, many of whom had relatively little contact with Roma organisations in Europe or within their own countries until very recently.

I was born in Romania to a Roma (Gypsy) father and a Romanian mother and lived in Romania until 2002. My father was brought up within the Roma community but left that 'world' behind when he married his non-Roma wife – my mother. Like the members of many minorities worldwide my father became acculturated to the 'majority' culture in Romania and tried to leave his original identity behind. He tried to forget about his family's identity and to 'pass' within the majority culture. He believed that it was easier for himself and his wife and children to function and achieve socially within Romanian society if he denied where he had come from originally – in the process. Although this might seem to be an easy thing to do, in reality it is anything but easy to try and change your identity. Your identity or your background will always come to the surface at some point despite your best efforts. Ironically, although there is huge prejudice against the Roma in Romanian society, it wasn't in the 'outside' world that the question of my father's and our family's part-Roma ethnicity first came to the surface. In fact, it was in the confines of the family home that we children first became aware of it. Both my sister and I were brought up as normal 'advantaged' Romanians and our parents ensured that we were kept apart from all our relatives on my father's side of the family. Any discussion about where my father was from was a taboo subject which was avoided at all times except when it became a source of tension between my parents. Occasionally, if there were arguments between my parents, my mother would refer to my father's 'unhappy' background as the source of many of their problems. As a small child you do not question your parents but accept nearly everything which they tell you out of respect for them. Even while quite young however, I realised that when there was 'tension' between my parents – it was sometimes due to the fact that our grandparents and cousins on my father's side of the family all lived in 'țigănia din Frumușița' – the well-known and 'avoided' Gypsy settlement in Frumușița. This was a large community located only three kilometres away from the village in which we lived. I also remember my mother getting very angry with me once or twice when I was disobeying her and telling me that I was worse 'than my aunts' and that I was being bold because 'my blood is calling'. I felt the sting of these words without fully understanding what my mother actually meant.

Like every other youngster I assumed that my parents' decisions were for the best and never questioned why the relatives on only one side of our family ever came to visit. I assumed that the grandparents on my father's side of the family just didn't care about my parents, my sister and I and that they were simply busy with all of the many other cousins which we had but about whom we rarely heard anything. I only remember my Roma relatives from Frumușița coming to our house a couple of times during the holidays and I remember that my father was embarrassed and angry that they were there. He kept telling them that it was time for them to go home and that he didn't like the fact that they didn't have any employment and were always asking for money. Also, the fact that both my grandfather and grandmother smoked and drank alcohol would have been considered shocking if any of our neighbours were to find out and would have been regarded as 'lowering the tone' of the respectable village where we were living.

I became more aware of all of these 'issues' when I first visited my grandparents' house in Frumușița/Galați: when my grandfather died (RIP). I was about seventeen years of age then and for the first time in my life I met a whole range of different people who were my blood-relatives blood. As with all local Romanian people I knew that the 'țigănia' was a place where only the Roma people lived. I knew that they were a people who were considered 'different', 'inferior' to everybody else but also dangerous, and that they had come to that place sometime in the past and settled there in a community that was very separate from all other Romanians. On the day of the funeral I discovered a little bit more about my grandparents through my conversations with the relatives at the funeral. My father's parents had been travelling throughout Romania and as with many nomadic people it wasn't clear whether they originally had a particular village or region which they had considered their 'homeplace'. My father had been born while they were 'on the road' in a place called Bârlad/Vaslui which is in the North-East of Romania. After his birth, his parents had continued the travelling life, looking for work in different towns and villages until they had been settled in Frumușița when my father was around sixteen years of age. On the day of grandfather's funeral I got to see the small house on the hill where my father had grown up with the big groups of children from the *mahalle* running around it and playing in the street. I also met all of these people whom I didn't know, even if they were somehow familiar because they were related to me. That occasion was the first and last time that I saw that house and (almost) all of my cousins. I have been travelling through many countries as part of my job since then and have rarely been back to Romania in recent years. Of course the fact that this one visit – and on the occasion of my grandfather's funeral – was the only time I got to meet a whole generation of my relatives – on one side of my family – has been a source of great sadness to me as I became older. I have also felt sad for my father of course as I now realise why he made some of the decisions that he did in the past and I also realise how difficult it must have been for him to make the sacrifices which he did.

The reality I was kept away from had something 'unsolved' in it; what I knew I was and what I knew I might be was actually there with me all the time, but unclear, sad and spread away in two 'worlds'.

Some of my father's sisters and himself, as their father, have blue-greenish eyes. The other side from my father's mother, they are quite dark. Sometimes, when I was getting angry with my father I always 'screamed' inside of me to him: 'you made it, because you have blue eyes and you're white'. No other relative of ours from my father's side ever lived out of the tiganie's borders (either in Frumusita, or in other outskirts of different cities in Romania). Just my father 'made it out'.

As I became older I noticed that I had a certain facility of languages. I managed to find out about a programme that combined both my linguistic skills and aspects of the ethnic background I knew I somehow had and eventually became a student in the Romanian – Romani Languages Section of the Arts Faculty in the University of Bucharest, in the capital of Romania. I graduated from this University in the summer of 2002 but had already started working on Roma-related issues about two years prior to my graduation. Between 1998 and 1999 I made contact with the Roma Centre for Public Policies – also known as Aven Amentza – in Bucharest where I began to work on a number of Roma-related policy-making projects and advocacy issues. It was an exciting time to work here and to witness at first hand the evolution of the Roma 'Movement' and their various advocacy initiatives in Romania. Until 2002, my part-Roma ethnicity was not really a major 'issue' for me personally or for those others who were working with me on these various Roma-related projects. The debates that sometimes take place between Roma activists and non-Roma or part-Roma activists whose work concerns Roma-related issues and rights was not an 'issue' for me as relating to my own background. As with Roma and Traveller-rights organisations in many other countries the 'Who is Roma and who is not Roma?' question or 'dilemma' is still a 'contested' issue in the Romania Roma movement, one which can sometimes cause 'tensions' as relating to representation and advocacy work on behalf of different cultural groups.

For me all this experience was also like an effort to understand the Roma reality and myself in this new asserted context. Maybe unconsciously, the work I did or I was trying to do was a kind of a retribution/paying back for all that people like my father and my relatives who had to face difficulties because of what they were in a time when I lived unaware and carefree.

A defining moment for me, both on personal level and as relating to my career occurred when I first came into contact with the Turkish-speaking Muslim Roma in Romania – often referred to as the *Horahane Roma*. This Turkish-speaking community are, one can argue, a 'minority within a minority'. While they live in the same country as other Roma they nevertheless are considered 'different' and are sometimes subject to prejudice both from non-Muslim Roma in Romania, other Turkish diaspora populations (groups often referred to as Turks and Tartars) and from the broader non-Roma society in Romania.

In fact my ensuing work with this community was one of the primary reasons why I decided to leave Romania 'permanently' and move to Turkey or – 'the place of the Muslim Roma'. My interest in working with this group of Roma coincided with a small but burgeoning movements towards the social and cultural 'awareness-raising' amongst the various communities of Roma in Turkey – including the *Horahane Roma*. A group of people which included myself came together who were interested in helping various the various Roma communities in Turkey agitate for their rights and who wished to create an organisation which could do so. This small group but enthusiastic group of people – a group of whom I am very proud to be a part of – started this advocacy work in Turkey with the launch of the Romani Studies Network, a network which combines both fieldwork, academic research with awareness-raising/advocacy work throughout a range of Turkish Roma communities as relating to social, cultural and educational issues. In addition, I also continued with my academic studies and graduated with a Masters Degree (MA) in Political and Social Sciences, at Marmara University in Istanbul. My dissertation thesis concerned the (lack of) status of the Roma in

Turkey, particularly when compared with the social status occupied by other Roma groups in South-Eastern Europe. The context within which my thesis was set was of course the range of European and international bodies' rules and regulations regarding minorities in general, and the Roma/Gypsies in particular.

When I first arrived in Turkey, there were no Roma NGOs and there was a quite a strong reluctance to the concept of 'getting organized' in terms of social and cultural advocacy. The initial work in Turkey therefore meant travelling through different regions of Turkey and 'sitting-down' with different (informal) Roma leaders. As anybody who is involved in the initial stages of advocacy work with a group – like the Roma – who have been long-marginalised from the major organs of society will testify to – the first question that needs to be addressed in any advocacy initiatives is 'Why?' and 'What difference will it make?' Both my fellow-workers and I were frequently 'tested' and asked what 'getting organised' in a civic way – actually means and whether such forms of organisation and advocacy can really help in giving a 'voice' – maybe the only 'voice' or 'outlet' – for groups for whom decades of marginalisation, poverty and exclusion are the norms. Relating the experiences and successes of other Roma organisations and groups outside of Turkey – in parts of Eastern Europe – was a good starting-point for our endeavours. So too was the fact that policy changes as instigated by the Turkish government – particularly as relating to the drive for EU accession – meant that some Turkish Roma began to establish NGOs (Non-Governmental Organisations) for the first time. While it is widely acknowledged that Turkey is not a particularly 'liberal' country when it comes to issues pertaining to the cultural identity of various minority or ethnic groups, the desire for EU accession meant that some Roma communities now had, for the first time, the opportunity to circumvent the 'mainstream' Turkey population and argue for rights based on a stronger premise – than of the normal citizen requesting their everyday human rights.

Since 2002 I have worked as a moderator of an e-group entitled Roma in Turkey which works to support the communication and information-flow between Roma communities and activists within Turkey but also with other Roma 'scattered' throughout the world. In addition to our advocacy work, we, who were working with the Roma in Turkey realised that we needed to have the practical skills to deal with the 'new' opportunities and challenges that would now face us on the ground so that we could work with the Roma communities in implementing change that was clear and positive. In an effort to gain more practical and 'fieldwork' skills in this area, I began working with a Turkish-based international NGO in 2003, one which works primarily in relief aid, but also as addressing the development needs of a range of varied disadvantaged communities in Turkey and in other regions of the Middle East. My work with this NGO called IBC – International Blue Crescent Relief and Development Foundation began by initiating a number of small-scale projects addressing needs of the Roma communities in Turkey and with a specific focus on Roma children.

Following the December 2003 earthquake which devastated the city of Bam in south-eastern Iran, I coordinated the humanitarian mission to that city under the auspices of the IBC and worked there for one full year. In addition to destroying a great deal of the city, this earthquake killed over 43,000 people, injured 20,000, and left over 60,000 people homeless which meant that there was a lot of very hard work to be done. While in Iran I came into contact with another Roma group – known as 'the *Zargars*'. The *Zargars* are one of if not the only Roma group between the other many Dom and 'Gypsy-like' groups who live in Iran and other neighbouring Middle Eastern countries such as Pakistan and Afghanistan. The *Zargars* speak a dialect of Romanes which has retained the highly-inflected morphology as spoken by some Roma groups in Europe. Their dialect seems to be quite similar to a number of dialects spoken by Roma communities in Romania today but it also contains many words and influences from languages such as Farsi and Azeri Turkish. Gypsies (I call 'Gypsy' here the community of the Roma and other sub-groups derived from dom groups!) are a small minority in Iran with various estimates putting the entire Gypsy population of Iran at around 110,000 people out of a total Iranian population of 68,959,931 people. This contrasts with Turkey where the official number of Roma is given as 500,000 people. As with statistics relating to many Gypsy, nomadic and often-marginalised groups however, it is very difficult to know how accurate any of these estimates are. For instance, I have spoken to Roma leaders and spokespeople in Turkey who put the real figure for the Roma population in Turkey at five times higher than the estimated figure 2.5 million and there are others again who give different figures. Gypsy communities can be found throughout Turkey, and there are very significant Roma populations in the Thrace[1] and Marmara[2] regions (the Rom groups) and also in Anatolia[3] (Dom[4] groups) including areas such as Maras, Antep, Adana or Istanbul. Roma whose families originated in Bulgaria make their homes in areas such as Kayseri, Adana, Osmaniye, Sakarya and Çorum and as with Roma everywhere there are variants as regards group self-ascription and names/ascriptions as applied to these groups by non-Roma. In Çorum,[5] in the north of Turkey, for example, the 'settled' Roma living there, whose families originated in Bulgaria are often referred to as 'Haymantos', while in cities such as Erzurum, Artvin, Bayburt, Erzincan and Sivas the Roma are frequently given ascriptions such as 'Posha' or 'Bosha'. In Van, Hakkari, Mardin and Siirt, it is slightly different again and Roma in these areas are most often identified as 'Mutrib' – the word 'mutrib' or 'mɪrtɪp' meaning 'musician' in Arabic.

Two basic observations can be made in the Turkish context as relating to both the hetero-identification of Roma/Gypsies (i.e. the identification of the Roma by non-Roma) and self-identification – as indicated by the Roma themselves. Roma in Turkey *refer to themselves* as '*Roman*' or '*Çingene*' – a self-identification as relating to their ethnicity – or by using only the religious self-identification, for instance – referring to themselves as *Muslim*, *Alevi* or *Abdal*, a form of reference which is quite common amongst those Roma who are Shia. The latter form of self-identification is based on religious ascription and avoids any reference to Roma origins. The names given to the Roma are wide-ranging and vary from city to city and region to region. They are sometimes referred to as *Posha* (in Eastern Anatolia especially) or as *Mɪrti/Mutrib* in places such as Hakkari, Mardin, Siirt and in the southern part of Van). In Adana and Osmaniye Roma are frequently referred to by the terms *Kocer* and *Cono* – (pronounced 'djono') while in the capital of Turkey, Ankara, they are frequently called *Teber*. In Diyarbakır , south-eastern Turkey, the Roma[7] are known by a range of interesting names, some of which have not previously appeared in the literature relating to the populations and cultures of this area of Turkey. Some Roma here are referred to as *Kereçi/Karaci* (a Persian word meaning 'stranger' or 'foreigner') while others are referred to as *Ashik* or *Gelsin*. Christian Roma are referred to by a different name – i.e. *Balamoron* – although this term is limited to the identification of Greek Christian Roma only. As with Roma in other countries a frequent method of Roma ascription/categorisation relates to the different trades which particular families and communities have traditionally followed – e.g. *Elekçi* (sieve-makers), *Sepetci* (baskets-makers), *Kalayci* (Tinsmith), *Demirci* (Ironsmith), *Kemikci* (Kokalara – artisans who work in bone), *Bohcaci* (door-to-door pedlars), *Arabaci* (horse-carriages operators) etc.

In a country as large as Turkey, it is no surprise to discover that religious allegiances are diverse, a fact which makes the identification of different Roma groups more complex, particularly given that religious affiliation has a very strong influence on the self-identification of many Roma communities. For instance, the *Posha* groups from the Van area of Eastern Turkey are considered to be Muslims, while those Roma living in Tokat,[8] Eastern Turkey who are today frequently regarded as Muslims, identified themselves in the not-too-distant past as Christians. The Roma living in south-eastern Turkey appear to follow Islamic religious rites which are close to the religious beliefs of the Çuki, the Shia Muslims, the Alevi and the Abdal groups. It is also the case that some of the *Mırtip/Mırti/Mutrib* Roma, many of whom who live in Siirt, Hakkari, Mardin and Van are Muslims of the Shafi rite. It is generally acknowledged that the vast majority of the Roma in Turkey are Muslim and their religious affiliation lies amongst a range of 'groups' including the *Shafi Sunni Shafi or Hanefi, the Shia, the Alevi and the Abdal*.[9]

Turkey and the Roma: Some Future Issues for Consideration

Roma in Turkey face a similar set of social issues and problems in the present-day as many of their counterparts in both Western and Eastern Europe. Prominent concerns as expressed by Turkish Roma communities themselves include: employment, housing, education, health, legal provisions and prejudice in terms of society and the law. The fact that many large sections of the Turkish population live in very difficult social and economic conditions today is often used as an excuse or pretext for not addressing the needs of minorities and ethnic groups within Turkey who are considered to inhabit the margins of society.

While the Roma in Turkey do not face persecution in the form of torture etc. due to their Roma ethnicity, it is undeniably the case that their position in society involves considerable mis-treatment, particularly as related to their categorization and perceived 'Other' social status. The Roma, both historically, (and in the present-day) – are most often mentioned in terms which are negative and reductionist. They almost inevitably appear in regional and national ordinances and laws which mention such issues as – e.g. 'dealing with delinquency', 'dealing with beggars', 'preventing illegal acts' etc. as elucidated in official and state sources. While Turkish Roma have not faced the ugliness of ethnic cleansing and racially-motivated attacks as Roma have in many European countries, one only needs to scratch under the surface of the 'romantic/folkloric' toleration of the *Çingeneler* (Gypsies) by the majority (non-Roma) to find that the Roma and their identity is almost unilaterally rejected. They are subject to a 'silent' and institutional discrimination, a prejudice that is made overt in the a range of Ordinances and Laws that have been instituted since the beginning of the modern Turkish state, laws which call for the assimilation or 'ejection' of Roma from various regions and cities.

A small, but increasing number of Turkish Roma are aware of the international Romani movement and its struggle for the rights and self-identity of the Roma throughout Europe and the rest of the world. The number of these Roma who are as yet politically 'activated' or 'aware' is still very small but the situation is slowly improving. Their increased involvement in sustainable development programmes is a progressive step into the future as it is only through awareness-raising, enhanced community organisation and increased legal/societal representation that social change will be stimulated and Roma access to social and educational resources will be improved.

Endnotes

1. Today the name Thrace designates a region spread over southern Bulgaria (Northern Thrace), northeastern Greece (Western Thrace), and European Turkey (Eastern Thrace). Thrace borders on three seas: the Black Sea, the Aegean Sea and the Sea of Marmara. In Turkey, it is also called Rumeli. Ancient Thrace (i.e. the territory where ethnic Thracians lived) also included present day northern Bulgaria, north-eastern Greece and parts of eastern Serbia and eastern Republic of Macedonia. The European portion of Turkey, known as Trakya (Thrace), encompasses 3% of the total area but is home to more than 10% of the total population. Thrace is separated from the Asian portion of Turkey by the Istanbul Bogazi (Bosphorus Strait), the Marmara Denizi (Sea of Marmara), and the Çanakkale Bogazi (Dardanelles Strait).

2. The Sea of Marmara, also known as the Sea of Marmora or the Marmara Sea, is an inland sea that connects the Black Sea to the Aegean Sea, thus separating the Asian part of Turkey from its European part. The Bosphorus strait connects it to the Black Sea and the Dardanelles strait to the Aegean. The former also separates Istanbul into its Asian side and European side.

3. Anatolia is a large and, roughly-rectangular peninsula which is situated bridge-like between southeastern Europe and Asia. The Anatolian part of Turkey accounts for 97% of the country's area. It is also known as Asia Minor, Asiatic Turkey, the Anatolian Plateau. The term Anatolia is most frequently used in specific reference to the large, semiarid central plateau, which is rimmed by hills and mountains that in many places limit access to the fertile, densely settled coastal regions.

4. The Dom (or Domi) of the Middle East are frequently considered a section of the larger Roma (or Gypsy) ethnic population. They may also be related to the Domba people of India. They have a rich oral tradition and express their culture and history through music, poetry and dance. Their estimated population of 2.2 million is primarily spread across parts of Turkey, Egypt, Greece, Jordan, Israel, Lebanon, Iraq and Iran. The actual population, however, is thought to be higher as some Dom are excluded from national census and others label themselves in national terms rather than as Dom. Nowadays, many Dom speak the dominant languages of their larger societies, but Domari, their national language, continues to be spoken by more insular communities.

5. Çorum is a city with a population of nearly 180,000 people in the Çorum Province of northern Turkey. Historically, Çorum was associated with

the famous Ertuğrul family. Their Karadeniz (Black Sea) dynasty dated back to the early 12th century and the family ruled in Çorum for seven centuries until the establishment of the Republic of Turkey in the early 20th century.

6. Diyarbakır is a major city in southeastern Turkey situated on the banks of the River Tigris, and is the seat of the Diyarbakır Province. It is the second-largest city in Turkey's Southeastern Anatolia region, after Gaziantep, with a population of over 500.000 people of which a large Kurdish population.

7. Here, I use the term 'Gypsy' and not 'Roma' for the groups of South-Eastern Turkey and the Middle East in general, as they are not considered to be Roma. These groups are sometimes referred to as Dom or Lom or are known frequently given this ascription by others – both Gypsy and non-Gypsy. These latter groups often comprise other and varied nomadic groups whose mode of living is very similar to that of the stereotypical/archetypal 'Roma' / 'Gypsy' populations).

8. Tokat is a city in Anatolia. It lies inland of the central Black Sea region and is over 400 kilometres from Ankara, the Turkish capital.

9. This statement is made with the proviso that little research has, as yet, been completed, as relating to the range and diversity of nomadic and 'Gypsy-like' groups who live and work in South-eastern Anatolia and it often quite difficult to work out the exact religious affiliation of different groups.

References

Andrews, P. (1992) *Turkiye`de etnik gruplar* (Trans: Mustafa Kupusoglu), Istanbul: Ant Yayinlari, Tumzamanlaryayincilik

Arayici, A. (1999) *Ulkesiz bir alk*. Cingeneler, Istanbul: Ceylan Yayinlari,

Beuninghaus, R. 'Les Tsiganes de la Turquie Orientale' in *Etudes Tsiganes*, 1999, Vol. 1.

Marushiakova, E. and Popov, V. (2000) *The Gypsies in the Ottoman Empire*, UK: University of Hertfordshire Press (Interface Collection)

Marushiakova, E. and Popov, V. (1997) *Gypsies (Roma) in Bulgaria Germany*: Peter Lang Verlag

7.

Constructing the Romani 'Feminine': The Case of Colum McCann's *Zoli*

Micheál Ó hAodha

Zoli, the title character of Colum McCann's novel, is a Roma (Gypsy) woman who grows up in Slovakia just before World War II. Hers is a story of tragedy and forced migration, a story much of which is recounted by the central character to her grown daughter many years later in a world that is so different that the past is like mirage. Zoli's voice looks back to a time that once was and to the attempted annihilation of a people who have always been amongst Europe's most reviled and ostracised. McCann's eponymous heroine is 'a tall young woman ... not beautiful, or not traditionally so anyway, but the sort of woman who stalled your breath. She held herself at the door nervously, as if she were a bowl of water that would not be allowed to spill.' Her childhood is destroyed when she watches a group of fascist soldiers force her parents and extended family onto a frozen lake. The doomed Roma wait in the night as the frozen lake cracks around them, the sun rises, and their world disappears with the melt of breaking day. Zoli joins a small group of Roma families as led by her own grandfather group of Roma, a band who spend the rest of the War running from the Nazi persecution which threatens to engulf their entire culture. They live the lives of the invisible migrant, the hunted who hide in the forests and along the forgotten trails. This wandering of this group is a portent of the history that is the Roma, a group who have remained 'invisible' to the public record and yet have endured centuries of harassment, demonisation and the ultimate horror of the Nazi Porraimos.

The Holocaust saw the deaths of at least half a million Roma while under various communist regimes their culture was suppressed and they were forced from their caravans, deprived of social services and subjected to widespread policies of forced sterilisation. Zoli responds to this attempted oblivion by teaching herself to read and write, something then forbidden to many Roma women, and becomes a poet and a celebrated as a singer. In the process she becomes something of a custodian of Roma tradition, a 'voice from the dust', the expression of an age-old collective unease, the 'Other' which observes quietly on the margins. Ironically Zoli's adoption of the written word and her hesitant entry into the world of the *gadzo* or non-Gypsy is also a prelude to the annihilation of her own self. She meets Stephen Swann, a half-Irish, half-Slovak man who is on an idealistic search for his 'roots'.

He falls in love with Zoli, her singing talent and her poetry and begs Zoli to marry him, this despite the taboo against Roma women marrying outside their own community. Swann is an idealist and a dreamer who foresees the emergence of new era – one encompassing 'a world raised up in an immense arc and everyone beneath it looking up in admiration'. He convinces Zoli to have her poetry published and when she later changes her mind about this, he betrays her by having the poems published anyway. The Communist leaders in Slovakia then appropriate her poetry as propaganda for the attempted assimilation of the Roma population and the obliteration of their culture and language. This attempt at cultural elimination comes in the guise of a false embrace – an apparent dialogue with the outcast and the 'curing' of the Roma's 'backward' habits and tradition of non-literacy. Zoli soon finds herself in that liminal space that is the person who no longer belongs. Her talent is exploited by the denizens of the non-Gypsy community for propaganda purposes and she is condemned by her own community to 'Pollution for Life: The Category

of Infamy' and sent into exile. A Gypsy, she now becomes the per-
petual wanderer – 'I have sold my voice,' she says 'to the arguments of
power.' At the heart of McCann's evocative story is the destruction of
a woman's soul and the parallel renting of a self-contained universe,
whose 'politics are road and grass'. In its place appears the hermetic
post-modern society, the arid core of which is the re-fashioning of
the human impulse and the arid homogeneity of the post-war European consciousness. The principal narrative that we hear during the
course of this novel is Zoli's but McCann also tells his story from
several different perspectives at the same time, thereby performing
an astonishing feat of ventriloquism and mimicry. It dances along a
tightrope of guilt and shame and even drifts across countries in the
search for an inner calm. McCann does not fall into the trap that has
haunted so many writers who have written about the Roma to date
– i.e. the elevation of his heroine to the status of the 'noble savage'
who suffers the ultimate betrayal. Zoli's story is a hymn to the world
of modernity that is as individual as it is harsh and brutish. His prose
is graceful and evocative, a form of poetry that very few present-day
artists are capable of writing. McCann's literary sensibility embraces
us through his characters and their memory of sound and smell. His
gift is a haunting Irish sensuality that is both harsh and beautiful.

The 'Zoli' Interview: Colum McCann Speaks with Micheál Ó hAodha

What did you know about the Roma before you started writing the book?

Nothing. I came to the Romani culture empty-handed. That's interesting, now that I finally understand it. The *gadjo* (non-Gypsy) comes
in, swaggering, but is immediately apparent as empty-handed. What
an idiot he is. He thinks he can watch. Even worse, he thinks he can
understand. He has no background to trade on.

But then again there's a freedom in that, an open doorway, if
you're open to possibility. You walk into it cold. Then you pass through
a warm house. And you realise you've been somewhere special. And
then you understand that in a certain way, you, the changed one, have
turned your own clichés upsidedown. I was the one who went in with

nothing. This could be called begging, but it's not. It's searching. And, then, I was the one who came out – after four years of writing and researching – if not more knowledgeable, then at least changed.

I equate my initial ignorance with the general level of ignorance in the wider world. I'm no different to anybody else. I knew nothing about Gypsies. I didn't even know the word Roma or Romani. But my interest was piqued by the Isabel Fonseca book *Bury Me Standing* and I just wanted to know. I wanted to delve. I wanted to see if it was possible to tell this story that was largely untold. It was then I found my heroes … the Papuszas of the world, the Hancocks, the people in the Milan Simecka foundation, the community workers, the ones that effect a difference in the larger communities.

In relation to the novel, I know that I didn't get it all right. I know that. Who can? Who might want to? *Zoli* is a failure. All books are. But I tried to tell it in the most honest way possible. I tried to make a little footprint.

The thing I'd love is that a young Romani writer might look at *Zoli* and say – hey, that's okay, but it's not good enough, I need to write my own story. That would be a curious form of success for me. If it became the yeast for the bread that finally comes from the oven.

What was the catalyst for this book?

I was literally looking for a book that would form a peak to my ideas about exile. I have written about exile since my earliest collection, *Fishing the Sloe-Black River*, when I was in my twenties. It has – though I wasn't always entirely aware of it – been my obsession for two decades. And once I realised that it was my obsession, it was time to get rid of it. One last excursion into that particular darkness. And then my wife, Allison, told me about Papusza, whom she'd read about in Isabel Fonseca's book. I couldn't get rid of her. This poet. This exile. This Gypsy. In order to lose her, I had to write her.

It was, I hope, my most complicated statement about exile. But there's no point in me sitting down to try and make intellectual sense of it. That's for others. It should be emotional. It should be felt. By way of analogy, consider the writer as being disguised as a creek.

Eventually he or she meets other waters. That is the reader, or even the critic. Hopefully it hits a wider world.

Have you had much feedback from women about the book? How did they 'respond' to this story of an 'unusual' woman whose life experience and minority culture background would have been quite different to the average woman's life (in either Western or Eastern Europe back then?)

For whatever reason it seems that women have latched on to this book – and especially women who know what it is like to be marginalised. Perhaps they recognise her in a way. Some are frustrated by Zoli and her seeming lack of action in her middle age – and yet that's part of her attraction too. I can see that Zoli is frustrating as a fictional character … in a way she's meant to be … if you take it from a white European or American perspective, she never seems to fight back. She takes what comes to her. She walks away. She never entirely embraces where she has come from. And yet from a Romani point of view, what she does is extraordinary, and, I hope, true. She forges her own identity. She fights through, not back. And in the end it becomes a personal song of triumph. So much of the Romani experience seems to be captured there, or at least I hope it is.

She becomes someone else, something else, someplace else. She sees the value in the elsewhere but this time the elsewhere is an imaginative place, a written place – and finally it becomes a poem. I tried so hard to code all this in the book. It's strange, now, to confront it as an idea. I wanted Zoli to have an emotional life. I wanted people to believe that – perhaps – one might be able to go down to Northern Italy, today, of all days, and meet her. There she is, walking outside the coffee shop! There she is in that mountainside hut. I wanted that for the reader. To see Zoli as entirely real. And that's been the response. Readers seem to somehow know Zoli.

It's a book about gender, voice, distance, media. A friend of mine said that it wasn't hip, but it was hip-high. It struck him. And I meant for it to deal a blow to the solar plexus.

And yet many other readers thought that Zoli should have a triumphant halo around her at the end. Certainly I didn't want her to become a spectacle of disintegration. There's been enough of that. But

I didn't want to turn her into cliché. I didn't want for her to stand up at the conference in Paris and deliver a blow for Romani rights. No. Her victory was smaller – but no less significant – than that.

It has been noted by some readers that you are fascinated by the idea of the 'Other' or Otherness? Was this always the case – i.e. from your earliest writing – or is the exploration of Otherness something which has become more important to you and your work in recent times?

I'm a middle-class Dubliner now living in New York. I sound halfway between suburbia and silence. But I've tried all my life to value the story of the anonymous other. In this case – for Zoli – I didn't think that enough had been said. Is that arrogant? Maybe it is. Probably it is. But I'd rather die with my heart on my sleeve that end up some-one who patrols quietly around the perimeters. Watch those waters. They're tepid. I'm so sick of divorce stories and suburban triste. And so I thought, Slovakia, Roma, socialism, okay, I'll try that story. I'm not trying to excuse myself. I hear writers, when they're talking about minorities, giving the excuse that they're half this, or an eight that, or that their best friend is this shade of skin colour … as if that allows them the right to own the story.

I don't own any story. It's my job to intrude. And, always, in the back of my mind – whether I'm writing about homeless people in New York subway tunnels, or the gay underworld in the 1970s, or the teenagers caught in the Northern Ireland conflict – I'm aware of what I'm saying, or thinking, that I'm not that, what should I write about it, what right do I have? It's economically arrogant, culturally arrogant, sexually arrogant, socially arrogant. That's not me! That's not my life! But what am I going to do? Write about the pleasant Friday afternoon in 173 Clonkeen Road, Blackrock, County Dublin? Or the very nice chess game I just had with my kids on 86th Street in Manhattan? That's my immediate life, yes, but I'll leave that to a writer more talented than me. So … To be the voice of 'the other'? Fuck, yeah. Absolutely. No better compliment. Or to be a small cata-lyst of that voice? Wonderful! That's where I'm comfortable. That's where I'm best.

Do I claim to be that voice? No. Of course not. I write stories. That's another one of my jobs. I try for them to be good. I want them to be engaging. And on a certain level I want them to be social.

Some might argue that Irish fiction until recent decades was somewhat insular and fixated on themes relating to a rural Ireland that has virtually disappeared – and issues as relating to sex, religion, authority, poverty and the conflicts between different generations etc. It appears that Irish fiction and other media music/film has become more 'international' now – dealing with more 'universal' themes. How do you feel about this?

Fair enough – but then at some stage you go back to your own. *Zoli* is an Irish novel. How can it be anything else? I'm an Irish writer. And yet it must be everything else. I realise that I'm answering by evading, but that's the job of the poet. Then again, I'm not a poet. I'm a contrarian.

People have asked why I didn't write about the Irish Travellers. Well, because I think that story is in the process of being told by others who are more inside than me, more at the centre, with more access. They will, and some already have, told it better than I could.

Did you feel a burden of 'responsibility' in bringing the story/voice of somebody who is now dead but who was also a woman from a 'reviled' group who've been subjected to centuries of stereotype and many of whom have had no literary or public voice to date?

Yes, it was a massive responsibility. I didn't want it to be – or didn't even expect it to be a responsibility. But then I began researching and I was astounded. There were so few stories, so few novels. And they all came out the same. I wanted Zoli to fit in a certain box and yet for her to change that cardboard box utterly.

Early on in the novel I knew that it was the greatest social responsibility that I have had – as a writer – to date. I found that a lot of the scholarship was shoddy, particularly from people on the outside who wanted to impose their ideas on the Roma.

Is this the first book where you have written in the 'persona/voice' of a woman? How did you find that – was it more difficult than writing in the voice of a male narrator or the same?

I've written in a woman's voice before... My first published short story was 'Sisters' in a woman's voice. But this is the first woman I truly know as a character. I am quite convinced that Zoli is alive today and living in Northern Italy, although of course she is not. In this sense, I find her to be my truest character.

The Roma would be one of the largest minorities who have come to settle in Ireland in recent times – many with a view to making a life for themselves in Ireland permanently – was this in the back of your mind when you wrote the book?

It's a good question ... but it had nothing to do with the writing of the novel.

Again ... maybe someday I'll write the story of the Roma who have come to Ireland... I'm amazed that other Irish writers (apart from yourself) haven't had the gumption to do it... Why? I did at one stage flirt with the notion of bringing Zoli to Dublin, but she refused this option. She just wouldn't get on that ferry! I spent about a month writing that section and then, in the end, she tore up her first class ticket!

Did you find it difficult to balance writing somebody's story (albeit fictionalised to a great extent) and the duty of 'informing' people about some of the realities of Roma history and their development as an 'outsider' group?

A great question. I never felt it before. I never felt myself to be 'the uncreated conscience of my race' in any manner or means. I never felt a duty to 'represent' Ireland. But I felt it necessary – and maybe even imperative – to get the story of the Roma at least partway right. I mean, the thing is that I wanted to communicate that the Roma are as internally diverse as any other people. Fiction writing is about being able to hold the essence of contradiction in the palms of your hand. I wanted the story to have wide ripples. The thing is the troughs of silence run very deep. But once you penetrate them, many other voices will emerge.

You lived in a Roma settlement in Slovakia for a number of months?

I stayed in a few settlements, but I didn't live there. I was in Slovakia for two months altogether.

What did you find difficult about this experience and what was the most rewarding aspect of it?

The poverty in certain areas was brutal. Amongst the worst I've ever seen. And the racism was astounding. Then, to have such generosity around, that amazed me. I mean, these people invited me into their homes. They should have been berating me for my silence and igno-rance. They should have been taking up arms against the policemen who spat on them every day. That astounded me. And we would sit in at night and sing songs. I sang Irish ballads. And the kids would lean against me and sometimes go to sleep. Possibly because I sang so badly.

You must have heard some amazing stories while you were living there? Were there any that left a lasting impression on you?

All the stories left an impression on me. I can't remember and sepa-rate them now from the stories I created about Zoli. Hopefully her story contains their stories. I do remember that one day I was in Svinia, in what they call 'the dog eater's camp.' I saw a young boy sitting near a bridge, rolling a cigarette. The bridge was a mess, put together with planks, aluminum siding, rope, tree trunks, sodden cardboard, tires, that sort of stuff. The boy himself looked part of the bridge. He was sprinkling tobacco onto the paper. Then I noticed that he had torn a page from a book in order to roll the cigarette. When he lit the smoke, the paper flared a moment, and he smoked in quick sharp bursts. When he was finished, he tore the remaining pages from the book and stuffed them in the pocket of his jeans. He threw down the cover and it landed at the foot of the bridge. When he walked off towards a ramshackle shed, I strolled across to see what he had just smoked – it was a Slovak translation of the Rumanian writer, Emile Cioran. And I thought, well, that says it all, doesn't it? He had smoked the page.

8

'Writing Back into the Text': New Writing by Irish Travellers

Micheál Ó hAodha

In the recent past it was common to view post-colonialism and Irish culture through an inherited dichotomy of colonised/coloniser (or empowered/disempowered). This was a process which replicated to a large extent the imperialist power structures of old. But what of Ireland's postcolonial configurations with respect to the histories of social groupings once characterised as 'fragmented and episodic' (Gramsci, 1971: 55), Irish Travellers and migrant workers, included. In this essay I hope to provide a very brief overview of recent 'life writing' as produced by Irish Traveller writers, with a particular focus on one more recently produced 'life history' – '*The Turn of the Hand*': *A Memoir from the Irish Margins,* by Mary Warde.[1]

This brief essay also seeks to underscore the importance of re-thinking and inherited discourse or praxis within the Irish (post)-colonial context. Emphasized in the narratives described here is the reality that is the 'radically undecidable nature of the text' in addition to a general re-appraisal of our assumptions with respect to colonial textuality. In narratives such as Mary Warde's, contested ideas of Irish identity and nationhood as relating to both the Traveller and settled communities are played out through a deconstruction of textual authority whereby the discourse is shifted laterally, opening up a dimension beyond the binaries of what might be deemed 'traditional' or contested discourses'. The Irish colonial text is 'strained between representing the other and denying Otherness, giving authority and giving it away, the text becomes both the refuge of colonial ideology and repeated sign of its own ambivalence and incapacities as a discourse' (Graham 2002: 38). The text *is* the margin or limen, that special point of tension which is simultaneously both a border and a crossing point. In many life histories produced by the representatives of 'marginal' groups such as Travellers, it is where textuality and discourse are in a constant state of tension, the dichotomy between that which exists inside and outside the text. The image of the Traveller in Irish imaginary is both complex and contested. Traveller 'Othering' and the othering of 'outsiders' is redolent of many other aspects of Irish popular tradition and the way in which the Self/Other dichotomy has operated in Ireland with respect to small minorities until very recently.[2] Irish literature has a long history of encompassing various tropes and representative discourses as relating to portrayals of Irish Travellers and the figure of the societal 'outsider' generally.

It is a truism to say that Traveller character or tropes have never been 'at home' in the literature and visual culture of the Irish mainstream. A long-established or quintessential 'outsider', the image of the Traveller has long held a strong appeal for the Irish writers and artists a fascination which is evident in Irish language literature – both oral and written – for centuries but which appears to have reached an apex in Irish English-language writing during the late-1900s in particular. Writers as well-known and diverse as Synge, Yeats, Pádraic Ó Conaire, James Stephens, Liam O'Flaherty, John B. Keane, Bryan MacMahon, Jennifer Johnston and Richard Murphy have employed Traveller characters and Traveller tropes as have modern-day dramatists (Pat Shortt) and playwrights (Marina Carr). In many cases the Traveller image has tended to reflect a long-established or generic image or lore, one which is frequently a mirror-type of the colonial 'stage Irishman'. Various manifestations of this have included the happy-go-lucky vagrant, the criminal, the drunk, the storyteller, the fighter and the outcast.

Ironically, despite their 'marginality' to the narrative in many instances, the representations of Irish Travellers have in common with their European counterparts that their representational paradigm refers to a question that has obsessed the modern nation-state to a large degree, i.e. the question of ethnic or racial identity or affiliation and the question of origins. As Nord suggests, a people whose origins are not easily identifiable form the historical point of view often come to '... stand for the question of origins itself and to be used as a trope to signify beginnings, primal ancestry, and the ultimate secret of individual identity' (Nord, 2006: 30).

The 'Othering' of Irish Travellers has been influenced and energised by a range of discourses, whether fictional oeuvres in both Irish and English, drama, folktales, narratives or other texts, each of which can be said to encompass both hegemonic and counter-hegemonic impulses but which (in the main) constitute a discourse of negative 'othering' regarding the Travelling community. Similar to other traditionally migrant and diaspora peoples, Irish Travellers have however seen the construction and permeation of a wide range of reductionist representations and stereotypes (Hayes, 2004; Bhreathnach, 1998) in relation to their community, many of which have assumed the status of 'fact' within Ireland's collective conscience. Such frequently superficial representations of the Traveller have subsequently assumed a life of their own, a discourse which has subsequently become reified over time, forming itself into what Foucault (1977) defined as a 'regime of truth':

> *Chaque société a son régime de vérité, sa 'politique générale' de la vérité: c'est-à-dire, les types de discours qu'elle accueille et fait fonctionner comme vrais...* (Foucault, 1977: 25)

> Each society has its regime of truth, its 'general politics' of truth: that is, the types of discourse which it accepts and makes function as true... (Foucault cited in *Rabinow*, 1991: 43).

This primarily negative literary confluence traverses the linguistic divide and is evident in both the literature produced in Irish (Gaelic) and Irish literature as written in English. Neither can this tradition of cultural 'Othering' as relating to Travellers and other 'outsider' groups one be divorced from the European literary context where literary or visual representations of Gypsies or Roma frequently oscillate between a vague romanticism and downright hostility. Recent Traveller literature has emerged to challenge the 'fixed' or stereotypical discourses through which Travellers were reproduced culturally and ideologically in the past, however. This new 'canon' of literature is one which seeks to forge a 'place' for Travellers in modern Ireland, one that is no longer confined solely to the societal margins. Autobiographies, 'life histories' and memoirs as produced by Travellers themselves (e.g. Joyce, 1985; Donohue, 1986; Cauley, 2004; Dunne, 2004; Gorman, 2002; Ward: 2010) serve to challenge the 'traditional Western mode of self-representation in historical terms and is redolent of that change in genre and approach that permits a greater diversity in terms of self-representation – multi-voiced texts, life histories and 'testimonies' and newer autobiographical practices as representative of different cultural traditions.

An essential impulse of this literature type is the countering of the 'older' and more stereotypical ways that Travellers were represented in the Irish cultural imaginary until relatively recently. This 'new' literature has a strong autobiographical or semi-autobiographical aspect to it and frequently attempts to bring Travellers in from the margins of public discourse and deconstruct the near-monolith that were nineteenth and twentieth century literary representations of Travellers. Themes which occur strongly in this life writing include the importance of nomadism – or the 'nomadic mindset' as it is now more frequently referred to – within Traveller history and tradition and the pride felt in the ability of a community to survive and thrive on the margins despite poverty and the frequent assignation of pariah status to it. Also highlighted in more recent life writing are such concerns as the necessity for all younger Travellers to have pride in their genealogy and their own community, a re-writing (or a 'writing back into the record' as it were) of the roles which Travellers played in the historical development of Ireland and the struggle for independence, the large and hitherto-neglected role played by Travellers amongst the Irish diaspora and the often-fractious relationship that has defined Traveller-settled relations particularly since the urbanization of

Ireland gathered pace in the early 1970s. One area where a small number of Travellers felt the full rigor of the state was when certain Traveller children were taken away by the agents of the state – the courts or the 'cruelty' (Society for Prevention of Cruelty to Children) and sent to 'industrial schools', borstals and the like. An excellent account of the time two male relatives of Mary's spent in the 'notorious' Letterfrack Industrial School is provided in this volume in addition to some very rare photos from the era in which they were incarcerated there – the 1920s Indeed, the nexus that is Traveller/Settled relationships, particularly in an Ireland which has become culturally diverse but also where the Traveller and the settled communities intersect with one another one a very frequent basis – in sport, work, school, interactions with the social and educational institutions of the state, is one of the primary issues explored in *The Turn of the Hand*:

> We have lived beside each other for centuries on the small island that is called Ireland. We've lived within a stone's throw of one another – within spitting distance – and yet, there's never been as much misunderstanding and lack of communication. The same was true in the past and it's true to a certain extent even today. Because myth forms people's perceptions of one another. It's all they have, the only mirror where they can see the other who might be a stranger to them ... (Warde, 2010: 5-6)

> I'm tracing back now, drawing my way back through the well of the years to where the only history is what is passed down – from gather to cam (father to son). This is oral history now because it's all that we Irish were left with for the many centuries. All that we had. And a Ward family member, a Traveller Ward – he fought at the Battle of Vinegar Hill. He fought in 1798, spilled blood in the place where the blood flowed like rain. And from death and destruction came rebirth – he met a girl named Brigid Keefe. She was a settled girl, one of the many women who were involved in the rebellion and often-forgotten.... And they married in the place which they then called the 'hidden Church'. (Warde, 2010: 2)

A unique aspect of this life history is the research which went into the interface that is the oral and written traditions whereby Mary Warde spent a good deal of time in archives, both church and state-related, tracing family relationships in effort to discern whether the oral tradition with respect to genealogy and family history corresponded with the written record. In the main, her research showed that the two traditions reflected one another in a way that was uncannily accurate. The author provides a detailed family tree based on her researches and demonstrates the manner whereby many Travellers intermarried with 'settled' people in the past, an intermarriage pattern which saw a particular increase (mainly women from the settled community marrying men from the Traveller community) - both before and after the Great Famine. Like the vast majority of Irish families today, historical evidence and documentation relating to family history became much scarcer once one tried to trace back much further than the 1820s. Close linkages between Travellers and settled people could also be observed in relation to emigration and the Irish diaspora who 'took the boat' to Australia, England or America. The 'distinctions' between Traveller and 'settled' weren't maintained to the same degree once people emigrated there were strong linkages between both communities when it came to travelling to the USA by boat or where one person or family would 'sponsor' another in order that they might travel. So too was the case of the USA where many young Traveller women went into 'domestic service' similar to their 'settled' counterparts.

> Pat 'the Mun' went out to America a couple of times. Two of his sisters went out there too. He had an uncle in America who had gone out there when he was a very young man, just a teenager. He went out with a family from just outside Mountbellew, a family of small farmers whom he worked with. They did well in America near upstate New York. He stayed out there with the old man and his who had brought him out. When that farmer got old he gave the younger man some land and as time went on he built a house for him too. Afterwards the uncle 'claimed out' his nieces and nephews and got jobs for them, as was the Irish custom in those days. The extended family and one emigrant helping the next to get set up in their

new life. The girls generally worked as domestics in houses. They worked for Irish and Irish-American families as nurses and what they call 'au-pairs' today. Some of them were in Philadelphia, Chicago and Boston in addition to New York. My grandfather took the boat with two of his sisters, partly to protect them and look after them on that long journey. We who live in the age of the aeroplane and internet find it difficult to imagine what it was like, but in those days a journey by ship was one hell of a journey. We cant even imagine what it was like in those days for Irish people, young people in particular. My grandfather's sister Ellen went out to America on her own before that, she was only a bout 13 at the time and travelled out with another family from Tuam town (settled people) to meet her uncle. She then got work with a family and in turn sent back for my grandfather and her younger sister Margaret. My grandfather was only about twelve years old. He stayed out there until he was about fifteen or sixteen and he worked on the farm. My grandfather was a harum-scarum; he was a bit of a devil. He would got to visit Ellen who was living in Philadelphia with the family she worked for and he would have to be back to work on the Monday, but they mightn't see him for a month. On one occasion he got his wages and met up with a crowd of Irish lads that were coming home and he came home with them. He was seventeen or eighteen then and he stayed around Galway and Tuam for a while. His uncle then sent for his younger sister Jane who was only around 12 so my grandfather decided he'd go back out with her. His uncle sent out the passage for the two of them. So off he went again and back to the farmer he had worked for previously, looking after cattle. (Warde: 2010: 109-110).

The liminal margins of the 'text' present exciting new opportunities for analysis; in particular, they offer places where agency in the form of oral traditions influence the discourse, where the text is de-centred, loosened and re-contextualised and where older 'truths' are challenged:

My bits of research also showed that contrary to what some people might say many Traveller families moved in and out of houses during the course of their lives. There wasn't too many that spent the entire year on the road. They mixed-and-matched instead depending on the weather, the road conditions and the work opportunities. Maybe they would stay the winter in the houses and then once summertime came they would be off travelling. Of course they wouldn't have had the transport which Travellers have today at that time. Many Travellers were lucky if they had a jennet or a donkey and they would use the 'ass and sack' - as it was then called - for their travels. This was a big 'brand bag', a big bag that they would sew the mouth of and then cut one slit in the middle of. They would put this across the donkey's back and put all their goods in it and that's how they travelled with a couple of donkeys. They would have tied the wattles (the rods) for the tent to the donkey and maybe sat a child on top of it. In the summer then, they would camp under the cart, that's if they had a cart. Or else in against the ditch where they would make a shelter. A lot of us would have stayed in sheds and houses too, places that were known as 'cart-houses' or hay-sheds at that time. There was a lot of houses around the country that had been abandoned by 'settled' people who had emigrated and some would spend the night there. Country people would have relied on the Travellers to bring them news or to mend their pots and pans…If the weather was very bad in the winter and the children got sick the women would have gone into the County Home, but this was very rare.

The text begins to operate as a nexus where political resistance and social agency preclude any single meaning. Such a process is in line with the 'new' function of the literary or cultural critic as delineated by Barthes (1977) whereby the focal point is on the reader/audience – those who read/hear and interpret the text, as opposed to those who generate text. '…to mix writings, to counter the ones with the others in such a way as never to rest on any one of them' (Barthes 1977: 146). Texts are placed one against the other in order to challenge and alter the prevailing orders of power. As delineated by Foucault, such a process involves contextualizing the circumstances of narrator and audience and reader, in short everybody who generates and 'receives' the text, whether in oral or written form:

Perhaps it is time to study discourses not only in terms of their expressive value or formal transformations, but according to their modes of existence. The modes of circulation, valorization, attribution, and appropriation of discourses vary with each culture and are modified with each (Foucault 1984b: 117).

Endnotes

1. The phrase 'the turn of the hand' is a reference to the skill with which Mary Warde's relatives including her father Edward Warde worked the metal. Edward Warde who is a central figure in this book was exceptionally-gifted worker in metal and bronze and acknowledged as so by both the Travelling and 'settled' communities. He could work with any metal-type and in addition to all sorts of farm implements and household utensils he carved Crucifixes for churches, candle-holders and 'tilly lamps' during the era when paraffin oil was still in widespread use. The latter, which included a shutter, functioned much as a 'torch' would today and farmers were able to place a candle within it and use it to check on animals which were sick at night or cows and sheep that were about to give birth.

2. This is a dichotomy which is now likely to see significant change given the increasingly multi-cultural nature of present-day Irish society. Ireland has witnessed large-scale immigration within the past fifteen years or so, the majority of immigrants emigrating from eastern Europe and sub-Saharan Africa thus rendering a much less-homogenous society in terms of culture or ethnic affiliation.

References

Bhreathnach, A., 'Travellers and the Print Media: Words and Irish Identity', *Irish Studies Review*, 6, 3 1998

Cauley, W. and Ó hAodha, M. (eds.) (2004). *The Candlelight Painter: The Life and Work of Willy Cauley, Traveller, Painter and Poet*; Dublin: A. and A. Farmar Publishing

Dunne, P. and Ó hAodha, M. (eds.) (2004) *Parley-Poet and Chanter: A Life of Pecker Dunne*; Dublin: A. and A. Farmar Publishing

Foucault. M. 'Vérité et pouvoir', en L'Arc 70 (Aix-en-Provence, 1977), 25.

Gibbons, L. (1996) *Transformations in Irish Culture*, Cork: Cork University Press in association with Field Day

Gorman, B. (2001) *King of the Gypsies* (Bartley Gorman with Peter Walsh) Bury: Milo

Graham, C. 'Liminal Spaces': Post-Colonial Theories and Irish Culture

The Irish Review (Autumn/Winter), 1994, 16, pp. 29-43

Graham, C. and Kirkland, R. (1999) *Ireland and Cultural Theory*, London: Macmillan

Lanters, J. (2010) *The 'Tinkers' in Irish Literature: Unsettled Subjects and the Construction of Difference*, Dublin: Irish Academic Press

Ó hAodha, M. (2007) *Irish Travellers: Representations and Realities*, Dublin: Liffey Press

Ó hAodha, M. (2011) *'Insubordinate Irish': Travellers in the Text*, Manchester: Manchester University Press

Nord, D. E. (2006) *Gypsies and the British Imagination, 1807-1930*, New York: Columbia University Press

Rabinow, P. (ed.) (1991) *The Foucault Reader: An Introduction to Foucault's Thought*, London, Penguin.

Warde, M. (2010) *The Turn of the Hand: A Memoir from the Irish Margins*, Newcastle, UK: Cambridge Scholars Publishing

9.

Gulanyunung Pialla ('Our Talk'): An Australian Aboriginal Review of Irish Travellers

Dr. Dennis Foley

The author identifies as Aboriginal-Irish, my Aboriginal ancestors are the *Gai–mariagal* and the *Wiradjuri*, my Irish ancestors are said to have wintered in Bandon and summered at Dungarvan. In 2011 with the support of my employer, the University of Newcastle, together with the Australian Endeavour Foundation and the generosity of my host, Professor Thomas Cooney and the Dublin Institute of Technology (DIT), I was able to undertake a qualitative study of Travellers in the Republic of Ireland. This is a brief overview and summary of some issues raised in this study involving 150 interviews. The results are not that surprising for those with any contact or knowledge of the Irish Traveller, who in general are a resourceful ethnic minority who suffer many, if not the worst of the social inhibitors by the dominating – assimilating society.

In Australia, Canada, New Zealand, the USA, Hawaii and Japan it is relatively easy to delineate the Indigenous from the coloniser, or the assimilated from the assimilator based primarily on skin colour or facial features, family associations, surnames etc. One of the most enduring myths is that we as a group are 'lazy', 'indolent', 'erratic' and 'roving', who simply 'don't want to work' (Curthoys and Moore, 1995: 2). My time in Ireland revealed similar myths said of Travellers. Konish (2010) urges historians to come to terms with popular racist assumptions about Aboriginal work practices; I found her work also applicable to Travellers in Ireland. The more I researched; the similarities between our differing minority groups became clearer. In Ireland, surprisingly the 'settled' Irish can often determine a Traveller by how they dress, how they live and conclusively by how they talk. The issue of Irish Traveller identity however is becoming more complex in a country that is quickly embracing multiculturalism. Indeed Irish people in general are currently struggling to identify themselves for the 'Irish Paddy' and the 'Irish Cosmopolitan' are fast becoming detached from the reality of what it is to be Irish as the Irish settler reconstructs themselves through a hybrid process of regressive globalisation in an attempt to preserve a cultural concept conserving an 'old Irish spirit' which is possibly lost forever in the reality of the new modern, post-agrarian Ireland (O'Donovan, 2009).

The age old Irish values of community, kinship, sense of humour were perhaps partially devoured if not fatally mauled by the greed of the Celtic tiger; the cosmopolitan and global community of Ireland is now flooded by a tsunami of eastern European workers (Hughes, 2011), not forgetting the African and Asians who have changed the cultural landscape of Ireland forever. Indeed I would add that not only has the 'old Irish spirit' drowned in the cosmopolitan flood, it has fuelled a festering of racist views, primarily toward the Traveller and those who are culturally different to mainstream. Changes in population makeup, recessive globalisation and cosmopolitan multiculturalism in the post modernist society have impacted on the real and perceived cultural values of Ireland (Hughes, 2011; Gillespie, 1998). The resultant mindset has ascribed agency to the 'Irish People' to write history and cultural criticism in the first person, excluding the voice of the Traveller (Comerford, 2003: 267). The impact on the Traveller within Irish culture and the Irish identity is quickly disappearing. The population of Ireland has changed, and as previously mentioned so have its values yet it seems to be ignoring the symptoms of its societal problems, especially toward the Traveller. The United Nations in their first periodic review in October, 2011 put the Irish human rights record under scrutiny in Geneva (Kelly, 2011). The Minister for Justice Alan Shatter defended his government's performance and advised the UN Committee that he was giving serious consideration to conferring ethnic minority status on the Traveller community, yet a number of countries including Pakistan, Afghanistan and Slovakia challenged the Irish government on their track record of human rights towards Travellers (Mac Cormac and Stein, 2011). A dichotomy and social travesty when you consider the criticising countries own record on human rights, or does this action reflect just how bad Ireland is judged within the international community in the way it treats its Indigenous minority?

The answer is not simple; O'Connell's (1996) analysis of Irish society revealed major divisions in class, gender, power, wealth, education, beliefs and values. In fact it has been stated to the author by a leading academic at Trinity College (who wishes to remain anonymous) that when the British occupied the country the Irish were the 'pigs in the parlour', now the Irish bourgeois own the parlour and it's the Irish Traveller and the immigrants who are the new generation of parlour occupants. When this conversation was continued in Aberdeen recently in late 2011 at an international conference with several leading international social scientists including two outstanding Maori academics the view was debated that perhaps Irish society in general has a deficit complex or understanding towards its minorities including Travellers especially when one considers that its education system is monocultural and it has no political will to introduce anti-racist legislation and/or acknowledge the cultural identity of the Travellers (O'Connell, 1996). A conclusion that supports the United Nation's recent concern of the Irish government's track record on human rights towards Travellers despite Minister Shatter's new found consideration to confer ethnic minority status (Mac Cormaic and Stein, 2011). Or is the Irish Middle Class trying to remain tied to their blue-collar roots? As O'Donovan (2009) writes, is the struggle to maintain the identity of the 'Irish Paddy' and the 'Irish Cosmopolitan' in fact an attempt at racial solidarity, creating a perception of a monoculture working class society? If so, this is possibly more about the inability of the 'new' Irish middle class to adjust to their new found wealth and status, the legacy of the Celtic Tiger compounded by social depression as a symptom of the recession. Ignorance and lack of education however as to what is Ireland ensures that the Traveller remains defined as the 'other' and in so doing is stratified at the lower level of the social stratification ladder and remains the outcast.

The end result is a society that fails to acknowledge the ethnic status of its largest minority, and a minority that is Irish. Travellers are not imported, not an invader, they are an indigenous group yet are snubbed by officialdom who fails to acknowledge their ethnic minority status. As one elderly Traveller male advised the author, 'by not giving us ethnic status we don't exist, if we don't exist, then they wipe us from this land. They [the Irish Government] are no different than the English landowners' (September 2011).

The debate over ethnic minority status for Travellers is also difficult to understand or accept when one looks at the biased aggressive attitude of some sections of Irish society and academia. Indeed the debate over ethnicity in Ireland has similarities to an argument by the former Australian Howard government in their then refusing an apology to Aboriginal Australia and likewise successive Irish Governments refusal to recognise the ethnic identity of its own Indigenous minority. The Australian argument was based on a perceived liability, an intangible debt based on the 'what if' principle, if we say sorry then we have to compensate for all the things done wrong against them, why should the current generation pay for the actions done in the past. Are Ireland's lawmakers also worried about an intangible liability if they recognise Travellers as an ethnic minority? Or like former Australian policies of assimilation, is Ireland waiting for the liability to disappear? The smoothing of the dying pillow, in time if we ignore them [Travellers] long enough they will indeed die out. Sorry Ireland, it didn't work in Australia, we came back from extirpation, and I am sure based on what I have experienced, the tenacity and cultural fortitude by some Traveller groups will ensure what remains of Traveller heritage will indeed not disappear in a neoliberal economy and society that is trying its best to ignore them.

Size constraints have limited the depth of this brief paper however it is a summary of research and qualitative interviews made to ensure that it is representative of a broad sample base of the community from Cork to Sligo, and from Galway to Dublin. This paper is meant to be an introduction to an upcoming publication at DIT on my research, an insight into the development of Traveller entrepreneurship in an academic forum, which I hope in future, will be driven by Traveller researchers who will own their academic destiny. This ownership, or foundation, the ontological platform is best stated by one of the author's Indigenous mentors:

> [O]ur Ontology, as I understand it, is the reverential connections between the spiritual realms of operations of the universe and the material operating platform or the physical earth, of the treasured Mother; acting in accord beyond peaceful co-existence. The beyond is, I believe the unalienable tenure of relevance to life, birth, and death that engulfs the spiritual and material Mother in a cyclic pattern of perpetuity (West, 1998: 2).

Professor Japanangka Errol West is speaking of the Australian Aboriginal Ontology which, for Australian Aboriginal academics is their research foundation. When we speak of mother earth, the foundation of Aboriginal beliefs then there is a place to move from or return to. It appears the Travellers ontological space is not clearly defined. Perhaps it was the Traveller's acceptance of Catholicism as the substitution for their traditional beliefs and linkage to land, that ensured their ontological position was displaced within the process of colonianisation, a process that continues today with the current governments assimilation policies in mainstreaming education facilitation, maintaining a program of settler housing projects and the criminalisation of roadside camping as a few examples.

Traveller ontology and opinion appears mixed depending on the representative bodies and/or family groups interviewed. Oral history in some clans is vocal with some poor historical substantiation; others remain tight lipped allocating resources to family survival ensuring the oral history of their clans is not for outsider's interpretation. Research of literature also reflects incompatible opinion (Bhreatnach and Bhreatnach, 2006; MacLaughlin, 1995; McCann, O Siochain and Ruane, 1994).

The All Ireland Traveller Health Study Our Geels 2010 is an important example of seminal research methodology towards Traveller and is a template for research into ethnic minorities for both the Indigenous community and academics from around the world illustrating how the mainstream research community (settler) society and the ethnic (or Indigenous) minority can work together in grounded data gathering. It has been achieved to a degree in Canada, Aotearoa (New Zealand) and other Indigenous groups that are working towards their voice being heard within the academy. 'Our Geels' no doubt is one of many such projects in Ireland; it is mentioned for its positive impact on the author as a 'superior' methodological model to that which is normally driven by non-indigenous anthropologists and sociologists on Aboriginal Australia.

The research undertaken within the forthcoming DIT report often involved open Interviews acting upon opportunities to discuss and interview participants at times in an unstructured way to gain an insight into the world of the Traveller entrepreneurial activity and wider societal understanding and/or interaction. Semi-structured interviews were used in the majority of formal interview scenarios. Whenever possible snowball sampling was applied based on formal introductions similar to two decades of research undertaken developed by the author within Indigenous communities across the globe. No cold calling was used in respect of Travellers as interviewees were introduced to the researcher prior to contact to ensure they were comfortable with an interview following standard protocols ensuring respect is provided to the participant. This was done to ensure Indigenous protocols of respect both in gender and social positioning of males was practised. When a young Traveller woman was interviewed as an example, it was always in the company of a male or a senior woman, likewise when a senior woman was interviewed it was always in the company of another and in a public place. Likewise young males were in groups however senior males were respected as my 'Elder' and cultural 'kinship' respect was given. To my personal joy, the recorded interviews included several independent Traveller entrepreneurs who could be classified as 'transient' or 'nomadic', living in vans on holding sites or in temporary accommodation. They roughly follow travel patterns that have been established by their family for generations, deviating only when modernity places insurmountable hurdles in their way or opportunity recognition establishes new challenges and resources for their family to prosper.

Note the word 'transient' is used as an adjective not as a noun as it is deemed to be derogatory by some as is the word 'Pavee' and 'Tinker'. However, some Travellers do use all three words when describing themselves. In the south Pavee is acceptable to some, in the north and west some objected. In the west, transient is often used when delineating between a settled Traveller and one who still follows a semi-nomadic life or when referring to the ancestors who lived on the lanes and byways and led a transient existence, then the terminology is used in a positive and glowing way. The term 'Tinker' is generally deemed to be a negative stereotype however many used it when talking about their family, especially in a historical context. The word itinerant is not used by the author due to its stereotypical negative association; it's like calling my people a 'boong', or a 'coon'. Interestingly, among Aboriginal people we often call each other 'blackfella' and many other names; it's acceptable within our own circles yet when the non-indigenous refers to us in this way it is not accepted. I mention this as I found word associations, family linkages and kinships ties, reciprocal obligations and many more subtle interacting social actions/practices as standard urban Australian Aboriginal practice. I am not defining Irish Travellers as Aboriginal; however, ethnographically to the outsider, I witnessed a patriarchal system that has remnants of its historical beginnings in ancient clan structures that is reminiscent of my own culture.

In my research I was also fortunate to interview Travellers who were self-employed in enterprises, mostly living in public housing a few were property owners. Interviews were also undertaken with service providers to Travellers, Traveller leaders, Traveller network and community support staff, mainstream (settler) next-door neighbours of Travellers, farmers, publicans, shopkeepers, police officers, media persons, civil servants, bankers, educators (levels one two and three i.e. primary, secondary and tertiary level for the Australian readers) and average Irish citizens, many of whom were opinionated with something to say about 'Travellers'. Often these discussions were divisive based on racial negativity and groundless hatred. It would seem there are persons of disrepute in all groups, ethnic minorities and classes of society; I accept that there are Travellers who do not practice the Ten Commandments. However based on my street experiences, one thing that struck me having experienced poverty at times during my own life is that it is very easy to associate poverty with petty crime. Indeed hunger can force you to be desperate. I witnessed little fortitude by many people or the Irish Government to understand the causation of Irish Traveller poverty; rather I did witness a general attitudinal stereotyping by the settler population demonising the symptoms of Traveller poverty and a general unwillingness by sections of the settled population to consider any remedial action such as culturally acceptable education and health services. In fact whilst I was in Ireland government budget cutbacks ensured any support became almost non-existent.

Interestingly, several settler people who deal with Travellers on a regular basis either in community support or in business refused to talk to me as they 'had no opinions on Travellers'. Perhaps this was done to protect their commercial interests or as outlined by several Traveller representative groups, poor investigative journalism (some under the umbrella of academic research) has in the recent past not been objective and/or entirely honest in depicting Traveller culture. Indeed sensationalism by some members of the media and some academics has created a level of mistrust between Traveller people and researchers. I interviewed several TV people who openly acknowledged they were after sensationalism, not cultural accuracy. Thus building trust between the research participants required time, patience and skill. At the opposite end of the scale (and as previously mentioned), many settled people were vocally opposed to Travellers interaction within Irish society. To illustrate my experiences a popular hotel in Dublin evicted me and reimbursed me for the pint I was drinking when they found out after idle chatter with the Manager that I was researching Travellers. It just goes to show how racism is indeed a negative practice because not only had I not paid for that or the preceding pint; I had also not paid for the superb counter lunch. Often in idle conversation Hotel staff or the like would ask me where I was from, what was I doing in Ireland and this is where you had to be careful when to disclose that you were researching Travellers or not. I have had confirmed lodgings cancelled – evaporating when the 'T' word was mentioned. Yet when I rang just 15 minutes later they still had vacancies thus verify their racial bias. I have been shown the door in a Chemist shop in Sligo, told not to come back to a café in Galway, I have been denied service in Hotels saying we don't want your kind here, I was evicted from a Dublin cab in the pouring rain, and treated like a felon by the Irish Immigration, all because I mentioned I was researching Travellers. I do not regret it for if that's how a professional Australian academic is treated I can begin to understand the racial subjugation that is experienced by Travellers by mainstream Irish society and understand why so many are beginning to hide their cultural backgrounds when they can … its called survival!

Based on my observations and field research, it is safe to say that the Irish Traveller and Australian Aboriginal people seem to have cultural and socioeconomic similarities. One association is a commonality with the mainstream media where minor incidents seem to be front-page news if committed by a Traveller yet go unreported if allegedly committed by a settled person. Unfortunately this negatively impacts on the general public perception, reinforcing stereotypes and negative 'race based' perceptions. However the worse similarity between Traveller and Aboriginal is the shared statistics of short life expectancies, unacceptable levels of diabetes, increasing rates of coronary syndrome and thrombosis including myocardial infarction, preventable diseases, and infant mortality rates at 3.6 times that of the general population, unacceptable high suicide rates, overrepresentation in incarceration, poor education attainment, substance abuse, poor diets/obesity and extremely high levels of unemployment.

Any comparison conclusively reveals that the Irish Traveller and Aboriginal Australia are collectively the poorest, most uneducated, underemployed, socially marginalised groups within their respective countries. Another interesting research finding is the greatest impediment to Traveller enterprise and likewise Australian Aboriginal enterprise; is not the lack of capital, or subsequent working capital required in the lifecycle of the enterprise, and/or business expertise and experience, although the importance of any one factor should not be discounted. The single greatest impediment to business for Aboriginal and Traveller entrepreneurial activity is racism. Racism in Ireland practised by the dominant society towards the Traveller is institutional – overt - covert and accepted as a normal hurdle in the daily life of the Traveller entrepreneur. As in Australia, it is not until racism is physical or exclusionary that it is noticed by the victim as it is so common and indeed expected.

Traveller culture, history, language, song, dance, folk stories and life is rich which should be recognised by all as a national treasure, an asset to tourism and Ireland's collective cultural heritage. Yet Paddy's ignorance deprives future generations. In conclusion not all settled Irish people are racist towards the Traveller, it brought great happiness to my heart after several weeks of negative interviews when a sprightly semi-retired 93 year old farmer over a cup of tea in a regional town told me wonderful stories of his families association with Traveller clans describing them as the 'salt of the earth' in their interaction with his family over several generations. Indeed, in contrast not all Travellers are thieves or con-men. However whilst the dominant society stereotypes, perpetuates negativity ensuring ignorance allowing poverty, then they create the breeding grounds of despair and desperate people.

References

Bhreatnach, C. and Bhreatnach, A. (Eds.) 2006, *Portraying Irish Travellers: Histories and Representations.* Cambridge Scholars Press: Newcastle, UK.

Comerford, R. V. 2003. *Ireland: Inventing the Nation.* New York: Oxford University Press Inc.

Curthoys, A. and C. Moore, 1995, Working for the white people: An historiographic essay on Aboriginal and Torres Strait Islander labour. *Labour History*, Vol. 69:1-29.

Gillespie,Paul. 1998, Multiple Identities in Ireland and Europe. In *The Expanding Nation: Towards a Multi-Ethnic Ireland.* Ronit Lentin (ed.) Conference at Trinity College Dublin, 22-24 September, 1998. Department of Sociology: Trinity College, Dublin.

Hughes, Gerard. 2011. Free *Movement in the EU: The Case for Ireland.* Study. Freiedrich Ebert Stiftung, Berlin, Germany.

Kelly, Mark. 2011. UN review puts Irish human rights record under scrutiny. *The Irish Times*. October 6. http://www. Irishtimes.com/newspaper/opinion/2011/1006/1224305 Accessed 11 October, 2011.

Konishi, Shino. 2010, Idle men: the eighteenth-century roots of the Indigenous indolence myth. In Frances Peters-Little, Ann Curthpoys and Peter Docker (Eds.) *Passionate Histories: Myth, Memory and Indigenous Australia*, The Australian National University E Press: Canberra.

Mac Cormaic, Ruadhan and Michelle. Stein, 2011, State Questioned on Human Rights. *The Irish Times*. October 6. http://www. Irishtimes.com/newspaper/breaking/2011/1006/breaking Accessed 11 October 2011.

MacLaughlin, Jim. 1995, *Travellers and Ireland: Whose Country, Whose History*. Cork University Press: cork.

McCann, May. Seamas. O Siochain, and Joseph. Ruane, (Eds.) 1994, *Irish Travellers: Culture & Ethnicity*. The Institute of Irish Studies, The Queens University of Belfast: Belfast.

O'Connell, John. 1996, Ethnicity and Irish Travellers, in *Irish Travellers: Culture & Ethnicity*. May McCann, Seamas O Siochain and Joseph Ruane (eds). Institute of Irish Studies, The Queens University of Belfast for The Anthropological Association of Ireland: Belfast. pp.: 110-129.

O'Donovan, F. 2009. *Socheolas: Limerick Student Journal of Sociology*. Vol. 2(1): 95-115.

School of Public Health 2010, The All Ireland Traveller Health Study Our Geels. University College Dublin.

West, Japanangka Errol. 1998, Speaking Towards an Aboriginal Philosophy. Indigenous Philosophy Conference, Linga Longa April 1998.

The Chharas and Their Drama of Liberation

Dakxin Bajrange Chhara and Brian Coates

Introduction

In the history of British India, many scholars have been attracted to the history of India's de-notified tribes, often branded 'Criminal Tribes'. Schwarz (2010) explores the historical account of British regulations in India; in 1772, under Warren Hastings he notes that 'article 35 of general regulations allowed for the punishment of offender's family and village on the argument that Indian criminals were such, by profession and hereditary, and members of like-minded fraternities' (2010: 4). He goes further into an account of the formation of criminal tribes finding that 'Regulation XII of 1793 was directed towards groups of criminals by profession and wandering gangs whose whole families were either put to work on roads or otherwise were forced to settle down' (ibid). He argues that these regulations inspired British officials to compile lists of wandering tribes who could be useful to the State and to introduce legislation to control their movements and to enable forced sedentarization.

During the mid-nineteenth century, the British began to widen their tax net to include the remote areas of India. The State started to tax Adivasi tribal communities, who lived in inaccessible forests and mountains under the land revenue system,. The revenue system disrupted several social practices of the tribal people and brought repressive intermediaries such as tax collectors and Jagirdars (landlords) to collect revenue on behalf of the British regime. Colonial economic policies gave rise to many conflicts between tribal people and the British state. The repressive system and conflicts also inspired tribal communities to take an active part in the 1857 rebellion against the British (Chauhan, 2009: 74-75). In the late nineteenth and early twentieth centuries, as the colonial regime faced increasingly serious resistance and revolt from various sections of Indian society, socio-biological theories, such as Francis Galton's theory of eugenics, influenced a range of theorists all over the world. The theory of eugenics suggested that an inclination to commit crime was a hereditary trait and could be controlled by re-engineering society on a biological, rather than a political basis (Friedman, 2011). Within eugenic theory, there was a strong school of thought put forward by criminologists and scientists, which held that crime was inherited over generations in a family through the genes of a parent or ancestor (TAG Report, 2006: 54).

Many leading public figures including John Maynard Keynes, Winston Churchill and Arthur Balfour, believed in eugenics. This added to the reasons adduced by the British administration for classifying a section of the people in India as criminal classes. Additionally, the notion that members of these tribes were born criminals was also a part of the most frequent criminological theories, which dovetailed with the Italian school headed by Cesare Lombroso. His idea of the born criminal, a 'biological throwback', found a ready target in the itinerant tribes, whose unsettled and unconventional ways were little appreciated amongst the educated elites of India (Verma, 2002). In the wake of such theories being believed by scholars and intellectuals in the Britain, the British policy makers, baffled by the indigenous wandering ways of some of the tribes and nomad groups of India, fixed them in the category of hereditary criminals (Marriott and Mukhopadhyay, 2006). This may be a reason for the focus in Victorian England on lower social strata as a means of creating a category of 'lower order species, which might undermine social stability' (Nijhar, 2009: 2), described as 'dangerous' (Nijhar, 2009: 5) classes. It also accounts for the introduction of the Habitual Criminal Act in

1869 in England and the later introduction of the Criminal Tribes Act in 1871 in Imperial India (Nijhar, 2009: 2). Such laws coupled with newly imposed forest laws and revenue policies made many of the nomads destitute, leading them into petty crime for sustenance, which reinforced the idea of hereditary criminal traits. This was one of the 'techniques' (Fanon, 1990; 34) of the colonialists to dominate colonized masses/natives and brand them as suspect people on their own land.

The Criminal Tribes Act (CTA) of 1871 provided the legal mechanism to incarcerate adivasi communities in reformatory settlements. Sher (1965) notes the historical accounts of settlement provisions under the CTA which stated that if any member of a registered criminal tribe who committed a crime under the Indian Penal Code specified in the first schedule, was convicted of the same offence for a second time they would be convicted 7 to 10 years imprisonment. But on the third crime they were sentenced for transportation for life. Strangely, for the same offence non-criminal tribe members were imprisoned for just 3 to 6 months or even set free. 'Therefore, the Criminal Tribes Act was completely an act of genocide on the criminal tribes of India' (Sher, 1965: 247). The CTA also instituted various forms of spatial control and restrictions. Criminal Tribes' members had to report to the local police station or to the village headman for roll-call, called *hazri*, to prove their presence in the specified area. Sometimes, the time for reporting was from 11.00 pm to 3.00 am. Criminal tribe members had to come for *hazri* (roll-call) three times a day and this rule went on for 10 to 15 years. These awkward timings, year after year, generated frustration among criminal tribe members as they 'compelled some people to sleep at the police station and led to some deaths due to excessive cold' (Sher, 1965: 246). He also notes that due to this inhuman legal treatment, innocent people sometimes actually became criminals. This regulation also increased the sexual exploitation of so-called criminal tribe women by village headmen or local police authorities. The settlements were meant to reform criminal tribe members and the administration of settlements was given to a Christian Missionary organization, the Salvation Army, which profited from the enterprise. They paid low wages to criminal tribe members for their extremely hard work (Sher, 1965: 253). Vishvanathan (2009) ironically states that, 'The criminalization of tribes was a great achievement of law which was the invention of bonded labour' (p. 65). Sher (1965) asserts that according to the Bombay Enquiry Committee of 1939, the Christian missionaries began to convert young girls and send them to distant places without the knowledge of their parents or guardians. It seems, at every level, the colonial regime wanted to crush potential threats to their rule, or those who resisted them during the colonial period.

Figure 1 (Trivedi, 1931)

The colonial regime's inability to understand Indian communities led them to look upon wandering tribes as criminals. Schwarz (2010) observes that these were people who appeared by their nature to wander beyond the boundaries of settled civil society: sanyasis, sadhus, fakirs, dacoits, goondas, thugs, pastoralists, herder and entertainers. Entertainers, who were nomads in nature and traditional performers by profession, were also placed in confinement. They became suspicious people for the police, placing them in an uneasy relation to authority which resulted in an alarmingly high rate of incarceration. Laddoben, an 85-year old Chhara woman living in Ahmedabad, in an interview with one of the authors (Dakxin Bajrange, Chharanagar, Ahmedabad, India on 17 April 2011) recalled how nomadic communities used to be entertainers in the state of Maharashtra, including the Kanjar tribe and they performed songs and dance on the streets but *patel* (policeman) arrested them and put them into settlements. The picture below is of the open camp-life in the Bhavnagar district of the Gujarat state where Adodiyas (Chharas) were kept under police surveillance.

These settlements were highly fenced areas intended to keep tribespeople inside, with round-the-clock security. Males were not allowed to go outside and females could go only to purchase vegetables or items of daily use from a nearby market on short term licence. They did not know of any reason why the police put them in incarceration in this way. There were hard punishments if a person ran away from the settlement. In the documentary film Actors are born here (2008) Dadi, a woman from the Kanjar tribe from the state of Maharashtra described how they used to be street entertainers and sung songs such as Zhumka Gira Re, Bareli Ke Bazzar main… (An ear ring fallen, in the market of Bareli…) and people used to give them grains so that they could eat something. But once they were arrested by police without any charges and put in settlements, their lives became worse (*Actors Are Born Here*, 2008). The law not only restricted their movement to certain areas but made them vulnerable to all sorts of brutality. The arrests of street entertainer communities could be a result of section 26 of the CTA:

Any eunuch so registered who appears, dressed or ornamented like a woman, in a public street or place, or any other place,
with the intention of being seen from a public street or place,
or who dances or plays music, or takes part in any exhibition,
in a public street or place or for a hire in private house may
be arrested without warrant and shall be punished with imprisonment of either description for a term which may extend
to two years, or with fine or with both (TAG Report, 2006,
p. 227).

The above section of the CTA illustrates how the colonial administration marginalised the traditional arts and talents of nomadic
communities and categorised the performers and artists as criminals.
Under section 26 of the CTA, children were separated from their
parents to avoid hereditary crime. These provisions increased crime
among notified members as they hurt children and parents both,
emotionally and psychologically, and their reform after these experiences was almost impossible (Sher, 1965: 248). Between 1871 and
1924, amendments to the CTA tended to emphasise the more oppressive provisions of the Act. The police, judiciary and village headmen got more power to control notified tribes. The last amendment
to the CTA in 1924 increased the power of village headmen. Their
tainted history as nomads, forced sedentarization and social stigmatization, gradually reduced them to a level of extreme disadvantage,
while making them compete for employment and education with
other marginalized groups.

According to documents in the India office section at the British
Library, the Bill to repeal the CTA of 1924 was introduced in the
Legislative Assembly on 6 February 1947 by Venkatasubba Reddiar.
To repeal the CTA, the statement of objections and reasons issued by
Reddiar and others were as follows:

The Criminal Tribes Act, 1924 is oppressive and inhuman.
Instead of improving the moral of the backward communities; it has the tendency to make them deteriorate mentally
and morally. The Act is a blot in the statute book and should
not be allowed to stand in it anymore (Reddiar et al., 1947).

The Bill was aimed to be effective immediately in the whole of British India. But sadly, nothing happened in this regard and the Act continued in place for years, even after independence. After independence, India was so disturbed due to the bloodshed of partition between India and Pakistan, that decisions were delayed in relation to the CTA's abolition. Sher (1965) explores the Government of India's appointment of The Criminal Tribes Act Enquiry Committee in 1949-50 to decide whether the Act should be repealed or not. The independent government took many years to consider whether members of so-called criminal tribes should be released. The Enquiry Committee members toured all over India for consultation with activists, policemen, community members, etc. They recommended that CTA was unconstitutional in free India and that all the people under this act must be freed immediately (Sher, 1965: 264). However, it took a long time to free the innocent inhabitants of the settlements. After five years and seventeen days of independence, the Government of India repealed the CTA on 31 August 1952 with the Criminal Tribes Laws (Repeal) Act, 1952 (Sher, 1965; 264). People of ex-criminal tribes were categorised as De-notified Tribes (DNT). In Hindi they were named *Vimukta Jatis* (Especially-free communities). However, there is an argument that this marginalized section of Indian society has been neglected within Indian politics and left without constitutional safeguards or development policies. People who fought hard against the colonial invasion for their natural resources like forests, rivers, mountains, were once again made to disappear into the forests, mountains and margins of villages. The Act was repealed but the stigma of 'born criminals' remained and DNT communities continued to be subject to repressive state policies.

After independence, de-notified tribes became, arguably, an 'indistinct mass' (Fanon, 1990: 34). for elite politicians and instead of rehabilitation or welfare policies for de-notified tribes, the independent government of India replaced the CTA with the Habitual Offenders Act (HOA) in 1959. The ex-criminal tribes again came under state scrutiny and suspicion, now with another name, habitual offenders. Due to their tainted history as Criminal tribes they again became scapegoats for the police. The enactment of the HOA empowered the police to investigate habitual offenders without warrant which resulted in abduction, interrogation, illegal detention, custodial deaths and false arrests of de-notified tribespeople. Devy (2006) studied this de-notification and how it was followed by the substitution of a series of Acts, the most important being entitled the Habitual Offenders Act (HOA). De-notification should have ended the vulnerability of DNTs caused by the CTA but instead, HOA preserved some provisions of the former CTA, 'except the premise implicit in it that an entire community could be born criminal' (Devy, 2006; 22). HOA handed power to the police to investigate habitual offenders without warrant and ex-criminal tribes became soft targets for the police. After reviewing India's 15th – 19th periodic reports, on 9 March 2007, The UN's Committee for the Elimination of Racial Discrimination directed India to repeal the HOA and to rehabilitate the de-notified tribes (Mohapatra, 2007). After many presentations by the Gujarat based group, the De-notified and Nomadic Tribes Right Action Group (DNT-RAG) in the National Human Rights Commission of India and despite the commission issuing orders to the state governments to repeal HOA 1959 immediately, this act prevails in most of the states in India leading to the suffering of marginalised communities, whom Devy (2006) describes as, 'invisible people … on the run for decades, halted for a while …(they) looked up to us with some hope' (31). Devy (2006) speaks of his meeting with a member of the eunuch community (included in CTA), who said to him: 'Sir, I have heard it is said that India is now a free country with her own laws. Is it true?' Devy comments, 'This is the question in the mind of every Indian nomad, called a thief' (p. 35).

The Chhara Tribe

The Chhara tribe exemplifies the points made above. It was nomadic and notified as a Criminal Tribe in the CTA. The Chharas are known as Sansis in Delhi, Punjab and Rajasthan, Kanjar and Kanjarbhat in Maharashtra, and Adodiyas in Bhavnagar district of Gujarat. Chharas live in a place called Chharanagar in the suburb area of Ahmedabad city in the state of Gujarat which is in the western part of India. The population is approximately twenty thousand, there is almost 90 per cent primary education and in every family there are graduates

Figure 2: The Picture of Chharanagar where the Chhara tribe lives (Budhan Theatre, 2010)

but due to the stigma of being an ex-criminal tribe member, very few find jobs. Because of this, many Chhara youth aspire to become lawyers, since law, as an independent business is a self-sufficient occupation. This also helps the educated people of the Chhara tribe to live a non-discriminatory life. As one Chhara lawyer put it, 'I felt that if they are going to keep calling us thieves I might as well learn what the law is' (Friedman, 2010). There are more than 170 advocates in the community. However, almost 60 to 70 per cent people brew liquor for their livelihood in the community; liquor is illegal in the dry state of Gujarat. Around 20 per cent earn their livelihood by committing petty crimes. It does not matter in this work if they belong to an ex-criminal tribe. This may be a reason why Chharanagar is an infamous area of the city which most non-residents are afraid to visit. The area where the Chharas live is stigmatised and creates a negative mindset within mainstream society. Most people do petty jobs to educate and feed their children. After independence, in the absence of any policy framed by the government for their socio-economic alleviation and acceptance by mainstream society, the Chharas continue to live a stigmatized existence even after several decades of being de-notified. They have no option but to revert to thieving or brewing illicit liquor. Brewing illicit liquor, known as Daru, was a traditional art but in absence of any respectable livelihood after independence, became a profession of the community. Until the 1970s, almost all the people of the Chhara community were engaged in thieving or brewing illicit liquor but during the 1980s, people started sending their children to the schools because they did not want them to follow the same work for their livelihood. Instead, they wanted their children to secure good jobs, via education and to live a respectable life. The writer and playwright Dakxin Bajrange recalls:

> ...following my grandfather, my father also used to be a thief but he never wanted me to follow his profession; instead, he gave me and my siblings the best possible education for our future. During the 1980s, every parent wanted this change in for the next generation.

This is a unique and significance element of transformation through education in the Chhara tribe's history.

Traditionally, Chharas used to be traditional entertainers, such as street singers and dancers. However, for the colonial administration, these street performers were always under surveillance; the authorities believed that the women of the Kanjar tribe (Chhara) entered into the town or village in parties, sang and danced to gather information which they then passed on to their males so that they could plan a robbery (Gunthorpe, 1882; 84). In contrast, Dadi, a Kanjar (Chhara) woman stated in the documentary film *Acting like a Thief* (2009) that they were nomads and for livelihood they danced by putting a pot on their head and sword in the hand and in return people gave them grains. In this honest occupation, they could feed their families. Gunthorpe's somewhat imaginative observation may have led to the Kanjar tribe's notification as a Criminal Tribe. Even after independence, their colourful traditional dance attracted many mainstream people and scholars: Ragini Devi, a renowned Indian classical dancer from the United States was attracted by the Chhara women's traditional folk dance talent while on her visit to Ahmedabad city during the 1960s. She invited Chhara women to put on a dance performance in town and soon after the show finished, the headman of the community asked for a certificate of performance to show to the local police, as it was already sunset and they were told by police to go back to their camp before sundown (Devi, 1972; 19). Even after independence, Chharas had to prove their presence to the local police station because they were members of ex-criminal tribes.

In the section above, I have discussed historical accounts of India's nomadic tribes and the colonial imagination/politics behind their definition as criminal tribes under the Criminal Tribes Act. I have also talked about the so-called reformatory settlements where they were kept as bonded labourers in the name of rehabilitation and were exploited physically, emotionally and economically. I have also fleshed out a brief history of the Chhara tribe as, historically, an entertainer community and its current social and political status as a criminal tribe which was imposed by the history. Another chapter remains to be told: the way in which the Chhara people joined with the Indian social theatre movement and used their traditional skills and theatre arts to overcome historical stigma; the story of the Budhan theatre movement which the Chharas originated shows how theatre can act as a vital force in the liberation of oppressed communities. This will entail a short history of modern theatre in India in order to place the Budhan movement in a social theatre context.

Liberation Drama

During the eighteenth century, there were many nomadic communities in India which used to travel from one place to another to entertain people. For example, Nats for acrobats, Kanjars for singing and dance, Nayak for Bhavai (Folk Theatre), Charans for religious singing, Snake Charmers for snake shows, Kalandars for monkey shows, etc. They lived a nomadic life and carried their cultures and traditions wherever they travelled.

In most of the country the professional mummers who were nomads would travel in the village, like the potters or the weavers, form a caste on their own, variously named Bhands, Nakals and Mirasia. They were itinerant players who visited the houses of the peasants on marriage, birth, and festival, regaling the audience with jokes and songs and recitals for which they were paid in kind, but kept at an orthodox distance, being regarded more or less as untouchables (Anand, 1950: 13).

Srampickal (1994) also mentions that nomadic people carry with them, their oral traditions and culture, and share a cultural heritage, described variously as folk culture. Entertainer tribes were the only source of entertainment for rural audiences and they always welcomed them.

> Some tribes had greater talents than the others in representations of scenes and could stir up emotions in the audience as well, rouse in them love and war, or make them laugh. In the interplay between the actors and the audience, the theatre was born (Anand, 1950: 19).

In India, Calcutta was the first city which was ruled by the British where the enactment of the Permanent Settlement Act in 1795 created a new class of absentee landlord popularly known as the Bhadra log. (Srampickal, 1994). The British imported writers and producers to produce British classical plays in India. Indians, educated in Western pedagogy, began to produce and write English plays. The purpose of promoting English culture was 'to create a class of people who would be Indian in blood and colour but English in taste, opinions, values and intellect' (Macaulay, 1945). This was a planned act by the colonial regime to invade Indian culture and impose their language and theatre culture. Only *Bhadra log* (elite people) were allowed to see theatre. *Bhadra log* means those people who were English speaking Indians and were under the influence of British culture. This cultural invasion was unbearable for Calcutta-based writers and, in 1833, Bengali theatre was founded in the house of Nabin Chandra Basu with the performance of *Neel-darpana*, written by Dinbandhu Mitra in 1833 based on socio-political realities and struggles. People found new expression in the play. The play was highly successful and welcomed by the common men. Following these kinds of patriotic plays, in 1876, the Great National Theatre produced the play titled *Gajadananda O Yubaraj* (Gaja and the Prince) and performed it on 19 February in the same year (Bharucha, 1983: 21-22). He explores how the play criticized Bengali lawyer Jagadananda Ray who had invited the Prince of Wales to visit his house and meet his family members in Calcutta. A stir among Bengali intellectuals was that Jagadananda permitted the Prince to see ladies in his house who welcomed him in an Indian traditional way. Culturally, this was intolerable in the, then, Bengal and the Prince's visit was mercilessly criticized in the Great National Theatre production. It was obvious that the British administration of India could not tolerate satires about the Prince of Wales and soon after first performance, the then viceroy, Lord Northbrook issued an ordinance on February 29, 1976 to authorize the Bengal government to 'prohibit certain dramatic performances which are scandalous, defamatory, seditious, obscene or otherwise prejudicial to the public interest' (Bharucha, 1983: 23). However, theatre was so effective that the regime had to introduce the Dramatic Control Act in India. It was the first non-violent cultural resistance against the British regime who were politically threatened by the effects of performance art in India.

Post-colonialism and the Theatre of the Street

The first political theatre movement during the 1940s was not inspired by the independence movement but rather by Marxist ideology. Theatre became a nationwide movement with the foundation of the Indian People's Theatre Association (IPTA) in 1942 which was the cultural wing of the Communist Party of India (Srampickal, 1994). The model of the IPTA was folk theatre but IPTA members faced many problems in working with rural folk forms, as they were ignorant about the condition of life in the villages and also they did not know the languages spoken in rural areas (Bharucha, 1983). Meanwhile, Bengal faced terrible famine which was a result of negligence on the part of the ruling class in which 3 million people died. Based on the famine, Bijon Bhattacharya, founder of IPTA, wrote the play *Nabanna* (New Harvest) in 1944 which became a milestone of Indian socio-political theatre, which Bharucha (1983) describes as being 'radical in form and content, terrifyingly honest in its depiction of suffering, and daringly innovative in its use of language and stagecraft' (p. 44). Unfortunately, IPTA could not sustain itself long and was disbanded after Independence in 1947. It also split from the communists due to political differences and turned into small units nationwide. The tradition of IPTA was carried forward by some of its key members and well known theatre practitioners like Habib Tanveer, Sarveshwar Dayal Saxena, Tripurari Sharma and Badal Sircar who later began to develop community theatres (Srampickal, 1994).

During the 1950s to 1970s, IPTA members used street theatre to raise consciousness among people for socio-political issues. Badal Sircar called this theatre form 'third theatre' to differentiate it from westernized proscenium theatre and folk theatre, but drawing from both' (Srampickal, 1994: 105) and all over India this form was considered the 'epitome of conscientious and experimental theatre' (Srampickal, 1994: 105). The street theatre form was one of the easiest and the most powerful theatre forms to broadcast the voice of the common citizen's social and political issues. It is a theatre form which is 'inexpensive, flexible, portable, yet imaginative, challenging the aesthetic notions and social sense of the audience' (Srampickal, 1994: 109-110). Normally, street theatre performances happen in a circle which Southern (1965) argues was the original and natural shape of theatre. A circle allows the audience to feel that the performer or performance is not different from them, that both are on the same level. Srampickal (1994) states that, in India, which is a diverse country, and where there are hundreds of languages and dialects and a high degree of illiteracy, street theatre is 'versatile and adaptable, cheap and mobile and has tremendous potential' (101) and has become a voice of the common people.

During the 1960s-70s, theatre activists felt that workshops were too short of communities and had an inadequate follow up and that 'the villagers initial enthusiasm soon runs dry and conscientization remains only skin-deep' (Srampickal, 1994: 51). A good solution for this was the Social Action Groups (SAGs) founded by young people in the villages. The SAG plays were 'the simplest, short, open-ended pieces, performed in villages and usually addressing topical and local areas of concerns' (Srampickal and Boon, 1998: 137). Theatre was made in villages with the help of peasants who performed shows on a regular basis. These groups accepted theatre as a larger organizational process of development for the people and they involved communities directly in this process for social and political change (Srampickal, 1994: 51).

IPTA member, Habib Tanveer developed SAG theatre with the tribes of Chhattisgarh, who could not read or write. He named his community theatre 'Naya Theatre' (New Theatre). Naya Theatre began a new trend in the commercial theatre which was performed by non-trained traditional peasant actors. Due to Habib Tanveer, peasant actors also got space on mainstream stages as well in rural Indian performing platforms. These people followed Freire and Boal's two dimensions of action and reflection theories in which peasants (the oppressed) come into a dialogical process with their oppressors, those whom they traditionally thought of as superior; the question is raised of how to find a voice to break the vicious circle of oppression (Freire, 2005: 65-66). Through action and reflection, a dialogue was initiated that engaged community people in 'participation, democratic decentralization and collective management' (Srampickal, 1994: 165) of theatre processes which led them towards liberation. In this way, the entire process became one of education and an essential element in the act of consciousness raising of actors and spectators. There were many issues related to SAGs in the villages including funding, factions within a village, the quality of production, its entertainment quality, violence from landlords or political goons and the livelihood issue of low caste actors in the upper caste and landlord dominant society. Despite all these issues, SAGs were very much active till the 1980s. This grassroots movement created enormous energy among peasants to speak, perform and have open discussion about their social and political problems (Srampickal and Boon, 1998: 137).

The journey of community theatre, in a larger sense, began in 1998. Tribal activist and literary critique Ganesh Devy and Bengali writer Mahasveta Devi came to Chharanagar. They started a small community library with the help of the community's youth. Meanwhile, a judgement from the Calcutta High Court about the killing of Budhan Sabar appeared in the quarterly magazine called *Budhan*. Budhan was a person who belonged to the Sabar de-notified tribe of the West Bengal and was brutally beaten up by West Bengal police and then sent to judicial custody, where he died due to severe injuries in the head and chest (Devi, 1998: 69). The judgement came that

Budhan Sabar had been brutally beaten up in police custody and that this beating was the cause of his death. The police officers involved were suspended and compensation was awarded to the widow of Budhan Sabar. (ibid). This judgement was remarkable for the de-notified tribes in sustaining their faith in the Indian judiciary. The founder of Budhan Theatre, Dr. Devy, suggested that the Chhara youths prepare a play based on the judgement. The community youth came together in the small library and started rehearsals. They adopted the street theatre form, which they had learned during the making of previous plays. From the community group, Dakxin Bajrange was assigned to write the play. Budhan's brutal killing and the community's daily encounter with the legal system and judiciary emerged from similar circumstances. For Dakxin, the writing out of the incidents related to Budhan Sabar was similar to writing daily notes of his observations and of the discrimination suffered by his parents. Dakxin recalls that the Budhan group were not financially sound and needed to arrange for the money, props, lights, costumes, make-up and space which were required for the play, that the group only had their bodies and voices to express Budhan's killing and their daily encounter with the legal system and the judiciary. Grotowski (1968) explained the very nature of poor theatre form, that the reception of poverty in theatre, uncovered all that is not indispensable to it, exposed to us not only the backbone of the medium, but also the deep richness of the art form (p. 21). Unknowingly, we were following Grotowskian (1968) idea of the poor theatre against 'synthetic theatre' which includes 'literature, sculpture, painting, architecture, lighting, and acting (under the direction of a metteur-en-scene)' which he calls 'nonsense' (19). He suggests avoiding any 'bag of tricks' and the use of techniques of the 'trance' during performance, by 'ripening' of the actor, which is expressed by a tension towards the extreme, by a complete 'stripping' down, by laying bare of one's own intimacy (Grotowski, 1968: 16). He asserts:

Can the theatre exist without costumes and sets? Yes, it can.
Can it exist without music to accompany the plot? Yes.
Can it exist without lighting effects? Of course.
And without a text? Yes. The history of the theatre conforms this.
But without Actor, it doesn't. It can't (32).

They had only actors and their bodies to express their historical stigmatization – a situation which had caused Budhan's death. Along with community people and many eminent people around the world, Ganesh Devy witnessed the first performance of the play *Budhan* on 31 August 1998 when the first International Convention of De-Notified and Nomadic tribes was organised at Chharanagar. In an interview in the documentary film titled *Actors Are Born Here* (2008), Devy stated about the play *Budhan*:

> I believe that it was not an enjoyable play or it was not the play to perform on the stage, in fact, I don't believe that it was the play at all. I think the play was associated with the life experience of the community and slowly, it was getting the voice and that voice had dramatic form.

He further explained that in the first performance of *Budhan*:

> There was hardly anybody in the audience who did not feel profoundly moved to see the Chhara youths enacting the entire Budhan Sabar case, with what passion, with what easy do they act, these Chhara boys and girls! (Devy, 2006: 26).

The Chhara youth got the medium to express their socio-political issues, thoughts; the theatrical events acted as a non-violent weapon in the struggle to resist the state and to ask for their constitutional rights; constitutional rights such as freedom of movement, social, political and economic citizenship, dignity and security of their human rights. Accustomed to being imprisoned, beaten, extorted and humiliated over the decades, a cumulative anger has always burned within the Chharas (Malekar, 2009). Punished once by the past, and twice by the people who unkindly keep in mind their history, Chhara youth are to a great extent looking for a path to break through the inhuman circle of a criminalized identity.

The play became more significant when at the end of it Chhara actors asked the audience thrice in a chorus, 'are we second class citizens?' and then they asserted their appeal to their audiences, 'we want respect' (Bajrange, 2010: 30). Devy (2006) notes:

> *Budhan* had become a myth and symbol of India's vast community of vulnerable and victimised. A man, a name, and a

108

symbol: Budhan. So do myths spring up and grow. And so do they carry within them such pain! (p. 27).

References

Acting Like a Thief, 2007. Documentary film. Directed by Shashwati Talukdar and Kerim Friedman, USA: Nine and half productions.

Actors Are Born Here, 2008. Documentary film. Directed by Dakxin Bajrange. India: Information Department of Government of Gujarat.

Agency, 2011. Budhan Theatre to offer two IGNOU-recognised courses. [online]. [Accessed on 2nd Aug. 2011]. Available from: http://www.dnaindia.com/india/report_budhan-theatre-to-offer-two-ignou-recognised-courses_1546654.

Aiyappan, A. 1948. *Report on the Socio-Economic Conditions of the Aboriginal Tribes of the Province of Madras*. Madras: Government Press.

Anand, M.R. 1950. *Indian Theatre*, London: Dennis Dobson Ltd.

Bajrange, D. 2010. *Budhan*. India: Bhasha Research and Publication Centre.

Budhan Theatre. 2010. *Photos Album of Budhan Theatre*. Ahmedabad: Budhan Library.

Bharucha, R. 1983. *Rehearsals of Revolutions*. Honolulu: University of Hawaii Press.

Bharucha, R. 1993, *Theatre and the World Performance and the Politics of Culture*. London and New York: Routledge.

Brook, P. 1968, *The Empty Space*. England: Penguin.

Chauhan V. 2009, 'From protest to movement: Adivasi Communites in History, Society and Literature'. In: S. Chew, F. Becket, S. Durrant, L. Hunter, J. McLeod, S. Murray, B. Nicholls, J. Plastow, and D. Richards. eds. *Moving Worlds, CHOTRO, Adivasis Voices and Stories*. Leeds: University of Leeds.

D'Souza, D. 1998. What A Fall Was This. [Online] Rediff on the net. [Accessed on 23 July 2011] Available from: http://www.rediff.com/news/1999/may/05dilip.htm.

Da Costa, D. 2010. 'Subjects of Struggle: Theatre as space of political economy', *Third World Quarterly*, 31(4), pp. 617–635.

Dave, D. P. 2011. Chharas teach theatre to IIMA students. [online]. [Accessed on 30 July 2011]. Available from: http://www.ahmed-abadmirror.com/index.aspx?page=article&sectid=3&content id=201102102011021003012174871284341.

Desai. S.D. 2008. Why Rangaparva is no child's play. [Online]. [Acessed on 27 July 2011]. Available from: http://articles.timesofindia.indiatimes. com/2008-10-15/ahmedabad/27897407_1_communal-violence-girls-theatre.

Devi, M. 1998. Justice. Budhan Newslatter of Denotified and Nomadic Tribes Rights Action Group. III(4). pp. 69-71.

Devi, R. 1972. *Dance Dialects of India*. Delhi: Motilal Banarsidass

Devy, G. 2006. *A Nomad Called Thief*. India: Orient Longman.

Faleiro, S. 2005. Thieves who steal a chance in life. [Online]. [Accessed on 31 July 2011]. Available from: http://www.tehelka.com/story_main15. asp?filename=hub112605thieves_who.asp.

Fanon, F. 1990. *The Wretched of the Earth*. Penguin: England.

Freire, P. 2005. *Pedagogy of the Oppressed*. New York and London: Continuum.

Friedman, K. 2010. A look at why Chharanagar is the land of lawyers. DNA [online]. 8 January [Accessed on 18 June 2011]. Available from: http:// fournineandahalf.com/blog/2010/01/08/a-look-at-why-chharanagar-is-the-land-of-lawyers/.

Friedman, K. 2011. 'From Thugs to Victims: Dakxin Bajrange Chhara's Cinema of Justice'. *Visual Anthropology* 24(3), pp. 1-34.

Government of India, 1949. The Constitution of India. [Online]. [Accessed on 11 Aug. 2011] Available from: http://aptel.gov.in/pdf/constitution-of%20india%20acts.pdf.

Grotowski, J. 1968. *Towards a Poor Theatre*. New York: Simon and Shuster.

Gunthorpe, E. J. 1882. *Notes on Criminal Tribes Residing in or Frequenting the Bombay Presidency, Berar and The Central Province*. Bombay: The Times of India Steam Press.

Jadav, J. 2011, 'The community of thief has 36 arts of stealing'. *Gujarat Samachar*. 27 March 2011. p. 10.

Katakam, A. 2008. Dramatic Turn. Frontline magazine [online] [Accessed on 31 July 2011]. Available from: http://www.hindu.com/fline/fl2520/ stories/20081010252008600.htm.

Macauly, L. 1945, *Report of the Delhi Rural Broadcasting Scheme 1944-45, India Office*, London: The Education Secretary in Lord Bentinck's government (1828 to 1848).

Malekar, A. 2009. Budhan Bolta Hai. Info change article [Online]. [Accessed on 31 July 2011]. Available from: http://infochangeindia.org/agenda/multiculturalism-and-intercultural-dialogue/budhan-bolta-hai.html.

Marriott, J., Mukhopadhyay B., and Chatterjee, P. eds. 2006. *Justice, Police, Law and Order, Britain in India, Criminal Tribes' Act, 1871. Act XXVII.* London: British Library, Oriental and India Office Collections.

McConachie, B. A. 2006. 'A Cognitive Approach to Brechtian Theatre', *Theatre Symposium*, (14), pp. 9-24.

Mohapatra, S. 2007. Repeal the Habitual Offenders Act and affectively rehabilitate the denotified tribes, UN to India. [Online]. [Accessed on 20 July 2011]. Available from: http://www.asiantribune.com/index.php?q=node/4972.

Nijhar, P. 2009. *Law and Imperialism: Criminality and Constitution in Colonial India and Victorian England* (Empires in Perspective. London: Pickering and Chatto.

Parekh, B. 2001. *Gandhi: A very short introduction.* UK: Oxford.

Please don't beat me Sir, 2011, Documentary film. Directed by Shashwati Talukdar. USA: Half and Nine Pictures.

Rebello, J. 2008. Art of the 'Criminal Tribe'. [online]. [Accessed on 31 July 2011]. Available from: http://timesofindia.indiatimes.com/home/sunday-toi/Art-of-the-Criminal-Tribe/articleshow/2986932.cms.

Reddiar, V. et al. 1947. Statement of Objects and Reasons, IOR:L/PJ/7/12165, Indian Office. London: Legislative Assembly Department.

Read, B, and L. Iyar. 2002. History, Institutions and Economic Performance: The Legacy of Colonial Land Tenure Systems in India. Available from: http://www.nyu.edu/gsas/dept/politics/seminars/banerjee.pdf

Schwarz, H. 2010. *Constructing the Criminal Tribes in Colonial India - Acting Like a Thief.* UK: Wiley-Blackwell.

Sher, S.S. 1965. *The Sansis of Punjab – A Gypsy and De-notified Tribe of Rajput Origin.* India: Munshiram Manoharlal

Shor, I. and P. Freire. 1987. *A Pedagogy For Liberation – Dialogues on Transforming Education.* Westport, Connecticut and London: Bergin & Garvey.

Southern, R. 1965, *Seven Ages of Theatre*, London and Boston: Faber and Faber.

Srampickal, J, 1994. *Voice to the Voiceless – The Power of People's Theatre in India*, New Delhi: Manohar Publishers and Distributers.

Sureshkumar, C. 2008. Ill-Will in Society. [online]. [Accessed on 27 July 2011]. Available from: http://www.thehindu.com/todays-paper/tp-features/tp-metroplus/article1461097.ece.

TAG Report, 2006. Recommendations of Technical Advisory Group. [online]. [Accessed on 24 of August 2011]. Available from: http://www.scribd.com/doc/933435/TAG-Report.

Trivedi, R.K. 1931. *Bhavnagar State Census – Report Part 1*. Bhavnagar: Government Press.

Vermaq, A. 2002. 'Consolidation of the Raj: Notes from a police station in British India, 1865 to 1928'. In L.A. Knafla, ed. *Crime Gender and Sexuality in Criminal Persecution, Criminal Justice History*. CT: Greenwood Press.

Vishvanathan, S. 2009. 'Listening to the Pterodactyl'. In: S. Chew, F. Becket, S. Durrant, L. Hunter, J. McLeod, S. Murray, B. Nicholls, J. Plastow, and D. Richards. eds. *Moving Worlds, CHOTRO, Adivasis Voices and Stories*. Leeds: University of Leeds.

Part Two

TRAVELLER LIVES AND CULTURE

11.

Introduction

Mary Moriarty

My name is Mary Moriarty. I worked with Clare County Council from 2001 to 2008 as a Liaison officer to help with the programme for the Traveller community in County Clare. There are around 800 Traveller families in County Clare. The main area would be Ennis, with the majority of families living within the co-ordinates of Ennis. Some living in Ennistymon, Shannon but through the programme there are now families that have been accommodated in Milltown Malbay, Coonfuna, Ruan, Corofin, Quin and Six Mile Bridge. There are also quite a lot of families in mainstream housing in Shannon and other parts of the county. The site in Shannon was already up and running with seven families of McDonaghs when I started work in Clare.

One of my main jobs was to bring people together, to come up with ideas that would work towards their own advantage for better accommodation for themselves and their families. Clare had received a lot of bad publicity for not providing accommodation for Travellers. There was a couple of sites built in the 1970s and 80s, a court order had closed one of those down which was Drumcliffe because of anti-social behaviour and overcrowding on the site. The residents of the area took a court order against the council and were successful through the courts. This meant that for three years nothing could be done on the provision of sites for Travellers. Over a seven-year period, the Government and Clare County Council spend €20 million in providing accommodation in County Clare for Travellers. There was one site in Shannon,

Five sites in Ennis, three sites in Ennistymon and the upgrading of another site. Those consisted of group housing, mixed housing and bays. We were very successful in getting mainstream accommodation around Ennis for Travellers. We got some families to move to smaller areas which was are successful. Clare is a county with many different family groupings. You have McDonaghs, Mongans, Joyces, Keanes, McCarthys, Sweeneys, Wards, Sherlocks, Maughans and Dohertys. So with a wide range of different family groups it's hard to get a happy medium. One of the big things was to get Travellers involved in the managing of their own sites and getting involved in the work ethos. Clare County Council employed quite a lot of Travellers during the boom times. They had men working in Ennis Town Council and women working in Clare County Council. There were many training projects through St. Joseph's Training Centre and a very successful after school project. The Community Development Project (CDP) started in Ennis during this time and had Travellers involved. We had the Women's Primary health care programme which trained women to work in their own community. We had Travellers working in schools helping children mix between with their settled pairs.

Attitude is very important when working with Travellers and getting to know the people and that you can build a trust with them. I had many happy days in Clare working with settled and Traveller people. One of the successful projects that I worked with is The Shannon Horse Project which was run in conjunction with Travellers and Settled people.. I travelled with Helen McDonagh to Tralee to visit the horse project there. We had people from the Clare County Council and John McDonagh from Shannon and Auld Frank (John's father). We met the people involved with the horse project including some Travellers on the site adjacent to the project. The project, the first of its kind in County Clare is the result of long negotiation and huge effort between local Travellers and Clare County Council. The result is a 33 acre site accommodating 12 horses and twelve foals for eleven months of the year. There is a sand arena on the site, and stables. The project is very beneficial for young Travellers to work alongside their peers and to care for animals and bringing different family groups together. This is a very good project for young people to get involved in as it is keeping them off the streets and out of trouble and teaching skills to look after animals.

I worked with a lot of different people and made many friends one in particular was Pat Galvin. He has done trojan work for the past 40 years in supporting young and older Travellers. He was involved with the first training centre in 1974, he was involved in soccer and handball and spent many years going to Kilrush to play handball. He was involved with the housing project and travelled to meetings all over Ireland in the 1970s and 80s and transported travellers to these meetings. He even did a voluntary driving instructor for a time. In the early 2000s when we couldn't get a patch of ground to put anyone onto, Pat took seven families onto his front lawn at Ross Ruan. A lot of people thought that the families wouldn't stay 48 hours but they stayed for years until they we eventually accommodated. He made a lot of friends through having them in his front lawn and a lot of the Traveller men helped him on his land. This was a god send when we could not accommodate them anywhere else. Pat is now retired but still involved with offering support and advice to people who call to him.

Below is an article from *The Sun* newspaper, 29 February 2012, which I found very interesting:

Travellers' Kids Lose

Just over half of Traveller children make it to secondary school, according to a report on gypsies in the EU. The report found that laws criminalising the entering on to public or private land, together with limited housing options, has disrupted their schooling. It also shows discrimination against Travellers is widespread. Thomas Hammarberg, Council of Europe Commissioner for Human Rights said: 'In many European countries, Roma and Travellers are still denied basic human rights and suffer blatant racism.'

In spite of Travellers being one of the biggest employers in Ireland over the last 60 years and the amount of money that has been spent, I would ask the question did we get benefit out of it. The answer would be yes and no! As we still have people in their 20s and 30s who cannot read and write even though they have been through the school and training system. Now that our training centres have gone we are in the situation where we have to compete with everyone else for a place in a training project. And due to lack of education we will be tipped at the post by people who are now coming out of school within the wider community with a full education, in spite of the fact that every child is equal according to the Constitution. It will take many decades before we are fully in line, if ever, with our counterparts within the settled community. And this will be down to the interest of Traveller parents to send their children to school on a daily basis and with extra help and support within the school system and the support of the authorities in keeping check and in attendance records and the support of principals and teachers to make sure that none attendance be passed on to the appropriate authorities.

The idea for this book came from memories of people who took part in supporting Travellers and helping Travellers to adapt to a new way of live in changing times. Having worked through the years with Travellers I have seen many changes, some good and some not so good. A lot of sadness and a lot of happiness. It is very important that we should never forget the people who struggle and live at the edge of our town throughout Ireland and abroad.

I asked a lot of organisations and individuals for their views to take part in this book in the last 18 months; a lot did come back to us and a lot didn't. This could be due to a number of reasons such as time constraints and the pressure of daily life, but I am most grateful to those who did respond. I have complied many of these works into the following section of the book.

I would like to say thanks to all the people who did respond and a special thanks to my daughter-in-law Ashling for all her hard work in proof reading and typing, and to my daughter Aaron for all her help and support. Also to Nicole and Siobhan for their help.

12.

Remembering Mrs Biddy Warde of Galway

Patricia Moloney

Early Years

Although she died nearly twenty years ago Mrs Biddy Warde (RIP) is still remembered with great affection as one of the great old characters of Galway. Mrs. Biddy Warde (née MacDonagh) was born in Cragga, County Roscommon in 1914 into a family of skilled tinsmiths, (tinkers in the real sense of the word) who made their living selling working tin and selling pots and pans to the settled population. During her teens she was married to John Warde (also known as 'Galway John') who worked as a tinsmith and chimney sweep, following a match arranged by their mothers in the traditional fashion. As a girl with lots of experience caring for younger brothers and sisters, she was regarded as a 'good catch' who would make a good wife and mother. John Warde was a brother of Edward Warde of Tuam (also a tinsmith and chimney sweep). They were sons of Pat 'the Mun' Warde whose family lived in Cloonthoo near Tuam for a while and were forced to take to the road again due to the 1886 evictions in Cloonthoo Road.[1]

John and Biddy Warde had twenty-one children together (of whom ten survived) and in time they became one of the most famous and well-regarded traveller families in Galway city and county. Biddy Warde became well-known in Connemara as well as in

Galway city, as she travelled around selling their produce of tin pots and pans, holy pictures, blessed statues, rosary beads and holy medals. She was regarded as having the 'gift of the gab' and it is said that she would not be allowed to leave some houses she visited giving the household a song. In Galway they often camped in Lough Atalia Road near the Galway docks and also in the Rahoon area.

'Big John' Warde became one of Galway city's best known chimney sweeps and carried his equipment of brushes and sticks around the city on a big bicycle. However the arrival of central heating had an impact on his business and by 1970s he was one of the last traditional chimney sweeps left in the country but ironically the oil-crisis of the 1970s appears to have helped his situation and given him some hope for a recovery of business. A newspaper article in November 1976 quoted a 'happy Galway John': '[C]entral heating had me nearly finished,' he said, but 'people are going back to fires and chimneys.'[2]

Supreme Court Case

In 1972 John and Biddy Warde hit the headlines when a front page story in the *Galway Advertiser* reported that John Warde was to appeal his case to the Supreme Court backed by the Galway Branch of the Itinerant Settlement Committee in an attempt to have a Galway Corporation bye-law declared invalid. In accordance with the 1948 Sanitary and Services Act which prevented landowners from erecting or allowing temporary dwellings on their land without a licence from local authorities, in 1953 Galway Corporation listed seventeen roads in the Borough and passed a bye-law outlawing the erection of temporary dwellings there under the following headings: (a) a hazard to public health; (b) interfering with the amenities of an area: (c) if the dwelling constitutes a danger to traffic and (d) if the dwelling was within 100 yards from the road.[3] John Warde was prosecuted for 'constituting a danger to health and amenities' in Seamus Quirke Road, Newcastle, he was fined and ordered to pay £3.15 costs. He appealed to the Circuit Court and shortly before Christmas 1971 Justice Durkan decided that the case should be heard in the Supreme Court.[4]

This action was the culmination of a series of incidents at the time concerning travellers and the Galway local authorities. In 1967 John Warde was convicted of having a temporary dwelling (one horse drawn caravan and a camp) at Rahoon Road on the 17th January of the same year but the summons was later dismissed by Justice Burke. In April 1967 John and Biddy Warde were issued with a summons for an act likely to cause obstruction to traffic under a Galway bye-law, as it was alleged that at William Street West on the 4th December 1966 they 'did stand on the footpath for a period longer than was necessary for passing or repassing'. Mr. Comerford of Messrs. H. Concanon and Co, Solicitors for the defence described this action as: '... a form of persecution. They are not only moved from pillar to post by the Local Authority but they are prosecuted for standing on the side of the road.'[5]

In August 1969, in a notorious incident, a traveller encampment at the intersection of Rahoon Road and Cloran's Road was attacked by a mob of over thirty people, some armed with hurleys and claiming to be supporters of the Rahoon Residents' Association. Contemporary newspaper accounts report that the mob tore down tents and at-

tempted to drag away three caravans. A standoff which lasted three hours ended when the Gardai advised the travellers and their twenty-three children to 'move on'. The nine traveller families then moved to set up camp at Lough Atalia Road, near Galway Docks and one of the children, nine and a half year old Eamonn Warde was brought to the Regional Hospital Galway for medical treatment. Mr. Paul O'Donovan, an official of the Itinerant Settlement Committee, was later quoted as describing it as the 'Bogside all over again, as a mob attacked defenceless people'.[6] The final outcome of this situation was that the case of *Galway Corporation v John Warde* was not progressed because Galway Corporation did not wish to proceed.[7]

Protest March

On 5 November 1976 the a group of travellers in Galway city marched through the city to campaign for housing and to protest against the scrapping of an earlier proposed itinerant village of 'tigeens'. They were supported by a small group of students and Mrs. Warde watched the march from Eyre Square and gave support from the sidelines as the group made its way to the Corporation offices in Dominick Street.

There, the four member deputation of Bernadette Higgins, John and Martin Warde and Tom Sherlock presented a letter to the Acting town clerk which was addressed to the Mayor of Galway and which concluded with the statement, 'Please make the Corporation change their minds and let us have our houses - Galway Travelling People'.[8]

Later Years

John and Biddy Warde were later housed in Corrib Park and in Camillaun Park, Newcastle where they lived out the rest of their days. In later years in Camillaun Park 'Mrs Warde was known universally by all the children as 'Big Mammy' as they waited for her return from town with sweets and fruit.[9] One of the most recognisable figures in the city of Galway, a photograph of her visiting one of her regular haunts, the Galway market, was published in the *Connacht Sentinel* as early as 1974 with the caption, 'A familiar face at the Galway market, Mrs. Biddy Warde.'[10] Other regular haunts over the years included many of the old pubs in Galway: Whelan's now the Stage Door and Murphy's now the Goalpost in Woodquay, and Hogans in Bohermore where the horse and cart would be tied up outside the door during the 1940s.

She was a regular in Neachtain's of Cross Street when it was run by the Maguires. Her personality and good humour resulted in her to

being treated with respect by all that knew her. Of the many stories remembered about her, one favourite concerns the occasion when a 'wino' was foolish enough to try to get some money from her by telling her that he hadn't eaten in three days: Her response: 'Haven't you great will power?' is remembered as one of the great put-downs of all time.[11] She was also rumoured to have the power to curse and whatever the truth of this, it meant that even drunks took extra care not to offend her in any way.

She enjoyed music and singing and her favourite ballads included 'John O'Reilly' and 'The Galway Shawl'. On a pilgrimage to Lourdes with the Galway diocese she became famous for out-singing Bishop Casey at the sing-song and a video of this pilgrimage survives.[12] She was very religious and always carried her rosary beads and holy water with her and like many of her generation she was also a great believer in *pisreogs*. 'Chattering magpies would be a sign for her that there would be a fight before the day was over, redheads were enough to make her turn in her path and black cats and howling dogs were portends of bad tidings.'[13]

Her favourite haunt of all was the Quays pub in Quay Street which she visited first when she was sixteen years old. On 21st February 1994 her custom of over sixty years was celebrated when a portrait of her by Joe Boske was unveiled by the then Minister for Arts, Culture and the Gaeltacht, Michael D. Higgins. Mrs. Warde could still remember her first visit in the 1920s when it was run by Martin and Mary Lydon: 'I was in with my mother and I had a glass of lemonade. I had five children before I took my first glass of stout' she said.[14] Mrs. Warde celebrated with a glass of Satzenbrau, a choice of drink to which she had switched when she was obliged to give up Guinness twenty years earlier after being diagnosed with diabetes. 'I always had the run of the place right from the early days. I could come in and light the fire and pull a pint for myself and I've always been made welcome since' she said.

When Lydons ran the bar, Biddy often helped out by pouring drinks and lighting the fire and she was known to chastise the staff if they did not tend the fire properly, telling them that 'the fire was the heart of the pub'.[15] At the unveiling, Seamus McGettigan, manager of the Quays, who commissioned the portrait, said that it was 'a

'2 Galway Advertiser, 24th February, 1994

THAT'S ENTERTAINMENT

The Quays Honour an Authentic "Old Galwegian"

If a city is measured by its people, then Galway is definitely a city of "characters" and one of these "characters" was honoured by The Quays Pub on Monday of this week when Minister for Arts, Culture and the Gaeltacht, Michael D. Higgins T.D. unveiled a wonderfully true-t0-life portrait of Biddy Ward done by artist Joe Boske.

Biddy Ward has been as much a part of the Galway scene as the statue of Pádraig O'Conaire in Eyre Square for many years, as was her husband, who was familiarly known as "Galway John".

Biddy has been a "regular" in The Quays Pub for many years. Indeed, she would have known it as "Lydon's Bar". The streets have changed a lot since those days, but The Quays still retains much of the character of the pub Biddy would have known back then. And certainly her welcome is as warm as it has ever been!

Michael D., in his remarks, spoke of his own memories of Biddy Ward, and said that he was delighted to be asked to unveil Joe Boske's splendid portrait of her. Joe Boske's portrait arose directly out of an invitation from The Quays.

Biddy Ward now "hangs" just over the fireplace in the pub she's been frequenting for many years. Make sure you stop in and have a look - and drink a toast to Biddy Ward while you're at it!

● Michael D. Higgins, Minister for Arts, Culture and the Gaeltacht, with Mrs. Biddy Ward and artist Joe Boske

nice way to pay tribute to one of the pub's most loyal customers'. The portrait hangs over the fireplace near her favourite seat which was reserved for her for the many decades of her long life.

With her distinctive dress of shawl, skirts, rings and 'beady pocket' with buttons sewn on it, Mrs Warde was much photographed during her lifetime. After her death, her 'beady pocket' was framed and hangs near her portrait in the Quays Bar. Mrs Biddy Warde died at Merlin Park Hospital on Friday, 23 September 1994, and after a special funeral Mass at Galway Cathedral attended by many hundreds of mourners, she was buried at the New Cemetery, Moneenageisha alongside her husband John who died in 1980. During a lifetime which was not without its troubles; 'good times and bad times' she gained the respect of all who knew her. On 25 September 1994 John Francis King, on his popular Sunday morning show on Galway Bay FM, read out his own tribute, a poem entitled 'Biddy Warde's Last Chapter'. The final verse of the poem reads:

So we'll close this book of memories
Of a person as well known
As we say God rest you Biddy,
You were one of our own.[16]

Ar dheis Dé go raibh a h-anam dílis.

Acknowledgements and Copyright

Sincere thanks is extended to Patricia Codyre for permission to use two of her photos of Biddy Warde.

Endnotes

1. Rice, Sean Edward, 'Last of the tinsmiths and chimney sweeps remembers', *Connacht Tribune*, 7 April 1989; O'Donoghue, Paul, 'Proud and upright men', Indreabhan, 1987; Warde, Mary *'The Turn of the Hand': A Memoir from the Irish Margins.*

2. *Connacht Sentinel*, 9 November 1976

3. *Galway Advertiser* 6 January 1972 front page

4. *Galway Advertiser* 6 January 1972 front page

5. *Connacht Sentinel*, 7 March, 1967, Solicitor Hits Summons as 'form of Persecution', *Connacht Sentinel*, 25 April 1967

6. *Connacht Sentinel* 26 August, 1969

7. *Galway Advertiser*, Thursday 7 December 1972

8. 'Why have you attacked us and called us thieves?' *Galway Advertiser*, 11 November 1976

9. Mulqueen, Eibhir, *City Tribune*, 30 September 1994

10. *Connacht Sentinel* 20 August 1974

11. A.G., *Tuam Herald*, 1 October 1994

12. Thanks to Dr. Eithne Conway-McGee for this information

13. Mulqueen, Eibhir, *City Tribune*, 30 September 1994

14. Biddy is honoured by her local of 60 years, Farragher, Francis, *Connacht Sentinel*, 22 February 1994

15. Mulqueen, Eibhir, *City Tribune*, 30 September 1994

16. *Galway Advertiser* 29 September 1994.

13.

Travellers' Personal Experiences

Martin Ward

I was born in Galway in the 1960s; I come from a large family of 15 – 7 boys and 8 girls. My father's name was Paddy Ward and my mother's name was Mary.

My grandfather on my paternal side was also Paddy Ward; he was in the Militia in his younger days. He was fondly known in the Tuam area as 'Paddy the Basket' because he used to sell trinkets from a basket, or 'Paddy Larry' because his father's name was Laurence. My paternal grandmother was Ellie Ward, who was a daughter of Davie Ward and Mary Gill, Davie made his living as a drover.

My maternal grandfather was Davie Ward; he died in 1937 at a very young age of 28 years. Family lore has it that he was a strong man and this led to his death. One day while passing Killminion graveyard he came across a group of men trying to shift a heavy stone from a grave. He went into the grave and lifted the stone out with little bother but it damaged his heart. He died shortly afterwards.

My maternal grandmother was Ann Connor, who had two daughters, my mother Mary and my aunt Winnie. My grandmother died in Manchester in 1960 and is buried at Southern Cemetery as is my aunt Winnie. I have put this piece in as it is something that has motivated me all my life and I often think of the hardships my parents and poor grandparents went through. They had a very hard and sometimes sad life. I have left a lot out of my family background and someday I hope to put the whole thing in print.

Moving to Gilmartin Road and School

We moved to 48 Gilmartin Road, Tuam in 1966 from Cloontua Road, Tuam or the Suilleen as it was better known. My father sold his barrel top wagon to Dave Sweeney the day we moved. I can still remember the day fairly well. Our cart was packed up with all the belongings and was taken to the house which was about a mile away from where we camped. The house was quite basic with an open fireplace and no furnishings. My parents had to purchase the furnishings themselves. For the first few weeks we used straw as mattresses until beds could be got.

I went to Mercy Primary School with my siblings when I was 6 years old. My father brought me for the first week or so. I recall my father arranging for my sister May to take me to school one morning, she did as she was asked, but she took me to the wrong school. She took me to the Presentation Primary School and enrolled me there. May thought this was the school I went to. My father knew it was the Mercy so we had a problem and I wasn't squeaking to no-one, as I would have got May into trouble and I didn't want that because she could give an awful clout if you crossed her, so nothing was said. My father did find out about a month later and he's word were: What type of amadauns am I rearing who get lost going to school? There was never another word said about this technical embarrassment.

I did enjoy my years in the Presentation school with my cousins and friends. We had some great teachers such as Sister Catherine McHugh, Sister Leo, and Sister Phildailis and of course Sister Kevin. Some have gone to their heavenly reward. They were great Sister's, each and every one of them. I enjoyed my time there for the fun and craic. As a youngster I did not learn too much educationally as my literacy was basically writing my name when I left 1st class.

I was transferred into the Christian Brothers School (CBS) in the early 70s. I was now with the big boys. New comers could get a hard time back then but I wasn't worried because some of my older brothers were there to look out for me. My first teacher at the CBS was Mrs Harte; I had a good year there and went on my first school trip to Bunratty Castle and Shannon Airport. It was a new experience for me. I remember being in 4th class with Brother Maine's, he was a great teacher and he got me really interested in the educational process something which I am still interested in today. I learned more from Brother Maine's in that one year than I did in all my other years at school. I left school in 6th class, something I still regret today. Well, I suppose you just can't put an old head on young shoulders experience provides that.

Work

I started work a few weeks after leaving school with Homelee Bedding which was owned by a Cork man the Late Dan Buckley. I worked with them for about 12 years and I loved every minute of it. Dan was a great mentor and tutor. I learned a lot from him. He was a pure gent. I am glad to say Dan Buckley's family were likewise great people. I was always treated with respect and I developed a strong work ethos there. Dan had a tremendous singing voice, he was a great tenor and he's speciality was the 'Banks of My Own Lovely Lee,' staff had great respect for this adopted Tuam man. I was glad and privileged to have known and worked with him.

When I left Homelee Bedding I was on the Brew, nothing happening and not much to do. This was the 80s and a lot of factories were closing and there was no work around. I recall my wife Teresa telling me in June 1981, that Mary Moriarty wanted to know if I would have an interest in setting up a Youth Club for young Travellers. I contacted them and also Owen Ward and asked him if he was interested. The rest is history. We completed a youth leader training course with the Galway Youth Federation and set up a Youth Club called St Christopher's. The club is still functional today, nearly 24 years later and has regular attendance.

I worked as a volunteer with Mary's group which was the Tuam Travellers Support Group for a number of years. I started driving a mini bus in September 1990 for Tuam Travellers as they had set up a preschool and I did this job for 10 years. I started as a youth worker with the group in 2000; this was a full time position. Prior to this I was a part time youth worker for 6 years and during those years I developed the whole youth project with the help of others in Tuam. Today, I am proud of what we have developed, we have our own youth hall, boxing gym, computer room and adequate equipment for our youth projects which I feel is essential for any youth service provision. I strongly believe that youth work has made a difference and has impacted in a positive manner to the individual and to society in general. I took over the role of Manager of the Western Traveller and Intercultural Development Ltd in June 2006. I find this role challenging and demanding at times. I have responsibility for 50 employees and various projects and programmes within the Organisation. This work would not be possible without the great team of co-ordinators and supervisors who support the whole project and insure the smooth running of all projects. I have found as Manager and from previous experience that you are only as good as the team around you and we have an excellent team of people.

We took on the running and ownership of Parkmore Childcare Community Crèche from 1 January 2011. The Tuam Community Resource Centre approached us and requested our support in insuring the continuing of the child care centre. We were negotiating for nearly a year and got great support from the County Childcare Committee insuring the transfer happened. We took it over and increased the attendance from 25 kids to 72. That was a major achievement in less than a year. Today the Organisation I work with is the biggest community group and service provider in the Tuam area.

Further Education

Over the years I have attended further education courses and training programmes, I feel it is important to develop ones skills and potential. I have also worked with Westtrav and insured with the support of staff and agencies that other Travellers and the general public could avail of these educational opportunities. I have availed and completed the following courses:

- Higher Cert in Youth Work Studies
- Diploma in Community Development
- Higher Cert in Business Enterprise
- Train the Trainer
- Fetac level 5 Community Addiction Studies

- Putting the Pieces Together
- BA in Business Enterprise and Community Development.

I have also completed other educational programmes and required training.

Town Council

I was elected to Tuam Town Council on 11 June 1999, in which I took the fifth seat, and was elected early. I was elected Mayor of Tuam in 2003 to 2004 and I was elected again in 2007 to 2008. I was elected again for a third term in June 2009. I stepped down in May 2010 due to health reasons.

* * *

Joyce Shouldice

Joyce Shouldice was born in Tipperary. She was a teacher in the Protestant School in Galway.

From the *Voice of the Traveller* in 1986 I was always interested in Travellers but a bit afraid, I felt sorry for them because of the conditions they lived in, I remember, in 1967, reading something in the hairdressers about two men in Dublin, Victor Bewley and Fr. Fehily saying that two Traveller children dies to every one among the settled community because of the conditions they lived in. I went in to the Mayor and asked him was anyone doing anything for Travellers in Galway. He was absolutely astonished that anyone would ask him a question like that. He said that there was a woman going out preparing them for their first Holy Communion and Confirmation. I got in touch with her and two of us formed a committee. We asked the Mayor if he would hold a public meeting and bring down Victor Bewley and Fr. Tom Fehily to talk. He did and we had quite a large public meeting. Victor showed slides of what they were doing in Dublin. There was a great interest in the situation of the families we had Galway at the time.

Joyce Shouldice was Accordance for Accommodation like Sister Colette in 1974. Sister Colette was appointed Co-ordinator for Education. I met Joyce in her first visit to Tuam when she visited my late father and mother (RIP). I knew her for many of years she was a very kind person and was well known to the Galway Travellers in particular and still fondly remembered today. She was particularly great friends with Biddy Warde and her husband the late Galway John. Joyce had a great fondness for Biddy and they spent many happy hours together. She knew all the Galway Travellers personally and she was involved with the Saint Vincent de Paul in the 60s.

It was very bad weather this one Christmas Eve when they were packing boxes of food for Travellers as Christmas hampers and to settled people who were in need also. Joyce was working with the Mayor of Galway Bridie Flaherty at the time that was well known figure in Galway politics. They were both very tired at 9.00 o'clock and their last call was to the Traveller families on the roadside in Rahoon. Galway John, Biddy, Tom McDonough (townie Tom) and his wife Ann where among the families. Joyce and Bridie parked in the middle of all the families. Joyce took one end of the road and Bridie took the other, delivery boxes, they were starving with the hunger at this stage and the smell of the fry been cooked made things a lot worse for them. The last call they made was to John and Biddy. Biddy had a lovely dinner ready and Joyce was asked to stay for something to eat, she was that hungry she sat down by fire and had her dinner with a big mug of tea. After she finished she felt a lot better but felt guilty for Bridie so she went to look for her. She found Bridie with John and Biddy Warde tucking into soup, meat and bread. She was enjoying the meal. Joyce was so shocked to see Bridie and the grease running down her face. Biddy asked Joyce to come in and have something she replied no thanks I already ate but I will have a mug of tea and a bit of cake. The main families we worked with at that time were the Wards, Mongans, McDonaghs, Sherlocks and Maughens.

Joyce told the story of one of the battles she had to go through when the Corporation decided, under pressure from us, to put up a halting site at Rahoon. The workmen were blocked by residents. Then residents took sticks and hurlers to drive out Travellers. Paul Donovan nearly ended up in hospital. We got television cameras out to let

the country see the violence. We were abused and received nasty letters in the post. They used to surround my house in large groups and
shout insults. There were some nasty phone calls and they tried to get
my husband sacked from his job. He was called to Dublin to explain
his wife's actions. I met him at the station.

'Have you got the sack?'

'No.'

'Did they ask you to get me stop working for Travellers?'

'Yes.'

'Do you want me stop?'

'No.'

When he died in 1971 my Traveller friends marched up the aisle
of the church and kissed my cheek. They gave me such a wonderful
feeling even though it was a very lonely time for me. The fact that
we were Protestants made no difference. They came to our church
anyway.

Another very difficult time was when Teresa Mongan was given
a house in Bohermore along with two other Traveller families. Residents wouldn't let her go in but they let other two in. We pressured
the Corporation and they agreed that she would get the next house
that came up in Mervue which was the area she wanted to be in. The
Garda got her in but the residents held her prisoner. They wouldn't let
anyone in or out. We were trying to get food into her. We got abused.
My car was kicked. I was really afraid but called the television report-
ers and the pressure forced the residents to lift the siege.

This was a problem for people working with Travellers all over
Ireland from the general public. The good thing about the entire situation was that the dedication and hard work from all the voluntary
people paid off. The Travellers in Galway that Joyce worked with are
still there today. Their children and grandchildren are around Galway
and have done well for themselves and for their families through
education and training while the majority live in houses today; they
still value their customs and culture as Traveller people.

I myself worked with Joyce for many years and she always felt
that the Traveller children were well able to look after themselves
and others from a very young age because of all the training they
got from their parents and grandparents. I came across one situa-

tion which proves this point to me. One evening I got a phone call that one of my friends that had gone into hospital to have a baby. Her husband was in prison at the time so myself and another lady rushed up to the house to see what we could do to help. We found the eleven year old looking after the children and a sleeping baby in a cot. The first thing we did was to ask the child what was needed in the house. I left my friend there to mind the children as I went off to the shop and bought everything that was needed for the house until their mother came home. When I arrived home I looked into the cot, I remembered I didn't get anything for baby so I asked the little girl what the baby would eat she paused and pointed to the shelf and said he eats that it. It was a Cow and Gate can so I rushed back to the shop to get two tins of it, when I returned to the house I found the grandparents there looking after the children. The baby was standing up in the cot with a slice of bread in one hand and ham in the other. Imagine my shock; I knew then that the child only wanted us out of the house because she had sent for her grandparents. We laughed all the way home. God Rest their Souls, a lot of them are gone but their families are still around Galway and they always stop for a chat when I see them.

Joyce Shouldice with Sr Colette Dwyer

134

People were generous to hand out money so as long as you didn't put a Traveller into their housing estate or put a site beside them. We had three sites in Galway but it took many years to get the fourth and it was a proud day when we got it. Things have changed since that. Travellers usually get houses now but there is still a lot of hatred against the sites. Sometimes if there isn't proper planning or the wrong families are put in and it doesn't work. It has cost a fortune to the Government and Local Authorities with sites getting damaged and if too many families are settled in the one area. It takes a long time for families to gel together and even sometimes that doesn't happen. Some families will tell you that they have said it to Local Authorities but nobody listens. If you have families working together, they are better left to themselves to solve their own problems. They don't trust people that they don't know to get involved but as soon as they get to know that person who is trying to help the trust will build and they will work together.

Joyce and people like her were put through a lot of abuse from the wider community but they still carried on supporting the poor and I have the greatest respect for them.

* * *

Memories of Sister Colette Dwyer

By Mary Lalor
Given at the Memorial Mass

In memories of Sister Colette Dwyer who passed away recently at the age of 94. Colette was born in Cork in 1917. She came from a rich family, her father was an Irish man and her mother was a French woman. She studied English in Oxford. She was teaching from 1944 to 1951. From 1951 she was the Headmistress in Combe Bank in Kent and from 1956 to 1967 she was the Headmistress of the school at Mayfield, Sussex.

In 1967 Sister Colette Dwyer returned to Ireland until her death. She was the Reverend Mother of Killiney. She realised the need of education to the Travelling people and encouraged the sisters to teach them. She saw the need for development of housing in Sal-lyoggin and the need of education to girls at secondary level.

Sister Colette supported the two schools in Killiney and Sal-lyoggin. She moved to County Clare where she lived for many years then to County Galway for 16 years where she worked with Travellers for the education and training of young people. She has set up many training centres, visiting teachers and was in contact with social workers all over the country.

Dick Grogan said in *This Week* magazine October 1, 1970. Education is the key factor for children in the Travelling community and that still stands today in 2012 more important than ever. Dick quotes in page 25, 'The itinerant child is like no other child in our society', he was at a disadvantage from day one. Sister Colette is pictured with Mr Paudge Brennan in page 26.

A report in 1984 Education of Travelling people ten years on from her time of work with Travellers stated 'many Travelling children are still missing out on education'. The single greatest reason for non- attendance, without any shadow of doubt, is the lack of settled place for Traveller families to live and this still stands today in a lot of cases where families don't see education as important.

Myself and Mary Moriarty happened to work with Sister Colette for 20 years. I started working with Sister Colette in the late 70s. The work was tough. Sister Colette Dwyer was a great leader. Sister Colette chose the religious life instead of marriage, entering the Society of the Holy Child Jesus in 1938 .She had many happy memories of her life in England but a lot of sad ones too. We visited convent schools, workshops, sites, Travellers houses and Travellers living on the side of the road. She started the 3RD training centre in Ireland for young Travellers in 1975. The first training workshop started in Ennis in 1974. It was a shed at the back of the Mercy Convent which is now the Temple Gate Hotel. It was broken into after a year but restarted on the Gort road where it still is today.

I learned a lot from Sister Colette, she was used to getting her own way with everything so it could be difficult working with her at times because I like to get me own way as well. I learned very quickly the best way to let Sister Colette know I disagree on something she would say is being very quiet and not talking than she would know I wasn't happy with what she was saying and in the end would let me give my own opinion. She was a very hard working woman, would start early and not finish until late.

We had our funny times and our sad times. I have great respect for Sister Colette for all she has done. She drove a small fiat car and she was well known in the south for speeding. But she would always get away without a fine with her sense of humour by pretending the Guard who pulled her over was a Sergeant. I tried it one day when I got pulled for speeding and I got away with it. She was dangerous driver but she had no fear, where I would be scared to death in the car with her.

She would go visit a training centre, schools, and Traveller's site all in one day and would never stop to get something to eat our think of herself. She created work for a lot of people around her and got jobs for many. But she wasn't always a good judge of people and if I was to say one thing in Sister Colette's memory it is that she worked hard all her life and got money to help schools and training centres. It was difficult to understand her way of working. If there was elections happening in the Government, Sister Colette would go to Barry Desmond who was in the Government at the time to introduce us to all the Ministers.

Sister Colette had no fear. I arrived up to Clare one time to give her a report and she had just come back from mass, she was getting out of the car without pulling the hand break and the car reversed back into the lake with Sister Colette half in and half out of the car. She was not hurt only a few nettle stings. When she was brought back to the house she asked me what did

I see and I replied the funniest thing I've ever seen in my life. I and Sister Colette spend many days travelling the roads, rain or snow, arriving home late at night and out early the next morning again. The last ten years I worked on my own and reported back to her. Sister Colette made many enemies as well as many friends. She would always find a way to support education to Travellers from childhood to adulthood.

Times are changing now and Travellers are well able to stand on their own feet and know that education is the best for their children. Because of work that was done in the early days we now have young

Traveller's in second and third level education. In the Traveller community we now have two young people studying medicine; we also have people training in college for teaching. There are many young Travellers working in health and education and many other's in key positions but unfortunately because of the stigma around the Travelling community they can't come out and admit they are Travellers because of their jobs and this is sad.

There will always be a difference to the way Travellers are treated because they are different.

* * *

Katherine Ward

My name is Katherine Ward and I am a Traveller. Those last ten words may tell you a lot about me and at the same time they tell you very little. They whisper the lineage I was born into, the culture I grew up within and carry the associations others are often quick to identify me with but in reality they tell you very little about 'me'.

When Mary asked me to write about my life I found the idea a little daunting, unsure if I had much if anything at all to say, so it has taken me a while to put pen to paper. Not wanting to get too lost in writing I've decided to touch gently on some things we all embrace in common. Hopefully they might show others and remind myself that difference is something we all possess and that the root of any conflict is when we forget we truly do belong to one another. Punishing others due to a difference is punishing ourselves, as we limit our horizons and experiences; cut ourselves off from the greater life, one that is filled with wonders beyond words.

Few know of the intricate complications that exist between a person so heavily categorised by their origins and the task that is in attempt to navigating a way past cultural identity, to the ever present yet subtle presence of a person behind the words. In a way right now my life above all other labels has found a warm glow in that of motherhood. My child, Oisin, who is almost five has renewed my life's direction, purpose and within the world, my place of belonging.

His father and I are still together but marriage is an option I have yet to take. I chose to find the man before the altar, a diversion from the cultural norm that has certainly being noticed. As too was my choice to remain in education, employment and other aspects of independence and empowerment.

I have had the blessing to inherit many beautiful gifts, not only the deep love and support of my family but the knowledge of survival and an untold strength. Sadly, I have also inherited the discrimination and ignorance felt by those who came before me, which is something I pray will not be passed onto my child.

It is a cruel fate that for a majority of my family and my own life; that no matter how hard I work, how well I behave or how bright I shine, I am still made somewhat dim by the ignorance of others.

My dreams are the dreams of all people, that of security, happiness, fulfilment and health. While I could break them down to such things as wanting to own my own home, having enough financial freedom to holiday twice a year, the appreciation of the small things and other such thoughts, they are still never the less just reflections of that deeper human spirit.

My culture has guided my life but like a compass it's a guide and not the journey. I have learned that no power can make us see what we don't want to see, that no words will ever convince anyone of something they don't want to be convinced of, that discrimination knows no creed or community but shackles us all and that I do not need the moving road beneath my feet to honour my past and empower my future.

In a way I guess my story is just a story, unique as it is mine but common as it is a part of yours, my culture is an aspect of who, one in which I am proud of, not only in words but in actions but it is not all that I am, so I hope next time, whoever you are and wherever you're from, that if you meet a Traveller . . . try to see the person behind the word.

* * *

Brigid Sherlock

I am a young Traveller woman. I was born and raised in Clare. I am from a large Traveller family. From a young age my mother and father sent me to school to get an education. In the early years of primary school I never felt the difference or knew the difference between Travellers and Settled. I was raised in a house all of my life, I lived the same as everyone else. It wasn't till I was 11 or 12 years old that I became aware that there was a difference. I was never invited to parties, sleepovers, outings etc. I used to be upset but I got over it very quickly.

When I went to secondary school that's when it really stood out. If I had a disagreement with someone the first thing I would be called was a Knacker. I didn't really know the meaning of Knacker but I knew it was something they called Travellers if they didn't like them. When I would be called that name I felt a load of different emotions. I felt hurt, annoyed, angry but also confused why I or any other Traveller would be called this and wondered where this name came from.

When I left secondary school in my third year, I went to work in a hotel. The hotel management knew I was a Traveller and had no problem with it. They had a Traveller employed with them for a few years when I started working there. So the feedback and experience had been very positive.

I decided after about a year that I wanted to do more and applied to FÁS for a computer course. At the time everything was about computers and if you could use a computer you had a good chance of getting a job in an office. I did a full time course with FÁS for six months and then applied to the Health Service Executive (HSE) for a job that had been advertised. The job was to work alongside a Development Worker to develop a positive and healthy programme for Traveller women. I stayed employed for 18 months before I decided to leave and try something else. I started a two year programme in Childcare with the Vocational Education Committee (VEC). I did this for one year and decided it wasn't for me. About one year later I applied to Clare County Council for a position as a Clerical Worker. I stayed with the Council for two and a half years. My experience there was very positive. The people I worked with in that section knew I was a Traveller but never made an issue of it. Anyway my way of thinking was, when I started working with people I would tell them from the start that I was a Traveller and if they liked it fair enough, if not that was their own look out. I was employed to do a job and that's what I am going to do. I left there to get married and move away from Clare. I didn't last very long away and I always regretted leaving the Council.

I was married about 10 months when a job for an office assistant came up with a Traveller Company who supports Travellers in seeking employment or self-employment. I had been there 21 months when the company closed down due to no funding been available. This was very disappointing not just for me but for all the other Travellers that had been supported with this company. The organisation that I had been working with for 21 months had been established 4 years previously. A lot of hard work and commitment went into this project to make it successful. A lot of interaction would have taking place with Travellers and employers to overcome the negative perception that Settled and Travellers had of each other. At this stage I would like to acknowledge the work and commitment of my employer and I feel without his openness and support this project would not have been as successful as it was.

Traveller children are our future and progression through primary, secondary and on to third level education with support not just from services that are available to them but from their families is essential. I would like to see Travellers giving themselves as much options in life and prove to themselves that they are the same as anyone else and to give their children in time a good future. If Travellers are to take their rightful place alongside everybody else in the New Ireland of the future, interaction needs to continue.

* * *

Owen Ward

There has been ample effort provided to identify the origin of the Irish Traveller, and yet there is a distinct difference of opinion within the Travelling community, that purports the opinion that we are an ethnic group. I agree that there are arguable possibilities that can quell the best of opinions when one considers the language and the cultural differences between the two communities. However the cant or shelta as a dialect has distinct and specific connections to the old Irish language. I believe that as two separate communities, such as we are, possibly, were one community at one time or another. The old Ireland of yesterday boasts of the travelling tradesmen, such as the cobbler, the tailor, the tinsmith, the annual harvester, the travelling musicians and the blacksmith. Trades that have long since faded due to progression and modernisation. Yet, the romantic attraction to living with nature is best served with a good dwelling and a sound education that can allow the community to progress onto the next step of social and community development.

There is an opinion within the Irish Travelling community that we should hold on tight to the faded past. That we should respect the olden ways, that we should remember them and respectfully apply them to our daily living as traits of importance and value. That is true of many things within the Irish Travelling community, but not all. Cultures change that is their acceptable practice since their conception. However there are individuals and organisations within Ireland that want to live as in the past. In the fast changing world of today, where the rights of the children are paramount, in relation to the right of education and safety of the most vulnerable within our society. It is difficult to see a way of living for anyone that wishes to live in the past while we brush shoulders with the advancing wheel of modern progression while clinging to a faded past. The Irish Traveller will not disappear from the island of Ireland as many would have us believe. We will continue to progress with the world around us and if we wish to progress as a nations community we must contribute as our forefathers did. We must learn again, we must discipline ourselves to the understanding that we can only survive as a community if we contribute to the wider community as a whole. We should not allow ourselves the privileged thought that we deserve the understanding of others to accept our heritage and culture, while we refuse to recognise that their modern culture is the fold of development that we will progress towards, what else is there?

Regarding our right to be accepted as members of an ethnic minority group, because Europe says we tick all the boxes is questionable. Firstly, the Irish Traveller living on British soil and our own Northern Ireland have been accepted as members of an ethnic minority group, primarily because they are living in a country that is not of their origin. Presently we have an educated opinion that says that we should partake of the same opportunity, but with a distinct difference, we will become ethnic minority Irish within our own country. While we accept ourselves as been members of the minority group, I believe that the stop towards obtaining an ethnic status can be both dangerous and detrimental to the Irish Traveller. Firstly, the tag of ethnicity has a price that can divide communities further. If we observe and recognise that we have a shared history with other occupants of this country, we might come closer to accepting that we are but a simple fragment of Irish society that for one post-colonial practice or another, coupled with several famines and foreign landlordism that shared the purpose of the thought that they could divide the countrymen of Ireland. Then they have succeeded many years after their colonial rule has stopped. Some might regard it as a delayed political response to yesteryears opinion within our past.

The Irish Traveller purports to be of old Irish stock, part of the originals, as old as the shamrock itself. Then where is our staunch individualism that Irishmen are world renowned for? We have survived as a community because we learned to adapt. We must further continue to adapt if we are to consider our progress. We must accept that our very nature of existence depends on our young being educated, our old being cared for and our young and able workforce seeking gainful employment that can only provide a better future for our children. The feared excuse that we will conform, is an idiotic opinion, best residing in its own wallow. The fear that the Irish Traveller will disappear from within the world unless the tag of ethnic status is obtained, is an opinion that is best left in the minds of those that want legal change without community change. To further highlight the legal status of the ethnic rule. It is a status that communities have had to obtain to provide social protection, by promoting division by way of legal isolation.

In our efforts to obtain the ethnic status we tend to drift closer into the category of foreign communities that have found a good way of life in Ireland. All foreign nationals that have found a home in Ireland live reasonably well and contribute to the community as a nation. The ironic exception to the understanding is the Irish Traveller. There are facts of proof that acts of discrimination towards the Irish Traveller are still in practice. However, that same practice has dwindled over the years. But the other edge of the sword of discrimination is swinging in the direction that the Irish Traveller has the justifiable right to further infringe its own development by opting for ethnic status, simply because we tick all the boxes of recognition that define an ethic group. Therein lays the conflict. The Irish Traveller does not need to acquire the status that will further divide them from their own countrymen. As a community we would be better suited to accepting the mind set that we need to educate ourselves further and deliver that opinion to the children of Travellers. It is only with a status of an educated community that we can fold the past away and obtain a better understanding of today's Ireland.

Our community needs to acknowledge that we are still in our infancy as regards education. We need to promote the understanding that we need to contribute to the State as a viable workforce within the Irish Travelling community. We need to be blinkered in our vision of progress and strive towards professional status as a competent, reliable, hardworking community. At present we purport the opinion that we need everything in place before we can progress as a community of people. However, if we stand shouting for change to be enforced on others, without complementing the obvious need for change within ourselves as a community then I believe that we are only adding further fuel to the fire of indifference. Having to access an ethnic status will provide further isolation for the Irish Traveller. Our final point, Europe like the rest of the world has not got a good record in caring for ethnic minority groups. In times of economic change such groups become the first casualties of hard times. I would advise caution to anyone that wishes to grasp for the choice of ethnicity without first having knowledge on the status as a subject.

* * *

Rosanne Sweeney Ward

My name is Rosanne Sweeney Ward and I am a member of the settled Travelling Community. I am 25 years old and I am married to Michael Sweeney since the 23rd of October, 2009. Both myself and Michael have lived in Tuam our whole lives. I come from a family of nine, my father, mother, three brothers and three sisters and there are five in Michael's family, his father, mother and two sisters.

I am currently working for the Parkmore Community Childcare Crèche in Tuam for the last 12 months but I am based in the Western Traveller and Intercultural Development where I was on their FÁS Community Employment scheme for 4 years. I am responsible for the Administration and Accounts for the crèche and I am also responsible for the FÁS account along with all record keeping, management of files etc. I have completed my Junior and Leaving Certificate exams. I then completed my Manual and Computerised Payroll course and various other courses in the line of Accounting and Payroll.

Although I am now working with accounts and finance, and enjoy it immensely, I cannot always say that this was my ideal job. When I was younger, I wanted to become a hairdresser! My mother got me into a FÁS course in Hairdressing which was running in Galway at the time and I had to go on the bus every morning at 7.30 am and come home on the bus at 4.00 pm. Although this was seen as a normal procedure to get into Galway if you were not driving, many members of the Travelling Community outside of Tuam would not approve of this as it was not seen as a respectable thing to do if you were a single girl. I would disagree with this way of thinking as my father has worked in the same line of work for over 45 years and has never been 'on the dole' and I would like to think that I could be very proud of myself in saying that nobody pays my way for me. This cannot be said for all members of the Travelling Community and indeed the settled community as the common misconception of Traveller girls and women is that they are home makers, not workers.

Throughout my time working with the Western Traveller, I have met an array of Traveller women from different counties in Ireland. Many of these are strong willed and independent women who will fight for what they believe in and what they want. I think that this is the way forward for Traveller women as the days of the men going out getting a few pound are over. Along with the state of the economy, people will have no choice but to go out and look for work. This will also break any boundaries and stereotypes against Traveller women working which may be the best thing that ever happened for Travellers!

* * *

Francis Barrett

Francis Barrett was a young boxer, boxing out of a container in Hillside, Galway as was his younger brothers and many other Travellers. Chick Gillen was his trainer from the age of 11. Chick Gillen described Francis as a great guy who always had a pleasant smile and a great personality. Chick said Francis was totally dedicated to the sport and actually trained for fun and anything Chick advised him to do, he would do it. He was the first young Traveller to represent Ireland in the Olympics in Atlanta, Georgia. It was a proud day for Travellers in Ireland when one of their own carried the flag for Ireland. He has made a good future for himself and his family in London where he lives and works. He is still involved in boxing and working with young people. His most recent event was Blood of the Travellers.

The documentary *Blood of the Travellers* won an award at the 9th Annual Irish Film & Television Award for TV Documentary.

Below is an extract from *Voice of the Traveller* magazine:

> The origin of Ireland's Travelling people is a subject that has been debated for many years. Some say they are related to Romany gypsies or some other ethnic group that arrived here over the past 1000 years, others say they have been a community in Ireland long before the arrival of the Celts and subsequent invaders, while more say they are 'settled Irish people' who 'took to the road' during times of famine and eviction in the years since Oliver Cromwell. Now for the first time this subject has been approached using the tools of DNA technology. Over the past year Olympian Francie Barrett has

collected 40 Traveller DNA samples from every corner of Ireland. This DNA has been analyzed by a team of scientists from The Royal College of Surgeons in Dublin.

In 1996 a nineteen year old Francie Barrett captured the imagination of the Irish general public. Forbidden since he was a child to join the boxing club because he is a Traveller, he trained in the back of an old container on an unofficial site without running water or electricity. He dreamed of getting respect for the Travelling people by qualifying for the Olympic Games where he was told everybody was treated equally. When he qualified for the Atlanta Olympics he won the hearts of the nation. When he was given the honour of carrying the Irish flag in the opening ceremony it was a defining moment in Traveller history. With the boxing gloves now hung up and the relationship between the 'settled' and 'Traveller' community a difficult one, Francis had a new quest. He wanted to uncover the history of his people and in doing so try to understand why their culture is in danger of being wiped out today.

There are many great young sportsmen, including Joe Ward who made a great dash at the Olympics this year but sadly was tipped at the post. A great young boxer who will go far in which ever path he chooses in life. We wish him all the best and I'm sure whatever he try's his hand at he will achieve. We wish him luck in the future at whatever he decides to do and he has the support of a great family behind him.

There are many other young Travellers who have made a great impact to sport, not forgetting the Handball players of the past. In the past we had many people in the field of sport and music. I wish them all well in the future through further education and a better understanding of the cultural differences. I'm sure we can achieve a lot more.

* * *

Caroline Canny

My name is Caroline Canny. I have worked as a Primary Healthcare Coordinator with Western Traveller and Intercultural Development (WTID) Tuam for almost four years. WTID is a Traveller led organisation whose aim it is to enhance the educational, cultural, economic, and political development of the Travelling community & marginalised groups in Tuam town and its environs.

I am originally from a nursing background and have always had a keen interest in women's health and education. I have always believed in the philosophy that if a woman has access to information not alone with their own health and quality of life improve but so too will that of her children and partner.

My day to day work on the Primary Healthcare Programme consists of working directly with seven Community Health Workers (CHWs) who are Traveller women that during their training completed modules on women's health promotion; healthy meal planning; importance of physical activity; mental well-being; effects of drug and alcohol misuse and environmental health issues. My role includes mentoring and guiding these women to increase health awareness within their own community; encouraging individuals to access their own lifestyle behaviours; acting as signposting agents to relevant health service providers; coordinating information sessions on topical health issues; informing individuals of the importance of regular health check-ups and facilitating on site screening.

I also act as a Traveller representative at various fora such as the National Traveller Health Network and Travellers Drugs Networks held at Pavee Point; Traveller Midwifery Gynae Working Group and Western Regional Traveller Health Network. The National Cancer Screening Service, local mental health service providers, Western Region Drugs Task Force and the Diabetes Clinic based at University Hospital Galway are services that the programme links closely with to help ensure that the health needs of Travellers are on the agenda. The CHWs and I are always keen to assist members of the community; we work with the community to help itself. Again I feel this goes back to empowering women as women are usually at the coal face rearing children; ensuring their families are cared.

The Reverend Monsignor Thomas Fehily

By Mary (Warde) Moriarty

The Reverend Monsignor Thomas Fehily was born the 28th of October, 1923 in Ballineen, County Cork. He died the 2nd of January, 2010 and was buried in Ballineen in County Cork. He was ordained on 29th May, 1949 at the Holy Cross College, Clonliffe and appointed Monsignor by Pope John Paul II on 2nd June, 1980.

He was involved in many things, organisations and societies throughout his working life. The one he will be remembered best for is organising the Pope's visit to Ireland. He had only two months to organise for the Pope's visit but it was a job well done.

I remember him best for his work with the Traveller community. I met him first in the early 60s when I was only a teenager. He was travelling the country meeting Traveller people and setting up groups to work with us. He was a great help to the Traveller community and when he visited us in County Galway he talked with the young and the old people. He asked me and some of my teenage friends who were babysitting would we like to get a job and work our maybe go to school. I replied that I was in school before and I didn't like it. He asked me why I didn't like school and I told him because the other girls at school would pull my hair and he said why did you not pull her hair back? I told him there was too many of them and I was by myself.

I met him later in the 70s when I worked with Sister Colette. There was a funny story told when himself and Victor Bewley travelled the country. Thomas always drove because Victor was a very slow driver. They would set off on a Friday night to different counties to meet groups. People from religious organisations and anybody else who was willing to sit within a community, willing to promote the cause. Thomas used to write to the Bishop of Diocese to let him know what county they were going to next. On one occasion he notified the Bishop of an up-coming visit. The Bishop received the letter and proceeded to notify the priest and religious orders not to let those communists into the county, not to meet with them or talk to them because they wanted to destroy the Travellers. When they drove to the convent which was the Head of the Mercy Order, they were hussed around the back where they were brought in. They talked and afterward had mass. They went to visit Travellers not knowing what opposition that was against them. In the end it turned out alright. Instead of keeping them out of county it brought everybody together. Both Thomas and Victor were a very odd mix but they were the best of friends and did great work.

I remember another occasion when we were at a conference in Galway at the University. Thomas Fehily and Victor Bewley travelled by train from Dublin to the conference and would return home on the 3 o'clock train on Sunday afternoon. But Thomas needed to get back to Dublin early to attend a funeral at 5.15 pm and the 3.00 o'clock train would not get him there on time. Victor asked me did I know anybody who was going back to Dublin and I replied that Sister Colette had to go back for a meeting in the morning. He asked Sister Colette did she have room for Thomas, she said she did but they would have to leave straight away. We all said goodbye and watched as Thomas rushed after Sister Colette, to get a lift in the car. Victor said it will be interesting to find out at the meeting on Wednesday how Thomas's trip to Dublin with Sister Colette went!!

14.

'I Hear the Bells that Mark Her Passing'

Ann Sweeney

I hear the bells that mark her passing
So much sadness in the sound
I see white birds the sky ascending like a banner above the town.

We camped around Corradulla until I was ten. They were happy years, lots of friendly people. I remember hot summers watching men cut turf, turn and sack it.

In autumn we'd pick apples and sell them. Sometimes grandparents would pull in, aunts and uncles from Dublin for a week or two but we stayed and went from shelter tent and horse to a trailer and van.

Winters were cold, storms rushing across the open ground. One time we had to leave the trailer and shelter down a boreen under blankets in the van. I was one of eventually fifteen children and father often pointed out the need to find our own way in the world.

The teachers in the school were lovely, Miss Hindley and Miss Whin. I remember the communion procession to the church in simple white dresses. Afterwards our uncles helped to spend the money in the village. We used to get milk from Pa Glynn and one of the Murphy's, dairy farmers. They were great to us.

When I was ten we moved to Ballybritt, a four tigeen site with running water and a twin tub washing machine. My mother was greatly helped with these facilities. After two years we moved to a mobile home on the Tuam road and then into a house in Castlepark with an upstairs and a downstairs. I didn't go on to second level. In those days traveller children were expected to help at home, help the family economy. I just met Sister Brigid when she called to the trailer with Kay Savage the social worker. When she started the Fairgreen training centre in 1976 some of my sisters worked there so I knew the lie of the land before I started.

It was great to meet other girls from across the town. My father and mother were always strict about bringing us and collecting us from places. So we had plenty to talk about. We would clock in at nine and carry on with the work in hand-machining tartan skirts for Staunton's, patchwork quilts and jeans. Two girls cooked and washed up in a rota. It was great having our own few bob. We'd put some into the house and save some for the time we'd be married. Travellers married early. Sister Brigid kept an eye on us. We'd look to see if she had a smile on her face coming in the door. If not there could be thunder. After lunch we were allowed across the road to the chapel to light a candle but some girls would go off around the town. She didn't like to be fooled. The centre was called 'Flags and Banners' when we specialised in those.

I moved to Sandy Road into an industrial bay. I started to work for Sister Rose in a club for single girls. Our family went back and forth to England. Then when I had my own family around me in Galway I worked with Louise in the club and I'm still there twenty years later, teaching the children of the girls I first taught.

Looking back I see that Sister Brigid gave women the first step into getting out and doing things for themselves, making a living, learning to drive, having confidence and pride in our traditions.

15.

Rokkering on the Drag

Alex Smith (English Gypsy Showman)

Edited and transcribed by Micheál Ó hAodha

My name is Alex Smith and I am a Romany Gypsy who has spent much of his life working as a Travelling showman on the fairgrounds of Britain. As this book is the story of the people and languages of the Crossroads and as I spent most of ninety-two years living at the Crossroads of the world I am very happy to share with you readers a few brief life experiences and some information about my language.

Let me introduce myself. My name is Alexander William Smith. My second name is William but I've never used the William part. I've done this to cause confusion at times in my dealings with authority and with the law. I've been knocked off, from time to time, you see. There were times in the past when I was an outlaw. In fact you could say that I've lived outside the law for most of my life in a manner of speaking. Why is this? Because I am a Traveller. I'm a Travelling Showman. A Romany Travelling Showman to be exact. I'm a Smith one of the last of my breed. The way society has been organised up until now myself and other people like me have been left outside the 'system'. We've been shouted at and told to move, to shift and to get lost. We've been ignored in the hope that we'll go away, that we'll disappear quietly to be remembered in the museums and the 'old photograph albums. I am 92 years of age now and I've seen a lot of life. And I'll be honest with you. I've mixed with good and bad through the years. And I prefer to mix with the good. I've seen the ups and downs, the good days and the hardship days. And when times were very tough, I had no option but to go with the bad. If it meant the difference between my children starving on the side of the road there was no choice for me to make. I was always a fighter and a survivor. I was a wanderer too. I did what I had to do.

I was born on the eighteenth of February, 1911, in Yorkshire. I was born in a pub. And I've loved a good drink to this day. Is there a connection between the two?! My father was a Romany Gypsy horse-dealer and breeder by the name of William Smith. His name was William but he was always called Bill or Darkie, the latter because of his thick black curly hair. It is from him that the William comes from in my own name. And it is from my mother's side that the Alexander comes. My mother was Russian and so she named me Alexander since many of the Russian royal family was named Alexander. Over the years and in my different dealings with authority I've given different years for the year in which I was born so that sometimes I have been listed as born in 1911, sometimes in 1912, 1913 or 1914 and so on. Sometimes I even got muddled up myself! But I've always remembered that the eighteenth of February was the date. I have it here written on some of my official documents that I was born at Epsom Downs but not even those official documents have got it right. That I was born at Epsom Downs is just another tale that I told over the years when it the need arose. There's no doubt that there were many Smiths Travellers and Gypsies born at Epsom Downs over the course of the past century, but I was never one of them! My mother and father told me that I born in my grandfather's pub at Beadale in Yorkshire and I have no reason to doubt their story. They should know after all!

Father

I'll tell you a bit my father now. Bill Smith was his name. He was the eldest son in a family of thirteen children. His grandfather and grandmother raised seven sons and six daughters. I remember hearing that when my father was born it was touch and go for a good while. In them days many children used to die in the first months of their lives. And some women died too. Luckily, the medical field has improved a lot in the meantime. He nearly died – that's what I heard – and if he hadn't been a survivor – I wouldn't be here telling this story now! I can't recall now what it was that had him laid low but whatever happened they managed to get him over it eventually. They say it was my grandmother who got him through. She had her old Gypsy tricks – the old herbs and rubs and all the rest of it. The older people then had a great knowledge of herbs and the different plants that they could use for healing. They had to really. There were no hospitals worth talking about and you needed a lot of money to see a doctor then. They had no option but to use their own medicine. With my grandmother's help my father got over those first few months until he was out of the danger zone. She built him up until – and this is according to my uncles and aunts – he actually turned out to be the strongest and the hardiest of the thirteen in the end. Like every Gypsy boy then my father was learning the Gypsy skills and trades from a young age. He was working with his own father from when he was knee-high, learning the horse-dealing and horse-doctoring. And even when he was small, his father, and my grandfather were giving him bits of advice that would stand him in good stead later on. When they were discussing the ways and of the horse-dealing my grandfather always advised him as follows:

'Mix with the gentry son and you won't go wrong. If you want to be a good horse-dealer do your dealing with the Lords, the Ladies and Gentlemen.'

My grandfather's advice was to have a big influence on my father's life. Right down to the fact of his marriage. Because if it hadn't been for buying and selling on behalf of the English and Russian aristocracy my father would never have met the woman to whom he eventually got married. The woman who was to be my mother. How he met her is an interesting story. My father worked regularly for the Duke of Leeds as a horse-dealer, horse-doctor and as a breeder of dogs. The dogs were used for hunting and for dog-baiting and fighting. One day the Duke of Leeds called my father aside and said to him. 'Darkie my friend, the grand-duke Nicholas Nicolaievich of Russia is coming over to buy some greyhounds for bear-baiting. You could put him wide (in the know) about which animals would be best for him to buy. The Grand-Duke Nicholas came to England and bought the animals he was looking for. He was so impressed with the knowledge that my father and grandfather had about animal- rearing and training that he asked them to come to Russia for a few months so as to help him in his animal-dealing over there. He paid their fares to go to Russia that winter and they spent a few months at his family's winter palace in a place called Toola, near Moscow.

So grandfather and father lived there at the Archduke's palace for the best part of three months. They worked for the Archduke and showed him the tricks of their trade. They met him every day and taught him the skills of the horse-breeding and the horse- doctoring. They studied the temperaments of the different animals and worked out which of the horses were best for breeding and which were best for trading. And they experimented with the dogs too. And it while they were there at the palace that my father set eyes on my mother and I think he fell head over heels in love with her from the first time that he saw her.

Sometimes I wonder what that first moment must have been like. What it was like that first time that my father saw my mother. She was a beautiful woman and I have this image in my mind of a Russian winter with the snow ankle-deep on the ground. And there's somebody walking across the snow. It's a woman making her way slowly across the courtyard and she leaves her footprints in a line behind her in the snow.

And there's a man peering out from one of the windows of the palace. The man is my father and he's looking out to see what the weather is like. He spots the snow and the long line of footprints. Then he sees my mother.

Mother

My mother's father was the Head Huntsman for the Grand-duke Nicholas Nicolaievich of Russia. His surname was Asmarov and my mother was known as Maria Asmarov. It may be that she had Gypsy or Romany blood herself because I've heard since that many of the aristocracy in that part of the world employed Gypsies in many positions of authority in their household. Gypsies have always been employed as court musicians and entertainers for example in the royal courts in Eastern Europe and Russia. And clearly the Grand-Duke didn't have any issue with employing my father and my grandfather as horse-trainers and dog-trainers even though they were Gypsies. In fact I've heard that many of the aristocracy in the former Eastern Bloc have intermarried with the Gypsies over the centuries and so have Romany blood mixing with their own 'blue blood'.

My father was five years older than my mother when he got to know my mother first. She was only a teenager and there was no chance for them to get married or to run away together. And so he came back to England again with his own father when their time was up. I'd imagine he must have been a bit sad the first time. But he was nothing if not determined my father. From the very first weeks of his life he had showed himself to be a fighter. He never forgot the girl who was to become my mother. He was smitten, as they say. And so he made it his business to use whatever means he could to make sure that both he and his father got some more work in Russia. Their first trip there was very successful and it wasn't too long before the Archduke was writing to his friend the Duke of Leeds and asking for the two Smiths to be sent over again for another stint of work. They came and went like that, once or twice a year, for the next five years. When five years had passed my father went over there again and he and my mother got married. Then they came back to England then and made a life for themselves here.

Myself

As with many a Gypsy and Travelling Showman I've done a thousand things to make a living on the road. I've worked on the buildings. I've worked at the totting (scrap) game. I've collected and recycled copper cable from building demolition jobs and motorways. I've bought and sold second hand goods that were left in the rubble of the flats and the houses that were reduced to rubble during the blanket bombing of the Second World War. I've polished and rebuilt stoves, engines, gates every garden ornament under the sun and sold them at the dawn markets up at Club Row in the city of London. I worked as a greyhound trainer as a young boy down at the White City near Shepherds Bush, London. I even worked as a bookie at the greyhound tracks for a period of time. I've worked in the Merchant Navy and travelled around the Horn of Africa. I've visited Ghana and South America and seen storms in the seas of Brazil and Argentina that would put the fear of God in somebody. I've tarmacked the driveways of *cénas* (houses) from London to Manchester and from Newcastle to Hull.

I've even been a burglar for a while. When times were tough before the Second World War and there was no unemployment benefit I had no option but to go screwing (stealing) from houses of the rich so that my *chavees* (children) had a bit in their mouths.

I spent short stretches in Wormwood Scrubs and Dartmoor for 'motor vantage' and 'smash-and-grab'. This was when I was in my early in my early twenties. I met criminals and 'wide' boys in the drinking dens of the East London and the West End and I could tell you stories if I had time. I found myself in the mansion of Billy Chandler one rainy winter afternoon. He was the king of the London Underworld then and the man who arranged some of England's biggest bank robberies. I drank whiskey with him and saw him press a button so that his fireplace moved to reveal the famous 'peter' (safe) where he kept his guns, his jewels and his money. This was in the era before anyone had anything automatic. I was on the edge of the London underworld then but I never went in too deep. I never wanted to. The times that I chored it was a case of 'needs must'. That is to say that as soon as there was work available again I went back on the road and earned good money. But the most of my life was spent on the fairgrounds of England and Wales. For years I had a juvenile (a roundabout) and a stalls and I worked the fairs and the carnivals of every town and village. You can name a street-fair, horse-fair or fairground and I've worked there – Stow-on-the-Wold, Appleby, Stratford-on-Avon Street Fair and Pewsey Carnival.

Like many another Romany Gypsy I spent many months travelling around Ireland in the old days. When I was only a little mush (boy) I travelled to many horse-fairs in Ireland with my father. The fairs were held then in the streets and in the town square in those days. Ireland was a very rural country then and there was a great interest in the *grai* (horse) both as a working animal and as an animal for breeding and dealing. I remember the Fair of Clonmel in County Tipperary in the early 1930s as if it was only yesterday. Men with ash plants surveying the horses as the trotters flashed up and down the road with shouts of mind your backs' to any sleepy spectators. The harness-men polishing their silver harness until it was glinting in the sun. The shoes of the horses throwing up sparks as their hooves clatter down the road. The groups of men buying and selling – dealers, drovers and blockers gathered in groups around the best-turned out horses. There were other Romanies there apart from ourselves and you could find anything for sale there – stoves, bicycles, cutlery, carpets, curtains, candy floss, popcorn – even a canary in a cage.

What Being a Gypsy and a Travelling Showman Means to Me

Sometimes people ask me what makes me a Gypsy? And I tell them that it's part of my breed. It's my breed of freedom. And the fact that I never want to be domineered and dominated by others in society. It's the instinct in you that never wants to be crushed down. You've got a certain amount of freedom in your life as a Gypsy. Or at least you have it in your heart even if the authorities wish to wipe out our way of life. You have it in your mentality and in your particular outlook on life. I'm an amicable person. I like to be friendly to be fellow-man and they to me. But if somebody tried to hold me down and tread me down and thought they were better than me, I wouldn't be slow to respond. I wouldn't be slow to retaliate. No. I'd say. No. Don't crush me down I am me. I am me! You're not going to brainwash me into your way of living. I'm following a way of life that has been followed by a community of people for centuries. I've followed it and I've been proud of making my living on the road. Why is that you ask? Because I've been me! I've done what I've wanted to do.

I've been true to myself and my blood. Myself and my breed and my people. If I've done wrong I've considered it and suffered the consequences. Fair enough – I might have made mistakes in the same way as the next man. But if it's been right – to me, and my way of thinking - it's been right. It is always worth remembering. Right might be wrong in the eyes of the law. But at least I can say that I have lived my way. I haven't been ground down. When people have tried to belittle me or imply that they were better than me that is when I have risen up. That's when I have prided myself on my freedom of living – my freedom of life – my freedom of everything.

I am an old man but I have always remained a free man. You're free man or woman now and for always. That to me is the true definition of a Gypsy. You're a free man. In my opinion – that is the true definition of your breed as a Gypsy.

The Gypsies in Ireland

The 1940s saw many Gypsy people moving out of the big cities in England. They did this because they didn't want their chavees (children) to be killed in the terrible bombing that was going on then. They didn't want to have bad memories haunting them for the rest of their lives. Some of them went to Ireland where they intermarried with the Irish Travellers. There's Irish Travellers today who have the blood of the Smiths, the Rileys, the Boswells, the Prices and a hundred other Gypsies flowing in their veins.

The last time I travelled in Ireland was during the late 1950s. In a way I was like the Gypsies who had travelled there in big numbers a decade before me. My dear first wife Lil had died shortly before then and my youngest girl (who was travelling with me) were still in mourning for her. We couldn't have gone to a better place than Ireland at that point. The country was still very rural then and there was much more respect for the Travelling man. I remember the Gardaí (Irish police) coming up to me outside my wagon and sitting beside our *yog* (fire) to have a cup of tea. I remember the town of Galway where I camped beside the Spanish Arch which was right in the centre of that lovely city. The people there were the nicest people I met anywhere in Ireland. Those people in the west of Ireland were what

I consider the true Irish people. While I was in Galway I met some English show people whom I knew from back home – the Tofts. They told me they were making a good living there and encouraged me to stay in Galway for a while. But I couldn't. I was young and I was a wanderer. I had a lot more road left to travel then. I know that the Tofts are still in Galway to this day and I wish them all the best.

Rokkering

Although I am a half-Russian/half-English Romany Gypsy by birth, the form of Romany that I speak is a language that was spoken at many an Irish crossroads and on the drags (roads) and tobys (fairground) in Britain, in America, Canada, New Zealand and Australia. My dialect is a mixture of Romany as spoken by the English Gypsy and the Fairground Speech of those Gypsies or Travellers known as the Show people. Although I often referred to myself over the years as a Romany Rai (Romany gentleman) I suppose it would be more accurate to call me what in the language of the Romany Traveller would be known as a *poshie gorgja* (half-breed). Russian was my first language. I still speak Russian fluently to this day. Only the other day I spoke to some Polish immigrants, in Russian, some men who were here working as labourers on the roads. I never learnt Romany as a full language because my father wished me to adapt to the 'settled' life as he had did at a young age. I picked the Romany and the Fairground speech up as I went along.

My Granny Digby was an excellent Romany speaker and I remember her speaking fluent Romany to me when I was a young boy. She taught me bits and pieces and I use the Romany to this day when I run into older Travelling men and Gypsies. But like the road-life it seems to be dying out amongst the younger generation. The language isn't used much now. When we use it we mix it in with English but even then the lives of the younger Gypsies has changed. It is a different life now, a more sedentary life and there doesn't seem to be the same use made of the Romany. When I travelled the roads of England, Wales and Scotland you heard different families with different dialects. I remember working up in Wales and I found it difficult to understand the Welsh Gypsies at time because their Romany was so

161

different from my own. From what I heard, the Romany language originated with the Romany or Roma (Gypsy) people who were a tribe that migrated out of India originally. They left India many centuries ago and they have been travelling the world ever since. That's why the Romany has a lot of words in it – like *parni/pani* (water) – that you can still hear in India to this very day. That's what I heard from all the old people and the language experts can back me up I'm sure. Thieves also had their own Cant in days gone by. I heard it many a time as a young man when I worked in the greyhound racing game and when I socialised in the West End drinking dens of times past. I heard it too when I worked in the markets up in East End – up around Hackney and Bethnal Green – the places where people like the Kray brothers came from. I heard it spoken by the lags when I was in the *staripen* (prison) for short stretches too. Maybe they still have a language of their own today. I don't know because I've been on the right side of the law for the best part of fifty years now! I'm living the quiet life now! I'm a quiet man now, waiting for whatever is on the other side. If you can't live the quiet life when you are nearly a century old, then you never will!

My Gypsy Dialect – Mostly Romany and Fairground Speech

Strides – trousers
Tilt – tent cover
Dik – to see, to look
Bori – big (also means 'pregnant')
Kushti – good, happy
Grai – horse
Yek – one
Choring – stealing
Scimisched – drunk
Dukkering – fortune-teller
Drag – road
Staripen – prison
Tumble – understand
Parni – water

Lubbeni – loose woman
Rai – king
Romany Rai – Romany gentleman
Wide – clever, knowing
Clobber – clothes
Reef – collapse (e.g. our tilts (tents) reefed (collapsed) in the gale.
Yog – fire
Toby – fairground
Roomered – married
Flatties – non-Travellers
Gorgjas – non-Travellers
Vardi/Vardo – caravan, trailer
Rakli – girl
Mush – man
Stook – neckscarf (Romany men often wore stooks in the past)
Drag – road
Rokkering – speaking (Romany)
Juk – dog
Shushi – rabbit

Some Criminal Slang – From Times Gone By

Badge – steal, hide
Screw – steal
Drumming – burgling (different houses)
Peter – safe
Blagging – selling (usually exaggerating about a product to make it sound saleable)
Telling the tale – telling lies (inventing a story)
Grass (verb) – to learn, know
Grass (noun) – informer, snitch
Groyn – Sovereign
Lag – prisoner
Little Bow Peep – sleep
Apples and pears – stairs
Barnet – hair

16.

Johnny Keenan and Aspects of the Traveller Musical Tradition

Micheál Ó hAodha and David Tuohy

In the first rushing, I thought it was Doran who was playing! The style and 'dialect' are very close to him and this was a reel greatly favoured by Johnny himself. The version and harmony accompaniment are practically identical with what he used to have, but Keenan's personal style is noticeable throughout, especially in the tight fingering. As with Johnny, he is gentle and skilled in his harmony accompaniment. I am familiar with this reel as 'The Mountain Lark' (O'Neill No. 1244). 'McLeod's Reel' is well known, but here Paddy's piping is worth hearing and having to hand. Slip Jig: Drops of Brandy … he told me he was making keys with silver spoons … and he was making reeds out of bits of cane … he used to do all his own work with his pipes, anything would go wrong with them he was able to do them. – Mrs. M Cash, a close relative of Johnny Doran, *The Long Note* (1988)

In this essay we examine some aspects of Paddy Keenan's musical style and discuss some aspects of his music that are often considered typical of what is sometimes termed the 'Traveller style' of Irish pipe music. We also outline a number of ways in which Paddy Keenan has contributed to the development and of certain technical facets of the uilleann pipes as they continue to evolve within the category of music known worldwide as traditional Irish music. Generally acknowledged as the most accomplished uilleann piper performing today, Paddy Keenan is certainly one of the most brilliant musicians of his generation, a generation which has seen traditional Irish music scale unprecedented heights in terms of global appeal and recognition and a step further in recent decades by Paddy Keenan. *The Long Note* was a series of music programmes on RTE Radio 1 which were broadcast in 1988.

Travelling Style: Some Aspects of Johnny Keenan's Pipe-Playing

Paddy Keenan is also unique in that he has inherited an enduring musical legacy from a minority within Irish culture – the Irish Travellers. In the pantheon of Traveller musicians he can rightfully claim his place alongside such piping legends as fellow Travelling musicians John Cash and Johnny Doran. Paddy Keenan was born in Trim, County Meath, in the heart of the Irish midlands. His father, John Keenan Sr., from neighbouring County Westmeath was a very well-known musician in his day as was his father before him. His mother was from County Cavan, an area closer to the border with Northern Ireland. Her maiden name was Mary Bravender. Paddy was about ten years of age when he first began playing the uilleann pipes and four years later he had his first major public performance when he took part in a concert at Dublin's famed Gaiety Theatre. He later played with the rest of his family in a group called The Pavees. At seventeen, Paddy left the traditional music scene and Ireland behind and travelled around England and throughout Europe where he concentrated on playing blues and rock with a number of bands. He then returned to Ireland after a couple of years and began playing music with two well-known traditional singers and musicians Tríona Ní Dhomhnaill and her brother Mícheál Ó Domhnaill. Dublin fiddler Paddy Glackin, who was to join Paddy Keenan as a founding member of the world-renowned Bothy Band at a later date, joined the this trio who later became five when they were joined by flute player Matt Molloy. Within a short space of time the group was augmented by the arrival of two other seminal influences in the Irish traditional music 'revival' of the 1970s – accordion player Tony MacMahon and guitarist/bouzouki player Donal Lunny. These various musicians combined to form the group 'Seachtar'. The Bothy Band were also considered seminal in 'modernising' Irish traditional music through the amalgamation of a driving rhythm section with traditional Irish tunes in new and innovative manner that had never been heard prior to this. To see the band playing live was considered quite an event, an experience which one music reviewer referred to as quite similar to 'being in a jet when it suddenly whipped into full throttle along the runway!'

One area in which Keenan has contributed more than most to the 'revival' and development of the Irish uilleann piping tradition relates to the construction and enhancement of certain technical innovations as relating to the instrument itself. In this aspect Keenan is drawing on a very old and as yet little-acknowledged aspect of Irish traditional music whereby Traveller musicians such as the Cashes, Dorans, Dohertys, Dunnes and Keenans to name but a few, brought their skills as Travelling craftsmen to the service of the tradition. That Traveller musicians, in particular, made a substantial contribution to the development of many technical aspects of instrument-making is a fact that surfaces consistently in the margins of the few essays and books that have been written to date, where the influence of the Traveller tradition on Irish music is discussed.

Traveller John Doherty, who is probably the most famous fiddler ever to have come from County Donegal, a county which has specialised in producing talented fiddlers from one generation to the next, in addition to being a consummate tinsmith, was also known as a good maker of tin fiddles. These which were ideal for beginners who did not wish to spend a lot of money on the purchase of a new instrument but who nevertheless wished to find out time whether the fiddle suited them as an instrument, as indicated in the following account by 'Pecker' Dunne:

> There aren't too many musicians today who could make their own instruments. They are all factory-produced and made to certain specifications. However, that wasn't the way with the older Travelling musicians. I could make a fiddle even today if

I had to. Many is the time that my father and I made our own fiddles when we were young. It was a skill that all the good Traveller musicians had. We were able to make anything else that could supplement our income. You name it and the Traveller musician could make it when needs must. Horses reins and harnesses, fishing rods, tin cans, filters, poteen stills, uilleann pipes, fiddles and whistles. They were all the same to us. There was a great fiddler in Donegal called Johnny Doherty who used to travel that county in the 1930s and 1940s. He was able to make fiddles from tin which were ideal for beginners who were interested in learning the fiddle but were not sure whether they would be able to make a 'fist of it'. The Romany Gypsy musicians in England called the Boswells made their own fiddles as well. They made wooden box fiddles that were a similar style to the Dunne fiddles. Sometimes you would get an old fiddle that was broken up and take the neck out of it. And then you'd make the square box part of the fiddle and mould the two together. I often made them when I was young and my uncle Briany Dunne was a great man to make a fiddle (Cited in Dunne and Ó hAodha, 2004, 47).

Patrick 'Pecker' Dunne, another renowned Irish Traveller musician, who played with such luminaries of the Irish 'Folk Revival' as the Dubliners and balladeer Margaret Barry, has also acknowledged the contribution of Travellers such as his own family to the instrument making process:

My father broke his bosh one night when he was in Waterford. He was after having an argument with my mother. He had a few drinks on him and he got mad and danced on the fiddle… Anyway she took up the broken bits of the fiddle from the floor of the pub and brought them home. And the next morning my father and I got up and went down the town to find a few bits of timber. We found these boards that people used to call stuff boards. They were the boards that would have had cloth wrapped around them. They were great pieces of timber with which to make a box fiddle because they were well-seasoned. We brought home three or four of these boards and

167

set to work on making a new fiddle. The next day we headed into Waterford again, my father with his new box fiddle under his arm. We played the town the same day.... One time I was travelling in County Cavan myself and I broke the strings on my banjo. I had no spare strings, nor did I have the price of any new ones. So I went into a bicycle shop and asked the owner of the shop for some cable wire. This was the cable wire that they used to change the bicycle gears with years ago. He gave me a new pack of the stuff, fair play to him and I opened it up and made strings out of it. It didn't sound anything as good as a real set of strings but it did the job. I played away on them until they got me the price of a new set of strings. 'When needs must' as they say (Dunne 2004, 47-48).

That this tradition of continuous innovation and development in terms of the construction of the musical instrument itself is clear from the big contribution which Paddy Keenan has made to development of the uilleann pipes. While every uilleann piper would probably say that their instrument is unique and particular to themselves as a musician there is no doubt that Paddy Keenan has contributed hugely to the technical enhancement of the uilleann pipes both in terms of its physical construction and the texture and range of sound that can now be achieved with the instrument. The body of Paddy Keenan's uilleann pipes was found by Keenan's father, John, in a second-hand shop on Capel Street in Dublin many years ago. It is made up of three drones and regulators which are constructed of blackwood and ivory and silver mounts. The chanter was made by famous Dublin pipe maker and musician Leo Rowsome in the early 1930s. This is made from ebony and the wood is said to have come from the west coast of India. It is said that there is an actual historic link between this chanter and the Doran family, a Traveller family who are acknowledged as seminal influences not only on the Traveller piping tradition but on the Irish uilleann piping tradition as a whole. The oral tradition has it that the chanter originally belonged to one of the Dorans who were the first to begin a process of filing and under-cutting of the chanter, a process which has continued and evolved after the chanter passed into the Keenan family. Interestingly, the pipes' bellows were actually made by the Keenans, Paddy's father John Sr. constructing the bellows and the bag being made by Paddy himself. Although he belongs to the current generation of Traveller uilleann pipers in an era when musical instruments are frequently 'factory-produced' or made by machine, Paddy himself has made an important contribution to the construction of the bag. Traditionally the bag which accompanies the uilleann pipes was made out of basil although Traveller musicians who were always versatile often used a range of other materials when they were available, if they give a better sound or when the products they preferred were scarce. For example Paddy's father was not unusual in creating a bag out of an old piece of rubber such a as the tube of a lorry or a trailer.

Vinyl was a product which increasingly came to be used for the construction of the bag from the 1970s onwards; in particular a type of vinyl known as leatherette and Paddy Keenan was one of the first pipers to use this new product. Vinyl has brought a new elasticity to the bag and helped regulate the air pressure which the piper forces out of the bag while playing. Greater elasticity has helped further develop the quality of sound and the nature of the notes that can be produced with the bag and the uilleann pipes as the rate at which the piper is able to force out the air pressure greatly affects the tone which the chanter produces. The bag itself as constructed originally by the Keenans is also a new departure in terms of uilleann pipe design. In the past a single bag was prone to splitting or bursting under the huge pressure which is applied by the piper as his elbows work the bellows. The Keenans came up with the idea of creating a bag inside a bag – a double bag effect – whereby the vinyl seams are tougher and more durable under pressure. The older and more traditional skills of the 'smith' have also come into play as regards the manner in which the bag is attached to the rest of the instrument.

While in the past craftsmen tended to use waxed hemp to attach the main stock and the blow pipe to the bag, the Keenans and Paddy in particular have modified this process by the actual soldering of a small plate onto the back of the main stock and the fitting of a screw attachment there. This has ensured an enhanced durability in the instrument whereby it is virtually impossible to burst the bag irrespective of how much pressure is applied to it during the playing process.

This is an important innovation in relation to the construction of the uilleann pipes as in the past it was the tradition to ask a tailor or somebody with a 'good eye' to stitch the bag by hand. This stitching process, while an art form in itself also meant that the bag of the uilleann pipes was left vulnerable to leaks as it involved the piercing of the actual leatherette or vinyl. Today the seams of many of the bags are glued to the instrument as opposed to being stitched, a fact which renders the potential for leakage negligible.

Another innovation which has had a significant effect on the widening sound-range and tone of the notes that can be produced with the pipes, the adoption of which has been driven primarily by Paddy Keenan applies to the reed of the uilleann pipes and in particular, the construction of the reed. This aspect of the instrument's evolution almost certainly owes a significant debt to those generations of Keenan family pipers who went before Paddy, in addition to Paddy Keenan himself. While the reed is one of the smaller physical attributes of the uilleann pipes, it is nevertheless one of the most vital as the standard of the reed has a huge influence on the quality of the sound which a particular piper is capable of producing. It is also more often than not the exemplar of a piper's individuality as an artist and the source of his 'style', or that particular sound that is recognisably his/hers. In the case of Paddy Keenan, the stories regarding his propensity for experimentation as pertaining to the construction of the reed have nearly achieved 'mythic' status in musical circles. Like many Traveller musicians before him, including his own father John, Paddy Keenan has experimented with the shape, texture and craftsmanship of the reed from his earliest days playing the uilleann pipes. It is said that his father was actually teaching him to fashion reeds of different shapes even prior to his first lessons on the pipes. Keenan's propensity of experimentation was such that he often received 'strange' looks from his neighbours when he hung his range of freshly lacquered reeds from the branches of a tree in the family's back yard. A description of the intricacies of his reed-making process would form the basis of another paper but a few outline aspects of the process can be noted.

Keenan generally uses pieces of cane for his reeds and has a certain preference for Californian cane which – as he lives mainly in the US – he has access to reasonably easily. He sands the cane down using a circular object, usually a glass bottle, wrapped in sandpaper. This process is enhanced by the use of sandpaper and then Keenan shapes the blades of his reeds by 'eye' only as opposed to using measuring devices such as micrometres as used by other reed makers. When the blades of the reed are shaped to his satisfaction he ties them together and inserts a staple made from a metal tube into the reed. He then binds this staple to the tube with shoemaker's thread which is airtight and very strong. Further sanding and shaping takes place and the reed is regularly tested for its sound – a process known by pipers as 'crowing the reed'. Once the desired 'crow' or pitch of sound is reached a thin belt of copper known as a bridle is fitted to the reed. Keenan tends to go for flexibility and elasticity in all of these technical materials so that when he blows his different notes – it is possible for him to achieve different sound levels, sound pitches and textures of sound. Elasticity in the construction of both the reed and the bag is a vital element in Keenan's approach to both uilleann pipe construction and playing with the consequence that many other pipers who 'give it a go' with his pipes say that they find it very difficult to play his chanter in tune or get the same sound from it that Keenan does.

Many aficionados of Irish music and the uilleann pipes in particular state that Keenan's musical style – often referred to by the term – 'flowing' can be attributed to the his own ethnic heritage and the preference of a number of Traveller piping greats such as Johnny Doran for the open-fingered style, a style which is often said to be a hallmark of the Traveller piping style, one incorporating the use of flowing sequences of triplets. Seoirse Bodley, a noted composer and one-time Professor of Music at University College Dublin, summarised the 'open' Travelling style with particular reference to the piping of Johnny Doran as follows:

> ... in the reels you have this ... flowing series of triplets that just flow up and down in the easiest way and I think it's the most striking aspect of his style in many ways (*The Long Note*, 1988).

A closer examination of Johnny Keenan's piping technique however reveals that while his style is indeed predominantly an open one – incorporating a particular fondness for intricate ornamentation and the use of flowing segments of legato triplets being the style 'marker' – his style also incorporates significant elements which cannot be defined as open at all, including the use of staccato triplets and 'new' triplets which lie in the 'ambiguous' area is between both the legato and staccato styles. While the open-fingered style is today considered most 'typical' of the Traveller style of piping, it is arguable that this is only so because the great Johnny Doran, who was to have such a huge influence on succeeding generations of Irish pipers both Traveller and 'settled' chose to play predominantly in this style. As there are so few recordings extant of Traveller pipers it is very difficult to say with any certainty whether the open-fingered style incorporating the use of (predominantly) legato triplets was ever really the most typical style of all Irish Traveller pipers. Although often compared to Doran, it is worth noting that Paddy Keenan was already in his early twenties by the time he was to hear a tape of Doran's playing.

Consequently, Keenan's musical dialect or style was already at a very well-formed stage in piping terms before he had even had the opportunity to hear Doran's sound for the first time. It is also almost certain that Paddy Keenan has had access not only to a much wider and diverse range of musical influences – e.g. jazz, rock, country-western – than Johnny Doran ever did, but also to a wider range of pipers and piping styles. These include the acknowledged influence of 'staccato' piper Liam Walshe and legendary New York-born piper Patsy Touhey, both of whom were musicians from the settled community and both of whom had a preference for a more staccato style of piping as opposed to an entirely open-based style. Ironically, it may be that those people who claim that a direct 'line' between Johnny Doran's 'Traveller style' of piping and Paddy Keenan's may be correct in their assumptions but not necessarily for the reasons that are most commonly claimed. In fact Doran may have been a strong catalyst for innovation in uilleann pipe piping and as applied to the playing of triplets in particular, innovations which have been carried a step further in recent decades by Paddy Keenan. Incredible as it may seem there is in existence only one recording of Johnny Doran who is widely acknowledged to have been one of the greatest Irish pipers ever, a recording which was completed very shortly before his death (RIP) in 1950.

Attentive listening to the uilleann-pipe techniques of both Doran and Keenan reveal the existence of a range of 'new' or 'different' notes which can be defined as neither staccato nor legato. While these notes are clearly articulated they do not identifiably belong to either category, a fact which has resulted in these notes being termed 'defined triplets' by some musicians and musical theorists (Ring 1992, 55). These triplets are played by using a type of close fingering but in a manner which is still less forceful or 'defined' than that which is the norm during staccato fingering.

Conversations with Traveller relatives of Johnny Doran and other pipers suggest that this was style of triplet was also a regular, if relatively unacknowledged, aspect of Johnny Doran's musical technique also although most people would argue that Paddy Keenan has brought non-legato/non-staccato style to a new level in terms of sound and development. There are many musicians who would argue that the repetition (often at incredible speed) of successions of triplets – whether legato, staccato or 'defined' – is another hallmark of the Traveller piping style. Whether this is true or whether this categorisation of the Traveller style is another 'stereotype' which has assumed the status of 'truth' is a source of debate which would need a much longer essay than our current one to tease out.

What is beyond doubt however is that Paddy Keenan has set new 'markers' in terms of triplet playing for uilleann pipers through his range and mastery of the playing of sequences of triplets. In fact, his triplet playing on some traditional Irish music tunes is so exceptional that it has arguably become a showcase for his own absolute mastery of the instrument. A close analogy – albeit as related to a completely different instrument and musical genre – would be with the absolute control of his musical instrument expressed by renowned trumpet-player Miles Davis on 'defining' albums such as *Kind of Blue*, *Bitches' Brew* and *Sketches of Spain*. Keenan's total mastery of the uilleann pipes comes to fruition in another aspect of his musical style for which other pipers frequently express their admiration and (sometimes) envy! It is an aspect of his style which we can only briefly allude to within the framework of this essay but which is so characteristic of Keenan's 'sound' that no discussion of his piping could not fail to mention it. This technique known as 'backstitching' involves the rhythmic repetition – albeit that each repetition is accompanied by different and more intricate forms of the same notes – of the particular triplets as a tune progresses sometimes using a particular note as a primary reference point – the note C# is a particular favourite of Keenan's.

'Backstitching' is a term used (see Mitchell and Small, 1986: 25) for another explanation of the technical term initially by and in relation to some of the older Irish pipers who emigrated to the US at the turn of the century – hugely influential musicians such as Patsy Touhey, who would take a particular triplet – e.g. G, F# and E – and continue referring to it throughout the progression of a tune while using one particular note as their primary reference point or 'base' – so as to avoid getting 'confused' or 'lost in any way. For those readers who wish to investigate this aspect of Keenan's style further it is worth listening to the manner in which he plays a well- known Irish tune such as 'Harvest Home' on the various albums he has produced to date. On this tune and others Keenan frequently uses the 'backstitching' to maximum effect while using C# as his reference point, thereby utilising a musical 'turn' which gives him the freedom to demonstrate his virtuosity, speed and explosive power in terms of triplet playing and improvisation.

Conclusion

In this essay we have examined some aspects of Paddy Keenan's musical style and technique which act to distinguish him as an Irish musician and as a musician drawing on the musical well that is the Traveller piping tradition. We have outlined a number of ways in which Keenan has contributed to the development of certain technical facets of the uilleann pipes in the modern era. We have also discussed some aspects of his music that are often considered typical of what is sometimes termed the 'Traveller style' of Irish pipe music and pointed to some of the difficulties inherent in definitely categorising or 'boxing in' the particular style of a musician who has absorbed a very diverse range of influences, including traditional Irish music styles as developed by both Traveller and non-Traveller musicians. While it can be argued that Keenan's playing technique as outlined in the use of legato and 'defined' triplets has been strongly influenced by the Traveller style, and Johnny Doran in particular. It is also equally true that other aspects of his style, his virtuosity on staccato notes being a prominent example is as much indebted to the non-Traveller Irish musical tradition.

Keenan has continued to develop and mature his style in the years since the break-up of The Bothy Band as he has pursued a solo career. He continues to record and to play at many of the major annual festivals throughout the US, Canada, Britain and Ireland and more local-based sessions or ceilis. One of his most recent albums, *Na Keen Affair*, is available on the Hot Conya Records label and details of his tours can be found at http://www.paddykeenan.com.

Acknowledgements

The authors of this essay would like to thank the many musicians (both Traveller and non-Traveller) who generously shared their insights into the pipe music of both Paddy Keenan and Johnny Doran for the purposes of this essay. A special word of thanks is extended to Paddy Keenan and the members of the Doran and Rooney Traveller families in England for the generosity of their help in the background research for this essay.

References

Breathnach, B. (1977) *Folk Music and Dances of Ireland;* Cork: Mercier

Buckley, A. (1979) *Considerations in a Stylistic Analysis of Uilleann Pipes;* Stockholm: Musikhhistiriska Museet

Garvin, W. (1978) *The Irish Bagpipes: Their Construction and Maintenance;* Belfast: Blackstaff

Mitchell, P. and Small, J. (1986) *The Piping of Patsy Touhey;* Dublin: Na Píobairí Uilleann

O'Canainn, T. (1978) *Traditional Music of Ireland;* London: Routledge and Kegan Paul

O'Neill, F. (1987) *Irish Minstrels and Musicians;* Cork and Dublin: Mercier

Ring, B. (1992) 'Travelling style: The Uilleann piping of Paddy Keenan'; (M.A. Thesis), Cork: UCC.

17.

Victoria (Vic) Loving and the Travellin 'Revues': Some Recollections

Mícheál Ó hAodha

They entered in this order: first a boy with a lighted torch; then two beating drums; then the maskers two and two; then another torch. One of the maskers carried a dirty pocket-handkerchief with ten pounds in it, not of bullion but of the new money lately coined, which has the harp on one side and the royal arms on the other. They were dressed in shirts with many ivy leaves sown on here and there over them, and had over their faces masks of dog-skin with holes to see out of, and noses made of paper, their caps were high and peaked (in the Persian fashion) and were also of paper, and ornamented with the same leaves (One of the earliest references to Travelling 'players' as recorded in the English language and in Ireland – cited by R. Foster in Johnson 1980, 33).

The impact of a travelling theatre show on an unsophisticated audience in the days before television is difficult for a twentieth century student to recreate. The average modern child has already experienced a wider range of drama – plays, puppet shows, animated cartoons and documentary films – through the medium of television than his great-great grandparents saw in their whole lives. His critical reactions are already more sophisticated than theirs, and his expectations higher. To recapture the attitudes and reactions of any nineteenth century theatre audience requires, then, an effort of the imagination; even more so in the case of popular entertainments, for which there is less written evidence (Traies 1980, 11).

'On with the Show'

'Ladies and gentlemen, allow me to introduce to you our show,
With song and dance and story, nothing dull or slow.
Two hours of entertainment is the pattern we wish to weave,
Two hours of pleasure, what we hope to achieve,
So relax in your seats while we let ourselves go
For it's up with the curtain and (yes, you've guessed it)
On with the show.'
  – A typical opening 'spiel' as employed by the Travelling 'Fit-ups')

In this essay I provide an overview of a type of public entertainment that was very popular in Ireland as late as the 1970s, particularly in parts of rural Ireland. These were the 'Fit-ups' or the travelling road shows as performed by groups of Traveller show-people whose theatrical companies once toured Ireland and 'fitted' their scenery together in large tents and marquees thereby creating a fantasy world of exotic costumes, sets, variety and drama – in the pre-television era. This essay also provides a brief overview of the career of one the 'characters' of the fit-ups, an actress who ran her own touring show and who was a household name in the Ireland of the 1940s and 1950s – i.e. Victoria (Vic) Loving.

With the passing of each decade the number of people who remember those travelling theatres, which toured Ireland during the late 1900s and the early half of the twentieth century, becomes smaller. These shows, sometimes referred to as 'spots', 'road shows' or simply 'travelling shows' toured Ireland in large numbers in the pre-industrial era and seemed to reach their apex during the 1940s. These theatre groups included entertainers of all kinds including singers, dancers, comedians, magicians and acrobats. Many people, young and old, would walk for miles to see these performers of the 'touring class' including Vic Loving, Chic Kay, Mae Mack, Pat Lindsay, George Daniels and Frank Macari – to name but a few – artists who alternatively made them boo, cheer, clap or who simply made them laugh or cry. Whether it was Ireland's island status or the late arrival of 'rural electrification' and the television, Ireland always seems to have been a fertile venue for travelling shows.

The Little We Know

The history of Ireland's 'itinerant players', 'strolling players' or the *Lucht Siúil* (Travellers) who travelled Ireland's roads in the centuries prior to our own is still very much a matter of conjecture. As with the early history of Irish theatre itself, it is a subject that has, as yet, been little-explored in the scholarly literature. Some of the earliest sources in the Irish language mention travelling troubadours, musicians and a very wide range of entertainers, magicians, mummers, poets and acrobats, but the relationship between these earlier travelling artists and later troupes of travelling actors is an area of Irish life that is a fertile one for future scholars of Irish social and theatrical history. Under the Gaelic system known as Brehon Law, which was a hierarchical and caste-based system, it is likely that many travelling bards and entertainers were reliant on the permission and patronage of the Gaelic chieftains to travel through particular territories and follow particular trade 'circuits'. The Gaelic system of 'hospitality' would also have dictated that a reciprocal arrangement of mutual reliance and respect existed between performing troupes and their 'local' chiefs. By the time the nineteenth century came along, that 'reciprocal' arrangement as existing between 'patron'/ manager and performer was on its last legs as a consequence of an increasingly capitalist system for the organisation of the economy and the spread of local government regulation and state control generally. We know that the by the late-1800s the Music Halls had become increasingly subject to a vast raft of regulation and legal ordinances, a plethora of 'red-tape' which reached its high point as the nineteenth century came to a close. Changes to licensing laws made a music and dancing licence a requirement for virtually every public spectacle and music halls increasingly subject to the same legislation and standardisation of design and performance that the theatre was then subject to.

The late 1800s also saw the arrival of a number of 'waves' of moral and social reformers, many of whom belonged to various Protestant sects of a Calvinist hue, many of whom were opposed to drinking and entertainment in any shape and form. These reformers saw the increasing state control and legislation and the regulation of people's lives and public entertainments as an opportunity to challenge the existence of entertainment forms such as Music Hall and other types of theatre, a move which, 'on the surface' was disguised under a 'concern' for the style and operation of the Music Halls generally. Increased regulation and licensing gave the opportunity for the biggest Music Hall owners to 'buy out' some of the smaller venues and companies. These syndicates soon took over the Music Hall scene with the result that the majority of halls were now in the control of just a few proprietors. This new commercialisation meant a decline in the working conditions and pay that many performers were able to secure. Now that a few proprietors controlled the majority of the halls there was a strong tendency to extract the maximum work for the minimum pay from the various performers. Unsurprisingly, the performers began to look for ways to circumvent this situation so as to improve their own circumstances. Some of the braver performers bought tilts and 'fit-up' paraphernalia and took to the road, returning on a full-time basis to the 'strolling' life of their forebears, a nomadic life that they were well-accustomed to anyway.

As time went on, traditional Music Hall as it had once been known, went into decline and actually became known by its earlier name of 'Variety'. The theatrical landscape was to witness vast changes, all within the space of just a few short years. Over the next couple of decades, technological advances heralded the arrival of cinema and radio, both of which would put the final 'nail in the coffin' for Music Hall. By the time the Second World War was over, the theatrical landscape had changed beyond all recognition.

Some Early Twentieth-Century Shows

One of the earliest touring companies mentioned in twentieth-century Irish local history sources was 'The Bohemians', owned by Tommy Conway, a multi-talented performer who had joined Barry's Circus at an early age thereby gaining a taste for the stage. Conway later went into Music Hall, touring both England and Ireland, and formed his own travelling show in the late 1800s. A highly talented man, he wrote his own sketches and monologues, performed acrobatics, and was also a dab hand at scenery painting. Today Tommy Conway is best remembered for his prolific song-writing including, amongst others, 'The Moonshiner' and 'Hello Patsy Fagin'.

The four decades that spanned the 1920s and the late 1960s saw the road shows thrive in Ireland and at one stage there were more than eighty of these touring companies criss-crossing the country. These 'Fit-ups' shared similarities with those shows sometimes referred to as 'The End of the Pier' shows in Britain, a form of theatre which was also often peripatetic in nature. As in Britain, these touring shows were to provide the training ground for actors and actresses who would later 'make it big' in 'legitimate' theatre (Broadway) and in film and television. Some of the luminaries of Irish stage and screen who first 'trod the boards' and learned their trade in the Travelling 'Fit-Ups' were actors and entertainers as well-known (both nationally and internationally as Cyril Cusack, Anna Manahan, Hal Roach, Milo O'Shea, Barry Cassin, Bob Carrickford and Sandy Kelly.

In addition to this 'home-grown' talent, the years prior to the Second World War saw the arrival in Ireland of many showpeople and their companies who had frequently carved out a living for themselves in British music hall, repertory or 'end of pier' shows but who now wished to strike out for themselves, form their own companies, and discover 'pastures new'. Many of these showpeople moved to Ireland during the 1930s and 1940s and never went back to Britain.

Amongst the ranks of such artistes was Vic Loving, whose shows were known throughout Ireland, and in the Munster region in particular. Vic Loving was said to have been born in Madrid in 1889. Her passport, however, listed her birthplace in the 'less-exotic' location of Manchester. Her parents were circus folk who ran their own

Big-Top before moving to Lancashire in the north of England. It was only naturally that Vic would grow up wanting to 'entertain' and as a child, she and one of her friends (a young Gracie Fields) sang and danced outside the English working men's clubs; the people queuing outside the clubs throwing the occasional penny in their direction. Those early days were where she would 'learn the ropes' and it wasn't long before Vic was on her way to 'treading the boards' by way of the Music Hall. The Music Hall was like 'one big family' back then and included amongst Vic Loving's friends were other such greats as Ella Shiels, Little Tich, Gertie Gitana and Vesta Tilley. Male contemporaries of hers, some of whom were to make a name for themselves – initially in the silent pictures and then in the 'talkies' – were Peter Piper, Charlie Chaplin and Stan Laurel who was a vaudeville star of the 'Halls' and a member of one of Fred Karno's troupes which went by the name of 'The Mumming Birds'. Laurel's speciality was with marionettes, but he also played piano sleighbells and worked on a 'novelty aeroplane' act which he himself patented.

Like Stan Laurel, Vic Loving was an experimenter in terms of the theatrical form and was never one to shy away from risk. After a number of years 'treading the boards' she decided to take a different direction by engaging a chorus line, some musicians and taking them on tour. In the 1930s she and her husband decided to visit Ireland where there were many 'untapped' venues and a large and appreciative audience for the road-shows. They formed a bigger show and joined forces (like many other artists at this juncture) with another company, in this case, Harry Lynton for the summer season. Vic realised that she needed a large tent – known as a 'booth' – with which to accommodate her productions, the chorus line and a small orchestra, and as Harry had been running his Hippodrome Circus, prior to the two companies joining together, his tent was the perfect choice. Vic was one of those showbiz 'characters'. A woman with a flamboyant nature both in dress and demeanour, she was considered 'eccentric' to say the least! She was very fond of fur coats, richly-coloured clothes and diamond jewellery. Her taste for the eye-catching and the exotic also extended to her living accommodation. She had two caravans, one of which was her living quarters and the other, known as the 'White Caravan', which she used for entertaining her visitors. The latter got its name because everything in it was white – white carpets, white curtains, white upholstery, even the tea-service was white! It was in this caravan that she would regale her visitors, with show-biz gossip, her stories concerning the 'business' and the trials and tribulations of touring Ireland with the 'road-shows'. Vic was also known as a bit of a 'drill sergeant' when the shows were on tour. Wherever the travelling theatre set up its base had to be kept spick-and-span at all times and many actors and actresses recall long walks to find the local 'pump' (water pump) in the most rural of villages and towns in an effort to keep the *tóhbar* (area around the travelling theatre and its vehicles) in pristine condition.

The Ireland of the 1930s and 1940s was quite a conservative and rural-based country and a deeply ingrained clericalism meant that some Irish clergy – on occasion – took it upon themselves to 'denounce' these troubadours and their circus peformances/variety shows. Vic had her fair share of 'altercations' with local officials and clergy during her 'touring' years on Ireland's roads. In Cappamore, County Limerick, she was once denounced from the pulpit with the words – 'that show should be called Flesh Parade and not 'Flash Parade'!! – but resistance on the part of the clergy was vigorously rebuffed by the showpeople who generally went 'on with the show' no matter what the circumstances, and the population of the local villages who never seemed to be 'put off' by these admonishments, the shows being packed out every night in this, the pre-television era. Vic's husband, Peter, died when her son Brian – who went under the stage-name the 'Chicago Kid' – was just fifteen years of age and was buried in Lismore, County Waterford (RIP), where Vic and her troupe had made many friends including Adele Astaire (otherwise known as Lady Cavenish). The latter it was who famously classed Brian – (or the 'young Chicago Kid' or 'Chic' as he was often known) – as 'the pocket Fred Astaire', since Chic performed a top-hat and tails act which emulated the fabulous Fred.

Over time, Vic expanded her repertoire and her troupe's accommodation to include a specially designed tent which mirrored a real theatre. This was custom-built in a rectangular shape rather than the usual circular style. Her son Brian became the lynchpin of the show and once again changed his name – this time to Chic Kay – a name which is still remembered fondly by people today. He became the comedian of the Flash Parade, a multi-talented showman who could sing, dance and was also an accomplished multi-instrumentalist. Plays which they brought to the length and breadth of Ireland included such eagerly-awaited dramas as *Maria Marten, Murder in the Red Barn, Night Must Fall, The Informer* (based on Liam O'Flaherty's book and John Ford's 1935 film), *Little Old New York, East Lynne* and *Peg o' My Heart*. Vic Loving brought colour and gaiety to the Irish travelling shows with a cornucopia of costumed revues, scenes, variety and drama. In addition to being an extremely talented singer and actress she was constantly innovating. She tried to push the genre forward and was unafraid to try out new 'inventions' – such as special effects. Her show was one of the first in the country to use ultra-violet light or 'black lighting' as it was then called. She insisted on authenticity for all her productions and gleaned props and costumes from 'Big House' auctions. It is reported that Vic travelled with some 2,000 costumes, costumes whose style ranged from the Victorian period right up to the 1950s. This was in addition to the chorus line dresses which she designed and made herself and which gave her the nickname – 'the Sequin Queen'. Having such a large number of costumes and repertoires meant that she could completely change the whole look of her show on a nightly basis. In this way she was able to entertain the viewing public with a completely different show on a nightly basis, an audience, many of whom would walk or cycle great distances each night to enjoy the shows.

When Vic finally decided to retire – in large part due to the advent of television – she moved first to Drogheda, County Louth and then to Shankill in Dublin. She continued to do 'spots' until a year before her death in 1974. She represented the end of an era – the era of the Road Shows – an era which is gone but not forgotten.

Acknowledgements

With special thanks to Vikki Jackson and all the other showpeople who contributed their memories of the 'Spots' and especially Victoria Loving.

Endnote

1. The Fit-Ups were a natural progression from two previous types of entertainment from which they had originally evolved. These were the 'itinerant players' or 'strolling players' whose antecedents lay in the Medieval era and before and the Music Halls where so many latter-day stars of stage-and-screen originally 'made their name'.

References

Easthope, A. (1993) *Contemporary Film Theory*; New York: Longman

Fitz-Simon, C. (1994) *The Boys: a Biography of Micheál Mac Líammóir and Hilton Edwards*; London: Nick Hern Books

Gibbons, L., Hill, J., Rockett, K. (eds.) (1988) *Cinema and Ireland*; London: Routledge

Gibbons, L. (1996) *Transformations in Irish Culture*; Notre Dame: (University of Notre Dame Press in association with Field Day; Cork: Cork University Press

Jackson, V. and Ó hAodha, M. (2008) *Gags and Greasepaints: A Tribute to the Irish Fit-Ups*; UK: Cambridge Scholars Publishing

Pettitt, L. *Screening Ireland: Film and Television Representation*; Manchester: Manchester University Press, 2000

18.

The Everlasting Rose

Brigit Mongan

If the Everlasting Rose was the heart of one I loved to see it in the
winter would warm me like a glove.
I would reach my hand and touch it as if it was your face and feel
the sadness leave me in God's eternal grace.

There was a small building with a pool table where the boys
played and me and a few girls used to stand outside and torment
them. I was about eight years old. Paddy would come out and ask us
to sing a few songs to keep us from mischief. Two years later he heard
me singing 'Hopelessly Devoted to you' and said, 'You can sing.' He
used to teach my father the guitar so I asked him to teach me. And
that's how music began for me.

I practised the chords and strums, and a few months later I said,
'Sing me a song you wrote'.

He thought for a minute and said, 'You like country music. This
is about a friend of mine telling her partner he'd have to change his
ways.' And he sang 'Time Makes It Clearer'.

I said, 'I want to learn that.'

He wondered, 'Is it a bit grown-up for you?'

When I learned it off he said I sounded like a young Dolly Par-
ton. I could see he meant it. One day we went to Eugene Kelly and
recorded it. I learned how a track is built up instrument by instrument over what they call a guide vocal. Then finally I went into the

small place with a glass window, the cams over my ears so I was sing-ing with backing until Eugene, Paddy, my father and my mother were nodding their heads.

There was an audition for *Star Search* for RTE in Flannery's Ho-tel. I went into a room with my guitar facing two cameras and sang 'Time makes it clearer' standing up. I passed and the following week we were in RTE Donnybrook in a studio with three or four cameras and a heap of lights. My nerves! It was on the telly for a couple of weeks but a young one dressed as a witch passed me out.

The next year I walked into the music room and told Paddy that my mother and I had written part of a song about my grandmother's death, God rest her. It was called 'The Everlasting Rose'.

Paddy said, 'There's no such thing as an everlasting rose.' Then he said, 'Play it for me anyway.'

So I played the verse and chorus and he looked at me and said, 'It's good. Would you not write another verse?'

I told him I couldn't think of more so he said, 'okay, write this down' and in the space of minutes it was finished. By and by we went out to Eugene and he made it sound great. Everybody seemed to like it. We arranged a photo shoot for the cover. Then I wrote a song completely on my own and recorded that too.

A few weeks ago Eugene died unexpectedly. He was playing some gigs in America. I was very sad. He was a great man and the time I spent in his studio was incredible.

19.

The Road to Ennis

Words and Music by Paddy Houlahan

The books you read at school do not mention me
Because I am the invisible man in this country's history.
But I knew the farmer, I traded him a mare
I picked his beet and shaped his tins and I was welcome there,
I was welcome there.
No more call for my trade, everything's plastic made.
No more travelling around, I'm living on the edge of your
    town.
I'm living on the edge of your town.

Once a year, in springtime a shawled woman with a small child would knock on our door in Armagh. 'Would you have a few coppers sir'? I'd call my mother, who was kind. Then in December 1973, I was hiking through Ennis on route to my sister's home in Ennistymon. I glimpsed a couple of shelter tents at the top of what I found out later was Watery Road. The image stayed with me and I wrote a short poem 'Reflection on the Nativity'.

Flesh the word, a baby's cry in a house made of rags and boards along the
roadside where Traveller families lie in winter

A few days after Christmas the local priest, Fr. Ned Crosby was going to visit someone in hospital in Ennis. I went along for the spin.

Afterwards we called into a local authority house for a cup of tea with the Little Sisters of the Assumption. A week after I went back north a letter come in the post asking would I be interested in opening and running a training centre for young Travellers. My mother said, 'Go down and see what they want.' I hiked down again. The Watery Road had flooded and some families were sleeping in the Community hall. I took a camp bed and swapped stories, played a few Elvis songs on my guitar. I liked them. They were friendly and curious. Was I a protestant from the north?

Next day Sister Frances drove me around the sites, from shelter tents and huts to caravans and tigeens and a barrel wagon or two. The local committee, Hawley Keane, Pat Galvin, Sister Anne Kirane; later replaced by Sister Margaret McFadden; and others had worked hard to provide accommodation for people who had lost a way of life in rural Ireland and drifted into towns.

At the interview we didn't take about wages. I was part of the 60s generation who wanted to make a difference. Words like 'human rights', 'community', 'individualism', were banners in my mind.

I had waded through the political and religious routes of the conflict in the North and walked away from it. I would always be one of the 'boys from County Armagh' but I wasn't motivated like those. I admired John Hume, Austin Curry and Gerry Fitt to stay and help to reconcile the tribes.

We began by renovating a room and courtyard provided by the Sisters of Mercy. It had been an orphanage. Around twenty teenage boys and girls, paid by Anco, came every day nine to five. It was communal, we cooked and ate together, established a template of metal working, including traditional tin smithing, craftwork/sewing and machining, carpentry and literacy.

We formed a handball club and later entered a soccer team into the local league. I pushed to have four Travellers in the management committee. That was a struggle. A few years later, I was angered by local hotels refusal to admit a girl to her first dance. I decided we'd have to take a constitutional test case to establish the right of admission.

They called me a name, it wasn't mine
from an age long before my time
Hung a label on me, a whole identity
to stop me from crossing their line

We worked with the Irish Council for Civil Liberties until after 18 months their representative left the job. I found another solicitor but another year later he informed us that all our documentation had been lost. It was a bitter disappointment. Then I was part of a National Council delegation pressing the issue with the Attorney General. We were served tea and a quality biscuit. It went no further.

I was responsible for the literacy unit. One day I asked the group to write about their travels in Ireland. A lad wrote a short piece about his father losing a house and, looking for it, asked the King Ward had he seen it. The King Ward told him to 'f-off' whereupon a fight ensued, his father emerging victorious. I loved the colour of it and got some old typewriters from the VEC and we began to type up these stories.

Some were like telegrams. Literacy skills varied from none to fluent. Bye and bye we brought out a collection. It was titled 'Young Travellers, Many Voices One Community'. We made enough to buy some drums, electric guitars, microphones and a PA. I had been teaching music on acoustic instruments. They had appeared on *The Late Late Show* singing 'Travelling Family', our own song. We played for weddings, dances and at National Association AGMs. I wrote songs with Pat Sherlock, our guitar player, and then when the lads married and went to England, kept on hearing themes in the talk of the centre and memories of Mary Warde en route to meetings.

My father rises early, makes a sup of tea
he lights the kitchen stove and then he call me.
His days are often empty nothing much to do
So he tells stories of the travelling life he knew

In the evening they would meet down lonely country lanes
a field away you'd hear a collie bark
and they'd pass the time away with talk about the day
standing round the campfire in the dark

The more I thought about the harsh conditions their forebears had endured for hundreds of years the more I wanted to salute their perseverance.

I think about them sometimes, walking in the town
The lives that were linked together before mine came around
They were the Travelling People struggling to survive
And the name the buffers call me can't take away my pride

We were leaves in the wind; we watched the trees go bare
We were leaves in the wind; we shook the frost out of our hair
We were leaves in the wind, we heard the owl we saw the lark
We were leaves in the wind, we sang round camp fires in the dark.

In the mid-80s one of the lads pulled into Dublin for a month. We listened wide-eyed when he told us about one aspect of the life there, 'They bring in cars at night and burn them', stolen motors. Ennis had been a quiet place. The following year I moved to Galway and it was happening in Ballybane.

Almost every night a car gets burned out on the site
almost every day the shades drive in to make us pay
and Daddy says nothing at all
whatever time the boys come to call
I go where I want but I wonder is it better this way?

Times were changing.

Part Three

TRAVELLER ISSUES AND CHALLENGES

20.

Irish Travellers, National School and the Educational Experience

Micheál Ó hAodha

This essay gives a brief overview of a unique and exciting piece of research as undertaken by a group of Traveller women from Limerick city, in recent years, the findings of which were published in a book entitled *Whiddin to the Gauras: Talking to Our Own* (2005). Most important of all however is the fact that it gives a small glimpse into what it is like to be considered 'different', 'other' or labeled as a 'problem' in modern Ireland.

There is widespread acknowledgement amongst both the Travelling and settled communities that education is a crucial asset in order for young people to live their lives with dignity in present-day Ireland. Achieving a certain level of education is necessary to accomplish many of the most mundane and tasks that each citizen of the State undertakes on a daily basis, for example, taking the correct exit onto the motorway; passing the exams to be gain a haulier's licence or negotiating the numerous roundabouts which seem to have mushroomed on the approach to every Irish town since the days of the 'Celtic Tiger' economic boom! Having appropriate access to an education also aids a person's development in terms of their identity and the ability that each individual has to affirm or negate resistance to that identity. This is particularly true of individuals who are members of a small minority ethnic group such as the Irish Travellers.

As a group who have been primarily a non-literate community in recent generations educational access is a more pressing issue for this minority than for many others in present-day Ireland. Although more and more Traveller children now complete primary school, very few go on to secondary education and only a handful complete third level. This means, among other things, that policies affecting Travellers, and the research on which they are based, are framed and implemented by outsiders, policy-makers who are frequently not familiar with Traveller culture and way of life. While it has been the case that the Traveller community have been researched in a variety of ways over recent years, it has generally been the case that outside 'experts' have been commissioned to analyse or explore a particular aspect of Traveller culture or life. While this research has sometimes had a collaborative element and involved the Traveller community in its research process, it has more often been the case that there has been little or no consultation with the Traveller community.

This project was an attempt to redress this balance. Four Traveller women from Limerick – Mags Casey, Bridgie O'Donoghue, Ann O'Donoghue and Ann O'Driscoll – trained as qualitative researchers with project leader Eleanor Gormally, a lecturer in Education from Mary Immaculate College. The research, which was designed and carried out in a collaborative manner, focused on interviews with a small group of Limerick Traveller children about their lives, and especially school. As is customary with many community development projects, the manner in which the project was carried out was accorded just as much importance as the project outcomes. This is reflected in the structure of the book, with the first two out of three sections dealing with the women's/Traveller parents reflections on their own educational experiences and on the methods they used while conducting their research. The third section discusses the content and implications of what the children said during the interviews.

The book charts the ongoing process that were the training and intercultural dynamics of the project and makes clear that working with minorities such as Travellers in a collaborative manner – where the members of the minority are the subjects as opposed to the objects of the research – can be a very productive and successful research process. The book gives an overview of the complex relationship that exists between Traveller parents, Traveller children and the Irish educational process, and outlines the extent of Traveller educational inequality within the Irish educational system today. The second half of this qualitative study makes for particularly interesting reading as it gives a very clear insight into where Traveller parents and children have concerns as regards their interaction with the educational system. These concerns are cumulative and are a consequence of the experiences of a number of generations of Travellers within Irish society, the general thrust of which has been assimilative and generally ignorant of most aspects of Traveller identity and culture.

Parental involvement is undoubtedly a key element in the education of children and the establishment of a successful and ongoing relationship between home and school. While there are exceptions, this project shows that for the majority of Traveller parents, active participation in the provision of education to their children remains a formidable task. Many Traveller parents have had limited often negative experiences of the educational system themselves and consequently feel intimated when crossing the threshold of the school gates. As outlined in this book, many Traveller parents' estrangement from the educational process is compounded by a sense that they themselves are personally alienated from the school set-up and the perception that they are unskilled or unable to provide the support and supervision which their children need to succeed at school. A number of core themes emerge from this book, all of which impinge on the Traveller/school interface as it currently operates. They include:

- Discrimination against Travellers
- The implementation of the integration policy in the provision of Traveller education
- Withdrawal of Traveller children for learning support (especially during Irish language classes)
- Promotion of Traveller culture by the education system
- Provision of relevant and ongoing education support for Traveller parents

- Relationship and communication between Traveller and school personnel
- Visibility of Traveller 'voice' within the education system
- Inclusion of Traveller culture in school textbooks or syllabi.

The research sample for this project was drawn from five local primary (first-level) schools in the Limerick city area, two of which are situated in areas designated as disadvantaged. The Traveller children interviewed for the research were living in a diverse range of accommodation including: in houses on a Traveller site; in chalets on a Traveller site; in trailers on site or in trailers on the side of the road. A quick review of the interview data as transcribed in this book makes it possible to highlight a number of culturally-specific aspects of Traveller life which still hold strong currency amongst the community. Most of the activities which Traveller children tended to participate in outside of school tended to relate to the Traveller community, extended family and the maintenance of Traveller culture. The training and management of horses and family and childcare tasks were much higher on the day-to-day agenda for Traveller children as compared with children of a similar age from the 'settled' community.

For many Traveller children their sense of self appeared to be strongly related to their ability to perform certain tasks within the extended family. These tasks normally involved some degree of responsibility and were more often than not central to Traveller life and culture, a fact which was remarked upon by some of the Traveller researchers themselves as they undertook the project. The researchers discovered that for many Traveller children their overall sense of self-worth was, as with many non-Traveller children, strongly dependant on their parents' attitudes towards them. This interaction was slightly different from the same process as it occurs in the settled community as in many cases, Traveller children were more likely to elicit praise from their parents for what they could do (or indeed not do) as opposed to who they were.

A strong respect for the family was very evident in the responses of all the Traveller children who engaged with the project and family in Traveller culture was clear in encompassing extended family and in particular, grandparents. Many children pointed to the strong affinity they had with their grandparents and the large role played by grandparents and the elderly generally within the Traveller community. As one researcher pointed out, 'the children would be murdered for giving back cheek to a grandparent'. This would certainly contrast with the inter-generational experience of many 'settled' children where the placing of the elderly in nursing home care has become increasingly common.

Other aspects of Traveller culture as recounted by Traveller children – some of which would differ as to their extent and significance amongst a peer group in the settled community – also revolved around the elderly to one extent or another. For instance, attendance at Anniversary Masses, prayers for the dead, for the sick and the visiting of holy places or holy people were all highlighted by Traveller children as an integral part of their social and religious formation. Children in most Traveller families were expected to participate fully in religious family events, many of which also involved the elderly members of their community. The majority of children expressed negative views about where they lived, a fact which is indicative of the huge ongoing challenges that still remain as regards the provision of adequate and appropriate accommodation for Travellers in Limerick and most other Irish cities. Unsurprisingly, many Travellers in Limerick have sought accommodation in areas that facilitate involvement in 'traditional' Traveller activities such as horse-trading and scrap. Few local authorities in Ireland however provide facilities which include accommodation for scrap storage, horse management or living quarters for the extended family. As a consequence, the Traveller children's responses as relating to accommodation highlighted the 'dirt', overcrowding and danger that they associated with the environments around the trailers and chalets where they lived. Preference for a particular type of home varied among the children. Some children indicated a preference for living in a trailer particularly as this mode of living made it easier to move and travel when necessary. These children were in the minority however and the experience of travelling was unfamiliar to many. This was not surprising in view of the absence of transient sites for Travellers in Ireland and the 'boulder' policy that prevents most traditional Traveller stopping places from being accessed.

Interestingly, when describing his identity, one boy said he considered himself a Traveller but described his family as 'settled' for the simple reason that 'we don't travel round anymore'. Some of the interviews led Traveller children to discuss what they would like to be when they grew up and it was apparent from the responses that most children wished to follow in the footsteps of their parents and grandparents. For example, one boy stated that he wanted to have 'loads of horses', so many that he would be a 'farmer of horses', the same boy being adamant that he did not wish to own lots of land and thereby be a 'farmer' in the traditional meaning of the word.

Aspiring to motherhood remained very high on the list of life's milestones as outlined by Traveller girls indicating a contentment with the role model set by Traveller mothers within the community. The traditional desire of a young girl to become well-skilled in caring for the family, find a good husband and have a family of her own was reflected in the responses of many Traveller girls, some of whom already had considerable and responsible roles within the community as regards the care of the elderly including grandparents. The welfare of siblings, parents and grandparents was still seen as a essential role as fulfilled by the daughters and daughter-in-laws within Traveller families.

In some of the interviews, conversations around the notion of friendships in the school environment developed into a discussion of relationships between the sexes within the Travelling community. The responses from the Traveller children indicated a strong awareness of what was deemed appropriate behaviour and emphasised a strong moral code which would have been more prevalent amongst their settled peers in times past. The children who brought up this topic described the importance of maintaining an appropriate distance between Traveller boys and girls, particularly as children approached their early teens. Completely 'free' interaction between Traveller boys and girls was deemed unacceptable by most respondents and many children pointed out the preference for Traveller children from one site to interact only with the boys and girls from their own sites as opposed to other Traveller sites. Play between the sexes was discouraged unless the children were related to one another and Traveller girls were told by their mothers to – (in the words of the Traveller researchers) – 'stay away from the boys' and to mind their 'character'. Mixing with non-family boys would incur disapproval from many Traveller parents and as one child stated, a girl would get 'a bad name'. As a Traveller girl's future could depend on her 'reputation', a daughter would normally be chastised by her father or mother if she was playing with 'bauld boys'.

The experience of Traveller boys was very different from that of the girls with boys generally being encouraged to branch out into the 'men's world' of scrap and horses from an early age where they would associate 'only with the boys' from then on. Some boys did mention however that it was in this male world of the Traveller men that they first learned how to 'spot the girls'! The researchers noted that the children's responses echoed traditional conceptions of the gender/employment roles within the Traveller community, this despite the fact that changing gender roles and high male unemployment levels within the general community have already impacted to some degree on traditional Traveller values and their way of life.

The main findings of this research project, as elucidated by the Traveller researchers, make for interesting reading and would be worthy of consideration by any future policy-makers in Ireland's statutory bodies, local authorities and amongst Traveller organisations at all level. Of particular concern and as highlighted by the Traveller researchers on a number of occasions is the failure of the Irish primary school system to meet their children's needs and the disengagement from the educational process that this has engendered amongst many Traveller families. The primary thematics findings of this research project can be summarised as follows:

- That family was central to the Traveller children's life.

- That the Traveller children took on responsibilities in the home.

- That school was not talked about enthusiastically by the Traveller children.

- That the school day was perceived by the Traveller children as long and boring.

- That teachers were most liked when they were fair, let the children out to play and did activity related subjects with them.

- That some Traveller boys' relationships with the school principal, in the main, revolved around reprimand and punishment.

- That both the Traveller boys and the Traveller girls talked passionately about horses.

- That the Traveller children were hesitant to explore topics of a personal nature.

- That the school world did not appear to be connected with the Traveller child's world.

- That the Traveller children wished for improved standards of living accommodation.

Conclusion

The authors of this book acknowledge that the fact that the qualitative nature of their project meant that the sample of parents and children who worked on the project which culminated in *Whiddin to the Gauras* on a continuous basis was a small one. There is no doubt however that the experiences outlined in this book and the conclusions that can be drawn from these experiences will resonate with Travellers and other minorities on a much greater scale and well beyond the educational precincts of Limerick city.

Perhaps the most fundamental conclusion as outlined in this book and the most valuable is its elucidation of what happens to a community of people who have to hide their true identity in order to engage with a so-called tolerant and multicultural society as modern Ireland would proclaim itself to be. The Irish government's 1995 Task Force on Travellers was tasked with the job of charting policy and future objectives as pertaining to the Irish Traveller community. One objective which all Traveller and Roma and Sinti groups across Europe would endorse as an initial step forward would be the simple acknowledgement of Traveller and Gypsy identity. As this book makes abundantly clear, there is little hope for progress in any societal sphere including education until the identity denial, which has pervaded many aspects of Irish life as applied to the Traveller community is negated once and for all. Identity denial as a discriminatory tool has no place in good educational practice anywhere and can only compound already existent problems that traverse a wide range of domains as relating to social disadvantage, drug abuse, lack of self-esteem and poor social support. No amount of books and reports can replicate the violence that is inflicted on a people who are labeled a problem from the moment of their birth. The Traveller children interviewed in this book have given an eloquent account of what it is like to watch your parents deny their own identity in order to apply for a job or go into a pub. They have hinted at the feelings of self-inferiority that can overcome a young person who is aware that their entire community is considered dirty and troublesome or who have to remove their earrings before attending a school in order that they are not singled out for discriminatory behaviour. That Traveller children are aware of the 'distinction' that is made between their own community and the 'majority' community at an extremely early age is one of the most poignant messages to emerge from *Whiddin to the Gauras*.

Acknowledgements

A special word of thanks is extended to both Eleanor Gormally and Mags Casey for their input and help when preparing the above essay.

Whiddin to the Gaura: Talking to our Own – (Traveller Researchers Talk to Limerick Traveller Children) (2005) (Authors: Mags Casey, Bridgie O'Donoghue, Ann O'Donoghue, Ann O'Driscoll, Eleanor Gormally) is published by Veritas Publications, Dublin, www.veritas.ie.

References

Cauley, W. and Ó hAodha, M. (eds.) (2004). *The Candlelight Painter - The Life and Work of Willy Cauley, Traveller, Painter and Poet*; Dublin: A&A Farmar Publishing

Collins, M. (1994) 'The Sub-Culture of Poverty - A Response to McCarthy.' in *Irish Travellers: Culture and Ethnicity*. S. Ó. Síocháin et al. (eds.) Belfast: The Institute of Irish Studies, The Queens University of Belfast

Cottaar, A. et al. (eds.) (1998) *Gypsies and Other Itinerant Groups - A Socio-Historical Approach*; London: Macmillan Press

Court, A. (1985) *Puck of the Droms: The lives and literature of the Irish tinkers*. California: University of California Press

Dunne, P. and Ó hAodha, M. (eds.) (2004) *Parley-Poet and Chanter - A Life of Pecker Dunne*; Dublin: A&A Farmar Publishing

Harper, J. (1977) 'The Irish Travellers of Georgia' M.A. University of Georgia

Helleiner, J. (2000) *Irish Travellers: Racism and the Politics of Culture*; Toronto: University of Toronto Press

Hyland, J. (ed.) (1993) *Do You Know Us at All?*; Dublin: Parish of the Travelling People

Joyce, N. (1985) *Traveller: An autobiography*; Dublin: Gill and Macmillan

Kenny, M. (1996). 'The Routes of Resistance - Travellers and Second-level Schooling'. PhD. Trinity College Dublin

Kenrick, D. and Puxon, G. (eds.) (1972) *The Destiny of Europe's Gypsies*; London: Sussex University Press in association with Heinemann

Lee, J. (1989) *Politics and Society in Ireland, 1912-1985*; Cambridge: Cambridge University Press

McCarthy, P. (1994) 'The Sub-Culture of Poverty Reconsidered.' in S. Ò. Síocháin et al. (eds.) *Irish Travellers: Culture and Ethnicity*; Belfast: Institute of Irish Studies, Queen's University

McDonagh, M. (2000) 'Nomadism' in E. Sheehan (ed.) *Travellers - Citizens of Ireland*; Dublin: Parish of the Travelling People

21.

Traveller Education:
A Primary Teacher's Perspective

Cristín Wilkinson

By way of introduction I am a primary school teacher from Midleton, County Cork. On graduation from Mary Immaculate College in 2009 I have worked as a mainstream class teacher. Drawing on my recent studies and experience to date I have been asked to contribute to this book.

It is my intention to outline educational ideas that are important to increase the level of Traveller education in our society. The main objective is to impart the necessary tools to Traveller children so that they can progress through the education system reaching third level. It is also necessary to instil a positive attitude in them about education. Throughout my training in Mary Immaculate College we were reminded that 'the child is first and foremost a child', they should not be defined by their background, nationality, religion or disability. Therefore we must also tackle our own perceptions and stereotypes in society to ensure that the Traveller child, in particular, is treated fairly and respected. Drawing from my own experience I have witnessed this first hand in my classroom, a classroom of multi-cultural foreign nationals has provided me with further insights into the perceptions of Irish children and how they perceive foreigners/Travellers.

In the Primary School Curriculum, Department of Education and Science, 1999), it states the three general aims of the education system is to:

- Enable the child to live a full life as a child and to realise their potential as a unique individual

- Enable the child to develop as a social being through living and cooperating with others and so contribute to the good of society

- To prepare the child for future education and lifelong learning.

These aims are significant in ensuring that the children in our schools have a positive learning experience in primary school.

Important for Traveller children in particular is the last aim, 'preparing the child for future learning'. This is the aim for all who are striving to create a better relationship between the travelling community and education and for the progressing to third level education. The Traveller Access Initiative set up in Limerick has helped greatly with this process. As John Heneghan (2007) remarked in 2001, when he searched for Traveller students sitting the Leaving Cert that there were none and in that year there were no Traveller students enrolled in the University of Limerick. With the help of different support groups such as the homework club, adult and young women's group and the secondary school integration there were almost 20 teenagers with a great possibility of progressing to third level. This is an example of the possibilities that exist for Traveller students who have the adequate support and resources in place.

It is obvious that this support must come from the educational bodies in this country. There are systems already in place for Traveller children such as the Home School Community Liaison Scheme and Visiting Teacher for Traveller Service in school. The Visiting Teacher for Traveller Service overall function is to promote, facilitate and support the education of Travellers from pre-school to third level access. If all these support groups were effectively collaborating with the Traveller Access programme put in place throughout Ireland, I think this would be a major benefit for the Traveller student and would help in tackling the negative attitudes that still appear in our society towards this group. As Michael Hayes (2006) remarks, Travellers are at a disadvantage in society when trying to negotiate their struggle for their own identity and gaining recognition in a society where image is principal. They have not had much impact on how their way of life is portrayed due largely to the fact that literacy was and still is for some a major obstacle, having little primary written sources of their culture. Being traditionally excellent storytellers, a lot that was passed down during generations was passed through word of mouth. This can be used to its advantage and I think for the initiative to succeed we need to begin changing the image we have of Travellers in Ireland at present.

I feel that the first level of education a child receives is of immense importance as it shapes their attitudes and view of education and what they want to get out of the learning process. As a teacher, it is essential to present to them with a positive, fun and safe learning environment, one in which they will enjoy and benefit from through every aspect of their lives. Having had a lot of experience teaching non-national children, I have seen how important it is to differentiate the curriculum for the needs of the particular class and children of that class. For a Traveller child (as with any child), it is important that they feel included and welcome in their classroom and that the teacher is approachable and empathic to their needs. We also need to help children to feel empathy to all members of society. In the curriculum it acknowledges that children are a part of society and that their personal development is deeply affected by their relationships at home, in school and with other people. It is therefore necessary to ensure that each child feels equal and a respected member of our society.

When working with children who's first language is not English or children who struggle with literacy, the use of visual aids and clear instructions are effective. Setting children achievable goals is essential especially for the Traveller child as if they perceive a task is too difficult they will feel they cannot complete it and feel even less confident in themselves. Setting goals that are challenging yet the child can feel like it is achievable will help in motivating the child. It is not about the being the best but doing the best they can do. If the child feels incapable or alienated from tasks school can be very stressful and that is why differentiation and inclusion is so important. If you build on the child's interests they will be more involved and active in their own learning. The curriculum promotes the child being an active agent in his or her own learning. As young children are very much interested in their own world and are egocentric, they relate everything to themselves. Building on this we can encourage them to see the similarities between them and others. This is essential in tackling the negativity that still surrounds Traveller's and if these children do not feel like they belong in the classroom around children that are settled then they will not have a positive relationship with school and education. Bringing the child's interest and experiences into the classroom will allow them to feel confident in expressing themselves.

During my time in Mary Immaculate College, we had a number of lectures focused on teaching Traveller children. The lectures emphasised the importance of building on what Traveller children know and love, in particular their love for horses. Encouraging the children to do a specific project in groups or individually would educate themselves and others. While in my second year teaching fifth class girls, I read to them the novel *The Blue Horse* by Marita Conlon McKenna (1993). This story is told through the voice of a young Traveller girl and her experiences with stereotypes in society. It was amazing how well the children reacted to some of the issues in the novel and their responses were ultimately empathic to the Traveller girl. They could see how the girl was treated unfairly just because of her culture, and having children in my class from different cultures, countries, religion and colour, this promoted a feeling of equality and empathy in the classroom. There were no Travellers in that particular class but there were in the school and I felt that approaching the subject like this would be worthwhile in creating a positive attitude towards minority groups and encourage them to maybe read more of the novel themselves.

An interesting initiative that is appearing in schools in Ireland is the Building Bridges programme (Courtney and Gleeson, 2007). This is a programme that uses picture books as a method of teaching valuable comprehension and literacy skills through prediction methods, making connections and synthesising. This programme works particularly well with children who have English as a second language and children who have difficulties with literacy. This is a programme I feel would work very effectively with Traveller children as it is all about responding to visual stimulus and interpreting stories. As a culture of storytellers, this would appeal to them.

The academic aspect of school is of extreme importance but of equal importance is the social aspect. As a Traveller child may feel alienated or like an outsider, it would be a positive experience for them to be involved in extra-curricular activities. From sports to the arts, activities outside the classroom environment can help children to find something they are good at. Involvement in extra-curricular activities such as team sports should be encouraged. Team work allows the child to discover skills and create friendships. It would be a great place for the Traveller child to express themselves and have something that they can relate to with other children of the same age.

It is also of great importance that the parents are involved with their child's learning experience. Keeping the parents informed and helping them with ways to assist their child will build their confidence as well as the child's. The parents of Traveller children today may not have had a positive experience in school and this negativity may be passed onto their child unknowingly. As children spend 85 per cent of their time in the home they need the home support to succeed in school. With the Traveller Initiative in Limerick, there is a keen emphasis on educating the parents also to enable them to help their own children. I believe literacy is key in accessing education and fulfilling the learning experience. With a history of poor literacy skills, this has impacted the education of Travellers to date. It is difficult for some Traveller parents to help their children when it comes to the task of homework. Having set up Homework Clubs for the Traveller initiative, this allows children to gain support when it might not be available at home. These clubs have been set up in many disadvantaged areas and I think this is a critical resource for both the pupil, parent and teacher.

Conclusion

In light of the above we have seen how if the correct resources are put in place and utilised, that Traveller children and parents do understand the importance of education in their community. An educated Traveller community will not only benefit them as a minority in society but will also benefit the wider community, as Travellers and settled people will be able to integrate and co-exist in a more equal way.

From my experience education is still not at the forefront of every Traveller parents mind and this is an area I think we need to channel further resources in. I have found that group talks work in bringing to light underlying issues that might exist in a community and this could be the means to bring Traveller parents together to discuss their children's education needs. By tackling the negative attitude that Traveller parents may still have about the Irish education system (which may have failed them), it will enable Traveller children to participate fully in their education with teachers and parents working together for the benefit of the child.

Although my experience to date has been primarily with non-nationals, I have seen many similarities between the two groups. The challenge faced by us teachers has increased due to the growth of the multi-cultural classroom forcing us to tackle our own perceptions to ensure the inclusion of every child.

Bibliography

Conlon McKenna, M. (1993). *The Blue Horse*. O'Brien Press. Dublin

Courtney, A. and Gleeson, M. (2010) Building Bridges of Undestanding, Curriculum Development Unit, Mary Immaculate College, Limerick.

Department of Education and Science. (1999) Primary School Curriculum Introduction, Dublin, National Council for Curriculum and Assessment.

Heneghan, J. (2007) 'Travellers and access: The "Empathy and Mechanisms" Model at the University of Limerick' published in *The Stranger in Ourselves: Ireland's Other* (edited by Ó hAodha, M., O'Donnell, D. and Power, C.) Dublin, A&A Farmar.

Hayes, M. (2006) *Irish Travellers: Representations and Realities*, Dublin, The Liffey Press.

22.

'What Is the Use of a Book without Pictures or Conversations?'

Arts-based Educational Research in Adult Education

Richard Hannafin

It's very easy to do research if you think research is just finding out what nobody knows. Well, that's not good enough; if you want to do research, you want to do research that would have some influence. A lot of research is done which sure adds to our knowledge, but it adds to our knowledge in ways that we didn't find very useful. The best research is done with a shovel, not tweezers (Needham, cited in Gray and Malins, 2004, p. xii).

As I push the buttons on my personal 14' Mac Book Pro in the small hours on yet another wet balmy night in late July, I enter my password, take a sip of my coffee and patiently wait while my Mac opens all those locked doors in cyberspace to let me in to my virtual office. I fire up my search engine, enter another password which grants me access to the reams of documents which I'm assured by massive multinational organisations is kept safe and sound in a security box somewhere out there in their failsafe cloud in cyberspace.

Every time we jump through the digital matrix of passwords that, certainly in today's world, protects much of our personal information we are in fact making use of research conducted by Roger Needham in 1966. Considered a genius in computer security, operating systems design, memory management systems and networking, as well as being the founding director of Microsoft's Cambridge Laboratory he was a true pioneer in an age of digital revolution, especially so because of his vision of research (Press, cited in Gray and Malins, 2004).

Mike Press addresses the role of art research by describing the 'diverse family of creative disciplines' as having the 'potential to explore questions of great significance' in a 'dangerous, damaged and uncertain world'. Drawing on Needham's analogy of research being done with a shovel as opposed to tweezers, Press calls on researchers to 'get digging'. At times I feel that my own research into the role of the arts in adult and further education has indeed been done with a shovel, although now, maybe the use of a tweezers would be appropriate in the analysis of that research. My role as a teacher is in a constant state of flux. I am privileged to have the opportunity to work with a wide variety of groups from a broad spectrum of socio-economic, multicultural and diverse ethnic backgrounds. The common thread in all of my work is a visual approach to the field of adult education. My practice over the last 12 months has been concerned with the implications and possibilities which the arts hold for further and adult education. My journey as artist/researcher/teacher in the field of further and adult education began to gather momentum with an arts-based educational research (ABER) project based on the site of the Riverside Senior Traveller Training Centre (RSTTC) in the town of Rathkeale County Limerick from April to July 2011.

Arts-based research in education is a relatively new approach which employs new assumptions and methods as well as utilizing the established modes of inquiry. (Eisner, 2007, pp. 16-27). Elliot Eisner, professor of art and education at the Stanford University School of Education describes his initial interest in an arts based response to educational research as an:

> ... ambition of mine, to develop an approach to the conduct
> of educational research that was rooted in the arts and that

used art forms to reveal the features that mattered educationally . . . (ibid, p. 18)

There are of course issues surrounding the legitimacy of this kind
of approach, the main one being that arts-based research is considered by many in the sphere of educational research as a 'soft form' of
qualitative research. The positivist tradition which has informed western philosophy for the first half of the twentieth century describes the
arts as 'ornamental' and 'emotive' in their nature rather than bastions
of truth and knowledge. The arts are experienced, enjoyed or admired,
they do not provide the raw data needed to dissect or analyse in our
eternal quest for knowledge (Ayer, cited in Eisner, 2008). Plato regarded the human senses which are stimulated through the arts as a
distraction from the truth as they 'lead one away rather than toward
that form of critical rationality upon which truth depends' (Eisner,
2008, p. 4). Plato's theories about mind, knowledge, and rationality
are the building blocks upon which the modern concept of science
is based. Aristotle however takes a different approach by dividing
knowledge into three categories; the theoretical, the practical and
the productive (Mckeon, cited in Eisner, 2007, p. 4). Research conducted in diverse contexts has to consider the circumstances of that
context when addressing the aims and objectives of the research. In
differentiating the kinds of knowledge, which can be secured, knowledge subject to the conditions of the environment in which it is constructed, Aristotle provides an argument, which advocates a broader
approach to qualitative research. This widening of the playing field
encompasses the singular view of knowledge whilst at the same time
recognizes a multiple viewpoint which the literature relating to arts-
based research advocates.

> Aristotle cautions us that an educated man expects only as
> much precision as the subject matter will admit. It is as fool-
> ish to seek approximations from mathematicians as exacti-
> tudes from poets (McKeon, cited in Eisner, 2008, p. 4).

McCarthy (2007) contends that art making is the most 'fundamental human thing we can do', it is a process 'by which each person,

acting in the world in a social context, in a very real and literal sense, creates, revises, enriches and expresses his or her own mind' (p. 9). Comprehensive studies have already examined the role the arts have to play in society (Moore, 1997) and (Kelly, 1999, pp. 17-21). Francois Matarasso (1997) conducted a comprehensive study, which examined the impact of arts programmes on Britain's cultural and economic life. The study is primarily targeted at policy makers in the arts and social fields; it is a major study, which examines the role of the arts in a wide variety of contexts from education through to community regeneration. Fifty social impacts of participation in the arts are drawn up in order to provide a 'range of social outcomes' produced by active engagement with the arts. A sample of these outcomes shows that participation in the arts can:

- Increase people's confidence and sense of self-worth

- Extend involvement in social activity

- Give people influence over how they are seen by others

- Stimulate interest and confidence in the arts

- Provide a forum to explore personal rights and responsibilities

- Contribute to the educational development of children

- Encourage adults to take up education and training opportunities

- Help build new skills and work experience

- Contribute to people's employability

- Help people take up or develop careers in the arts (Matarasso, 1997, p. 14).

Over the course of 12 weeks I delivered a printmaking project in collaboration with the students of RSTTC. All involved with the exception of one individual were female, adult Travellers from the town of Rathkeale and the nearby town of Askeaton. With the support of the staff and director of the centre as well as the consent of the participants I initially embarked on a project which explored the themes of identity and ididviduality through the medium of fine art printmaking. At a time when these themes were being explored/exploited by various media organisations, most notably Channel 4's *My Big Fat Gypsy Wedding*, I wanted to gauge a visual response to Traveller Culture by allowing the group to research images which they felt underpinned their identity. I wanted students to explore their own culture in a considered , meaningful way so that they as a marginalised segment of society could take responsibility and ownership of how they were perceived in wider society. I was acutely aware at this point in time that my own role in the research process was blurring the margins between that of a community artist and an art tutor. Community arts do however echo some of the theories of adult education by referring to the critical pedagogies of educationalists such as Paulo Freire, bell hooks and Henry Giroux (Henderson, 2004, pp. 159-178). Focusing on Freire, concepts such as praxis and dialogue are particularly prevalent themes in community art literature.

The printmaking project in Riverside echoes many of the sentiments provided by the literature advocating the role of the arts in education. Dialogue became an increasingly prevalent theme over the course of the project. Visual techniques such as collage and concept mapping initiated class debates as to what were the dominant factors that informed Traveller culture. The collages (Figure 1) provided a platform for meaningful dialogue, which centered on how Traveller culture and identity is experienced by those who are part of the culture and perceived by those who are not.

Figure 1.

The collages produced by the students stimulated debate and provided a focus for the project, conversation surrounding the issues of female identity in modern day Traveller society came to the fore. Themes such as family, religion and fashion dominated discussions. The role of religion in christenings, communions, confirmations and marriages were discussed. The prints (Figure 2) reflected the ongoing dialogue in the class and dialogue was advanced in the class discussions relating to the prints.

Figure 2

With the project nearing completion, Mary Immaculate College made the use of their printmaking equipment available the class. This was a unique opportunity for the students to spend a day on campus in order to print their work using professional print making equipment. The resulting art works were to form a significant proportion of an exhibition showcasing the work of the students from the Riverside Senior Travelling Training Centre. The exhibition, entitled 'Riverside', was officially opened by Jimmy Deenihan Minister Department of Arts Heritage and the Gaeltacht on Friday, 24 February 2012.

The printmaking project in Rathkeale was an initial venture into the sphere of arts-based educational research. As a project, I feel that it succeeded in exploring themes within Traveller culture by gauging and documenting a visual response to Traveller identity as experienced from the perspectives of female Travellers. More importantly, the art work opened up lines of communication needed to further explore my own research theme of the role of art in education. A mutual relationship of trust and respect was fostered throughout the research process which was to form the basis of a more focused inquiry into the role of art in adult education. This focus culminated in a collaborative learning experience where one of the participants of the printmaking project, engaged in an Access programme in the University of Limerick, utilised her newly acquired printmaking abilities in order to address a complex sociology assignment. Kristina had attended lectures in UL for a semester in 2011. As a student, she was engaged, enthusiastic and determined. Kristina enjoyed the lectures and had a good grasp of the sociological concepts being discussed. However there were obstacles which stood in her way when she was required to submit an essay at the end of term. The texts and readings accompanying the lectures were beyond Kristina's level of comprehension. The assignment would prove a step too far as regards meeting the academic standards required at this level. But yet Kristina was well able to verbalise the content of the lectures. With the intervention of Annmarie Garahee of the VEC and John Heneghan, a lecturer at UL and Coordinator of Educational Access for Travellers at UL, who were both instrumental in the provision of this Access programme, a different approach to recognising the learning experience in UL was discussed. Kristina had already displayed an impressive aptitude for art through the printmaking project and was clearly adept at attaching meaning from her own culture to visual representations. Her work throughout the course of the printmaking project was now to form the vehicle for Kristina to complete her assignment by articulating her thoughts visually. With the support of the staff in Rathkeale STTC and UL, as well as Kristina's consent it was decided that we would work in collaboratively exploring the possibilities of the role of art in addressing the educational obstacles facing Kristina. The resulting work which consisted of a series of prints and a support sketchbook addresses the question:

Sociologists reject the idea that behavioural differences between men and women are biologically determined. Outline the key grounds for this rejection and discuss what this means for a sociological understanding of gender.

The work contained within the sketchbook offers a unique insight into how sociological concepts are broken down by reinterpreting the terms in relation to Traveller culture. The prints which were all created by Kristina bridge the gap between an academic understanding of sociological terms such as gender, socialization and social learning theory with a visual response informed by stories of Traveller life. The question provided the challenge, the stories unraveled the meaning and the prints display an understanding of complex sociological terms in the context of Traveller culture. Indeed even the collages created by Kristina for 'homework' offer a tangible link between the academic terms and her own understanding of them (see Figure 3).

Figure 3

Working with Kristina over the course of this project was a privilege, it served to strengthen my resolve advocating the role of art in adult education. Whilst the many studies and government policies support, encourage and recognise the positive effects of the arts in education, I feel that in general the focus is narrow, although the language is used with broad brush strokes. I am of course in favour of art for arts sake but as educationalists we need to be open to the possibilities the arts hold for our chosen field. In a time of austerity where arts budgets have been decimated I would argue that now more than ever we need to pursue inquiries which explore the contribution the arts can make to a society in economic recovery. If that means that a visual approach can be used as a strategy to advance the learning possibilities of adults accessing the world of further education will this not have a positive effect on the fabric of our society? Encompassing Gardner's theory of multiple intelligences as well as Freires' thoughts on visual images as a powerful means of communication I believe that the research undertaken in collaboration with Kristina is evidence of the role of art in advancing learning in adulthood. As relevant as the research is, it is as of yet but a stepping stone, one in the right direction for further arts-based inquiry. Echoing the sentiments of Hedy Bach, a practitioner in the field of visual narrative 'what indeed is the use of research without image and story'.

> Alice was beginning to get very tired of sitting by her sister on the bank, and having nothing to do: once or twice she had peeped into the book her sister was reading, but it had no pictures and conversations in it, 'and what is the use of a book,' thought Alice, 'without pictures or conversations?' (Carroll, cited in Bach, 2007, p. 281).

References

Bach, H. (2007) 'Composing a Visual narrative Inquiry', in Clandinin, Jean D. (ed.) *Handbook of Narrative Inquiry: Mapping a Methodology*, London, Sage, 280-307.

Eisner, E. (2007) 'Persistent tensions in arts-based research' in Cahnmann-Taylor, M. And Siegesmund, R. (eds.) *Arts-Based Research in Education: Foundations for Practice*, New York, Routledge, 16-27.

Eisner, E., (2008) 'Art and Knowledge' in Knowles, Gary J. and Cole, Ardra L. (eds.) *Handbook of the Arts in Qualitive Research: Perspectives, Methodologies, Examples and Issues*. London, Sage Publications Ltd., 3-12.

Freire, P. (1996) *Pedagogy of the Oppressed*, London, Penguin.

Gardner, H. (1991) *The Unschooled Mind: How Children Think and How Schools Should Teach*, New York, Perseus.

Giroux, Henry A. (1989) 'Schooling as a form of cultural Politics: Toward a Pedagogy of and for Difference' in *Critical Pedagogy, the State, and Cultural Struggle*, Giroux, Henry A. and McLaren, Peter L. (eds.), State University of New York, pp. 125-151.

Gray, C. and Malins, J. (2004) *Visualizing Research: A Guide to the Research Process in Art and Design*, England and USA: Ashgate, x–xii.

Henderson, R. (2004) 'Community arts as socially engaged art' in Fitzgearld, S. (ed.)., *An Outburst Of Frankness: Community Arts in Ireland – A Reader*, Dublin: Tasc, 159-178.

Kelly, E. (1999) 'Community Arts and Community Development' in Bane, L. (ed.), *The Adult Learner*, Aontas, Dublin, p.17-21 Available: http://www.aontas.com/download/pdf/adult_learner_99.pdf (Accessed 3 Aug 2012).

Matarasso, F. (1997) Use or Ornament? The social impact of participation in the arts. Available: http://www.disseminate.net.au/files/webfiles/OrnamentMatarasso.pdf (Accessed 3 Aug 2012).

McCarthy, C. (2007) 'Art and the Creation of Mind' accepted for Conference Presentation © 2007 Philosophy of Education Society of Australasia, Available: www.pesa.org.au/site/page//papers/2007papers/mccarthy2007.pdf (Accessed 1 Aug 2012).

Moore, J. (1997) Poverty: Access and Participation in the Arts Available: http://www.artscouncil.ie/Publications/Poverty_Access_and_Participation_in_the_Arts.pdf (Accessed 3 Aug 2012).

23.

Irish Traveller Families' Struggle for Healthcare in England: An Irish Answer for an English Problem?

Colm Power

Abstract

This article explores obstructions to health care access and delivery for Irish Traveller families in Britain. The sources of these barriers are usually related to their cultural and ethnic disqualification and the resultant pariah status of Irish Travellers that persists in much of mainstream society. This pariah status in society is often reproduced both structurally and professionally in health services, resulting in poor service provision and delivery to Travellers. Consequently, Traveller's specific health care needs are rarely met either sensitively or adequately through mainstream support and delivery mechanisms. Travellers' multiple disqualifications also have a negative impact on Irish Travellers' perceptions of, and engagement with, health services. This piece focuses on restrictions to health care access and support provided by general practitioners (GPs) and National Health Service (NHS) hospitals in Britain. While highlighting the stark disparities in health and mortality statistics between settled people and Travellers through secondary sources, this article concentrates on the environmental, cultural and social parameters that influence access to health care for Irish Travellers. In this context, the article uses a detailed illustrative study from the 'Room to Roam: England's Irish Travellers' research project to discuss access to health services for Irish Travellers in England, whether nomadic, living on trailer sites, or living in settled forms of accommodation. Finally, almost no Primary Care Trusts (PCTs) and social care providers in England employ specialist staff to work with Travellers on their specific health and social care needs. This article suggests that a successful Irish health development, based on training Travellers to become health care assistants in their own communities, could be successfully adapted to English conditions.

Introduction

This chapter explores the barriers to access and delivery of healthcare for Irish Traveller families in England and is based on a three-year 'Room to Roam' research project that highlights some of the key issues prevalent for Irish Traveller families when attempting to engage with and use healthcare services (see Power, 2004). Detailed background information about Irish Travellers in England is presented from this particular research, while also using knowledge from the author's extensive research experience in both Ireland and Britain, and incorporating substantial references to other relevant secondary sources . An illustrative study based on the reflexive practice of a settled primary health care worker from 'Room to Roam' is then used to represent and explain some of the key exclusions and discriminations experienced by Irish Traveller families in England in relation to healthcare access and service delivery. It also illustrated the challenges for settled primary health care workers coming to terms with difference (Ibid). All respondents' names referred to in this paper have been fictionalised to protect their identities.

The physical, psychosocial and mental health of Irish Travellers has been of particular concern over the last two generations as assimilation policies the author underpinned by criminalising laws have put huge stresses on all people of a nomadic disposition in England, and Ireland. These policies coupled with poor and/or coercive implementation have been responsible for overcrowding, evictions, poor sanitation, vermin and accident prone environments on both illegal encampments and poorly maintained official Traveller sites. But assimilation and criminalising policies are also increasingly resulted in Irish Travellers living in inappropriate forms of housing that fail to take into account their extended family, economic needs and cultural aspirations, leading to Travellers suffering the mental stress of sedentary living conditions, associated racism, isolation from family and clan supports, family breakdowns and deprivation. Settled forms of accommodation also mean having to interface with other unfamiliar cultures without any intercultural supports or mediation, and this has sometimes resulted in social friction, violence and the intimidation of Traveller families (Power, 2003, 2004).

Irish Traveller men tend to delegate responsibility for their family's healthcare to the mother, wife or matriarch as the culture tends to be very patriarchal in nature. Traditionally, many Traveller men's attitude to institutional healthcare is one of avoidance and denial of health dangers rooted in a strong culture of masculinity (see Power, 2004). Women generally shoulder the burden of responsibility for children's primary health and accessing healthcare systems. The delegation of healthcare by men to women in Traveller culture does not mean that the men are not interested in healthy families. Children's welfare and generational renewal are the lynchpin of Irish Traveller culture from both female and male perspectives, but the traditional division of responsibilities usually allocates family health to women and economic well-being to men. It is not the extended family, or indeed its patriarchal nature, that can limit the resources and capability of Traveller families to access formal healthcare, but the social and cultural tensions that can lead to structural dilution or breakdown (and resultant impoverishment) of the extended family through settlement in unsuitable urban sedentary accommodation. The cohesion of the clan is diminished and the social fabric of the family may unravel as their struggle for survival is compounded by the increased prevalence of drug addictions, alcohol abuse, domestic violence, desertion of families by patriarchs, and criminalisation, particularly of young men (Ibid, 2003, 2004; Mac Gabhann, 2011).

Irish Travellers have problems registering with GPs for a number of reasons including reluctance by some surgeries to take on so-called 'high maintenance' patients and the 'unintentional' impact of health service related legislation and policy in England. Irish Traveller families (particularly in urban settled situations) have multi-factorial health problems that centre on poverty, literacy problems, cultural taboos, the geographical specificity of health services, cultural estrangement from settled norms, and the impact of forced assimilation on mental health and loss of extended family supports (Greenfields, 2008; Power, 2004). Women's health suffers particularly as they prioritise the needs of large dependent families, often without a husband or the traditionally supportive extended family. Irish Traveller women have particular problems accessing specialist services in hospitals and clinics for both cultural and logistical reasons related to poverty, overwork, poor literacy, inflexible health service regimes, lack of understanding of bureaucratic and institutional functions, and lack of supportive health advocacy services.

Irish Travellers in England

Irish Travellers have been part of British society for centuries according to historical sources (Adams et al., 1975: 172-173). In contrast to the situation in the Republic of Ireland, they are recognised as a distinct ethnic group in England under the Race Relations Act 1976 and the Race Relations Amendment Act 2001. Historically, Irish Travellers were employed in horse trading, seasonal farm-work, rural crafts, selling domestic goods door-to-door (hawking), busking, and as tinsmiths and tradesmen. They filled vital niches in the economy of pre-industrialised Ireland and parts of rural England up to the 1950s. Many Irish Traveller extended families had established regular annual migratory patterns that included travelling between Ireland and various parts of Britain. Urbanisation, mass production of cheap disposable plastics, and the mechanisation of agriculture undermined the traditional basis of the Traveller economy. A combination of social exclusivity, nomadism, cohesive extended families and clans, and a strong resistance to regular wage-labour underpinned the nature and structure of the Irish Traveller culture and economy.

Travellers' entrepreneurial skills adapted as the 'mainstream' economy changed post 1945 and many migrated in large numbers to major cities in England. Access to motor vehicles created new opportunities for commercial nomadism, but also brought Travellers into contact with state regulatory agencies. As a consequence of modernisation the Irish Traveller economy has shifted to casual building work, tarmacing, market stalls, gardening and scrap metal collection, while some have developed successful businesses dealing in antiques and furnishings (Power, 2004; Adams et al., 1975). Many Travellers interviewed for 'Room to Roam', particularly those in urban sedentary forms of accommodation, survived on social security payments.

Demographics

Accurate statistics about Irish Travellers are difficult to obtain as they are not yet specifically defined as a separate ethnic grouping on census forms in England. Government population estimates are based on local counts of trailers on official sites, or other 'known' unauthorised encampments, carried out by local authorities. The 'total population' is extrapolated from the 'estimated' occupancy per trailer. This reporting procedure is non-mandatory and far from rigorous - no information is collected on actual Traveller population numbers, age, gender, or ethnicity. In effect, no accurate government statistics exist for Irish Travellers in Britain (Hickman and Walter, 1997: 20-21). Government figures for England and Wales (Office of the Deputy Prime Minister, 2001) indicate that 13,802 trailers were counted by local authorities. Of those, 3,346 were in unauthorised camps, indicating that just over twenty-four percent of all 'counted' Travellers have no legal or secure place to reside and live under threat of eviction.

These government estimates do not include the large numbers of Irish Travellers who are living either temporarily or permanently in settled forms of accommodation (Power, 2004). Many 'settled' Irish Travellers have been forced from their traditional nomadic way of life due to lack of trailer sites and the virtual outlawing of nomadism in England and Wales by the Criminal Justice and Public Order Act (CJPOA, 1994). No official data are collected on 'settled' Travellers, but these supposedly assimilated 'invisible' Travellers still 'travel' through private, social, and local authority housing stocks, often moving between or within cities up to five or six times a year. Many Irish Travellers are now seasonally nomadic, preferring to winter in housing while risking the vagaries of travelling for work, cultural and family related reasons (births, marriages, sickness, funerals, fairs etc.) during the Summer months (Power, 2004). Large disparities in population estimates are partly explained by high internal mobility rates, but also by the (largely un-researched) phenomenon of Irish Traveller seasonal and periodic migration between Britain and Ireland, and also continental Europe (Ibid).

Travellers' Health in England

There is a lack of specific health research on Irish Travellers in England. All Traveller groups in England suffer poorer health and lower life expectancy than is the norm in the settled community (Power, 2004; Parry, Van Cleemput, Peters, Moore, Walters, Thomas and Cooper, 2004). The health gap between settled people and Travellers is illustrated by comprehensive research (Abdalla, S. et al., 2010; see also Barry, Herity and Solan, 1989) carried out in Ireland specifically with Irish Travellers in 2010 which indicates that on average Traveller women live 11 years and Traveller men live 15 years less than the general population, while infant mortality rates are three and a half times the national average. Traveller men have four times, while Traveller women have three times the mortality rate of the general population. Suicide amongst Travellers is 6 times the rate of the general population accounting for about 11 per cent of all Traveller deaths. The infant mortality rate for Travellers is 3.5 times the rate of the general population. Of those Travellers interviewed for the 'Our Geels' research (All Ireland Traveller Health Study Team, September 2010), over 52 per cent aged 40-60 years had been diagnosed with high blood pressure, and over 42 per cent had been diagnosed with high cholesterol in last year, compared to 30 per cent and 35 per cent respectively of the general population in the same period.

This research allows the reader some appreciation of the gap between Irish Traveller and sedentary health status generally, though carried out in Ireland both north and south. Barry, Herity and Solan's earlier research (1989; for similar English statistics on all Traveller groups see Parry et al., 2004; Morris and Clements, 2001) reported that Irish Travellers indices of fertility were approximately 250 per cent more than the rate for the settled population. The stillbirth rate was 19.5 per thousand total births, perinatal mortality rate was 28.3 per thousand total births, and the infant mortality rate was 18.1 per thousand live births. Hennink, Cooper and Diamond's (1993) research emphasised the specific health needs of Irish Travellers citing discrimination experienced at clinics and health centres, and identifying high incidences of infectious disease, alcoholism, cardiovascular illness and mental illness.

Contemporary survival for all nomadic and semi-nomadic Traveller existences in England are characterised by various negative determinants: lack of basic hygiene facilities, insecurity on roadside and temporary (illegal) camps, regular forced eviction and harassment, and frequent conflict with local authorities, police, landowners and sections of sedentary society (Hawes, 1997; Hyman, 1989). The stark reality on legal municipal and private sites usually manifests in poor sanitary conditions, overcrowding, lack of tenure, and stigmatisation and criminalisation by local settled residents and sections of the police. Travellers in settled types of housing often suffer stress through separation from extended family supports, overcrowding, and local intimidation. Also, poor nutrition and dental care, tobacco and alcohol abuse, and to a lesser but increasing extent drug abuse can be factors in all Travellers' poor health record. Chronic illnesses such as respiratory diseases, rheumatism and digestive illnesses are also common to all Traveller groups in Britain (Power, 2004; Parry et al., 2004; Hyman, 1989).

Travellers can suffer high levels of anxiety, distress and depression due to the pressures of leading an outlawed nomadic lifestyle, or living on a 'ghettoised' overcrowded authorised site with no security of tenure, or being confined to inappropriate settled housing in run-down areas of cities and towns. All these modes of accommodation can undermine extended family support structures with possible dire consequences for communal and individual physical and mental well-being. The breakdown of traditional Traveller economies and the erosion of cultural self-esteem severely undermine the health and life-chances of Irish Travellers (Ibid). There are long-term mental health implications for Traveller women and men trapped on overcrowded and poorly resourced municipal sites or inappropriate housing with no prospect of resuming a nomadic lifestyle, or obtaining more culturally appropriate accommodation (Power, 2004). Evictions and related vicissitudes often result in cursory treatment of medical symptoms rather than determining actual causes, and can result in possible misdiagnosis and late detection of abnormalities and lack of continuity in care and treatment (Morris and Clements, 2001; Hawes, 1997; Hyman, 1989). In the Republic of Ireland specifically, Heron, Barry, Fitzgerald and MacLachlan (2000) argued in their health study that state accommodation policies (different but not dissimilar in consequence to those in England) have contributed to psychosocial breakdown in the Traveller community and found that about a third of mothers linked being an Irish Traveller to poor health due to their living conditions. Assimilation, criminalisation and accommodation policies in England have had similar consequences for Travellers generally. Irish Travellers' endurance has to a large extent been contingent on the group's internal solidarity and cohesion, and the uniqueness of their nomadically based culture, coupled with a refusal to conform to sedentary society's mores (Power, 2004; Heron et al., 2000).

Qualitative research carried out in Ireland indicates that the curtailing of nomadic lifestyles and forced settlement in housing has had a negative impact on the mental health of Irish Travellers bringing on feelings of isolation, confusion and loss of identity, loneliness and claustrophobia (Ginnetty, 1993; Abdalla et al., 2010). Immigration, urbanisation, poor settlement conditions, low self-esteem and the breakdown of extended families has taken its toll on Travellers' mental health in Britain (Parry, 2004; Power, 2004). The pressure and social tensions of overcrowding on official sites as the next generation matures but have nowhere to go has built up much negative stress and anxiety in communities. Young Traveller families who have never travelled or only moved seasonally, have few options as lack of site space forces them to accommodate elsewhere, while coercive anti-nomadic legislation (CJPOA, 1994) militates against travelling. But many are also excluded from the housing market through mortgage exclusion, relative poverty, and a reluctance to abandon the extended family. This can leave them with no options but severe overcrowding or the rough end of the private rented sector.

Lack of knowledge of bureaucratic systems, widespread illiteracy, and difficulties with 'settled' timeframes, and the failure of health and other organisations to recognise and address these issues, impede Irish Travellers' access to services. Rutter (1997: 10; also Parry et al., 2004) maintains that bureaucratic structures and procedures exclude all Travellers from services: 'Public services are offered on condition of settlement, e.g. signing on [social security], GP registration, Education. All instil the virtues of regularity, punctuality and responsibility'. As a result, these bureaucratic regimes serve to exclude many nomadic Travellers, but even ostensibly settled Travellers suffer exclusion from health services due to cultural blindness, illustrated by some of the research evidence below.

Care has to be taken when comparing international health research data as the political, cultural, policy and service contexts can differ considerably.

But, though Travellers are located in some of the most economically 'developed' nations, the comparative international population pyramids for Irish Travellers consistently resemble that of poor developing countries with high infant mortality, a burgeoning youth and young adult population and abnormally small numbers of elders by western standards. The following sections will examine provision, access and delivery of healthcare services to Irish Travellers in England.

The Healthcare of Irish Traveller Families

Irish Traveller women face discrimination as Irish people, as Travellers, as women, and as Traveller women in England. Therefore, promotion of gender equality, both internally within their own community, and externally in the wider social context, is fundamental to their health and empowerment. Traveller women's use of family planning, developmental screening, immunisation, and antenatal care services is very low in relation to other minority groups and society in general (Pahl and Vaile, 1986; Power, 2004). This can, to some extent, be explained by the traditional family mores and Catholicism of many Irish Traveller women. But Traveller women's lack of access to family planning services, pre and post natal healthcare, the impracticality or cultural insensitivity of clinics and staff, and lack of childcare facilities also echoes the experiences of other excluded black and ethnic minority women. There is a tendency by service providers to blame the victim or presume that they have choices, and the 'user friendliness' of the service is rarely considered from a clients perspective, particularly those clients who are severely marginalised (Papadopoulos et al., 1998; Department of Health, 1999).

Three focus groups (see Power, 2004) carried out with Traveller women reflected some key issues around their marginalisation in healthcare and illustrates a lack of understanding about their needs as Traveller women:

- Lack of access to regular GP services due to nomadic living – huge impacts on children's welfare and health needs. For example, immunisations for babies. Many Irish Traveller women said that they only accessed health through accident and emergency services.

- No systematic approach to transferring health records of Traveller families who move frequently, so they can miss vital family healthcare appointments.

- Settled Irish Traveller families felt that GPs did not understand their culture or their health needs, sometimes supplying them with medication they did not need.

- Great insecurities around Traveller women expressing their needs in a health arena, such as making themselves understood to receptionists and staff in doctor's surgeries and hospitals. Many women found it difficult to be understood because of their accents and this made them feel embarrassed and frustrated.

- Lack of knowledge about how health systems work, therefore Irish Traveller women struggle to engage with them.

The key themes outlined above add significantly to other stresses and strains for Traveller families. For example, eviction is a key feature (and/or fear) for nomadic Traveller families and underlines how health becomes de-prioritised in the struggle to survive as a family on the move. This discussion now looks at specific instances of eviction and will discuss this in the context of healthcare.

Manchester Environment Department's Mr. Player (cited in Ibid, 31, 41) has responsibility for evictions from Council property. He described how Traveller evictions had changed over the last fifteen years from a 'gung ho' approach where Travellers were moved quickly without any welfare considerations, to a more sensitive policy that involved co-operation with Health Visitors and others to ensure that the Traveller family's health and welfare were paramount. Health Visitor Gorman (cited in Ibid: 42) describes her first experience of visiting an illegal Irish Traveller encampment in Manchester:

> I remember being a little terrified really because it was my first visit to a site.' [Interviewer's question] Why so frightened? [Gorman's answer] 'I don't know, fear of the unknown.... I am used to knocking on people's houses, flats. Walking onto a site that looked chaotic by virtue of the scrap metal, the dogs... Lots of children around, not knowing which caravan door to knock on, simple things.... [C]arrying an official looking bag [and] looking much smarter ... makes you feel ... like an outsider.... So you have to get something going with the first person you spoke to.

Though Gorman's interview is highlighted in this paper because of her insightful comments, her fearful reaction was reiterated by many health service provider respondents in the 'Room to Roam' research. For example, the focus group held with service providers in Manchester, highlighted that their initial fears and prejudices' about Travellers were usually unfounded in practice over time.

Health Visitor Gorman (cited in Ibid) describes her part in an attempted eviction:

> I'd been asked to visit by Environmental Health [Manchester City Council] and there were a couple of caravans [on] an expanse of grass stuck in the middle of an area of housing.... Whoever wanted to evict this family couldn't because

the [woman] was seven months pregnant and she was within her rights not to be made to move on. They wanted me to … confirm that she was heavily pregnant and needed to stay there to access care…. I had to walk across this muddy field - it was just a nightmare…. I am an outsider, a professional and another agency [Travellers] are not used to dealing with…. I have to say why I have come and I was taken to the caravan which was absolutely pristine and … she did need to stay long enough to have the baby.

Highlighted in the Room to Roam focus groups and in-depth interviews with Irish Traveller women was a lack of consistency in their access to healthcare. It was emphasised that it was not easy to transfer health records to different geographical locations and this created many problems for Traveller families when accessing healthcare – with some families giving-up unless a dire emergency occurred. But lack of continuity in treatment, and also with health records is not confined to fully or partially nomadic Irish Travellers. Most housed Irish Travellers are not sedentary, but move regularly through the housing stock or sometimes switch to trailers in summertime and so present health professionals with similar challenges as Gorman (cited in Ibid) explains:

The other families I visited lived in houses. Once I'd been notified … I keep records on that child until they move out of the area. Then if I know where they've gone to my records follow them on to their respective Health Visitor whichever part of the country they live in'. [Interviewer's question] You give them a card with their health? [Gorman's answer] 'Most families wouldn't show that card to the new Health Visitor…. We usually rely on Health Visitors … to ask that mother where they'd come from. That Health Visitor then contacts the previous Health Visitor and says: 'Can you send me the record you've got on this child.' They should really then have one Health Visitor record in the country following them around. Of course it does not work like that but it's up to each Health Visitor to do a good tracking job…. With the Travelling families [you] are more likely to ask the last three addresses, who the three GPs were and did they meet the Health Visitor. If I then request records from their last address, and [the Health Visitor] never even knew they were there, at least we could request the record from the previous address or the one before ... you just have to work that much harder.

There are still many districts where some form of self-held record is given out to Travellers who want one. Children do (or should) have a 'parent held record' in the form of what's colloquially known as the 'red book' to health outreach professionals. This is generally used by Health Visitors, particularly for recording immunisations. For adult Travellers' health records, it depends on local practice. Gorman insists that the system of self-held 'health-cards' is ineffective, it would require compliance by all Travellers which she doubts would occur. At present some detective work is required by committed Health Visitors to trace families but Mrs. Gorman (cited in Power, 2004: 42) comments:

> I imagine some Health Visitors might just make a temporary record and never send that on.... When a Travelling family moves on and you don't know where they have gone you file it in a 'no trace' section so that when the next Health Visitor has sussed the family out they will request it from you ... you just hope that someone picks up on them and requests the records. But obviously with a highly mobile family ... you need to keep a history following them because a Health Visitor [may have] done valuable assessment work or input with that family and it is such a shame to have that wasted.... [W]ith the two caravan families, I had no previous records, I had nowhere to pass them onto when they moved. I had a really good relationship with one particular Traveller mother and I managed to wangle the mobile telephone number. She went to London so ... I managed to speak to her on the mobile ... so I sent my records on to the London Health Visitor.

Trust is difficult to establish between Irish Travellers and health outreach workers. The focus groups with Traveller women – whether nomadic, sited or housed – highlighted that their experiences with health and social services had been largely negative and they now found it difficult to place any trust in them. Consequently, Health Visitors control the Traveller's health data but often struggle to pass on vital contextual information to the Traveller's next destination, because this information is usually privy to the Travellers themselves. This lack of trust and information sharing interrupts continuity of support and treatment, but also undermines the professional dissemination of good health practice with particular Traveller families and can undermine the maintenance of detailed case histories that should enhance prevention, diagnosis and treatment.

Hawes (1997) and Hyman (1989) identified heavy tobacco smoking and poor diet as negative factors in Travellers health. Health Visitor Gorman (cited in Power, 2004: 43) agrees, but adds that in her Manchester experience overcrowding and inappropriate housing, combined with the pressures of single parenthood impact particularly on Irish Traveller women, many of whom are poor, often dependent on meagre state benefits and isolated on run-down council estates or in poorly maintained private housing:

> When you think about the effects of chronic stress, constant overcrowding, the difficulty in accessing Health Services, and the fact that there is no time to meet their needs or they don't go and have [necessary] operations done, or they are heavily dependant on cigarettes, have a poor diet and [drink] lots of caffeine.... I wouldn't like to generalise but the Traveller I am working with at the moment lives on loads of cigarettes and coffee, doesn't sleep too well, hardly eats and is depressed ... no way could her life expectancy not be affected. It's a combination of prioritising the kids and their crutches are the coffee and the cigarettes. These will be adding to her stress levels unfortunately, but they will give her an instant buzz, but then later on they will negatively affect her stress levels... And also ignorance about the value of good diets – having a cream cake for tea and missing out on two meals will make her feel ill enough. But there is no time for her to tackle that because the other needs of the family are so great...

Poor family support mechanisms and lack of culturally sensitive Social Service teams condemn many Irish Traveller mothers to poor mental and physical health through overwork, poor health education and a dearth of resources forcing them to rely on readily available stimulants and cheap sugar based 'foods' in order to prioritise their children's needs. This can also lead to inter-generational poor health as children learn their mothers' unhealthy coping strategies. Gorman cites (Ibid: 43) the case of a woman with nine children and no adult support at home who needed urgent medical treatment:

> ... because she had a bad uterine pro-lapse – she hadn't sought medical attention and the uterus was literally hanging out.... [T]he barrier to her having that surgery, the sterilisation and the pro-lapse repair was basically: 'How would she look after the kids?' Her eldest, he was seventeen ... he was dabbling in drugs ... so this mother never really got that healthcare she needed ... [her] needs are de-prioritised whether it is because they are overwhelmed with everybody else's needs or whether it is just that they accept their situation as their lot. Its multi-factorial ... why they don't get the help they need.

According to this evidence, Irish Traveller women, particularly when coping alone, have to sacrifice their own well-being for that of the children. Traveller women's health issues can also be concealed due to a reluctance by some Traveller women to speak about these issues to health practitioners who are strangers or have not developed a relationship of trust with the particular woman concerned (this issue was emphasised in focus groups with Irish Traveller women in 'Room to Roam' and other research the author has conducted since). Large families exacerbate this situation where mothers have to cope with siblings ranging from dependent infants to young adults in high risk urban situations and often without the support of a husband or the traditional extended family that has increasingly fractured under the pressures of rapid and often forced pseudo-assimilation into over-crowded inappropriate housing. Irish Traveller mothers are forced by circumstances to make short-term decisions for the good of their children that will adversely impact on their own health and may also rebound on the wellbeing of their children if the mother can't cope in the long-term due to ill-health, premature disability or death. Under such stresses, usually exacerbated by poverty, its hardly surprising that women often use the most readily available and inexpensive drugs (cigarettes, alcohol, cheap processed sugar-laden food etc.) to ameliorate stress and keep them going in their constant struggle to cope.

Families' Access to Secondary and Specialist Healthcare in Hospitals

Pahl and Vaile (1986, also Power, 2004) asserted that Travellers used hospital Accident and Emergency (A&E) services very frequently. Mrs. Gorman (cited in Power, 2004: 44), a PCT funded Health Visitor, discusses the consequences when A&E services are accessed regularly by families:

> [A]ny child that attends A&E under the age of four and a half, a copy of the medical records is sent to the Health Visitor.... It could be that a child [or] the parents need some support ... or health education because they have not got a fireguard or a safety-gate. And if they have had repeated A&E attendance we would act on that and ... sometimes a sister or doctor on A&E will phone us.... If they are not [GP] registered its sent to a Health Visitor or school nurse that covers that area, so somebody health-wise has a responsibility for a family.

The National Association of Health Workers with Travellers (NAHWT) (cited in Traveller Law Research Unit, 1997) believe that Travellers face difficulties and barriers obtaining referrals to secondary healthcare and when dealing with specialist medical services. Gorman (cited in Power, 2004: 44) describes the difficulties encountered by a single parent Traveller woman and her large family when accessing specialist healthcare in hospitals:

> I've just got one Travelling family at the moment – eleven children in a two-bedroomed house. Privately rented, she is desperate to try and get a more stable address, presumably a council one. The council are aware, yet when she was recently offered a property – the offer was quickly rescinded because

they magically found some arrears from years ago that she owed.... But she just seems to have that many hurdles put into her way ... chaos to do with schooling, offending behaviour in the children. They can't read or write so she just can't keep appointments or follow instructions, finds it difficult to act on advice given by [agencies] because they didn't know she couldn't read or write and they haven't had the nous to be able to explain things in her terms.

Gorman's narrative encapsulates the difficulties faced by many Irish Traveller women struggling desperately, often as the only responsible adult, to manage the complex logistics of large families in inappropriate accommodation. Gorman recognises that this particular Traveller woman is finding it difficult to understand and keep up with multiple agencies and bureaucracies whilst trying to care for her children. This Traveller woman was also trying to deal with hospital appointments because one of her children needed treatment. As Gorman (cited in Ibid: 44) explains:

For example, she goes to hospital to see a paediatrician with her child ... who prescribed some very important medicine for a chronic condition and his dosage is increased because his problem isn't well managed and she is given a hospital prescription. But nobody thought to tell her verbally that it had to be given in to the hospital pharmacy.... So she gives it in the local chemist and they say: 'I'm sorry this has to be taken to the hospital.' Well that's a massive task for her to get back to that hospital because the boys are such bad offenders that she can very rarely leave them unattended. They are aged from two years to seventeen and so the actual practicality of getting down to the hospital which was two buses [away] is horrendous and ... she can't afford it.

Poverty and lack of social supports condemn this Traveller woman and her family to a constant round of crises no matter how hard she tries. It is common for Travellers to have literacy problems. Therefore this Traveller woman should be given direction about what to do with the prescription by hospital staff, but this was not provided. Gorman (cited in Ibid: 44) continues her narrative:

> So I said to her: 'Well if you can come back later with the hospital prescription ... I'll hopefully persuade [the GP] to write you [a duplicate] prescription...' But she didn't come back because she couldn't get anyone to look after the boys and so the child is minus his very vital epilepsy drugs having fits. But that's a typical problem and of course from a GPs perspective he might just see a harassed mother with poor communication skills and might not, without my intervention, be willing to write that prescription.... Whereas I understand her better ... and spell it out for her to the GP. So I fill the gap between the patient and the GP if they are chasms apart, which they often are. Part of my job is to empower parents, to improve the health status of their children and help her understand a better way of getting something out of the GP... She's built more trust with me ... she might listen more carefully next time I say to her: 'Look Mrs. X this is how you need to tackle this.'

Gorman explains that it is important for her to build trust with the Traveller families she comes into contact with. She shows an unusual awareness and human sensitivity to Travellers – something not displayed in many of the other interviews with service providers. Most Traveller women come from highly patriarchal families and many suffer from low self-esteem, poor literacy and can be deeply embarrassed by their accents in the company of settled people (Ibid, 2004). Health Visitor Gorman (cited in Ibid: 44) continues her story:

> Just ... getting her to get the kid to his appointment is a massive task and getting her to convey ... a clear history to the paediatrician.... They feel that disadvantaged they don't have the confidence to speak up. Who knows what the paediatrician will ask her ... and if necessary ask her to say it again five times if he hasn't understood? She would need to remember [she might see different staff every time she has an appointment] every time she saw a doctor, the senior registrar, the

registrar ... the nurse in out-patients, to say to every-one of them: 'Look I have a difficulty, I don't read. Can you tell me what to do with this?' And it takes a brave person to say that to lots of different people each time they go back if the child's got a chronic condition. But that is something that I am in a prime position to try and help her do. But because there are so many problems, you often can't get down to giving her advice on those levels.

Therefore, even the logistics of getting to a hospital can be horrendous for Traveller families, but low self-esteem and poor literacy among Traveller women or men can be compounded by the insensitive bureaucracies of large hospitals when it comes to accessing and understanding treatment. All nurses have a duty to act as advocates for their patients but there is an almost total absence of specialist knowledge about Travellers or advocacy services in hospitals where staff could seek advice about the particular ethnic or cultural needs of minorities (Ibid). Medical treatment can be intermittent, understanding of medical conditions, dosages and treatment regimes poor or nonexistent – this can be a recipe for catastrophe when treating serious illness or disability.

Travellers need an appropriate health education programme that is practical and deliverable (Hennink et al., 1993; Pavee Point, 2005). But health education programmes can be excessively individualised and tend to shift responsibility for health back to the person looking for support. What is needed are models that would develop people's capacities to know and assert their rights, while addressing their particular socioeconomic difficulties, and also provide them with the support and skills to cope with ongoing problems in a healthier way. The insight and commitment of frontline health outreach workers like Health Visitor Gorman above (and the allied good practice of some dedicated voluntary Traveller services in England) should be utilised to train Traveller health workers as the active advocacy interface between their communities and health service professionals (who should also have in-service training concerning the culture and specific needs of Travellers) and bureaucracies.

Conclusion

Good practice in health work with Irish Travellers in England is at present mainly dependent on the initiative and commitment of interested Traveller support organisations and/or individual health professionals, rather than on regional and/or nationally co-ordinated policies developed by Primary Care Trusts (PCTs) or the National Health Service (NHS). There are no specific policies and systems developed to improve Travellers' access to health care throughout the country, and a lack of accessible and appropriately designed and targeted health information materials. Amongst the key recommendations that 'Room to Roam' suggests are that knowledge sharing and co-operation between health professionals is needed to assist in moving health policy forward to support Irish Travellers and their families. For example, dedicated Health Visitors (and other key workers) with valid experience of Irish Travellers can help ameliorate these obstacles, but for PCTs to deliver a culturally sensitive and responsive healthcare service to Irish (and other) Travellers, well-trained and motivated Health Visitors and community nurses are required who have access to specialist cultural knowledge and are trusted by communities.

PCTs commission primary, community and secondary care from providers including hospital and mental health services from NHS Trusts and the private and voluntary sectors. They also fund general practitioners and medical prescriptions. PCTs have a duty to develop healthcare services that support and empower extended families and minority ethnic communities like Irish Travellers. PCTs have a duty to improve practice and delivery through persuasion or sanctions on aberrant GPs, dentists, hospitals and other health service providers where poor delivery or inappropriate practices occur. Parry et al (2004) argue that the few dedicated Traveller PCT sponsored health workers in England were valued by the Travellers they served and significantly improved their access to and use of health services. Parry et al. (2004: 74; see also Power, 2004) claim that:

> Specialist provision would address inequities, involve capacity building and support community development, and should

include housed Travellers in the job descriptions, as these needs are so often overlooked.

Also, culturally sensitive health education materials in appropriate formats should be developed by PCTs covering areas such as first aid, immunisation, cancer, smoking, alcohol and drug abuse, preventative medicine, consanguinity issues and made available at and distributed by voluntary support groups, hospitals, health visitors and GPs (see Chapter 6 in Power, 2004).

But Traveller health delivery in England needs to move beyond specialist provision by settled professionals and embrace true capacity building in the Traveller communities by training Travellers to be health workers. This author suggests, having observed the training, development and health outreach work of Traveller health workers in Ireland that the World Health Organisation commended Irish model developed initially by Pavee Point and the Eastern Health Board and then extended throughout the Republic could be relatively easily adapted to English conditions. A few British based Traveller support groups have carried-out local community health audits, developed user-friendly leaflets on health issues, engaged in health capacity building amongst community projects, and carried-out cultural competence training within a minority of PCTs. But most of this work is localised and concentrates on Gypsy communities who tend to be more settled, rather than Irish Travellers. A small number of locally based health projects have been developed in England by Traveller groups building on models such as the 'Primary Health Care for Travellers Project' (PHCTP) pioneered in Ireland with varying degrees of funding support and success (Greenfields, 2008: 29-31). These projects and previous research have found that Travellers are more likely to discuss their health needs with members of their own community who share their cultural understandings, and so provide cultural safety and improved health access (Power, 2004; Parry et al., 2004). Consequently, PCTs across England should begin to develop and fund a strategy in conjunction with local Hospital Trusts and local support groups to develop a programme for training Travellers to become qualified health workers in their own communities.

In Ireland PHCTPs have been deployed on a county basis following a four year primary healthcare training programme for the Travellers involved. The projects are funded by the Health Service Executive (HSE) and managed by multi-agency partnerships. Community Development Health Workers co-ordinate projects with HSE support, and part-time Community Health Workers (predominantly women) from the Traveller community are recruited and trained. The overall aim of the PHCTPs is to improve the health and life expectancy of Travellers by creating opportunities for Traveller women to develop skills, participate in primary healthcare and get paid employment to support their families. These projects when active then identify the gaps, needs and health status of the local Traveller community and thus inform services to respond appropriately. The trained health workers establish Traveller participation in health promotion; liaise between Traveller and healthcare providers to improve access and delivery; and help develop strategies to encourage co-operation and direct communication between Travellers and Primary Care Teams. PHCTPs are also supported and informed by a National Traveller Health Network (NTHN).

PHCTPs offer 'a national model that has been operating effectively now for a considerable period' (CAN Action Learning Group, 2009: 6). PHCTPs health impacts are tangible already as Pavee Point (2005: 21) argue:

> [Travellers] attitudes to the health system have changed through the provision of information, training and resources. This, in turn, has brought about a change in their ability to access the system. Travellers are making greater demands on the health services and have greater expectations that they be provided in culturally appropriate ways.

In England PCTs, though now proposed for abolition in 2013, are organised regionally with a remit to commission healthcare for excluded groups. The delivery structures and health expertise, and local support and multi-agency groups exist in many regions of England to enable the PHCTP model to be adapted if given adequate planning, deployment, training and community development work similar to that afforded the 'model' in Ireland in order for it to become a success. What it now needs is a lobbying campaign by Traveller support groups in England for government and the institutional health players to engage positively to adapt, but not dilute the PHCTP model. Train Irish Travellers to work with Irish Traveller communities, and replicate similar dedicated schemes for other Traveller groups. Pavee Point (2005: 22) insist that though the PHCTP model has inspired other organisations working with marginalised groups to take its core principles on board while adapting the model in other areas that:

> *Replication of the 'Project' must be based on the application of the principles, not the outcomes of the 'Project'* [author's own emphasis].

PHCTPs are a success story for Travellers, improving Travellers' access to health care and enhancing the general health of Traveller families. Consequently, PHCTPs are also a success story for the hard pressed Irish health services involved. PHCTPs are also empowering Traveller women through education, training and employment, while building capacity in the community generally and pointing to positive routes for young Travellers in their futures. The resourcing of PHCTPs must continue in Ireland despite cutbacks in government expenditure, and the model should be adopted and adapted by health providers in England and beyond to benefit their Traveller communities.

Bibliography

Abdalla, S. et al. (2010) *All Ireland Traveller Health Study, Summary of Findings*, School of Public Health, Physiotherapy and Population Science: University College Dublin.

Adams, B. et al. (1975) *Gypsies and Government Policies in England. A Study of the Travellers' Way of Life in Relation to the Policies and Practices of Central and Local Government*, London: Heinemann.

All Ireland Traveller Health Study Team (September 2010) *Our Geels, All Ireland Traveller Health Study Summary of Findings*, Dublin: School of Public Health, Physiotherapy and Population Science, University College Dublin.

Barry, J. et al. (1989) *The Travellers' Health Status Study, Vital Statistics of Travelling People, 1987*, Dublin: Health Research Board.

CAN Action Learning Group (2009) *Model of a Community Health Worker*, Dublin: Combat Poverty Agency.

Department of Health (1999) *Reducing Health Inequalities: An Action Report*. London: HMSO.

Durward, L. (ed.) (1990) *Traveller Mothers & Babies: Who cares for their health?* London: Maternity Alliance.

Ginnety, P. (1993) *The Health of Travellers: based on a research study with Travellers in Belfast*, Belfast: EH & SSB.

Greenfields, M. (2008) *Exploring Gypsy and Travellers' Perceptions of Health and Social Care Careers: Barriers and Solutions to Recruitment, Training and Retention of Social Care Students*. Buckinghamshire New University: Faculty of Society and Health.

Hawes, D. (1997) *Gypsies, Travellers and the Health Service - A Study in Inequality*, Bristol: The Policy Press.

Health Worker, Dublin: Combat Poverty Agency.

Hennink, M. et al. (1993) Primary Healthcare Needs of Travelling People in Wessex (Working Paper 95-01), London: University of Southampton/ Department of Social Statistics.

Heron, S. et al. (2000) The Psychosocial Health of Irish Traveller Mothers, in M. MacLachlan and M. O'Connell (eds.) *Cultivating Pluralism: Psychological, Social, and Cultural Perspectives on a Changing Ireland* (pp. 93-116). Dublin: Oak Tree Press.

Hickman, M. and Walter, B. (1997) *Discrimination and the Irish Community in Britain*. London: Commission for Racial Equality.

Hyman, M. (1989) *Sites for Travellers: A study in five London Boroughs*. London: London Race and Housing Unit.

Linthwaite, P. (1983) *Health and Health Care in Traveller Mothers and Children*, London: Save the Children Fund.

Mac Gabhann, C (2011) *Voices Unheard, A Study of Irish Travellers in Prison*. London: The Irish Chaplaincy in Britain

Morris, R. and Clements, L. (2001) *Disability Social Care, Health and Travelling People*, Cardiff: University Press.

Office of the Deputy Prime Minister (2001) (accessed on 15 April 2006) 'Gypsy/Traveller Counts' www.housing.odpm.gov.uk/information/index14.htm, London: ODPM.

Pahl, J. and Vaile, M. (1986) *Health and Health Care Among Travellers*, University of Kent: Health Research Unit.

Papadopoulos, I., Tilki, M. and Taylor, G. (1998) *Transcultural Care: A guide for Health Care Professionals*, Wiltshire: Quay Books.

Parry, G. et al. (2004) *The Health Status of Gypsies & Travellers in England*, Sheffield: The University of Sheffield, School of Health and Related Research.

Pavee Point (2005) *A Review of Travellers' Health using Primary Care as a Model of Good Practice: Pavee Point Primary Health Care for Travellers' Project*, Dublin: Pavee Point.

Power, C. (2003) Irish Travellers: Ethnicity, Racism, and PSRs. *Probation Journal*, 50(3), 252-266.

Power, C. (2004) *Room to Roam: England's Irish Travellers – a Report of Research*. London: Community Fund/AGIY.

Rutter P. (1997) *From the Margins to the Mainstream: An Effective Management Strategy to Increase Access by the Haringay Traveller Community to Council Services*, Haringay Council: Work based Project.

Traveller Law Research Unit (1997) Traveller Law Reform: TLAST/TLRU conference and consultation report, Cardiff: TLRU, Cardiff Law School, University of Wales.

24.

Where Does Policy Go From Here? A Comparison of Urban Aboriginal Peoples in Canada and Travellers in Ireland

J.M. Heritz

Why compare? Comparisons involve an assessment of the similarities and differences that are key to comprehending and interpreting diverse historical situations and their significance for understanding current institutional realities (Ragin, 1987, p. 6). In the case of urban Aboriginal peoples in Canada and Travellers in Ireland the initial overarching similarities are that they are both nomadic groups, indigenous to their respective countries and they relied on oral traditions to preserve their cultures. What is noteworthy as well, are the differences between Canada and Ireland in regards to the stages in the development of public policy for Aboriginal peoples and Travellers respectively. Even though both governments treated these groups as separate from mainstream society, their policy approaches were quite different. Historically, government dominated their relationship with Aboriginal peoples with legislation that controlled their life ways, while Travellers were ignored by the state and laws that may have been applicable to them, for the most part, were not enforced. It was when these groups began transitioning to urban centres starting in the mid twentieth century that government policy in both countries changed and took on similarities starting in the 1960s. What is remarkable is that both countries made similar changes in policies in the 1980s and 1990s. However, these coincidences bifurcated in the 2000s. While urban Aboriginal policy is moving toward collaboration with Aboriginal organizations, Traveller policy is becoming increasingly controlled by the state. Another noteworthy similarity is the emergence and growth of advocacy groups in the last twenty-five years in facilitating programs and services for these groups. Starting with Canada, then Ireland, this chapter will compare public policy for urban Aboriginal peoples and Travellers in three stages. The first stage will illustrate how diverging policies had similar outcomes for both groups up to the mid-twentieth century. The second stage will assess the period starting in the 1960s and ending in the 1990s when public policy for these two groups followed similar paths: assimilation in the 1960s; reaction to assimilation in the 1980s; and recognition in the 1990s. The third stage will look at the bifurcation in policy directions that the two governments have undertaken in the new millennium. The conclusion will comment on the impact of public policy on the ability of both groups to make choices regarding their life ways in the twenty-first century.

Divergence

Despite their similarities as indigenous nomadic groups, urban Aboriginal peoples and Travellers were subjected to policies that were quite different. This section will provide a brief background to illustrate the divergences in policies for these two groups up to the mid twentieth century. There are three aspects of government policy that directly impact on urban Aboriginal peoples in Canada. The first is that Aboriginal peoples were subjected to colonial rule, formalised in proclamations and laws starting in the eighteenth century. The Royal Proclamation of 1763 established the relationship between the British Crown and Canada's Aboriginal peoples (and remains the legal source of Aboriginal rights in Canada to the present day)

(RCAPv1, 1996, p. 114). The Constitution Act 1867 that created Canada gave the federal government responsibility for 'Indians and the Lands reserved for the Indians' (section 91 (24)) and gave the provinces responsibilities for public lands, health, welfare, education and municipal institutions (section 92). What this means is that even though the Constitution Act 1867 delegated responsibility for Indians to the federal government, over time they rescinded this responsibility: first to the Metis; second to non-Status Indians as set out in the Indian Act; third to those residing off reserve; and fourth to the Inuit (Aboriginal peoples who live in Canada's far northern territories) (Graham and Peters, 2002, pp. 5-6). This meant that federal policy for Indians extended to the delivery of services to those on reserve only. This policy failed to acknowledge responsibility for Aboriginal peoples off-reserve, which meant those who would eventually live in urban centres. Secondly, the Indian Act 1876 empowered government to administer the affairs of Aboriginal peoples to the extent that they could not manage their own lands on reserves, or their money. Each reserve was under the supervision of federally appointed Indian agents who carried out policies developed in Ottawa (RCAPv1, 1996, p. 278). The Indian Act made rules regarding who was an 'Indian.' For example, if an Aboriginal woman married a non-Aboriginal she and her children would lose their status, but if an Aboriginal man married a non-Aboriginal woman she and their children would gain status. Having status meant that the person was registered as an Indian with the government, could reside on the reserve and was entitled to the provisions of the Indian Act.

The implications of these rules still affect the status of Aboriginal peoples in the present day. European settlers dominated their relationship with Aboriginal peoples and this control severed them from their traditional livelihoods. Thirdly, residential schools illustrate the domination that government had over Aboriginal peoples. Established in 1870 by the federal government and assisted by various denominations of Christian churches, residential schools were established to assimilate Aboriginal children into mainstream society. Children were forcibly removed from their homes and some were sent to institutions hundreds of miles away. The schools attempted to assimilate children by punishing them severely if they spoke their native languages. Children were taught English or French and the prevailing domestic and industrial skills that sought to re-socialize Aboriginal children: 'the "savage" was to be made "civilized"' (RCAPv1 1996, 335). These practices were compounded by the failure to provide adequate food, clothing, and medical services and to keep children safe from teachers and staff who abused them physically, sexually and emotionally (RCAPv1, 1996, 379). Having their children removed from their homes, not knowing when and if they would be reunited, parents lived in despair. When children returned to their homes they had difficulty communicating with their families and lacked the traditional skills required for community life. Residential schools and the irresponsible and dysfunctional parenting that resulted from these experiences are responsible for the issues of alcohol, drug and sexual abuse, family violence and mental abuse confronting Aboriginal peoples in the present day (Proulx, 2003; Warry, 2007). In summary, Aboriginal peoples have been subjected to government control for centuries. This control empowered government to set the boundaries of its jurisdiction, determine the identity of Aboriginal peoples, and assimilate them into mainstream society by sending their children to residential schools.

Historically, there was a sharp contrast in the colonial control of Aboriginal peoples in Canada compared to a somewhat nebulous relationship between government and Travellers in Ireland. The nature of Traveller nomadism, accommodation patterns and lifestyle could be affected by many departments but no one department was specifically responsible for Travellers. Bhreatnach explains that even though the School Attendance and Street Trading Acts of 1926, the Road Traffic Act 1933 pertained to Travellers, the regulations flowing from these laws were not enforced on them. When the Department of Local Government and Public Health extended regulations over its citizens into the 1960s, Travellers were ignored (2006, p. 90). From 1925 to 1960 most Dáil deputies addressed their complaints against Travellers to the Minister of Justice demanding legislation for trespassing animals, campsites, begging and public disorder. In 1950 the Minister for Justice explained that his department did not believe a solution existed: '6,000 of these persons whose people have been on the roads for centuries and that they have a prescriptive right to be on the roads' (Bhreatnach, 2006, p. 92).

In summary, the brief exploration of their historical backgrounds demonstrates drastic differences in policy for the two groups. Aboriginal peoples were increasingly controlled by government policies and legislation which determined and rescinded their identity and status. Even though the federal government was initially responsible for all Aboriginal peoples it increasingly took responsibility for those on reserves only. Residential schools were attempts to assimilate Aboriginal children, the scars of which are still felt in the Aboriginal community in the present day. In contrast, Travellers were not specified in policies or legislation and as such were ignored by government. Despite these contrasts when Aboriginal peoples and Travellers transitioned to urban centres in the mid twentieth century they emerged as marginalised groups and continued to be distanced from mainstream society.

Parallel Policies

The second stage of this analysis uncovers the remarkable coincidences in policy undertaken by both governments starting in the 1960s and ending in the 1990s. During these forty years government policy was directed at assimilating both groups. Reaction to assimilationist policy charted a course that moved toward the cultural acknowledgement of these groups in the 1980s. This trajectory of acknowledgement was incorporated into national commissions of inquiry that took place in the 1990s that recognized the life ways of urban Aboriginal peoples and Travellers.

Assimilation

Starting in the mid-twentieth century both groups began residing in urban centres in greater numbers. Emerging from different policy approaches, Aboriginal peoples were colonially controlled by government whereas Travellers were relatively ignored. However, both groups remained marginalized by mainstream society. Despite the contrasts in policy up to this time, both governments developed policies of assimilation to remedy the disparities faced by these groups.

248

The acceleration of government intervention in Aboriginal affairs was attempted by an overhaul of Indian policy in the 1960s. In 1969 the Canadian government published its policy paper, Statement of the Government of Canada on Indian Policy aka The White Paper. It argued for the elimination of the Indian Act and proposed equal participation of Aboriginal peoples in the cultural, social, economic and political life of Canada in exchange for their special status. The White Paper was rejected by Aboriginal peoples as assimilationist (Warry, 2007, p. 35) and was retracted by the federal government (Russell, 2003, p. 77). What the White Paper did however, was bring awareness to Aboriginal peoples of where they stood in their relationship with government and to themselves. Aboriginal organisations became established, including the National Indian Brotherhood (Assembly of First Nations) in 1968 and the Native Council of Canada (Congress of Aboriginal Peoples) in 1971.

The Commission on Itinerancy was established by the government of Ireland in June 1960 and published its report in August 1963 (Report, 1963, p. 11). The terms of reference set out to inquire about, 'the problem arising from the presence in the country of itinerants in considerable numbers' and to consider steps that might be taken 'to promote their absorption in the general community' (Report, 1963, p. 11) The commission was chaired by the Hon. Justice Brian Walsh of the High Court. The nine Commissioners included the Chief Medical Officer, a representative from the Farmers Association, Garda Síochána, the Catholic Church, health and education authorities. Travellers were not represented in the Commission. Of the 15 voluntary organisations and associations the commission invited to submit memoranda for the Commission's information no Travellers organisations were listed as none were formally established at this time. Even though the Commission admitted 'Travellers as they prefer themselves to be called' (Report, 1963, p. 37) it referred to them as itinerants throughout the report. The 166 page document reported on the travel habits, health, education, economic aspects, accommodation, social and ethical behaviour, criminal offences and the attitude of the settled population to itinerants. The commission portrayed the Traveller issue as one of improving their lower socioeconomic status by means of assimilation as indicated by the following excerpts from the Terms of Reference: 'the problem arising from the presence in the country of itinerants in considerable numbers'; 'to examine the economic, educational, health and social problems inherent in their way of life'; 'to consider what steps might be taken … to promote their absorption into the general community; pending such absorption, to reduce to a minimum the disadvantages to themselves and to the community resulting from their itinerant habits' (Ireland, 1963, 11; O'Connell, 1997). Despite its general thrust to absorb Travellers into mainstream society the commission provided information on the general state of Travellers in Ireland. As such it dispelled some myths about Travellers. For example, it stated that the notion of leadership of Travellers headed by 'kings', was an untruth perpetuated by newspapers (Report, 1963, pp. 37-38).

Reaction to Assimilation

In the 1970s policy reacted to models of assimilation by moving toward acknowledging Aboriginal peoples and Travellers. This was facilitated by consultation with advocacy groups that moved toward awareness of cultural difference. With input from the National Indian Brotherhood and the Native Council of Canada the Canadian government acknowledged Aboriginal peoples in Sections 25 and 35 of the Charter of Rights and Freedoms. There are two aspects to the repatriation (which eliminated ratification by British Parliament of some of the amendments in Canada's Constitution Act 1867) of the constitution that resulted in the Constitution Act 1982 and the Charter of Rights and Freedoms that are relevant to urban Aboriginal peoples specifically. Section 25 of the Charter of Rights guaranteed Aboriginal rights recognized by the Royal Proclamation of 1763. And Section 35 of the Constitution Act 1982 acknowledged 'the existing aboriginal and treaty rights of the aboriginal peoples of Canada' (Canada, 1982).

While the Irish constitution did not recognize Travellers in the manner that Canada's constitution entrenched Aboriginal rights, what the Irish government did in the 1980s was revisit its assimilationist stance in its report of the Review Body. Twenty years after the Commission on Itinerancy, the Travelling People Review Body

(Review Body) established in 1981 by the Ministers for the Environment and for Health and Social Welfare, reported in 1983 (Task Force, 1995, p. 54). The 133 page document acknowledged (lower case t) 'travellers' in its report. Walter MacEvilly, former Chief Executive Officer of the Southern Health Board was Chairman of the Review Body. Three Travellers, members of the National Council for Travelling People, were included in the 23 member commission which included representatives from the Departments of Health, Labour, Education and the Environment, the Garda Síochána, Society of St Vincent de Paul and County Councils (Report, 1983, pp. 1-2).

The Review Body acknowledged that the concept of Traveller absorption into society was unacceptable due to the loss of Traveller identity and 'suggested that it is better to think in terms of integration between the traveller and the settled community' (Report, 1983, p. 6). The Review Body set out six objectives. The first was to improve the well-being of Travellers. The second was to providing housing for Travellers who wished to be housed: 'Travellers who are not so accommodated cannot hope to receive an adequate education. Nor can they avail satisfactorily of services such as health and welfare which are of such significance in the life of all people. Nevertheless, the wishes of those Travellers who choose to remain on the road must be respected and serviced sites must be provided to allow them to continue that form of life with such dignity and comfort as it allows' (Report, 1983, p. 15). The third, fourth and fifth objectives were to ensure the availability of education and training, the provision of health care and special welfare needs. The sixth objective was to reduce hostility to Travellers by the settled population by identifying the causes of hostility and by 'public education designed to give the settled population a better understanding of travellers and their problems and to give the travellers an understanding of, and the reasons for, the settled person's attitude' (Report, 1983, pp. 15-16).

The Review Body traced the progress made since the Report of Itinerancy by reproducing sections of the 1963 report and commenting on its current status. Education and accommodation were given more scrutiny compared to health by the Review Body. Travellers experience difficulties in making the transition to settled living: 'inability to cope with financial and other commitments of settled living; claustrophobia and restlessness; loneliness; unsuitable location; subtle ostracisation or frank intimidation from neighbours' (Report, 1983, p. 38). Despite efforts to provide Travellers with standard housing, the number of Traveller families on the roadside grew from 1,142 families in 1960 to 1,149 in 1980. One reason given for the lack of Traveller accommodation by local authorities was the attitude that 'if they do too much, travellers from other counties will come 'flocking in'' (Report, 1983, p. 39). The Review Body dismissed this notion: 'It has been fairly well established by now that families remain in, or move into, areas or towns for their own good reasons, but never because of the facilities offered' (Report, 1983, p. 40). The final recommendation the Review Body made was for the creation of a corporate body that would: promote the welfare of Travellers; work toward the elimination of discrimination; monitor the effectiveness of programs to assist Travellers; coordinate services carried out by government departments; and 'promote a greater appreciation between traveller and settled people of each others rights and concerns' (Report, 1983, p. 109).

In the 1980s both governments reacted to their assimilationist policy stances of the 1960s by moving toward acceptance of the life ways of these groups. Canada entrenched guarantees of rights for Aboriginal peoples in its Charter of Rights and Freedoms in its repatriated constitution. Ireland's Review Body reacted to its former assimilationist policies by integrating Traveller life ways into recommendations. Constitutional negotiations in Canada and the Review Body included representation from organisations advocating for Aboriginal peoples and Travellers respectively. The reactionary shift away from assimilationist policies facilitated the following stage of recognition in the 1990s.

Recognition

Just five years after the repatriation of Canada's Constitution, Prime Minister Brian Mulroney and the premiers of Canada's ten provinces met at Meech Lake to address lingering antagonisms from the 1982 Constitution Act negotiations, a major one being to include the French-speaking province of Quebec in the constitutional fold.

Negotiations for the Meech Lake Accord witnessed further attempts for constitutional reform by the Assembly of First Nations and their advocacy for the right of Aboriginal self-government. Elijah Harper, an Aboriginal Member of the Legislative Assembly of Manitoba, was a pivotal actor in his veto of the ratification of the Meech Lake Accord just before the expiry of its three-year deadline in June 1990 (Valpy, 1990). Also in 1990 the Oka Crisis drew national attention when the Mohawk First Nation of Kanesatake staged an armed protest against the development of a golf course that encroached on their sacred burial grounds. From these events the Royal Commission on Aboriginal Peoples (RCAP) was commissioned in 1991 to 'investigate the evolution of the relationship among Aboriginal peoples ..., the Canadian government, and Canadian society as a whole' (RCAP v1, 1996, p. 669). The commission was co-chaired by Mr Justice René Dussault of the Quebec Court of Appeal and Georges Erasmus, former leader of the Assembly of First Nations. RCAP was the largest and at a cost of nearly $60 million, the most expensive public inquiry carried out in Canadian history. RCAP reported first by publishing Aboriginal Peoples in Urban Centres in 1993, a ninety-nine page document generated by the National Round Tables held in June 1992, that concluded:

> Aboriginal participants in the round table identified the problems they face in urban centres across Canada.... Participants described the social problems as a combination of ills: poverty, powerlessness, racism, joblessness, poor housing, family violence, abuse, AIDS, lack of child care, and low education and literacy levels. These problems are widespread and severe (Report, 1993, p. 62).

The major RCAP Report condensed hundreds of interviews and scholarly submissions into five concentrated volumes (Andersen and Denis, 2003, p. 379) that was published in 1996. Of the five volume RCAP Report, Chapter Seven in Volume Four, 'Urban Perspectives' (RCAPv4, 1996) reported on Aboriginal peoples in urban centres. RCAP identified three main problems urban Aboriginal people encounter due to jurisdictional disputes: first, they receive a lower level of service compared to First Nations on-reserve; second, they have difficulty accessing provincial programs available to other Canadian citizens because provincial governments will not accept responsibility for providing services; and third, they lack access to culturally appropriate services and services delivered in Aboriginal languages (Graham and Peters, 2002, p. 18; Warry, 2007, p. 19; Hanselmann and Gibbins, 2005, p. 80). RCAP noted the disparities in services to Aboriginal peoples living in urban centres to the extent that public policies had been overlooked as a result of disagreements over jurisdiction (Canada House of Commons, 2003, p. 6). This resulted in: a lack of program coordination; the exclusion of municipal governments; and Aboriginal organisations from policy discussions and confusion about the political representation of Aboriginal peoples in urban centres. These factors have negatively impacted on the ability of Aboriginal peoples to access appropriate services in urban centres (RCAPv4, 1996, p. 551). Of the many submissions made to the RCAP, critical issues for Aboriginal peoples in urban centres included the 'challenges to their cultural identity, exclusion from opportunities for self-determination, discrimination, and the difficulty of finding culturally appropriate services' (RCAPv4, 1996, p. 520). Despite its expense and media attention when the report was released, very little was done regarding the recommendations contained in the final report. Since its release in 1996 very few of its recommendations have been implemented (Andersen and Denis, 2003, p. 381).

The Task Force on the Travelling Community was established in July 1993 by the Minister for Equality and Law Reform to 'examine, advise and made recommendations on the needs of Travellers and on Government policy generally in relation to the Traveller community' (Task Force, 1995, p. 55). Senator Mary Kelly chaired the 18 member Task Force comprised of representatives of the major political parties, the Conference of Religious of Ireland, Departments of Education, Environment, Health and Social Welfare, the Minister for Equality and Law Reform, and Dublin County Council. Five members represented the following Traveller organisations: Pavee Point; National Federation of Travelling People; Irish Traveller Movement; and National Association of Traveller Training Centres. The 300 page Report of the Task Force on the Travelling Community was published in July 1995. According to the Task Force the recommendations that were made under three principal areas to meet its terms of reference included:

> ... key policy issues of relevance to Travellers namely accommodation, health, education and training, and economic development including the co-ordination of policy approaches by the relevant statutory agencies; relationships between Travellers and 'Settled' people; [and] the experience of Travellers with a particular focus on culture and on discrimination (Task Force, 1995, p. 57).

Of the seven Terms of Reference in the Task Force Report, four are significant to this comparison. The first is the coordination of national and local government in the areas of Housing, Health, Education, Equity, Employment, Culture and Discrimination. This coordination sought to define the roles and functions of the statutory bodies relevant to the needs of Travellers to facilitate the provision of services in all local authority areas. It is only in the terms of reference regarding coordination that discrimination against Travellers is addressed. Second is the provision of permanent caravan (halting) sites for all Traveller families who required them, by the year 2000. Third is the development of 'mechanisms including statutory mechanisms to enable Travellers to participate and contribute to decisions affecting their lifestyle and environment' (Task Force, 1995, p. 10). Fourth is 'to analyse nomadism in modern Irish society and to explore ways whereby mutual understanding and respect can be developed between the Travelling community and the settled community' (Task Force, 1995, p. 10). Excluded from the Terms of Reference, but included in the Recommendations, are provisions for the inclusion and participation of Traveller women and the organisations that represent them (Task Force, 1995, pp. 274-276).

While the Task Force definition of Traveller culture stated that '[t]he Traveller culture lies in the values, meanings and identity that the Traveller community shares' (Task Force, 1995, p. 71), it is only under the heading of 'Visible Manifestations' of Traveller culture that the Report stated: 'Traveller nomadism, the importance of the extended family, the Traveller language, and the organisation of the Traveller economy' (Task Force, 1995, p. 72). Nomadism was not addressed generally by the Task Force, but was addressed within the context of these various issues. The Task Force was informed that the Electoral Act of 1992 states that residence within a constituency is a prerequisite for registration, so that nomadism can disenfranchise Travellers (Task Force, 1995, p. 93). Nomadism was addressed two times in specific recommendations: nationwide access to patient records for improving continuity of care for nomadic Travellers (Task Force, 1995, p. 147); and a text book exchange system for primary school children who change schools because of the nomadic way of life (Task Force, 1995, p. 179). 'Traveller families who are provided with accommodation ... one local authority cannot expect duplicate provisions to be made by other local authorities, save where they avail of transient halting sites, for stays of short duration' (Task Force, 1995, p. 18). The Task Force tended to underplay nomadism by not addressing it as specific to Traveller culture. Attention to halting sites as accommodation for Travellers steered away from any ideological discussion of nomadism.

Not all members of the 1995 Task Force were in agreement with the content of the Report. The minority report (labelled 'Addendum' in the Report), was signed by four of its eighteen members. The three councillors and one local government official who signed the minority report were elected officials. Although Travellers were identified in the upper case in the Report, they were identified in the lower case in the minority report (and in the Terms of Reference (Task Force, 1995, p. 10). The minority report stated that government policy should consider alternatives to: 'the nomadic way of life in view of: the disadvantages of the current life-style of the traveller community; the changing pattern of work opportunities available to the traveller community; the increasing conflict with the settled community which arises mainly from the consequences of the nomadic lifestyle; the inordinate cost to the exchequer of catering for this way of life' (Task Force, 1995, p. 289).

The Irish government monitored the progress of the Task Force by publishing First Progress Report of the Committee to Monitor and Co-ordinate the Implementation of the Recommendations of the Task Force on the Travelling Community in 2000 and a second progress report in 2005. While a significant number of recommendations from the Task Force never came to fruition, some measures were taken involving coordination of authority, halting sites, inclusion and nomadism. Notwithstanding its centralizing tendencies (Norris and Winston, 2005, p. 818) regarding coordination of jurisdiction authority, the national government was unwilling to centralize Traveller accommodation despite the fact that Traveller organisations have advocated for a national agency to oversee its implementation (O'Connell, 2006). Involving the coordination of authority, the government did take measures against discrimination that were embodied in 1998 and 2000 Equality legislation. Regarding halting sites, the 1998 Housing (Traveller Accommodation) Act created the Local Traveller Accommodation Consultative Committee (LTACC) to advise the government regarding any general matter concerning accommodation for Travellers (Housing Act 1998). The Committee reported that few planned accommodation units for Travellers had been delivered by 2000. Only 89 families were allocated places on halting sites between 1995 and 2000, despite the Task Force recommendations that 2,200 permanent units be provided (Norris and Winston 2005, 809). In 2000 the number of families on the roadside had increased since 1995 and one in four Travellers did not have access to toilet facilities or running water (Garner 2004, p. 144). In summary, the Task Force on the Travelling Community addressed the disparities between the Traveller and Settled communities in Ireland. It sought to come to terms with health and education issues as well as accommodating Travellers in proposed halting sites. The Minority Report indicated that not all of its members were supportive of considerations for the Traveller community. Even though Travellers were recognized in the Equality Act and included in LTACC, legislation passed after the Task Force report drastically curtailed nomadism. Equality legislation, the LTACC and legislation subsequent to the Task Force impacting on nomadism are elaborated on below.

The Employment Equality Act 1998 prohibited discrimination on nine distinct grounds, including membership in the Traveller community (Equality Authority). Equality Authority annual reports indicate 'Travellers' report the highest number of cases of discrimination (Garner, 2004, p. 64). The Equal Status Act 2000 provided an outlet for Travellers to officially file complaints with the government of which the largest number of complaints were from Travellers. The Equality Authority annual reports indicate 'Travellers' report the highest number of cases of discrimination (Garner, 2004, p. 64). In an effort to curtail Traveller complaints to the Equality Authority, the Vintners' Federation of Ireland (VFI) campaigned to exclude Travellers from the Equal Status Act. As a result, the Equality Authority lost its powers to investigate allegations of discrimination against Travellers by owners of hotels and public houses (Fanning, 2009, p. 44). This meant that any action Travellers had regarding being refused service in a pub would no longer proceed as a complaint before the Equality Authority tribunal. It would now be subject to Vintners legislation and heard in the district courts where legal representation is required.

The Housing (Traveller Accommodation) Act 1998 created the Local Traveller Accommodation Consultative Committee (LTACC) to advise the government regarding any general matter concerning accommodation for Travellers (Ireland Housing Act 1998). The Act entrenched the inclusion of Travellers in local decision making for the allocation of Traveller housing which included halting sites and social housing. Regarding the inclusion of Travellers in housing policy, Norris and Winston revealed that most authorities failed to canvass Travellers' opinions regarding the option of transient halting sites while researching Traveller accommodation programs required by the 1998 Act. Forty per cent of the local authorities did not offer any type of options for halting site accommodation and 34 percent of the programs failed to make any provision for transient halting sites (2005, p. 814). An evaluation of the LTACC stated that members felt they had less input and were not satisfied with the content of accommodation programmes.

In summary, by the mid-twentieth century as both groups were migrating to urban centres, their governments sought to solve the problems of their marginalization, amongst other policy issues, by recommending the assimilation of both groups into mainstream society. In 1969 the Canadian government released the White Paper and in 1963 the Irish government released its Report of the Commission on Itinerancy 1963. Increasing advocacy for these groups brought about a reaction to assimilationist policies that was redirected toward entrenchment of Aboriginal rights in the Canadian constitution and acknowledgement of Travellers culture in the Report of the Review Body 1983. Of significance is that both governments included representatives from Aboriginal and Traveller advocacy organisations to bring about these changes. In the 1990s both national governments commissioned inquiries that made recommendations for the recognition, accommodation and improvement of the life ways of both groups. What RCAP did achieve was a discussion of critical issues that included challenges to their cultural identity, self-determination, discrimination, and the difficulty of finding culturally appropriate services for urban Aboriginal peoples. In Ireland, the Task Force made recommendations that included coordination of authority, halting sites, inclusion, discrimination and nomadism. Towards the end of the 1990s discrimination against Travellers was included in the Employment Act, and the Housing (Traveller Accommodation) Act 1998 created LTACC which made provision for the inclusion of Travellers in local housing committees. The end of the 1990s marked the end of the forty year parallel in government policies for urban Aboriginal peoples in Canada and Travellers in Ireland.

Bifurcation

This third stage looks at the bifurcation in policy directions that moves toward collaboration between urban Aboriginal peoples and government while placing increasing restrictions on Travellers in Ireland.

The Urban Aboriginal Strategy was created by the federal government in 1997 to partner with other governments and community organisations in response to the needs of Aboriginal peoples living in selected urban centres. Even though the federal government devolved its responsibility for Aboriginal peoples living off reserve (which includes urban centres) it created the UAS to coordinate the delivery of services to provide choices for urban Aboriginal peoples. The Federal Interlocutor for Métis and Non-Status Indians is charged with implementing the UAS to bring together Aboriginal organisations in urban centres to establish priorities and work together to fill gaps in social services (Canada, 2011).

While policy at the end of the twentieth century appeared to move toward recognizing Traveller culture by creating defences against discrimination under the Equality Act and including Traveller input through the LTACC, legislation in the new millennium ventured in a direction that resulted in curtailing Traveller life choices. The 2002 Housing (Miscellaneous Provisions) Act made it a criminal offence to trespass on and occupy public or private property. The amendments to the act authorizes police to impound caravans parked on unofficial sites, confiscate property and impose penalties of €3,000, imprisonment of one month or both (Housing (Miscellaneous Provisions) Act 2002, pp. 21-28). According to Fanning, the Act 'was passed with unseemly haste by an overwhelming cross-party majority and without any evaluation of the adequacy of current Traveller Accommodation plans, discussion of the needs of Travellers or consultation with Traveller organisations' (Fanning, 2009, p. 66).

In its concluding observations in 2005, the CERD Committee recommended that the newly established institutions in the field of human rights and non-discrimination be provided with adequate funding; it also commended the Irish Government for the adoption of the first National Action Plan against Racism, the establishment of the Irish Human Rights Commission, the Equality Authority and the NCCRI. Since then, the Irish Government has attempted to dismantle the equality infrastructure. In the October 2008 and subsequent budgets: the Traveller budget within the Department of Justice, Equality and Law Reform was halved; the National Consultative Committee on Racism and Interculturalism (NCCRI) was dismantled; the National Action Plan Against Racism was discontinued; there was a 24 percent budget cut for the Irish Human Rights Commission; and there was a 43 per cent budget cut for the Equality Authority (Pavee Point 2011, p. 2).

Conclusion

While Aboriginal peoples and their identity were historically controlled by government legislation, Travellers, in contrast, were not directly controlled by a specific act or a statutory department. For the most part legislative acts and regulations that did pertain to Travellers, regarding the education of Traveller children, were not enforced. The second half of the twentieth century witnessed remarkable similarities in policies in Canada and Ireland that initially sought to resolve problems of marginalization of urban Aboriginal peoples and Travellers by assimilation. Reaction to assimilationist policies took an ideological turn that moved toward recognizing these groups and their life ways. The new millennium witnessed a divergence in the parallel of Canada and Ireland's accommodation of life ways for atypical groups. While urban Aboriginal policy remained a provincial and local responsibility the nationally instituted Urban Aboriginal Strategy continued to work at collaborating with all levels of government to fill in program gaps at the local level. In Ireland Traveller nomadism was severely curtailed and penalized by enabling legislation. Even though the legislated LTACC arrangement is designed to include Travellers in housing decisions, it remains to be seen whether this model meets the expectations of either government or Travellers. And changes in equality legislation made it more onerous for Travellers to dispute evictions from public houses.

Informed by a historical comparison of public policy for urban Aboriginal peoples in Canada and Travellers in Ireland, my research presently leads to observe that despite government's moving toward recognition of Travellers in the 1990s, they are increasingly restricted in their ability to make choices, especially those regarding nomadic life ways. As increasing numbers of Aboriginal peoples are transitioning to urban centres government policy is moving in the direction of collaborating with Aboriginal organizations to facilitate their life ways. Despite growing awareness of and advocacy for Travellers in Ireland they face more challenges in the new millennium, including the potential of increasing government intervention to restrict their lifeways, legitimised by a climate of economic austerity.

References

Andersen, C. and Denis, C., 2003. Urban Natives and the Nation: Before and After the Royal Commission on Aboriginal Peoples. *The Canadian Review of Sociology and Anthropology*. 40, pp. 373- 390.

Bhreatnach, A., 2006. *Becoming Conspicuous: Irish Travellers, Society and the State 1922-70.* Dublin: University College Dublin Press.

Canada. 1993. *Aboriginal Peoples in Urban Centres.* Ottawa: Ministry of Supply and Services Canada.

Canada. 1982. Constitution Act, being Schedule B to the Canada Act 1982 (U.K.), 1982, c. 11 Ottawa: Publications Canada.

Canada. 1996. Report of the Royal Commission on Aboriginal Peoples. Looking Forward Looking Back Voume.1. Restructuring the Relationship. Volume 2 Part 1. Perspectives and Realities Volume. 4. Ottawa: Canada Communication Group.

Canada. Parliament. House of Commons. 2003. Standing Committee on Human Resources Development and the Status of Persons with Disabilities. Building a Brighter Future for Urban Aboriginal Children: Report of the Standing Committee on Human Resources Development and the Status of Persons with Disabilities. Ottawa.

Fanning, B., 2009. *New Guests of the Irish Nation.* Dublin: Irish Academic Press.

Garner, S., 2004. *Racism in the Irish Experience.* London: Pluto Press.

Graham, K. A. H. and Peters, E., 2002. *Aboriginal Communities and Urban Sustainability.* Ottawa: Canadian Policy Research Networks Inc.

Hanselmann, C. and Gibbons, R., 2005. Another Voice Is Needed: Intergovernmentalism in the Urban Aboriginal Context. In *Canada: The State of the Federation 2003: Reconfiguring Aboriginal-State Relations,* ed. Michael Murphy. Montreal and Kingston: McGill-Queen's University Press.

Ireland. 1963. *Report of the Commission on Itinerancy.* Dublin: Stationery Office.

Ireland. 1995. *Report of the Task Force on the Travelling Community.* Dublin: Stationery Office.

Ireland. 1983. *Report of the Travelling People Review Body.* Dublin: Stationery Office.

Norris, M., and Winston, N., 2005. Housing and Accommodation of Irish Travellers: From Assimilation to Multiculturalism and Back Again. *Social Policy & Administration,* 39, pp. 802-821.

O'Connell, R., 2006. The Right to Participation of Minorities and Irish Travellers. *Studies in Ethnicity and Nationalism,* 6, pp. 2-29.

Pavee Point Travellers Centre. 2011. Irish Travellers and Roma. Shadow Report. A Response to Ireland's Third and Fourth Report on the International Convention on the Elimination of All Forms of Racial Discrimination (CERD). Dublin: Pavee Point Travellers Centre.

Proulx, C., 2003. *Reclaiming Aboriginal Justice, Identity, and Community*. Saskatoon, SK: Purich Publishing Ltd.

Ragin, C.C., 1987. *The Comparative Method*. Berkeley: University of California Press.

Russell, P., 2003. Colonization of Indigenous Peoples: The Movement toward New Relationships. In: M. MacMillan and F. McKenzie, eds. *Parites Long Estranged: Canada and Australia in the Twentieth Century*. Vancouver: UBC Press.

Urban Aboriginal Strategy. 2011. Canada. Treasury Board of Canada Secretariat. Available at: <http://www.tbs-sct.gc.ca/hidb-bdih/plan-eng.aspx?Org=2&Hi=47&Pl=237> [Accessed on 20 June 2011].

Valpy, M.,1990. Mulroney's Promise Far From Fulfilllment. *Globe & Mail*, 15August A7.

Warry, W., 2007. *Ending Denial: Understanding Aboriginal Issues*. Peterborough: Broadview Press.

25.

The Parish of the Travelling People

The Parish of the Travelling People started in 1980 with a growing need to support Travellers in the whole of Dublin where at the time there were very few sites to speak of. The first Parish priest was Fr. Michael McCullough. People were living in dreadful conditions all over the city and county, being moved at all hours of the day or night. The Parish of the Travelling People stretches across the length and breadth of the Dublin city and county.

There were over 8,000 Travellers in this area at the time. In 1980 the Vincentian Community was asked by the Archbishop of Dublin to respond to the pastoral needs of Travellers throughout the diocese. These needs are physical, emotional and spiritual. We in the Parish take a holistic view of the person and community. Today the Parish is made up of men and women, Traveller and settled, cleric, lay and religious, working together to create a more inclusive, just and respectful church and society.

Our response to the Traveller community, who are excluded from Irish society and for whom discrimination is a daily occurrence, is one of solidarity. This relationship of solidarity prompts us to act as an agent of change, working with Travellers to have their rights realized, facilitating their participation within church and society and in this way contributing to the overall well-being of both Traveller and settled communities.

The Church plays a very important part in the life of the Traveller community. The key word is relationship. We build up relationships with certain individuals. Priests are very important to our community. They are there for us at times of birth, through our lives and at times of death. A relationship develops with those that are open.

The Parish of the Travelling People poses a challenge to local Parishes to acknowledge Travellers as people who are as much a part of local Parishes as their settled neighbours, and to ensure the participation of its neighbours, both Traveller and settled, in its life and activities.

While Travellers have moved into standard accommodations, which are halting sites, group housing, mainstream housing and private housing there are still a lot of families with nowhere to live.

The Parish met the needs of Travellers at Christenings, Communions, Confirmations and Weddings. They also travelled around the country to final resting places and participated in the masses. The Parish arranged pilgrimages around Ireland and also abroad. They would also arrange events to involve young Travellers in activities. A lot has changed since 1980.

I was asked some time ago by Fr. Derek Farrell, who now heads up the Parish, if there was still a need for the Parish of the Travelling People after 30 years. Having thought about this, I answered him that the need was still there but maybe in a different role. A lot of the people now living in standard accommodation are in line with their Parish churches. I see a need still for the Parish but in a more outreach level, because there is a lot of isolation among older Travellers, who now worry about their young people drifting away from the church. We are living in changing times within the church. The Traveller community feels sometimes isolated, and an outreach programme, which the Parish should head up, is one way of bringing a greater understanding in our changing world. Times have changed and people have moved on. We too have to move on if we are to stay focused within our community and outside of it in today's ever changing world.

Article taken from *The Light Within*, 2000.

26.

Traveller Heritage Project

In many ways Traveller history can be described as a 'hidden history'. Although in recent years the number of publications and resources about Travellers has increased there is still a wealth of information waiting to be discovered. Attempts to define Traveller history and culture is made more difficult by an absence of documents written by people from the Traveller community.

Traveller culture is based around oral tradition, with stories being passed down from generation to generation.

There are a wide range of sources that can be used to uncover and interpret Traveller history, these include parish records, such as baptism, marriage and burial registers; poor law records including settlement examinations; as well as census returns and photographs.

Traditionally, Travellers lived and worked in the rural areas of Ireland. Many came to work with farmers and local industries. Some of these families have settled in houses whilst retaining their cultural background. Other families moved on to local authority managed sites in counties or bought land themselves and set up small private sites.

There are a lot of families who still travel around Ireland. 'The Cant' language is still used by some families. Their sense of family is very strong and they often feel isolated from the settled communities around them.

Many farmers relied on Travellers to assist in harvesting certain crops, as there wasn't enough manpower available locally to bring them in on time. When paid work was unavailable, Travellers turned their hands to crafting items from raw materials that could be sold from door to door as they travelled.

Before living wagons became available in the 1830s, a tent was the usual mode of accommodation when travelling, or night shelter was found in barns and outhouses. Tents varied in style. Benders, consisting of a frame of bent hazel rods covered in whatever material was available – tarpaulin, old army blankets, sacking – could be easily dismantled and transported on tiltcarts to the next stopping place.

A lot of Traveller families love to hear stories from days gone by and we would hope to be able to document some of the history of Traveller families from the Tuam Area

Project Proposal

We propose to look at the history and genealogy of four Traveller Family names from the Tuam area. We will follow these four family groupings from present day to as far back as is accountable.

The aims of the programme are:

- To create family trees for the four family names

- To research and document Travellers history, previously unrecorded, and to develop an appreciation of Travellers' cultural heritage

- To promote Travellers' positive identity as a group and to enhance Travellers' identity and self-determination

- To resource the traditional skills of Travellers as well as stimulate the creative development of these arts

- To archive and produce photos, old stories and poems.

Management of the Project

The project will be managed by Western Traveller and Intercultural Development. A steering committee will be set up to oversee the project. The project will run for two years and will be located in Bru Bhride, Church View, Tuam, County Galway.

27.

The Traveller Education Framework at the University of Limerick – 'An Architecture for Social Inclusion'

John Heneghan

Introduction

Any approach to the study of Travellers, their culture, their experiences and their place in Irish society is hugely informed by the personal engagement between the researcher and Travellers themselves. This seems to be such an obvious statement to make that it borders on the superfluous. And yet, this engagement may be the catalyst in invoking change if the lives of Travellers are to be improved. Recent research and activities involving Travellers such as the All-Ireland Health Study (Department of Health, 2010) and the Primary Healthcare Programme run by the HSE in the Mid West area document significant interaction between researchers and educators and members of the Traveller Community. Many Traveller leaders comment that their community is 'researched out' (Heneghan, June 2010) and that research triggers little positive impact. That sentiment is not altogether justified. The disclosures in the Department of Health report that suicide accounts for 11 per cent of deaths among

Travellers or that 62 per cent of Travellers experience discrimination should spur on policy makers and community leaders, both settled and Traveller to work together in solving these issues. These two issues alone are of national concern. I would argue that the engagement with Travellers documented in the report(which was completed by UCD researchers) reflects an empathy that facilitated the emergence of these statistics and underlines their credibility. This quality of empathy, along with other qualities forms the components of the framework to be discussed below. The framework suggests that these qualities are needed in order to successfully pursue key goals for improving the quality of life of Travellers and thereby address the implications of the report. It will be argued here that interventions put in place by educators and agencies are not sufficient in making last change or improvement in the quality of life of the Traveller Community. The 'siloed' approach arising from individual agencies meeting their obligations has a limited effect if it proceeds without a collaborative element involving other agencies. For all providers, both statutory and non-statutory, a sense of sympathy may bring operators to the front line, but it is empathy that facilitates meaningful change. These observations have implications for the Strategic Plan 2011-2015 of the University of Limerick (2011). One of the four goals of the plan declares the University's commitment to its hinterland:

> We will be renowned for the excellence of our contribution to
> the economic, educational, social and cultural life of Ireland
> in general and the Shannon region in particular.

Accordingly, any discussion on educational access must address progress on meeting this goal.

The Traveller Education framework at the University of Limerick (UL) emerged out the Traveller Access Initiative funded by the Irish Higher Education Authority (HEA). It was the result of an iterative process in the sense that like many social inclusion programmes there was ongoing learning from what worked/what did not work. Concurrent with the activity however was a growing rapport between the University and Travellers so that as the years went by deeper ties and a growing trust facilitated more ambitious projects. What commenced as operational mechanisms such as homework clubs for children, equine classes for men and literacy classes for women, all operational in nature facilitated in time an atmosphere conducive to developing a strategic approach. Today, the Traveller Access Initiative is engaged with more than 140 Travellers and throughout Limerick City and County. What accounts for this sustained engagement? This may have been assisted by business experience, teaching skill and academic research training of those running the initiative but it only partly explains any of the successes achieved.

Genesis

This writer grew up in a household where both parents were dedicated on-the-ground community activists (ReHab and St Vincent de Paul). This was a major influence in charting the journey from aspiration toward action, which came about for me in 2001 with an EU-sponsored project involving employment policy and civil and social dialogue. Travellers were specifically mentioned in the equal opportunity 'pillar' of the EU-mandated National Action Plan and this provided a context in which to encourage education among the Traveller community.

The challenges however, were formidable. In a search of the entire document Supporting equity in higher education – report to the Minister for Education and Science (2003) the word 'Traveller' does not appear at all – not even once! Clearly 'Traveller access' to third level education was not at the top of the political agenda. A look at more recent statistics from the HEA underlines the sense of urgency that now exists in tackling illiteracy in the Traveller Community. The 2011 Census reports that 29,573 of the Irish population are members of the Traveller community. Unfortunately, less than 2 per cent of Travellers have a higher education qualification (2011 Census) which contrasts with the 23 per cent for the general population. This figure should be viewed in the context of CSO data which shows that only 2 per cent of Travellers have completed senior cycle at second level (compared to 23 per cent of the general population for all age groups) (HEA, 2004: 24). The obvious point here is that access to third level is determined by the completion rates at second and first levels. There is a vast difference in the levels of attainment between Travellers and their settled peers; among children whose ages were known, 62 per cent per cent of Traveller children dropped out of full-time education before they were 15 years of age compared to the national rate of 15.4 per cent (Pavee Point, 2005). By 2004 there was a noticeable change in the approach to educational access at government level. The Higher Education Authority(HEA), the entity that supervises higher educational structures in Ireland produced the 2005–2007 Action Plan for encouraging people from socially and economically deprived backgrounds to enter third level education including Travellers. There are 16 references to the word 'Traveller' in the document. The HEA set targets for Travellers accessing higher education and thereby reflecting that making education accessible to Travellers is firmly part of the Irish government's policy of educational access. This development complements a nationwide strategy for providing services in general to Travellers with plans generally being prepared every 36 months. This strategic approach sets goals for accommodation, health, education and employment that guide and inform Inter-agency Steering Groups for Traveller Services set up in every county council authority in Ireland. These goals have been integrated into the framework for the Steering Group in County Limerick.

The HEA continued with its funding of the Strategic Initiative Scheme in 2006 that addressed what it perceived as under-represented groups in higher education. It also included efforts at working with postprimary school students who are at risk of dropping out of school. Of course the areas that the HEA wishes to address such as student retention, economic and social obstacles and so on are not confined to the Traveller community. This is a challenge to the HEA as it carries out its remit in a time of economic austerity that has gripped the Irish economy since the onset of the financial crisis in September 2008 and the Traveller community is no less immune to the resulting cut backs to educational access. Dramatic cut backs to educational and social programmes threaten existing initiatives. The Visiting Teacher Programme was cancelled in 2011 a decision which can be expected to set back the education of Traveller children. The number of resource assistants in primary schools is being reduced and the ability to run specifically designed in-class initiatives for both Traveller and settled children is curtailed due to lack of funding. It should also be noted that problems of Traveller access are often considered as mainly cultural and historical and thereby adding to the complexity of implementing educational access for Travellers. That being said, the observations above and the involvement of the government-led educational initiatives today, contrasts with Irish government policy in the 1960s that was based on the questionable assumption that there was no such thing as Traveller culture. Policies that flowed from such an assumption were bound to be disastrous. Expecting that the provision of housing or enforcing school attendance would work while dismissing centuries of a 'way of life', was naive and unenlightened in the extreme. Thankfully, things have moved on. The HEA does not attempt to impose structures but rather allows and encourages players to develop their own programmes which are then assessed periodically by an independent assessor. This pragmatic approach allows for the development of best practices by participants that fit the local contexts. The framework presented here represents one example of a best practice.

The Traveller Access Initiative at UL

The right to an education is a fundamental civil right as indeed is the right to a roof over one's head should one wish it. The EU advocates a triangular relationship between Economy, Civil Society and Polity that facilitates a society to view all its citizens as participants. This is a subtle but powerful view because participation includes all social strands including those who are marginalised for whatever reason. Citizenship may invoke a person's responsibility to society but it is the concept of participation that calls on society to address the needs of the citizen. Educational and employment policy are integral parts of Irish social policy. Moreover, Irish education policy recognises that some students are disadvantaged not only because of social and economic circumstances but also due to cultural and historical factors. These policies carry the aspiration and hope for a greater quality of life. In Ireland the National Action Plan for Economic and Social Sustainability contains 'pillars of employment' one of which, 'equal opportunity' as mentioned above, specifically mentions Travellers as a group for social inclusion. This reflects the emergent, if belated, recognition of Traveller culture within Irish society. As Martin Collins, Pavee Point, put it when addressing the opening session of the National Seminar of Traveller Parents and Learners:

> Education needs to be about liberating Travellers, not about domesticating them. True education will give Travellers the tools to challenge their oppression rather than teaching them how to become acceptable in a settled world (Pavee Point, 2005).

Looking around County Limerick and Limerick City in 2001 I could not find very many Traveller students sitting the Leaving Certificate or going online on the Internet to register for third level courses via the central applications office (CAO). How many Travellers entered the mainstream at UL in 2001? None. Further, and more pointedly, there did not appear to be any students 'in the pipeline'. In time two local entities were contacted and offered help. These two organization, the Limerick Travellers Development Group (LTDG) and Limerick Youth Services (LYS) were anxious to address the dearth of pupils at secondary level. The LTDG strove to encourage Travellers to engage the educational process while LYS sought out schools willing to assist teenage Travellers to enter the process. Our arrival provided a catalyst by inviting adults to come in 'through the white gates' of UL and attend specially designed classes and programmes that addressed their interests. Advice from Traveller leaders, such as Bridget Casey, of the LTDG guided the Initiative in these first attempts at engaging with Travellers :

> Traveller men are concerned about their horses, and the women worry about hygiene, and education can never be separated from the accommodation issue. (Interview, Bridget Casey, Interim Director, LTDG).

Local Traveller Willie O'Reilly put it more succinctly when he said 'education is no burden'.

These insights influenced the creation and direction of educational activities for Travellers through the UL initiative. The men took lessons in equine care and driving theory. The women pursued lessons in healthcare, food hygiene and communication. A class in site management addressed hygiene and fire safety. The strategy was simple. By creating a positive attitude to education and making the participants feel welcome at UL, we were able to persuade the adults to support the homework club idea for their children. The pursuit of an effective programme for the schools, both at primary and post-primary would have failed had it not been for the assistance of the Visiting Teacher Service. The VTS engaged with school management and teachers during school hours and communicated with Traveller parents on homework, discipline and attendance issues, often during after-school hours. This engagement often led to personalised tuition and ongoing assistance together with children from the settled community. This is creating a 'culture of expectation' (Lynch, 2004) and more importantly a culture of achievement which may persuade Travellers to consider pursuing a third level education. Although the LTDG does not exist today, the relationship with many Travellers from those early interventions continues to endure.

Working with parents in this strategic fashion is not new, of course, as such an approach has long been in operation with the Dublin-based Pavee Point. The UL initiative confirms Pavee Point's contention (2005) that engaging with Traveller parents is critical to parents' involvement in the education of their children. Taking all of these interventions as a whole, it becomes clear that the central core shown in Figure 1 shows the mechanisms for progressing children along the educational continuum, a longitudinal approach that also provides educational activities for adults.

It also demonstrates interventions being pursued concurrent to the school engagement in support of the Initiative. Research, publications and working with individual candidates with potential for progressing toward third level seemed then and continue to be so viewed as compatible with the goals of educational access. They address Maeve O'Byrne question(2004, p. 37) 'Why is it in all our interests to promote access?' and imply perhaps that her question must be addressed continually.

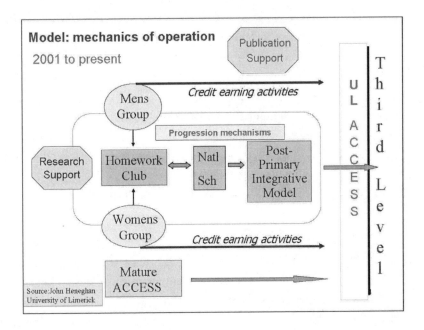

Figure 1. Model with Mechanisms

Before progressing, it must be mentioned that the Initiative decided earlier on to pursue a publications strategy prompted by the observation that Traveller culture was often referred to by Travellers but not many could articulate it. The publication of several books, some of them accessible to school-going children, removed once and for all for me the myth that such a culture did not exist. Two of these feature the lives of Travellers, the musician Pecker Dunne (2004) and the painter Willie Cauley (2004), who has since passed away. A third book is a collection of drawings and paintings that emanated from Traveller children's perceptions of their surroundings and the fourth is a dictionary of the Traveller dialect, Cant (Cauley, 2006). The editing, structure and publication of all of these were overseen by Dr. Michael Ó hAodha, who is an expert on Traveller history and culture and a member of staff of the Glucksman Library at the University of Limerick. His book *Irish Travellers: Representations and Realities* (2006) was supported by the Library and the subsequent reprint supported by the Initiative. That book together with his editing (along with David O'Donnell and Colm Power) of the *Stranger in Ourselves:*

Ireland's Others (2007) and *Postcolonial Borderland* (2008) with Christine Walsh, mark important contributions to both academic and social research of Traveller culture.

To the Traveller community, these books, particularly the two biographies, are viewed as 'one of our own' and it is to be hoped that all such publications will feature in schools in the years to come to enhance a greater understanding of Traveller culture and history. This present collection of essays continues that effort.

Emerging Qualities for Successful Engagement

In approaching the access challenge for Travellers at UL we sought to build a rapport with the Traveller community as a prerequisite to pursuing any form of an educational initiative. This was aimed primarily, not at young Traveller students, but at adult members. The strategy also pursued collaboration with key players involved with Travellers. In addition to the Visiting Teacher Service, the Initiative began to work closely with the Community Garda programme of the Garda Siochána, the Health Services Executive and the Vocational Educational Committee. In February 2007, UL accepted an invitation to join the Limerick County Inter-agency Group for Traveller Services, overseen by Limerick County Council and which provided a forum to contribute in a strategic way to delivering services to Travellers. Collaborating with new partners such as the Department of Education and Science, Department of Social Protection, NGOs West Limerick Resources and Ballyhoura Development brought an immediate advantage of shared resources. The Inter-agency membership also allowed UL to bring its involvement with Limerick Institute of Technology and Mary Immaculate College into the picture and increase the potential for non-traditional educational activities. Accordingly, by 2008 the Initiative at UL had developed sufficiently that it was feasible to reflect on and analyse the progress made.

From Model to Framework

The plans and mechanisms put in place resulted in an expansion of the initiative in three respects.

Firstly, there was expansion by Partnership. Joining the Steering Group for Limerick County essentially trebled the number of entities to collaborate with. Many of these entities such as the County Council, the VEC and FAS have statutory obligations to service the Traveller Community. UL's role is non-statutory but its rapport with Travellers contributed significantly to the collective effort of the Steering Group. Collaboration with Limerick Institute of Technology resulted in two programmes, woodwork and metalwork (and both credit-earning) being delivered to 16 men. Most significant of all, was the addition of Travellers to the Steering Group, some of whom had pursued educational qualifications at UL with assistance from the Initiative.

Secondly, there was a geographic expansion. The Initiative expanded beyond Limerick City and its environs to fund homework clubs in primary and postprimary schools in West Limerick and Cratloe in County Clare. In 2010 Bray Traveller Development Group accepted an invitation from UL to complete a Leadership programme that ran for six months. A significant development in this initiative was a presentation by the Travellers to the Garda Minority Liaison Unit for Munster, presently based in Limerick City.

Thirdly, there was an expansion in dialogue. The progressive and deepening relationship with Travellers that resulted from the Initiative's interactions allowed conversations to take place regarding behaviour and personal development. Sensitive Issues such as depression, loneliness, perceptions of self-worth and the threat of suicide featured in conversations among Traveller adults in classroom settings and in subcommittees of the Steering Group. In the opinion of this writer, an empathy emerged from this development and facilitated Travellers to express themselves openly and to be listened to with compassion. Empathy also facilitated discussions on how Travellers might engage more positively with the settled community and particularly with their neighbours. A meaningful two-way dialogue was now possible.

These developments had their genesis in the mechanics that were put in place to facilitate educational access for Travellers. The homework clubs, the credit earning activity, Travellers participating in the Interagency Steering Group and engagement with 140+ Travellers reflect success but they do not explain how or why these successes emerged. An examination of the framework presented below attempts elicit insights on what has now emerged as a strategic approach to managing services generally and educational access specifically, for the Travellers community.

The Framework

The preceding section gave a glimpse of certain qualities that emerged from several years of engagement with the Traveller Community. UL's involvement with the Inter-agency group for Traveller Services for County Limerick brought the University into contact with agencies statutorily mandated to provide these services and the Initiative at UL was informed by the expertise of these agencies and the challenges they face in carrying out their work. The graphic below in Figure 2 presents a structure that shows goals and the qualities required to successfully pursue those goals.

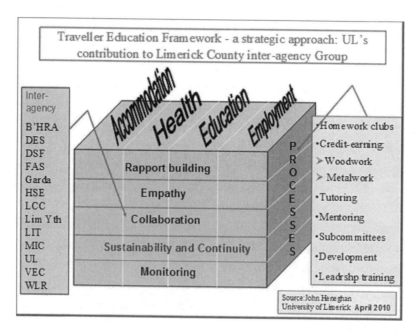

Figure 2. Traveller Education Framework at UL

These qualities are rapport building, empathy and collaboration. Two additional qualities, sustainability and continuity and monitoring contribute a management dimension that is consistent with the strategic aspect of the framework. To grasp their relevance, these qualities should be viewed as enablers in the pursuit of the four goals or objectives suggested by government strategy. In the opinion of this writer, the successes and progress by the Limerick County steering group were due largely to the presence of these qualities. This engagement has all the attributes of civil and social dialogue.

The very concept of participation has resulted in what the German philosopher Jurgen Habermas (1984) describes as being accepted into the others' lifeworld, This occurs because of a process of co-creation, where deliverer and recipient proceed beyond the exchange to create a structure that possesses the commitment of all the parties. It is the presence or absence of these qualities that transforms the engagement into a relationship. Engagement in the form of individual interventions be it a 5-week class in woodwork or a 10-week class in healthcare is temporary. A relationship offers the potential for a commitment to do more. The former is dictated invariably by available funding whereas the latter relies on a mutual respect that recognises a willingness to help even when resources have dried up.

To make a fundamental and substantive improvement to the living and social conditions for any disadvantaged group, a model based on operating mechanisms is not sufficient. The framework presented here is designed to overcome the shortcomings of a mechanical and finite process that engages with participants but may fail to create a lasting relationship. As professor of management Dr. Mike Morley at the Kemmy Business School has commented (Heneghan, 2010), the framework has implications not just for the Traveller community but for other disadvantaged groups and should be regarded as 'an architecture for social inclusion'. This matching of enablers with objectives of any socially isolated or disadvantaged group facilitates a strategic approach in such activity. As a result, it is reasonable to view it as applicable in pursuing the fourth goal of the University's strategic plan.

Research

Traveller leaders often bemoan the amount of research carried out in their communities – and the lack of action ensuing from same. In the UL initiative, however, research is deemed crucial. Having access at ground level to Traveller discussants and converting findings into creating best practices in a non-intrusive manner with Travellers themselves makes this a pragmatic exercise. Research activity is carried out along three strands: 1) monitoring the progress of learning activities and assisting at a distance – where our presence is not necessary we do not intrude; 2) collaborating with an international project on labour market access with colleagues in Canada, France and Scotland (Saha et al., 2008); and 3) contributing to publications on Traveller culture. The byword on research here is co-creation between members of the University initiative, the member agencies in the steering group and Travellers to generate critical input to the Initiative. Analysis of student educational progress, labour market survey, publications articles in the media all serve to inform the Initiative. This forces our Initiative to look outwards yet to remain tied to local conversations as to how and where one might best assist or intervene, directly or indirectly, to attain our common goals. It also provides an opportunity to train Travellers in researching themselves (Gormally, 2005). A milestone in these efforts was the opening of the Traveller and Roma Resource Room, located in the Glucksman Library in UL. This resource has become a collection of materials and a place of study for Travellers and non-Travellers alike and a step towards the creation of a Centre for Traveller Studies.

'Education is No Burden'

The Traveller Access Initiative at UL can take great pride in the progress to date. The homework club/secondary school activity now engages with first and second level schools and colleges in Limerick City and in County Limerick. We do not name these schools and colleges here due to the idiosyncratic nature of information disclosure within the Irish first and second level education systems; that said, these schools and colleges are in the vanguard and fully committed to achieving the goals of the initiative in partnership with the University and with the Traveller community. And yet, the most potent contribution to date to meeting the challenge may have come, fittingly, from a Traveller parent, Willie Reilly, who asserts to his children that 'Education is no burden'. It is a rallying cry and when allied to the key roles played by all the collaborating partners, it drives the educational goals and provides support systems that are crucial to progressing Traveller students toward third level and entering on their own merits.

Conclusion

Obtaining a certain educational level, whether the Junior Certificate or a degree, is an achievement but what happens afterwards is just as important. Successful graduates will need help in securing employment, particularly in the case of non-traditional students. Their experiences and indeed their success or failure regarding employment after they leave college matters, not just for the students individually, but for the community in which they live. If students from working-class communities attend college but make no apparent gain from this, it can have a negative impact on others' expectations. The student's position after college contributes to local perceptions (positively or negatively) about college itself (Lynch, 2004).

One can state an identical argument for Traveller students. The Employment Equality Acts prohibit discrimination in the workplace. The Equal Status Acts prohibit discrimination in the provision of goods and services, accommodation and educational establishments. Both Acts cover the nine grounds of gender, marital status, family status, age, disability, sexual orientation, race, religion and membership of the Traveller community (Crowley, 2004). To enact welcome legislation is unquestionably a positive achievement; to put the letters of such law into action is quite another in what is, in demographical and diversity terms, a very different country from 40 years ago. UL, in partnership with the Limerick Traveller community and members of the Limerick County Inter-agency group for Traveller Services is striving to deepen 'the level of interaction between our students and community groups'(UL, 2011). The framework facilitates that goal.

Acknowledgements

I must express my appreciation to the following: Equine Science Department (Dr. Bridget Younge, Head); History Department (Dr. Bernadette Whelan, Head and Dr. Ruan O'Donnell); Kemmy Business School(Dr. Philip O'Regan, Dean); Sociology Department(Dr. Eoin Devereux, Head); UL Library(Gobnait O'Riordan, Head Librarian); Dr Micheál Ó hAodha, librarian and Traveller/Roma and Migration Collection; David O'Donnell, Intellectual Capital Research Institute of Ireland; Governing Body, University of Limerick, Access and Student Affairs Sub-committee Student and Social Welfare (Breda Deedigan, Chair); Dr. Pat Phelan, Assistant Vice President, UL; Dr. Bernadette Walsh, Director, Student Affairs, UL; Patrick Hoey, Access Manager, UL; Anne McMahon, Norrie O'Connell, Natalie O'Neill, Rosemary Taylor, ALL of the Visiting Teacher Services (now disbanded); members of the Limerick County Inter-Agency Steering Committee; and of course, Limerick Travellers themselves.

References

Cauley, William (ed. Micheál Ó hAodha) (2004) *The Candlelight Painter*. A & A Farmar, Dublin.

Cauley, William (ed. Micheál Ó hAodha) (2006) *Canting with Cauley*. A & A Farmar, Dublin.

Crowley, Niall (2004) 'Taking action for equality – A response to Kathleen Lynch.' In HEA 2005, pp. 22-25. Department of Education and Science (2003) Supporting equity in higher education – A report to the Minister for Education and Science. May, Department of Education and Science, Dublin.

Dunne, Pecker (ed. Micheál Ó hAodha) (2004) *Parley-Poet and Chanter*. A & A Farmar, Dublin.

Gormally, Eleanor (2005) *Whiddin to the Gauras: Traveller Researchers talk to Limerick Traveller Children*. Veritas Publications, Dublin.

Habermas, J. (1984) *The Theory of Communicative Action*, Vol. 1. Boston: Beacon Press.

Hayes, M. (2006) *Irish Travellers: Repesentations and Realities*, Dublin: Liffey Press.

Heneghan, J. (2007) Travellers and access: The 'Empathy and Mechanisms' Model at the University of Limerick in Ó hAodha, M. et al. (eds.) *The Stranger in Ourselves: Ireland's Others*. Dublin: A & A Farmer.

Heneghan, J, (2010) The Traveller Education Framework at the University of Limerick. Education as a Catalyst for Regeneration conference, June 2nd.

Higher Education Authority (2004) *Achieving equality of access to higher education in Ireland: Action Plan 2005-2007*. National Office for Equity of Access to Higher Education, Higher Education Authority, November.

Higher Education Authority (2005) *Achieving equity of access to higher education: Setting an agenda for action in Ireland*. Proceedings of a conference in Kilkenny on 6-7 December, 2004. National Office for Equity of Access to Higher Education, Higher Education Authority, Dublin.

Lynch, Kathleen (2004) 'Neo-liberalism, marketisation and higher education: Equality considerations.' In HEA 2005, pp. 9-21.

O'Byrne, Maeve (2004) 'Access agenda for action: A presentation on behalf of access made accessible (AMA).' In HEA 2005, pp. 36-40.

Pavee Point Travellers Centre (2005) The Traveller education strategy: A new vision for Traveller education. Web: http://www.paveepoint.ie/ EducationStrategy.html6

Saha, S.K., O'Donnell, D., Patel, T. and Heneghan, J. (2008), A Study of individual values and employment equity in Canada, France and Ireland. *Equal Opportunities International*, Vol. 27 No. 7, pp. 629-645

University College Dublin (2010) *All Ireland Traveller Health Study*. School of Public Health, Physiotherapy and Population Science.

University of Limerick (2011) Pioneering & Connected, Strategic Plan 2011-2012.

Walsh, Christine and Ó hAodha, Micheál (2008) *Postcolonial Borderlands*. Cambridge Scholars Publishing.

The Road to Freedom

Julia Sweeney, Galway

I am a Traveller born
to be free,
Stripped of a culture
For no more will I see.

I have travelled the country
through hail wind and snow,
with me horse and me wagon and
all of me load.

I have camped on the road side,
I have camped in the fields,
I have roamed wild all over
even down by the sea.

I've heard many a story,
I have sang many a song,
by the campsite fires
when the days were so long.

Now the old way of living
Has come to an end,
for the Traveller has settled
but the road was my friend.

Contributors

Dakxinkumar Bajrange (Chhara) is a theatre practitioner and film maker. He graduated in Theatre and Global Development at the University of Leeds on the Ford Foundation International Fellowship in 2011 and currently works as a director at Budhan Theatre, a cultural wing of Bhasha Research and Publication Centre in India. He has written and directed 10 plays and supervised more than 30 plays at the Budhan Theatre. He made 43 short films on tribal music instruments for the Government. of India and made 25 films on various social and political issues of India. He won the South Asia Livelihood Documentary award, Jeevika 2005. He is an author of the book *Budhan Bolta Hai* (Budhan speaks) in the Hindi language, published by Bhasha.

Francis Barrett, born February 7, 1977 in Galway city, is a well-known boxer who now lives in England. Barrett came to worldwide attention when, as the youngest member of the Irish team (19), he became the first Irish Traveller to carry the Irish flag and box for his country during the 1996 Summer Olympics in Atlanta, Georgia. He is now retired from boxing and works in the construction industry in England.

Majella Breen is LTI Coordinator with Bray Travellers Community Development Group in County Wicklow.

Caroline Canny is a nurse working with Travellers in County Galway. She currently works with the Traveller Primary Health Care programme.

Dr Brian Coates retired from the post of Senior Lecturer in English at the College of Humanities, University of Limerick in 2005, and then worked as Director of Cultural Studies at the Bhasha Research and Publications Centre, Gujarat, India and as Senior Research Fellow in Cultural Studies at the Interaction Design Centre, University of Limerick, a post which he continues to occupy. His interests include Radical Philosophy, Feminism, Postmodernism and the cultures of artistic practice. He has also been involved in an education project in Lesotho and visited the country in February 2010 with the Kerry-based charity ActionLesotho.ie.

Martin Collins has been a Traveller activist for 28 years and is a founding member of Pavee Point Travellers Centre, of which he is now Co-Director. He has represented Pavee Point and Irish Travellers both nationally and internationally and is presently the Irish delegate to the European Roma Traveller Forum in Strasbourg. He represented Pavee Point on the Irish Human Rights Commission (IHRC) from 2001-2007. He also represented PP on the Task Force Report on the Travelling Community, which was published in 1995 and is generally regarded as a milestone in offering an innovative analysis on Traveller issues and how they might be addressed. He also has extensive experience in providing anti-racism/intercultural training for both the statutory and voluntary sectors.

Professor Dennis Foley lectures in the School of Humanities and Social Science, University of Newcastle, Australia. He researches and teaches across numerous academic fields related to Indigenous Australians. He directs his main research focus towards the emerging discipline of Indigenous enterprise and entrepreneurship.

Richard Hannafin is currently studying for a Masters in Adult Education at Mary Immaculate College Limerick. His research is primarily concerned with the implications the arts have for furthering learning. Engaging with adults from a wide spectrum of multicultural and socio-economic backgrounds, his work has resulted in projects in Limerick City and County ranging from festival floats with Asylum- Seekers to introductory printmaking classes for adult learners.

John Heneghan is a lecturer in the Kemmy Business School, University of Limerick. He is also the Coordinator of the Traveller ACCESS Initiative at the University of Limerick. The Initiative has helped to fund in-school initiatives, homework clubs and research resources in the area of Traveller, Roma and Migration Studies including this publication. John represents the University of Limerick on the Limerick County Inter-Agency Group for Traveller Services.

Willis's
Practice and Procedure
for the Quantity Surveyor

Willis's
Practice and Procedure
for the Quantity Surveyor

Eleventh Edition

Allan Ashworth
Keith Hogg

b

**Blackwell
Science**

Blackwell Science Ltd, a Blackwell Publishing company
Editorial offices:
Blackwell Science Ltd, 9600 Garsington Road, Oxford OX4 2DQ, UK
    Tel: +44 (0) 1865 776868
Blackwell Publishing Inc., 350 Main Street, Malden, MA 02148-5020, USA
    Tel: +1 781 388 8250
Blackwell Science Asia Pty Ltd, 550 Swanston Street, Carlton, Victoria 3053, Australia
    Tel: +61 (0)3 8359 1011

First published by Crosby Lockwood & Son Ltd 1951, Second Edition 1957, Third Edition 1963, Fourth Edition 1966, Fifth Edition (metric) 1969, Sixth Edition 1972, Seventh Edition by Crosby Lockwood Staples 1975, Eighth Edition by Granada Publishing 1980, Reprinted 1981, Reprinted by Collins Professional and Technical Books 1985, Ninth Edition 1987, Reprinted by BSP Professional Books 1990, 1992, Tenth Edition by Blackwell Scientific Publications 1994, Eleventh Edition by Blackwell Science Ltd 2002, Reprinted 2005

Library of Congress Cataloging-in-Publication Data

Ashworth, A. (Allan)
    Willis's practice and procedure for the
    quantity surveyor / Allan Ashworth, Keith
    Hogg, and Andrew Willis.—11th ed.
    Rev. ed. of: Practice and procedure for the
    quantity surveyor/Christopher J. Willis, Allan
    Ashworth, and J. Andrew Willis. 10th ed. c1994.
    Includes bibliographical references and
    index.
    ISBN 0-632-05334-8
    1. Building—Estimates—Great Britain.
    I. Title: Practice and procedure for the quantity
    surveyor. II. Hogg, Keith. III. Willis,
    Andrew. IV. Title.

TH435.W6853 2001
692'.5'0941—dc21   2001037963

ISBN-10: 0-632-05334-8
ISBN-13: 978-0632-05334-6

A catalogue record for this title is available from the British Library

Set in 10/12.5pt Palatino
by DP Photosetting, Aylesbury, Bucks
Printed and bound by Replika Press Pvt. Ltd, India

For further information on Blackwell Publishing, visit our website:
www.thatconstructionsite.com

Contents

Preface

The first edition of this book was published over 50 years ago, in 1951. This edition therefore celebrates its half centenary. It has throughout its existence provided a much needed source of information and analysis to generations of quantity surveyors. It is a book that is on the reading list of surveying courses throughout the world. The book also uniquely represents the work of three generations of quantity surveyors, the Willis family, the book being originally conceived and written by Arthur J. Willis.

Arthur J. Willis was a household name among quantity surveyors. He was responsible for the first two editions that were published in 1951 and 1957. His son, Christopher J. Willis, who was equally well known and was the President of the Quantity Surveyor's Division of the Royal Institution of Chartered Surveyors in 1978–1979, then jointly authored the next six editions. Allan Ashworth joined Christopher in writing the ninth edition and J. Andrew Willis, the grandson of the original author, joined Christopher and Allan in writing the tenth edition.

Throughout the book's life, it has sought to reflect upon the changing aspects of practice and procedures. These changes, as in all walks of life, have never appeared greater in society than they do today. Anyone who has any doubts as to just how much the profession of quantity surveying has changed should compare this edition with the first edition!

This current edition of *Practice and Procedure for the Quantity Surveyor* has sought to capture the wider role and activities of today's quantity surveyors. Like changes in society, this role has been under constant evolution since quantity surveyors were first employed well over two centuries ago. However, even before that time the work of the quantity surveyor was being carried out by someone, just as in some countries today, where the name of quantity surveyor may be unfamiliar, the important work is nevertheless carried out under a different title.

When *Practice and Procedure for the Quantity Surveyor* was first published, the role of the quantity surveyor concentrated on the measurement of building quantities, the preparation and agreement of final accounts and valuations of work under construction for interim certificate purposes. How vastly different are practices and procedures today. There has, for example, been a paradigm shift in quantity surveying practices from one concerned solely with cost to one that now places increased emphasis on value. But this is not entirely a late twentieth century phenomenon. Value has always been important, even though the emphasis might not always have been so explicit.

It was John Ruskin who, towards the end of the nineteenth century, said, 'It is not the cheaper things that we want to possess, but expensive things that cost less'. The importance of adding value in the construction industry cannot be over-stated or over-realised.

During the writing of this book there has been much debate among ourselves and the publisher as to whether the title of the book still remained appropriate and relevant in the twenty-first century. Many quantity surveying practices, both large and small, have diversified, and even with those who still only practise quantity surveying, their work, role and practice extend beyond that which the title alone describes. Some quantity surveying practices have changed their titles and designations in an attempt to reflect their skills, knowledge and understanding, and to capture other sources of work. Most of the other professions also suffer the same difficulty in name and title. We have considered titles that more accurately capture the practices and procedures that are involved. We have looked to the Royal Institution of Chartered Surveyors and its new faculty structure for some guidance, but like many quantity surveyors we do not see 'Construction' as being in any way a clearer, better or indeed a preferred title.

The book seeks to cover the work of a twenty-first century quantity surveyor and to describe the various activities carried out by quantity surveyors, giving worked examples and ideas where appropriate.

Allan Ashworth
Keith I. Hogg

Preface to the First Edition

The first thought of a writer putting pen to paper is (or should be): who will be my readers? It is only by constantly bearing them in mind, their requirements and their limitations, that one can so focus the writing that it becomes a readable book. The mere exposition of one's thoughts without this concentration on the reader produces a blurred image so often exemplified by dreary writing.

Who then is likely to be interested in the subject on which I have embarked? Not, I think, the established quantity surveyor in practice. He has explored the subject himself in the development of his practice, not in theory but by thought and experience. Not that any amount of reading will dispense with the need of both thought and experience for the successful practitioner. However, just as it is easier to make one's way through thick undergrowth in a wood if one can follow where someone has been before, so the path may be made easier for the practitioner of the future if he can follow footsteps: if he can see two or more tracks all the better; he can pick his way by whichever seems at the moment the most suitable, and it may be that in places the tracks will coincide and make the path still easier.

I have, therefore, visualised as my readers the student in his fourth or fifth year working for his final examination who has an interest beyond the limits of his syllabus, the surveyor who, having passed his final, may feel that he never wants to see another textbook, yet sees the need to extend his knowledge of the profession, and the practitioner in embryo or new-born, who has during his employment seen little of 'how it works'.

Offices vary considerably in size, type and even quality, and practice differs accordingly, as well as with the ideas (and idiosyncracies) of the individual surveyor. Bearing in mind my probable readers, I have concentrated on the smaller office and the requirements of the younger man. Other readers must not mind if they find the picture a little out of focus from their own standpoint.

Some of the subjects touched on – office organisation, finance, partnership – are not peculiar to quantity surveying, but, as in most cases the young surveyor will not have made any particular study of them, I felt that it was essential to outline something of their principles.

It is, perhaps, obvious to say when speaking of practice that what I have found, chosen or decided is not necessarily the experience, choice or decision of others. I must not, therefore, be read as laying down rules, but rather as putting forward suggestions.

Having started my professional training late, thanks to a little matter of a war, and practice rather early because opportunity knocked at the door, I felt that I lacked the variety of experience necessary to write authoritatively on professional practice. I am, therefore, particularly grateful for the help I have received from Mr E.W. Leaning, MA, FRICS, and Colonel J.B. Marks, OBE, FRICS, who have both made valuable suggestions for amendments, alternatives or additions, the latter being of particular assistance on the subject of public service. Further, without legal support I would not have dared to write on law, and I have to thank Mr D.A. Grant, DSO, barrister-at-law, for reading my first effort, correcting my misconceptions and giving me his most helpful advice. I must add thanks to my partner, Mr D.T.C. Thompson, FRICS, and several members of our staff, who have also pointed out errors and made numerous suggestions.

One cannot acknowledge all the sources of one's knowledge of practice, but I should particularly like to mention the value to me of those two textbooks on which I was brought up – Leaning's *Quantity Surveying* and Fletcher's *Quantities*. Between them they did much to lay the foundation of the two chapters on law.

A.J.W.
October 1950

1 The Work of the Quantity Surveyor

Introduction

In 1971, the RICS published a report titled, *The Future Role of the Quantity Surveyor*, which defined the work of the quantity surveyor as:

> 'ensuring that the resources of the construction industry are utilised to the best advantage of society by providing, *inter alia*, the financial management for projects and a cost consultancy service to the client and designer during the whole construction process.'

The report sought to identify the distinctive competencies or skills of the quantity surveyor associated with measurement and valuation, in the wider aspects of the construction industry. This provides the basis for the proper cost management of the construction project in the context of forecasting, analysing, planning, controlling and accounting. Many reading this will reflect that this is no longer an adequate description of the work of the quantity surveyor.

From the 1970s onwards the profession began to evolve rapidly and, in 1983 the RICS prepared another report that would explore further the work of the quantity surveyor and at the same time attempt to assess its future potential and directions. This report, *The Future Role of the Chartered Quantity Surveyor*, identified a range of skills, knowledge and expertise provided by the quantity surveyor and indicated a greater expansion of possible services that could be provided both inside and outside of the construction industry. This report began to examine the changing and shifting scene, the requirements of clients and their dissatisfaction with the services provided by construction professionals generally and their frequent disappointment with the products that they received.

Almost ten years later in 1991 the Davis, Langdon and Everest consultancy group produced *QS2000* on behalf of the RICS. This report began to describe the threats and opportunities that were facing the profession at the end of the twentieth century. Again its key message related to change and in ensuring the services provided recognised that the status quo no longer applied. Clients were demanding more for their fees. The changes identified in this report included:

- *Changes in markets:* outlining the previous performance and trends in workloads across the different sectors and the importance of the changing international scene, particularly the challenges arising from the deepening European Union.

- *Changes in the construction industry:* through the changing nature of contracting, an emphasis upon management of construction, the comparison with other countries abroad and the competition being offered from non-construction professionals.
- *Changes in client needs:* with an emphasis in terms of the value added to the client's business; they want purchaseable design, procurement and management of construction.
- *Changes in the profession:* noting employment patterns, the growth in graduate members, the impact of fee competition, the ways in which the quantity surveyor is now appointed, and changes in their role and practice with changing attitudes and horizons.

Towards the end of that decade, the former Quantity Surveyor's Division of the RICS produced a report titled, *The Challenge of Change* (Powell 1998). This report provided stark warnings to the profession, almost as a final warning that if the profession did not adapt to change then it would not exist in the future. This would also be the last report from the Quantity Surveyor's Division, since this marked the end of the divisional structure within the RICS. The report focused on five important areas, as follows.

Business world

This suggested that there would be economic stability in many countries around the world, thereby implying and encouraging construction activity to take place in the early part of the twenty-first century. Economic analysis suggested an end to boom and bust philosophies, and the greater stability that would allow the industry to prosper. The distinction between the contracting and professional services functions will be less well defined.

Customers

The clients of the industry will remain diverse but the larger ones will increase their international perspective. They will require all of their business partners to add value, take risk and in some cases probably share equity as well.

Projects

Information and communication technology will raise the expectations amongst all client groupings. They will expect improved value, higher quality and earlier completion. This will apply to all types of project and will not be restricted to capital cost projects alone.

Skills

The requirement for skills is both changing and increasing. Some of the technical functions will be transferred to computer applications and the distinction between technical and professional roles will become more emphasised. A broader knowledge of construction and property, increased communication abilities and a greater commercial acumen will become necessary along with some specialisation. The importance of life long learning will be fundamental to career prospects.

Information and communication technology (ICT)

The ICT revolution will continue to develop at an exponential rate. This will help to increase productivity and expand the range of information available and the services provided by quantity surveyors. The integration of computer applications will save time and increase speed. The application of consistency within the overall process and at every stage will generally increase the overall efficiency and effectiveness.

A changing industry

The prospects of the construction industry are intrinsically linked to those of a country's economy. In times of recession the industry's major employers are reluctant to invest and this has an immediate knock-on effect on the fortunes or otherwise of the construction industry. As a proportion of GDP, the output of the construction industry in the United Kingdom is comparatively stable at about 6%. The construction industry, for example, has not suffered the considerable decline of engineering, especially ship building and coal mining.

However, the industry is changing shape. As a result of privatisations over the past 20 years the share of the public sector's construction portfolio has been considerably reduced. At its peak in the 1970s this represented almost 50%. It is now less than half of this figure. Coupled with this have been strategic changes in the procurement of public sector building and civil engineering projects, through for example the introduction of the Private Finance Initiative (PFI). This has assisted the industry to refocus on longer term measures, such as the consideration of whole life costing. There is also an increasing use being made of design and build, a trend that is likely to continue.

In 1994, the Latham Report, *Constructing the Team*, was published with far reaching consequences on the construction industry and those employed in it, including quantity surveyors. Its chief aim was to attempt to change the culture of the industry and thus increase the performance of construction activities and the final product. The Latham Report, for example drew comparisons with motor car manufacturing and how this had changed to improve the product for the customer. By comparison the construction industry had not changed significantly or fast enough and was being regarded by some as little more than a handicraft industry (Harvey & Ashworth 1997). Other reports followed with similar and uncomfortable themes. These included a report by the Royal Academy of Engineering (Barlow 1996) and *Rethinking Construction* (Egan 1998). In order to achieve the objectives set out in the above reports, the whole design and construction process, including the work of the quantity surveyor needs to be re-engineered.

Characteristics of the construction industry

The total value of the construction output in the UK is currently £60bn, which is approximately 6% of GDP. The industry offers direct employment to around two million people and to others in supporting occupations. It is the fourth largest construction industry in Europe and represents about 9% of total output. The public sector includes a diminishing share of the work in the UK. In addition many UK firms and practices, including quantity surveyors have an international perspective often through offices overseas or through associations with firms abroad. There has, for example, been an increasing and expanding role of activities on mainland Europe. Approximately 80% of the UK workload is on building projects as distinct from engineering works. New construction projects account for about 50% of the workload of the industry. The repair and maintenance sector will remain an important component for the foreseeable future as clients place greater emphasis upon the improved long-term management of such major capital assets. A detailed analysis of the industry can be found in Harvey and Ashworth (1997).

The industry is characterised by the following:

- The physical nature of the product
- The product is normally manufactured on the client's premises, i.e. the construction site
- Many of its projects are one-off designs in the absence of a prototype model
- The traditional arrangement separates design from manufacture
- It produces investment rather than consumer goods
- It is subject to wider swings of activity than most other industries
- Its activities are affected by the vagaries of the weather
- Its processes include a complex mixture of different materials, skills and trades
- Typically, throughout the world, it includes a small number of relatively large construction firms and a very large number of small firms
- The smaller firms tend to concentrate on repair and maintenance.

Construction sectors

Within the construction industry quantity surveyors are involved in the following four main areas of work.

Building work

The employment of the quantity surveyor on building projects today is well established. The introduction of new forms of contract and changes in procedures continues to alter the way in which quantity surveyors carry out their duties and responsibilities. They also occupy a much more influential position than in the past, particularly when they are involved at the outset of a project. In some cases, they may be the client's first point of contact.

Quantity surveyors are the cost and value experts of the construction industry. Their responsibilities include advising clients on the cost and value implication of design decisions and the controlling of construction costs. Great importance is now attached to the control of costs on the majority of projects. Clients and designers are prone to making changes after the contract has been signed, and to order additional works that were not envisaged. This sometimes gives the incorrect impression that the quantity surveyor has not done the work correctly.

Building engineering services

Whilst this work is very much a part of the building project, it has tended to become a specialist function for the quantity surveyor, especially on large complex projects. An ever-increasing amount is expended on the elements that constitute this work. Traditionally, much of this work was included in bills of quantities as prime cost sums. It was largely presented in this way for three main reasons: building services engineers often failed to provide the appropriate details in time for quantification purposes; traditionally it was not the custom to measure this type of work; and contractors often preferred to offer lump sum quotations on the basis of drawing and specifications only. More enlightened clients realised that this approach was not very satisfactory in determining where the actual costs for this work are being expended. Whilst there is sometimes resistance to detailed quantification from some building services consultants, there is now a clear preference for a systematic breakdown of costs that can be properly compared and evaluated.

It is also accepted that to provide a rigorous cost control function for only part of a building project is unsatisfactory. The building services engineering work is frequently more extensive and expensive and its costs, value and cost control must be as rigorous as the methods applied on the remainder of the construction project. Quantity surveyors employed in this discipline have had to become more conversant with engineering services in their science, technology and terminology, in order to interpret engineering drawings correctly.

Civil engineering

It is difficult to define the line of demarcation between building and civil engineering works. The nature of civil engineering works often requires a design solution to take into account physical and geological problems that can be very complex. The scope, size and extent of civil engineering works are also frequently considerable. The problems encountered can have a major impact on the cost of the solution, and the engineer must be able to provide an acceptable one within the limits of an agreed budget, in a similar way that buildings are cost planned within cost limits. However, because of the nature of civil engineering works, they can involve a large amount of uncertainty and temporary works can be considerable, representing a significant part of the budget.

Civil engineering projects use different methods of measurement. In the UK, this might be either the Civil Engineering Standard Method of Measurement or Method of Measurement for Roads and Bridgeworks, although, in addition, other methods are also available. Different forms and conditions of contract are also used. These to some extent represent the different perception of civil engineering works. The work is more method-related than building works, with a much more intensive use of mechanical plant and temporary works. Bills of quantities, for example, comprise large quantities of comparatively few items. Because much of the work involved is at or below ground level, the quantities are normally approximate, with a full remeasurement of the work that is actually carried out. Also as there is not the same direct relationship between quantity and costs, contractual claims are potentially a more likely event.

Quantity surveyors working in the civil engineering industry provide similar services to those of their counterparts working on building projects. In addition to the methods of measurement and conditions of contract, quantity surveyors must also be conversant with the different working rule agreements, daywork rates and other documents such as *Civil Engineering Procedure,* which is published by the Institution of Civil Engineers.

Quantity surveyors have been employed by civil engineering contractors and design consultants since the turn of the century. Engineers also value the advice that quantity surveyors are able to provide on costs, value, contractual and other relevant matters. Engineers recognise the benefits of the quantity surveyor's specialised skills and knowledge in respect of the cost and financial aspects of construction. Many promoters, the civil engineering client, rely on pre-contract and post contract services provided by quantity surveyors.

Heavy and industrial engineering

This work includes such areas as onshore and offshore oil and gas, petrochemicals, nuclear reprocessing and production facilities, process engineering, power stations, steel plants, and other similar industrial engineering complexes. Quantity surveyors have been involved in this type of work for some time, and as a result of changing circumstances within these industries a greater emphasis is also being placed on value for money. In an industry that employs a large number of specialists, quantity surveyors, with their practical background, commercial sense, cost knowledge and legal understanding, have much to offer.

The work involved is generally classified as cost engineering. Modern-day cost engineers may come from a variety of different professions but a considerable number have their roots in quantity surveying. The professional cost engineer is widely employed in the USA and many countries of Europe, and this continues to be a growth profession. The RICS and the Association of Cost Engineers prepared a Standard Method of Measurement for Industrial Engineering Construction (SMMIEC) in 1984. Standard forms of contract are also published by the Institution of Chemical Engineers among others.

The basic methods employed are similar to those used in other quantity surveying work. They may be more numerically based and offer different forms of analysis which lend themselves to computerised measurement and cost administration systems. Bills of approximate quantities are often produced from sketches and drawings provided. Otherwise, performance specifications or schedules of rates or one of the variety of cost-reimbursable contracts may be employed. Alternatively take-offs may be prepared for the purchase of materials only.

Essentially, quantity surveyors who are employed on this type of work must be able to adapt to new methods of measurement, cost analysis, contract procedures and cost engineering practices. There is also a likelihood of being involved in a wider range of activities than those encountered on building projects.

The role of the quantity surveyor

Traditional role

The traditional role of the quantity surveyor has been described elsewhere and in previous editions of *Practice and Procedure for the Quantity Surveyor*. The history of the quantity surveyor from the middle of the seventeenth century is briefly described in Seeley and Winfield (1999) and in Ashworth and Hogg (2000). This traditional role, that is still practised by some, can be briefly described as a measure and value system. Approximate estimates of the initial costs of building are prepared using a single price method of estimating (see Chapter 6), and where this cost was acceptable to the client then the design was developed by the architect. Subsequently the quantity surveyor would produce bills of quantities for tendering purposes, the work would be measured for progress payments and a final account prepared on the basis of the tender documentation (see Fig. 1.1). The process was largely reactive, but necessary and important. During the 1960s, to avoid tenders being received that were over budget, cost planning services were added to the repertoire of the duties performed by the quantity surveyor employed in private practice. Hence the term private quantity surveyor (PQS). The contractor's surveyor was responsible for looking after the financial interests of the contractor and worked in conjunction with the PQS on the preparation of interim payments and final accounts. On occasions, contractors felt that they were not being adequately reimbursed under the terms of the contract and submitted claims for extra payments. This procedure was more prevalent on civil engineering projects than on building projects, although the adversarial nature of construction was increasing all the time.

Pragmatism and realism are some of the qualities most highly valued by clients in quantity surveyors (Davis, Langdon and Everest 1991). Some will argue that the distinctive competence found in quantity surveyors relies heavily on their analytical approach to buildings and that this stems directly from their ability to measure construction works. Furthermore, the detailed analysis of drawings leads to a deep understanding of the design and construction which enables them to contribute fully to the process. This intimate knowledge of projects is at the root of the contribution the quantity surveyor can make to the value of the client's business through the provision of the services shown in Fig. 1.1.

- Single rate approximate estimates
- Cost planning
- Procurement advice
- Measurement and quantification
- Document preparation, especially bills of quantities
- Cost control during construction
- Interim valuations and payments
- Financial statements
- Final account preparation and agreement
- Settlement of contractual claims

Fig. 1.1   Traditional quantity surveying activities.

Evolved role

In response to the potential demise of bills of quantities, quantity surveyors began exploring new potential roles for their services. Procurement, a term not used until the 1980s, became an important area of activity, largely because of the increasing array of options that were available. Increased importance and emphasis were also being placed upon design cost planning as a tool that was effective in meeting the client's objectives. This coupled with whole life costing (Chapter 7), value management (Chapter 8) and risk analysis and management (Chapter 9) were other tools being used to add value for the client. As buildings became more services orientated increased emphasis was being placed on the measurement, costs and value of such services. Quantity surveyors had historically dealt with this work through prime cost and provisional sums, but in today's modern buildings to describe the work in this context is inadequate. Other evolved roles have included project and construction management and facilities management (see Fig. 1.2). Because of the inherent adversarial nature of the construction industry they are also involved in contractual disputes and litigation.

Some practices became very nervous about the apparent demise of bills of quantities. It remains an apparent demise since at the commencement of the twenty-first century they still represented a significant proportion of work and associated fees. The wheel may have turned in some respects since

- Investment appraisal
- Advice on cost limits and budgets
- Whole life costing
- Value management
- Risk analysis
- Insolvency services
- Cost engineering services
- Subcontract administration
- Environmental services measurement and costing
- Technical auditing
- Planning and supervision
- Valuation for insurance purposes
- Project management
- Facilities management
- Administering maintenance programmes
- Advice on contractual disputes

Fig. 1.2 Evolved role.

instead of preparing bills for clients, quantity surveyors were preparing bills for contractors. This was the practice used during the nineteenth century! Also countries that hitherto had not yet embraced quantity surveying, and the number of these countries is continuing to decline, were beginning to see the benefits of schedules of quantities for tendering and contractual administration purposes.

Significant interests in the techniques of life cycle costing (recently renamed whole life costing) and value management were being actively pursued by practices and supported by academic research.

Developing role

The future development of quantity surveying services is likely to be influenced by the following important factors:

- Client focus
- Development and application of information and communication technologies
- Research and its dissemination
- Graduate capability
- Practice size.

Client focus

The construction costs of capital works projects will always be an important component for clients in their decision to build. These costs will include whole life costs. There can be only a few clients with the motto of Cheops, the builder of the great pyramid, who said, 'I don't care how much it costs or how long it takes!' Consultants are sometimes seen as adding excessive costs to projects and contractors, offering services that are late, of poor quality and of indeterminate high costs. Clients will always be prepared to pay for services that are able to demonstrate a financial benefit. The basic requirements of clients are shown in Fig. 1.3.

- Reduced time scales
- Practical completion must mean total completion, not 'nearly ready'
- Simplified process
- Complete understanding of the procurement process
- Comprehensive service including mechanical and electrical installations
- Excluding the exclusions
- Effective change management
- Solutions not projects

Fig. 1.3   Basic requirements of clients (*Source:* Powell 1988).

- Choice
- Co-investment and risk taking
- Commitment
- Credibility
- Competence
- Clarity and accountability
- Consistency

Fig. 1.4   Client needs – the seven C's (*Source:* Powell 1998).

The client needs of the early part of this century are broadly identified in Fig. 1.4.

Experience suggests that whilst improvement amongst the leaders in the construction industry can be expected to match the best in the world, the improvement generally will take time and will involve radical changes in culture and probably its structure. Barlow (1996) has suggested some of the examples of best practices that can be learned from the manufacturing industry sector (Fig. 1.5). There is a lack of understanding of best practices or even an awareness in some situations that change is the order of the day and urgent. There is a determination to survive but a lack of realisation of international competition.

Development and application of information and communication technologies

The implications associated with information and communication technologies are considered in Chapter 5.

- **Focus on customer satisfaction.** Recognise that clients want buildings and support after completion, at the right price, to the appropriate quality and standards, on time and meeting their needs.
- **Attention to the process as well as the product.** Product design has now become a byword in manufacturing industry, where the process used has contributed towards increasing the appropriateness of the product. Research is necessary in the construction industry in process analysis.
- **Concept of total quality approach and attitudes.** The total quality approach should not be confused with total quality management or quality assurance, which are now widely accepted in the industry. Total quality programmes are often expensive to implement relying on extensive training to bring about a shift in culture. It represents a continuous improvement programme.
- **Benchmarking.** The practice of benchmarking all of a company's activities against the best competition or against organisations who are known to be industry leaders is now commonplace in some quarters (see Chapter 18). A characteristic of many of these companies is their willingness to share knowledge with others.
- **Team-working and partnering, including supply chains.** This aims to make every individual feel worthwhile and as such it leads to greater pride within a company. It aims to harness the intelligence and experience of the whole workforce. It also extends beyond the individual company to include consultants, contractors, subcontractors and suppliers. For large clients they are also often part of the team (see Chapter 10).
- **Information technology.** The construction industry must welcome the more widespread use of information technologies and embrace the current Technology Foresight Initiative.

Fig. 1.5 Learning from manufacturing industry (Barlow, 1996).

Research and its dissemination

The importance of research and its dissemination is fundamental to any profession, especially one that is facing a change in direction and its practices. These are also considered in Chapter 5.

Graduate capability

The number of graduates in quantity surveying is unlikely to change significantly from the reduced numbers experienced in the late 1990s. The relative shortage in supply has already had the effect of increasing graduate salaries. Those graduates who have a good technical understanding, a broader use of business skills and a commitment towards life long learning are likely to be in high demand. For other graduates they will need to make themselves either more valuable to practices and contractors or less expensive.

The issues facing the future of the construction industry and in attracting able graduates to its various professions including quantity surveying, are many and varied and include the following:

- Under capitalisation exacerbated by fragmentation and the large numbers of small firms
- Low technology, labour intensive and traditionally craft based
- Litigious basis for settling differences and disputes
- Lack of prototype development resulting in untested and ill-specified components and technologies
- Low level of computing and use of information technology
- The use by government of the construction industry as an economic regulator contributes towards a cyclical workload
- High number of company business failures
- Poor image, working practices and employment conditions
- Difficulties of recruiting, training and retaining a skilled and committed workforce

Practice size

The particular advantages of small firms are their in-depth understanding of the local market and their low cost base. The traditional small practice has historically relied on document preparation and traditional quantity surveying activities. In order for these practices to survive in the longer term they will need to diversify and develop stronger links with a larger number of clients. Some small practices have been able to develop specialist activities by directing their activities away from the traditional work towards niche areas, such as taxation, dispute resolution and information technology for the industry. There is a view (Powell 1998), that many of the smaller firms will increasingly work on a subcontract basis for the larger firms, although the evidence for this at the present time is not convincing. Strategies might include some of the following:

- Being responsive to change and having the capability to move into new markets
- Developing links with a wider client base
- Investing in modern information communication technologies
- Managing the needs of the local market
- Seizing opportunities afforded by on-line working.

In growing a practice from a small firm to a large firm, one of the biggest hurdles to overcome is that of being a medium sized firm. Many of the larger firms have already diversified into multiple discipline practices. The difficulty for the medium sized firms is the retaining of high quality staff, forging links with larger clients and competing with the smaller firms with their lower overheads. The larger clients, for example, are likely to want to work with those practices that are able to offer the more comprehensive services, in essence a single point of professional responsibility. Strategies to overcome this difficulty might include some of the following:

- Avoiding competition with larger firms
- Developing market strategies to differentiate them from the larger firms
- Specialising and developing in-depth knowledge
- Forming alliances with overseas partners
- Entering joint ventures with complementary firms.

The large practices are expected to grow in size through expansion and mergers. They are likely to continue to diversify as the role of the quantity surveyor develops. The particular education, training and expertise will be used to increase the range of services that are provided. They will begin to challenge other established firms and in some cases will become management consultants to the construction industry. They will retain the specialised knowledge to allow them to compete with other disciplines that have established themselves with large clients. This move of providing broad based business solutions will continue despite the increasing competition from contractors and other large consultancy organisations.

The role of quantity surveyors in the public sector will continue to be threatened by private consultants, through fee competition and best value solutions. The smaller public sector quantity surveying departments are likely to disappear entirely as capital works are either carried out by the larger county authorities or awarded to private consultancies. Within the larger public sector organisations, longer term business solutions will become increasingly important and comparative benchmarking practices used more widely in order to establish best value solutions.

The clear differences between contracting and consulting have already become blurred. This process is likely to continue until demarcation lines between roles, activities and practices and the best attributes become more distinctive in newly divided sectors. The smaller contracting firms are all but disappearing, as subcontracting has become the normal pattern. These firms however will continue to use in-house surveyors to perform a wide range of managerial functions. The number of larger firms is becoming fewer and more of these are becoming part of multi-national organisations. The remainder of contracting firms will become more specialised focusing on a limited range of activities, product specifications or type of project that they carry out.

Historically private and public practice and contracting have frequently been seen as the two distinct parts of the profession. The work undertaken by each was also considered to be different in terms of the practices involved and the ethical considerations of doing the job. Increasingly clients have and are opting for single-point responsibility solutions through, for example, design and build and other contractor orientated practices such as PFI. In the past there might have been considered possible conflicts of interest by working for clients as well as for contractors. Such a concept has now all but disappeared.

The developing role of the quantity surveyor in these various and different organisations will be an expansion or further expansion in the areas of activities that are shown in Fig. 1.6.

- Automated measurement and quantification
- Environmental and sustainability analysis
- Advice on information and communications technology
- Taxation and investment advice relating to projects
- Supply chain management
- Facilities management
- Legal services
- Quality management
- Niche markets

Fig. 1.6   Developing role.

Skills, knowledge and understanding

The Royal Institution of Chartered Surveyors published a report in 1992, titled *The Core Skills and Knowledge Base of the Quantity Surveyor*. This examined the needs of quantity surveyors in respect of their education, training and continuing professional development. This reflected the requirements in the context of increasing changes and uncertainties in the construction industry and more importantly within the profession. Since the publication of this report, there have been a number of government and educational initiatives with regard to the implementation of life long learning. All subject disciplines have in recent years placed an increasing emphasis on the development of generic and specialist skills within their respective curricula. A course audit of such skills was first initiated by the Business and Technology Education Council (now EDEXCEL) and has since been accepted as an important component on all undergraduate and postgraduate courses in every university. The RICS report identified a range of skills that the profession would need to continue to develop if it wished to maintain its role within the construction industry. The report identified a knowledge base that includes:

- Construction technology
- Measurement rules and conventions
- Construction economics
- Financial management
- Business administration
- Construction law.

and a skill base that includes:

- Management
- Documentation
- Analysis
- Appraisal
- Quantification

- Synthesis
- Communication.

All of these remain valid requirements ten years later, although their relative importance has changed to suit changing needs and aspirations. The report also sought to set out and to identify the present market requirements and to anticipate expectations in the future. It also examined constraints that might in some way inhibit quantity surveyors from achieving their full and expected potential.

The report developed earlier themes from reports published by the RICS and others. These included *The Future Role of the Quantity Surveyor* (1971), *The Future Role of the Chartered Quantity Surveyor* (1983), *Quantity Surveying 2000* (1991) and *Quantity Surveying Techniques: New Directions* (1992). The report examined key trends in the demand for construction activity and the needs of professional services. The report also made reference to the wider opportunities that may lie beyond the horizon of construction, where the skills and knowledge base could be applied.

In analysing the knowledge base and accepting that this would be incremental and on a need-to-know basis, the report identified four key areas:

- *Technology:* This relates to process used and the product achieved
- *Information:* The requirement for sources and information management
- *Cultural:* The organisational and legal framework context
- *Economic:* The increasing importance of business and finance.

The report discusses the differences between skills and techniques. Quantity surveying has developed its own repertoire of techniques. Skills occur in respect of the levels of ability required to apply these techniques in an expert way. The different array of skills is assimilated with the knowledge base through education, training and practice. Whilst there is a general agreement about the skills and knowledge base required, different surveyors will place different emphases upon the relative importance in practice. The report concludes with a forecast of the future importance of the different core skills and knowledge requirements in a changing environment.

Powell (1998) further emphasised the importance of skills required of the chartered quantity surveyor tomorrow. Tomorrow has now already arrived! This report emphasised the need to:

- Develop a greater understanding of business and business culture
- Develop strong communications and ICT skills
- Challenge authoritatively the contributions of other team members
- Understand that value can be added only by managing and improving the client's customers and employer's performance
- Develop skills to promote themselves effectively
- See qualifications only as the starting point

- Recognise the need to take action now
- Become champions of finance and good propriety.

The skills of the quantity surveyor that were very important 40 years ago still remain important but their relative importance has declined to be replaced by new skills. This is evident across a whole range of industries and professions. The skills of today will also need to be enhanced as demands continue to evolve and change.

What's in a name?

The name 'quantity surveyor' conjures up a variety of different images in people's imaginations. For some, the term quantity surveyor is an outmoded title from the past. It certainly no longer *accurately* describes the duties that are performed. When the term was first applied to the profession, the work of the quantity surveyor was vastly different to that now being carried out and anticipated in the twenty-first century. New titles have been suggested which include 'construction cost consultant', as being the most preferred. 'Building economist', 'construction accountant', 'contractual and procurement specialist' are others that have been disregarded.

Some practices have also deleted cost entirely from the title, describing themselves simply as 'construction consultant', or 'construction management consultant'. Others have added a multiplicity of titles aimed at reflecting the practice's work and capturing new work from clients. Some practices have also opted for the now somewhat vague title of 'chartered surveyor', but this title has little to recommend it, unless the practice is solely practising in the United Kingdom or a commonwealth country. Even then it is confusing, since the title 'chartered surveyor' conjures up different meanings. To the man on the Clapham omnibus it is invariably confused with an estate agent, since these are the surveyors with whom the general public have the greatest contact! Project management is also a desired title by some practices, but this title too is imprecise, since it might reflect a wider scope than the construction industry alone. 'Management consultant' is an all-embracing term and is used by at least one of the large *former* quantity surveying practices. Quantity surveyors have perhaps been slow to work in this area of commerce and industry.

Adopting a title is important, but it must also seek to reflect the work carried out by the particular practice. In an age of diversification it may be desirable to use two or more titles to describe the work that is undertaken. Interestingly, the recent reorganisation of the RICS has moved away from divisions into faculties. The former Quantity Surveyor's Division, which was the second largest, has re-branded itself primarily as the Construction Faculty. This shift in title was not supported by everyone in the profession. No doubt fierce debate took place before the faculty title was finally agreed. There are increasingly some regrets about the dissolution of the former Institute of

Quantity Surveyors in the mid-1980s. The Construction Faculty is currently now the largest faculty in the RICS. Quantity surveyors are, of course, involved in a number of the other faculties within the RICS.

Contractors' surveyors have found a new title perhaps easier to acquire. Commercial management appears now to be their preferred description and title. This is a good title, reflecting well the work that they carry out for a construction company.

It should also be accepted that this dilemma of name is not unique to the quantity surveying profession. Many other professions have also diversified from their initially intended roles to offer commerce and industry a broader and sometimes all-inclusive service. The large accountancy practices have grasped the opportunities of management consultancy on a big scale. In fact most of the professions, including accountants and solicitors, with whom surveyors are sometimes grouped, now undertake work that is far removed from the simple dictionary definition of their description. It is also becoming increasingly common to find quantity surveyors at work in these multi-disciplinary, multi-industry practices.

So the debate on the name for the quantity surveyor will continue. There are no prizes for the best title, but the authors of this book would be interested to hear the views of its readers.

Bibliography

Ashworth A. and Hogg K. *Added Value in Design and Construction*. Pearson. 2000.

Barlow J. *A Statement on the Construction Industry*. The Royal Academy of Engineering. 1996.

Brandon P.S. (ed) *Quantity Surveying Techniques: New Directions*. Blackwell Science. 1992.

Davis, Langdon and Everest *Quantity Surveying 2000*. Royal Institution of Chartered Surveyors. 1991.

Egan J. (1998) *Rethinking Construction*. Department of Industry and the Regions. 1998.

Harvey R.C. and Ashworth A. *The Construction Industry of Great Britain*. Butterworth Heinemann. 1997.

ICE Civil Engineering Procedure. Institution of Civil Engineers. 1996.

Latham M. *Constructing the Team*. HMSO. 1994.

Pountney N. *The Right Formula*. Royal Institution of Chartered Surveyors. 1999.

Powell C. *The Challenge of Change*. Royal Institution of Chartered Surveyors. 1998.

QS Strategies. The Builder Group. 1999.

RICS *The Future Role of the Quantity Surveyor*. Royal Institution of Chartered Surveyors. 1971.

RICS *The Future Role of the Chartered Quantity Surveyor*. Royal Institution of Chartered Surveyors. 1983.

RICS *The Core Skills and Knowledge Base of the Quantity Surveyor*. Royal Institution of Chartered Surveyors. 1992.

Seeley I. and Winfield R. *Building Quantities Explained*. Macmillian. 1999.

2 Education, Training and Employment

Introduction

Courses in quantity surveying are offered at various levels and modes in universities and colleges in the United Kingdom. These courses are also replicated in many of the former commonwealth countries around the world. They are typically undergraduate courses of three (full-time), four (sandwich) or five (part-time) years' duration. Two-year technician courses are likely to be replaced with foundation degrees and these may allow for advanced entry to the undergraduate programmes.

Historically, quantity surveying courses were offered on a part-time basis through day release studies or through correspondence courses or distance learning. Students from these courses then sat the professional examinations of the Royal Institution of Chartered Surveyors or those of the former Institute of Quantity Surveyors until these professional bodies merged in 1985. The examinations were in three parts and these to some extent replicated the three years of undergraduate degrees offered by universities. However, since a majority of the study was on a part-time basis it usually took at least five years to complete the final qualifying examinations.

The undergraduate degree is the typical course that is studied by the majority of those who wish to become quantity surveyors. However it must be one that is recognised in partnership with or accredited by the Royal Institution of Chartered Surveyors. These courses allow students who obtain such a degree to become eligible for corporate membership, upon passing the Assessment of Professional Competence (APC). Programmes accredited by the RICS can be found in universities throughout the United Kingdom and in many parts of the world (RICS 1999).

Chronology of quantity surveying education 1960–2000

The historical development of quantity surveying has been well documented by Ashworth (1994) and this is summarised in Fig. 2.1. Surveyors traditionally entered the profession through an articled pupil scheme, whereby a partner or senior surveyor would personally supervise the embryonic surveyor. This system was later augmented through correspondence courses and day-release at a local college for preparation for professional examinations for institution membership.

The 1960s

- Quantity surveyors study on a day release basis from employment or through correspondence courses for Institution's examinations
- National Joint Committee is formed for technician qualifications
- Designation of the Council for National Academic Awards (CNAA)
- Introduction of full-time exempting quantity surveying diploma courses
- Initial debate on two-tiered profession

The 1970s

- 30 polytechnics formed in 1970
- RICS introduces its centres of excellence policy
- Development of full-time degree courses
- Part-time exempting diploma courses mainly for IQS qualifications
- Control of course expansion through the Department of Education and Science (DES), Her Majesty's Inspectorate (HMI), CNAA, and RICS
- Limited new course developments, although high demand by students

The 1980s

- Merger of the RICS and IQS
- Part-time degrees replace diplomas and external examinations
- Quantity surveying courses are mainly sandwich and part-time
- Recruitment and development of courses continues to expand

The 1990s

- Polytechnics become universities
- Popularity of quantity surveying courses among students
- Continuing professional development for all surveyors
- Development of higher degrees in construction management
- Continued role of accreditation in the UK and overseas

The 2000s

- Over-provision of quantity surveying courses
- Poor demand from prospective students
- University partnerships established with the RICS
- Continued expansion of courses overseas to meet local demands
- The technician body, MSST, merges with the RICS and a new class of membership is formed
- Further debate on the need for a two-tiered profession
- Consideration of higher degree for membership of the RICS

Fig. 2.1   Chronology of quantity surveying education.

The introduction of full-time and sandwich degree courses in quantity surveying did not occur until the late 1960s, and even then in only a small way. The widespread introduction of surveying undergraduate programmes took place in the 1970s. In parallel with these developments an expansion in higher education was also taking place in other subjects.

The development of undergraduate courses in quantity surveying should not be underestimated. While at the time of their introduction only 10% of the population had degrees, today that figure is now approaching 40%. To have attempted to develop such programmes today would have been much more difficult. It should also be recognised that the introduction of undergraduate courses in replacing the Institution's own external examinations was not simply a change in name. The focus of study moved from one that was concerned with relatively narrow training to that which provided a broader and more rounded education. Figure 2.2 illustrates the expectations to be received from a university education.

The development of the trained mind, which includes:

- critical thinking and reasoning skills
- ability to think conceptually
- intellectual perspective and independence of thought

The acquisition of knowledge through the:

- exposure to different domains of knowledge
- respect for cultural traditions
- use of knowledge to form sound judgements

Personal development which includes:

- moral, social, aesthetic and creative dimensions of personality
- development of attributes and skills

Development of a base for life long learning:

- learning how to learn

Fig. 2.2   Expectations from a university education.

Education continues to evolve rapidly in a changing world. The subject content, for example, is considerably different to that of 50 years ago. Changes have occurred in the relative importance of subjects and knowledge, new skills have been introduced and research has increased considerably. There has been a discernable shift towards problem solving and away from a reliance on memory recall. There is an emphasis towards understanding and the application of knowledge and use of a wider range of key and transferable skills. The delivery of programmes is also now more clearly focused on student centred learning and the development of study skills. The assessment of students places some importance, not just on an end of course examination, but on a combination of this and continuous assessment through a more holistic approach.

Partnership and accreditation

The RICS has, since the introduction of undergraduate degree courses in the 1960s, had a process of accrediting such courses. This allowed students from such courses to be exempt from the former RICS external examinations and to become corporate members upon satisfying the requirements of the Test of Professional Competence which subsequently became the Assessment of Professional Competence (APC).

Under its Agenda for Change initiative (Kolesar 1999), the RICS has attempted to review every aspect of the surveying profession. During this review it found that the status of the profession was in decline and that measures were needed to attract more able entrants to the profession. Whilst the accreditation of its courses was set to maintain standards in education suitable for the profession, the RICS believes that this existing process is unlikely to achieve continued improvement in quality without a radical change.

In response to this the RICS is in the process of revising its accreditation policies and replacing these with partnership arrangements with selected universities. This new policy, which will be introduced in 2001, applies currently only to the UK. In the longer term it will be extended to exempting RICS courses overseas. In order for a university to be eligible to form a partnership with the RICS, four criteria will be considered, as shown in Fig. 2.3. Each of these criteria must be met in full, regardless of how well other criteria may be achieved. The scale or reputation of a department or school must be of a sufficiently high standard in respect of research and teaching quality in order to attract the right calibre of staff and students. In order to remain a significant

Student entry	Average GCE A-Level points scores for entrants for the top 75% of entrants on to each relevant course.
Research	This is based on the latest research estimate scores or their equivalent which is currently defined in the Research Assessment Exercise (RAE) being carried out in 2001 in the United Kingdom.
Quality	The latest Teaching Quality Assessment (TQA) or equivalent. This generally refers to that which was carried out in 1996–98.
Employment	The Higher Education Statistical Agency (HESA) scores for the destination of graduates.

Whilst there are current targets for these four criteria, they will be kept under constant review in order to meet the changing needs and demands of the profession.

Fig. 2.3   RICS partnership criteria.

partner they must be capable of keeping pace with the RICS's drive towards higher standards of achievement.

The aims of each individual partnership arrangement will be to:

- Maintain standards
- Attract bright entrants to the profession
- Promote research in surveying related areas
- Respond to the needs of the profession with course development
- Improve profession and educational links.

In addition, individual partnership agreements will seek to develop niche areas of activity of an education provider.

The RICS partnership and accreditation board, in respect of the UK partnerships, will be responsible for:

- Analysing the total provision across the UK in respect of needs and demands
- Spreading best practices
- Approving and briefing practitioner external examiners
- Monitoring the threshold agreements.

Courses in quantity surveying have been accredited by the RICS in Hong Kong, Australia, New Zealand, Sri Lanka, Singapore, South Africa, Malaysia and China. Professional reciprocal agreements also exist with the respective national professional bodies, whereby members of a national professional body who practice in the UK can also achieve an RICS qualification. Courses in quantity surveying exist in all former commonwealth countries, although some may have only a limited relationship with the RICS.

Non-cognate disciplines

The RICS (Venning 1989) has long recognised the importance of recruiting members from a wide range of different disciplines. Whilst the majority of its recruitment will come from applicants who have studied on surveying courses, a number will be recruited from graduates in a non-cognate subject. Postgraduate courses have been developed to meet this need. These are essentially intensive fast track courses that enable such students to become chartered surveyors. Upon the completion of these courses, the students need to pass the APC.

National vocational qualifications (NVQ)

The NVQ framework is aimed at creating a coherent classification for qualifications across five levels, from level 1 to level 5. The highest level corresponds to graduate or professional level. The curriculum is a modular structure and is designed to facilitate transfer and progression. Core skills are included in all qualifications to enable recognition of aspects of achievement that may, in the past, have been unacknowledged. Outcomes are based on skills, knowledge, understanding and ability in application. The skills, or competence tests are as far as possible conducted in the workplace although this has sometimes been found to be unrealistic in logistical terms.

The design and structure of the NVQs on a unit basis has meant that a variety of routes to the qualification are available. This, in turn, means that the curriculum can be offered as flexible learning programmes unlike the more rigid traditional programmes. Students can negotiate the units that they wish to achieve, the order in which they achieve them, and their pace of study. Thus, learning programmes are tailored to individual needs. The development of the NVQs has resource implications although co-operation between institutions may reduce the overall increase in resource demands. The unit structure of the NVQs lends itself to credit accumulation and transfer systems and, in particular, the effective exploitation of the accreditation of prior experience and learning (APEL). Advantages of the NVQs are:

- A flexible programme of study
- A nationally recognised qualification
- Prior experience and learning can be accredited
- Study may be undertaken at a pace chosen by the student
- Transfer and progression are facilitated
- Core skills are integrated into programmes of study.

Disadvantages of NVQs are:

- The emphasis on competence skills has been at the expense of knowledge
- Competences are too narrow and simplistic
- An increased level of resources is required.

Assessment of professional competence (APC)

The different professional bodies continue to test the professional capabilities through the form of a single examination which is designed to assess an individual's competence to practice. In the RICS, this is the Assessment of Professional Competence (APC) and is more concerned with training than education. It is now widely accepted that training is only effective *on the job*. Whilst some colleges have provided simulated work experience of good quality, this could not replace the experience gained in a surveyors' office or on site with a contractor. Simulation is never the real thing!

Good training programmes offer the trainee a variety of different experiences. The RICS training log expects this to be the case, and trainees whose experiences have been too narrow may be requested to resubmit their log books after a broader experience has been achieved. The training programmes provided by contractors are often more varied and are frequently beyond those activities that can properly be described as quantity surveying.

Ideally, the experience offered should give to the trainee an opportunity to develop professional practical skills, put theory into practice, make decisions, solve problems and evaluate the functioning of the industry. The RICS Recorded Experience separately identifies building from engineering and subdivides the latter between civil engineering and mechanical engineering. There are five areas of approved experience to be gained and these include:

- Cost advice and cost planning
- Contract documentation
- Tendering and contractual arrangements
- Contract services
- Specialisations.

The latter covers a wide range of activities including taxation, insurance, litigation, technical audits, etc.

In deciding whether an individual meets the requirements for corporate membership the following are assessed:

- Application of theory into practice
- Awareness of the RICS Rules of Conduct and the possession of integrity
- Importance of accuracy to safeguard employers and clients
- Able to communicate orally and in writing.

In addition, the young surveyor is expected to develop to be a good ambassador for the profession, professionally and commercially aware, clear on clients' and employers' objectives, up to date with knowledge and skills, a team member, and able to work confidently without supervision.

The RICS Practice Qualification Group (formerly the Inter-Divisional APC Committee) introduced in October 2000 the need for all APC candidates to be employed in an organisation having a structured training framework or, at the very least a competency achievement plan. Competencies are designated as levels 1, 2 and 3. A good spread of level 1 competencies with some at level 2 can be achieved through sandwich work placements. Competencies at level 3 are probably achievable for students having considerable relevant experience. Before registering on the APC it is strongly recommended that employers and students are familiar with the latest requirements from the RICS. These requirements are described in the following publications:

- *APC Candidates and Employers Guide* (fourth edition)
- *APC Requirements and Competencies* (fourth edition)

In addition an employer is also recommended to become familiar with the following:

- *APC Guidance to Developing a Structured Training Framework*

The following guides are also available:

- *A Guide to the Recruitment and Selection of Graduate Trainees*
- *A Guide to the Induction of Graduate Trainees*
- *A Guide to the Coaching of Graduate Trainees*

The RICS has a number of regional training advisers who can offer help and assistance to employers. The training of staff is also recognised as a qualifying continuing professional development (CPD) activity and they can thus obtain personal benefits in developing a structured training framework.

Continuing professional development (CPD)

It used to be the pattern of practice that once the final examinations were passed then the formal education of the quantity surveyor was complete. It was recognised that through practice there would be a continuous development and that this would be stimulated by the demands and changes in practice and project experience. The general updating would be left to the responsibility of the individual surveyor. Those who were dedicated sought their own personal development through further study, or perhaps the acquisition of additional qualifications. Training programmes or formal staff development were not generally provided through employment.

With the pace of change in the industry accelerating, many of the professional bodies in the construction industry have recognised the importance of CPD and life long learning. It became mandatory for corporate membership of the RICS in 1984. It was accepted that if it was to become effective for the profession and the individual, then some form of registration was necessary. This requirement ensured that the benefits of institutional membership could only be retained if an adequate amount of CPD was undertaken over a period of time. The benefits claimed for CPD include higher productivity and profitability, lower staff turnover and absenteeism, innovation, improved client services, higher quality and improved job satisfaction.

Changing work patterns

The pattern of quantity surveying employment and work patterns is being affected by many factors in the early part of the twenty-first century. For example, the implications of information and communication technologies and the application of added value services will become of increasing importance. Powell (1998) has suggested that those who are committed to life long learning to ensure that their knowledge and skills are up to date and relevant will have the greatest opportunity of meeting the needs of clients and employers. Changing employment patterns was also a major theme in *QS2000* (Davis, Langdon & Everest 1991).

The vast majority of quantity surveyors are employed in private or public practice or in a contractor's organisation. In addition, quantity surveyors have been appointed to a variety of executive positions throughout the construction and other industries. In many instances, although their education and training as a quantity surveyor have been an asset in attaining a particular position, the role which they now perform may well have little or nothing to do with surveying practice.

Private and public practice

Traditionally, the principal difference between private and public practice was that whereas private practices are businesses, the main function of public practice was to ensure the accountability of public finances. This difference has narrowed considerably over recent years with the privatisation of many local and central government quantity surveying departments and those of the former statutory authorities. The aims and functions of the two sectors are therefore now similar to some extent. They are now able to compete against each other for work, and their livelihoods depend upon their performance measured against a range of indicators.

The status of the quantity surveyor is such that there is a need to provide clear, impartial and unequivocal professional cost and contractual advice. This means that a balance has to be drawn between maximising profits and maintaining a good service to clients. For those in the public sector this also includes accountability for public spending.

Private practice

Traditionally most quantity surveying firms have practised as partnerships. However, following changes in the RICS by-laws, some practices have decided to operate as limited-liability companies. The principal differences between the two are summarised as follows.

Partnership

Where two or more persons enter into partnership they are jointly and severally responsible for the acts of the partnership. Further, they are each liable to the full extent of their personal wealth for the debts of the business. There is no limit to their liability, as there is for directors of a limited company, to whom failure may only mean the loss of their shares in the company. All partners are bound by the individual acts carried out by each partner in the course of business. They are not, however, bound in respect of private transactions of individual partners. Partnerships come into being, expand and contract for a variety of reasons:

- As a business expands there is a need to divide the responsibility for management and the securing of work
- Through pooling of resources and accommodation economy in expenditure can be achieved
- The introduction of work or the need to raise additional capital may result in new partners being introduced.

The detailed consideration of partnerships falls outside the scope of this book. Suffice it to say that while it is not a legal necessity, a formal partnership agreement should be in place which legally sets down how the partnership will operate and covers such details as partners' capital and profit share.

Limited liability

Formerly the by-laws of the RICS prohibited members from parting with equity or shares to parties not actively involved in the practice. Increasingly it was felt that chartered quantity surveyors should be able to structure their practices so as to allow them to raise finance in ways that would enable them to improve their efficiency and effectiveness. It was also considered that both large and small firms would benefit from such a change and be better able to compete more effectively with other organisations which represent a fast-growing competition in their markets. Consequently, in 1986 the RICS removed the restrictions on limited liability. The changes involved the following:

- Removing the requirement for issued and paid-up share capital of the company to be not less than £25 000
- Bringing the professional indemnity insurance requirements for surveyors practising with limited liability into line with the requirements of other surveyor principals
- Removing the restrictions on the transfer of outside share capital in surveyors limited-liability companies, and on accepting instructions from outside shareholders
- Removing the requirement for surveyors wishing to practise with limited liability to apply to the Institution for permission to do so
- Imposing on surveyors who are directors of either limited or unlimited companies a requirement to ensure that they have full responsibility for professional matters
- Imposing an obligation on such surveyor directors of companies to include clauses in their memorandum and articles of association which provide for matters to be conducted in accordance with the Institution's Rules of Conduct.

Several leading quantity surveying practices had already begun to practise as limited-liability companies prior to these changes being implemented.

Deregulation allowed them a great deal more flexibility in the running of their companies, and led to more practices electing to operate in this way.

Limited liability partnerships

A recent development has been the promotion by the UK Government of the concept of a limited liability partnership (LLP), which came into force in April 2001. The key features of LLPs are:

- They will be separate legal entities distinct from the owners (members)
- Members of LLPs will not be jointly and severally liable in the normal course of business
- They will be treated as partnerships for the purposes of UK income tax and capital gains tax
- A partnership which evolves into an LLP will not undergo a 'deemed cessation' for income tax purposes
- They will have to file audited public accounts similar to a limited company
- They will require two or more designated members who will carry out tasks similar to those of a company secretary, for example, signing the annual return.

Therefore, the new LLPs combine certain crucial structural features of both companies and partnerships, the general intention being that the LLP will have the internal flexibility of a partnership but external obligations equivalent to those of a limited company. In common with partnerships, the members of an LLP may adopt whatever form of internal organisation they choose. However, they are similar to limited companies in that the members' liability for the debts of the business will be limited to their stakes in it and, therefore, they will be required regularly to publish information about the business and its finances (including the disclosure of the amount of profit attributable to the member with the largest share of the profits). Also, they will be subject to insolvency requirements broadly equivalent in effect to those that apply to companies.

Public service practice

The same general principles of practice and procedure apply to both private and public practice, with the obvious exception of the financial responsibility of the principal and the differences in the character and requirements of the respective clients.

For many years the amount of building work for which public authorities were responsible grew continually, until by the mid-1970s it represented almost 50% of the nation's construction output. Since then the workload in this sector has declined considerably. There has been some reduction in the requirement for public buildings following privatisation, and public sector housing is now to a large extent managed by housing associations. The effect of all this has been a large reduction in the number of persons employed in public service. However, the service still exists, and what follows highlights the significant differences between public and private practice.

Organisation

Public practice tends to reflect the organisation of the large private firm, and staff are subdivided by their job function.

The difficulty of private practitioners spreading their work evenly is solved in the public service by engaging only a proportion of the staff required to deal with the total requirements of the particular office. The remainder of the work is then outsourced to the private sector.

The range of quantity surveying functions undertaken by public practice offices varies according to policy, volume of work and staff available. The function most commonly assigned to the private practitioner is the preparation of contract documentation, but any or all of the various functions may be so assigned whether for a proportion or for all projects. In some instances the estimating, cost planning, valuations and final accounts are carried out by the department surveyors, but only a small proportion of the contract documentation required is prepared by its own staff. At the other end of the scale the surveyors in some offices act as coordinators of the activities of private surveyors, to whom all work is let.

The introduction of fee competition and the requirement to comply with the EC Directives on Public Supplies, Works and Services has led to all publicly funded work being advertised and fee bids invited. The recent introduction of best value for public sector projects, although an excellent ideal, is difficult and bureaucratic to administer. This principle also extends to the public departments themselves. Whilst in theory it removes the need to award projects on the basis of initial costs alone, and this is admirable, its application in practice is complex.

Conditions of employment

Private practices pay market rate salaries in order to attract and retain their staff. In the public sector a surveyor's salary depends on the grade point on appointment and the limit within a published scale. The grade payable is subject to the provisions for frequent reassessment of salaries to take account of changes in responsibility, additional experience and qualifications. Alterations to or improvements in the pay and grading structure are the subject of negotiations between representatives of a staff organisation and the employer's side. In most local authorities the negotiating body is the National Association of Local Government Officers (NALGO) but in the Civil Service different trade unions act for staff on different grades. The trade union bodies are responsible for a whole range of staff in addition to surveyors. Appointments and promotions in the public service require a formal interview before an examining board.

Duties

The extent of the work carried out by surveyors in public practice is to a large extent the same as that of surveyors in private practice. They are responsible for projects from inception to completion. In some authorities, the close collaboration between the different government officers may mean that the quantity surveyor is involved in the project at the very beginning.

In 'controlling' government departments the surveyor's work is restricted to the examination of estimates prepared by surveyors for subordinate authorities, and of the tenders subsequently received with a view to the department's approval being given.

Forms of contract

Most local authorities and statutory bodies use the Standard Form of Contract (JCT 98) or one based on that form. Central government work, however, is carried out under the GC/Works/1 Form, which may be used for both building and civil engineering work. Under this form of contract, the quantity surveyor performs duties that are similar to those under the Standard Form of Contract.

No matter how elaborate or comprehensive a building contract is thought to be, there are frequently unforeseen circumstances which require individual judgement and the client's approval. When dealing with an individual private client it is easier for the surveyor to discuss the matter with a view to recommending a course of action. The client is not likely to be creating a precedent and will therefore generally make a quick and usually reasonable decision. With government and, to a lesser extent, local authority work, the quantity surveyor's recommendation (whether it be a private firm or staff surveyor) often has to be referred to a contracts directorate or a committee. This is important since it may have repercussions on other projects being carried out by the authority concerned. The spending of public funds and their subsequent auditing may result in the quantity surveyor's calculations and recommendations being subject to considerable scrutiny. Whereas an individual client may be ready to meet a payment that is justifiable on moral grounds, officers in public service, who exercise the client's functions, will be reluctant to depart from the strict interpretation and guidelines of the contract, irrespective of the surveyor's recommendation. When they do apply these judgements, the payment is invariably described as ex-gratia to avoid creating a precedent.

Public service as a client

Such differences as exist between practice for a private client and for a public body largely result from the safeguards concerned with public spending and the possibility of fraud or corruption. Because of this, administrative procedures have been established to consider, examine and approve building projects and their estimated costs. This creates a requirement for professional people, including surveyors, to submit proposals in a prescribed form.

The accepting of tenders, honouring of certificates and paying of final accounts, require methods of financial control to ensure that every process has been properly authorised, within the amount approved, and with little possibility of fraud or wilful negligence taking place.

The administrative and financial controls are operated by staff who have limited training and little knowledge of quantity surveying or building contracts, beyond what they gradually acquire through their experience. Yet they find themselves answerable to committees and district auditors in local government or, in central government, to the Treasury, Select Committee on Estimates, Exchequer and Audit, the Public Accounts Committee and even Parliament itself. It is often the case that what seems a straightforward case to the surveyor may take a considerable time to reach settlement. The system of controlling public expenditure, particularly in government service, is over 100 years old, and some administrators and economists think that fundamental changes are now due. Whatever the procedure, the surveyor must provide the information, advice and help considered necessary in the interests of the public purse.

Two requirements of the public service as a client particularly affect the surveyor, and no distinction is made between the surveyor in private practice or in public service. When a project is financed from public funds a specified sum is allocated for the purpose. The sum is set within cost limits, which generally should not be exceeded, and the surveyor is expected to assist the architect or engineer in keeping the cost of the project within the allotted sum. If additional money is required, a special case has to be fully substantiated and approval obtained before the authority is committed to the additional expenditure. This is particularly important when successive Chancellors of the Exchequer aim at reducing public expenditure. With private clients, although the aspect of cost control is of equal importance, the obtaining of additional funding is unlikely to be subject to such rigorous procedures. The second requirement that affects the surveyor is that of audit. Most public offices, other than government departments, have their accounts audited twice a year, once internally by members of the finance officer's staff and then externally by independent auditors. The officers who carry out the audit are mostly accountants, but others without financial or quantity surveying training are also employed. Their task is to ensure that the financial provisions of the contract have been strictly adhered to, that all payments have been properly made, and that any unexpended allowances have been recovered.

The purpose of auditing is to ensure that the correct procedures have been properly followed. In addition, the auditors must be aware of the possibilities of negligence or fraud. Because of these responsibilities it is necessary for quantity surveyors to prepare the final account in strict conformity with the conditions of the contract. They do not have the same latitude as with a private client, and cannot always use the 'give-and-take' methods of balancing trifling or obvious self-cancelling variations. Only an experienced quantity surveyor can judge the fairness of 'give-and-take' methods, and the auditor cannot be expected to have this skill. As public money is being spent, each account and payment must not only be correct but be seen to be correct.

Comparison of public and private practice

Surveyors in public service have different concerns and anxieties to those in private practice. They may not have the difficulties of securing the necessary capital, finding offices, ensuring a flow of work and avoiding financial losses. But the public sector is subject to the whims of government and its ministers, and ideas are sometimes implemented for political rather than for practical or purposeful gain.

Though the variety of work in some public offices may be limited, there is some satisfaction in being concerned in a continuous programme of national or local public works and, though the 'client' may always be the same, at least the surveyor may have a better understanding of their requirements. In the larger offices the work is varied, but if the staff is specialised, surveyors may be confined to a limited range of duties and responsibilities. The surveyor's great responsibility in the public service is that of controlling the expenditure of public funds, money placed at the disposal of departments who must assume that this is being expended wisely and carefully.

Contracting surveying

The organisation of building and civil engineering companies varies considerably from firm to firm. Some of the larger firms, for example, may almost be general contractors, while other firms with comparable turnovers of work may do very little of the construction work themselves, relying almost entirely on subcontractors. The smaller firms will often expect a wider range of skills from almost everyone they employ. The contractor's surveyor may in some companies undertake a specialised range of tasks, but in other firms may be expected to undertake work that is normally outside the periphery of quantity surveying. The size and type of the contracting firm is therefore a very important influence on the surveyor's work.

The second important factor affecting the surveyor's work is the management structure of the firm. In some companies quantity surveying is seen as a separate function and is under the direction of a surveying manager. In other firms the quantity surveyors work with other disciplines under the authority of a contract manager.

Conditions of employment

The conditions of employment for the majority of quantity surveyors working for contractors are different to those of their counterparts employed in professional practice or public service. The most obvious difference is that a contractor's surveyor is likely to spend more time on site. In many cases they may be resident surveyors on a single project, or use this as a base for a number of smaller contracts.

Being a member of the contractor's project team also means more inter-disciplinary working at all levels of the surveyor's career. They may, for example, share an office with someone from a different profession, and therefore have the opportunity of gaining a better understanding of other people's work in the industry.

Many contractors also expect their quantity surveyor to work the same hours as their other employees on site. This often means an earlier start and a longer working week than those surveyors employed by the professional consultants. Furthermore, it is unusual to receive overtime payments on those frequent occasions where it is necessary to work late in the evenings or at weekends.

Contractors' surveyors do, however, tend to enjoy a greater amount of freedom in which to do their work, and they may also receive extra respon-sibilities earlier in their careers. Some contractors do, in addition, pay a site allowance, especially in those circumstances where the surveyor may have to live away from home. Contractors' surveyors are generally thought to be financially better off than surveyors working in private practice. This will, however, vary at different times during a career, and will need to take into account the various differences in the respective conditions of employment.

For a contractor's surveyor who works with one of the large national companies, there may also be the disadvantage or advantage (depending on how one looks at it) of needing to be more mobile. It will be necessary to move to where the work is located, and this could require the family moving house frequently throughout a career. The building industry tends to be more regional in nature and it may therefore be reasonable to expect only to work on sites within a certain location. Many of the small to medium sized firms tend to work only within a limited region. Civil engineering works tend to be more nationally organised, but these larger projects may tend to offset the otherwise more frequent mobility. Contractors' surveyors working on industrial engineering projects are often confined to those areas where these industries are located.

Role

The role of the contractor's quantity surveyor is somewhat different from that of the professional or client's quantity surveyor. They are unashamedly more commercially minded, and sometimes the financial success or failure of a project or even a company is due in part at least to the work of the contractor's surveyor. While the client's quantity surveyor may claim impartiality between the client and the contractor, the contractor's surveyor will be representing their own employer's interests. Prudent contractors have always employed quantity surveyors to look after their commercial and financial interests, and have particularly relied upon them in the more controversial contractual areas.

Function

Contractors employ quantity surveyors to ensure that they receive the correct payment at the appropriate time for the work done on site. In practice the quantity surveyor's work may embrace estimating and the negotiation of new contracts, site measurement, subcontractor arrangement and accounts, profitability and forecasting, contractual disputes and claims, cost and bonus assessment, site costing and other matters of a management and administrative nature. The various activities of a contractor's surveyor may include; estimating, financial management, site costing and bonusing, contract management, negotiation with suppliers and subcontractors, interim certificates and payments, contractual matters and the preparation and agreement of claims. The detailed aspects of the contractor's surveyors work are further considered in the relevant chapters.

Design and build

There are now many construction companies who are actively engaged in design and build, speculative development and similar sorts of ventures. Contractor's surveyors in these companies are now more likely to become more involved in precontract work in some way or other. They may be responsible for advising the designer on the cost implications not only of the design but also of the methods which the firm may use for construction on site. They will also be consulted on the contractual methods to be used and the documentation that is required, and will recommend the ways in which the scheme might be financed, taking into account the speed of completion.

The importance and increased trend towards single point responsibility from clients in the construction industry have made everyone more aware of this aspect of procurement. Private practice quantity surveyors are often heavily involved, either directly on behalf of the client or through the engagement of contractors who request their services in documentation preparation for tendering purposes.

Work for subcontractors

Since a large amount of work is now undertaken by subcontractors, this section of the construction industry benefits from using quantity surveyors. The surveyors who work for these companies will undertake a far wider range of duties and may well be concerned with all aspects of a financial nature, including negotiating with the bank, the submission and agreement of insurance claims, VAT and dealing with the companies' accountants. In other capacities they may be responsible for general management, the allocation of labour to projects, planning their work and dealing with their wages.

Future prospects for contractors' surveyors

The future prospects for the contractors' surveyors are seen to be very good, for several reasons:

- The increase in the direct employment of contractors for design-and-build arrangements and management contracts places a greater onus and more emphasis on their work. In these circumstances it may become necessary for them to become more involved in precontract activities.
- The fact that contracting margins are very small. Companies tend to rely upon the surveyors for expertise to turn meagre profits into more acceptable sums, and loss-making contracts into profit.
- Because of their proven performance there are now wider opportunities for them amongst a whole new range of firms who can utilise their skills.

Contractors' surveyors are employed at the highest levels within firms, which in itself emphasises their importance and their potential for the future. Many contracting firms now have at least one director whose professional origins have been in quantity surveying. Such a director may be responsible for the surveying and estimating departments in a company or more commonly a role in commercial management, and is likely to be concerned with the financial decisions and management of the construction company. Many medium-sized firms have seen the importance of giving their chief quantity surveyors considerable responsibility in financial matters, with their importance overall in the firm being recognised by a directorship.

Relationships and the client's quantity surveyors

The contractor's surveyor's first contact with the client's quantity surveyor will probably be in raising queries on the contract documentation, particularly if it is the surveyor who has priced the work. Upon receipt of the acceptance of the contractor's tender, the contractor will inform the architect of the names of the contracts manager, agent, quantity surveyor and other senior personnel who will be responsible for the project.

The contractor's surveyor and the quantity surveyor would then normally meet to discuss points that were raised at tender stage or during a post-tender meeting. These would include matters relating to the correction of errors in pricing, the procedures to be followed regarding remeasurement and financial control, and the dates of interim valuations.

The relationship between the two surveyors will usually start amicably enough, and this is the way it usually ends, but there is always the possibility of deterioration in the relationship developing. This may occur because one party does not feel that the other is being as fair or as scrupulous as they ought to be.

It needs to be remembered that the two surveyors are trading in a very desirable commodity: money. While fairness is an excellent motive to follow and should help to reduce the number of potential problems arising, it must also be remembered that there is a contract to be considered, and auditors will need to be satisfied that correct procedures have been followed. Each party to the contract, the client and the contractor, have employed their respective surveyors to ensure that their own interests are properly protected. On matters of dispute the advice may well be to settle these differences on a give-and-take basis.

It is all too common nowadays for disputes to lead to adjudication or arbitration or indeed to litigation. Before this happens both surveyors should warn their employers of the considerable financial costs of legal disputes.

The professions

The professions are one of the fastest growing sectors of the occupational structure in Britain. At the turn of the twentieth century they represented about 4% of the employed population. One hundred years later, at the start of the twenty-first century, this had risen to 20% of the working population, although the definition had become much broader. Several reasons are given for the rapid growth of the professions, such as an increasing complexity of commerce and industry, the need for more scientific and technical knowledge and an improved desire for greater accountability.

However, the professions are vulnerable as information and communications technology continue to develop and advance. Some of their more repetitive functions have already been subsumed and much of their specialist knowledge can already be readily accessed. The understanding and application of this knowledge is more difficult, but progress continues to be made through the use of, for example, expert systems. Easy access to tele-communications will allow their work to be carried out in the most economical parts of the world. In addition, the blurring of professional boundaries means that non-specialist disciplines are now competing for a share in the workload.

The built environment professions

The built environment professions in Britain are many and varied; they represent a distinctiveness about the industry and are a matter for much debate. There are in the order of 300 000 members and students amongst the seven main chartered professional bodies who work in the construction industry. In addition to these chartered bodies there are a further 20 non-chartered bodies competing for a share of the work. The RICS is the largest professional body in construction and property with a membership of over 100 000 members.

It is sometimes argued that the difficulties which arise in the industry are due, at least in part, to the many different professional groups which are involved. Others argue that the services which the construction industry provides are now so specialised that one or two different professional groups would be inadequate to cope with the complexities of practice. Whilst the UK is different in this respect to many countries around the world, there is no standardisation of practice and considerable differences exist, even across the different countries of western Europe.

The quantity surveying profession

There were approximately 35 000 members of the former Quantity Surveyors' Division of the RICS. It is difficult to estimate how many other quantity surveyors there are in the UK and around the world, but the figure is probably in excess of 300 000. These include members of other professional bodies, such as the Chartered Institute of Building in the UK, various professional bodies overseas and quantity surveyors who have no professional affiliation.

There has been a shift in employment patterns from the public sector towards contracting (Fig. 2.4). Whilst the profession weathered the economic storm of the early 1990s better than many other professions, it has nevertheless suffered in terms of both employment and remuneration.

	1981	1991	2001
Private practice	54	53	48
Public service	22	15	12
Contracting	17	20	26
Commercial	5	10	12
Education	2	2	2

Fig. 2.4 Employment patterns of quantity surveyors (%) (*Source:* RICS).

In comparison with other professions, such as engineering, accountancy and law, quantity surveying private practices are relatively small. The largest quantity surveying practice has about 1500 staff world-wide, and this is exceptional. By comparison the largest British engineering consultant has almost 4000 staff world-wide. On an international scale some of the larger accountancy, law and management consultancies employ in excess of 10 000 staff. At the other extreme the smaller practices with fewer than ten staff account for between 50 and 60% of quantity surveying private practices. There has been a trend to develop multi-disciplinary practices over the past decade.

Pacific Association of Quantity Surveyors (PAQS)

The Pacific Association of Quantity Surveyors is an organisation of quantity surveyors located around the fast developing Pacific rim countries. They share information and have intentions to develop common accreditation procedures that allow accreditation by one of the professional bodies to be accepted by the remainder. The membership of PAQS is shown in Fig. 2.5. Other quantity surveying institutions around the world are associate members.

The future of the built environment professions

The built environment professional bodies grew steadily, both in number and in membership, throughout the twentieth century. It can easily be argued that

- Australian Institute of Quantity Surveyors
- New Zealand Institute of Quantity Surveyors
- Singapore Institute of Surveyors and Valuers
- Institution of Surveyors in Malaysia
- Japan Institute of Quantity Surveyors
- Sri Lankan Institute of Quantity Surveyors
- Hong Kong Institute of Surveyors

Fig. 2.5   Membership of PAQS.

there is a proliferation of professional bodies working in the construction industry in the UK. Their future is influenced by:

- The diversification and blurring of professional boundaries often including non-built environment professions such as those involved with the law and finance
- Their role as learned societies
- The education structure of courses in the built environment
- The pressure groups both within and outside of the construction industry
- The desire in some quarters for the formation of a single construction institute, to unify all professionals involved in construction and property
- The need to maintain standards and codes of professional practice.

Role of the RICS

The Royal Institution of Chartered Surveyors remains the premier institution for quantity surveyors. This is due largely to history and also to size. The RICS remains one of the largest professional bodies around the world. In terms of construction professional bodies in the UK, the RICS is by far the largest and most influential with a total membership of over 100 000. Quantity surveying professional bodies also exist in several countries around the world, most notably those that were members of the former commonwealth. The RICS liaises with these bodies at different levels and there are many RICS members who hold dual qualifications. Powell (1998) identified the following as key requirements expected of the RICS and other local surveying bodies:

- Improving education and entry level to respond to challenges likely to be met by individuals and firms
- Change from protectionism to facilitator
- Provide leadership in a fragmented construction industry
- Accept that it is the commercial world that is the leading edge but use its position and authority to influence and create and spot trends
- Reflect the need for individuals to remain champions of propriety and fairness and uphold the charter

- Constantly upgrade professional skills, business skills and knowledge to a level which is envied by other professions
- Promote the benefits of employing a chartered surveyor so that the currency value of belonging to the RICS is as high as possible
- Improve communication and develop the single profession culture amongst its members.

Bibliography

Ashworth A. *Education and Training of Quantity Surveyors*. Chartered Institute of Building. 1994.

Davis, Langdon and Everest *QS2000*. RICS. 1991.

Hubbard C. *Investing in Futures*. The Education Task Force Final Report. RICS. 1999.

Kolesar S. *The values of change*. Presidential address. RICS. 1999.

Powell C. *The Challenge of Change*. RICS. 1998.

RICS. *Degrees and Diplomas Accredited by the RICS*. Royal Institution of Chartered Surveyors. 1999 (and subsequent updates).

Venning P. *Future Education and Training Policies*. RICS. 1989.

3 Organisation and Management

Introduction

Setting up and expanding a practice or business, together with general management and finance, are all subjects adequately dealt with in the many textbooks on business management. However, there are certain specific aspects of organisation and management relating to the work of the quantity surveyor that are worthy of consideration in some detail. They include:

- Staffing
- Office organisation
- Marketing
- Management of quality, time and cost
- Education and training
- Finance and accounts.

Staffing

The staffing structure within a quantity surveying practice, public service or contracting organisation will comprise members of staff carrying out the quantity surveying or other specialist service and those providing the necessary support services such as administration, accounts and information technology. The overall staffing structure will differ from one organisation to another, but certain general principles will be similar.

Private practice

The way an office organises and carries out its surveying work will to some extent be determined by the size of the practice and the nature of its commissions. The larger the practice, the more specialised the duties of the individual surveyor are likely to be. There are essentially two modes of operation, as shown in Fig. 3.1. Type (a) separates the normal surveying work on a project into the cost planning, contract documentation, final account work and specialist services, e.g. value management, taxation advice. Some coordination will be necessary between the phases of a project, as different personnel will carry out the work in each. This type of organisation gives staff the opportunity to develop their expertise in depth

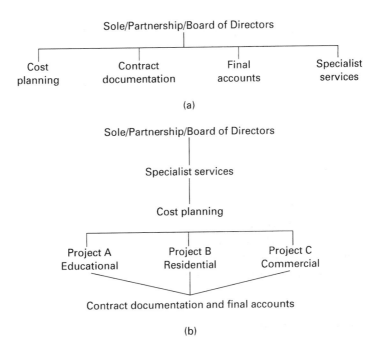

Fig. 3.1   Modes of operation of office organisation.

and, with regard to the growing range of specialist services in larger practices, this may be essential.

Type (b) allows the surveyors to undertake all aspects of the project from inception to final completion and provides the surveyor with a clearer understanding of the project. This alternative will often allocate the staff to teams, who then become specialists in certain types of project, depending of course on the type of work undertaken and the workload at any one time. This model does not easily accommodate the development of specialist service expertise, which requires concentration of activity rather than a more generalist approach.

Most practices today also carry out other work that may be incidental to their main work, possibly because of the interest or particular skills and knowledge of members of staff. In other instances specialist work represents a major source of work for the practice.

Whichever procedure is used by the office for carrying out its work, some programme of staff time will be necessary if the services are to be carried out efficiently to meet the project requirements. The first management aid needed to plan and control the work is a planning and progress chart. This is a linear timetable, which breaks down the project into its various parts, and to be complete it must take into account all aspects of the project, including the preparation of interim valuations and the final account. It may be desirable in the first instance to prepare the chart on the basis of pre-contract work alone, but for overall planning purposes some account must also be taken of the other duties that have to be performed. The type, size and complexity of the project will need to be taken into account in planning the work that has to be done.

The overall management of the practice and the well being of the employees are the responsibility of the partners/directors. Each project will be the responsibility of an associate partner/director, or at least one of the senior surveying staff who, having identified the work that needs to be carried out within a particular time, will determine the resource level required to perform the various tasks, either using staff within the office or calling on freelance staff as necessary. This is likely to be a necessary aspect of calculating the fee when bidding for work or negotiating with clients. It is also essential to pre-plan resources in order to budget costs against anticipated fee income. A major problem often facing the practice is the restricted time available to produce tender documentation and the like. Being at the end of the design process, they have to rely upon the other members of the design team to supply their information in good time. This emphasises the importance that should be attached to an adequate programme of work, by identifying the work that has to be done, who will do it, and the date by which it should be completed.

Support services

In addition to the surveying and other specialist staff within an organisation there will also be the support staff necessary for its efficient operation. These will include secretarial and administrative support as well as the finance and accounts and information technology departments (information technology is covered in Chapter 5 and elsewhere in this book). However, the ever-increasing influence of computer systems on the quantity surveying and office administrative functions means that the balance of the general staffing structure is continually changing.

Office organisation

General organisation

Quantity surveyors, whether in private practice or in a support department within a contracting organisation, provide a service, and therefore the direct staff costs and indirect costs (such as employers' National Insurance contributions and pension contributions) form the largest part of the cost of running the practice or department.

The general establishment, expanding and equipping of an office are outside the scope of this book. However in addition to staffing costs there are significant further costs associated with the running of an office, and it is worth noting the main items that constitute the general office overhead.

The major component of overhead expenditure is likely to be the office accommodation in terms of rent and the cost of furniture and general equipment, IT equipment (which has a very high rate of obsolescence) and communications necessary for the office to function efficiently. Other items of overhead expenditure are likely to include administrative costs, marketing and general expenses.

Specialist stationery

In addition to general stationery, there is specialist stationery for use by the surveying staff in performing various tasks. The extent and format of this will be dependent upon the level of use of information technology and the scale of activities. Pro-formas and specialist paper will be required for most activities including cost planning, measurement, final accounts and specialist services such as value management. When selecting such materials, thought should be given to the ability to photocopy, store and use it in IT systems.

Reference books and information

A characteristic of a quantity surveying office or department is the specific need for reference books and cost and technical information to assist the surveyors or specialists in performing their duties. Reference libraries will have been developed over a number of years and it is important that they be kept up to date to ensure that the staff can be fully aware of current developments in all aspects of the construction industry.

The core material that is required for reference, and which will need frequent updating, includes the following:

- Textbooks on the principal subjects encountered in the office
- British Standards Institution Handbooks
- Construction price books
- Building Cost Information Service (BCIS) cost information (also available as a computer application)
- Current editions of all forms of contract
- Wage agreements
- Plant hire rates
- EU directives/publications
- Professional and general construction industry journals
- Technical literature on products, materials and components
- Specifications.

Increasingly, much of this information is becoming available on-line although hard copy formats are preferred by many surveyors in practice. The management of information is a major and important task and should not be done casually.

Building costs records

A certain amount of keeping of records is essential in any office, though there is a tendency to delay preparing them because they are not directly productive. They have a habit of never getting done when the information is fresh. The surveyor's own cost records will be of much greater value than any amount of published cost data. They relate to live projects and can be stored in a manner that easily facilitates retrieval. Some care, however, needs to be exercised when using them because there could have been special circumstances which may or may not need to be reflected in any re-use of the information. It is, however, more likely to reflect the pricing in the local area and therefore in this context it is more reliable.

It is good practice to prepare a cost analysis of every tender received, and these analyses will form a bank of useful cost records. If prepared in accordance with the principles of analysis prepared by the BCIS then some measure of comparability with their cost analyses can be achieved. Different clients may require different forms of cost analysis to suit their particular purpose. Supplementary information on market conditions and specification notes should also be included. These will be necessary in any future comparison of schemes. One of the outcomes of changing procurement trends, in particular the increased use of design and build in lieu of the traditional method, is the reduction in quality of information for analysis purposes.

It is important when compiling cost records to maintain a constant basis. The use of the BCIS principles will greatly assist in this. For instance, it may be desirable or necessary to omit external works, site clearance or preparatory alteration work from the price. The analysed tender sum must, however, make this omission clear.

Refurbishment projects do not lend themselves so well to records of this kind, and it is therefore preferable to provide an analysis in a rather different way, perhaps by identifying the cost centres for this type of project. Although these types of scheme are commonplace today in the UK, a standard form for their cost analysis has yet to be devised. Their unique nature, in terms of existing design, condition and constraints, is such that estimating by means of previous cost analysis will in any event require considerable adjustment and frequently reversion to resource based techniques.

When the building scheme is complete a final cost can be recorded, and this may also be calculated as a cost per functional unit or superficial floor area. No attempt should be made to recalculate the cost analysis, as the project costs by now will be largely historic and the allocation of the final accounts to elements is very time consuming.

Building Maintenance Information (BMI) have a form of cost analysis for the maintenance and running costs of buildings. Surveyors concerned with costs-in-use or the occupancy costs of buildings may need to refer to or prepare analyses in this way.

Employer's responsibilities

There are certain health and safety and insurance issues to be addressed by employers.

Health and safety

There are continuing amendments to the statutes concerned with health and safety matters that are relevant to offices, and employers should establish the current legislation and ensure adherence. In general terms, there is responsibility on the employer in respect of the safety, health and welfare of employees and this incorporates a wide range of obligations including the following:

- The employer must ensure that any plant or equipment is properly maintained
- The employer must ensure that the systems of work are safe
- The employer must ensure that the entrances and exits are easily accessible
- Relevant instruction or supervision should be provided where required to avoid misuse of equipment, etc
- In addition to employees, the general public visiting the premises must also be properly safeguarded from any risks
- The need to provide adequate heating, lighting, ventilation, sanitary conveniences, washing facilities and drinking water
- The provision of minimum space standards to prevent overcrowding, making allowances for space occupied by furniture, fittings and equipment
- The need to provide reasonable means of escape in the event of fire for all office premises.

In some buildings some of the occupier's responsibilities are transferred to the owner of the premises, who is also responsible for complying with the provisions of legislation for the common areas, such as entrances, passages, stairways and lifts. Environmental health officers from the local authority are responsible for enforcing the legislation in private offices.

With regard to the current fire precaution related legislation, where premises fall within the relevant Act an application must be made to the fire authority for a fire certificate. The authority will then visit the premises to assess the means of escape and other fire prevention measures and make recommendations where necessary.

This is by no means a comprehensive review of health and safety related matters. The demands on employers are increasingly onerous and failure to comply with health and safety requirements may lead to both corporate and personal prosecution. There are also changing work practices, which need attention. For example, one aspect that is becoming a major concern relates to the extensive and concentrated use of workstations and VDUs. This practice may result in health problems to users requiring consideration of several factors including workstation ergonomics, light quality and background noise. There are several comprehensive web pages that may now assist in updating on health and safety matters, including those of the Health and Safety Executive and the HMSO (e.g. for details of the Fire Precautions (Workplace) Regulations 1997).

Fire insurance

Insurance of the building will usually be the landlord's responsibility, but the tenant will need to cover the contents of the office against damage by fire and burglary. The general furniture and stationery will present no difficulty; however, a serious consideration in the event of a fire is the replacement of documents in the office, particularly those referring to contract documentation in the process of preparation. If everything is destroyed there may be no alternative to beginning again. The client of course will not pay a double fee. It is therefore advisable to insure the documents in the office under a special item. It will be very difficult to assess a figure but it should be substantial, the premises being a comparatively small matter when the contingent liability is considered. Only the cost of their replacement as it relates to salaries and overhead costs will be covered, unless a 'loss of profit' policy is taken out.

The impact of damage or theft relating to IT installations is likely to be very significant. Suitable provision should be made to minimise such risks including adequate back-up systems, preferably in separate and secure locations.

Employer's liability insurance

An employer is liable to pay compensation for injury to any employees arising out of and in the course of employment, caused by the employer's negligence or that of another member of staff. In order to be able to meet these obligations the employer is required by law to take out a specific insurance under approved policies with authorised insurers. Premiums are based upon the type of employee and the salaries that are paid.

Public liability insurance

An owner or lessee of premises may be liable for personal injury or damage to the property of third parties caused by their negligence or that of a member of staff. The insurance cover should be sufficient to cover the different status of individuals, and actions by both principals and employees not only on the premises but anywhere while on business, and in countries abroad if this is appropriate.

Professional indemnity insurance

A conventional public liability policy does not normally cover any liability where professional negligence is involved. There is a requirement for members of the RICS to maintain approved professional indemnity insurance.

Marketing

In the current climate of changing professional roles and status within the construction industry, the marketing of quantity surveying and other construction-related professions has taken on added importance. The marketing of professional services is a difficult task, however, as it involves selling a service rather than a product.

As quantity surveyors look to diversify the services they offer, it is necessary for them to recognise their specific strengths and weaknesses and those of their competitors, and to identify potential clients (in both existing and new market sectors) together with their needs and requirements. The services provided can then be tailored to meet these requirements and a marketing strategy can be targeted accordingly.

It is essential to have a clear marketing plan, to develop the marketing and presentational skills of key individuals within the organisation, and to maintain an awareness of potential business growth.

Corporate image

Quantity surveying practices, whether consciously or not, present an image of themselves: both to others employed in the construction industry and to new and existing clients. This image may be developed from the way the firm's partners or directors see the future role of the profession of quantity surveying. Some practices, particularly smaller ones, are therefore content to see themselves in a traditional role, offering a service that is still in demand. Others have developed new skills and services and offer a much wider portfolio of advice and surveying services to meet the expanding needs and expectations of their clients, which in turn are being changed by active marketing from within the industry.

The image of the firm is therefore reflected to a large extent by the aspirations of the partners or directors and their collective experience, together with the commissions that they have undertaken. The expertise of the other members of the practice must also not be underestimated, as they are able to contribute to and enforce this image. It is important to have available details of staff development and achievements to reinforce the image. The important qualities to be portrayed are those of integrity, reliability, thoroughness and consistency.

The types of project, services provided and methods of working are important aspects to consider, and ones in which future clients are likely to be interested. Clients will also want to know how the practice keeps to programmes and costs and how good generally its advice has been. They will wish to identify its various strengths and weaknesses, and will be interested to know how the practice has managed changes in technology and perhaps how this will affect the future method of working. Surveyors should recognise areas of service that may be used by clients as performance indicators and should ensure that their related output is to a high standard. For instance, accuracy with estimates will be seen by most clients as vital, as will work affecting the achievement of deadlines in design and construction programmes. Perhaps some practices have in the past concentrated on other issues of professional practice at the expense of those that are seen as more important by clients.

The firm's track record, future potential and ability to solve problems should be conveyed in such a way that the practice demonstrates that it is the most appropriate to undertake the client's work, will suit the client's method of working, and will provide the quality of service commensurate with the fee charged.

Public relations and marketing

The surveying profession generally has done little in the past to advertise its skills to the public. The majority of the public therefore still presume that surveying equates with land surveying, and among the other established professions outside the construction industry quantity surveying is still largely unknown. The increasing diversity of surveying activities has also made it difficult to clearly identify a common role. Some practitioners are involved in the traditional areas of the profession whilst a growing number are involved in the provision of a much wider range of services. In addition, the role of the contractor's surveyor, which in some respects has been previously neglected by the profession, is also diverse and a growth area.

The RICS Quantity Surveyors' Division in recent years has attempted to redress this imbalance by carrying out studies amongst clients and by publicising its ever-widening range of services, with questionable success. However, the RICS Agenda for Change, rapidly coming into effect at the time of publication of this book, has recognised the shortcomings, and via its new policies, will hopefully be more successful in promoting the profession. It has invested, and intends to continue to invest, in the promotion of all areas of surveying and, with the introduction of more activity focused 'faculties' in place of discipline focused divisions, has attempted to reflect the many functions of the surveyor within the construction sector. The Institution has adopted a more positive and proactive role in support of its members than its hitherto relatively passive position. It now seeks to ensure that the major financial institutions, development banks and aid agencies are continually aware of the surveyor's essential contribution to the development and construction process. It would be of even greater advantage to ensure that the quantity surveyor's services are properly understood and appreciated by those with whom contacts are first made. Client organisations must be encouraged to make full use of quantity surveying services and be convinced that they do provide value for money in all commercial and contractual aspects of construction.

In 1991 the RICS published *Quantity Surveying 2000: The Future Role of the Chartered Quantity Surveyor*, which through research studies reviewed the changing markets, the changing nature of the construction industry, the changing profession and concluded with how the profession should respond to these changes through diversification into new markets and provision of new services. The publication predicted that services such as facilities management and value management would be major surveying activities, by the year 2000 if taking the title of the publication literally. Whilst these predictions are far from reality, there is some good evidence to show that the movement of the profession is in this general direction.

The regulations on advertising and publicity for the function of quantity surveying have been significantly relaxed by the RICS over the years. However, care must still be taken to ensure that all statements made about a firm are an accurate representation. Advertisements must not seek to explicitly solicit instructions, nor compare a firm's services with those of others.

Public relations and marketing are seen as vitally important to the recruitment of able young people into the profession, including women and ethnic minorities, who within the construction sector generally are greatly under represented. The current levels of recruitment into the quantity surveying profession may be at a critical level. Most major practices and contracting organisations are finding it difficult to recruit from a dwindling supply of graduates and many initiatives are emerging to help redress this situation.

Practice brochures

The general easing of advertising restrictions presented both the quantity surveying profession and individual firms with new ways of marketing their services and seeking new clients. One of the most effective ways of achieving this is the preparation of a brochure that describes the practice and the services that it has on offer. It can be sent out in response to enquiries or distributed when the opportunity arises. It may be necessary in the first instance to prepare the brochure in conjunction with a marketing agency in order that the correct balance and effect is achieved.

The type of brochure available varies from something prepared internally by the practice and assembled into an appropriate folder, to the elaborate, professionally prepared booklet which comes complete with colour illustrations. Some practices provide a variety of literature and other material, which seeks to emphasise the different specialist services that they offer. Other practices, in addition, provide a quarterly contract or cost review or newsletter, which aims to keep their name firmly in their client's mind.

The production of a brochure must be done with care and skill to create the correct corporate view of the practice. It should not be dull and uninteresting but should give the appearance of something that demands to be read. The information must be factual, but its presentation should be persuasive and emphasise the qualities and skills of the practice. The information may include the origins and development of the practice, partnership details, services provided, projects completed, office addresses, lists of clients and photographs of partners and projects.

Presentations

A considerable proportion of new commissions are obtained through fee competition, which often involves preparation of pre-qualification documents, details in support of a fee tender submission and in certain instances formal presentation to clients in person.

Although the format of presentations will differ depending upon the specific client, the project and the services to be provided, the main aim is to get across to the client general details of the practice, specific previous relevant project experience and (most importantly) the capability to carry out the required role. Likewise, contractors are increasingly being required to pre-qualify for inclusion on tender lists. In addition to general company information and experience, they need to identify their approach to the important aspects of management strategy and programming capability.

In recent years, the opportunity to improve the quality of presentations has greatly improved with the assistance of information technology. Use of presentation software, for instance Microsoft Powerpoint, in conjunction with a laptop computer and a compatible projector, will greatly enhance presentation quality. Whilst cynics may frown upon the trend toward what they may see as over elaborate presentations, absence of such quality may reflect negatively upon an organisation.

Internet

Many organisations have now developed their own web pages, which may be used to market their services and provide general information to clients. How successful this device may be as a marketing tool within a very traditional industry is unknown; however, its importance will clearly grow in the coming years. In designing a web page, the care and attention required to portray the correct image, as in other areas of marketing, is very important. Other factors that should be considered include ease of use, links to other appropriate web sites and currency and quality of information provided.

Quality management

Quality management systems

Considerable attention is given nowadays to the aspects of quality of the service provided by consultants and contractors to their clients. Increasingly clients in all sectors of the construction industry are demanding that consultants and contractors operate a quality management system and obtain third-party certification to demonstrate compliance with ISO 9001.

Practices and companies wishing to obtain certification following assessment by one of the certification bodies need to demonstrate that their procedures comply with the Standard. The scope of services for which registration is sought has to be clearly identified on the application for assessment and evidence demonstrating this scope has to be presented at the time of assessment.

Quality of documentation

While quality management systems set procedures to be followed to ensure quality of service provided, another aspect that is worth considering is the quality of documentation leaving the office, as this is the chief means of communication with other organisations. There will be correspondence in the form of letters or reports issued on every project, from the first letter of instruction to a final letter sending in an account for fees. The science and art of letter and report writing constitute a subject well worth studying, but only a few points can be mentioned here.

The object of writing is to convey the ideas of one person to the mind of another, who is not present to be addressed verbally, and at the same time to make a permanent record of the communications. The writer must convey by words alone both the emphasis required and the tone in which the letter or report is written. Words and phrases must, therefore, be very carefully chosen.

Without going into the subject too deeply, a few suggestions may be made:

- Be sure that the points made are clear
- Be as brief and straightforward as possible and do not use two words where one will do
- Start a new paragraph with each new point
- If a long letter develops, consider whether it is not better to put the matter in the form of a schedule or report, with only a short covering letter
- Be sure to write with the reader in mind; do not use technical terms when writing to a non-technical client
- Avoid commercial clichés, journalese, Americanisms and slang
- Avoid spelling mistakes and bad grammar; they give a poor impression to an educated reader
- Avoid the impersonal.

Surveyors, particularly recent graduate surveyors, will find many letters appropriate to a variety of situations that have been prepared on past and present projects and are held on file. Use of these previous communications, either directly or as a basis for a letter in a new situation, will save much time and should normally reflect a mature and professional style.

Time and cost management

In the increasingly competitive fee and tender market the management of time and cost is of significant importance. There is a need for staff to be managed in as efficient a way as possible. To assist in this, detailed records of time expended and thereby costs incurred need to be monitored on a regular basis.

Resource allocation

Resources need to be allocated to specific tasks on one or more project depending upon their size and complexity. Teams may be assembled for document preparation or post-contract administration on large projects. The overall resource allocation needs to be regularly monitored. Certain work will be indeterminate or require immediate attention, which can cause problems in overall planning. Agreement of design and documentation production programmes with members of the design team can assist in preplanning the timing of resource requirements.

Individual time management

Each member of staff needs to manage his or her time as efficiently as possible. This is particularly important when they are involved on a number of projects at any one time. Effective time management, although achievable in theory, becomes more of a problem in practice.

Individual tasks should be prioritised, with the most urgent (not the most straightforward) being addressed first. Where deadlines are critical, a timescale should be applied to each task to provide a target for completion.

Staff time records

It is also necessary to plan and coordinate the individual staff members' time. This information can be presented on a bar chart for each member of staff. It needs to take staff holidays into account, to be revised at regular intervals, and to be reviewed weekly.

Whether or not an organisation has a full job costing system, it is necessary that detailed records be kept of the time worked by each member of staff. See the sample weekly time sheet relating to a traditional quantity surveying practice in Fig. 3.2. This may be required as a basis on which to build up an account for fees for services that will be charged for on a time basis, or to establish the cost for each particular project. Such costs will be used primarily to establish whether a particular project is making a profit or a loss, but may also be used to estimate a fee to be quoted for similar future work.

Each member of staff needs to keep a diary in which to record not just movements, meetings and other matters but also time spent on each project. It is essential that entries are made on a daily basis and entered up before leaving the office. In addition to identifying the project worked on, notes of specific activities, such as cost planning and preparation of interim valuations, need to be identified in order for time sheets to be comprehensively completed.

Progress charts

The keeping of charts showing the work in the office and its progress is useful for management purposes. It can also identify future commitments in work-

Weekly Time Sheet

	Name	Grade	Location	Staff No.	Week Ending:

Job Description	MON		TUES		WED		THUR		FRI		SAT		SUN		TOTAL		CODE		
	BASIC	O/T	BASIC	O/T	BASIC	O/T	BASIC	O/T	BASIC	O/T	BASIC	O/T	BASIC	O/T	BASIC	O/T	JOB NO.	WORK CODE	CH/NC
Office Administration																			
Training/Study Leave																	FOR ANALYSIS OF WORK		
Public Holidays																	CODES SEE BACK OF		
Annual Holidays																	THIS DOCUMENT		
Sick																			
Others (Specify)																			
TOTAL																			
Signed (Staff)						Approved (Partner/Associate)													

WORK CODES

CODE	DESCRIPTION
A	PRE CONTRACT ESTIMATES AND COST CONTROL
B1	TENDER AND CONTRACT DOCUMENTATION INCLUDING REPORTS
B2	NEGOTIATIONS
C1	POST CONTRACT – VALUATIONS AND COST REPORTS
C2	POST CONTRACT – FINAL ACCOUNTS
D	CLAIMS
E	OTHER QS SERVICES eg Liquidations, attendance at additional meetings, etc
F	PROJECT MANAGEMENT
H	FACILITIES MANAGEMENT
I	OTHER eg Insurance valuations, expert witness work, arbitration, etc

Fig. 3.2   Sample weekly time sheet.

load, although these may only be tentative. The form of a progress chart may be similar to that used for construction works, different jobs taking the place of the stages in a building contract.

The progress chart may also be useful in helping to decide whether to look for additional staff or whether there is an under-utilisation of staff for which work in the long term will need to be forthcoming.

Education and training

The various methods of entry into the profession are described in publications by the RICS.

Whether staff are selected from school-leavers, who will then attend a university on a day-release basis, or directly from an undergraduate university degree course, will depend on availability and the practice's preference. There are advantages in both cases. Professional practice is really only something that can be learned by experience, and this argument favours the school-leaver/part-time student who has the opportunity to link learning with practice, and of course, the advantage of being paid throughout the training period. However, intensive study of theoretical knowledge may provide the young surveyor with a wider view of the profession. Full time study, albeit frequently interrupted by work placement opportunity within the typical sandwich course structure, provides a different working environment which some students find preferable. In either case the surveyors of the future who wish to achieve chartered status are required to undertake some type of RICS exempting course, and professional membership of the Institution will be via the Assessment of Professional Competence (APC).

The underlying objective of academic study, therefore, should be to develop in the student an understanding of the principles and concepts relating to the process of quantity surveying. Although this should contain some technical training, this responsibility is largely left to the professional offices and contracting organisations. Recognition as a qualified surveyor will still be in the hands of the Institution.

Upon qualifying, the surveyor should not consider this to be the end of studies. Regular continuing professional development (CPD) must be undertaken as a requirement of RICS membership. This may mean attending courses or further study for specialisation in a particular aspect of the profession, such as management. It may also incorporate postgraduate courses and research. Education and training are more fully described in Chapter 2.

Finance and accounts

Generally, the subject of finance and accountancy is not seen as an essential part of some undergraduate surveying courses. However, it is a fundamental and important business skill and as such is important to the quantity surveyor in general. This has been recognised by some universities, which in response are expanding the business content of their courses. Larger practices and companies will have finance and accounts departments with specialist accountancy staff, whereas within smaller organisations senior management deals with all financial matters.

The accounts

The primary purpose of keeping accounts is to provide a record of all the financial transactions of the business, and to establish whether or not the business is making a profit. The accounts will also be used:

- In determining the distributions to be made to equity holders
- In determining the partners' or company's tax liabilities
- To support an application to a bank for funding
- To determine the value of the business in the event of a sale
- As a proof of financial stability to clients and suppliers.

All limited companies are required under the Companies Acts to produce accounts and to file them annually with the Register of Companies in order that they are available for inspection by any interested party.

The principal accounting statements are the profit and loss account and the balance sheet.

Profit and loss account

The profit and loss account records the results of the business' trading income and expenditure over a period of time. For a surveying practice, income will represent fees receivable for the supply of surveying services; expenditure is likely to include such items as salaries, rent and insurance. After adjustments have been made for accruals (revenue earned or expenses incurred that have not been paid or received) and prepayments (advanced payments for goods or services not yet provided), an excess of income over expenditure indicates that a profit has been made. The reverse would indicate a loss.

The preparation of the profit and loss account will enable the business to:

- Compare actual performance against budget
- Analyse the performance of different sections within the business
- Assist in forecasting future performance
- Compare performance against other businesses
- Calculate the amount of tax due.

An example of a simple profit and loss account is shown in Fig. 3.3.

Profit and loss account for the two months to 28 February 1993		
	£	£
Income		
Fees received		300 000
Expenditure		
Salaries	150 000	
Rent	50 000	
Others	30 000	
Depreciation	20 000	250 000
Profit for the period		£50 000

Fig. 3.3   Example profit and loss account for QS practice.

Balance sheet

The balance sheet (Fig. 3.4) gives a statement of a business' assets and liabilities as at a particular date. The balance sheet will include all or most of the following:

Balance sheet as at 28 February 1993

	£	£
Fixed assets		
Fixtures and fittings		200 000
Less: Depreciation		20 000
		180 000
Current assets		
Fees receivable	60 000	
Cash at bank	60 000	
	120 000	
	50 000	
Current liabilities		
Net current assets (working capital)		70 000
Net assets		£250 000
Capital		200 000
Retained profits		50 000
		£250 000

Fig. 3.4   Example balance sheet for QS practice.

- *Fixed assets:* those assets held for long-term use by the business, including intangible assets
- *Current assets:* those assets held as part of the business' working capital
- *Liabilities:* amounts owed by the business to suppliers and banks
- *Owner's capital:* shareholders' funds (issued share capital plus reserves) in a limited company, or the partners' capital accounts in partnership.

The various types of asset and liability accounts are considered in more detail below.

Assets

The term assets covers the following:

- *Intangible assets,* which include goodwill, trademarks and licensing agreements, usually at original cost less any subsequent write-offs
- *Fixed assets,* which include land and buildings, fixtures and fittings, equipment and motor vehicles, shown at cost or valuation less accumulated depreciation
- *Current assets,* which are held at the lower cost or new realisable value. Current assets include cash, stock, work in progress, debtors and accruals in respect of payments made in advance.

Depreciation, referred to above, records the loss of value in an asset resulting from usage or age. Depreciation is charged as an expense to the profit and loss account, but is disallowed and therefore added back for tax purposes. Depreciation is recorded as a credit in the balance sheet, reducing the carrying value of the firm or company's fixed assets. For tax purposes, depreciation will be considered under the provisions of the Capital Allowances Act.

Liabilities

Liabilities include amounts owing for goods and services supplied to the business and amounts due in respect of loans received. Strictly they also include amounts owed to the business' owners: the business' partners or shareholders. Note that contingent liabilities do not form part of the total liabilities, but will appear in the form of a note on the balance sheet as supplementary information.

Capital

Sources of capital may include proprietors' or partners' capital or, for a limited company, proceeds from shares issued. Capital is required to fund the start-up and subsequent operation of the business for the period prior to that period in which sufficient funds are received as payment for work undertaken by the business. The example in Fig. 3.4. identifies an initial capital investment of £200 000; however, this investment is soon represented not by the cash invested but by the business.

To illustrate the movement of cash in terms of receipts and payments, a simple example of a summarised bank account statement is included in Fig. 3.5. This statement is produced periodically, usually monthly, and is the source of the cash postings to the other books of account.

Receipts	£	Payments	£
Capital introduced	200 000	Salaries	150 000
Fees received	240 000	Rent	50 000
		Other expenses	30 000
		Fixtures and fittings	150 000
		Balance carried forward	60 000
	£440 000		£440 000

Fig. 3.5   Bank account summary statement.

Finance

There are several ways in which a business can supplement its finances. The most common way is by borrowing from a bank on an overdraft facility. The lender will be interested in securing both the repayment of the capital lent and the interest accruing on the loan. The lender will therefore require copies of the business' profit and loss account, balance sheet and details of its projected cash flow.

Cash forecasting and budgeting

It is necessary for a business to predict how well it is likely to perform in financial terms in the future. Budgets are therefore prepared, usually on an annual basis, based on projected income and expenditure. Once a business is established, future projections can be based to a certain extent on the previous year's results.

As mentioned above, in the event that it is the intention to borrow money from a bank then the bank is likely to request a cash-flow forecast for the next six or twelve months. The preparation of cash-flow forecast is a relatively easy process and in practice a computerised spreadsheet package or accounting software will be used to project the likely phasing of receipts and payments.

The example cash flow forecast in Fig. 3.6 illustrates the starting-up of a professional business. It identifies the initial introduction of capital, the borrowing facility requested and the projected effect of expenditure and receipts over the period. It can be seen from the forecast that an additional £10 000 of funding will be required in April and a further (£25 000 − £10 000) = £15 000 in May.

	January	February	March	April	May	June
Capital introduced	200 000	—	—	—	—	—
Fees received	60 000	180 000	50 000	110 000	100 000	200 000
Asset sales	—	—	—	—	—	—
Receipts	260 000	180 000	50 000	110 000	100 000	200 000
Salaries	75 000	75 000	75 000	75 000	75 000	75 000
Rent	25 000	25 000	25 000	25 000	25 000	25 000
Equipment	100 000	50 000	20 000	30 000	—	—
Others	15 000	15 000	15 000	15 000	15 000	15 000
Payments	215 000	165 000	135 000	145 000	115 000	115 000
Movement in cash	45 000	15 000	(85 000)	(35 000)	(15 000)	85 000
Balance brought forward	—	45 000	60 000	(25 000)	(60 000)	(75 000)
Balance carried forward	45 000	60 000	(25 000)	(60 000)	(75 000)	10 000
Borrowing facility	50 000	50 000	50 000	50 000	50 000	50 000
Additional requirement	—	—	—	10 000	25 000	—

Fig. 3.6 Example cash-flow forecast.

This cash flow is typical of a business start-up, when substantial sums are spent in advance of income being received. Provided the business is run profitably the outflow should be reversed before too long.

Books of account

The underlying books of account are likely to comprise the general ledger (which will include all general items such as salaries and rents) and totals from the subsidiary ledgers such as the sales ledger (fees or other income receivable), the bought ledger (accounts payable), the cash book (a record of the bank transactions) and the petty cash account. Other books, such as fee and expenses books, may also be kept.

In addition to the books of account, businesses must retain vouchers such as receipts, invoices, fee accounts and bank statements to support the accounting records. These are required by businesses' auditors and for VAT purposes.

Use of IT in accounting

Accounting functions have become less time-consuming through the use of computers for the regular and routine entries and calculations that are necessary. Entries can be allocated to different accounts, and up-to-date information can be retrieved quickly and efficiently in a variety of formats to meet particular needs. This greatly assists in the financial management of a business.

Annual accounts/auditing

At the end of a business' financial year a set of 'end of year' accounts are prepared bringing together all the previous year's financial information in the form of a profit and loss account and balance sheet as described earlier. In most circumstances an independent accountant will audit accounts; indeed this is a requirement for all larger limited companies under the Companies Acts. Audited accounts will carry more authority with the Inspector of Taxes and are also useful to prove to third parties, including prospective clients, that the financial status of the business has been independently scrutinised.

Bibliography

Barrett P. *Profitable Practice Management for the Construction Professional*. E. & F. N. Spon. 1993.

British Standards Institution. ISO 9001, *Quality Management Systems: requirements*, 3rd edition. BSI 2000.

Davis, Langdon and Everest. Quantity Surveying 2000: *The Future Role of the Chartered Surveyor*. RICS. 1991.

Jennings A.R. *Accounting and Finance for Building and Surveying*. Macmillan Press. 1995.

Kolesar S. *The Values of Change*. Presidential address;. Royal Institution of Chartered Surveyors. 1999.

Park A. *Facilities Management: An explanation*. Macmillan. 1998

Powell C. *The Challenge of Change*. RICS. 1998.

Websites

Health and Safety Executive (HSE) [online] available at: http://www.hse.gov.uk accessed on 17/4/2001.

Her Majesty's Stationary Office (HMSO) [online] available at: http://www.hmso.gov.uk/legis.htm accessed on 17/4/2001.

4 The Quantity Surveyor and the Law

Introduction

The purpose of this chapter is to describe in general terms how the law affects the quantity surveyor in practice, concentrating on the form of agreement between the quantity surveyor and the client, the impact of the demand for collateral warranties and performance bonds, the requirement to maintain professional indemnity insurance cover and the Employment Acts as they relate to the employment of staff. The wider issue of construction law is a complex and ever-changing area, the detail of which falls outside the scope of this book.

The quantity surveyor and the client

The quantity surveyor in private practice provides professional services for a client. The legal relationship existing between them is therefore a contract for services. The nature of this contract controls the respective rights and obligations of the parties. So far as the quantity surveyor is concerned it determines the duties to be performed, powers and remuneration for the particular work undertaken.

Agreement for appointment

There is no legal requirement that the agreement or contract between the surveyor and the client should consist of a formal document nor even, indeed, that it be in writing. Nevertheless, given that it may be crucial to establish the precise nature of the relationship in the event of a dispute, it is desirable that the understanding reached be confirmed in writing. If differences subsequently arise and proceed to litigation, the court will be faced with the problem of ascertaining the true intentions of the parties from the available evidence. Clearly a written record will, in these circumstances, be a great deal more persuasive than the possibly disputed recall of the contending parties.

The existence and nature of the agreement can be established by an exchange of correspondence or by the use of a standard form of appointment, such as the Form of Agreement, Terms and Conditions for the Appointment of a Quantity Surveyor which is published by the RICS. It cannot be overstated that whatever practice is adopted, there is a need to ensure that a valid, comprehensive and adequately evidenced contract exists between the respective parties.

Professionals can sometimes find themselves in difficulty if they undertake work relying only upon an incomplete agreement, in which important items remain to be settled. Given the real pressures to acquire business, it is easy to succumb to this temptation without adequately weighing the risks involved. However, the law does not recognise the validity of a contract to make a contract and, where any essential element is left for later negotiation, the existing arrangements are unlikely to be recognised as a binding agreement.

In *Courtney & Fairbairn Ltd* v. *Tolaini Bros (Hotels) Ltd* (1975) 1 AER 716; 2 BLR 100, the defendants, wishing to develop a site, agreed with the plaintiffs, a firm of contractors, that if a satisfactory source of finance could be found, they would award the contract for the work to the plaintiffs. No price was fixed for the work but the defendants agreed that they would instruct their quantity surveyor to negotiate fair and reasonable contract sums for the work. Suitable finance was introduced, and the quantity surveyor was instructed as agreed. The quantity surveyor was unable, in the event, to negotiate acceptable prices, resulting in the contract being awarded elsewhere. The plaintiffs sued for damages, claiming that an enforceable contract had been made. It was held that the price was a fundamental element in a construction contract and the absence of agreement in that regard rendered the agreement too uncertain to enforce. This case was, of course, not directly concerned with the provision of professional services but the legal principle illustrated is of general application.

A persuasive incentive to take care arises from the fact that the ability to recover payment for work done will usually depend on the existence of an appropriate contract. Performance alone does not automatically confer a right to remuneration, although where a benefit is conferred, the court will normally require the beneficiary to make some recompense, possibly by way of a *quantum meruit* payment, meaning, as much as is deserved.

In *William Lacey Ltd* v. *Davies* (1957) 2 AER 712, the plaintiff performed certain preliminary work for the defendant, connected with the proposed rebuilding of war-damaged premises, in the expectation of being awarded the contract for the work. The defendant subsequently decided to place the contract elsewhere, and eventually sold the site without rebuilding. The plaintiff sued for payment for work already done. In this case it was held that in respect of the work done, no contract had ever come into existence but, nevertheless, as payment for the work had always been in the contemplation of the parties, an entitlement to some payment on a *quantum meruit* arose.

In this context it is reassuring, from the quantity surveyor's point of view, to note that, where professional services are provided, there is a general presumption that payment was intended. In *H.M. Key & Partners* v. *M.S. Gourgey and Others* (1984) I CLD-02-26, it was said: 'The ordinary presumption is that a professional man does not expect to go unpaid for his services. Before it can be held that he is not to be remunerated there must be an unequivocal and legally enforceable agreement that he will not make a charge'. However, while some recovery of fees may be possible without the formation of a binding contract, the lack of such an agreement enhances the possibility of disputes and litigation. Moreover, if the basis of enforced payment is to be *quantum meruit*, there is no guarantee that the court's evaluation of the services provided will correspond with the practitioner's expectations.

Given that all relevant terms are settled and agreed, and incorporated in a formal contract, the intentions of the parties may still be frustrated by a failure to express the terms clearly.

In *Bushwall Properties Ltd* v. *Vortex Properties Ltd* (1976) 2 AER 283, a contract for the transfer of a substantial site provided for staged payments and corresponding partial legal completions. At each such completion 'a proportionate portion of the land' was to be transferred to the buyer. A dispute arose as to the meaning of this phrase. It was held that in the circumstances, no certain meaning could be attributed to the phrase; that this represented a substantial element in the contract; hence the entire agreement was too vague to enforce.

However, if a valid contract exists in unambiguous terms, the court will enforce it. It is therefore vital to ensure that the terms are not merely clear but do in fact represent the true understanding of the parties, both at the outset and as the work progresses. When the actual work is in hand with all attendant pressures, it is all too easy to overlook the fact that the obligations undertaken and remuneration involved are controlled by the contract terms. Departure from or misunderstanding of the original intentions, unless covered by suitable amendments of those terms, may have very undesirable consequences as the following case illustrates.

In *Gilbert & Partners* v. *R. Knight* (1968) 2 AER 248; 4 BLR 9, the plaintiffs, a firm of quantity surveyors, agreed for a fee of £30 to arrange tenders, obtain consents for, settle accounts and supervise certain alterations to a dwelling house on behalf of the defendant. Initially work to the value of some £600 was envisaged, but in the course of the alterations the defendant changed her mind and ordered additional work. In the end, work valued at almost four times the amount originally intended was carried out; the plaintiffs continued to supervise throughout and then submitted a bill for £135. This was met with a claim that a fee of £30 only had been agreed. It was held that the original agreement was for an all-in fee covering all work to be done; the plaintiff was entitled to only £30.

The moral is clear: avoidance of difficulty and financial loss is best ensured by accepting engagement only on precise, mutually agreed and recorded terms, setting out unequivocally what the quantity surveyor is expected to do and what the payment is to be for so doing. If, as often happens, circumstances dictate development and expansion of the initial obligations, the changes must be covered by fresh, legally enforceable agreements. Oral transactions, relating to either the original agreement or later amendment of it, should always be recorded and confirmed in writing. This is more than an elementary precaution, for it should be borne in mind that what is known as the parol evidence rule will normally preclude any variation of an apparently complete and enforceable existing written contract, by evidence of contrary or additional oral agreement.

The agreement for appointment of a quantity surveyor, whether a standard or non-standard document, will encompass certain general provisions including the following:

- Form of agreement/particulars of appointment
- Scope of services to be provided
- Fee details
- Payment procedures
- Professional indemnity insurance requirements
- Assignment
- Suspension
- Copyright
- Duty of care
- Dispute procedures.

Other provisions such as limitation of the quantity surveyor's authority, communications and duration of appointment, might be included.

The agreement can be executed either as a simple contract or as a deed. There are important differences, two of which are the most significant as far as the quantity surveyor is concerned: the need for consideration and the limitation period.

In a simple contract there must be consideration. This is a benefit accruing to one party or detriment to the other, most commonly payment of money, provision of goods or performance of work. The period in which an action for breach of contract can be brought by one party against the other is limited to six years. In a speciality contract, a contract executed as a deed, however, there is no need for consideration and the limitation period is 12 years. The significance of the latter is that a quantity surveyor who enters into an agreement as a deed, doubles the period of exposure to actions for breach of contract.

Responsibility for appointment

What has been written so far assumes that the quantity surveyor's appointment arose from direct contact with the client. Additional problems may occur where the appointment arises indirectly from the retained architect or project manager. In such cases the power to appoint on behalf of the client may subsequently be called into question. There is no general solution to this problem. The actual position will depend on the express and implied terms of the other consultant's contract with the client. If they have express power to appoint, then, of course, no problem arises and the appointment is as valid as if made by the client in person. However, reliance on their possessing an implied power to appoint would be very unwise. It is clear that the courts do not recognise any general power of appointment or delegation as inherent in an architect's or other consultant's contract with a client.

In *Moresk Cleaners Ltd* v. *T.H. Hicks* (1966) 4 BLR 50, the Official Referee stated bluntly that 'The architect has no power whatever to delegate his duty to anyone else'. That case concerned the delegation of design work but it would seem equally applicable to other unauthorised appointments.

This absence of a general implied power to appoint does not preclude the possibility that in particular circumstances it may be held to exist. There is, for example, some rather dated authority for the proposition that, where tenders are to be invited on a bill of quantities basis, such implied authority may be present.

Potential difficulties in the matter can be easily avoided, by the simple expedient of ensuring that, where the employment of the quantity surveyor is negotiated by another consultant, the terms of the appointment are conveyed in writing to the client and the client's acceptance thereof similarly secured. Ratification by the client will then have overcome any deficiencies in the consultant's authority.

Responsibility for payment of fees

Where an effective contract exists between the quantity surveyor and the client, provision will be contained relating to the payment of the professional fees involved. No real difficulty should be experienced where the appointment has been made by a duly authorised agent, or the client has ratified an appointment purported to have been made on their behalf. The position where no valid agreement exists has already been mentioned, and it was suggested that even in such unfortunate circumstances some remuneration, probably by way of a *quantum meruit*, will usually be forthcoming.

However, if the authorised agent has made the appointment in excess of their powers, the quantity surveyor will have to look elsewhere than to the client for payment. In such circumstances it will usually be possible to bring an action against the agent personally. Such a claim would normally lie for warranty of authority, either where the agent had misunderstood or exceeded the authority granted by the client, or had not actually purported to act on the client's behalf. The existence of a legal remedy is nevertheless of doubtful consolation if the debtor is unable to pay.

If there are any reservations regarding the financial standing of a potential client, the surveyor must make enquiries, perhaps by taking up bank references, and then trust to commercial judgement. In this connection, it is vital to ensure that the documentation accurately reflects the true identity of the client. This may seem too obvious to mention but misunderstandings can and do occur, particularly in dealings with smaller companies controlled by a sole individual. It is easy to confuse the individual acting on behalf of a company and acting in a personal capacity. The unhappy result may be dependence for payment on a company of doubtful solvency, having imagined that one was acting for an individual of undoubted substance. Finally, it is chastening to reflect that monies owed in respect of professional fees are in no way preferred in the event of insolvency.

Amount and method of payment

Actual fees and fee rates are now a matter for negotiation, since recommended scales do not exist. Entitlement depends on the terms of the agreement under which the services are provided, and any negotiations are constrained by practical rather than legal considerations. However, where the work involves advising on matters connected with litigation or arbitration, for example in respect of claims, it is not permissible to link the fee to the amount recovered. In *J. Pickering* v. *Sogex Services Ltd* (1982) 20 BLR 66, arrangements of that nature were said to savour of champerty – that is, trafficking in litigation – and as such to be unenforceable as contrary to public policy.

Where possible it is prudent to make provision for the payment of fees by instalments at appropriate intervals. The payment of a series of smaller amounts while services are being provided tends to be more readily accepted than the settlement of a substantial bill when the work has been completed. Moreover, failure to pay on time may be a useful guide to the state of the client's finances. If the worst happens and the client is rendered insolvent, there is some comfort in being an ordinary creditor for only the balance and not the entirety of the fee. Failure to pay on time should be treated seriously and, if necessary, legal steps taken promptly for recovery. In these matters patience and understanding are more likely to lead to disappointment than to reward.

Negligence

Where the law is concerned, negligence usually consists either of a careless course of conduct or such conduct, coupled with further circumstances, sufficient to transform it into the tort of negligence itself. As stated earlier the extent and nature of the duties owed to the client by the quantity surveyor, as well as the powers and authority granted to the client, will be determined by the contract for services between them.

It has always been implied into a professional engagement that the professional person will perform duties with due skill and care. This requirement is reiterated by provisions in the Supply of Goods and Services Act 1982. Lack of care in discharging contractual duties is, and always has been, an actionable breach of contract.

As late as the mid-1960s, when it was so held in *Bagot* v. *Stevens Scanlan & Co* (1964) 3 AER 577, the existence of a contractual link between the parties was believed to confine liability to that existing in contract and to exclude any additional liability in tort. Since then, the position gradually changed and the courts appeared to recognise virtually concurrent liability in both contract and tort. Thus an aggrieved contracting party was able to sue the other contracting party or parties both in contract and tort. This was illustrated by the decisions in *Midland Bank Trust Co Ltd* v. *Hett, Stubbs & Kemp* (1978) 2 AER 571 and, more immediately relevant to the construction industry, in *Batty* v. *Metropolitan Property Realisations Ltd* (1978) 7 BLR 1.

Liability was also considered to exist independently, where there is no contractual link between the parties, enabling a third party to sue in the tort of negligence. A plaintiff suing in negligence must show that:

- The defendant had a duty of care to the plaintiff, and
- The defendant was in breach of that duty, and
- As a result of the breach the plaintiff suffered damage of the kind that is recoverable.

In the first place, the plaintiff would try to show that the defendant owed a duty of care. From the principles established in *Donoghue* v. *Stevenson* (1932) AER I (the celebrated 'snail in the bottle' case), the courts tended to find the presence of a duty of care in an ever-increasing number of circumstances.

The tentacles of the tort of negligence even extended well beyond normal commercial relationships, at least so far as the professional person was concerned. Since the well-known case of *Hedley Byrne & Co Ltd* v. *Heller & Partners Ltd* (1963) 2 AER 575, any negligent statement or advice, even if given gratuitously, seemed in certain circumstances to afford grounds for action.

In more recent times in the case of *Junior Books Ltd* v. *The Veitchi Co. Ltd* (1982) 21 BLR 66, the House of Lords held that a specialist flooring subcontractor was liable in negligence for defective flooring to the employer with whom the subcontractor had no contractual relationship. Almost immediately, however, the courts began to retreat from the position by means of a long string of cases which culminated in *Murphy* v. *Brentwood District* Council (1990) 50 BLR 1 which, among other things, overturned the 12-year-old decision in *Anns* v. *London Borough of Merton* (1978) 5 BLR 1.

The tortious liability for negligence is therefore reduced, which in itself has led to the growth in the use of collateral warranties.

There is little case law concerning the negligence of a quantity surveyor. However, it is always advisable to limit the risk involved. The best safeguard is discretion and a reluctance to express opinions or proffer advice on professional matters, unless one is reasonably acquainted with the relevant facts and has had the opportunity to give them proper consideration.

Death of the quantity surveyor

Whether the liability to carry out a contract passes to the representatives of a deceased person depends on whether the contract is a personal one. That is, one in which the other party relied on the 'individual skill, competency or other personal qualifications' of the deceased. This is a matter to be decided in each particular case.

In the case of a quantity surveyor with no partner, the appointment must be regarded as personal, and the executors could not nominate an assistant to carry on with business unless the respective clients agreed. With a firm of two or more partners the appointment may be that of the firm, in which case the death of one partner would not affect existing contracts. But the appointment may be of one individual partner, as an arbitrator for example, where another partner in the firm could not take over, even though he or she may be entitled to a share of the profits earned by the partner in the arbitration.

The fact that a contract between a quantity surveyor and the client is a personal contract, if that is the case, does not mean that the quantity surveyor must personally carry out all the work under the contract; this is unless it is obvious from the nature of the contract, for example a contract to act as arbitrator, that the quantity surveyor must act personally in all matters. In other cases, such as the preparation of a bill of quantities and general duties, the quantity surveyor may make use of the skill and labour of others, but takes ultimate responsibility for the accuracy of the work.

Death of the client

The rule referred to in the previous paragraph as to a contract being personal applies equally in the case of the death of the client. Here the contract is unlikely to be a personal one, and the executors of the client must discharge the client's liabilities under the building contract and for the fees of the professional people employed. The fact that the appointment of the surveyor was a personal one will not be material in the case of the death of the client.

Collateral warranties

A collateral warranty, or duty of care agreement, is a contract that operates alongside another contract and is subsidiary to it. In its simplest form, it provides a contractual undertaking to exercise due skill and care in the performance of certain duties which are the subject of a separate contract. An example of this would be a warranty given by a quantity surveyor to a funding institution to exercise due skill and care when performing professional services under a separate agreement between the quantity surveyor and the client. The purpose of a collateral warranty is to enable the beneficiary to take legal action against the party giving the warranty, for breach of contract if the warrantor fails to exercise the requisite level of skill and care in the performance of the duties.

It used to be the view that such an agreement was not very important, because it merely stated in contractual terms the duties that were owed by the quantity surveyor to a third party in tort. That view is no longer tenable.

There is a fundamental contract principle that only the parties to a contract have any rights or duties under that contract. The principle is called *privity of contract*. For example, in a contract between a client and quantity surveyor, each has rights and duties to the other. The quantity surveyor has a duty to carry out specific duties but has no duty to any third party. That would be the case even if the contract stated that there was such a duty.

At one time the third party would have been able to overcome this kind of problem by suing in the tort of negligence if there was no contractual relationship. However, this is no longer the case. This has been stated earlier in connection with negligence and the law in this regard has changed over recent years, culminating in the case of *Murphy* v. *Brentwood District Council* (1990) 50 BLR 1.

As a result of the fundamental changes in the law, collateral warranties are now of significant importance to clients. These have therefore proliferated in recent years. It is now common for contractors, nominated and domestic subcontractors and suppliers and all the consultants to execute a collateral warranty in favour of the client, the company providing the finance for the project and/or prospective purchasers/tenants.

There are standard forms of warranty to be given to funders and purchasers or tenants published by the British Property Federation (BPF) which have been approved by the Royal Institute of British Architects (RIBA), RICS, ACE (Association of Consulting Engineers) and the BPF. There are also a great many other forms of warranty, some of which have been especially drafted by solicitors with a greater or lesser experience of the construction profession and the construction industry generally.

The party requiring collateral warranties in connection with a project would probably gain maximum benefit from those provided by the design consultants. It is more likely that a claim under a warranty will be related to design matters. However, it is common for warranties to be requested from all consultants on a project, including the quantity surveyor. It is important to ensure that all consultants enter into a warranty on the same terms, with the exception of clauses relating to the selection of materials (see below).

The following are specific issues that should be considered by quantity surveyors when called upon to sign a warranty.

Relationship to terms of appointment

Prior to agreeing any warranty terms, it is essential to have full written terms of appointment as described earlier. Unless the duties to be undertaken by the quantity surveyor are fully detailed, the standard warranty term that 'all reasonable skill and care be taken in the performance of those duties' leaves it open to argument as to the definition of such duties if a claim is brought under the warranty in the future.

The warranty should refer specifically to the terms of appointment – and it is important that the terms and conditions of the warranty are no more onerous than those contained in the appointment.

Materials

The standard forms of warranty include provisions regarding taking reasonable skill and care to ensure that certain materials are not specified. This clause should be deleted from quantity surveyors' warranties as it relates primarily to design consultants.

Assignment

The warranty is likely to make provision for the warrantee to be able to assign the benefits to other parties. The more restrictive the assignment clause, the better as far as the quantity surveyor's potential liability is concerned. Much of the value of the warranty is the ability to assign, and therefore if a quantity surveyor agrees to an assignment clause it should be limited in terms of number of assignments and time-scale: for example, assignment only once within a limit of three years subject to the quantity surveyor's consent.

Professional indemnity

The warrantee will be concerned with the level of professional indemnity insurance cover carried by the quantity surveyor, and the required level of cover will be stated in the warranty. It is important that all warranties are passed to the insurers before being signed or the insured could be at risk.

A requirement to maintain professional indemnity insurance cover at a level for a specific number of years is impractical. A requirement to maintain cover should be limited to using best endeavours to maintain cover as long as it is available at commercially reasonable rates.

Complete records should be kept of all warranties given, as it is necessary to disclose these annually to the insurers at the time of renewal of the policy.

Execution

The essential differences between a simple contract and a deed have been highlighted earlier. If the quantity surveyor is requested to enter into a warranty agreement as a deed, whereas the terms of appointment are executed as a simple contract, the quantity surveyor's period of liability to the third party will be twice as long.

Performance bonds

There is an increasing demand for consultants to provide performance bonds, particularly on major projects. Although it is a concern that clients consider it necessary to require such bonds in the pursuit of work, the quantity surveyor may not be in a position to object.

The conditions of the bond are likely to be similar to those required from a contractor. The value is calculated as a percentage of the total fee, 10%, for example, and the conditions under which it can be called upon are stated. In certain instances 'on demand' bonds are being requested, whereby payment by the surety can be demanded without the need to prove breach of contract or damages incurred as a consequence. It is therefore important to check the conditions in detail and to ascertain the cost of providing the bond prior to agreeing fee levels and terms of appointment.

The common sources of protection are bank guarantees and surety bonds. The terms bonds and guarantees have similar meanings and are used synonymously within the construction industry. Guarantees are documents that indemnify a beneficiary should a default occur. They are usually provided by banks. Performance bonds are usually issued by insurance companies. A performance bond assures the beneficiary of the performance of the work involved up to the amount stated. Performance bonds are three-party agreements between the bondsman, beneficiary and the principal debtor.

Professional indemnity insurance

It has always been prudent for quantity surveyors to protect themselves against possible claims from their clients for negligence, for which they may be sued. Such mistakes may not necessarily be those of a principal's own making but those of an employee. The RICS by-laws and regulations make it compulsory for practices, firms or companies to be properly insured against claims for professional negligence. Minimum levels of indemnity are specified. Premiums are calculated according to the limit of indemnity selected, the number of partners or directors, the type of work that is undertaken and the fee income. The policy chosen must be no less comprehensive than the form of the RICS Professional Indemnity Collective Policy as issued by RICS Insurance Services Ltd.

The policy covers claims that are made during the period when the policy is effective, regardless of when the alleged negligence took place. Claims that occur once the policy has expired, even though the alleged event took place some time previously, will not be covered. A sole practitioner is therefore well advised to maintain such a policy for some time after retirement. Recent court cases suggest that a professional person may be held legally liable for actions for a much longer period than the normal statutory limitation period would otherwise suggest.

Contracts of employment

There are certain legal requirements relating to the employment of staff. The basic relationship between the employer and the individual employee is defined by the contract of employment. This is a starting point for determining the rights and liabilities of the parties. Although these rights originated from different statutes, they are now consolidated in the Employment Protection (Consolidation) Act 1978, though further amendments were introduced in the Employment Act of 1990. An Employment Relations Act was introduced in 1999. An important feature of these rights is that they are not normally enforced in the courts but in employment tribunals.

The Department of Trade and Industry has an Employment Relations Directorate that seeks to develop legislation on:

- Hours of work
- Pay entitlement
- Public holidays
- Employment agency standards
- Individual employment rights
- Redundancy arrangements
- Employee consultation
- Trade unions and collective rights
- European employment directives.

A contract of employment must be given to each employee within 14 days of commencing employment. It should cover matters regarding the conditions of employment, including hours of work, salary, holiday entitlement, sick leave, termination, and the procedures to be followed in the event of any grievance arising.

Other Acts worthy of note are the Sex Discrimination Act 1975, whereby a person cannot be discriminated against because of his or her sexual orientation or marital status, and the Race Relations Act 1976, which considers discrimination on the grounds of colour, ethnic or national origins or nationality. These Acts cover not only recruitment but also promotion and other non-contractual aspects of employment. The Equal Pay Act 1970 covers contractual terms *and* conditions of employment in addition to pay, making it unlawful for an employer to treat someone differently because of their sex.

An employer must give the employee the amount of notice to which he or she is entitled under the contract of employment. This will relate to the employee's length of service up to a maximum of 12 weeks, although the contract may specify a longer period. Employees may be dismissed for acts of misconduct, but the employment tribunal must be satisfied that the employer acted reasonably should a complaint be brought to them. Some of the following might be considered as misconduct:

- Absenteeism
- Abusive language
- Disloyalty
- Disobedience
- Drinking
- Using drugs and smoking
- Attitude
- Personal appearance
- Theft or dishonesty
- Violence or fighting.

In order for an employee to bring a case for unfair dismissal, an employee must be able to show at least one of the following:

- Employer ends employment without notice
- A fixed term contract ends without being renewed

- An employer forces an employee to resign; this is known as constructive dismissal
- An employer refuses to take back a woman returning to work after pregnancy
- An employer gives a choice of resignation or being dismissed.

An Employment Tribunal will investigate whether the employer was acting reasonably after investigating all of the facts of the case. It will want to establish that:

- Warnings were given
- Adequate notice was provided for a disciplinary hearing
- The employee had the opportunity to comment on the evidence
- A decision was not made by someone who had not heard the employee's view
- An appeal was decided by someone who was not already involved.

Sometimes a job comes to an end because the firm has no more work or because the kind of work undertaken by the employee has ceased or diminished. In these circumstances the employee will normally be entitled to redundancy payments. In order to establish a claim the employee must have at least one year's service, be between the ages of 20 and 65, and have been working for a minimum number of hours per week, depending upon the length of service.

Bibliography

Cecil R. *Professional Liability*. Legal Studies and Services (Publishing). 1991.

Comes D.L. *Design Liability in the Construction Industry*. Blackwell Science. 1994.

Dalby J. *EU Law for the Construction Industry*. Blackwell Science. 1998.

Dugdale A.M. and Stanton, K.M. *Professional Negligence*. Butterworth. 1989.

Griffiths M. *Partnerships and legal guide*. CLT Professional Publishing. 2000.

James P.S. *Introduction to English Law*. Butterworth. 1994.

Jess, D.C. *Insurance of Professional Negligence Risks*. Butterworth. 1989.

RICS *Caveat Surveyor: Negligence Claims Handled by the RICS Insurance Services*. RICS Books. 1986.

RICS *Direct Professional Access to Barristers*. RICS Books. 1989.

RICS *Caveat Surveyor II*. RICS Books. 1990.

RICS *Compulsory Professional Indemnity Regulations*. RICS. 1993.

Ryley M. and Goodwyn E. *Employment Law for the Construction Industry*. Thomas Telford. 2000.

Speaight C. and Stone G. *The AJ Legal Handbook*. Architectural Press. 1996.

Walmesley K. *Butterworths Company Law Handbook*. Butterworths Tolley. 2000.

Webber L. *The impact of the Woolf reforms on surveyors*. College of Estate Management. 2000.

5 Research and Innovation

Introduction

The wider role of quantity surveying is concerned with best use of scarce and available resources. Traditionally many of its practices have been applied to the construction industry, although the techniques and skills have a much wider application. A majority of the practices and procedures that are used have been developed in practice from a pragmatic approach to meet the needs and requirements of clients and the construction and property industries. Whilst there is much that can be described as research and development, little has been carried out in a structured manner and then only by a relatively few members of the profession. Time is short and there is a fundamental need to verify that the practices being used are the most effective for the job. At the same time the profession does not stand still and there is the need to develop its full potential. These two statements are both valid but are frequently seen as a dichotomy.

One of the most frequent criticisms of quantity surveyors has been their narrowness of vision. Problems are considered in the context of construction costs with only a limited appreciation of the other project attributes. Until recently the context of the quantity surveyor's work was restricted to costs, with hardly any consideration of value. Davis, Langdon and Everest (1991) suggested that it was simpler to cost engineer a design solution to a pre-determined cost target, than to ensure a proper balance of expenditure throughout the building to maximise the client's benefit or to add value. However, the history and development of the quantity surveyor (Ashworth and Hogg 2000) clearly shows that there has been a paradigm shift in thinking and practice from cost to value. Also, as new techniques and methods have been added to the quantity surveyor's portfolio, there has been an incremental shift in this direction.

Research and development work is now seen by some of the larger professional practices to be an important part of their activities. In some practices it forms a distinctive feature of the practice's profile and portfolio of work and as a source for income generation. It achieves this in two ways: by supporting the work of the practice and through providing high quality publications for business and industry. Work within the profession:

- Provides a framework within which quantity surveying research and development is encouraged to take place

- Raises an awareness amongst quantity surveyors of the importance and role of research and innovation
- Further develops a dynamic research and development community
- Seeks to persuade government and other agencies of the importance of such research and development and the need for its proper resourcing
- Stimulates debate on the future direction of the profession and the role of research and development within it.

Role of the RICS

The RICS in 1999 launched a Research Foundation recognising a rapidly changing world and work environment. The Foundation will support and enhance the profession through an accurate and rigorous understanding of the way in which the natural and built environments behave. Research is critical to this understanding. The RICS Research Foundation's objectives are to:

- Act as the leading international body in the understanding of all matters relating to the development, management and use of the built and natural environments
- Provide leadership on the major debates that are taking place
- Contribute to the more effective and efficient use of built and natural environment, to the benefit of everyone involved
- Disseminate this to the widest audience.

The Research Foundation will seek to achieve this in three ways:

Setting the agenda for debate
- Using focused and rigorous research to bring about a clearer under- standing and analysis of the major policy issues
- Acting to bring about a consensus on the key issues to be addressed by policy and research development
- Influencing policy and strategy at the highest levels.

Promoting the latest thinking
- Identifying innovative solutions and ideas
- Putting forward best practices in the implementation of new techniques and processes
- Developing a clearer understanding of the operation of the property, construction and development markets.

Supporting an active research community
- Developing world class research capabilities in the built and natural environments
- Encouraging the exploitation of new thinking and approaches to the key

issues that we face in the effective management and development of our built and natural environments.

The RICS is committed to a research and development programme which combines long term strategic studies aimed at determining the future shape and direction of the profession in the construction and property industries and targeting those projects which support Institution policy developments. It awards a number of small research grants, often, but not necessarily, to those employed as academics. It publishes and distributes summaries of these research findings, so that debate and policy can be informed by the latest research and analysis. A full list of these is available from the RICS. Reports have included, for example:

- *Procuring property consultancy in an age of change: the role of the intelligent client.* (College of Estate Management)
- *Design and build: Can it put a cost on good design?* (Liverpool John Moores University)
- *Does competitive fee tendering affect the service quality of construction profes- sionals?* (University of Salford)
- *Building the web: the internet and the property profession.* (College of Estate Management)
- *Computerised maintenance management systems: do they do the job?* (University of Greenwich)
- *Learning to succeed, or how firms in the surveying profession can learn to stay ahead.* (Sheffield Hallam University)

In 1991, the RICS undertook a survey to help determine the extent of these activities in the universities and published a report, *The research and develop- ment strengths of the chartered surveying profession: the academic base.* The infor- mation included in the RICS report provided an overall profile of research activities, general areas of capability and specific research expertise, research links with the profession and details of external research contracts.

Classification of research and development

The research process is illustrated in Fig. 5.1 and usually commences with a desire or need to find out or verify existing knowledge. The initial starting point is to set out the objectives in the form of a research proposal. Often such proposals are too broad resulting in a superficial analysis and understanding and a failure to achieve the expected outcomes. The better proposals are those which relate to a problem, where the researcher already has some prior knowledge and experience. Whilst the objectives that are set at the start of the process may be clearly understood, it is not uncommon for these to be altered as the research proceeds. It may be necessary to reappraise the problem after an initial investigation and once a thorough literature survey has been com-

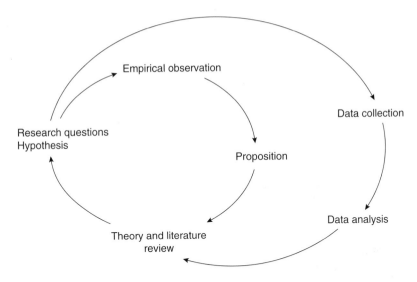

Fig. 5.1   Research circle.

pleted. Academic research that can be carried out in collaboration with practice is a useful combination to be pursued. Research may be classified under the following headings:

Basic research   Experimental or theoretical work undertaken primarily to acquire new knowledge of the underlying foundation of phenomena and observable facts. Undertaken without any particular application in mind.
Strategic research   Applied research in a subject area which has not yet advanced to the stage where eventual applications can be clearly specified.
Applied research   The acquisition of new knowledge which is primarily directed towards specific practical aims or objectives.
Scholarship   Work which is intended to expound the boundaries of knowledge within and across disciplines by in-depth analysis, synthesis and interpretation of ideas and information and by making use of rigorous and documented methodology.
Creative work   The invention and generation of ideas, images and artifacts including design. Usually applied to the pursuit of knowledge in the arts.
Consultancy   The development of existing knowledge for the resolution of specific problems presented by clients often within an industrial or commercial context.

Research and development in the construction and property industries

Research and development takes place in all industries including the construction and property industries and its associated professions and is important for the following reasons:

- Technical change is accelerating and progressive businesses tend to quickly adopt new techniques and applications
- Research and development is inseparable from the well-being and prosperity of a country and of the separate businesses within the country
- Research and innovation are inseparable
- Research and development are necessary to maintain international competitiveness and success, particularly as the craft based traditions of construction diminish and the technological base expands
- This background of constant change and challenges demands an effective research and development base to introduce change effectively and efficiently
- The expenditure on research and development, within the construction industry, is small when compared with our competitors overseas and with other British industries
- Whilst the expenditure on research in the construction industry is lagging behind that in other industries and countries, it is far ahead of that in surveying.

The expenditure on research and development in the construction industry in Britain amounts to about 0.65% of the construction output. Construction companies, for example, contribute about 10% towards this sum, which is approximately one-third of that of our competitors in France, Germany and Japan.

The RICS (1991) Report stated that for research and development activities to fulfil their potential within an area of activity, it was necessary to stimulate a 'virtuous circle' of research. This is typified by the following features:

- There is sufficient awareness and confidence in the capabilities of the research base to encourage the profession to be prepared to commit funds to research
- The flow of funds into research is perceived by the profession as being of great benefit to them
- The profession sees the value in supporting research activities and is willing to continue to invest
- There is a sufficient flow of funds into research in order to support and maintain a high-quality research base.

When a profession achieves this virtuous circle, then it is very likely that it will be extremely well supported by research and development. It will be proactive, dynamic and forward looking. In order to bring this about, one of the most important issues is how to overcome the barrier of lack of knowledge of the research and development capabilities that already exist. For those who still doubt the wider benefits to be achieved from research and development, it is worth noting what the Centre Scientific et Technique du Batiment said in 1990:

'The stronger the research and development effort of a sector, the better its image; even in a fragmented sector. Just look at the image of doctors!'

Changing role of the quantity surveyor

The role and work of the quantity surveyor have changed considerably, particularly over the past two decades (see Chapter 2). These changes in direction and practice are expected to be overshadowed by the accelerated developments which are likely to take place in the immediate future. A major theme of the report *QS 2000* (Davis, Langdon & Everest 1991) is the changes facing the profession. The much later report by Powell (1998) was more alarmist but sent the same message. Perhaps the quantity surveying profession had failed to heed the warning of *QS2000*? The RICS presidential address in 1999 (Kolesar 1999) further reiterated the importance and inevitability of change. Heraclitus (c.540–480 BC) stated: 'Nothing endures but change!' The RICS presidential address in 2000 (Harris 2000) continued with a similar theme, with the desire to elevate the status of the profession. Research and development have important roles in this vision of the future. The following represent some of the issues which, in the absence of appropriate and relevant research and development, may allow opportunities to be missed or to be ineffectively undertaken:

- Blurring of professional disciplines, both within the surveying profession generally but also with other professional groupings
- Wider range of services offered to present clients
- Application of quantity surveying expertise to new markets
- More extensive and intensive use of information and communications technology to improve efficiency and effectiveness
- Changes in the professional structure
- Multi-discipline working and development
- Increased emphasis on continuing professional development
- Geographical dispersion of work to allow for the most economical methods of working
- Forecasted shift between professional and technician activities.

Harris (2000) has further argued that to persist in prescribing tight definitions of our expertise in an attempt to safeguard our work from our competitors will not be successful. He further argues that we will also not succeed through our technical superiority alone.

As with all professions, quantity surveying has evolved and will continue to do so for the foreseeable future. This evolution has been a response to changing demands and services expected from clients and the developing skills and knowledge base of practitioners coupled with the wide implications of information technology. Fig. 5.2 indicates some of the changes to the profession which have occurred since the middle of this century. The majority of

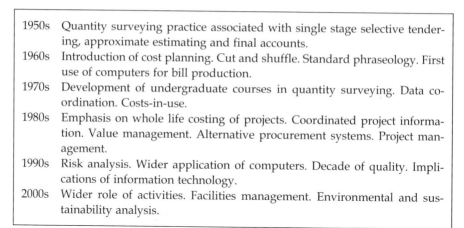

1950s	Quantity surveying practice associated with single stage selective tendering, approximate estimating and final accounts.
1960s	Introduction of cost planning. Cut and shuffle. Standard phraseology. First use of computers for bill production.
1970s	Development of undergraduate courses in quantity surveying. Data co-ordination. Costs-in-use.
1980s	Emphasis on whole life costing of projects. Coordinated project information. Value management. Alternative procurement systems. Project management.
1990s	Risk analysis. Wider application of computers. Decade of quality. Implications of information technology.
2000s	Wider role of activities. Facilities management. Environmental and sustainability analysis.

Fig. 5.2   Trends in quantity surveying practice.

these changes have happened as a result of the pragmatic needs of practice in response to changes in the needs of clients and technology, rather than through any formal development or research.

Research and development in quantity surveying practice

Several of the larger quantity surveying practices have now established research and development sections as an integral part of their practices. This has been done both in an attempt to diversify and also to be at the leading edge of the profession. Some practices have been able to recoup income from work that is broadly described as research and development. Others have joined in collaborative ventures with universities, become members of research advisory teams or have allowed researchers access to non-sensitive data and information. Such activities are also able to provide a useful spin-off for public relations and publicity. Research and development is therefore seen as being important for the following reasons:

- Improving the quality of the service provided to clients
- Increasing the efficiency of work practice
- Extending the services which can be provided
- Developing a greater awareness of new technologies
- Providing a fee earning capability from research and development contracts
- Enhancing public relations and practice promotion.

Data collection and analysis

In some practices, research and development departments evolved from the routine collection of cost and contract information for their own regular use in cost planning and cost forecasting associated with new commissions. It is well understood by all surveyors that the best information available is that which is collected by the practice itself, relying only upon other sources, such as the BCIS, price books, etc. as secondary sources of data.

Market trends

Since construction costs and prices are associated with productivity and market conditions it is important for surveyors to be informed of current trends in practice in order that clients can be properly advised. Whilst the national published data is again valuable, this will form only a secondary source to the specific market information and trends which are retained by the surveying practice.

Practice expertise

A practice that has an extensive involvement with a particular type of construction project is able to provide detailed analyses on the different project components, so that the full extent of any changes in design or specification can easily be assessed. Such a practice is then able to develop a detailed expertise with a particular type of construction or procurement arrangement.

Objective and speculative research and development

It is also important to develop a research data base prompted by the needs of the individual surveyors in order to allow for possible future surveying services to be developed. On this basis clients can be provided with information which in the future might generate new commissions for the surveyor. Development of this type may be undertaken with specific objectives in mind or be speculative, attempting to forecast changes in the market or in the demand for surveying services. It may also be done to meet identified client needs for specific surveying services.

Fee earning capability

In addition to the more usual surveying services, research and development activities are able to generate their own contracts for commissioned research. Some practices, for example, have developed a part of their own research and development expertise to publish the systematic collection and analysis of their data. Surveying practices are also able to submit research and development ideas or bids to government or research bodies for research and development contracts. This has in the past been done in association with a university or college as a collaborative venture.

Information and communication technologies (ICTs)

'Information technology' is a relatively recent addition to the English language. It has its counterparts in the French, 'Informatique', and the Russian, 'informatika'. For many, information technology is synonymous with new technology such as microcomputers, telecommunications, computer controlled machines and associated equipment.

The use of computers has had a dramatic influence upon human behaviour and development since the early 1990s. Computers have also had a major impact upon the profession of quantity surveying, in respect of the role and function of the professional activities. Whilst the capability of computers and their associated software continues to increase, their relative and real price decreases. Reliability is now generally good and their use has become easier as simplified and user-friendly procedures have been introduced. The use of information and communication technologies has also created wide ranging implications. From a social point of view ICT has changed the way in which we communicate and reach decisions, manage our work and store information.

Computer literacy

Computer literacy requires an understanding of the following two related areas of computer knowledge:

- *Knowing computer capabilities and limitations:* General understanding of the organisation, capabilities and limitations of the various machines, i.e. the hardware.
- *Knowing how to use computers:* Familiarity with the common uses or applications of computers. Comfortable working with pre-written software.

Additional competence is gained by mastery of the following two additional areas:

- *Knowing how computer software is acquired:* General idea on how individuals and organisations develop custom made programs and information systems.
- *Understanding the computer's impact:* Aware of the impact that computers and information systems are having on people and organisations.

Information technology continues to develop at an exponential rate. Virtually everyone involved in the construction industry now has extensive access to this technology. What can be imagined will be achievable, if this is desired. Many aspects currently not imaginable will also be achieved, probably in a shorter term than envisaged. There is a tendency to over-estimate what will happen in the next couple of years, but to under-estimate what may take place in the medium term.

Quantity surveying practice

Information technology has been shown to be an effective tool for a wide range of applications in the construction industry. These have included computer aided design (CAD) and drafting, and assisting manufacturers of building materials. The use of CAD by design professionals has been able to demonstrate considerable success in the modelling of design solutions. Although information and communication technology applications are capable of achieving high work levels and have been reported to offer time savings of up to 40%, they sometimes do not always meet the expectations for increased productivity and product quality in the construction industry. The opportunities are substantial. The following areas lend themselves to the development of information technology in construction applications:

- Design and production techniques which incorporate design aids, robots, energy management, commissioning of buildings and education and training
- Information systems which employ data bases, quantities, drawings and models, specifications, property data and electronic data interchange
- Hardware and software which include interfaces, expert systems, standards, integration of applications and software techniques
- Communications which apply to intelligent buildings, wide area networks, local area networks, integrated services digital networks, optical fibres and wiring, radio technology and security.

Survey findings amongst quantity surveyors suggest that a majority are ICT literate. It is impossible to complete a quantity surveying degree course without the use of ICT for a wide range of applications. These will include the general applications such as word-processing and spreadsheets and the more specialist software such as digitised measuring packages, BCIS on-line, estimating and tendering software and integrated databases. Quantity surveying consultants use a complete range of software, but there is often a lack of an overall strategy for its implementation and investment and for on-going training.

In order to integrate the client, team and process more fully, supporting ICT networks will become increasingly adopted. However, the continuing problem with the construction industry remains its lack of standardised data and information and the lack of compatibility between different programs. EDICON and CITE are standards that are readily available and quantity surveyors should take full advantage of these. The multi-disciplinary and design and build environments are the most conducive to the development of integrated IT facilities.

Figure 5.3 provides an indication of the use of information technology in quantity surveying practices. Whilst the use of IT continues to grow owing to its efficiency and effectiveness of operation, in some areas of work manual methods still remain competitive in terms of familiarity and the speed of

Application	Percentages
	10 20 30 40 50 60 70 80 90 100
Development appraisal	******************#######
Early cost advice	****************************######
Measurement	************************######
Digitisers	********************####
Documentation production	***####
Post contract	******************************########
Cash flow forecasting	*****************************########
Project management	********************####
Word-processing	***
Spreadsheets	***####
Databases	******************######
Desk top publishing	*********#####
Internet	*****************************############
Electronic mail	***

***** Current use
Projected use

Fig. 5.3 Extent of use of information technology by quantity surveyors.

application. In other cases, computerised systems have been able to improve the quality of service provided to clients and to produce information that was not previously available or was too difficult to obtain from manual systems. In some quantity surveying practices IT has progressed so far that they no longer see the necessity for extensive secretarial support, since their surveyors access most of their information and data directly from the computer. However, typically only about 60% of practices currently have staff with some formal computer training.

The likely future methods of working according to Powell (1998) suggest the following in respect of information and communication technologies:

- Greater access to international and non-local markets and projects
- Use of low cost third world resources
- Cooperative team working
- Shared contributions to managed process
- Information becomes a commodity
- Concurrent engineering
- Tele-working
- Hot-desking.

Major ICT issues

Machiavelli made this comment in the sixteenth century:

- Poor image, working practices and employment conditions
- Difficulties of recruiting, training and retaining a skilled and committed workforce.

There is a general lack of understanding of best practices or even an awareness in some situations that change is the order of the day and urgent. There is a determination to survive but a lack of realisation of international competition.

Innovation

Innovation is about the introduction of the new in place of the old, especially changes in customary practices. Innovation involves developing a strategy which involves people, practices, processes and technology to deliver high added value.

A great deal of technological change passes unnoticed. It consists of the small-scale progressive modification of products and processes. Such has been the description of the construction industry. Freeman (1987) has described such changes as incremental innovations. They are important, but their effects or shock-waves are only felt within the immediate vicinity. More important are the radical innovations or discontinuous events which can have a drastic effect upon products and processes. A single radical innovation will not have a widespread effect on the economic system. Its economic impact remains relatively small and localised unless a whole cluster of radical events are linked together in the rise of new industries or services, such as the semiconductor business. These are the more significant changes. The following five generic technologies have created new technology systems:

- Information technology
- Biotechnology
- Materials technology
- Energy technology
- Space technology

These represent new technology systems that change the style of production and management throughout the system. The introduction of the electronic computer is an example of such transformations.

The concept of long-wave developments, each of less than 50 years duration, is generally associated with the work of the Russian economist, N.D. Kondratiev. Figure 5.5 is a highly simplified picture of the sequence that might be commonly envisaged. Four complete K-waves are identified with the implication that we are currently entering a fifth. Each wave has lasted approximately 50 years and appears to be subdivided into four phases: prosperity, recession, depression and recovery. Each wave seems to be associated with significant technological innovation associated with production, distribution and organisation.

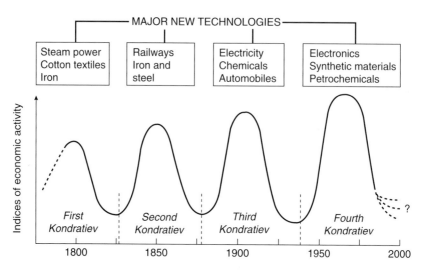

Fig. 5.5 Kondratiev long waves of economic activity and associated major technologies (*Source:* Freeman 1987).

The fifth Kondratriev cycle, which appears to have begun in the early 1990s, is associated primarily with the first of the five generic technologies listed above. Information technology is around which the next wave of technological and economic changes will cluster (Freeman 1987). The development of information technology originates from communications technology and computer technology.

Innovation in the quantity surveying profession should seek to:

- Identify important innovations which have contributed to construction quality cost effectiveness and added value
- Educate industry leadership in the importance of innovation within their respective companies and associations
- Encourage architects, engineers, contractors and surveyors to develop and implement processes for innovation to occur
- Recognise important innovations within the industry, once achieved, through awards, publications, etc.
- Develop financial support for further innovations within the construction industry and its varied services.

The Construction Productivity Network (CPN) was formed as a result of the Latham Report (1994) and is under the auspices of the Construction Industry Board (soon to be superceded by the Strategic Forum for Construction). This is a partnership of the construction industry, its clients and government working together to improve efficiency and effectiveness in construction. The Board aims to secure a culture of co-operation, teamwork and continuous improvement in the industry's performance. CPN exists to promote the sharing of knowledge and the benefits of innovation across all sectors of the contractor selection or tendering purposes. However, the advice will be especially crucial during the project's inception. During this time major decisions are taken affecting the size of the project and the quality of the works, if only in outline form. The cost advice given must therefore be as reliable as possible, so that clients can proceed with the greatest amount of confidence. Where the advice is inaccurate, it may cause a client to proceed with a project that cannot be subsequently afforded or, because of a too high forecast of probable costs, may result in a project being prematurely aborted.

Quantity surveyors are the recognised professionals within the construction industry as cost and value consultants. Their skills in measurement and valuation are without equal. It should be recognised that clients and designers who are either unable or unwilling to provide proper information by way of brief, quality or budget, must therefore also expect the cost advice to be equally imprecise! The quantity surveyor must also realise the importance of providing realistic cost information that will contribute to the overall success of the project. In this context it is important to have an awareness of both design method and construction organisation and management. Quantity surveyors are the industry's experts on building costs and must perform their duties to appropriate professional standards. The client when paying for a professional opinion requires this to be sound and reliable. Failure to carry out these duties properly, in the context of an expert, could provide grounds for liability for negligence. Surveyors must therefore avoid giving estimates 'off the cuff'. It is also preferable during the early stages of a project to suggest a range of prices rather than a single lump sum. The quantity surveyor should also remember the maxim that the first estimate of cost is always the one figure that the client remembers.

Precontract methods

The methods that can be used for pre-tender price estimating are shown in Fig. 6.2. Although they are often referred to as approximate estimating methods, this needs to be read in the context of the way in which they are calculated rather than in terms of the intended accuracy of price alone. The degree of accuracy will depend upon the type of information provided, the quality of relevant available pricing information and the skills and experience of the quantity surveyor who prepares the estimate of cost. Familiarity with the type of project and the location of the site are important factors to consider.

Most of the methods are reasonably well known, but only those that are current or have possible future use have been described.

Unit method

The unit method of approximate estimating consists of choosing a standard unit of accommodation and multiplying this by an appropriate cost per unit. The technique is based upon the fact that there is usually some close

Method	Notes
Conference	Based on a consensus viewpoint, often of the design team.
Financial methods	Used to determine cost limits or the building costs in a developer's budgets.
Unit	Applicable to projects having standard units of accommodation. Used as a basis to fix cost limits for public sector building projects.
Superficial	Still widely used, and the most popular method of approximate estimating. Can be applied to virtually all types of buildings and is easily understood by clients and designers.
Superficial perimeter	Never used in practice. Uses a combination of floor areas and building perimeters.
Cube	This used to be a popular method amongst architects, but is now in disuse.
Storey-enclosure	Is largely unused in practice.
Approximate quantities	Still a popular method on difficult and awkward contracts and where time permits.
Elemental estimating	Not strictly a method of approximate estimating, but more associated with cost planning; used widely in both the public and private sectors for controlling costs.
Resource analysis	Used mainly by contractors for contract estimating and tendering purposes. Requires more detailed information on which to base costs.
Cost engineering	Mainly used for petrochemical engineering projects.
Cost models	Mathematical methods which continue to be developed

Fig. 6.2   Methods of pre-tender estimating (*Source:* Ashworth, 1999a).

relationship between the cost of a construction project and the number of functional units that it accommodates. The standard units may, for example, represent the cost per theatre seat, hospital bed space or car park space. Such estimates can only be very approximate and vary according to the type of construction and standard of finish, but in the very earliest stages of a design they offer a guide to a board or building committee. Apparently the cost per prison cell is higher than a bedroom unit in a five star hotel!

Superficial method

This type of estimate is fairly straightforward to calculate and costs are expressed in a way that can be readily understood by a typical client. The area of each of the floors is measured and then multiplied by a cost per square metre. In order to provide some measure of comparability between various schemes, the floor areas are calculated from the internal dimensions of the building: that is, within the enclosing walls.

The best records for use in any form of approximate estimating are those that have been derived from the quantity surveyor's own previous projects and past experience. However, extensive use is also made of cost databases to provide, if nothing else, a second opinion on the estimated costs. These are also especially useful where a quantity surveyor has no previous records on which to base an estimate. In these circumstances the Building Cost Information Service (BCIS) database may need to be consulted. The BCIS *Quarterly Review of Building Prices* is also a useful guide to which further reference can be made. This type of information must, however, be treated with considerable caution since it can easily produce misleading results. It can also rarely ever be used without some form of adjustment. Buildings within the same category, such as schools or offices, have an obvious basic similarity, which should enable costs within each category to be more comparable than for buildings from different categories.

It is important to consider varying site conditions. A steeply sloping site must make the cost of a building greater than it would be for the same building on a flat site. The nature of the ground conditions, and whether they necessitate expensive foundations or difficult methods of working, must also be considered. The construction design and details to be used will also have an important influence. A single storey garage of normal height will merit a different rate per square metre from one that is constructed for double-decker buses. Again, a requirement for, say, a 20 m clear span is a different matter from allowing stanchions at 5 m or 7 m intervals. An overall price per square metre will be affected by the number of storeys. A two-storey building of the same plan area has the same roof and probably much the same foundations and drains as a single storey of that area, but has double the floor area. However, the prices for high buildings are increased by the extra time involved in hoisting materials to the upper floors, the danger and reduced outputs from working at heights and the use of expensive plant such as tower cranes.

The shape of a building on plan also has an important bearing on cost. A little experimental comparison of the length of enclosing walls for different shapes of the same floor area will show that a square plan shape is more economical than a long and narrow rectangle, and that such a rectangle is less expensive than an L-shaped plan. There are, however, exceptions to these general rules.

The standard of finish naturally affects price. There will be clients who require office blocks with the simplest of finish and there will be others to whom, perhaps, more lavish treatment has advertisement value: they may want expensive murals or sculpture.

In projects offering different standards of accommodation it will be preferable to price these independently. A variety of rates may therefore be required, depending upon the different functions or uses of the parts of the building. There may also be the possibility of the need to include items of work that do not relate to the floor area, and these will have to be priced separately.

Approximate quantities

These provide for a more detailed approximate estimate than any of the other methods. They represent composite items, which are measured very broadly by combining or grouping typical bill measured items. In practice only items of major cost significance are measured. For example, strip foundations are measured per lineal metre and include excavation, concrete and brickwork items up to damp proof course level. A unit rate for this work can be readily built up on a basis obtained from a cost database price book or priced bills of quantities from previous projects. Walls may include the internal and external finish, and the total costs of the windows and doors can be enumerated as extra over.

This method does provide a more reliable means of approximate estimating, but it also involves more time and effort than the alternative methods. No specific rules exist, but the composite items result from the experience of the individual quantity surveyor. In order for the quantities to be realistically measured, more information is required from the designer. Specially ruled estimating paper is available, which is designed particularly for approximate estimating purposes.

Approximate quantities should not be confused with a bill of approximate quantities. The latter would usually be based upon an agreed method of measurement, but since the design is not at a sufficiently advanced stage, the quantities must therefore only be approximate. Also, the approximate quantities used for precontract estimating are simplified, since several of the bill items are grouped together to form a single composite description.

The use of approximate quantities for precontract cost control can create some costing and forecasting difficulties, as by the time the drawings have reached the required stage many of the matters of principle have already been settled. Often these cannot be altered without a major disturbance of the whole scheme.

Cost planning

Cost planning is not simply a method of pre-tender estimating, but seeks also to offer a controlling mechanism during the design stage. Its aims in providing cost advice are to control expenditure and to offer to the client better value for money. It attempts to keep the designer fully informed of all the cost implications of the design. Full cost planning will incorporate the attributes of whole life costing and value management.

Two alternative forms of cost planning (RICS 1982) have been developed, although in practice they have been combined into a single method. Elemental cost planning was devised by the then Ministry of Education (subsequently Department for Education and Employment (DfEE)) in the early 1950s. It was developed largely in response to the extensive school building programme in which there was found to be a wide variation in cost throughout the country. Also costs needed to be monitored and controlled more effectively than had must, however, be aware of all current published trends. These publications will include those specifically for the construction industry as well as publications of a more general nature.

The accuracy or reliability of the estimate is of prime importance. On average, $\pm$ 10% is the typical sort of estimating accuracy that is expected in the construction industry. This percentage will be much higher at inception, when only vague information is available (Ashworth and Skitmore 1986). Forecasts are unlikely to be consistently spot-on, as by definition estimates will always be subject to some degree of error. Estimates should be shown as a range of values rather than as a single lump sum. Alternatively, confidence limits could be offered as a measure of estimates' reliability. The following factors are said to have some influence upon the accuracy of estimating:

- Quality of the design information
- Amount, type, quality and accessibility of cost data
- Type of project, as some schemes are easier to estimate than others
- Project size, as accuracy increases marginally with size
- Stability of market conditions
- Familiarity with a particular type of project or client.

Proficiency in estimating is the combination of many factors, including skill, experience, judgement, knowledge, intuition and personality (Ashworth and Skitmore 1986).

Preparing the approximate estimate

The method to be used for the preparation of an approximate estimate will depend to some extent on the type of project and the amount of information provided by the designer and the client. The more vague the information, the less precise will be the estimate.

The estimate for a complicated refurbishment project could be prepared on the basis of the gross internal floor area, but this would require a large quantity of other calculations on the part of the quantity surveyor. Of course, if the surveyor was familiar with the type of work, the designer and the client, then this approach would be satisfactory. A more useful method would be to use some form of approximate quantities. Once the estimate is acceptable, it will form the budget for the project. *Precontract Cost Control and Cost Planning* (RICS 1982) provides useful information on preparing approximate estimates.

The first part of the process is to quantify the project using one of the methods described earlier and then to price these quantities using current cost information. The cost information can be obtained from previous projects, from cost analyses, or from some published source. It is usual to add on a contingency amount to cover unforeseen items of work. The amount of this is highest at inception and it gradually reduces as the design becomes more certain. The contingency amount is not removed entirely until the completion of the final account.

As the project is priced at current prices some addition is required to allow for possible increased costs. This is normally added as two separate amounts – the first up to tender stage in order to allow for comparison with tenders, and a second to allow for increased costs during construction. The forecasting of these sums in periods of high inflation is difficult.

Approximate estimates of construction costs normally exclude VAT, even on those projects where VAT will be charged. This can represent a considerable item so this should be clear to the client. Even this total sum will not represent the full costs of construction to the client. Professional fees for the architect, engineer and quantity surveyor, and other charges for planning approval, must also be added. The professional fees will always attract VAT, unless the practice is very small. The estimate should also be clear as to items that have been excluded altogether.

Whole life costing

It has long been recognised that it is unsatisfactory to evaluate the costs of buildings on the basis of their initial costs alone (Ashworth 1999a). Some consideration must also be given to the costs-in-use that will be necessary during the lifetime of the building. Whole life costing is an obvious idea, in that *all* costs arising from an investment decision are relevant to that decision. The primary use of whole life costing in construction is in the evaluation of alternative solutions to specific design problems. The whole life cost plan is a combination of initial, maintenance, replacement, energy, cleaning and management costs. Whole life costing must take into account the building's life, the life and costs of its components, inflation, interest charges, taxation and any consideration that may have a financial consequence on the design (Flanagan and Norman, 1993). Many of these are indeterminate. Whole life costing is considered in more detail in Chapter 7.

Value management

Value analysis or value engineering was developed as a specific technique during the 1940s, and has been extensively used for a variety of purposes, particularly in the USA. It has been described as a system for trying to remove unnecessary costs before, during and after construction. It is an organised way of challenging these costs and is based upon a functional analysis that requires the answer to the six basic 'what if' questions of value analysis. In essence, the technique seeks to improve the value for money in construction projects by improving their usefulness at no extra cost, by retaining their utility for less cost, or by combining their improved utility with a decrease in cost. This technique has been renamed value management (Kelly and Male

2000), with an emphasis on it being a more proactive tool. It is considered in more detail in Chapter 8.

During the 1950s value engineering started to penetrate European manufacturing industries and it is today recognised as a means of efficiency-oriented management. It has only in recent years begun to be applied in the UK construction industry. Value management is seen to complement current quantity surveying practice and procedure.

Risk analysis

Quantity surveyors have traditionally presented their clients with single-price estimates, even though it was apparent that on virtually every project differences would occur between this sum and the final account.

The construction industry is subject to a greater amount of risk and uncertainty than most other industries. Also, unlike other major capital investment, construction projects are not developed from prototypes. Many schemes represent a bespoke solution, often involving untried aspects of design and construction, in order to meet an individual client's requirements. All construction projects include aspects of risk and uncertainty (Flanagan and Norman 1993).

Risk is measurable and can therefore be accounted for within an estimate. For example, quantity surveyors involved in forecasting the costs of a new project will have access to different sorts of cost data and this, coupled with their expertise, will enable a budget price range to be calculated within specified confidence limits. It is desirable to offer an estimate in this way rather than to suggest a single price. Uncertainty is more difficult to assess, as it represents unknown events that cannot be even assessed or costed. Different techniques can be applied, such as Monte Carlo simulation, to assess the risk involved. The risk will of course not be eliminated but at least it can be managed rather than ignored.

Best value

In examining the evolving role of the quantity surveyor there is no doubt that there has been a paradigm shift from thoroughly assessing the costs of construction towards adding value (Ashworth and Hogg 2000). The importance of value for money in building and engineering design is not new. Cheapness in itself is of no virtue. Added value is the new watchword. In its simplest sense it is a term that is used to describe the contribution a process makes to the development of its products.

Best value (DETR 2001) is a concept that has come out of the Local Government Act 1999 which sets out the requirements that are expected. The key sentence in the Act is, 'A Best Value authority must make arrangements to secure continuous improvement in the way in which its functions are exercised, having regard to a combination of economy, efficiency and effectiveness'. The so-called 3Es (efficiency, effectiveness and economy) concept has been in existence for some time. The concept of best value applies equally as well in the private as in the public sector. Best value aims to achieve a cost-effective service, ensuring competitiveness and keeping up with the best that others have to offer. It embraces a cyclical review process with regular monitoring as an essential part of its ethos. The best value concept for local authorities is being managed through the Audit Commission.

Best value extends the concepts of value for money that have been identified by Gray (1996), Egan (1998), Powell (1998) and Ashworth and Hogg (2000). Egan for example, defines value in terms of zero defects and delivery on time, to budget and with a maximum elimination of waste. In order to show that best value and added value are being achieved, it becomes essential to benchmark performance including costs. It is also necessary to benchmark the overall cost of the scheme so that improved performance in the design can be assessed against its cost. The sharing of information underpins the whole best practice process. Even the leaders in an industry need to benchmark against their competitors in order to maintain that leading edge. Whilst the aspiration of best value is both admirable and essential, its demonstration in practice presents the challenge.

Taxation

The implications of taxation can have an important effect on construction projects. Whilst it is unlikely to be the main aim of a client, tax efficient design must be considered. It has implications on the construction, fitting out, repairing, running and maintenance costs of buildings. The designing of buildings to be optimally tax efficient can yield substantial benefits for owners and occupiers. Several years ago a House of Lords judgment stated, 'No man in this country is under the smallest obligation, moral or otherwise, to arrange his affairs as to enable the Inland Revenue to put the largest possible shovel into his stores'. Taxation avoidance, rather than evasion, is within the law, and is a necessity bearing in mind the high and diverse incidence of taxation.

The influence of taxation and its effects on buildings and property are constantly changing owing to revisions in taxation principles and the introduction of new measures or rates by the Chancellor of the Exchequer. This is often incorporated as part of the annual budget presentation. Clients cannot expect full guidance on these matters from their accountants, since their technical knowledge of the construction process and its products is limited. In this respect quantity surveyors are well placed to advise the client on these matters, perhaps working in conjunction with an accountant. Every project has its own peculiarities and will require an individual analysis.

All taxes have some bearing on buildings and property. Stamp duty, for example, is a tax on documents and is charged on the transfer of ownership of all land and buildings above a certain value. Council tax and non-domestic rates (business tax) are annual charges relating to the ownership of buildings. With each of these taxes there is little room for reducing the taxation burden. In connection with the latter, clients considering building in a general location may be advised to build in an area that has lower local taxes. This will have to be balanced with the need to be in a particular location, the availability of sites and their respective charges.

Value Added Tax (VAT)

VAT is charged on the supply of goods and services in the UK, and on the import of certain goods and services into the UK. It applies where the supplies are taxable supplies made in the course of business by a taxable person. This tax was introduced to the construction and property industries through the Finance Act 1972. It is a direct result of the UK joining the European Union. The principal legislation is now embodied in the Value Added Tax Act 1974.

Building work is either standard-rated, currently 17.5% or zero-rated. Examples of zero-rated works include residential buildings, which include children's homes, old people's homes, homes for rehabilitation purposes, hospices, student living accommodation, armed forces' living accommodation, religious community dwellings and other accommodation which is used for residential purposes. Certain buildings intended for use by registered charities may also be zero-rated. Buildings which are specifically excluded from zero-rating include hospitals, hotels, inns and similar establishments. The conversion, reconstruction, alteration or enlargement of any existing building are always standard-rated. All services which are merely incidental to the construction of a qualifying building are standard-rated. These include architects', surveyors' and other consultants' fees and much of the temporary work associated with a project. Items which may be typically described as 'furnishings and fittings', e.g. fitted furniture, domestic appliances, carpets, free-standing equipment, etc. are always standard-rated irrespective of whether the project may be classified as zero-rated. The VAT guides provide examples, but throughout these documents, individuals are advised to check their respective liability with the local VAT office. The ratings of some items are arbitrary whereas others will need to be tested by the courts.

Corporation tax

Profits, gains and income accruing to companies who are resident in the UK incur liability to corporation tax. The level of such liability is governed by the profits, gains or income for an accounting period.

Capital and revenue

Capital expenditure is money that is expended in acquiring assets, or for the permanent improvement of, addition to or extension of an existing asset. Such assets must generally have a useful life beyond one year and include items of buildings, machinery and plant.

Revenue expenditure is concerned with the maintenance of such an asset whilst it is in use. It is, by definition, those costs which cannot be classified as capital expenditure. It includes local taxes, annual water and sewage charges, energy, cleaning, insurances and minor repairs.

Capital expenditure will result in increased amounts for fixed assets on a balance sheet, whereas the revenue expenditure is chargeable to the trading or profit and loss account.

Capital allowances

The taxable profits of a company may be reduced through applying allowances against capital cost expenditure. The law on capital allowances is contained in the Capital Allowances Act 1990, together with provisions for future amendment through subsequent Finance Acts. The allowances are calculated on the basis of the following:

- *Initial allowance* This is an initial sum that is allowed against the expenditure of an item in any financial year.
- *Writing down allowances* These are sums that can be offset against taxable income on an annual basis for a specified term of years. These may represent, for example, the theoretical depreciation of an asset.
- *Balancing allowances* These are charges or additional allowances made at the end of an asset's life. Their intention is to balance the allowances against the actual amounts.

Industrial buildings

Industrial buildings are treated differently to the majority of other types of buildings, being broadly defined as buildings used for the processing or manufacture of goods. They include buildings that are used for the storage of materials before manufacture and for goods after production. They must have a direct link with production and as such, wholesale warehouses are excluded. The offices that form a part of the factory are included if they do not exceed 25% of the total cost.

The full costs of construction including professional fees are allowed. Whilst land costs are excluded, the costs of any site preparation may be included. The full costs of the purchase of a building from a builder are allowed. Costs expended on existing buildings, plant and equipment are also included. There is an allowance of 4% per annum, calculated on a straight line basis, until the costs have been fully written down (i.e. 25 years). In the event of a sale, a balancing adjustment is applied.

Where the location of the building has been designated as an Enterprise Zone, expenditure incurred on buildings can qualify for an initial allowance of 100%. Where fixed plant and machinery are an integral part of the building, this is treated as a part of the building in respect of claiming Enterprise Zone allowances.

Plant and machinery

The treatment of capital expenditure on plant and machinery is very complex. Whilst the definition regarding machinery is generally understood, plant is not and has come before the courts on many occasions. It may include 'whatever apparatus is used by a businessman for carrying on a business'. This will exclude stock-in-trade which is bought or made for sale, but will include 'all goods and chattels, fixed or moveable, alive or dead, which are kept for permanent employment in a business'. This legal opinion was stated in *Yarmouth* v. *France* (1887). The main problem lies in distinguishing the apparatus with which a business is carried out from the setting in which it is carried on. Lifts and central heating systems are treated as plant, but plumbing and electricity systems are not. Specific lighting to create an atmosphere in a hotel and special lighting in fast food restaurants have been held as plant.

In *Jarrold* v. *Johngood and Sons* (1963), it was stated that items need not be subject to wear and tear, in this case movable metal office partitioning. The maintenance of plant is always an allowable revenue expense. Builder's work specifically required for the installation of plant items is deemed to be part of the capital cost item.

Computer hardware is a capital expenditure item and allowances are usually claimed under the short life asset rules. Where software is purchased at the same time the Inland Revenue have suggested that this should also be treated as part of the capital cost. Licences to operate software are treated as a revenue expense.

Plant and machinery costs, for taxation purposes, are not treated in the same way as the buildings that house them. First year allowances are from time to time 100% of their capital cost. The full amount of taxation relief can therefore be gained immediately on these items. However, it is more usual to allow a first year allowance and thereafter a writing down allowance of 25% in subsequent years.

Financial assistance for development

In building development some consideration must also be given towards the financial assistance that may be available.

Whilst the various planning regulations are able to prevent undesirable development from taking place, they are unable to encourage socially desirable development to be undertaken. As a part of the planning process the government and its agencies can suggest to a developer that certain specified works are carried out as a part of the approval for development. These might include, for example, leaving part of proposed housing development as a public open space. However, in order to encourage desirable developments to take place in unattractive locations, some form of financial assistance may be necessary.

The intention of such financial assistance is to support projects in areas where they might otherwise not take place, or in circumstances where there may be little obvious economic benefit to a developer. Such assistance may be offered from a local or regional authority or from a central government department. Major considerations are given to the effective co-operation between the public sector, local and central government and private business and voluntary organisations. Financial assistance may arise for one of the following reasons:

- Urban renewal programmes
- Regeneration of industrial areas
- Investing in jobs to benefit areas of high unemployment
- Land reclamation schemes
- Property improvement, such as housing improvements
- Slum clearances and derelict land clearance.

The aim is to encourage private companies or public managing agents to develop areas either as a means of improving the standards and amenities, or through investing in projects that will help in wealth creation. At the same time unemployment in a region may be able to be reduced. Financial assistance is therefore targeted in areas where it may otherwise be difficult to encourage companies to invest. Whilst financial assistance is available for a variety of different purposes, it is in the designated areas where the size of grants is the largest.

Investment grants are made by the government to manufacturing and extractive industries only, in respect of new buildings or adaptations and plant and machinery. The grants are treated as non-taxable capital receipts. Loans are treated in a similar way and may be free of interest. Loans are sometimes offered to companies who for a variety of reasons cannot secure finance in the normal conventional ways through commercial banks. Financial assistance may be a combination of:

- Taxation allowances on capital expenditure for buildings and plant. The company in receipt of such an allowance must in the first instance make a profit to secure the benefit.
- Low rents or business rates, offered by a local authority as inducements to locating in their area. These may be offered only for a limited number of years.
- Grants of up to 50% for capital items to assist firms in new developments.
- Extending, converting and improving industrial and commercial property.

- Amenity grants of up to 100% of the costs associated with providing access roads, car parking and other amenities.
- Bridging finance to close the gap between developing a building and its market value.
- Interest relief grants to offset some of the costs of borrowing finance.
- Building loans. As well as acting as a guarantor for bank finance for building, up to 90% of the market value of land and buildings may be met through loans charged at preferential rates of interest.
- Enterprise Zone benefits, which include 100% tax allowances for money invested in commercial and industrial buildings and exemption from local property taxes.
- Enterprise Zone status providing simplified planning procedures for developments.
- Subsidies paid to companies who employ additional employees in specified occupations.

Regional initiatives

Regional industrial policy operates within a general economic framework designed to encourage enterprise and economic growth in all areas of Britain. However, in some areas specific additional help is provided under the Regional Initiative. Help is thus focused on the assisted areas, which are designated intermediate and development areas.

The areas are those that have high unemployment caused by the demise of traditional industries or the loss of major employers. In order to obtain assistance, projects must create or in exceptional circumstances safeguard jobs within a designated area. Projects must have a good chance of long-term viability. In addition, the greater part of the project costs must be financed by the applicant or from private sector sources. Applicants must also be able to show that without this assistance the project would not take place at all. A further criteria is that improved economic efficiency and greater security of employment should result. Grants are based on the fixed capital costs of new buildings or adaptations of existing buildings, plant, equipment, machinery, vehicles, etc. Grants are available under a number of schemes such as, Regional Selective Assistance, Regional Enterprise Grants, Enterprise Initiative, Training and Research Grants and the European Community.

Post-contract methods

The cost control of a construction project commences at inception and ends with the agreement of the final account. A variety of methods are used to control the costs of construction during the post-contract stage. If the cost control is to be effective then any changes that might affect the contract should be costed *prior* to instructions being issued to the contractor.

Budgetary control

Budgets are used for planning and controlling the income and expenditure. It is through the budget that a company's plans and objectives can be converted into quantitative and monetary terms. Without these a company has little control. A budget for a construction project represents the contract sum divided between a number of different subheadings or work packages.

The contractor will have a costed work programme for the project, although this can be disrupted through changes (variations) to the scheme or the acceleration or the deceleration of activities.

The client's budget represents the time-scale of payments and the availability of funds for honouring the contractor's certificates. Clients with several projects under construction will need to aggregate the amounts of interim certificates from different projects to obtain the total funding requirements. In addition, clients are concerned with the total forecasted project expenditure. The ability to control this depends upon the sufficiency of the pre-contract design, the need for subsequent variations, the steps taken to avoid unforeseen circumstances, and matters which are beyond their control, such as strikes.

The contractor's budget provides a rate of expenditure and a rate of income throughout the project. The contractor's funding requirements represent the difference between these two items, and the amount of capital required at the different times can then be calculated. Contractors also need to aggregate this information from all their current projects in order to determine the company position. Budgetary control compares the budgets with the actual sums incurred, explaining the variances that arise. In common with other control techniques, budgetary control is a continuous process undertaken throughout the contract duration.

Client's financial reports

Financial reports are prepared at frequent intervals throughout the contract period, depending upon the size and complexity of the project, to advise clients on any expected changes to the contract sum. An example of a typical financial statement is shown in Chapter 13, where such reporting is covered in more detail.

Client's cash flow

In addition to the client's prime concern with the total project costs, the timing of cash flow is also important, since this will affect borrowing requirements. The client's quantity surveyor will prepare an expenditure cash flow profile based on the contractor's programme of activities, and any subsequent changes or revisions to this programme. On large and complex projects, and in periods of high inflation, the timing of payments, based upon different constructional techniques and methods, might result in a different contract sum representing a better economic choice for the project as a whole.

Contractor's cost control

The contractor, having priced the project successfully enough to win the contract through tendering, must now ensure that the work can be completed for the estimated costs. One of the duties of the contractor's quantity surveyor is to monitor the expenditure, and advise management of action that should be taken. This process also includes the cost of subcontractors, as these are likely to form a significant part of the main contractor's total expenditure. The contractor's quantity surveyor will also comment on the profitability of different site operations. Wherever a site instruction suggests a different construction process from that originally envisaged, then details of the costs of the site operations are recorded. The contractor's quantity surveyor will also advise on the cost implications of the alternative construction methods that might be employed.

Discounting the fact that estimators can sometimes be wide of the mark when estimating, even with common work items, contractors need to satisfy themselves if wide variation between costs and prices arise. This will be done for two reasons: first, in an attempt to recoup, where possible, some of the loss; and secondly to remedy such estimating or procedural errors in any future work. There are various reasons why such discrepancies may arise:

- Character of the work is different from that envisaged at the time of tender
- Conditions for executing the work have changed
- Adverse weather conditions severely disrupted the work
- Inefficient use of resources
- Excessive wastage of materials
- Plant standing idle for long periods
- Plant being incorrectly selected
- Delays due to a lack of accurate design information.

Often when the project is disrupted by the client or designer this can have a knock-on effect on the overall efficiency and output of the contractor's resources. Contractors may sometimes suggest that they always work to a high level of efficiency. This is not always the case, and losses occur due to their own inefficiency. Costing systems that indicate that a project or site operation has lost money are of limited use if a contractor is unable to remedy the situation. A contractor needs to be able to ascertain which part of the job is inefficient and to know as soon as it begins to lose money. The objectives therefore of a contractor's cost control system are to:

- Carry out the works so that the planned profits are achieved
- Provide feedback for use in future estimating
- Cost each stage or building operation, with information being available in sufficient time so that possible corrective action can be taken
- Achieve the benefits suggested within a reasonable level of administration charges.

Contractor's cash flow

Contractors are not, as is sometimes supposed, singularly concerned with profit or turnover. Other factors also need to be considered in assessing the worth of a company or the viability of a new project. Shareholders, for example, are primarily concerned with the rate of their return on the capital invested. Contractors have become more acutely aware of the need to maintain a flow of cash through the company. Cash is important for day-to-day existence, and some contractors have suffered liquidation or bankruptcy not because their work was unprofitable but because of cash flow problems in the short term. In periods of high inflation, poor cash flows can result in reduced profits, which in their turn reduce shareholders' return. A correct balance between the objectives of cash flow, profit, return and turnover is required. In addition, inflation and interest charges will also have an impact on these items.

Bibliography

Aqua Group The *Pre-contract Practice for the Building Team.* Blackwell Science. 1992.

Ashworth, A. Cost *Models, Their History. Development and Appraisal.* CIOB Technical Information Service No. 64, Chartered Institute of Building. 1986.

Ashworth A. and Skitmore M. *Accuracy in cost estimating.* Proceedings of the Ninth International Cost Engineering Congress, Oslo. 1986.

Ashworth A. *Cost Studies of Buildings.* Longman. 1999a.

Ashworth A. Cost modelling. In *Building in Value* (eds Best R. and De Valence G.) Edward Arnold. 1999b.

Ashworth A. and Hogg K. I. *Added Value in Design and Construction.* Pearson Education. 2000.

Barrett F.R. *Financial Reporting, Profit and Provisions.* CIOB Technical Information Service No. 12, Chartered Institute of Building. 1982.

Brandon P.S. (ed.) *Quantity Surveying Techniques: New Directions.* Blackwell Science. 1992.

Cooke B. and Jepson W. *Cost and Financial Control in Construction.* Macmillan. 1982.

DETR. *Best Value.* Department of the Environment and the Regions. 2001.

Egan J. *Rethinking Construction.* Department of the Environment, Transport and the Regions. 1998.

Ferry D.J., Brandon P.S. and Ferry B. (2000) *Cost Planning of Buildings.* Blackwell Science. 2000.

Flanagan R. and Norman G. *Risk Management in Construction.* Blackwell Science. 1993.

Flanagan R. and Tate B. *Cost Control in Building Design.* Blackwell Science. 1997.

Fortune C. and Lees M. *The relative performance of new and traditional cost models in strategic advice to clients.* RICS. 1996.

Gray C. *Value for money: Helping the UK afford the buildings it likes.* Reading Construction Forum. 1996.

Kelly J. and Male S. *Value management in design and construction.* E. & F.N. Spon. 2000.

MacPherson J., Kelly J. and Male S. *The Briefing Process: A Review and Critique.* The Royal Institution of Chartered Surveyors. 1992.

Nellis H.G. and Parker D. *The Essence of Business Taxation.* Prentice Hall. 1992.

Powell C. *The Challenge of Change.* Royal Institution of Chartered Surveyors. 1998.

Pullen L. *What is best value in construction procurement? Chartered Surveyor Monthly,* February. 2001.

Raftery J. *Principles of Building Economics.* Blackwell Science. 1991.

RICS *Precontract Cost Control and Cost Planning.* The Royal Institution of Chartered Surveyors. 1982.

Saunders G. (ed.) *Tolley's Taxation Planning.* Tolley Publishing Company Ltd. 2000.

Somerville D.R. *Cash Flow and Financial Management Control.* CIOB Surveying Information Service No. 4, Chartered Institute of Building. 1981.

7   Whole Life Costing

Introduction

Whole life costing is not new. It is typically adopted by owners as part of a strategic reassessment of their facilities. It influences the procurement of new buildings and engineering structures and the choices about renewal, refurbishment and disposal. It is becoming much more important as long-term building owners start to demand evidence of their costs of ownership. PFI consortia must, as a matter of course, attempt to assess the financial risks of taking on long-term responsibility for building and engineering operation and maintenance.

It has long been recognised that to evaluate the costs of buildings and engineering structures on the basis of their initial costs alone is unsatisfactory. Some consideration must also be given to the costs-in-use which will accrue throughout the building or structure's life. The use of whole life costing for this purpose is an obvious idea, in that all costs arising from an investment are relevant to that decision. The image of the whole life of a building or structure is one of progression through a number of phases, with the pursuit of an analysis of the economic whole life cost as the central theme of the evaluation. The proper consideration of the whole life costs is likely to result in a project which offers the client better value for money. The earlier that whole life costing is considered, the greater will be the potential benefits.

There are a number of definitions and descriptions of whole life costing. The one that currently best describes it is, 'the systematic consideration of all relevant costs and revenues associated with the acquisition and ownership of an asset' (Construction Best Practice Programme 1998).

Anecdotal evidence suggests that for every unit of capital cost spent on the construction of a building, over a 30 year period there will be ten units spent on maintaining and 100 units on staffing the business activity. Improvements obtained through adopting a whole life cost approach can make a big difference, particularly when expressed in terms of the core business activity (Construction Best Practice Programme 1998).

Each building has a useful life. Planning costs in terms of that usage is as important as establishing costs at the inception. However, the prediction of whole life costs is problematic and often insufficiently used in the design process as an advisory tool.

There are a variety of factors that influence the whole life costs of buildings. These include the:

- Identification of costs incurred during a building or engineering structure's life and the inter-relationship with its use and maintenance
- Appreciation of forecasting techniques available and their use as a planning tool
- Consideration of the effects of time on the accuracy of cost advice with particular regard to technological advancement, government policy and fashion
- Understanding of the importance of the application of risk analysis techniques in the validation of cost advice
- Importance of long life, loose fit and low energy in managing the flexibility of designs during the life of buildings.

Whole life costing applications

The following are some of the advantages of using whole life costing:

- It gives an emphasis on a whole or total cost approach undertaken during the acquisition of a capital cost project or asset, rather than merely concentrating on the initial capital costs alone
- It takes into account the initial capital costs, repairs, running and replacement costs and expresses these in comparable terms
- It allows for different solutions of the different variables involved and sets up hypotheses to test the confidence of the results achieved
- It is an asset management tool that allows the operating costs of premises to be evaluated at frequent intervals
- It allows, for example, changes in working practices, such as hours of operation, introduction of new plant or machinery, use of maintenance analysis, to be properly evaluated as tools of facilities management.

Whilst there has been an emphasis upon the use of whole life costing during the pre-contract period, its use can be extended throughout every phase of a building's life, as follows.

At inception   Whole life costing can be used as a component part of an investment appraisal. The technique is used to balance the associated costs of construction and maintenance with income or rental values.

During the design stage   It is used to evaluate the different design options in order to assess their economic impact throughout the project's life. It is frequently used alongside value engineering and other similar techniques. The technique focuses on those areas where economic benefits can be achieved.

During the construction stage   During this phase there are many different areas that can be considered for its application. It can be applied to the contractor's construction methods, which can have an influence upon the timing of cash flows and hence the time value of such payments. The contractor is able to apply the principles to the purchase, lease or hire of the construction plant and equipment. Construction managers and contractors' surveyors are able to offer an input to the scrutiny of the design, if involved sufficiently early in the project's life to be able to identify whole life cost implications of the design, manufacture and construction process.

During the project's use and occupation   It is a physical asset management tool. Costs-in-use do not remain uniform or static throughout a project's life, and therefore need to be reviewed at frequent intervals to assess their implications. Taxation rates and allowances will change and have an influence upon the facilities management policies being used.

At procurement   The concept of the lowest tender bid price should be modified in the context of whole life costing. Under the present contractual and procurement arrangements, manufacturers and suppliers are encouraged to supply goods, materials and components which ensure their lowest initial cost, often irrespective of their future costs-in-use. It is now accepted by many clients that a greater emphasis should be placed upon the overall economic performance of the different components.

In energy conservation   Whole life costing is an appropriate technique to be used in the energy audit of premises. The energy audit requires a detailed study and investigation of the premises, recording of outputs and other data, tariff documentation and appropriate monitoring systems.

Whole life costs

In addition to initial capital construction costs, other costs accrue as changes occur throughout the project's life (Fig. 7.1). The costs associated with the major refurbishment of an existing project are sometimes classified as initial costs, particularly where an existing project is undergoing extensive works or a change in building use.

In addition to the items shown in Fig. 7.1, there are many other costs-in-use that must also be considered in connection with the whole life costing of a project. These include:

- Fuel for heating, lighting and communications
- Facilities management
- Business rates and insurances
- Redecoration (much of this will coincide with an aspect from Fig. 7.1)
- Cleaning

Main factors to consider

Building life

Over time existing buildings decay and become obsolete and require maintenance, repair, adaptation and modernisation. There also lies a varied pattern

Terminology description

Maintenance	Regular ongoing work to ensure that the fabric and engineering services are retained to minimum standards. It is frequently of a minor nature.
Repairs	Associated with the rectification of building components that have failed or become damaged through use and misuse.
Renewal	The upgrading of a building to meet modern standards.
Adaptation	Frequently includes building work associated with conversions, such as a change in function and typically includes alterations and extensions.
Renovation	Repairing and rebuilding.
Retrofitting	The replacement of building components with new components that were not available at the time of the original construction.
Conservation	Building works carried out to retain the original features or restore a building to its original concept.

Fig. 7.1   Building renewal.

of existence, where buildings are subject to periods of occupancy, vacancy, modification and extension. Figure 7.2 identifies some types of building life.

The useful life of any building is governed by a number of factors, such as the methods of construction envisaged at the initial design and the way that the building is cared for whilst in use, e.g. the amount of wear and tear and the levels of maintenance that are applied. The life of buildings can be assessed in different ways and these are briefly considered later in this chapter.

The design must also recognise the difference between those parts of the building with long, stable life and those parts where constant change, wide variation in aesthetic character and short life are the principal characteristics. There seems to be little merit in including building components with long life in situations where rapid change and modernisation are to be expected.

Component life

The life span of the individual materials and components has a contributory effect upon the life span of the building. However, data from practice suggest widely varying life expectancies, even for common building components (RICS 1992). Whole life costing is concerned not so much with how long a component will last, but for how long a component will be retained. The particular circumstances of each case will have a significant influence upon component longevity. These will include:

- Correct choice of component specification
- Use of appropriate design details

Condition	Definition	Examples
Deterioration		
Physical	Deterioration beyond normal repair	Structural decay of building components
Obsolescence		
Technological	Advances in sciences and engineering results in outdated building	Office buildings unable to accommodate modern communications technology
Functional	Original designed use of the building is no longer required	Cotton mills converted into shopping units, chapels converted into warehouses
Economic	Cost objectives are able to be achieved in a better way	Site value is worth more than the value of the activities current on the site
Social	Changes in the needs of society result in the lack of use for certain types of buildings	Multi-storey flats unsuitable for family accommodation in Britain
Legal	Legislation resulting in the prohibitive use of buildings unless major changes are introduced	Asbestos materials, Fire Regulations
Aesthetic	Style of architecture is no longer fashionable	Office building designs of the 1960s

Fig. 7.2 Building life and obsolescence (adapted from RICS 1986).

- Installation in accordance with the manufacturer's directions, relevant Codes of Practice and British Standards
- Compliance with the conditions of any relevant third party assurance certificates
- Appropriate use by owners, users and third parties
- Frequency and standards of maintenance.

The management policies used by owners or occupiers are perhaps the most crucial factors in determining the length of component life. There is a general absence of such characteristics in retrieved maintenance data (Ashworth 1996b).

Discount rate

The selection of an appropriate discount rate to be used in whole life costing calculations depends upon a wide range of different factors. The discount rate to be chosen will depend to some extent upon the financial status of the client. For example, public sector clients are generally able to obtain preferential

theory. The problem of its application in practice is twofold: the known or predictable and the unknown or uncertain.

The first real difficulty, and this should not be underestimated, is the application of statistical analysis to life expectancies, discount factors and other data to be used in the calculations. This is the assessment of risk, where the use of techniques such as probability and sensitivity analysis can be used to interpret the results and provide confidence limits to such assessments.

The second problem is much more difficult to deal with. This concerns the possibility of events not being imagined at the inception stage of a project that may have a total life of 100 years. Such events are in the realms of uncertainty and fantasy and cannot be measured or evaluated. During the past 50 years society has been under rapid change. This change is expected to accelerate in the future. It is therefore difficult to predict what influence such changes will have on the validity of whole life costing, even for a few years ahead.

Whole life costing does however offer potential. Its philosophy of whole cost appraisal is preferable to the somewhat narrow initial cost estimating approach. The widespread efforts so far expended in its research and development are a positive move. Whole life costing is at best a snapshot in time in the light of present day knowledge and practice and anticipated future applications.

Bibliography

Ashworth A. Life cycle costing: Predicting the unknown. *Journal of the Association of Building Engineers*, April. 1996a.

Ashworth A. Estimating the life expectancies of building components in life cycle costing calculations. *Journal of Structural Survey*, **14** (2). 1996b.

Ashworth A. Data difficulties of building components for use in whole life costing. The Surveyor. *Journal of the Institution of Surveyors Malaysia*, fourth quarter. 1996c.

Ashworth A. *Obsolescence in buildings: Data for life cycle costing*. Chartered Institute of Building Technical Information Service. 1997.

Ashworth A. and Skitmore M. *Accuracy in Estimating*. Chartered Institute of Building. 1982.

Building Maintenance Information. *Occupancy Cost Planning*. Building Maintenance Information Service. 1992.

Construction Best Practice Programme. *Whole life costing*. Department of the Environment, Transport and the Regions. 1998.

Flanagan R., Norman G., Meadows J. and Robinson G. *Life Cycle Costing: Theory and Practice*. Blackwell Science. 1989.

Gordon A. The three 'Ls' principle: Long life, loose fit, low energy. *Chartered Surveyor Building and Quantity Surveying*, Quarterly. 1977.

Hoar D. and Norman G. Life Cycle Cost Management. In *Building Cost Techniques New Directions* (ed. P.S. Brandon). Blackwell Science. 1992.

Housing And Property Manual. Component life manual. Spon. 1992.

National Building Agency. *Maintenance cycles life expectancies*. National Building Agency. 1985.

Property Services Agency. *Costs in Use Tables*. The Stationery Office. 1991.

RICS *A Guide to Whole life Costing for Construction*. Surveyors Publications. 1986.

Royal Institution of Chartered Surveyors and the Building Research Establishment. *Life expectancies of building components. Preliminary results from a survey of building surveyor's views*. Royal Institution of Chartered Surveyors Research Paper No. 11. 1992.

8 Value Management

Introduction

The opportunity that value management (VM) affords the practising surveyor to improve value to the client has now been well demonstrated for several years in the UK construction sector. Although this may be regarded as a specialist area, many quantity surveying practices provide this as one of the growing areas of professional service. Having said this, the development of value management within the profession, despite its recognised benefits, has been slower than ideal. In this chapter, value methodology is outlined and supported with examples that will aid the reader in understanding how the service may be performed and how value can be enhanced by its application. The execution of value management requires an understanding of the processes involved and an understanding of how to determine an appropriate VM approach. Whilst this knowledge is essential to the practice of value management, the principles and philosophy provide surveyors with additional tools and techniques, and possibly new ways of thinking, all of which may be used in other areas of professional activity. Knowledge of value methodology is important to the surveyor, either from the perspective of actual service provision, or from an appreciation of its benefits and application when advising clients.

The list of clients using value management in the UK contains many large organisations, and the high profile endorsement of the practice, at professional institution and government level, was fairly continuous during the 1990s. Value management has been recognised as an important component that is important to the success of projects in providing the foundation for improving value for money in construction. It therefore provides practitioners with an excellent opportunity of contributing further to the value added service they provide. This may occur at several points in the life of a project, for example, to assist in the development of a project brief or in response to a problem at any stage during design or construction. Value methodology may also provide the surveyor with opportunity beyond the usual boundaries of the construction industry, for example, prior to the decision to build, to examine a strategic problem that a company may face. In such areas of service provision, competition may be more apparent from management consultancies than construction professionals. Value methodology does not belong to the construction industry; in fact its origins lie elsewhere.

Background

Value management developed from the demands of the manufacturing industry in the USA during World War II. Lawrence Miles (1972), an electrical engineer with the General Electric Company, who adopted a functional approach to the purchasing requirements of his company, developed the value analysis concept. This involved the functional analysis of a component in terms of what it did and invited a search for an alternative solution to the provision of that functional requirement at a lower cost. The use of the concept further developed during the 1940s and 1950s and grew within the USA, becoming a procedure that could be used during the design or engineering stages. The term value engineering was initiated in 1954 by the US military, an organisation that has a long history of involvement with value techniques. Value engineering spread to the UK manufacturing industry during the 1960s and, at around the same time, was introduced to the US construction industry.

The value management concept was first used within the UK construction industry in the 1980s. Although manufacturers around the world today use value techniques, their use within the construction sector is largely restricted to the USA, UK and Australia. The status of value management is now recognised by legislation in the USA and New South Wales, Australia. In the UK, several bodies have issued documents providing recommendations and guidelines; however, the government has stopped short of any obligatory requirement. Several countries now have representative organisations that serve to promote the use of value methodology and control standards of service provided. A discussion on training opportunity and membership of relevant professional societies is provided later in this chapter.

Terminology

The terminology used in value management may be confusing to those being introduced to the subject for the first time. For example, the terms value management, value engineering and value analysis are frequently used synonymously, particularly value management and value engineering, to mean the entire concept. Although the semantics are considered unimportant, it is vital that the meaning of each term is understood in the context in which it is read or discussed. Therefore, the following definitions are provided as those used throughout this text:

Value management   This is the overarching term used to describe the total philosophy and extent of the practice and techniques. Value planning, value engineering and value analysis, shown below, together form a subset of value management.

Value planning   Value planning is carried out in the early part of a project before the decision to build or at briefing or outline design stage. Value techniques assist in arriving at a group decision in terms of the available criteria. It is a common misconception that the use of value management techniques is intended solely for the resolution of a problem, for example, for the reduction of planned expenditure in cases of a budget overrun following the production of a scheme design.

Value engineering   The use of value techniques when completed designs or elements of the design will be available for study during the detailed design and construction stages.

Value analysis   The use of value techniques that are carried out following the completion of a building.

When should surveyors use value management?

To examine this aspect, it is first important to define what value management is and what it is not, which may be considered subjective. Although value management does not provide a strict discipline or science to which every practitioner must rigidly adhere, it is considered to have some essential components, as follows.

- *The use of a structured job plan*   Central to the value management process is the structured workshop, or series of structured workshops, at which group decisions are made. An important aspect of the value management workshop is its structure that usually follows a five-phase process known as the job plan. This is described in detail below.
- *The involvement of a multi-disciplined team*   Value management is a *multi-discipline* exercise in that it ideally requires the participation of consultants from all relevant design disciplines and client representatives who share a common interest (and thus are *stakeholders*) in the success of a project. To be effective, and it is regarded as critical to the success of value management, the team should have an appropriate mix of experience, knowledge and skills and, dependent upon workshop objectives, a range of stakeholder perspectives. An important consideration when selecting a value management team is whether to use the existing design team members or an independent workshop team – although the lack of use of the latter in the UK suggests that this may be rather academic. The participation of independent design consultants would appear to be unusual other than in the US public sector. Use of the existing design team brings several advantages to the proceedings. Where existing project members are used, there is less likelihood of difficulties with the implementation of 'outsiders'' ideas, costs are curtailed, there is a saving in time due to the existing knowledge state of the project and it could prove to be a useful team building exercise. However, a potential major disadvantage could be the dominance of original design concepts (if these have been established), which may be strongly defended by designers. The prospect of this occurring is supported by research into design practice and it is something that facilitators are and need to be aware of.

- *Maintenance of the basic project function*   An often-made comment by quantity surveying practitioners is that they carry out value management as part of their traditional duties. This belief is held due to the contribution the quantity surveyor frequently makes relating to the establishment of cost reductions. This reveals a fundamental misunderstanding of value management. The task of reducing costs is usually carried out by the quantity surveyor, irrespective of function. Value management attends to the elimination of unnecessary costs, costs that relate to elements of a design that provide no function.
- *The management of a competent facilitator*   The facilitator is central to the success of the value management process. The role of the facilitator includes advising upon the selection of the VM team, co-ordinating pre-workshop activities, deciding upon the most appropriate timing and duration of workshops, workshop management and preparing reports. Workshop management can be a difficult challenge requiring a variety of skills. These include:
  - The ability to determine and adhere to an appropriate agenda
  - Identifying and gainfully using the characteristics of team members
  - Promoting the positive interaction of participants
  - Motivating and directing workshop activity
  - Overseeing the functional analysis process
  - Encouraging an atmosphere conducive to creativity whilst at the same time maintaining a disciplined structure.

Therefore, although value techniques may be applicable in many situations, the costs and time associated with a formal value management study incorporating the elements outlined above may restrict its use. In practice, value management tends to be utilised in high cost and more complex projects. However, since the savings achieved in a VM study are likely to be significant (say 5% to 15%), and external VM costs could be less than £5000 to £6000, VM is a feasible option on relatively small projects.

Examples of how value management may be used to the benefit of clients include the following.

To obtain a reduction in costs

Consider the value management approach compared to the normal quantity surveying approach:

At tender stage, a proposed library building is over budget by, say £250 000.

Traditional cost reduction exercise by the quantity surveyor

The quantity surveyor considers that the internal finishes element appears to offer scope for savings, and proposes for consideration a schedule of cost reductions. This includes a reduction in the specification of floor tiles (the substitute having a reduced life span, being more difficult to maintain and having a less attractive appearance) and the omission of access flooring from two floors. Clearly, the required budget can be achieved by this action, but with a loss of function that the client would have preferred to retain.

Value management approach

A facilitator co-ordinates a value engineering workshop with the objective of achieving savings of £250 000. The workshop team, using value techniques, ascertains that the function of 'accommodate staff' has been provided by the inclusion of personal office space for all members of staff based upon previous library practice. The workshop team find that the cost of this function (£750 000) can be halved, without loss of function, since, with the increased use of IT and 'hot desking', private staff accommodation can be provided on a staff ratio of 33%. It may be observed that if value management had been used early in the design process, this element of poor value would probably not have occurred. Since it is likely that the retrospective improvement to design is less efficient than *getting it right first time*, the beneficial use of value management early in a project's life is emphasised.

The difference between cutting costs and cutting unnecessary costs is fundamental to the value management approach (Ashworth and Hogg 2000).

The improvement of concept briefing

As referred to previously, value management is not restricted to the resolution of a problem that has occurred during design development but may be used to assist in the concept briefing stage.

Construction design is a complex task and in order to simplify the process, designers tend to adopt a strategy that results in the early production of sketch proposals. These early designs, often based upon relatively little information, are dominant in determining the final outcome of the eventual design. On the understanding that 80% of costs are committed at concept design, the opportunity to add value at this stage of a project is significant.

Value planning, which is carried out in the early stages of a project, before the decision to build or at briefing or outline design stage, provides good opportunity for a multi-discipline team (including client *stakeholders*). With the use of value techniques, the VM team will be supported in reaching a group decision in terms of the criteria for a proposed design. The production of a functional analysis diagram may be one of the methods used and the example in Fig. 8.4 indicates the use of this technique at a strategic level. This diagram, which can be weighted to indicate design priorities, will assist in directing members of the design team toward the project objectives and may be used to monitor design output. Value management can therefore be used to mitigate the well-known inadequacies of traditional concept briefing (Ashworth and Hogg 2000).

The application of value management

When examining the practice of value management, there is a tendency to focus upon the activities of the workshop and pay too little attention to the preparatory and completion stages. Since the essence of the value management philosophy is held in the workshop activities, this may be understandable. However it is important to stress the importance of both the pre and post-workshop activities of a value management study. For example, at the pre-workshop stage there is a need to identify the nature of workshop events, and during the post-workshop phase, action is essential if the client is to benefit from the achievements of the study.

Pre-workshop stage

The pre-workshop stage is necessary to:

- Establish why the client wishes to undertake a value management study, and the expected outcomes. Learning about the problem before action is taken is an important step in the value management process. Although a client may have identified a problem at the onset, a preliminary investigation may reveal a different problem to that outlined. For example, the reduction in building costs may be seen as the solution to a budget shortfall. However, the real problem may lie in the need to enhance project revenue and thus establish a higher project budget. Although this example is fundamental, the suggestion is also quite radical in terms of our traditional approach.
- Decide upon the nature of the workshop including duration, timing, core activities and location. Although the benefits of value management may be extended to any problem or decision-making situation, specific project needs and resources have unique demands. For example, the detail relating to a study at the concept stage for a new rail tunnel between Portsmouth and the Isle of Wight, will clearly be different from that required in connection with the need to attain savings, one week into an inner city refurbishment project. Factors such as project complexity, size, public profile, available resources and programme may all have a significant bearing.
- Determine the composition of the value management team. As stated, stakeholders' participation is a fundamental requirement of value management since value needs to be improved in terms of their perspectives, not those of consultants or a single client agent. The term stakeholder can be considered to incorporate any person with an interest in the proposed project. The composition of the team will vary with each project, not only in terms of personnel, but also the number and experience of participants. For example, in the above mentioned comparison between the Portsmouth/Isle of Wight Tunnel and inner city refurbishment project, the tunnel project would likely attract a greater number of stakeholders, many with little relevant experience. In such situations, briefing members of the

value management team prior to the workshop with regard to the project, study objectives and the value management process will be an important factor. In any value management study, briefing the participants of the study objectives will be beneficial.

- Collect information and circulate to the selected workshop participants. This may necessitate substantial research and the support of client representatives and members of the design team. Throughout the value management process, the support of senior management is seen as crucial to a successful outcome.

An example of the type of pre-workshop activity that may occur is shown in the scenario below.

Scenario

A cinema organisation proposes to construct a new multiplex cinema in a major city location. They have been advised to undertake a value management study at feasibility stage as a response to a lower than anticipated project return. A facilitator has been appointed. This term is commonly used in lieu of value manager and has been used throughout this example.

Following appointment, the facilitator meets with the client and ascertains the following information:

- A site has been obtained and outline planning permission has been given
- The client's architect has been appointed to the proposed scheme and has prepared an outline sketch proposal. The quantity surveyors have prepared a feasibility report.

It is agreed that a first value management workshop should be held two weeks hence. Following this initial briefing, the facilitator also recommends a two-day event that will be held in the business suite of a hotel located close to the proposed development.

Study team

In cognisance of the information obtained from the client, the facilitator recommends a value management team comprising:

- Project consultants: architect, quantity surveyor, structural engineer, services engineer. Each of these consultants has been involved in other cinema developments for the client
- Client stakeholders: commercial director, sales and marketing director, regional operations director.

An important aspect of the team composition in this study is seen as the presence of decision takers. Absence of the need to refer back or be concerned about the approval of a senior authority before giving advice or taking decisions will contribute to the successful outcome of the study.

Information gathering and briefing

The facilitator arranges a meeting with members of the design team and the client organisation to discuss details of the project. At this meeting, information required for the workshop is identified and key information is collected for distribution to all study participants. The design team are also briefed with regard to the study and its objectives. Their contribution to the workshop is outlined, namely brief presentations from each member at commencement of the study. The quantity surveyor is advised that cost advice will be required at key points during the workshop and is requested to review, in advance, the budget estimate and to provide an elemental cost comparison (see Chapter 6, Cost Control) with similar developments previously executed by the client. A spatial cost model showing a breakdown of costs for key areas in the cinema is also requested. The zones to be considered include entrance lobby, ticket sales, pre-entertainment areas, refreshment/merchandise areas, theatres, staff and management areas, ancillary space provision and general circulation space. It is agreed that an additional quantity surveying representative will also attend the workshop to assist with cost advice needed during the workshop.

In addition to briefing the participants as to the purpose and format of the workshop, the facilitator is able to obtain feedback with regard to particular views and perspectives of each stakeholder. This is important to the success of the study, allowing some forethought as to workshop management and identifying some items of focus.

It is of some importance to note that the arrangements for the workshop that have been outlined above can and should vary dependent upon individual situations. Some practitioners believe that a minimum study duration should be three days. Whilst it is possible that in practice many studies would benefit from more time, value can be gained from workshops of shorter duration. Clearly, the required scope and depth of the study will be major determinants.

Workshop stage

The structured job plan approach was developed by Lawrence Miles and, whilst academics and practitioners have refined and contextualised a variety of differing methods, it is normally adhered to in all approaches to value management in some form. Whilst this suggests a rigid approach, it should be regarded as an outline; situations and projects will differ and make their own demands on workshop approach and activity. For example, a workshop is perhaps more efficient when limited to the information, creative and evaluation phases (described below) where time is restricted or resources are not available, with provision for development and presentation in a follow up meeting. Likewise, the job plan structure indicates a logical and sequential path, which in practice may vary and necessitate iterative action. The stages of the job plan are discussed below.

The information phase

The workshop begins with an information phase in which particulars of the problem or project are presented to the value management team. If the value management study relates to a proposed building, this can include a contribution from the client's representatives, the architect, structural engineer, quantity surveyor and other members of the design team which will offer details of project background, aims (distinguishing between a client's needs and wants) and constraints (e.g. site, budget, time). Although the primary aim of the information phase is to provide all team members with sufficient detail to allow a good understanding of the project, it also serves as a team building opportunity that, if well managed, is useful in preparing a good base for the remainder of the workshop. A feature of this phase of the workshop is some form of functional analysis that is frequently carried out via the production of a function logic diagram (see the functional analysis section later in this chapter). This results in an enhanced project understanding and allows unnecessary costs to be identified in terms of cost worth (see functional analysis section) and forms a focus of further study. An example of a FAST diagram relating to the cinema scenario outlined above is also considered in the functional analysis section.

Creative phase

Once the VM team have a good insight into the project, including an understanding of its functional needs, the participants are requested, in the creative phase, to engender alternative solutions and ideas. This part of the proceedings is usually performed with the aid of brainstorming and other creative thinking methods to stimulate members to generate ideas that will improve value. With adherence to the key brainstorming rules – that as many ideas are produced as possible and that participants are reserved in their judgement of the suggestions until the creative phase is complete – a large number of suggestions will be generated for future evaluation.

The evaluation phase

There is a range of methods used during the evaluation phase to evaluate the merits of the proposals made during the creative phase. How best to obtain the agreement of workshop participants as to the selection of ideas for further development is a matter that needs to be resolved. Since the work carried out in the development phase is likely to be very detailed and time consuming, only those ideas able to demonstrate good value improvement should be selected. The method used to evaluate the ideas generated in the creative phase will be situation dependent (e.g. influenced by available time, workshop timing, workshop team, project complexity) and may rely on a democratic procedure or the facilitator's ability to get open accord. One technique that is occasionally used is 'championing' which depends upon team members volunteering to 'champion' a particular idea (i.e. accepting responsibility for its development). Therefore, ideas without champions are rejected and thus the best ideas retained. The outcome of the process, irrespective of the method used, is to carry forward the most beneficial ideas to the development stage.

One approach, which may be used to evaluate brainstormed suggestions, is to provide qualitative estimates as to the likely impact in terms of time, cost and quality, and ease of implementation for each proposal. This procedure will allow the identification of those items that offer high value gain and are relatively easy to incorporate within the design. An example of a value proposal evaluation form is shown in Fig. 8.1.

VMA VALUE MANAGEMENT ASSOCIATES							
Project:		**Sheet:**				**Date:**	
		Impact			Opp.		**Comment**
Nr	**Description**	**T**	**£**	**Q**		**Action**	
1	Redesign entrance/ticket dispensing area	2	5	3	5	D	
2	Reduce storey height	2	3	1	1	R	
3							
4							
5							
6							
7							
8							
9							
10							
11							
...							

Notes:
Impact (T = time, £ = cost, Q = quality): 1 = low; 5 = high
Opp. (i.e. Opportunity) – ease of implementation: 1 = impossible; 5 = easy
Action: Accept, Develop, Reject

Fig. 8.1   Value proposal: evaluation form.

In this example, the suggestion 'Redesign entrance/ticket dispensing area' is considered likely to have a very high impact upon cost and could be incorporated within the design easily. Alternatively, the suggestion 'Reduce storey height' is considered to have a much lower cost impact and will be impossible to achieve. Clearly, suggestion one will be worthy of development and suggestion two rejection.

The development phase

The evaluation of ideas generated in the creative phase has probably been based upon no more than an outline perception by this stage of the workshop. The development phase accommodates the further work that is necessary to establish whether an idea should become a firm proposal or, if the workshop is at briefing stage, to consider the incorporation of ideas within a revised brief. This detailed work is time consuming and will probably involve much technical input. It is nevertheless essential to execute this developmental work before the presentation of formal proposals. Because of the time involved during this development phase, it is often advantageous to complete the related work beyond the confines of the workshop and present it at a subsequent meeting. The work performed during this phase will include the preparation of alternative designs and cost exercises in order to justify the merits and feasibility of the new proposals. The services of non-consultant stakeholders are, therefore, unlikely to be required at this stage.

Whilst details of whole life costing techniques are outlined elsewhere in this book, it is important to further enforce their importance in the preparation of adequate value management proposals. In the life of a building, occupancy costs will be more significant than initial costs. Therefore, when considering alternative design proposals within the value management process, whole life costs must be considered to assist the decision making process.

It is usual to submit proposals on a pro-forma such as the one shown in Fig. 8.2. The form serves to illustrate the level and type of information that will be prepared in the development stage. In addition to the information contained on the form, additional detail in the form of drawings, calculations, etc. may also be relevant and necessary for the client to give full consideration to the design change proposed.

The presentation phase

The objective of the presentation phase is to present the team's proposals to the client representatives. The presentation of proposals, which will probably include adjustments to original design proposals, is something that may be very sensitive to consultants and possibly the client.

The presentation normally occurs at the end of the value management workshop process and is intended to communicate the proposals to the client representatives. Decisions relating to the proposals will probably be deferred until after workshop closure. Although the proposals may have been prepared in detail and with as much accuracy as possible, some review is likely to be necessary and further investigation and consultation may be required.

Post-workshop stage

The completion and monitoring of an implementation plan to ensure post study action is taken as an essential component of successful value manage-

VMA VALUE MANAGEMENT ASSOCIATES

| Project | New City Cinema | Date: 2/3/00 | Impact |
| Proposal: | Revise reception/entrance area | Ref: 21 A | considerations |

Detail:

The original entrance/reception area accommodates a ticket counter and lobby which is designed to handle all customers. With reference to the FAST diagram, the system to receive viewers/dispense tickets/ inspect tickets is high cost in terms of both designed accommodation and operation. There is an increasing trend toward auto-dispensers and inspection systems which is changing the space requirements and staffing location and levels.

The new design proposal shows a revised entrance layout which accommodates IT displays/ticket dispensers at 12 customer stations. Anticipated reduction in staffing – at reception, 1 at entrance.

Time:
No revision to exterior. Interior redesign: project at concept – minimal time implications

Resources:
No significant resource implications to implement

Rationale/advantages/disadvantages:

Entrance to the cinema is more rapid and comfortable and requires less space that can be dedicated to ancillary entertainment and sales. This will improve revenue and reduce running costs. As a result of reduced staffing levels, customer care may be seen to reduce and security problems may increase.

Action:

❑   **Reject**
❑   **Develop**
❑   **Accept**

Cost summary	Drawing refs:		Design status: Outline/ working		Implementation details:
	Initial cost	NPV running	NPV maintenance	Total cost	
Original design					
This proposal					
Saving/add					

Notes:

1. The accuracy of costs provided will depend upon the level of information and time available for the calculations.
2. The net present value of running costs and net present value of maintenance costs must relate to a realistic business life projection.
3. The proposal should be prepared in such a way as to allow various members of the design team and client organisation to understand the rationale.
4. In addition to providing details of the proposal, the form acts as a checklist and prompter of action and implementation.
5. When considering the proposal, consideration should be given to the impact of accepting the change in terms of time or resource implications, e.g. time to redesign and associated fees, planning approvals, delivery dates...

Fig. 8.2   Value management proposal form.

ment. Although the benefits of value management include team building and 'buy in' to a project, project value improvement necessitates action beyond words. Despite this, in some situations, the post-workshop stage may fail to fulfil the findings and undertakings of the value management study. These will be included in a detailed report, but reports do not guarantee action.

The post-workshop phase is improved if action determined in the value management study is fully accepted by participants (rather than imposed) and is carefully monitored. Personnel need to be identified to follow up the action outlined in the report and a post workshop meeting, at which the outcome of the action phase is reviewed, will promote success.

The activities included in the post-workshop stage include the following.

Report

Following completion of the value management study, it is necessary to prepare and submit a detailed report of the activities of the workshop. This will include a review of the value management process carried out, indicating key aspects such as project background, study objectives, value management team membership, information base, timing and duration, workshop activities, function logic diagrams and other supporting models and details of the workshop proposals.

Implementation

Irrespective of the level of success achieved during the workshop stage, the real measure of success in a value management study lies in the extent of implementation of the proposals. This will be dependent upon several factors including the level of client support and commitment, the attitude of members of the design team and the time available. The implementation of 50% of value management proposals may indicate a successful value management study (Norton and McElligott 1995).

Implementation will occur via a detailed response to the facilitator's report from the client body. This will indicate those proposals outlined in the report which are accepted, rejected or requiring further development before a decision can be made. Following this, it is good practice to hold a further meeting at which all outstanding matters can be clarified and confirmed.

Functional analysis

There is a range of opinion regarding the importance of functional analysis within construction related value management. Its benefits are well recognised and considered by some to be vital to the process. This is not a universal opinion however and some practitioners consider it of little value.

At this point, it is useful to reflect that functional analysis is a method of examining a product or process in terms of what it does rather than simply what it is. It is generally recognised as a distinguishing feature of value management, dating back to Larry Miles and value analysis. However, the analysis of function should not be seen purely as an integral part of the value management process but should be recognised as a useful methodology that may be used in the absence of the value management framework. For example, there is nothing to prevent a site team (or a single individual) examining a process or aspect of the design with the use of an internally executed functional analysis exercise. This may be relatively quick to perform and may be helpful in searching for value improvement or the mitigation of a problem. This is not to suggest that this is a substitute for a formally executed value management study. This informal approach to functional analysis will clearly have limitations; an individual or small and unrepresentative team will have a restricted view of function and in any event, it is only one part of the value management package which, as stated above, some practitioners now downplay in terms of construction related service.

The main reason for the use of the simple and effective technique of functional analysis is clear. When applying the method to a building component or element, the question 'What does it do?' as opposed to 'What is it?' is asked. Therefore, when looking for alternatives, we search for something that will provide the required function rather than try to find a substitute for the previous solution. Establishing the true functions of a product and considering the costs of each function identified can in itself be an illuminating exercise. The potential impact of the approach can be seen when considering the wristwatch. Most people would state that its function was to indicate the time. If this were simply the case, why do people pay a wide range of prices for such a function? If you can obtain this function for £3.50, why spend £2000. The answer lies in the additional functions required by some people; improving image (esteem function), extending life/providing date (additional use functions) may well justify to some, an additional expenditure of £1996.50.

Figure 8.3 shows the range of application of functional analysis, from the strategic level to that of the individual component. The applicability of functional analysis within the construction industry is determined by level of operation. Although a one week value management study examining, in detail, the design of a door closer may provide value gain to a manufacturer (in a production run of 100 000), there can be no place for such examination within the context of a new building. The relative costs involved are insignificant and in any event, suggested design changes are likely to lead to non-standard components resulting in cost increase rather than decrease. However, the application of functional analysis at a higher level of abstraction, for example a high cost element or entire building, is valid.

The matrix shown in Fig. 8.3 (Ashworth and Hogg 2000) further explains some of the principles of functional analysis. It shows a hypothetical analysis of the costs of a softwood window relative to functional requirements. Note that the values and function allocation indicated are entirely notional and are there purely to serve the explanation. The logic shown in the table is related to

Component	Permit ventilation	Control ventilation	Exclude moisture	Retain heat	Transmit light	Improve security	Reduce sound	Reduce glare	Extend life	Assist cleaning	Enhance appearance	Component cost £
					Function							
Lintol	15	–	–	–	15	–	–	–	–	–	–	30
Opening	10	–	–	–	10	–	–	–	–	–	–	20
Frame	–	5	5	5	5	–	–	–	10	–	5	35
Casement	–	15	15	15	15	–	–	–	30	–	35	125
Ironmongery	–	10	–	–	–	5	–	–	–	20	5	40
Glass	–	5	5	5	–	5	10	5	–	–	10	45
Paint	–	–	–	–	–	–	–	–	5	–	10	15
Function cost	25	35	25	25	45	10	10	5	45	20	65	310

Fig. 8.3   Functional matrix 'softwood window' (*Source:* Ashworth and Hogg 2000).

cost/worth and is based upon the convenient assumption that all costs can be allocated to some particular function. Worth is defined as the least cost necessary to provide the function. Thus if we focus upon the functional costs of the 'casement' we can observe the following:

- The minimum cost of a casement to serve the basic functions of 'control ventilation', 'exclude moisture' 'retain heat' and 'transmit light' is £60 (assumed to be present in all windows). This amount has been allocated in equal amounts to each of the functions.
- An additional cost of £30 is attributed to the increased specification of softwood – the function of which is to 'extend life' (and reduce the maintenance) of the window.
- An additional cost of £35 is attributed to the window style, say of Georgian appearance in small panes incorporating moulded sections, the function of which is to 'enhance appearance'.
- Function is not always as it first may seem. The function of 'permit ventilation' is achieved by forming an opening; with regard to ventilation, the purpose of the casement is to 'control ventilation'.
- The functions can be divided into: basic – those which are essential (shaded) in Fig. 8.3 and secondary – those which are not essential (but possibly unavoidable or necessary to sell the product), often provided in response to the design solution (e.g. reduce glare). The choice of what is basic and secondary may be subjective and dependent upon individual perception (hence the need for stakeholder participation). The separation of basic and secondary functions assists with the understanding of a project and may identify areas to target for value improvement.
- In terms of cost/worth, if we only require the basic functions as shown (as

stated above this is a subjective view), the window is only worth £165 (the sum of the shaded function totals). Thus, if we have expended £310 and do not require 'reduce sound', 'reduce glare', extend life', 'assist cleaning', and 'enhance appearance' (e.g. We live in a bungalow, in a quiet rural hamlet, surrounded by trees and have simple aesthetic tastes) we have not achieved good value.

This shows the way in which functional analysis may be used to identify unnecessary costs or to highlight a disparity of expenditure, possibly leading to substitution with a design alternative. The benefits of functional analysis in practice on a component such as a softwood window, will probably be minor and therefore not worthwhile; however, the benefits of the technique can be seen (Ashworth and Hogg 2000).

Functional analysis diagramming techniques

A common method of performing functional analysis is with the aid of functional analysis diagramming techniques such as FAST (functional analysis systems technique) or a value hierarchy. Please note that these diagrams are a means of carrying out and expanding the usefulness of a function analysis; functional analysis may be performed, as shown above, without such techniques.

   Functional analysis diagramming techniques can be used across the varying levels of a project development, for example at a strategic stage to possibly identify the building need, at built solution level to assist in the briefing process, and at elemental level to identify unnecessary costs. In practice however, within the construction domain, the use of the technique at technical level is doubtful. Examples of these, and how they may inter-relate, are shown in Fig. 8.5.

Cinema scenario

As part of the information phase of the value management study, a FAST diagram is constructed. A simplified example is provided in Fig. 8.4. The following notes describe the main features:

- The diagram is constructed by using the identified functions and applying 'How/Why' intuitive logic to develop a structured model. Functions are identified by the value management team and conveyed in the form of verb-noun descriptions. In practice, the use of Post-it Notes solves the problems associated with continual development and amendment of the diagram.
- Applying the questions 'How' and 'Why' to the relationship between identified functions tests the logic of the diagram. For example, the function 'show movies' is served jointly by 'project image' and 'accommodate people'; likewise, the reason for projecting image and accommodating

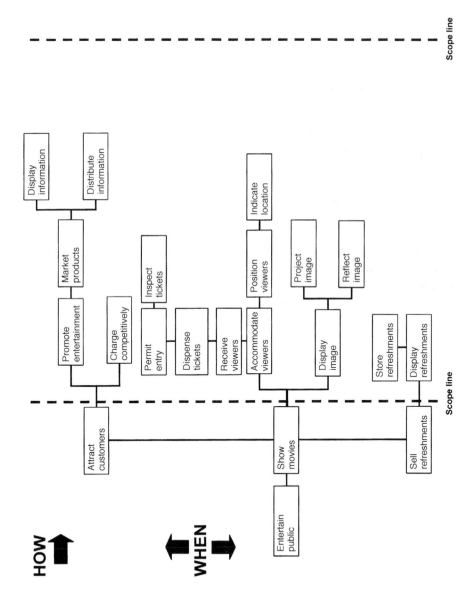

Fig. 8.4 FAST diagram.

people is to show movies. A further question which may also be used when constructing the diagrams is 'When?'. In the cinema example, 'When' accommodating viewers, there is also the need to receive viewers and dispense tickets. This approach assists in the practical construction of the diagram and also in the maintenance of the applied logic.

- The left scope line has been established with 'Show movies' as the basic function. This is effectively the limit of the study. Although a higher level of abstraction would provide the opportunity to analyse other alternatives to the function 'entertain public', or even beyond, e.g. 'improve profit', the core business activity of the client in this study is to 'show movies'.
- The scope line to the right of the diagram provides the limit at which further dilution to the question 'How' would serve no practical purpose. Design solutions generally appear to the right of this line.

The construction of FAST diagrams can be a difficult task and the notes above are intended to provide an outline explanation only. In practice, the use of FAST diagramming techniques will require training. Simpler forms of function/logic diagrams may be more easily used and are more common. These follow the principles of How/Why logic in the form of a tree diagram, but are generally looser in terms of adherence to convention. The outline examples shown in Fig. 8.5 are indicative examples.

The use of function logic diagrams helps to describe the problem environment and allows participants in a value management workshop to understand the relationship between project objectives and solutions. The application of costs to a function logic diagram will also assist in the identification of high cost functions, which may help in directing further value management activity.

Figure 8.5 shows the inter-relationship between the various levels of use of function logic diagrams.

Supporting the case for value management

General claims of the success of value management in financial terms suggest that for a value management fee of 1%, a 10% to 15% cost saving can be achieved. It is hard to imagine that practitioners and clients would not use value management, in the belief that this level of result could be attained. However, general and vague statements such as the one above are difficult to prove, particularly perhaps to quantity surveying practitioners who frequently achieve the same order of cost savings for clients in their traditional role.

Despite the acclaim given to value management, although its application within the domain of the large quantity surveying practice is increasing, the extent of its growth and application is inconsistent. Also, the application of value management within the domain of the smaller quantity surveying practice appears to be at a very low level. This may be due to several reasons including:

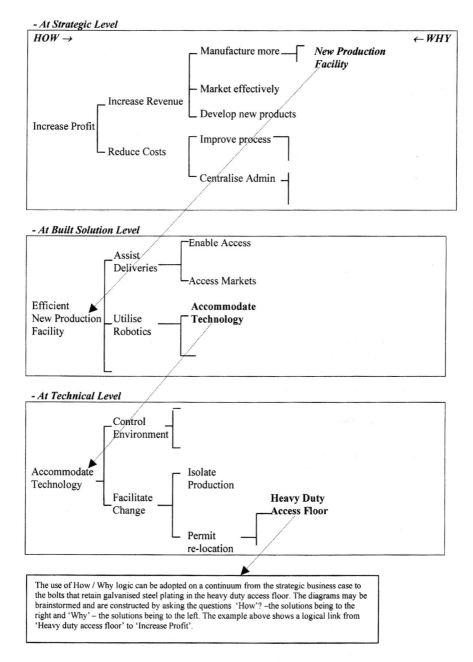

- At Strategic Level

HOW →   ← *WHY*

Increase Profit
- Increase Revenue
  - Manufacture more — **New Production Facility**
  - Market effectively
  - Develop new products
- Reduce Costs
  - Improve process
  - Centralise Admin

- At Built Solution Level

Efficient New Production Facility
- Assist Deliveries
  - Enable Access
  - Access Markets
- Utilise Robotics — **Accommodate Technology**

- At Technical Level

Accommodate Technology
- Control Environment
- Facilitate Change
  - Isolate Production
  - Permit re-location — **Heavy Duty Access Floor**

The use of How / Why logic can be adopted on a continuum from the strategic business case to the bolts that retain galvanised steel plating in the heavy duty access floor. The diagrams may be brainstormed and are constructed by asking the questions 'How'? –the solutions being to the right and 'Why' – the solutions being to the left. The example above shows a logical link from 'Heavy duty access floor' to 'Increase Profit'.

Fig. 8.5 The use of HOW/WHY logic and inter-relationships at varying levels of indenture (*Source:* Ashworth and Hogg 2000).

- There is insufficient time to carry it out
- Clients are unwilling to pay for the service
- Clients do not request the service
- The quantity surveyor provides the service already
- Value management skills are unavailable
- There is resistance from design consultants.

Research into the factors inhibiting the use of value management within the quantity surveying domain (Hogg 2000) indicates that practitioners who have had no previous involvement with value management consider each of the stated possible barriers to its use more highly than practitioners who have had direct value management experience. This may be the result of exposure to value management; however it could also indicate an existent negative view, prior to direct experience, that inhibits its application in practice.

If a major reason for the low use of value management is that clients do not request it, the reasons for this could include:

- It is likely that many clients may be unaware of value management, particularly those that are smaller and/or more occasional. It appears that many practitioners, both with and without value management experience, believe that the quantity surveyor already provides the value management function as part of the quantity surveying role. If quantity surveyors believe this, they may communicate it to clients, not by direct reference but by the exclusion of value management from services offered.
- Clients may not think the service warrants an extra fee. If this is the case then surely clients are failing to fully understand the cost/benefit trade-off – which can be expected to show a high return for any value management costs. It could also be that some clients expect that such a high value service should be part of the standard design team remit.

Within the design team, it is reasonable to believe that the quantity surveyor is in a position of great influence with regard to the implementation of value management. This is in some way demonstrated by the inconsistent growth and application of value management within the quantity surveying domain, which suggests that its use is influenced by advice from specific quantity surveying consultants.

Value management can add great value to a project and the quantity surveyor should appreciate the full nature of the process and provide opportunity for its application in practice.

Professional development and accreditation

There are several value management societies in various parts of the world that aim to assist value managers by promoting, developing and controlling standards of practice and qualifications. The Institute of Value Management in the UK has introduced a programme of formal training which provides practising and prospective value managers with the opportunity to obtain a recognised education and comprehensive training, resulting in a UK qualification.

Bibliography

Ashworth A. and Hogg K. I. *Added Value in Design and Construction.* Pearson Education. 2000.

Green S.D. *A SMART methodology for value management.* The Chartered Institute of Building, Occasional Paper No 53. 1992.

HM Treasury. *Procurement Guidance No. 2: Value for money in Construction Procurement.* The Stationery Office. 1996.

HM Treasury. *Central Unit on Procurement Guidance Note No. 54 Value management.* The Stationery Office. 1996.

Hogg K.I. *Value management; a failing opportunity?* RICS COBRA Conference Proceedings. 1999.

Hogg K.I. *Factors inhibiting the expansion of value methodology in the UK construction sector.* Society of American Value Engineers. 2000.

Kelly J.R. and Male S.P. *A study of Value management and Quantity Surveying Practice.* Surveyors Publications. 1988.

Kelly J.R. and Male S.P. *A critique of value management in construction.* CIB W55, Sydney. 1990.

Kelly J.R. and Male S.P. *The Practice of Value Management: Enhancing Value or Cutting Cost.* RICS. 1991.

Kelly J.R. and Male S. *Value Management in Design and Construction: The economic management of projects.* E & F N Spon. 1993.

Latham Sir M. *Constructing the Team.* The Stationery Office. 1994.

Male S.P., Kelly J.R., Fernie S., Grönqvist M. and Bowles G. *Value Management – The value management benchmark: A good practice framework for clients and practitioners.* Thomas Telford. 1998.

Miles L.D. *Techniques for Value Analysis and Engineering.* McGraw-Hill. 1972.

Norton B.R. and McElligott W.C. *Value Management in Construction – A Practical Guide.* Macmillan. 1995.

RICS. *Improving Value for Money in Construction: Guidance for Chartered Surveyors and Clients.* RICS. 1995.

9 Risk Management

Introduction

Risk management is a practice that many of us use on a regular basis. As an example, consider briefly our possible concerns and preparations relating to the purchase of a secondhand car, seen by many to be a risky investment. The level of risk involved will be relative to our incomes, the cost of the car, the characteristics of the seller of the car and so forth.

The major concerns and actions we take may include:

- Risk of false ownership? We may request a formal search to verify ownership.
- Risk of latent mechanical failure? In the first instance, we will probably examine the car thoroughly, perhaps with the assistance of an expert. We may also obtain some form of warranty against such failure.
- Risk of tampering with the stated mileage? We may invite a friend with a good knowledge of car mechanics or a professional advisor to inspect for signs of inconsistent wear and tear.

This example demonstrates the principles that we apply instinctively at a personal level. Whilst this level of risk consideration may be appropriate at an individual level, the importance of active risk management in construction demands greater attention. The complexity and scale of most building projects is such that good risk management in the construction industry requires more than purely common sense and instinct.

Construction projects are full of risks and include those that may relate to external commercial factors, design, construction and operation. The principles outlined in this chapter can, in the main, be transferred to any stage of a project development, although in this text we have largely focused upon risk management in the context of the construction phase.

An increasing number of companies, professional organisations, academics and risk management practitioners advocate the benefits of risk management, and the promotion of the practice at a high level continues. The success of risk management is supported by the growing list of clients using it within the UK, a list that contains many major organisations. Risk management is understood to be an important factor that is critical to the success of projects in providing a method with which to improve value for money in construction. It is therefore of great interest to the quantity surveying practitioner, in private practice or in contracting, in that it provides an opportunity of contributing further to the 'added value' service they provide.

When should surveyors use risk management?

Risk management is seen as a major element of project management and therefore it could be argued that this chapter belongs within that domain. However, most experienced surveyors will recognise that in many projects, perhaps most, the responsibility for project management is rather unclear. In some situations, a dedicated project manager will be appointed (frequently with a quantity surveying background), whilst in most projects the role is performed by a member of the design team, typically the project architect, or is informally shared by several of the client's consultants. Irrespective of the prescribed roles and responsibilities, the leadership and management of projects is often a natural consequence of the abilities, experience and personalities of the individual project team members. The quantity surveyor is well placed and possibly the most suited and motivated toward the management of risk amongst all client advisors. It should therefore be a service that can be provided at varying levels. The absence of a dedicated project manager should not mean the absence of risk management, although in practice this seems to be the case.

The scale of risk management applied to projects will vary in accordance with needs. In most situations, complex risk analysis is likely to be both unnecessary and impractical. A great deal can be achieved without major fee implications and therefore quantity surveyors should give careful consideration to the provision of a risk management service. Clients will benefit and professional reputations will escalate. In the most basic form, and dependent upon project size and complexity, great benefit will come from a half day workshop during which risks can be identified and analysed and management response determined. The technical skills required at this level are not great; the most important aspect is ability to communicate and understand the context and demands of the project.

The construction industry has a poor reputation that is due, in the main, to its perceived inability to meet the needs of clients in achieving project completion dates, completing projects within budget and providing a high quality product. The frequency of the failure of projects to meet the expectations of clients in terms of one or all of these factors is a long-term and continuing cause for concern within the industry. The application of risk analysis and management provides a means of improving this situation. Risk management provides the opportunity to control the occurrence and impact of risk factors and provides clients with better information upon which to make decisions.

An indication of the range of risk management opportunity within the domain of the quantity surveyor is outlined below.

To assist in the cost management process

One area of perceived weakness in the service provided by the quantity surveyor is in the calculation of the contingency amount. In practice, the methods of determination of an appropriate contingency provision generally appear to be very crude, including the use of a standardised percentage addition to the estimated contract sum. It is apparent that in many situations, the contingency fund, which is intended to be an all-inclusive risk provision, is ill considered. For example, at tender stage for a project with an estimated cost of £15 million, the consultant quantity surveyor may include a contingency sum of £150 000, perhaps with the general agreement of the client and architect, but generally on the basis of 'usual' practice, possibly accommodating some vague notion of the uniqueness of project circumstances.

The frequency and level to which the contingency provision is seen to be an inadequate device with which to protect clients against risk is such that many clients are likely to be dissatisfied at project outturn costs and may be critical of the level of cost advice provided by the quantity surveyor. This is irrespective of the likelihood that in situations, clients themselves may be responsible for varying amounts of the additional costs. It is, of course, not only under-provision that is a concern. It is also possible that in some situations, due to an unwarranted contingency allowance, tendered project costs may be considered to be in excess of the client's budget resulting in unnecessary and costly post-tender remedial action.

Since the contingency allowance is seemingly the only consideration given to risk in many projects, the application of aspects of risk analysis could be used to greatly improve its accuracy. This view is supported by research by Mak et al. (1998) which found that '...the use of the ERA [estimating using risk analysis] approach has improved the overall estimating accuracy in determining contingency amounts...'.

Risk analysis skills appear to exist within quantity surveying organisations, although in practice they are rarely used. There is good opportunity for the practising quantity surveyor to utilise these skills for the benefit of clients and for professional credibility. If clients, in challenging the reasons for cost overruns, are advised that they were due to unforeseen events for which the contingency provision has proved inadequate, are they entitled to ask how the contingency premium was calculated? This seems a reasonable request of professional quantity surveyors; unfortunately in many situations the anticipated response is likely to be less reasonable.

The benefits that risk analysis may bring to the cost management process are not restricted to the client. Contractors, particularly in light of current procurement trends, are well used to dealing with more than construction risk, including that relating to design. Contingency provision should therefore be a key concern to contracting organisations, and methods of calculation should reflect professionalism rather than pure instinct, although commercial pressures demand a different perspective.

To assist in the decision-making process

Generally when we give cost advice to clients, the one thing that we are usually sure of is that our advice is not given with certainty. At feasibility stage, when we advise a client that a project will cost £5 000 000, this is given as an approximation. As consultants, our estimates are given on the basis of a forecast of a yet unknown party's forecast of costs (the contractors) usually in an uncertain timescale and with uncertain design information. It is therefore common practice to provide range estimates, e.g. £4 800 000 to £5 200 000, and to bring our uncertainty to the client's attention. Nevertheless, the decision to progress with a project will be made upon the basis of this information and will require interpretation by the client. Simulation, discussed in detail later in this chapter, is a technique which provides clients with a much more comprehensive view of project risk. A probabilistic cost forecast provides an open view on outturn cost likelihood and reduces the relative vagueness associated with traditional single point estimating. Although this may be regarded as a tool that would normally be restricted to dedicated project management, the quantity surveyor should understand its application and benefits.

To assist in bidding for construction work

The use of intuition in accommodating risk when bidding for construction work is prevalent amongst building contractors. This approach may be seen as the only practical way of winning work since, in the face of competition, the need to obtain work will ultimately be the major factor in determining price. This intuitive approach may be one cause of the high failure rate of contractors to achieve an acceptable profit that in extreme cases leads to business failure. It seems reasonable to assume that the intuition of contractors will be influenced by market conditions. Irrespective of this, a more rigorous approach to project risk would be beneficial in providing a clearer picture of project demands. This in turn would facilitate a more effective risk response.

The discussions above relate to cost risks; however, contractors are frequently faced with schedule risks. If liquidated and ascertained damages for late completion are set at say £50 000 per day, the risk to a contractor of late completion is very large. The risk management process can be used to assist in establishing a fuller understanding of the risks and can provide a means of improving their management.

Recent trends in construction procurement frequently interfere with the traditional risk balance. The progress of the Private Finance Initiative (PFI) is one such example whereby the contracting organisation may find itself as both promoter, either solely or jointly, and contractor in the same scheme. In such situations, the contractor is faced with a different risk outlook than traditionally encountered.

The application of risk management

In principle, risk management is a straightforward process in that it requires the evaluation of risk and the execution of a risk management strategy. The assessment of risk first entails risk identification, followed by the analysis of risks identified. This imparts a level of understanding that is needed to facilitate the adoption of a suitable risk management response.

Risk identification

The customary method of carrying out a risk analysis is by utilising a workshop at which participants 'brainstorm' recommended risks that they consider could have an impact upon a project. The workshop forum, which brings together specialists from a variety of relevant disciplines, promotes a wide project viewpoint, which, if managed well, will lead to meaningful debate and communication. This should be considered as an exercise that is beneficial in itself. Brainstorming activity is not the only approach to risk identification. Historical data may be used, possibly using the experience of the participants' records, formal or otherwise. Also, the use of checklists may assist in providing structure to the thought processes used. An indicative example of such a checklist is provided in Fig. 9.1.

A checklist such as the one shown in Fig. 9.1 will be useful in directing attention to predetermined and recognised categories of risk and thus assisting with the identification of those which are project specific. The examples of categories given will incorporate a large range of risks; some categories in particular are wide in their potential scope. There is some danger with checklists that their use may limit deliberation to those categories contained in the list and it should be borne in mind that this could result in ruling out some major and possibly significant items.

The success of the risk identification process will depend on several factors including the level of experience and ability of the personnel concerned with the workshop, the amount of data readily available, the skill and experience of the analyst/facilitator, the time available and the timing of the workshop. It is important to realise that the process of risk identification is not likely to result in the discovery of all possible risks. This is not a practical objective.

When identifying risks, it is important to appreciate exactly what we are trying to establish. To facilitate the process of risk analysis and risk management, it is necessary to think about the possible sources of the risk, not merely the risk event. For example, if we consider the scenario of a basement excavation, one risk event could be that of the collapse of an adjacent road during the course of excavations. To allow proper risk analysis and risk management, the sources of this risk event should be understood. In this case, these may include inadequate direction of the workforce, accidental damage to an existing retaining wall, inadequate shoring design, inadequate shoring construction, or vandalism – all of which may be independently assessed and

Risk category	Indicative examples
Physical	Collapse of sides of trench excavations, surrounding infrastructure or striking existing services resulting in delays, additional cost and possible injury
Disputes	Disruption to a third party's business due to noise, dust, restricted access or construction traffic resulting in reduced sales, financial loss and possible litigation
Price	Increased inflationary pressures causing a severe increase in building costs and excessive financial loss; at present not a problem but consider 1970s and overseas
Payment	Delay in the payment by the main contractor to nominated subcontractors causing a reduction in works progress and resultant programme delays
Supervision	Delays in the issue of drawings or instructions by the architect resulting in abortive work, delays, additional costs and contractual claims from the contractor
Materials	Non-availability of matching materials required in a refurbishment project resulting in possible redesign, programme delay and additional expense
Labour	Non-availability of labour due to the construction of another nearby major project which causes a regional shortage of specialist sub-contractors
Design	Errors in the design due to lack of communications between structural engineers and architect resulting in abortive work, or possibly building failure

Fig. 9.1 Checklist of risk categories.

managed in some detail. Fig. 9.2 provides a summary of the existing risks and outlines possible considerations and actions with the assumption that this risk belongs entirely to the contractor.

Risk analysis

To begin with, it is important to be aware that problems in construction do not restrict themselves to cost, although in due course all problems may have a cost effect. In numerous situations, time or schedule risk is of more significance than pure cost and, in some cases, quality may be the most important priority. Therefore, it is essential that risk analysis addresses the needs of a given situation and centres upon applicable areas of concern.

There is a range of risk analysis tools that may be used to evaluate the identified risks. The choice of the most appropriate approach will depend on

Collapse of adjacent road during excavations		
Identified sources	Considerations	Possible actions
Inadequate direction of the workforce/ Accidental damage to existing retaining wall/ Inadequate shoring construction	All of these items more or less relate to one source, that of direction of the workforce, although each will require separate consideration. Potential high impact (in terms of time, cost and personal injury). Implications of Statutory Health and Safety transgression. Insurance?	Enforce quality control procedures. Allocate a reliable supervisor to the task. If subcontracted out, ensure the reliability and good standing of the subcontractor and that risk adequately transferred. Verify insurance provisions for such occurrences. Verify arrangements with municipal engineers as to condition of existing road, location of drains etc
Vandalism	Potential high impact as above, also inner city location suggests above average likelihood.	Strictly enforce health and safety procedures including proper protection of the site and the works. Verify insurance provisions for such occurrences
Inadequate shoring design	As above. The appointment of experienced engineers should reduce the likelihood.	Transfer the risk relating to the design of the temporary works, by appointing external consultants. Verify insurance provision.

Fig. 9.2   Scenario of a construction project – basement excavations to residential development.

project size, type and opportunity. Examples of some of the approaches, which may be categorised as qualitative, semi-quantitative and quantitative, are as follows.

The risk management workshop

The benefits of the risk management workshop have been highlighted earlier in this chapter. Without reference to any particular analysis technique, possibly the most simple and most effective aspect of risk analysis is the appraisal of risk that is possible during the course of structured workshop discussions. Workshops offer the means whereby risks may be identified, assessed and attended to; great advantage may be obtained without any element of more complex and demanding quantitative assessment.

Probability/impact tables (a 'semi-quantitative' approach)

One uncomplicated method of assessing risk is by the use of probability impact tables (P/I Tables). This simple process involves the weighting of a qualitative assessment and hence is termed 'semi-quantitative' analysis. An example of a P/I table – indicating the consideration of risks relating to a possible schedule delay – is shown in Fig. 9.3.

	Impact						1. Existing road collapse
	Very low	Low	Medium	High	Very high		2. Cut through gas mains
Probability							3. Cut through power supply
							4. Labour dispute
							5. Excavation equipment breakdown
Very high		5	9				6. Delay in piling rig delivery
High			8				7. Collapse of large sewer
Medium		2, 3	6				8. Delay due to vandals
Low				7, 10	1		9. Delays due to hard rock
Very low				4			10. Planning delays

Fig. 9.3 P/I table showing indicative consideration of schedule risk relating to the basement excavations outlined above.

To make the use of P/I tables more worthwhile a definition of the descriptors used in the table is required, for example, 'very high probability' equates to more than, say, a 75% chance of occurrence. It is clear that this technique should be designed and applied to meet the circumstances of specific project requirements. The example above, which examines aspects affecting time, may also be adapted and utilised to assess risks affecting cost and quality. Use of this simple technique permits risks to be positioned in terms of severity and therefore allows the management team to be more purposeful and focused upon the most significant issues. There is a need to concentrate upon those risks that have a high impact if they arise and have a high chance of occurrence. It is both inefficient and impossible to spend time on all risks, and matters that are inconsequential or of an extremely low incidence should be put to one side.

The case study example in Fig. 9.4 for a proposed lecture theatre shows the output from a combined value management/risk management workshop held in late 2000, relating to a short session focusing on project risk. Several key stakeholders, and the designated contractor and his designers, attended the workshop. The summary shows the identified risks, their evaluation in terms of simple P/I criteria and an outline response. Although the time allocated to the exercise was brief, it served a useful function in bringing to the fore several key issues in terms of both design and programming matters. It is important to appreciate that this is a summary; the workshop discussions allowed a wide range of views and concerns to be aired and resolved.

Nr	Risk	Evaluation		Response
		Prob.	Imp.	
1	Noise from roof	M	VHi	Client/contractor research. Client to request satisfactory design and back-up information from contractor
2	Climbing on roof	Hi	VHi	Eliminate by design. Client to request contractor to design this risk out
3	Lecture theatres too small	Lo/M	Hi	Client research; confirmation of additional seats required/provided following incorporation of VM proposals. Client to request details of cost implications from contractor
4	Exceed delivery time (in terms of academic programme 2002)	Lo	Lo	Client review. If deadline 2002 October, risk low; however, uncertainty exists re funding
5	Is this the wrong building?	Lo/M	Hi	Because of faculty requirements/split, no alternative
6	An uncomfortably cold building if emergency exit used as circulation	Hi	VHi	Research by contractor. Client to request satisfactory design and back-up information from contractor
7	Budget compromises client satisfaction	Hi	Hi	Client/contractor review. PR/ communication to be used to avoid dissatisfaction
8	Technology outstrips need for teaching	VLo	VLo	No action
9	Lack of user focus	Lo	VHi	No action
10	Future use/ uncertainty	VLo	VLo	No action
11	Savings/income generation not met	Hi	Hi	Client considers targets to be realistic, therefore no action. Risk may be reduced by internal review
12	Planning	VHi	Hi	Client reduce/contractor review. No contract or physical activity until planning permission obtained. Building location may change. Client to monitor this carefully and to review when further details known. A change in position may jeopardise client satisfaction.
13	Advice re incoming services	VLo	Hi	Client to eliminate by order of substation. Survey has reduced risks of problems associated with existing services.
14	Cost uncertainty (if back to square 1)	M	M	Client/contractor review. Budget must be maintained.

Contd

Nr	Risk	Evaluation		Response
15	Duration of tender	Hi	M	Client/contractor reduce. Several doubts exist re legal situation with contractor. Client to promptly clarify
16	Uncertainty re client's detail design	M	Hi	Client to resolve subsequent to outcome of VM study
17	Lack of funds to complete			Not discussed. See 15
18	Risks from noise (e.g. exams) .	Lo	M	Client/contractor review. Client accepts. Previously not a problem. No further action.
19	Subjective image	VHi	VLo	Client reduce by PR
20	Doubtful conference suitability	Hi	M	Client review. Considered not to be in doubt, provided adequate rain shelter provided
21	Under utilisation	Lo	Lo	Client accepts. No action
22	Programme			Previously discussed
23	Funding availability	VLo	VHi	Client review and monitor requirements of funding council and eliminate by compliance
24	Iterative design cost			Previously discussed. Reduce risks by obtaining fee quote for new design. NB. Not all VM outcomes are new designs, e.g. info/development re acoustics
25	Contractual disputes	Lo	VHi	Client/contractor review. Client to reduce by attention to contractual aspects, e.g. duration of tender
26	Lack of staff 'buy-in'	VHi	Lo	Client PR
27	Lack of faculty involvement and user 'buy-in'	VHi	Lo	See 26
28	Access to site/ designers' limitations	Lo	Lo	Considered low risk. No action
29	Lack of power back-up	Lo	Hi	Client accepts. Risks reduced by performance monitoring. Subdivision of boards to be considered by client to reduce risk
30	Unacceptable interior quality	Lo	Hi	Client accepts. PR as previous. Validity of design for conferences to be confirmed by client

Fig. 9.4 Example summary of risk evaluation and outline response – proposed lecture theatre.

Risk registers

As part of the approach to risk analysis, a list of identified risks may be produced and expanded to contain important information relating to each item. This database may be used as a management tool and will normally include key details of each identified risk with possible reference to:

- Description of the risk
- The predicted probability and impact
- 'P/I ranking' of the risk
- Identification of the owner of the risk
- Details of the strategy to be adopted to control both impact and probability
- Contingency provision
- An action window which identifies the period in the project when the risk may prevail.

The risk register acts as a control document and assists as a means of monitoring the management of risks throughout a project. For example, an identified risk in a refurbishment project may be the need to eradicate dry rot, which at the time of project design is not evident. Since, based on previous experience, the probability of its occurrence in the building is deemed high, and the potential impact large, as a precaution a contingency allowance is made for timber treatment throughout the building. In addition, the client's consultants include a contingency provision to allow for the replacement of timbers and additional work to the structure, where found necessary. The time that this possible expenditure would occur, if required, would be between month 3 and 4 of the contract. These and other details are retained in a risk register. At the closure of the 'action window', i.e. at the end of month 4, no dry rot had been found. At this stage, all areas of the building have been fully exposed and inspections carried out. No additional works are found necessary. This situation allowed the release of the contingency allowance, and the removal of this item from the monitoring process.

In addition, risk registers may be used as a reference tool for future project evaluation, with many of the included risks being relatively common in occurrence and very similar in content in most project situations.

Expected monetary value (EMV)

One method of bringing probability and impact together is by the use of the expected monetary value (EMV) technique. With this approach, possible outcomes are weighted by the expected probability of each occurring and combined to produce an aggregate result.

This approach can be used in several areas, for example, to produce an overall project outcome by application to independent elemental costs, or to calculate a sensitive rate in production of a tender. The EMV approach is demonstrated in Fig. 9.5, along with the limitations and dangers of its use.

Example: Earthworks Sub-Contract

An earthworks subcontractor is preparing a bid for a large infrastructure project that incorporates 20 000 m^3 of excavation. The subcontractor's estimator is aware that there is a range of possible ground/weather conditions which will influence productivity. From previous experience and records of past projects, the estimator is able to broadly categorise four different types of working condition that may exist during the summer months, each type carrying a different cost of excavation and removal:

Very dry/hard	£3.00/m^3
Dry/firm	£2.50/m^3
Wet	£3.50/m^3
Very wet	£4.50/m^3

The question to be answered is – Which rate is applicable?

Previous records show that in the past 10 years the ground was very dry for 15% of the time, dry for 25% of the time, wet for 40% of the time and very wet for 20% of the time.

Using an expected monetary value (EMV) approach, the following calculation was used to produce a composite rate:

£3.00 * 0.15	=	£0.45
£2.50 * 0.25	=	£0.63
£3.50 * 0.40	=	£1.40
£4.50 * 0.20	=	£0.90
EMV	=	**£3.38**

With this more analytical approach, the contractor may choose to use the EMV, i.e. £3.38, resulting in the following tender (excluding all other components such as profit etc.)

Tender: 20 000 m^3 @ £3.38 = £67 600

Unfortunately, the real world is not quite so simple. For example, what happens in the event that the ground is permanently wet?

Cost: 20 000 m^3 @ £4.50 = £90 000

A heavy loss of £22 400!

Is the contractor prepared to take this risk? This is likely to depend on several factors (see section 'Willingness to accept a risk' later in the chapter). If the contractor is a major national organisation able to withstand this level of loss and, at the same time, spread the risk across many projects, then perhaps so. However, if the contractor is a small regional organisation, unable to suffer the consequences of a very wet site for the duration of the project, then perhaps not.

This example illustrates the dangers of prescribing the outcome of a purely mathematical approach to risk.

Fig. 9.5 Expected monetary value.

Simulation: (quantitative risk analysis)

On most construction projects, it is likely that quantitative risk analysis is neither sensible nor needed due to the relative payback from the extra time and know-how required to complete such an appraisal. Simulation does however present a powerful and important method that may be appropriate to large and complex projects.

Construction is a complicated process involving a broad range of activities, each of which may go wrong during the course of a building project. As far as cost risk is concerned, Fig. 9.6 shows notional costs for a hypothetical project, which, for reasons of simplicity, has been reduced to four elements.

	Least cost (a)	Most likely (b)	Highest cost (c)
Substructures	150 000	170 000	245 000
External walls	325 000	335 000	345 000
Roof	185 000	195 000	240 000
External works	155 000	215 000	235 000
Totals	815 000	915 000	1 065 000

Fig. 9.6   Cost model showing a minimum, maximum and most likely cost (*Source:* Ashworth and Hogg 2000).

The costs shown in Fig. 9.6 have been produced following a workshop carried out in the early stages of a project's development. Discussions relating to the substructure element may have been recorded something like this:

...3.0   Substructure: The QS has produced a budget estimate amounting to £170 000. This includes the provision of £20 000 for excavation in bad ground (say hard rock removal). The architect advised that in a project constructed earlier in the year, on an adjacent site, no rock was encountered. The engineers agree with the architect that rock is unlikely, but are concerned that some piling may be required. No data from site investigations is available at present. The budget prepared by the QS is accepted as a reasonable provision for the substructures; however, a minimum cost and maximum cost are also identified.

Similar considerations have been made concerning each of the elements shown. A question to consider now is, 'Does the client have adequate finances to build the project?' Since this may depend on the amounts selected, which costs do we use? A negative client or client advisor may select the worst case scenario in each element resulting in a predicted total cost of £1 065 000. Whilst this approach to risk may be understandable in exceptional circumstances (where a 'fail safe' position is required), it is not in most construction projects. In the example used, there may be a 10%

chance of the worst case in each element. The chances of each occurring simultaneously are thus $0.1 \times 0.1 \times 0.1 \times 0.1$ with a consequential probability of 0.0001 (i.e. 10 000:1).

Further consideration of the above cost model will reveal other weaknesses: there is an unmanageable range of 'what-if' scenarios; the values given are discrete (i.e. 'in between' values are not accommodated – the model does not allow a substructure cost of £160 000); no allowance is made for the fact that the minimum and maximum values are distinctly less probable than the 'most likely' value.

Simulation allows us to model each element in terms of cost likelihood (costs being used in the example but this can be applied to schedule risk also). It allows for continuous values (as opposed to discrete) and accounts for the possibility of each value by using probability density.

Figure 9.7 shows triangular probability density distributions representing each of the four elements considered, where probability (P) is on the vertical axis and minimum cost (a), most likely cost (b) maximum cost (c) are on the horizontal axis (Ashworth and Hogg 2000).

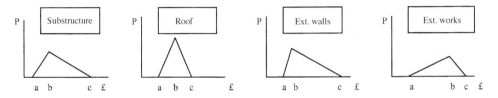

Fig. 9.7 Indicative probability distributions of the elements contained in the cost model (*Source:* Ashworth and Hogg 2000).

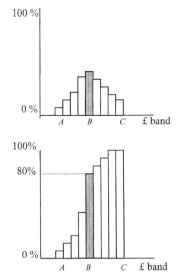

In this format, the **relative probability distribution** allows decision takers to see:
- that estimate 'B', although most likely, is unlikely to be exactly achieved
- the likelihood of occurrence of each cost band
- the minimum cost band 'A' and maximum cost band 'C'
- a 'risk profile' of project cost.

In this format, the **cumulative probability distribution** allows decision takers to see:
- that approximately 80% of the iterations produced a total cost estimate of value 'B' or less, which may be considered an acceptable degree of risk by a client (of a total of 500 randomly generated iterations, 400 resulted in a cost of 'B' or less).

Fig. 9.8 An illustration of output from a simulation exercise (*Source:* Ashworth and Hogg 2000).

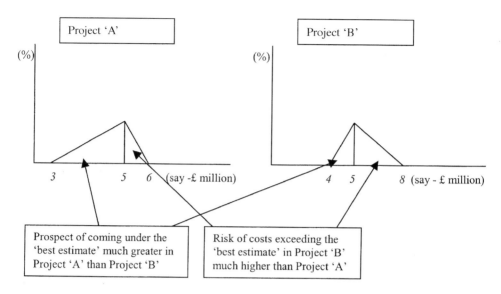

Fig. 9.9   Comparative simulation outputs (*Source:* Ashworth and Hogg 2000).

Following the construction of the elemental cost models in the form of probability density distributions, simulation software is used to randomly select elemental values that are collected to generate an estimate of total project costs. This exercise or iteration is repeated many times to produce, say, 500 estimates. Since, in each iteration, the selection of values is dependent upon each elemental probability density distribution, most of the elemental values will be selected about point 'b'. The frequency at which total project estimates will comprise elemental estimates tending toward values 'a' or 'c' is very low and the likelihood of an estimate being produced from the sum of four minimum elemental costs (point 'a') or four maximum elemental costs (point 'b') is mathematically unlikely. The output of the simulation exercise can be presented as a relative or cumulative probability distribution (Fig. 9.8). This information provides decision takers with a much clearer picture of the risks involved than by the provision of a single point estimate (Ashworth and Hogg 2000).

Information in this form allows clients and client advisors to see a full picture of possible project outcomes and therefore assists in decision-making. To illustrate the significance of this, consider below the relative probability distributions of two projects that have been generated from a simulation exercise (Fig. 9.9). Both have similar 'most likely costs' (i.e. £5 million, which in normal conditions one would assume would be the basis of project estimates traditionally reported to clients) but the risk profile of project 'B' is considerably less attractive than project 'A' (Ashworth and Hogg 2000).

Risk management

Following the identification and evaluation of the risk, the way in which the risks should be managed needs to be determined. The successful management of risk requires:

- Focus upon the most significant risks
- Consideration of the various *risk management options*
- An understanding of effective *risk allocation*
- An appreciation of the factors which may have an impact on a party's *willingness to accept risk*
- An appreciation of the *response* of a party if and when a risk happens.

Focus upon the most significant risks

Methods of deciding on the most important risks in a project have been outlined above. Whilst there are doubts about the need to artificially restrict the number of risks to be actively managed, it will be clearly advantageous to give attention to those risks which are considered to be high impact/high probability.

Risk management options

There are only a small number of risk management options available for consideration, which is helpful in simplifying the process. These may be categorised as follows:

- A risk can be *shrunk* or reduced by, for example, establishing more and better information about an unknown situation
- A risk can be *accepted* by a party as unavoidable and any alternative strategy may be considered as being inefficient or impossible to adopt
- A risk may be *distributed* to another party, for example, contractors usually distribute construction risk by selecting reputable subcontractors to carry out the work
- A risk may be *eliminated* by the rejection of a project or by the rejection of a particular part of the proposed works.

This may be presented to highlight a convenient Mnemonic (SADE): Shrink Accept Distribute Eliminate.

In so doing, there is no order of action suggested in the consideration of the four active risk management options. However, it is reasonable to consider the potential reduction of a risk before giving thought to further, perhaps more drastic action, since the level of the new risk may influence ensuing considerations.

There are two further passive alternatives in addition to the active options outlined above. It is possible to *monitor* risks without action (i.e. 'keeping an eye on the situation') or unintentionally *accept* the risk, the natural default situation if all other risk considerations are overlooked. Both of these alternatives should be considered as a poor response and both may result in disaster, particularly the latter.

To demonstrate the effect of the above risk strategy options, consider the following project scenario:

Project: the construction of a block of residential flats in which a double basement car park is required. The flats are positioned in a busy inner city location, surrounded on all sides by main roads/buildings in occupation. The ground is known to contain a significant amount of landfill, and existing services (including large Victorian sewers, gas mains and water mains) have been vaguely identified as close to the intended works. Clearly there is an abundance of potentially major risk events in constructing the basement car park, including earthworks collapse; cutting through existing services; damage to existing buildings and roads; problems of construction due to confinement of site and bad ground.

Consider the indicative appraisal of risk management options (considered from the perspective of the client) in Fig. 9.10.

Appraisal of risk management options

It is important to recognise that when risk management action is taken, in each case (including that of the 'elimination' option) secondary risks should also be considered. These risks, which are identified in Fig. 9.10, arise as a result of the selected risk management strategy.

There seems to be an opinion held by many occupied in the construction industry that the best way to manage risk is to pass it to another party. This is prevalent throughout the construction hierarchy: clients to contractor/consultants; contractor to subcontractor. This may be in the belief that such action results in the removal of the risk, which as shown in Fig. 9.10, is not the case. It is possible to enlarge risk by distribution and this should be appreciated. This can be shown by consideration of the design and build procurement option. The key aim of this method of procurement is single point responsibility; this includes the transfer of design risk from the client (and his consultants) to the contractor. Since the design process in design and build is likely to be carried out speculatively and in a relatively short duration, it is realistic to presuppose that at the point of contractual agreement, the design will be less complete than at a similar stage with the traditional procurement option. If it is acknowledged that the design is less firm, it should also be evident that the risks relating to the design will be amplified. Thus, with design and build procurement, design risk is enlarged, not eliminated. This does not refute the existence of client advantages of this risk transfer but demonstrates the requirement to fully recognise the effects of risk allocation (Ashworth and Hogg 2000).

Risk management option	Possible action	Possible secondary risks
Shrink the risk	Obtain more accurate information about the nature of the site and location of existing services. Relocate the car park. Direct a specific construction method e.g., contiguous piling	Additional information may be inaccurate. Relocated car parking may produce additional problems. Selected construction method may cause problems to contractor resulting in additional problems
Accept the risk	Allow a contingency to cover the eventuality. Insure against the risk. (Insurance in this case is seen as the contribution to a wider contingency fund. Some may classify this as distribution)	Contingency provision is inadequate. Risk acceptance by client promotes more 'carefree' attitude by contractor resulting in more risk eventualities. Insurance provision inadequate
Distribute the risk	Pass all associated risks to the main contractor. (Frequently it would seem, the natural default)	Excessive risk premium. Contractor loss resulting in aggressive attitude (e.g. claims) or insolvency. The latter will result in significant problems to the client
Eliminate the risk	Abandon the basement car parking. (This may not be a true option without the abandonment of the total project since planners may require the facility)	Location of new car parking causes new problems. Piling (bringing new risk) is a requirement of the new substructure design since the poor ground overburden is no longer removed during basement construction

Fig. 9.10   Identified risk – earthwork collapse say (– high probability, very high impact) (*Source:* Ashworth and Hogg 2000).

Considerations in risk allocation

As previously indicated in the consideration of the active risk management options shown in the above example (Shrink, Accept, Distribute, Eliminate), the most desirable method of management appears to be by distribution to a third party with acceptance by the existing owner being the least preferred. The effective distribution of risk is a key element of risk management and is a principal objective of contracts which should be arranged – from a client's perspective – to optimise his/her exposure to risk.

When taking into consideration the allocation of risk to another party, thought should be given to the following factors:

- The ability of the party to manage the risk
- The ability of the party to bear the risk if it eventuates
- The effect that the risk allocation will have upon the motivation of the recipient
- The cost of the risk transfer.

There are many examples of inappropriate risk allocation within the construction industry that occur due to the strong desire to minimise risk exposure at all costs.

Willingness of a party to accept risk

The readiness with which a party may be prepared to accept a risk will depend on several key factors including:

- Attitude to risk; a party who is risk averse is, in essence, someone less willing to accept risk than someone risk seeking. This fundamental will also be translated into the assessment of a risk premium.
- Perception of risk; a party who has recently experienced a serious injury on a construction site is quite likely to perceive the probability of a similar occurrence on a new project more highly than someone without the experience. This viewpoint may be translated into additional risk premium.
- Ability to manage risk; theoretically, a party unable to manage a risk due to lack of resources or experience should be less willing to accept a risk than someone with the necessary expertise. In practice, however, this may not occur on the basis that, occasionally, particularly where good management is lacking, 'fools rush in where angels fear to tread'.
- Ability to bear risk; theoretically, a party unable to bear a risk due to the lack of the necessary financial back-up should be unwilling to accept.
- The need to obtain work; this factor is likely to be the most significant of all. When the construction industry is in recession, a party is more willing to accept risk as a necessary means of business survival. Alternatively, when work abounds, a full consideration of project risk can be allowed for. Risk acceptance is therefore market sensitive.

Response when a risk eventuates

If and when things ultimately go wrong, and in construction they appear to do so a great deal of the time, a contracting party who has accepted the corresponding risk will be accountable for the related losses. Whilst this is understood, it is also quite possible that the party suffering the loss will be moved toward recovery in some way. In some situations, this may be manifested in contractual claims or a decrease in the quality of construction. This reality should be accepted and the mitigation of risk should be seen as desirable irrespective of who is in possession.

Merging risk management and value management opportunity?

In several important respects, the approach to risk analysis is comparable to that of value management. It typically involves a workshop which is managed by a risk analyst/facilitator; brainstorming and other techniques which help with the decision-making process; an ordered approach; and multi-discipline involvement. This relationship is recognised by some practitioners and organisations who now combine the activities of risk and value management into one comprehensive workshop. The use of project workshops committed to the consideration of value improvement and risk management appears to offer a good opportunity for adding value to the service provided to clients. This action should not be confused with the regular activities of design team meetings.

Bibliography

Abrahamson M.W. *Risk Management*. International Construction Law Review. 1998.

Ashworth A. and Hogg K.I. *Added Value in Design and Construction*. Pearson. 2000.

Byrne P. *Risk, Uncertainty and Decision Making in Property Development*. E & F N Spon. 1996.

Chapman C.B., Ward S.C. and McDonald M. *Roles, Responsibilities and Risks in Management Contracts*. SERC Research Grant Report; University of Southampton. 1989.

Hogg K.I. and Morledge R. Risks and design and build: keeping a meaningful perspective. *Chartered Surveyor Monthly*. RICS. May 1995.

Institution of Civil Engineers and the Faculty and Institute of Actuaries. *Risk Analysis and Management for Projects (RAMP)*. Thomas Telford. 1998.

Kelly J.R. and Male S.P. *Value Management in Design and Construction: The economic management of projects*. E & F N Spon. 1993.

Latham Sir M. *Constructing the Team*. The Stationery Office. 1994.

Mak S., Wong J. and Picken D. The effect on contingency allowances of using risk analysis in capital cost estimating: a Hong Kong case study. *Construction Management and Economics*, 16. 1998.

Raftery J. *Risk Analysis in Project Management*. E & F N Spon. 1994.

RICS. *Improving Value for Money in Construction; Guidance for Chartered Surveyors and Clients*. University of Reading for RICS. 1995.

Smith N.J. (ed.) *Managing Risk in Construction Projects*. Blackwell Science. 1999.

Vose D. *Quantitative Risk Analysis: A Guide to Monte Carlo Simulation Modelling*. John Wiley & Sons. 1996.

10 Procurement

Introduction

Procurement is the process that is used to deliver construction projects. The dictionary definition states that procurement is 'acquiring or obtaining by care or effort'. Clients who have made the major decision to build are faced with the task of procuring the construction works that they require. This may be a daunting prospect, given the level of financial commitment and other risks associated with the venture, the complex nature of construction and the possible perception of the construction industry as one that frequently underperforms.

A little over 30 years ago the clients of the construction industry had only a limited choice of procurement methods available to them for commissioning a new construction project. Since then there have been several catalysts for change in procurement, such as:

- Government intervention
- Pressure groups being formed to create change for the benefit of their own members, for example, the British Property Federation
- International comparisons, particularly with the USA and Japan, and the influence of developments relating to the Single European Market
- The apparent failure of the construction industry and its associated professions to satisfy the perceived needs of its customers in the way that the work is organised
- The influence of developments in education and training
- The impact from research studies into contracting methods
- The response from industry, especially in times of recession, towards greater efficiency and profitability
- Changes in technology, particularly information technology
- The attitudes towards change and the improved procedures from the professions
- The clients' desire for single point responsibility
- The publication of headline reports: in 1994, the Latham Report, and in 1998, the Egan Report.

This has resulted in a significant shift in methods of procurement used by clients.

Procurement trends

Although traditional procurement systems are frequently used, in recent years there has been a significant shift toward alternative strategies. Figures 10.1 and 10.2 indicate the trends in procurement methods used between 1984 and 1998.

It should be borne in mind that procurement preferences are likely to be linked to the levels of construction activity and that figures for one year should not be taken out of context. Notwithstanding this cautionary note, the data in Figs 10.1 and 10.2 does show that:

Procurement method	1984 %	1985 %	1987 %	1989 %	1991 %	1993 %	1995 %	1998 %
Lump sum – firm bills of quantities (BQ)	58.7	59.3	52.1	52.3	48.3	41.6	43.7	28.4
Lump sum – spec. and drawings	13.1	10.2	17.7	10.2	7.0	8.3	12.2	10.0
Lump sum – design and build	5.1	8.0	12.2	10.9	14.8	35.7	30.1	41.4
Remeasurement; approximate BQ	6.6	5.4	3.4	3.6	2.5	4.1	2.4	1.7
Prime cost plus fixed fee	4.5	2.7	5.2	1.1	0.1	0.2	0.5	0.3
Management contract	12.0	14.4	9.4	15.0	7.9	6.2	6.9	10.4
Construction management	–	–	–	6.9	19.4	3.9	4.2	7.7
Total	100.0	100.0	100.0	100.0	100.0	100.0	100.0	100.0

Fig. 10.1   Trends in methods of procurement – by value of contracts (*Source:* Davis, Langdon and Everest 2000).

Procurement method	1984 %	1985 %	1987 %	1989 %	1991 %	1993 %	1995 %	1998 %
Lump sum – firm bills of quantities (BQ)	34.6	42.8	35.6	39.7	29.0	34.5	39.2	30.8
Lump sum – spec. and drawings	55.7	47.1	55.4	49.7	59.2	45.6	43.7	43.9
Lump sum – design and build	2.4	3.6	3.6	5.2	9.1	16.0	11.8	20.7
Remeasurement – Approximate BQ	3.2	2.7	1.9	2.9	1.5	2.3	2.1	1.9
Prime cost plus fixed fee	2.3	2.1	2.3	0.9	0.2	0.3	0.7	0.3
Management contract	1.8	1.7	1.2	1.4	0.8	0.9	1.2	1.5
Construction management	–	–	–	0.2	0.2	0.4	1.3	0.8
Total	100.0	100.0	100.0	100.0	100.0	100.0	100.0	100.0

Fig. 10.2   Trends in methods of procurement – by numbers of contracts (*Source:* Davis, Langdon and Everest 2000).

- In 1998, the use of firm bills of quantities was not the main method of procurement (by value) and the decline in this form of procurement, which appeared to have steadied during the early 1990s, continues.
- The growth of design and build procurement appears to be continuing; in 1998 it accounted for approximately 41% of contracts let by value and 21% by number. The increased use of this method of procurement since 1984 is dramatic, as is the increase between 1995 and 1998.
- The statistics relating to management contracting and construction management – 2.3% by number, 18.1% by value – reflect the use of this type of procurement in high value contracts.
- The relatively low usage of both remeasurement and prime cost contracts in 1984 (approximately 11%) has further declined and in 1998 accounted for only 2% of contracts in use by value.

General matters

The wide range of procurement systems now available, and the understanding that procurement choice may have a significant bearing on the outcome of a project, signify both the opportunity and importance of meeting the procurement challenge with a well-considered strategy. The selection of appropriate contractual arrangements for any but the simplest type of project is difficult because of the diverse range of views and opinions that are available. Much of the advice is conflicting and lacks a sound base for evaluation. Individual experiences, prejudices, vested interests and familiarity, together with the need for change and the real desire for improved systems, have all helped to reshape procurement options available to us at the commencement of the twenty-first century. The proliferation of differing procurement arrangements has resulted in an increasing demand for systematic methods of selecting the most appropriate arrangement to suit the particular needs of clients and their projects. In recent years, the amount of research and publications within the field of construction procurement has also grown, as the bibliography at the end of this chapter indicates.

Whilst the main issue is that of satisfying the client's objectives, a matter examined in detail later, at an implementation level the following are the broad issues involved.

Consultants or contractors

These issues relate to whether to appoint independent consultants for design and management or to appoint a contractor direct. The following should be considered:

- Single point responsibility
- Integration of design and construction

- Need for independent advice
- Overall costs of design and construction
- Quality, standards and time implications.

Competition or negotiation

There are a variety of different ways in which designers or constructors can secure work or commissions, such as invitation, recommendation, speculation or reputation. However, irrespective of the final contractual arrangements that are selected, the firms involved need to be appointed. Evidence generally favours some form of competition in order to secure the most advantageous arrangement for the client. There are, however, many different circumstances that might favour negotiation with a single firm or organisation. These include:

- Business relationship
- Early start on site
- Continuation contract
- State of the construction market
- Contractor specialisation
- Financial arrangements
- Geographical area.

Also, the advent, development and promotion of partnering has changed the view of some clients toward the need for competition (see later in this chapter). In determining the need for competition, it must not be assumed that the choice between that and the option of negotiation is clearly defined, as each case must be decided on its own merits.

Measurement or reimbursement

There are in essence only two ways of calculating the costs of construction work. The contractor is either paid for the work executed on some form of agreed quantities and rates or reimbursed the actual costs of construction. The following are the points to be considered between the alternatives:

- Necessity for a contract sum
- Forecast of final cost
- Incentive for efficiency
- Distribution of price risk
- Administration time and costs.

Traditional or alternative methods

Traditionally, most projects built in the twentieth century in the UK have used single-stage selective tendering as their basis for contracting. With a wider knowledge of the different practices and procedures around the world, and some dissatisfaction with this uniform approach, other methods have evolved to meet changing circumstances and aspirations of clients. The following factors should be considered (these are examined in more detail later in this chapter):

- Appropriateness of service
- Length of time from inception to completion
- Overall costs inclusive of design
- Accountability
- Importance of design, function and aesthetics
- Quality assurance
- Organisation and responsibility
- Project complexity
- Risk apportionment.

Standard forms of contract

There are a wide variety of different forms of contract in use in the construction industry. The choice of a particular form depends on a number of different circumstances, such as:

- Client objectives
- Private client or public authority
- Type of work to be undertaken
- Status of the design
- Size of proposed project
- Method used for price determination.

Local authorities use different forms of contract from central government departments, while some of the larger manufacturing companies have developed their own forms and conditions. These often place a greater risk on the contractor and this is in turn reflected in the contractor's tender prices. The different industry interests continue to develop a plethora of different forms for their own particular sectors. A trend toward greater standardisation would be welcomed. As long ago as 1964, the Banwell Report recommended the use of a single form for the whole of the construction industry as being both desirable and practicable. The message has largely gone unheeded owing to the variety of interested parties involved.

Although the general layout and contents of the various forms are similar, their details and interpretation may vary immensely. Different forms exist for main and subcontracts, for building or civil engineering works, and according to the relationship between the client, consultants and contractors. The different versions of the JCT (Joint Contracts Tribunal) forms of contract are used on the majority of building contracts.

Practice notes

The Joint Contracts Tribunal from time to time issue 'practice notes', which express their view on some particular point in practice. While due account should be taken of such opinions, they do not affect the legal interpretation of the terms of the contract and are thus not finally authoritative. They are similar to a discussion in Parliament of the interpretation of an Act.

Methods of price determination

Building and civil engineering contractors are paid for the work that they carry out on the basis of one of two methods:

- *Measurement*   The work is measured in place, i.e. in its finished quantities, and paid for on the basis of quantity multiplied by rate. Measurement may be undertaken by the client's surveyor, in which case an accurate and detailed contract document can be prepared. With this method, the risk relating to measurement is carried by the employer and that for the rate by the contractor. Alternatively, measurement may be undertaken by the contractor's surveyor or estimator, in which case it will be detailed enough only to satisfy the contractor concerned. With this situation, the risk relating to both measurement and rate is carried by the contractor.
- *Cost reimbursement*   The contractor is paid the actual costs based on the quantities of materials purchased and the time spent on the work by operatives, plus an agreed amount to cover profit. Elements of measurement contracts may be valued on the same basis by the adoption of day-works.

Measurement contracts

The alternative forms of measurement contract which may be used in the construction industry are as follows.

Drawing and specification

This is the simplest type of measurement contract and is really only suitable for small or simple project work. There has, however, in the past, been some use of this method on inappropriately large projects, often based on misconceived ideas. Each contractor measures the quantities from the drawings and specification and prices them in order to determine the tender sum. The method is thus wasteful of the contractor's estimating resources, and does not really allow for a fair comparison of tender sums. The contractor also has to accept a greater risk, since in addition to being responsible for the pricing they are also responsible for the measurements. In order to compensate for possible errors, contractors will tend to overprice the work.

Performance specification

This method results in an even more vague approach to tendering. The contractor is required to provide a price based upon the client's brief and user requirements alone. The contractor must therefore choose a method of construction and type of materials suitable for carrying out the works. The contractor is likely to select the least expensive materials and methods of construction that comply with the laid down performance standards. Some design and build contracts (see section on procurement options later in this chapter) may be based on performance specification.

Schedule of rates

In some projects it is not possible to predetermine the nature and full extent of the works. In these circumstances a schedule is provided that is similar to a bill of quantities, but without the quantities. Contractors then insert rates against these items and these will be used to calculate the price based on remeasurement. This procedure has the disadvantage of being unable to provide a contract sum, or any indication of the likely final cost of the project. On other occasions, a comprehensive schedule already priced with typical rates is used as a basis for agreement. The contractor in these circumstances adds or deducts a percentage adjustment to all the rates. This standard adjustment can be unsatisfactory for the contractor, as some of the listed rates may be high prices and others low prices.

Bill of quantities

This provides the best basis for estimating, tender comparisons and contract administration. The contractors' tenders are therefore judged on price alone as they are all using the same measurement data. This is an efficient approach to the measurement of the works, since only one party is responsible rather than each individual contractor. As a negative, this type of documentation relies on the production of working drawings before tender stage and is time consuming to prepare. It is therefore not a practical approach where time is in short supply. Also, the employer's acceptance of the risk relating to measurement and design contributes to uncertainty of final cost.

Bill of approximate quantities

In some instances it may not be possible to measure the work accurately. In this case a bill of approximate quantities would be prepared and the entire project measured upon completion. This is a useful approach where an early start on site is required; approximate bills can be measured from incomplete drawings.

Cost-reimbursement contracts

These types of contract are not favoured by many of the industry's clients as there is an absence of a tender sum and a predicted final cost. This type of contract also often provides little incentive for the contractor to control costs. It is therefore only used in special circumstances, for example:

- Emergency work projects, where time cannot be allowed for the traditional process. For example, following a fire in the departure hall of a major airport, the key priority of the client would be to ensure passengers could use the airport without disruption as quickly as possible. Any possible additional cost arising due to the nature of the contract would probably be insignificant relative to the possible loss in revenue.
- When the character and scope of the works cannot really be determined. For example, this is frequently the case with elements of measurement contracts for which the works are valued on a dayworks basis.

Cost reimbursement contracts can take several forms. The following are three of the types that may be used in the above circumstances. Each of the methods pays contractors' costs and makes an addition to cover profit. Prior to embarking on this type of contract, it is important that all the parties concerned are fully aware of the definition of contractors' costs as used in this context.

Cost plus percentage

The contractor is paid the costs of labour, materials, plant, subcontractors and overheads, and to this sum is added a percentage to cover profits. The percentage is agreed at the outset of the project. A disadvantage of this method is that the contractor's profit is related directly to expenditure. Therefore, the more time spent on the works, the greater will be the profitability. In other words, lower efficiency leads to greater profit.

Cost plus fixed fee

In this method, the contractor's profit is predetermined by agreeing a fee for the work before the commencement of the project. There is therefore a possible incentive for the contractor to attempt to control the costs, because it will increase the rate of return. However, to counter this, it is also possible that since the fee is fixed, the contractor can improve his profitability only by reducing management costs, precisely what the client is seeking. In practice, because it is difficult to predict cost accurately beforehand, it can cause disagreement between the contractor and the client's professional advisers when trying to settle the final account, if the actual cost is much higher than that which was estimated at the start of the project.

Cost plus variable fee

The use of this method requires a target fee to be set for the project prior to the signing of the contract. The contractor's fee is made up of two parts: a fixed amount and a variable amount depending on the actual cost. This method provides an even greater incentive to the contractor to control costs, but has the disadvantage of requiring the target cost to be fixed on the basis of a very rough estimate.

Contractor selection and appointment

There are essentially two ways of selecting a contractor: through competition or by negotiation. This will apply to any working arrangement, including strategic partnering, which in the first instance requires the appointment of a contractor partner. Competition may be restricted to a few selected firms or open to almost any firm that wishes to submit a tender. The contract options described later are used in conjunction with one of these methods of contractor selection.

European legislation imposes restriction on tendering arrangements for the procurement of public goods and works. Where government related expenditure is involved above a prescribed contract value, it is necessary to invite tenders from member states by advertising the project in the *Official Journal of the European Communities.* The subdivision of contracts into smaller 'projects' with the intent of falling within the threshold value is not allowed. At present, it seems that this European initiative is not having a major effect upon competition for construction work in the UK. It does, however, impact significantly on securing publicly funded projects.

The Construction Industry Board (CIB) has developed a Code of Practice for the Selection of Main Contractors. This replaces the previous Code of Tendering Procedure issued by the National Joint Consultative Committee (NJCC). This publication, although not mandatory, does provide guidance and suggested good practice on the selection of contractors and the awarding of construction contracts. With reference to the CIB document, the key principles of good practice to be adopted when appointing contractors in competition (either by single or two-stage tendering) are:

- 'clear procedures should be followed that ensure fair and transparent competition in a single round of tendering consisting of one or more stages'
- 'the tender process should ensure receipt of compliant, competitive tenders' Where contractors feel it necessary to attach conditions to tender submissions due to their inability to fully comply with the tender documents, tender evaluation becomes more complex.
- 'tender lists should be compiled systematically from a number of qualified contractors'
  As stated, it may be necessary to consider European procurement law when compiling lists of tenderers. Considerations to be made when selecting the preliminary list of firms include: the firm's financial standing and record; its recent experience of building over similar contract periods; the general experience and reputation of the firm for similar building

types; the adequacy of its management; and its capacity to undertake the project. Although in some respects, the inclusion of some tenderers may appear to be automatic due to their size and previous record, consideration should be given to regional standing, resources and reputation which may differ from the national or another regional position. Generally, with a pre-qualified list of tenderers, there should be no doubt as to the ability of any of the tenderers to satisfactorily complete the contract.

- 'tender lists should be as short as possible'
  The code is prescriptive on this matter and the recommendations are shown in Fig. 10.3 below. Whilst the rationale for this guidance is not in doubt, in practice, clients must consider the possibility of collusion and breaches in confidentiality. The risks of this are increased where the list of tenders is very small, three for example. (See section on 'Selective competition' later in this chapter.)
- 'conditions should be the same for all tenderers'
- 'confidentiality should be respected by all parties'
- 'sufficient time should be given for the preparation and evaluation of tenders'
  The code is also prescriptive on this matter and the recommendations are shown in Fig. 10.4. These times clearly depend on situation and procurement type.

(It should be noted that both the preliminary list and preliminary enquiry in Figs 10.3 and 10.4, relate to a 'first' tender list and enquiry which will be subsequently refined on receipt of details relating to willingness to tender, available capacity, relevance of skills and experience, proposed project

Contract type	Preliminary list	Tender list
	Number invited to respond	Number invited to tender
Design and construct	Maximum 6, ideally 3 or 4	Maximum 3
Construct only	Maximum 10, ideally 4–6	Maximum 6, ideally 3 or 4

Fig. 10.3 Recommended number of tenderers (*Source:* Code of Practice for the Selection of Main Contractors (CIB 1997)).

Contract type	Preliminary enquiry	Tender
	Time to return preliminary enquiry	Time to return tender
Design and construct	Minimum 3 weeks	Minimum 12 weeks
Construct only	Minimum 3 weeks	Minimum 8 weeks

Fig. 10.4 Recommended tender periods (*Source:* Code of Practice for the Selection of Main Contractors (CIB 1997)).

team, and understanding and attitude toward the project. This is not to be confused with two-stage tendering discussed later in this chapter.)

- 'sufficient information should be provided to enable the preparation of tenders'
- 'tenders should be assessed and accepted on quality as well as price'
- 'practices that avoid or discourage collusion should be followed'
- 'tender prices should not change on an unaltered scope of works'
- 'suites of contracts and standard unamended forms of contract from recognised bodies should be used where they are available'
- 'there should be a commitment to teamwork from all parties'
  This is very much the essence of the way ahead for improving the construction industry, central to the partnering approach and desired in all forms of contracting.

Selective competition

This is the traditional and most popular method of awarding construction contracts. In essence a number of firms of known reputation are selected by the project team. The guidelines outlined above should be adhered to where relevant.

Open competition

Open competition, whereby details of the project are first of all advertised in local or trade publications inviting requests for tender documents, is not an efficient practice, and in consideration of the guidelines above, is not a recommended practice. Whilst the approach allows new contractors, or those who are unknown to the project team and the client, the possibility of submitting a price, the costs of tendering are high and the process of pricing the items lengthy. Where selective tendering is adopted with a list of six tendering contractors, the law of averages indicates that tendering costs for six projects will be absorbed in one successful submission. In open competition, this waste is much greater, depending on the total number of interested contractors, and is of course borne by clients. Some very reputable contractors may not be interested in tendering in such conditions.

The use of open tendering may relieve the client of the obligation of accepting the lowest price. This is because firms are generally not vetted before the tenders are submitted. Factors other than price must therefore be taken into account when assessing tender bids. It is generally accepted that a lowest price tender will be obtained by the use of this method.

Negotiated contract

The negotiated contract method of contractor selection involves the agreement of a tender sum with a single contractor. The contractor will offer a price using the tender documentation, and the client's surveyor then reviews this in detail. The two parties then discuss the rates that are in contention, and through a negotiation process a tender acceptable to both parties can be agreed. Owing to the absence of any competition or other restriction other than the acceptability of price, this type of contract procurement is not generally considered to be cost advantageous. It can be expected to result in a tender sum that is higher than might have been obtained by using one of the previous methods, although substantiation of the order of this is difficult to assert. Because of the higher sums incurred, public accountability and the possible suggestion of favouritism, local government does not generally favour this method.

A negotiated contract should result in fewer errors in pricing. It also accommodates contractor participation during the design stage, and this may result in savings in both time and money. It should also lead to greater cooperation during the construction period between the designer and the contractor. Where an early start on site is required, it clearly offers distinct advantages to a drawn out competitive tendering approach.

Two-stage tendering

The main aim of two-stage tendering is to involve the chosen contractor on the project as early as possible. It therefore tends to succeed in getting the person who knows what to build (the architect or engineer) in touch with the firm that knows how to build it (the contractor) before the design is finalised. The contractor's expertise in construction methods can thus be used in the architect's design. A further advantage is that the selected contractor will be able to start on site sooner than would be the case with the other methods of contract procurement.

In the first instance, an appropriate contractor must be selected. This can be achieved by inviting suitable firms to price the major items of work from the project. A simplified bill of quantities is therefore required that will include the preliminary items, major items and specialist items, allowing the main contractor the opportunity of pricing for profit and attendance sums. The guidelines published by the CIB are applicable to this stage in the process.

The contractor will also be required to state their overhead and profit percentages. The prices of these items will then form the basis for subsequent price agreement that will be achieved through negotiation.

Serial tendering

Serial tendering is a development of the system of negotiating further contracts, where a firm has successfully completed a contract for work of a similar type. Initially contractors would tender against each other, possibly on a selective basis, for a single project. There is, however, a legal understanding that several other similar projects would automatically be awarded using the same bill of rates. The contractors would therefore know at the initial tender stage that they could expect to receive a number of contracts, which could provide them with continuity in their workload. As an alternative, it may be that a 'series' of projects are awarded to a contractor who successfully tenders in competition on the basis of a notional 'master' bill of quantities that will include a comprehensive range of items and will be used to price each future project in a defined series. In either situation, conditions would be written into the documents to allow further contracts to be withheld where the contractor's performance was unsatisfactory.

Serial contracts should result in lower costs to contractors since they are able to gear themselves up to such work by, for example, purchasing suitable types of plant and would generally benefit from economies through the increased total contract size. Serial contracts are appropriate to buildings such as housing and schools in the public sector. This method may also be usefully employed in the private sector in the construction of industrial units. It has been successfully used with industrialised system buildings.

This arrangement for letting contracts, although having several advantages including that of promoting a good working relationship, is not to be confused with the concept of partnering which is discussed in detail later in this chapter.

Procurement options

There are several procurement options available to the client and within each broad type there are several variants, each of which may be possibly refined to accommodate particular client needs and project specifics. For example, within a traditional arrangement, it is normal to have some of the works carried out under a cost plus or remeasurement arrangement and possible also to let a portion of the works on a design and build basis. An appreciation of the operation and application of each of the procurement options is essential to developing a sound procurement strategy.

Traditional

In this approach, the client commissions an architect to take a brief, produce designs and construction information, invite tenders and administer the project during the construction period and settle the final account. If the building owner is other than small, the architect, traditionally the first point of client contact, will advise the client to appoint consultants such as quantity surveyors, structural engineers and building services engineers. Other consultants, particularly the quantity surveyor, may also be the client's first port of call. The contractor, who has no design responsibility (unless particular portions of the work are so identified), will normally be selected by competitive tender unless there are good reasons for negotiation. The design team are independent advisers to the client and the contractor is only responsible for executing the works in accordance with the contract documents. Fig. 10.5 shows the relationship of the parties.

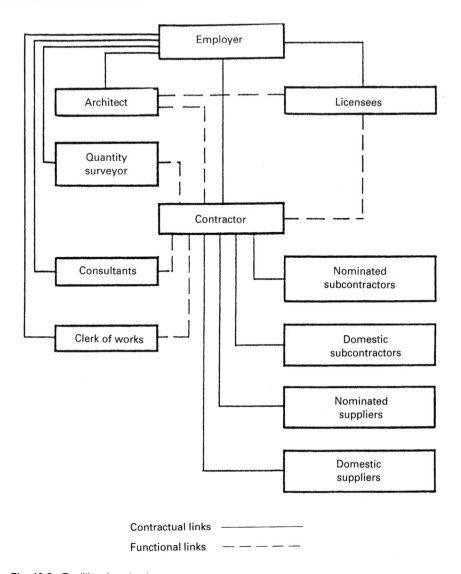

Fig. 10.5 Traditional contract.

The key feature of this form of procurement is the separation of design and construction. The client appoints a team of consultants, frequently led by the architect, to design the building and prepare tender documentation. The main advantages and disadvantages of this procurement option are as follows.

Advantages

- A high level of price certainty for the client. Since cost is known before construction commences, and providing the design process has been completed fully in the pre-contract stage, a high degree of price certainty exists.

- A low tender price.
- Accommodates design changes and aids the cost management process.
- Relatively low tender preparation costs. In addition, subject to the status of the tender documents, high tender quality.

Disadvantages

- A relatively lengthy time from inception to start on site.
- Problems relating to design error. The risk relating to the design lies with the client. Post-contract design changes are frequently abundant and resultant delays and disputes are common.
- Lack of involvement of the constructor in the design process.

Design and build

It has been suggested that the separation of the design and construction processes, which is traditional in the UK construction industry, has been responsible for a number of problems. Design and build (Fig. 10.6) can often overcome these by providing for these two separate functions within a single

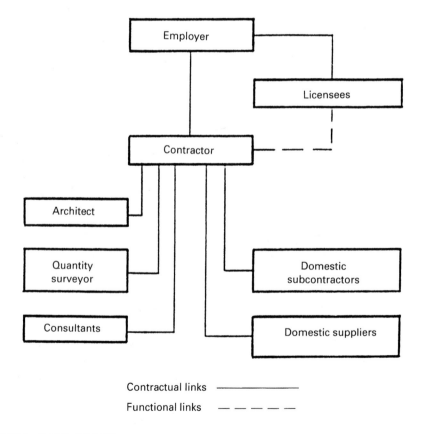

Contractual links

Functional links

Fig. 10.6   Design and build.

organisation. This single firm is generally the contractor. The client, therefore, instead of approaching an architect for a design service, chooses to go directly to the contractor. With this method of procurement, the contractor therefore accepts the risk for the design element of a project.

It is common for the client to initially appoint design consultants to develop a brief, examine feasibility and prepare tender documents that will include a set of employer's requirements. Contractors are invited to tender on the basis that they will be responsible for designing and constructing the project and will submit a bid, which will incorporate design and price information. The contractor's proposals will be examined by the client and the project subsequently let. An issue to be considered in the early stages of the project is the nature of the employer's requirements, which may vary significantly in terms of detail. Clients may need to balance their conflicting desires to both direct the design and transfer full design risk to the contractor.

Develop and construct is an approach whereby the client's consultants prepare a concept design and ask contractors to develop that design and construct the works. Frequently, the client attempts to transfer the risks associated with the early design by novation. With this approach, the client's architect and pre-contract designs are 'transferred' to the contractor who accepts the related liability as part of the contractual arrangement. This procedure is unpopular with contractors who are inclined to believe that in such situations the allegiance of the architect remains with the client.

There are several advantages and disadvantages to the use of design and build that should be considered, including the following.

Advantages

- *Single point responsibility* If problems arise during the works, the contractor is unable to place blame with the client's consultants and will be motivated toward the reduction of design problems and their mitigation when they arise.
- *Price certainty prior to construction* Provided there are no client changes, a high level of price certainty exists.
- *Reduced project duration* This is made possible due to the overlap of the design and construction phases.
- *An improved degree of buildability* This may be achieved since the contractor has a greater opportunity to influence the design, although in practice, this will depend on the level of design direction contained in the employer's requirements.
- *Fitness for purpose* The potential exists to extend design liability beyond reasonable skill and care to include fitness for purpose. Insurance difficulties re the increased design liability and the possible questionable ability of contractors to withstand the impact of a large claim in the event of failing to achieve the fitness for purpose requirement, are such that it will normally be preferable to forego this opportunity (Morledge and Sharif 1996).

Disadvantages

- *Client's reduced ability to control design*   The scale of this concern depends on the design and build approach adopted.
- *Commitment prior to full design*   In essence the client contracts to buy a building that is yet to be fully designed.
- *Difficulty in comparison of tenders*   The evaluation of the differing design alternatives contained within the contractors' proposals may add a significant complexity to the normal tender review process.
- *Cost management difficulties*   A much reduced level of price information is available to the client's surveyor, creating significant cost management problems.

Management based contracts

There are several possible variants to a management based procurement strategy. Each shares the main characteristic of the appointment of a party – usually a contractor – to manage the construction works (and in the case of design and manage, the design of the works also) in return for a lump sum or percentage fee. The scope of the management provision and methods of establishing contractual links in the construction supply chain provide differentiation between specific types. This approach to procurement is particularly suited to large, complex projects whereby it may be beneficial to reduce risk for the contractor (Murdoch and Hughes 1992).

Management contracting

Management contracting is a term used to describe a method of organising the project team and operating the construction process. The management contractor acts in a professional capacity, providing the management expertise and buildability advice required in return for a fee to cover overheads and profit. The contractor does not therefore participate in the profitability of the construction work itself and does not employ any of the labour or plant, except for the possibility of the work involved in the setting up of the site and the costs normally associated with the preliminary works. The works are let on a package basis, usually by competitive tender (although other methods of procuring individual works packages may be adopted), and contracts are between the management contractor and works contractors. Figure 10.7 shows the relationship of the parties.

Advantages

- *Early involvement of the management contractor*   Because the contractor is employed on a fee basis, the appointment can take place early during the design stage. The contractor is therefore able to provide a substantial input into the practical aspects of the building technology process.

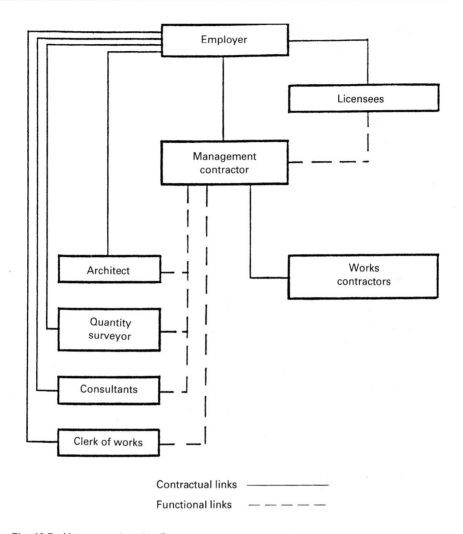

Contractual links   ——————————

Functional links   — — — — —

Fig. 10.7 Management contracting.

- *Reduced project duration* Construction work may start as soon as sufficient work has been designed.
- *Accommodates later design decisions* Some design decisions relating to work which may be sequentially at the end of the construction phase, may be deferred due to the letting of work in packages.

Disadvantages

- *Commitment prior to full design* Design is incomplete at the time of commencement and therefore aspects of price, quality and programme are uncertain when the client decides to proceed.
- *Increase in client risk* The risks relating to additional costs arising as a result of the faults of the works contractors (e.g. delays, defective work, claims from other works contractors) lies with the client.

Construction management

Construction management offers an alternative to management contracting and has been adopted on a number of large projects over recent years. Construction management shares a close similarity to management contracting; however the main difference is that the individual trade contractors are in a direct contract with the client.

The client appoints a construction manager (either consultant or contractor) with the relevant experience and management expertise. The construction manager, if appointed first, would take the responsibility for appointing the design team, who would usually also be in direct contract with the client. The construction manager is responsible for the overall control of the design team and trade contractors throughout both the design and construction stages of the project.

Because of the direct contract arrangements, additional client involvement is required and this approach is therefore not recommended for those without adequate experience and resources.

Design and manage

Design and manage is similar to management contracting in that a management contractor is paid a fee for managing the construction of the works; however, as the term may suggest, it extends the role to incorporate the management of the design of the project. The benefits and pitfalls of the system are also similar to those experienced in management contracting. The major difference relates to the additional design responsibility of the management contractor. To this extent the characteristics of this form of procurement bear similarity with design and build – the gain of single point responsibility and the loss of design control.

Contract strategy

In deciding on a contract strategy, recognition should be given to client priorities (and where possible, desires) in terms of project duration, cost and quality objectives. In order to determine an appropriate method, it is necessary to match the needs of the client with the most suitable approach available. To enable this, an understanding of both the client's objectives and the operation and relative attributes of the available procurement/contract types and methods of appointment, is required. The following points should be borne in mind.

Project size

Small schemes are not suitable for more elaborate forms of contractual arrangement. Such procedures are also unlikely to be cost effective. Small schemes will more likely use either selective or open tendering or a type of design and build. Medium to large projects are able to use the whole range of methods, with the very large schemes more advanced, and complex forms of procurement may be necessary.

Client type

Clients who regularly carry out construction work are much better informed, develop their own preferences and will not require the same level of advice as those who only build occasionally. They may, however, need to be encouraged to adopt more suitable and appropriate methods, and the quantity surveyor will need to convince such clients that the adoption of such suggestions will lead to improved procedures. Experienced clients may have a working knowledge of the construction industry, may retain the services of in-house construction advisors and will be able to contribute to the process throughout. Inexperienced clients may have unrealistic expectations and the tendency to inappropriately interfere rather than contribute.

There is a range of client types which, although each client will be unique, may be categorised by key characteristics. The categories of client that are likely to be encountered in practice include: public bodies, including local authorities, who are experienced and have a large and wide portfolio of construction needs; large commercial developers who build for profit; and large and small companies who build to improve and extend their business and are thus owner occupiers. These different client types will have different procurement needs.

The priorities of these groupings will generally differ in terms of the balance of time, cost and quality objectives, accountability and certainty of output. For example, public sector clients are likely to be driven more by the need for low cost, cost certainty and accountability than are private sector clients.

Client procurement needs

Time

Project duration or completion dates may be critical to the success of a project, and in some situations if not met could lead to total failure in meeting a client's objectives. Whilst most clients are likely to have a desire for an early building completion, it is important to distinguish between this and true need since attempting to meet the objective of early completion is likely to have consequences on other project requirements. The choice of procurement strategy can have a large impact on the duration of a construction project.

Cost

In the event that a limited capital budget is the prime consideration of the client, quality, in the form of a reduced specification, is likely to be restricted and project duration will be the optimum in terms of construction cost rather than client choice.

It is generally believed that open tendering will gain the lowest price from a contractor, although, as previously stated, this brings several possible problems and is therefore not recommended. Negotiated tendering supposedly adds about 5% to 10% to the contract sum although it is difficult to ascertain an exact premium. Projects with unusually short contract periods tend to incur some form of cost penalty. The introduction of conditions that favour the client, or the imposition of higher standards of workmanship than normal, will also push up costs.

The degree to which cost certainty is required prior to commitment to construction or at project completion, restricts procurement choice considerably. The risks associated with abortive design fees are also a factor of which clients should be aware.

Quality

The quality of a building is influenced by several factors including: the briefing process; the suitability of materials, components and systems and their interrelationships within the total design; and the quality control procedures that are in place during both design and construction. The choice of procurement strategy can affect the design process and means of control by which the client and his advisors can monitor both specification and construction activity. It should be noted that quality is a subjective issue, sometimes difficult both to define and identify; it may not necessarily mean a more complex building or a higher specification.

Accountability

Whilst organisations receiving public funding will naturally be concerned with accountability since they are subject to public scrutiny, it is often assumed that accountability is less of a concern for companies in the private sector. This assumption may be misplaced. Research carried out by Masterman in 1988 showed that 'private, experienced secondary clients, i.e. major and active manufacturers, retailers, service organisations etc...' indicated accountability as the most important criterion in ensuring project success (Masterman 1992).

Certainty of project objectives

Some forms of procurement (e.g. management contracting) incorporate an inherent facility to accommodate design development throughout a project and others are particularly unsuited to design changes (e.g. design and build).

Market conditions

The selection of the process to be used will vary with the general state of the economy and should also take into account the predicted changes to it within the project's life. When there is ample work available, contractors may be reluctant to enter what they perceive to be unsatisfactory relationships. When the market is at a low point, contractors will be more willing to accept risk, a situation which should be understood by the client for its negative effects as well as positive, since liquidations and claims are more likely to ensue in such conditions.

The relative strengths and weaknesses of the available options may be evaluated in terms of the above factors. Since each strategy will contain a differing balance of the various attributes required by clients, a prioritisation of key objectives is necessary to enable the most suitable choices to be made.

Partnering

Many of the problems that exist in construction are attributed to the barriers that exist between clients and contractors. In essence, partnering is about breaking down these barriers by establishing a working environment that is based on mutual objectives, teamwork, trust and sharing in risks and rewards.

Within the UK construction industry, partnering activity is relatively recent and has been given significant impetus by the Latham Report (1994) and the report by the Construction Task Force (1998): *Rethinking Construction (The Egan Report)*. The prominent recognition given to partnering in the late 1990s is a clear indication of the strong belief that the partnering approach can make a major contribution to improving value within the construction industry. However, it should also be recognised that significant negative opinion on the practice of partnering exists. A review of articles relating to partnering, published in 1997–1998, indicates the level of conflicting views.

Partnering relies on the principle that co-operation is a more efficient method of working than the approach resulting from traditional contracting in which each party is driven toward looking after their own independent objectives.

There is no universally accepted version of partnering and the range of definitions clearly demonstrates this. The version here (which it is important to add, has been subsequently revised by the authors) provides a relatively simple view, which should be easily understandable by all:

> 'Partnering is a management approach used by two or more organisations to achieve specific business objectives by maximising the effectiveness of each participant's resources. The approach is based on mutual objectives, an agreed method of problem resolution and an active search for continuous measurable improvements.'

> (Bennett and Jayes 1995)

It can be seen from this definition that there are three main components to a partnering arrangement: mutual objectives; an agreed method of problem resolution; an active search for continuous and measurable improvements.

The nature of partnering is such that it may take several different forms depending on the situation and the objectives of the parties involved. However, it is possible to broadly classify a partnering arrangement as either 'project partnering' or 'strategic partnering'. Although the differences between these two, which relate to scale and level of relationship, are significant, the essence of the partnering concept is the same in both.

Project partnering

As the name would suggest, project partnering relates to a specific project for which mutual objectives are established and the principles are restricted to the specified project only. The great majority of partnering opportunity is of this type since:

- It can be relatively easily applied in situations where legislation relating to free trade is strictly imposed
- Clients seeking to build on an occasional basis may use it.

Strategic partnering

Strategic partnering takes the concept of partnering beyond that outlined for project partnering to incorporate the consideration of long-term issues. The additional benefits of strategic partnering are a consequence of the opportunity that a long-term relationship may bring and could include:

- Establishing common facilities and systems
- Learning through repeated projects
- The development of an understanding and empathy for the partners' longer term business objectives.

The partnering process

Once the decision to partner has been made, the procedure of partnering principally involves a selection procedure, an initial partnering workshop and a project review.

The selection of a good client or contractor partner who is trustworthy and committed to the arrangement is fundamental to the process. Partnering can be used with traditional procurement methods in the initial selection stages. This is followed by a workshop that will be attended by key stakeholders and usually results in the production and agreement of a partnering charter that will be signed by all participants.

During the project implementation stage, performance will be regularly reviewed. This will incorporate all relevant project matters including quality, finance, programme, problem resolution and safety.

Advantages and disadvantages of partnering

The adoption of partnering – at a strategic level or for a specific project – is considered to bring major improvements to the construction process resulting in significant benefits to each partner. These may include:

- Reduction in disputes
- Reduction in time and expense in the settlement of disputes
- Reduction in costs
- Improved quality and safety
- Improvement in design and construction times and certainty of completion
- More stable workloads and income
- A better working environment.

However, in considering the use of a partnering approach, it is necessary to acknowledge the existence of some important disadvantages and concerns regarding its use. These may include:

- Initial costs
- Complacency
- Single source employment; Strategic partnering could result in either party becoming very dependent on one client and thus becoming extremely vulnerable should this source of work be threatened.
- Lack of confidentiality of client/contractor processes and systems; Disputes could occur in the event that information, which may be regarded as commercially confidential, were to be withheld from one or more of the partners
- The lack of competition; the accepted route to securing a 'good value' price is through the competitive tendering process.
- Absence of partnering through the supply chain; the benefits of partnering seem to be absent from the contractor–subcontractor relationship
- Concerns about legal issues; there is some doubt as to the legal status of the Partnering Charter.

The future of partnering is unclear. The prevailing culture that underlies the construction industry contains strong elements of mistrust, cynicism and resistance to change. These cannot be easily overturned. Market realities should not be ignored, nor can the importance of the need for the delivery of a well balanced education to future construction professionals (Ashworth and Hogg 2000).

The role of the quantity surveyor

It is of fundamental importance to clients who wish to undertake construction work that the appropriate advice is provided on the method of procurement to be used. The active selection of an inappropriate form of procurement, or the passive acceptance of a regularly used and hence 'comfortable' practice, can have a major impact on the success of a project.

Advice must be relevant and reliable and should be given independently, without the intrusion of individual bias. The advice provided should exclude considerations of self-interest. A client should not be faced with unwittingly selecting an inappropriate form of procurement as a consequence of selecting a particular consultant or profession as the first port of call.

Quantity surveyors are in an excellent position as procurement managers with their specialist knowledge of construction costs and contractual procedures. They are able to appraise the characteristics of the competing methods that might be appropriate and to match these with the particular needs and aspirations of the employer. Procurement management may be broadly defined to include the following:

- Determining the employer's requirements in terms of time, cost and quality
- Assessing the viability of the project and providing advice in respect of funding and taxation advantages
- Recommending an organisational structure for the development of a project as a whole
- Advising on the appointment of the various consultants and contractors in the knowledge of the information provided by the employer
- Managing the information and coordinating the work of the different parties
- Selecting the methods for the appointment of consultants and contractors.

Procurement procedures are dynamic activities that are evolving to meet the changing needs of society, the industry and its clients. There are no longer standard solutions; each individual project needs to be separately evaluated on its own individual set of characteristics. A wide variety of different factors need to be taken into account before any sound advice or implementation can be provided. The various influences, at the time of development, need to be weighed carefully and always with the best long-term interest of the client in mind.

Bibliography

Ashworth A. *Contractual Procedures in the Construction Industry*. Pearson Education. 2001.
Ashworth A. and Hogg K.I. *Added Value in Design and Construction*. Pearson Education. 2000.
Bennett J. and Jayes S. *Trusting the Team*. Centre for Strategic Studies in Construction. University of Reading. 1995.
Bennett J. and Jayes S. *The Seven Pillars of Partnering; a guide to second generation partnering*. Reading Construction Forum Ltd; Thomas Telford Publishing. 1998.

Bennett J. *Partnering in Action*. SBIM Conference Proceedings. 1999.

CIB (Construction Industry Board). *Code of Practice for the Selection of Main Contractors*. Thomas Telford. 1997.

Clients Construction Forum. *Survey of Construction Clients' Satisfaction 1998/99 – Headline Results*. Clients Construction Forum. 1998.

Construction Industry Board. *Constructing Success: Code of practice for clients of the construction industry*. Thomas Telford. 1997.

Construction Task Force. *Rethinking Construction (The Egan Report)*. Department of the Environment, Transport and the Regions. 1998.

Coulter S. Most clients yet to try partnering. *Building*, June, 1998.

Davis, Langdon and Everest. *Contracts in Use: A survey of Building Contracts in Use during 1998*. RICS. 2000.

Franks J. *Building Procurement Systems – A client's guide*. The Chartered Institute of Building and Longmans. 1995.

Janssens D.E.L. *Design – Build Explained*. Macmillan Education Ltd. 1991.

Latham M. *Constructing the Team*. The Stationery Office. 1994.

Long P. Partnering agreements: the legal knot. *Construction Law Bulletin*. Cameron McKenna. 1998.

McGeorge D. and Palmer A. *Construction Management – New Directions*. Blackwell Science. 1997.

Masterman J.W.E. *An Introduction to Building Procurement Systems*. E & F N Spon. 1992.

Morledge R. and Sharif A. *The Procurement Guide: A guide to the development of an appropriate building procurement strategy*. RICS. 1996.

Murdoch J. and Hughes W. *Construction Contracts: Law and Management*. E & FN Spon. 1992.

11 Contract Documentation

Contract documents

The contract documents for a building project, using JCT 98 (clause 1.3) comprise:

- Contract drawings
- Contract bills (or specification)
- Articles of agreement
- Conditions of contract
- Appendix.

In addition, immediately after the signing of the contract the architect will provide the contractor with other descriptive schedules and documents that are necessary for carrying out the works. The contractor will also provide a copy of the master programme (JCT 98 clause 5).

On civil engineering projects, using the ICE (Institution of Civil Engineers) conditions of contract, the following typically represent the contract documents:

- Conditions of contract
- Specification
- Drawings
- Bills of quantities
- Tender
- Written acceptance
- Contract agreement.

The range of contract forms have been referred to in Chapter 10. When the choice of form of contract has been decided, the next step is the preparation of the documents that will accompany the signed form of contract.

The contract documents for any construction project will include, as a minimum, the following information (Ashworth 2001):

- *The work to be performed* This usually requires some form of drawn information, including plans, elevations and cross-sections. Additional details will also be prepared depending on the complexity and intricacy of the project. This will provide information for the client and even a non-technical employer is usually able to grasp a basic idea of the architect's or engineer's design intentions. The drawings will also be required for planning permission and building regulations approval, where appropriate. On some projects drawings may be used as a basis for three-dimensional models and computer graphics.

- *The quality of work required*   The quality and performance of the materials to be used and the standards of workmanship must be clearly conveyed to the constructor, the usual way being through a specification or a contract bill.
- *The contractual conditions*   In all but the simplest projects some form of written agreement between the employer and the constructor is essential. This will help to avoid possible misunderstandings. It is recommended that one of the standard forms of contract should be used as discussed in Chapter 10. It is preferable to adopt the use of a standard form of contract rather than to devise separate conditions of contract for each project.
- *The cost of the finished work*   Wherever possible this should be predetermined by a firm estimate (tender) of cost from the contractor. This is best achieved through the use of some form of measured quantities of the work. However, it is recognised that on some projects it is only feasible to assess the cost once the work has been carried out. In these circumstances the method of calculating this cost should be clearly agreed.
- *The construction programme*   The length of time available for the construction work on site will be important to both the client and the contractor. The client will need to have some idea of how long the project will take to complete in order to plan arrangements for the handover of the project. The contractor's costs will be affected by the time available for construction. The programme should include progress schedules to assess whether the project is on time, ahead or behind the programme.

Coordinated project information

Research undertaken by the Building Research Establishment in the mid-1980s identified that the biggest single cause of quality problems on building sites is unclear or missing project information (Allott 1984). Another significant cause of disruption of building operations on site has been highlighted as shortcomings in drawn information. Much of the site management time is devoted to searching for missing information or reconciling inconsistencies in that which is supplied. This, together with a lack of compatibility in project information generally between the drawings, specifications and bills of quantities, is a major concern. The difficulty is partially due to the fact that the information is sourced from several different professional disciplines involved in the project.

In order to improve this situation, the Coordinating Committee for Project Information (CCPI) was established by the major bodies in the construction industry. After consultation they produced the following documents:

- Common Arrangement of Work Sections for Building Works (CAWS 2000)
- Project specification
- Production drawings
- Code of Procedure for Measurement of Building Works
- SMM7.

CCPI as a working committee has been disbanded but its work is now monitored by the Building Project Information Committee (BPIC). The purpose of CAWS is to define an efficient and generally acceptable identical arrangement for specification and bills of quantities. The main advantages are:

- *Easier distribution of information, particularly in the dissemination of information to subcontractors*   One of the prime objects in structuring the sections was to ensure that the requirements of the subcontractors should not only be recognised but should be kept together in relatively small tight packages.
- *More effective reading together of documents*   Use of CAWS coding allows the specification to be directly linked to the contract bills descriptions. This reduces the content in the latter while still giving all the information contained within the former.
- *Greater consistency achieved by implementation of the above advantages*   The site agent and clerk of works should be confident that when they compare the drawings with the contract bills they will no longer ask the question 'Which is right?'.

CAWS is a system based on the concept of work sections. To avoid boundary problems between similar or related work sections, CAWS gives, for each section, a list of what is included and what is excluded, stating the appropriate sections where the excluded item can be found. CAWS has a hierarchical arrangement in three levels, for instance:

- Level 1 R Disposal systems
- Level 2 R1 Drainage
- Level 3 R1O Rainwater pipes/gutters.

CAWS includes some 300 work sections commonly encountered in the construction industry. Although very dependent on size and complexity, no single project will need more than a fraction of this number, perhaps as a general average 25% to 30%. Only level 1 and level 3 are normally used in specifications and contract bills of quantities. Level 2 indicates the structure, and helps with the management of the notation. New work sections can be inserted simply, without the need for extensive renumbering.

Form of contract

This is the principal contract document and will generally comprise one of the preprinted forms of contract available to the industry. Such forms have the general agreement of the different parties involved. The form of contract, under JCT 98, takes precedence over the other contract documents (JCT 98 clause 2.2). The conditions of contract establish the legal framework under which the work is to be undertaken. Whilst the clauses aim to cover for any eventuality, disagreement in their interpretation frequently occurs. When disputes arise these should be resolved quickly and amicably by the parties concerned. Where this is not possible, it may become necessary to refer the disagreement to a form of alternative dispute resolution, adjudication or arbitration. The parties to a contract usually agree to take any dispute initially to adjudication rather than to litigation. This can save time, costs and adverse publicity which may be damaging to both parties. Where the dispute cannot be resolved, it is taken to court to establish a legal opinion. Such opinions, if held, eventually become case law and can be cited should similar disputes arise in the future. The majority of the standard forms of contract comprise, in one way or another, the following three sections.

Articles of Agreement

This is the part of the contract which the parties sign. The contract is between the employer (building owner) and the contractor (building contractor). The blank spaces in the articles are filled in with the:

- Names of the employer, contractor, architect and quantity surveyor
- Date of the signing of the contract
- Location and nature of the work
- List of the contract drawings
- Amount of the contract sum.

If the parties make any amendments to the Articles of Agreement or to any other part of the contract, then the alterations should be initialled by both parties.

In some circumstances it may be necessary or desirable to execute the contract as a deed (formerly under seal). This is often the case with local authorities and other public bodies.

Conditions of Contract

The Conditions of Contract include, for example, the contractor's obligations to carry out and complete the work shown on the drawings and described in the bills to the satisfaction of the architect (or supervising officer). They cover matters dealing with the quality of the work, cost, time, nominated suppliers' and subcontractors' insurances, fluctuations and VAT. Their purpose is to attempt to clarify the rights and responsibilities of the various parties in the event of a dispute arising.

Appendix

The Appendix to the Conditions of Contract includes that part of the contract which is peculiar to the particular project in question. It includes information on the start and completion dates, the periods of interim payment and the length of the defects liability period for which the contractor is responsible. The Appendix includes recommendations on some of this information.

Contract drawings

The contract drawings should ideally be complete and finalised at tender stage. Unfortunately this is seldom the case, and both clients and architects rely too heavily on the clause in the conditions allowing for variations (JCT 98 clause 13). Occasionally the reason is due to insufficient time being made available for the pre-contract design work or, frequently, because of indecision on the part of the client and the design team. One of the intentions of the SMM7 was to only allow contract bills to be prepared on the basis of complete drawings. To invite contractors to price work that has yet to be designed is not a sensible course of action. Tenderers should be given sufficient information to enable them to understand what is required in order that they may submit as accurate and realistic a price as possible. The contract drawings will include the general arrangement drawings showing the site location, the position of the building on the site, means of access to the site, floor plans, elevations and sections. Where these drawings are not supplied to the contractors with the other tendering information, they should be informed where and when they can be inspected. The inspection of these and other drawings is highly recommended, since it may provide the opportunity for an informal discussion on the project with the designer.

The contractor upon signing the contract is provided with two further copies of the contract drawings. These may include copies of the drawings sent to the contractor with the invitation to tender, together with those drawings that have been used in the preparation of either the contract bills or specification. In JCT 98, the contract drawings are defined in the third recital of the Articles of Agreement as those which have been signed by both parties to the contract. It will be necessary during the construction phase for the architect to supply the contractor with additional drawings and details. These may either explain and amplify the contract drawings, or because of variations identify and explain the changes from the original design. An information release schedule is to be provided (clause 5.4.1) and further drawings and details are the norm and are expected to be provided (clause 5.4.2).

Schedules

The preparation and use of schedules is particularly appropriate for items of work such as:

- Windows
- Doors
- Manholes
- Internal finishings.

Schedules provide an improved means of communicating information between the architect (or engineer) and the contractor. They are also invaluable to the quantity surveyor during the preparation of the contract bills. They have several advantages over attempting to provide the same information by way of either correspondence or further drawings. The checking for possible errors is simplified, and the schedules can also be used for the placing of orders for materials or components.

During the preparation of schedules the following questions must be borne in mind:

- Who will use the schedule?
- What information is required to be conveyed?
- What additional information is required?
- How can the information be best portrayed?
- Does it revise information provided elsewhere?

The designer must supply the contractor with two copies of these schedules that have been prepared for use in carrying out the works (clause 5.3.1). This should be done soon after the signing of the contract, or as soon as possible thereafter should they not be available at this time. The architect should supply the information release schedule as described in clause 5.4.1.

Contract bills

Some form of contract bills or measured schedules should be prepared for all types of building projects, other than those of only a minor or simplified nature. The bill comprises a list of items of work to be carried out, providing a brief description and the quantities of the finished work in the building. The bill may include firm or approximate quantities, depending upon the completeness of the drawings and other information from which it was prepared.

Purpose of contract bills

The main purpose of contract bills is for tendering. Each contractor tendering for the project is able to price the work on precisely the same information with the minimum amount of effort. This avoids duplication in quantifying the construction work, and allows for the fairest type of competition. Despite the predicted demise of contract bills a large proportion of all contracts awarded in the UK still use some form of firm or approximate quantities. Other procurement routes such as design and build and management contracting also require some form of quantification of construction work. However, contract bills are not appropriate for all types of construction work, and other suitable methods of contract procurement should be used. For example, for minor works drawings and a specification may be adequate, or where the extent of the work is unknown, payment may be made by using one of the methods of cost reimbursement.

In addition to tendering, contract bills have the following uses. These should be borne in mind during their preparation:

- Valuations for interim certificates
- Valuation of variations
- Ordering of materials if used with caution and awareness of possible errors and future variations
- Cost planning
- Planning and progressing by the contractor's site planner
- Final accounting
- Quality analysis by reference to the trade preamble clauses
- Subcontractor quotations
- Cost information (noting the provisions of JCT 98 clause 5.7).

Preparation of contract bills

Contract bills are prepared by the quantity surveyor, adopting best practice procedures. The items of work are measured in accordance with a recognised method of measurement. Building projects are generally measured in accordance with SMM7. Other methods of measurement are also available to the construction industry (Fig. 11.1). On mass housing projects it may be preferable to use a simplified version such as the Code of Measurement of Building Works in Small Dwellings. Separate methods also exist for work of a civil engineering nature and petrochemical plants. An international version is available from the RICS. Descriptions and quantities are derived from the contract drawings and SMM7 and are on the basis of the finished quantities of work in the completed building. The contents of contract bills are typically as follows.

Preliminaries

This covers the employer's requirements and the contractor's obligations in carrying out the work. SMM7 provides a framework for this section of the bill. It includes, for example:

- Names of parties
- Description of the works
- Form and type of contract
- General facilities to be provided by the contractor.

In practice, although the preliminaries may comprise over 20 pages of the contract bills, only a small number of items (10–15) are priced by contractors. The remainder of the items are included for information and contractual purposes only. The value of the preliminary items may account for between 8% and 15% of the contract sum.

Preambles

The preamble clauses contain descriptions relating to:

- The quality and performance of materials
- The standard of workmanship
- The testing of materials and workmanship
- Samples of materials and workmanship.

This section of the contract bills has in some cases now been replaced by a set of standard and comprehensive preamble clauses. The contents of the preambles section are usually extracted from a library of standard clauses. Contractors rarely price any of this section.

Measured works

This section of the bill includes the items of work to be undertaken by the main contractor or to be sublet to domestic subcontractors. There are several different forms of presentation available for this work, the most common of which are:

- *Trade format*   The items in the bill are grouped under their respective trades. The advantages of this format are that similar items are grouped together, there is a minimum of repetition, and it is useful to the contractor when subletting.
- *Elemental format*   This groups the items according to their position in the building, on the basis of a recognised elemental subdivision of the project, e.g. external walls, roofs, wall finishes, sanitary appliances. In practice contractors tend to dislike it since it involves a considerable amount of repetition.

Prime cost and provisional sums

Some aspects of a building project are not measured in detail but are included in the bills as lump sum items. These sums of money are intended to cover specialist work not normally undertaken by the general contractor (prime cost sum) or work which cannot be entirely foreseen, defined or detailed at the time that the tendering documents are issued (provisional sum). They are separately described as for defined or undefined work. Prime cost sums cover work undertaken by nominated subcontractors, nominated suppliers and statutory undertakings. They include lump sums that have been based on quotations for items of work such as electrical installations, lifts, escalators and other similar conveyancing systems, etc.

Appendices

The final section of the bill includes the tender summary, a list of the main contractors and domestic subcontractors, a basic price list of materials and nominated subcontractor's work for which the main contractor may desire to tender.

The form of tender is the contractor's written offer 'to undertake and execute the works in accordance with the contract documents for a contract sum of money', and will also state the contract period and whether the contract is on the basis of a fixed price. The tenders are submitted to the architect who will then make a recommendation regarding the acceptance of a tender to the client. If the client decides to go ahead with the project, the successful tenderer is invited to submit a copy of the priced bills for checking. The form of tender usually states that the employer:

- May not accept any tender
- May not accept the lowest tender
- Has no responsibility for the costs incurred in their preparation.

Methods of measurement

The quantifying of construction works is best done using an agreed set of rules or method of measurement. It is then clear to all users how the work has been measured and what has not been measured (deemed to be included in SMM terminology).

In 1912, a committee was formed to prepare rules for the measurement of construction works, resulting in the first edition of The Standard Method of Measurement of Building Works (SMM) in 1922 (Fig. 11.1). However, it should be noted that this was preceded by a SMM in Scotland that was published in 1915. A unified SMM for the whole of the UK was not agreed until 1965.

Historically, prior to this time, quantity surveyors or measurers as they were then described, prepared quantities and remeasured work using their own ideas and preferences. This often caused ambiguity, confusion and doubt, not to mention disagreement, on the part of the contractor's staff particularly the estimators and surveyors. Some surveyors would measure the work in detail, whereas others would adopt a practice of measuring only the cost significant items. When SMM7 was being developed, everyone wanted simplicity. This meant to those in private practice, fewer items to measure. Contractors wanted more precise, and probably more detailed, information.

1915	Scottish SMM for Building Works.
1922	Standard Method of Measurement of Building Works, 1st Edition.
1927	SMM Building, 2nd Edition.
1933	Standard Method of Measurement of Civil Engineering Quantities.
1935	SMM Building, 3rd Edition.
1945	Code for the Measurement of Building Works in Small Dwellings, 1st edition
1948	SMM Building, 4th Edition.
1953	SMM Civil Engineering Quantities (Revision).
1956	Code for Small Dwellings. (Revision).
1958	Scottish Mode of Measurement.
1963	SMM Civil Engineering Quantities (Revision).
1963	Code for Small Dwellings, 2nd Edition.
1963	SMM Building, 5th Edition.
1964	SMM Building, 5th Edition (Amended).
1968	SMM Building, 5th Edition (Metric).
1969	Method of Measurement for Roads and Bridgeworks.
1970	SMM Building, 5th Edition (with fitted carpet amendment).
1972	Standard Method of Measurement of Construction Engineering Works.
1976	Civil Engineering Standard Method of Measurement.
1979	SMM Building, 6th Edition (with Practice Manual).
1979	Code for Small Dwellings, 3rd Edition.
1979	Principles of Measurement (International) for Works of Construction.
1984	Standard Method of Measurement for Industrial Engineering Construction.
1984	SMM6, with amendments.
1985	CESMM, 2nd Edition.
1987	SMM7 Measurement Code.
1988	SMM7.
1991	CESMM 3rd Edition.
1998	SMM7 with amendments.
1999	SMM7 Measurement Code, second edition.

Fig. 11.1 Methods of measurement.

The main aim of the different SMMs is to provide a clear set of rules that can be used for measuring construction work. The rules apply equally to work that is proposed or executed. Some words and phrases in contract bills have developed implied meanings, trade customs and practices. Standard phraseologies have also been developed to standardise and clarify meanings of bill descriptions. However, the introduction of SMM7 largely reduced the need for these, since it was written with the dual purpose of measuring and billing in mind. SMM7 also has the advantage of being readily suited to the use of information technology.

SMMs have not been without their critics. Some have contested the technical adequacy of their rules, the ease of application and the overall value of measured analysis. Others have argued that it is inappropriate to value varied work in the way intended and recommended by the forms of contract. Some have suggested that the limitation of contract bills is as a direct result of the rigidities of SMMs. There has in the past also been criticisms of the time involved in measuring cost insignificant items. The introduction of SMM7 has largely remedied this.

In countries where quantity surveyors have been long established they have developed their own methods of measurement for building works. These have often been based on a UK SMM, and have been adapted to suit local conditions, such as different methods of construction and its associated technologies.

At the beginning of the twentieth century, no standard method of measurement existed by which construction work could be adequately measured. By the end of that century a multiplicity of different methods had emerged. The methods that are acceptable include the following facets:

- Technical adequacy of the rules
- Lacking in ambiguity
- Ease by which the rules can be applied
- Measurement only of items of cost significance
- Consideration of a wide variety of applications.

Contract specification

In certain circumstances it may be more appropriate to provide documentation by way of a specification rather than contract bills. The types of project where this may be appropriate include:

- Minor building projects
- Small-scale alteration projects
- Simple industrial shed type projects.

The specification provides detailed descriptions of the work to be performed, to assist the contractor in preparing the tender. A specification is used during:

- Tendering, to help the estimator to price the work that is required to be carried out
- Construction by the designer in order to determine the requirements of the contract, legally, technically and financially, and by the building contractor to determine the work to be carried out on site.

With the introduction of Coordinating Project Information (CPI), as described above, the specification has become more important than ever. BPIC in their publications make it clear that the specification is the key document from which all other information, either for drawings or contract bills, will flow. The writing and use of specifications is a subject in its own right and as such warrants separate study (Willis and Willis 1997).

National Building Specification

The National Building Specification (NBS) is not a standard specification. It is a large library of specification clauses from which to select relevant clauses. They often require the insertion of additional information. NBS thus facilitates the production of specification text specific to each project, including all relevant matters and excluding text that does not apply.

NBS is available only as a subscription service, and in this way it is kept up to date by issue of new material several times a year via disk and hard copy for insertion into loose-leaf ring binders. NBS is prepared in CAWS matching SMM7, and complies fully with the recommendations of the CPI Code of Procedure for Project Specifications. There are three versions of NBS, the Standard Version, an abridged Intermediate Version and a Minor Works Version.

Schedules of work

A schedule of work is a compromise between a specification and contract bills. It is more like contract bills and does not include any quantities for the work to be carried out. Its main purpose is therefore in valuing the items of work once they have been completed and measured. A schedule of rates may be used on:

- Jobbing work
- Maintenance or repair contracts
- Projects that cannot be adequately defined at the time of tender
- Urgent works
- Painting and decorating.

Master programme

It is the contractor's responsibility to provide the master programme. This shows when the works will be carried out (JCT 98 clause 5.3.1.2). Unless otherwise directed by the architect, the type of programme and the details to be included are to be at the entire discretion of the contractor. If the architect agrees to a change in the completion date because of an extension of time (JCT 98 clause 25.3.1), then the contractor must provide amendments and revisions to the programme within 14 days.

Information release schedule

This schedule is described in clause 5.4.1 (JCT 98). It informs the contractor when information will be made available by the architect. The schedule is not annexed to the contract. However, the architect must ensure that the information is released to the contractor in accordance with that agreed in the information release schedule. In practice the architect needs to coordinate the information release schedule with the contractor's master programme for the works.

Discrepancies in documents

JCT 98 clause 2.3 requires the contractor to write to the architect if any discrepancies between the documents are found. The form of contract always takes precedence over the other documents. The contractor cannot therefore assume that the drawings are more important than the contract bills. However, drawings drawn to a larger scale will generally take precedence over drawings that have been prepared to a smaller scale. JCT 98 clause 6.1.2 expects the contractor to adopt a similar course of action should a divergence be found between statutory requirements and the contract documents. Where discrepancies or differences result in instructions to the contractor requiring variations, these will be dealt with under clause 13. The contractor should not knowingly execute work where differences occur within the various documents supplied by the design team. However, it is not the contractor's responsibility to discover differences should they arise.

Bibliography

Allott A. *et al. Common Arrangement for Specifications and Quantities.* Coordinating Committee for Project Information. 1984.

Ashworth A. *Contractual Procedures in the Construction Industry.* Pearson Education. 2001.

Building Project Information Committee. *Common Arrangements for Works Sections for Building Works* (CAWS). 1987.

CAWS (Common Arrangement of Work Sections) Committee for Project Information. 2000.

CIOB *Code of Estimating Practice.* Chartered Institute of Building. 1997.

Willis J.A. and Trench W. *Willis's Elements of Quantity Surveying.* Blackwell Science, Oxford. 1998.

Willis C.J. and Willis J.A. *Specification Writing for Architects and Surveyors.* Blackwell Science. 1997.

12 Preparation of Contract Bills

Appointment of the quantity surveyor

The appointment of the quantity surveyor is likely to have been made at an early stage when early price estimates were under consideration. This may be before any drawings are available, in order to provide some cost advice to the client. Only on very small projects will a quantity surveyor not be required at all. Contractors should not be asked to submit tenders in competition without quantities being provided. These may take several different formats today. There may, of course, be special considerations that would justify such invitations for a larger contract and, equally well, similar considerations that could call for quantities being provided for a contract of a lesser value

It should not easily be forgotten that the abortive work involved is considerable if six or eight contractors are each asked to prepare their own quantities for estimating. The costs involved are high and must be borne by the industry and ultimately passed on to the client. The number of firms that might be involved in open tendering makes this point even more forcefully.

Under the EU regulations public sector construction contracts and private sector contracts financed by more than 50% by public authorities over 1 million currency units (ECUs) (approximately £3 500 000) must be invited and awarded in accordance with the procedures laid down in EEC Directive 89/440. The Directive provides for a 'restricted tendering procedure' which permits the selection of technically and financially competent contractors following the advertisement in the *Official Journal of the European Communities* circulating throughout member states. In such cases there might be five, ten or more contractors tendering, and the sum total of increased overheads if they had to prepare their own quantities would be prohibitive, to say nothing of the scarcity of qualified staff to do it. The different interpretations which each contractor may put on the same drawings and specification are a further disadvantage and a possible cause of difficulties at a later stage.

Receipt of drawings

The quantity surveyor will usually collect the drawings and any specification notes from the architect's office and at the same time discuss the job. General notes will be made of any verbal instructions given, but the more detailed questions will arise once some detailed examination of the documents has been made. A timetable for the completion of the contract bills will be agreed, along with dates when additional detailed drawings and information can be expected. It is likely that drawings of some sections of the work are incomplete, and a good deal of time may be wasted if the taking-off of that section is begun on the drawings available. A 1:20 detail may quite likely alter the 1:100 drawing, and an alteration, however slight, may affect a lot of items in the dimensions. If further drawings are to follow, it is helpful if the order in which they are being prepared can be agreed, having regard both to the architect's office procedure and the surveyor's requirements.

Study of documents

The drawings received should be stamped with the surveyor's name and date of receipt except, of course, originals that have to be returned. On a job of any size, a register of drawings should be completed, giving their reference number, scale and brief particulars (Fig. 12.1). The advantage of separate sheets is that each taker-off can have a copy, which will assist quick reference until thoroughly acquainted with the drawings. Particulars of any further drawings received should be added to the list when they come in.

The documents will then be examined by a principal or senior assistant in charge of the project and the takers-off will be allocated. The first things to be done are to:

- See that all the necessary figured dimensions are given, both on plans and sections

Project title: Southtown School			Project Nr: 00
Consultant: Architect			Sheet Nr: 1
Drawing identification			Revisions
Nr	Title	Scale	
1	Block plan	1:1000	
2	General plan	1:100	
3	Sections, elevations	1:100	
4	Classroom plans	1:20	
5	Cloaks, toilets plans	1:20	
6	Assembly hall plan	1:20	
7	Heating chamber	1:20	
8	Door details	full size	
10	Metal window schedule	1:50	
15	Drainage	1:200	
17	Classroom store fittings	1:20	

Fig. 12.1 Sample drawing register.

- See that the figured dimensions are checked with overall dimensions given
- Insert any dimensions that can be calculated and may be useful in the measurement
- Confirm any errors in figured dimensions with the architect, so that the originals can be amended accordingly.

Except on the smallest jobs the drawings should be supplied in duplicate, and on larger jobs there may be three or more copies. It is advisable to number the sets so that it can be seen at a glance to which set a drawing belongs.

It will make the rooms stand out clearly if the walls are coloured in on plan and section in the surveyor's office; moreover, the act of colouring them will give an early indication of the general construction. This can be done quickly with coloured pencil and will be found well worthwhile. There may also be manuscript notes, or even alterations in plan, made by the architect at the last moment on one copy, and these should be transferred to the other copies. It sometimes happens that plans and sections are hatched as a labour-saving device (as hatching will be printed on all copies) but the surveyor should superimpose his colouring.

It will also be found useful in a job of any size to mark on the general plan (usually 1:100) the positions of the parts that are detailed. A cross-reference in coloured pencil in both cases will stand out. There may, for instance, be a number of 1:20 details spread over several sheets: for example, entrance doors, bay windows, or particular points of construction. Sections can be referenced by normal section lines superimposed on the plan in a distinctive colour with the drawing number and section reference given. Elevations can be referenced in a similar way. It may be found frequently that sections on detail sheets are not given a letter reference by the architect, but have a title such as 'Section through kitchen'. The surveyor can give them a letter reference for the special purpose. The marking of the general plans in this way makes them serve as a key, so that a taker-off working on some particular part of the building can see at a glance what details are available.

A careful perusal should then be made of the specification or specification notes. By following through systematically the sections of the taking-off, gaps may be found in the specification which require information. These may be quite numerous when only notes are supplied, as 'notes' vary considerably in quality, thoroughness and extent. When a standard specification, such as NBS in one of its versions, is used then the opportunity can be taken to check that the correct alternatives have been chosen, that superfluous matter has been deleted, and that all the gaps have been filled in.

Schedules

Schedules are useful, both for quick reference by the taker-off and for eventual incorporation in the specification for the information of the clerk of works and site agent. They may be supplied by the architect with the drawings, or it may be necessary for the surveyor to draft them. Internal finishings should certainly be scheduled in a tabulated form, so that the finishes of each room for ceiling, wall and floors can be seen at a glance, with particulars of any skirtings, dadoes or other special features. Schedules for windows and doors would include frames, architraves and ironmongery. Those for manholes would give a clear size, invert, thickness of walls, type of cover and any other suitable particulars.

Some of the material on schedules may be otherwise shown on drawings, but the schedule brings the parts together and gives a clear view of the whole. The schedule of finishings, if not supplied in the form of a drawing, should be copied and given to each taker-off, as each will at some time want to know what finish comes in a particular place, when it is necessary to make deductions or allow for making good.

Taking-off

Query sheets

After drawings and specification have been examined a first list of queries for the architect or engineer will be prepared. These should be written on the left-hand half of A4 sheets, numbered serially and dated. The use of printed headed sheets can be prepared for the purpose. When a sufficient batch of queries has been collected, they can be communicated to the architect or engineer, asking for the return of replies, as soon as possible. It is often more convenient and expedient for the surveyor to meet the architect or engineer to discuss the queries, in which case the responses can be noted. On return to the office details should be sent to the architect or engineer for confirmation and clarification.

The queries should be given serial numbers, carried from one set to another, and the sets filed together as they are received so that the series is complete. Each taker-off should, if possible, have a copy and record the queries as they are dealt with. A final check should be made when the taking-off is completed to see that there are no gaps or overlaps.

It often happens that some proprietary material, of which the surveyor has never heard, is mentioned in the specification. If the name and address of the maker are not provided, the surveyor should find them out and send for a manufacturer's catalogue. At the same time material prices should be obtained and if possible the expected fixing or installation costs. In suitable cases it may be prudent to ask for a small sample, as the sight and handling of a piece of the material is often helpful in disposing of difficulties that may arise in describing the fixing.

A telephone enquiry to the Building Centre will almost always provide the name and address of the maker when only the trade name of a proprietary article is known. Lists of trade names with the names and addresses of manufacturers will be found in many reference and price books. The internet can also be used effectively to obtain such information.

The surveyor should *never* accept an unknown name without investigation. A material specified has, before now, been found to be obsolete, and to describe it in the contract bills not only looks foolish and reveals ignorance, but involves queries being raised by tenderers. Even when the surveyor knows a material, if there has not been an occasion to refer to it for some time, up-to-date particulars should be sought. Specifications may vary, new developments will occur and prices will fairly certainly have changed.

References to merchants' catalogue numbers or numbers of British Standards and Codes of Practice should be verified. An incorrect figure may appear in the specification either through error or through the writer not realising that the reference has become obsolete. Queries to an architect could take the form shown in Fig. 12.2.

Project Nr . . . .   **Southtown School**   Sheet Nr . . . .
Queries

Date

Ref   *Query*   *Reply*

1. Finish to floor of entrance hall   *Date*
   specified wood block, coloured as
   tile?

2. Should not dimension between piers
   on north wall be 5.08 not 5.03? (to fit
   the overall 56.85)

3. Dpc not mentioned in the spec.
   notes? ?lead cored felt

4. Should brick facing to concrete
   beams be tied back?

                  Etc. etc.

Fig. 12.2 Sample query sheet.

Division of taking-off

For a small project it is most satisfactory if one person does the whole of the taking-off. For larger buildings the amount of subdivision will depend on the time allotted for the job and the availability of takers-off. Where two are made available a subdivision might be:

- Carcase of the building
- Internal finishes, windows, doors and fittings.

Such sections as sanitary plumbing, drainage and roads are more or less independent of other sections, and could be allotted as one or other of the takers-off becomes available. When three takers-off are available, the third could start on these sections, and on buildings involving a lot of joinery fittings they might take responsibility for these. There are few projects on which it would be practicable to use more than four takers-off. The measurement of the carcase of a building would not normally be subdivided. The superstructure might be subdivided for a steel or reinforced concrete frame building. The frame, with floor, roof slabs and beam casings, would be the charge of one person, while the brickwork and roof coverings would be dealt with by another. Such a section as roofs could, if necessary, be separated. If possible, however, one person should see the whole structure through.

In the same way, the measurement of the windows and external doors can hardly be subdivided, as they are sometimes structurally combined and have similar finishings. It would be preferable for internal doors to be done by the same person, as many items such as lintels and plaster reveals will occur in both sections. Internal finishings can be done by someone else if a careful schedule has been prepared and there is close cooperation between the takersoff measuring finishings and openings. The Scottish method alleviates this problem by measuring the work on a trade basis.

The more the taking-off is subdivided the greater the risk of duplicating items or assuming that someone else will have measured specific items. There are certain items in which practice differs with different offices. For example, some surveyors measure skirtings with floor finishings and others with wall finishings. Some measure them net, others adjust for openings in the doors section. It is important, therefore, that clear rules are adopted and care is necessary to see that new or temporary takers-off, not used to the office custom, are informed.

A set of 1:100 and 1:20 or other general layout drawings should be available for each taker-off, and it is worth the surveyor paying for the extra prints if they are not supplied. Single copies of special drawings are usually sufficient, such as details of joinery fittings or layout of plumbing services and drainage. These are usually the concern of only one taker-off. If a second copy of the specification can be supplied it will be found to save a lot of time when two or more takers-off are involved. On a large contract it may be worth having copies of the specification or substantial extracts photographed, particularly when, as may be the case, it is supplied in draft. The amount of supervision of the taking-off necessarily varies with the expertise of the individual. A junior taker-off just starting to do this work may require a large amount of supervision and answering of queries. This is part of the training required. The beginner must learn but it must not be at the expense of serious mistakes. Quite a casual query may reveal unexpected ignorance, and with the inexperienced one must always be alert.

Computerised systems

Computerised methods of measuring vary from the traditional process of writing to the computer screen to the use of digitised or electronic measuring from computerised pad, to the wider use of computer-aided design (CAD) systems. These systems have now been in existence for over 25 years and there is the capability to generate automatic contract bills. Electronic data interchange (EDI) also allows the process to be taken even further by transferring the bills and other documentation directly into the contractor's own computer system. This allows for a form of automatic estimating, using a contractor's own pricing information. This can then be analysed and adjusted to suit the particular project conditions.

Buildings erected in stages

When buildings are to be erected in stages, separate prices may be required for each stage. If so, each stage will require an entirely separate bill or set of bills. It may be, however, that the division into stages is only for organisation of the work, for example, when part of a building must be completed before another part can be commenced. As far as the client is concerned only one price is required, but it would be much more convenient, both for interim certificates and final accounting, if each section were separately billed. Provisional sums, for specialist work, would be allocated accordingly.

Similar circumstances arise for housing estates where houses are completed and handed over one at a time or in batches. Though it is not necessary to have a separate bill for each type, this is valuable. In any case, some idea of the value of each type must be calculated for interim certificates and for the release of retention monies that may become due.

Elemental bills

Where the billing is to be by elements instead of by trades, the taking-off must be subdivided accordingly. The Building Cost Information Service (BCIS) publishes an agreed standard list of elements which can be used. The peculiar character of the job may mean that all in the list are not used, and it may be that a new element must be introduced. In the interest of more accurate cost analysis the standard list should he adhered to so far as possible. If it is found practicable to make the sections of the taking-off correspond with the elements, it will probably be possible to save time in writing the bills.

Until someone is used to taking-off by elements there is also the risk of something being missed or measured twice. There is nothing to prevent the normal order and classification of taking-off being followed, as long as it is clear to which element each item is assigned. It is useful to give code letters to each element, such as FDN for foundations, EXTLW for external walls or P for partitions. Dimensions can be marked up with these code letters prior to billing.

Numbering dimension sheets

It is advisable to mark every page at the top with the section of the dimensions to which it belongs and the serial number of the page, such as Roofs 24 or

Windows 38. On reference to any sheet one can then see quickly to what section it belongs. Sheets are also usually numbered serially right through, either on each page or on each column. It is important to ensure that sheets do not go missing. It is advisable to keep a running index to the dimension sheets as a check, giving at the same time, whenever referred to, an overall view of the status of the taking-off.

Alterations in taking-off

Alterations are sometimes made by the taker-off after the dimensions have been squared and perhaps even later when they have been carried through to the bill stage. It is important that such alterations are at the same time taken through all the stages involved. If the taker-off marks the alterations with a pencil cross and hands the sheet personally to whoever is responsible for the next stage this should ensure that the corrections are made. Alterations should not be made to the taking-off by others. There may be a reason for an apparent error. Often, after making what appears to be a correction, it is found that the dimensions were right the first time.

Contract bills

Standard descriptions

To the casual onlooker all bills of quantities may look the same, but a more detailed examination will reveal personal differences and preferences. Most quantity surveying practices have developed their own style for their bills of quantities. In an attempt to overcome misinterpretation by contractors and to ease the process of bill preparation, the use of standardised bill descriptions was developed in the 1960s. Also the effective use of computers for this purpose requires a standard library of descriptions. The bill items, instead of being written as a single description, are frequently composed of a group of phrases. The descriptions are built up by using levels of phrases or words; by combining these, an ordered description is compiled.

The introduction of SMM7 signalled the end of standard phraseologies since SMM7, as well as being a set of rules for measuring, also provided the key phrases for writing the bills. The use of this method has resulted in a much greater uniformity than otherwise existed for contract bills. This is helpful to contractors with their own processes of tendering, estimating and final accounting.

Specialist bills

Prime cost sums to be included within contract bills require estimates from specialist subcontractors. Bills of quantities can be prepared for such specialist work. Such bills should state that the specialist will be a nominated subcontractor, and should state the form of main contract to be used. It is usual to state the brief conditions of the main contract and the amount of cash discount to be allowed, since this may not agree with the specialist's normal practice. Similar bills can be prepared for the materials of nominated suppliers, although this is a less common practice.

Bills should be sent in duplicate, so that the specialists have a copy of their instructions. They will sometimes quote on their own form or letterhead. It is advisable to ask for a copy of the bill to be signed and returned as confirmation of the terms suggested.

Preliminaries and preamble clauses

If possible, before billing of the measured work commences, the preambles to each section covering materials and workmanship should be drafted from the specification, amplified if necessary by reference to previous bills. This should be done by one of the takers-off, who will by then have a comprehensive knowledge of the job. By writing the preamble clauses first, the biller can see how far the descriptions are already covered and make notes of any clauses which it is thought should be added.

If the project is for a public authority, the surveyor may be supplied with their typical preliminaries items clauses. Otherwise the surveyor will use a previous bill as a guide. Care should be taken to ensure that everything is applicable to the particular project. There may be clauses, parts of clauses, or even single words, which were inserted specially for the previous job and which, being in type like the rest, are not now evident as insertions. In the same way, owing to some particular circumstances, omissions may have been made previously that now need to be reinstated.

Everything that concerns price must be included in the contract bills. The unnecessary duplication of descriptions in specification and bill can be avoided by reference in the bill to clause numbers and headings of the specification, where there is a full specification prepared and issued with the bills. Where, however, the specification is not part of the contract, it is more satisfactory for the tenderer to have everything in the bills to save the extra effort spent in cross-reference.

Prime cost sums

Prime cost, or PC sums, are based on estimates received from potential nominated subcontractors or suppliers. Such estimates can be obtained on request from the firm concerned, who will have been appraised of what is required. While a submission of an estimate on its own is sufficient it is advisable to follow the procedures laid down by the JCT for nomination of a subcontractor. These procedures, as far as tendering is concerned, are as follows:

- NSC/T Part 1: the invitation to tender to be issued by the architect
- NSC/T Part 2: the form of tender to be submitted by each subcontractor

- NSC/T Part 3: the particular conditions to be agreed by contractor and subcontractor prior to entering the nominated subcontract.

These are subsequently followed by agreement, conditions, warranty and nomination forms.

Use of these procedures goes a long way to ensuring that the terms of the subcontract are clear and unambiguous. This greatly reduces the possible grounds for dispute.

A check should be made of all PC items with the subcontractors' or suppliers' estimates. The surveyor must also ensure that provision is made for any materials to be supplied by the contractor (for example, cement and sand for tiling). There may be other special conditions accompanying a specialist's estimate, often set out in small print on the specialist's standard form. These must be examined to ensure that they are acceptable. For instance, there may be a requirement from a steelwork or structural floor contractor for a hard standing alongside the new building to allow hoisting direct from lorries into the final position. Requirements regarding unloading vary, and these must be clear as far as the contract is concerned.

It is advisable to mark the estimate with any adjustments made, so that the build-up of the sum given in the bill can be traced. As the estimate may not be retained it will be found useful to note on the dimensions against the provisional sum the name of the firm, date and reference of estimate, amount and discount. If there are any blanks in PC prices, provisional sums or quantities on the draft, they should be marked in with a pencil cross so that they are not overlooked.

A schedule of all PC and provisional sums should be prepared showing how the figures have been calculated, with a copy sent to the architect in a form similar to that shown in Fig. 12.3.

Numbering items

Items in the contract bill can be serially numbered from beginning to end. Alternatively, each page can have items referenced from A onwards in order that an item might be referenced, as for example, item 50 C or 94 B. The latter is the preferred method, since if new items have to be inserted at a late stage the whole sequence of numbers does not need to be revised.

Schedule of basic rates

If the contract alternative is used, requiring recovery of fluctuations to be based on the rise or fall in prices of materials (an unlikely event in current practice), an appendix will be required to the contract bills, in which the contractor can set out the rates on which the tender is based. The appendix can contain a list of the principal materials (which the contractor can supplement if necessary) or it can be left to the contractor to prepare the list. Alternatively, a fixed priced list could be given of the principal materials, but it is preferable

Southtown Primary School

Schedule of PC and provisional sums

	Source of information	Amount	Included in bills
Nominated subcontractors			
Structural steelwork	Quotation: Steelright	92 560.45	95 000
Wood block flooring	Quotation: Floors asUlike	125 413.00	130 000
Nominated suppliers			
Sanitary fittings	Quotation: Sanitary PLC	62 354.67	65 000
Statutory undertakings			
Water connection	Letter from Southtown Water Authority		5 500
Provisional sums			
Planting	Specification notes		17 500
Fitted furniture	Specification notes		30 000

Fig. 12.3   Specimen schedule of PC and provisional sums. *Note:* Such a schedule might also be produced for named subcontractors under IFC 84, or subcontractors (subcontractors and suppliers) in the ICE Form.

to let contractors include their own rates, as one contractor may be better placed than another through being a large buyer, or for some other reason.

If the priced contract bills are not being returned with the tender, it is advisable to reprint the schedule of basic rates of materials as an appendix to the form of tender as well, so that it can be considered when tenders are compared.

Schedule of allocation

When the price adjustment formula for calculating variation of price claims is to be used, it is necessary when the contract bills are complete, and before they are sent out to tender, to prepare an allocation of all the items in the bills. This is done by preparing a schedule of all 49 work categories and then allocating all the bill items to the work categories. Preliminaries and certain provisional sums are included in a balance of adjustable items section.

When this allocation is complete it is included in the bills, and in submitting a tender a prospective contractor is deemed to have agreed to the allocation chosen by the quantity surveyor. It is unlikely that a tendering contractor will challenge the allocation, but if they do they must do so when submitting the tender. When the tender has been accepted it is a straightforward exercise to complete the schedule by filling in the appropriate amounts. The whole process is self-checking in that the end result must be the contract sum.

Completing the contract bills

The draft bills should receive a final careful read through, an overall checking of the quantities and editing prior to their issue. An examination should be made to see that all gaps in the text have now been completed, such as cross-references to item numbers or summary pages. The bills should have their quantities compared by cross-checking against similar quantity related items. This aspect of work is usually carried out by the principal or a senior assistant whose experienced eye should be able to detect any major discrepancies, if these are present. Someone not directly involved in the project will often be able to spot possible errors.

A final careful examination should also be made of the drawings and specification. All notes on the drawings should be examined in case any have been missed. 'Of course, you've taken this' may produce the answer, 'No, I thought *you* had!' The specification can be run through in pencil, clause by clause, in confirmation that each has been included, either by the takers-off measuring or by those who drafted the preliminaries or preambles sections. At some stage between completion of the draft bill and passing of the proof the whole of the dimensions and the billing process should be examined to ensure that arithmetical checks have been carried out and the process audited.

The number of copies required of the finished document will include the number sent out to tender and copies for the client, architect, quantity surveyor and contractor. Two copies are also usually required for the contract.

Proof reading

The reading through of a proof copy of the contract bills is an important task. One person comparing a draft and a proof will very easily miss differences and mistakes will occur. The best way is for two to check, one reading from the draft and the other following in the proof. Periodically the duties and documents should be changed to avoid the soporific effect of listening to the reading for too long. It is usual to read from the draft copy because this is slower than reading from the proof copy. A good way to simplify the reading through is to go through the quantities columns first to ensure:

- Correctness of figures, both of item numbers and quantities
- That they are in the right column
- That the m or m^2 or m^3 are correct.

Copyright in the bills of quantities

Copyright is established by the Copyright Act 1988 in every 'original literary, dramatic, or musical work'. It is not clearly established whether there is copyright in contract bills. The RICS has taken the opinion of counsel, and were advised that in his opinion copyright existed, on the ground that the bill was an original literary work within the meaning of the Act of 1911, which used the same wording. This is an expert opinion and it should be remembered that experts sometimes differ. This is a reason for actions in law. There are inevitably many clauses in a bill of quantities that are more or less standard and used in very similar form by many surveyors, but the quantities are undoubtedly original. There will be in all bills a number of items that are original and peculiar to that particular bill.

There might be those who would take advantage of an opportunity to reuse a surveyor's bill. The best protection is to have a specific reservation by surveyors in their agreements with their clients of the rights of reprinting and reusing bills. If, of course, the surveyor is advised, when instructed, that it is proposed to use the bill again as and when required, and the condition is accepted, there can be no redress. The difficulty is avoided if the RICS Form of Agreement, Terms and Conditions for the Appointment of a Quantity Surveyor is adopted without amendments. In clause 8 of that agreement, copyright in the contract bills is retained by the quantity surveyor.

The dimensions and other memoranda from which the contract bills are prepared are in a different category. These are the surveyor's own means to an end. It has been held that the surveyor is entitled to retain these documents, unless, of course, as is sometimes the case, the contract with the client provides otherwise.

Invitation to tender

The project team will usually prepare, often in consultation with the client, a list of firms to be invited to tender, in some instances by way of some form of pre-qualification such as interview. Guidance is provided in the Code of Practice for the Selection of the Main Contractor. The firms selected will be sent a letter of invitation in advance of the documentation to confirm that they are on the list of proposed tenderers. This letter will include the following:

- Name of client and architect
- Title and location of the job
- Approximate date when the contract bills will be issued
- The time to be allowed for tendering
- Where the drawings may be inspected or some description of the works
- The form of contract to be used.

A typical letter for such a case is given in Fig. 12.4, based on the CIB Code of Practice for the Selection of Main Contractors. Occasionally some of the requirements of the Code of Procedure are not necessary. The requirement that tenderers should have two copies of the bill is important if they must send a priced copy with their tender or even forward it on advice that their tender is under consideration. If, however, a blank copy is sent after receipt of tenders, the extra expense of two copies to all tenderers does not seem justified. The offer of additional copies of the bill, or of sections of it, which the above-mentioned code stipulates, is only likely to be necessary in large contracts.

Dear Sirs

Southtown Church of England Primary School

We are authorised to prepare a preliminary list of tenderers for the construction of the works described below.

Your attention is drawn to the fact that apart from the alternative clauses to the Standard Form of Building Contract as detailed below, further amendments to the Standard Form of Contract are annexed and will be incorporated in the tender documents.

Will you please indicate whether you wish to be invited to submit a tender for these works on this basis. Your acceptance will imply your agreement to submit a wholly bona fide tender in accordance with the principles laid down in the *Code of Practice for the Selection of Main Contractors*, and not to divulge your tender price to any person or body before the time for submission of tenders. Once the contract has been let we undertake to supply all tenderers with a list of the tender prices.

Please state whether you would require any additional unbound copies of the contract bills in addition to the two copies you will receive. A charge may be made for extra copies. You are requested to apply by [insert date]. Your inability to accept will in no way prejudice your opportunities for tendering for further work under our direction; neither will your inclusion in the preliminary list at this stage guarantee that you will subsequently receive a formal invitation to tender for these works.

Yours faithfully

- Job: Southtown Church of England Primary School
- Employer: Blankchester Diocesan Board of Finance
- Architect: LMN Chartered Architects
- Quantity Surveyor: RS&T Chartered Quantity Surveyors
- Consultants: None
- Location of site: Site plan enclosed
- General description of work: New Primary School
- Approximate cost range: £700–800 000
- Nominated subcontractors for major items: Engineering Services
- Form of contract: JCT 98 incorporating amendment 1
  - Clause 19.1.2: will apply
  - Clause 21.2.1: insurance is not required
  - Clause 22A: will apply
  - Clause 23.1: will not apply
  - Clause 38: will apply
- Percentage to be included under clause 38.7: 10%
- Examination and correction of bills: overall price to be dominant (confirm or withdraw)
- The contract is to be: under hand

(Contd)

- Anticipated date for possession: [date]
- Period of completion of the works: 65 weeks
- Approximate date for dispatch of all tender documents: [date]
- Tender period: 5 weeks
- Tender to remain open for: 4 weeks
- Liquidated damages value: £1000 per week
- Details of bond requirement: None

Fig. 12.4 Preliminary enquiry for invitation to tender.

Form of tender and envelopes

Except for clients who have their own standard tender forms, the surveyor will probably be required to draft one to be issued with the contract bills. Tenders are sent either to the client or the architect according to the designated arrangements made for the delivery, which must be adhered to by all tenderers. They are normally to be sent in an envelope marked with the name of the job so that they can be put aside on receipt and all opened together.

Contractors may be given the option to tender for work covered by prime cost sums, in accordance with clause 35.2 of JCT 98. Provisions should be made on the form of tender for tenderers to state what specialist work (if any) they would like to tender for. With the current emphasis on early planning, the architect may want to nominate some of the specialist firms provisionally when preparing the drawings. In this way the architect is able to obtain the benefit of consultation with them.

Some public and private authorities require the priced bill to be returned with the tender. Where this is required, a separate addressed envelope of a suitable size should be provided for its return. The priced bills will be delivered sealed, and only opened if they are to be considered for acceptance. The envelope must, therefore, be marked with the name of the project in the same way as that enclosing the tender form, and the tenderers should be instructed that each must put their name clearly on the outside. (See Fig. 12.5 for an example form of tender.)

Issue of drawings

The contractors who are invited to tender should each be issued with copies of the location drawings, the site plan and the main plans and elevations of the project. Where appropriate relevant component details and drawings should also be provided. During the preparation of the bill of quantities, if errors are found in the architect's and engineer's drawings these should be corrected. The architect or engineer should be advised of these in time to allow the necessary corrections to be made prior to issuing them to the tenderers.

TENDER FOR: Southtown Church of England Primary School

TO: LMN Chartered Architects

Dear Sirs

Southtown School

We having read the conditions of contract and the bills of quantities delivered to us and having examined the drawings referred to therein do hereby offer to execute and complete in accordance with the conditions of contract the whole of the works described for the sum of £1726517.00 and within 65 weeks from the date of possession.

We agree that should obvious errors in pricing or errors in arithmetic be discovered before acceptance of this offer in the priced bills of quantities submitted by us, these errors will be dealt with in accordance with the CIB Code of Practice for the Selection of Main Contractors – overall price to be dominant.

This tender remains open for 28 days from the date fixed for the receipt of tenders.

Dated this .... day of .... 20......

Name

Address ....

....

....

Signature ....

Fig. 12.5 Form of tender. *Note:* If used in Scotland a paragraph needs to be added confirming the tenderer's willingness to enter into a formal contract, and the signature requires two witnesses.

Dispatch of finished bills

A covering letter (Fig. 12.6), will be issued with the drawings and contract bills to the tenderers. It should state:

- What documents are enclosed
- The date, time and place for delivery of tenders, and that tenders are to be delivered in the envelope supplied
- What drawings are enclosed and where and when further drawings can be inspected
- What arrangements the tenderer must make for visiting the site, with whom an appointment should be made, or where the key can be obtained. If the site is open for inspection this should be stated
- A request for an acknowledgement of the tender documents.

[Date]

Dear Sirs

Southtown Church of England Primary School

Following your acceptance of the invitation to tender for the above, we now have pleasure in enclosing the following:
- Two copies of the contract bills
- Two copies of the general arrangement drawings indicating the general character and shape and disposition of the works, and two copies of all detailed drawings referred to in the contract bills
- Two copies of the form of tender
- Addressed envelopes for the return of the tender and priced bills of quantities together with instructions relating thereto.

Will you please also note:
- Drawings and details may be inspected at the offices of the architect
- The site may be inspected by arrangement with the architect
- Tendering procedure will be in accordance with the principles of the Code of Practice for the Selection of Main Contractors
- Overall price to be dominant (confirm or withdraw).

The completed form of tender is to be sealed in the endorsed envelope provided and delivered or sent by post to reach the architect's office not later than 12.00 noon on [date]. Please acknowledge receipt of this letter and enclosures and confirm that you are able to submit a tender in accordance with these instructions.

Yours faithfully

Quantity surveyor

Fig. 12.6 Formal invitation to tender. *Note:* In Scotland it is mandatory for the priced bills to be returned with the tender, elsewhere it is a desirable alternative to adopt the option of delivery within four days.

It is also advisable to state that the client (employer) is not bound to accept the lowest or any tender or to pay any expenses incurred by the tenderer in preparing the tender.

Care must be taken in arranging the documents for each contract, so that all have them complete and correct. They are probably best laid out in piles with their envelopes and checked as they are put into them. For a comprehensive checklist of the information to be provided with the tender information, refer to Appendix 1 of the Code of Practice.

Correction of errors

Once the bills are dispatched to the contractors for tendering purposes, a copy should be examined. Mistakes may still be found, even after careful checking has taken place, perhaps made in the rush to send out the bill in time. Queries may arise, too, from contractors tendering. Unless errors are of a minor nature, they should be circulated to all contractors in time for them to correct their copies before tenders are completed. An acknowledgement should be requested to ensure that all tenderers have incorporated the corrections. During the examination of the priced bills of the successful contractor it should be verified that these corrections have been made. A typical letter is shown in Fig. 12.7.

[Date]

Dear Sirs,

Southtown School: New Extensions

Will you please incorporate the following corrections in the contract bill:

Item 246. For 16 m^3 read '66 m$^{3\prime}$.
Item 356. For 'm$^{2\prime}$ read 'm'.

Please acknowledge receipt of this letter.

Yours faithfully,

RS&T

Fig. 12.7 Letter to contractors: corrections to the contract bills.

Receipt of tenders

Delivery and opening

In public authorities, tenders will probably be addressed to the secretary or principal chief officer. With private clients they are usually forwarded to the architect or the quantity surveyor. On the due date for receipt of tenders, the envelopes received will be counted to check that they have all been received, prior to being opened. After opening, the official concerned or the architect or quantity surveyor will prepare a list of the tendered amounts.

The practice sometimes adopted of not giving contractors the list of tenders, or giving the figures only without the names, is to be discouraged. Publication of the result is the least that can be done in return for the time, effort and cost that is involved in preparing tenders. It is recommended that tenders delivered late, after the due time, should be returned, unopened, to the contractors. Contractors do share information in a variety of ways and an unscrupulous contractor might take advantage of this. If the postmark showed the tender to have been dispatched before the time for delivery, this might be an exception to the rule.

Reporting of tenders

In considering the tenders received, factors other than price may be of importance and these should form part of the assessment criteria provided to tenderers. The time required to carry out the work, if stated as a requirement on the form of tender, may be compared. Time is frequently an important matter to the client. Although there may be reasonable excuses for failing to keep to the time agreed, and even justification for avoiding the liquidated damages provided for by the contract, the time stated by a reputable contractor may be taken as a reasonable estimate, having regard to the prevailing circumstances. The *Code of Procedure for Selective Tendering*, however, recommends that contractors tender only against price, since it is not known what value a client may place on time.

If the contract is subject to adjustment of the price of materials via the traditional method, the schedule of basic rates of materials must also be considered. The question should be asked, 'Has the tenderer assumed reasonable basic prices for materials?' If they are too low there can be an excessive increased cost on a rising market or too little in reduced costs on a falling market. Where tenders are very close, the schedules of basic rates may be compared, since the lower tenderer may have less favourable prices. Only a preliminary examination will be made at this stage to ascertain which tender or tenders should be considered for acceptance. A fuller report will be made later by the quantity surveyor.

The architect will rely extensively on the quantity surveyor for advice on these matters. A report will be prepared for the client or committee concerned, setting out clearly the arguments in favour of acceptance of one tender or another.

When tenders are invited from a limited number of contractors the lowest, or potentially lowest, should generally be accepted, although consideration must be given to other assessment criteria stated in the invitation to tender. However, tenderers are usually informed that the client has no legal obligation to accept the lowest or any tender or be involved in the costs of their preparation. But, in a limited invitation to tender (selective tendering) there is a moral obligation to accept the lowest, if any.

In open tendering, which is not recommended, there may be clear justification for rejecting the lowest tender on grounds other than cost. However, when the expenditure of public money is involved, there may be repercussions and the grounds for such rejection will need to be clearly demonstrated.

Examination of priced bill

Before acceptance of a tender, the tenderer whose offer is under consideration is required to submit a copy of the priced bills to the quantity surveyor for examination. If this has not been delivered with the tender, an additional copy should be sent to the contractor for this purpose. Sometimes, to save time, the original bills may be requested. However, the original bills are often marked with the estimator's pricing notes which would be injudicious to disclose. There is no justification for the certificate that is sometimes required that the copy of the bill has been compared and checked with the original. The tender is a lump-sum tender and the sole purpose of obtaining the pricing is to provide a fair schedule for the adjustment of future variations.

The first check is an arithmetical check. Clerical errors are common. It is important that the contract bills are as correct as they possibly can be prior to the signing of the contract. If, for example, an item has been priced at £0.50 per m and extended at £0.05, it will not be fair that either additional quantity or omission of the item should be priced out at the incorrect rate in adjusting accounts. All clerical errors should be corrected in the contract copy of the bills. The amount of the tender will of course not normally be altered. Any difference will be shown as a rebate or addition as an addendum to the summary (see Fig. 12.8). This addendum will be used for interim valuations and adjustment of variations, to all rates except prime cost and provisional sums.

Summary	£
Preliminary items	18662.00
PC and provisional sums	55408.00
Substructure	17479.06
	8131.16
Concrete work	~~8031.16~~
Brickwork and blockwork	19083.69
Roofing	4789.88
Woodwork	18103.97
	4392.36
Metalwork	~~4393.36~~
	1884.38
Plumbing services	~~1884.28~~
Plasterwork and finishings	8616.01
Glazing	1036.77
Painting	4302.74
Drainage	3728.98
External works	16445.98
	£182064.98
	~~£181965.88~~
Water and insurance 3.5%	6367.57
	£188432.55
	~~£188333.45~~
Tender submitted £188300.00	

Fig. 12.8   Corrected summary in contract bills.

In addition to the arithmetical check, a technical check is also made of the pricing by examining the contractor's rates and prices. Deliberate or accidental errors may be found. Items may accidentally have been left unpriced. Items billed in square metres may have been priced at what is obviously a linear metre rate, or vice versa. An obvious misunderstanding of a description may be noted. Corrections should be made so that a reasonable schedule of rates for pricing variations results.

A secondary reason for examination of the priced bill is to ensure that the tenderer has not made such a serious mistake that they would prefer to withdraw the tender. Under English law contractors may do this at any time prior to the acceptance of a contract. When such a serious error is detected, it is always advisable to bring this to the attention of the tenderer. The error will sooner or later be discovered, resulting in a risk that constant attempts will then be made to recover the loss, to the detriment of the client's interest. The contractor should, however, be recommended to stand by the tender that has been submitted.

Notwithstanding the guidance provided in the Code of Practice for the Selection of Main Contractors, if the correction of the error does not bring the tender under consideration above the next highest, the architect may feel that the client should be advised to allow amendment of the tender. Otherwise the next lowest tender should be considered. If a tender has been accepted and a contract formed, tenderers strictly cannot withdraw. However, this may not be a good policy to adopt for the above-mentioned reason. There are cases where a successful tenderer realises that the tender submitted is well below that of the other competitors. There is the temptation to adjust the bills, knowing that these will still be below other contractors' sums. To avoid this temptation occurring, the practice of submitting priced bills with the tender is recommended.

If priced bills are delivered with the tender by all contractors, only the bills of tenderers under consideration for acceptance should be opened. All others should be returned unopened. In the summary in Fig. 12.8, alterations have been made correcting clerical and other errors found in the priced bills. The increased total means that all rates except PC and provisional sums, (which the contractor has no power to reduce) will be subject to a percentage rebate. To calculate this percentage, extract PC and provisional sum amounts, as shown in Fig. 12.9.

The effect of this calculation is as follows. In the variation account all rates will be subject to addition of 3.50% for water and insurances, and all except PC and provisional sums and accounts set against these will also be subject to a rebate of 0.18%. The water and insurance percentage can be converted into a percentage on the contractor's own work instead of on the whole total as appears in this example. In that case the two percentages can be combined into a single percentage. However, in this case, since the contractor has expressed water and insurances as a percentage of the whole, they are so treated.

		£
Provisional sums		10000
Mechanical services		14850
Electrical services		8223
Wood flooring		2200
External staircase		4050
Metal windows		6500
Water mains		200
Ironmongery		550
Sanitary fittings		890
Daywork		2610
		£50073

The rebate to be expressed as a percentage is:

Errors	182064	
	181966	98

Rebate in tender	188433	
	188300	133
		£231

(This total equals the total difference between £188433 and £188300.)

The percentage is calculated as follows:

Corrected total without insurance, etc.	182064
Less PC and provisional sums	50073
	£131991

$$\text{Percentage} = \frac{231}{131991} \times \frac{100}{1} = 0.18\%$$

Fig. 12.9 Calculation of percentage rebate.

Correction of errors

Two alternatives are described for dealing with genuine errors in rates and prices. Where overall price is dominant the contractor either confirms or withdraws the tender. Where rates are dominant the contractor is allowed to confirm or correct. The difficulty is to decide what is a genuine error, particularly as, under JCT 98 clause 5.2, four days can elapse before the priced contract bills must be produced – a further reason to request that they are submitted at the same time as the tenders. The option to be adopted must be made prior to the tenders being invited.

Examination of schedule of basic rates

Where a contract is to be subject to price adjustment and exceptionally the formula method is not being used, a basic price list of materials must also be provided. This is usually requested at the same time as the bills for checking.

The basic price list only covers those materials for which an adjustment is required. All rates not supported by a bona fide quotation must be carefully checked. Some materials, such as Portland cement, have standard prices. Others, such as steel tubing or stoneware drainage goods, are often quoted at a percentage on or off a standard list. Current rate comparisons can be obtained from the trade association concerned. The majority of the basic rates will probably be compared with those in price books or from local builder's merchants. It is usual for only the major items to be included, to reduce the unproductive paper work of all concerned.

The prices will usually vary with the amount purchased. Quotations should be examined within a context of an expert knowledge of prices. It is not unknown for merchants to make mistakes against themselves in the price quoted. It will probably be some months before the quotation is accepted, and then only after further tenders have been obtained by the contractor in an attempt to reduce costs. The mistake being discovered, the contractor may claim the correction as increased cost. Under the normal forms of contract fluctuation in market price must be proved, so recovery of the amount of the error cannot be made.

The introduction of the price-adjustment formula, which is now generally preferred, negates this process and instead the quantity surveyor will be required to complete the schedule of allocation and the reduction of the work categories to the agreed number if required.

Addendum bills

The lowest tender is sometimes for a higher amount than the client is prepared to spend. It is usually possible to reduce the tender sum by changing the design in terms of either quantity or quality. However, the correct application of cost planning procedures should avoid this problem. An addendum bill is prepared in a similar way to the variation account referred to in Chapter 14. Changes to the design are measured and priced using the rates from the contractor's priced bills. The addendum bill is prepared prior to the contract being signed and the contract sum is hence based on the revised tender figure. The bill modifies the original quantities, and the quantities so modified become part of the contract. The adjustments are mostly omissions, but balancing additions are also required. Where there are no rates or prices for these in the bills, they are agreed with the contractor through a process of negotiation. Sometimes, if a variation is complex but its value can be estimated fairly accurately, the adjustment can be made on a lump sum agreed by the parties concerned.

Preparation of contract bill of quantities

A fair copy of the priced bills is required for signature with the contract. If a blank copy has been sent to the contractor to be completed, this can be used as the surveyor's office copy after making any alterations necessitated by the checking process. A corrected copy, for the contract, is made by the quantity surveyor. If necessary it should contain the schedule of basic rates of materials or the allocation of the items, so making them part of the contract.

The prices in the contractor's priced bill of quantities are confidential. They must be used solely for the purpose of the contract (JCT 98, clause 5.7). Though they naturally contribute to the quantity surveyor's knowledge of current rates and prices, they can only be referred to for the surveyor's own information. They should not, for example, be discussed with another contractor. Where contractors have submitted priced bills with their tenders, those not considered for acceptance are returned unopened. Their prices remain unknown to all but the contractor. It is not unknown for contractors to submit tenders out of courtesy, because they do not like to risk offending a client or architect. Their rates and prices will be kept unknown if this procedure is followed correctly.

Preparing the contract

The duty of preparing the contract by completing the various blank spaces in the articles of agreement is the responsibility of the architect, although the quantity surveyor is often asked to complete it. It is sometimes necessary to add special clauses to the conditions of contract and to amend other clauses. Where this is required they must be written in, and the insertion or alteration must be initialled by both parties at the time of signing the contract.

Extreme care must be taken if clauses within standard conditions of contract are to be amended, as specific alterations can affect other clauses. It is not recommended. It is usual to seek legal advice if it is intended to make substantial amendments. Any portions to be deleted must be ruled through and similarly initialled. All other documents contained in the contract, i.e. each drawing and the contract bills, should be marked for identification and signed by the parties; for example:

- This is one of the drawings
- This is the bill of quantities
- referred to in the contract signed by us this day of 20...

For the contract bills, this identification should be on the front cover or on the last page, and the number of pages can be stated. If the standard form with quantities is used the specification does not form a part of the contract. It will thus not be signed by the parties. If there are no quantities the specification is a contract document and must be signed accordingly. All the signed documents must be construed together as the contract for the project.

Contracts are either signed under hand, when the limitation period is six years, or when a twelve years period is required the contract is completed as a deed, formerly under seal. In the latter case it is important to ensure that this is duly recognised, as failure to do so could have serious implications.

Case law exists that illustrates the importance of ensuring that all the contract documents are in agreement with each other. In *Gleeson* v. *London*

Borough of Hillingdon (1970) EGD 495, there was a discrepancy between completion dates set out in the contract bills and completion dates in the Appendix to the JCT form of contract. Delays had occurred, and the question was raised with regards to the correct date to be used when calculating liquidated damages. The court held that under the relevant clause of the form of contract in use at the time (JCT 63, clause 12 (1)), the date in the Appendix prevailed. Litigation would not have occurred had the contract documents been properly checked for any inconsistencies.

Bibliography

Aqua Group. *Tenders and Contracts for Building*. Blackwell Science. 1990.

Aqua Group. *Precontract Practice for the Building Team*. Blackwell Science. 1992.

CIB. *Code of Practice for the Selection of Main Contractors*. Thomas Telford. 1997.

Dearle and Henderson. *SMM7 Reviewed*. Blackwell Science. 1988.

Nisbet J. *Called to Account: Quantity Surveying, 1936–1986*. Stoke Publications. 1989.

RICS *Appointing a Quantity Surveyor*. Royal Institution of Chartered Surveyors. 1999.

Willis J.A. and Trench W. *Willis's Elements of Quantity Surveying*. Blackwell Science, Oxford. 1998.

13 Cost Management

Introduction

The scope of the surveyor's involvement during the post-contract stage of a project will generally require the preparation of interim valuations, the preparation and agreement of the final account and the management of project costs throughout. Final accounts are discussed in the next chapter. It is usual for both the client and the contractor to employ a surveyor or team of surveyors during the post-contract phase. The successful execution and completion of the post-contract procedures and the final account very much depend on cooperation between the client's appointed surveyor and that of the contractor. Whilst the responsibilities of these differ, there are areas of involvement common to both and it is important that each side has an understanding of the process and possible approaches. This is further underlined by the developments in procurement and contract choice, which continue to emerge.

Depending upon the size and nature of the project, the post-contract administration may be undertaken by site-based staff involved on a full time or intermittent basis. Nevertheless the duties to be performed will be somewhat similar. Likewise, the degree of involvement may vary according to the type of main contract. For example, if the contract is awarded on an approximate quantities basis requiring re-measurement on site, there will be a need for additional surveyors to be involved to carry out the site measurement. Alternatively, if the project is design and build, it is probable that the demands upon the time of the client's surveyor will be much reduced.

The issue of contract choice and the impact it may have upon practice is somewhat of a difficulty to overcome in a book of this type. There are now many contract options available and it is impossible to accommodate the specifics of each. Furthermore, there will undoubtedly be additional choice by the time this book reaches the reader. For example, the publication of the ACA (Association of Consultant Architects) Project Partnering Contract (PPC 2000) will likely be encountered by surveyors in the near future. Therefore, in the interest of clarity and pragmatism, the emphasis of this chapter is on the practical rather than contractual. Where reference to the contract becomes a necessary part of the explanation, the main standard form used is JCT 98 Private with Quantities. Despite its relative decline in use over recent years, it is still considered to be the most commonly understood, and knowledge of it is a fundamental requirement for students and practitioners. Although only occasional reference to other forms of contract is made, much of the explanation and associated practice and procedure relating to JCT 98 can be transferred to these with little or no amendment. However, although strong similarities may exist – a great deal of the wording in some contracts may be identical, e.g. Standard Forms JCT 98 (Traditional) and WCD 98 (Design and Build) – there are also subtle and distinct differences which the reader should be wary of and research further where practice demands.

Since the contractual basis of this chapter generally relates to JCT 98, it accommodates the provisions of the Housing Grants, Construction and Regeneration Act (the Construction Act), which became effective in May 1998.

Valuations

The construction industry survives on cash flow and the role of the surveyor is of key importance in this regard. JCT 98 makes clear the duty of the client's quantity surveyor in this respect (clause 30.1.2.1):

> 'Interim valuations shall be made by the Quantity Surveyor whenever the Architect considers them to be necessary for the purpose of ascertaining the amount to be stated as due in an Interim Certificate.'

In addition, the contract states that where the use of the price adjustment formula applies (see later in this chapter), in accordance with clause 40, the quantity surveyor must prepare the valuation.

Most construction projects encountered by the surveyor will have contractual provision for the payment of the contractor for work done, at regular intervals during the contract period. The amounts involved in the construction of major works and the duration of most projects warrant this approach. Therefore, the contractor has a regular cashflow, which is vital to profitability within the construction industry. This issue of regular payment is a major feature of the Housing Grants, Construction and Regeneration Act 1996 (the Construction Act), the contents of which are reflected in the 1998 Standard Form of Building Contract.

Between the date of the first interim certificate, subject to agreement between the parties, and the issue of the certificate of practical completion, interim certificates must be issued at the regular intervals stated in the Appendix. The most common period of payment, and default situation if none is stated, is at one monthly intervals. If requested by the architect, which is the norm, it is the responsibility of the surveyor to calculate the amount of such interim payments. Following the issue of the certificate of practical completion, the architect may issue further interim certificates 'as and when further amounts are ascertained'.

Certificates and payments

In the course of a construction project for which interim valuations apply, an architect or contract administrator will be called upon to make decisions and issue a series of certificates that must be issued in accordance with the provisions of the particular contract. In so doing when acting in an arbitral situation, an architect is under a duty imposed by law to act fairly and impartially between the parties.

Where an interim certificate is required by the contract, and certainly under JCT 98, its issue is a condition precedent to payment. If the certificate is improperly withheld, entitlement to payment may be enforced in the absence of the requisite certificate.

The employer must pay the contractor no later than 14 days from the issue of the interim certificate. Failure to do so may result in the application of one or more of the remedies available to the contractor:

- Claim for interest on the late payment. In addition to the amount due to the contractor, simple interest will be due on the amount of late payment, calculated at a rate of 5% above the Base Rate of the Bank of England, current at the due date, for the duration of the delay in payment.
- Suspension of the works. If the employer fails to pay in accordance with the contract, the contractor may issue a notice to the employer, copied to the architect, to the effect that the works will be suspended after a further 7 days, allowing time for delivery. Once the employer has paid the amount due, the work should recommence within a reasonable time thereafter.
- Determination in accordance with clause 28 of the standard form.

The surveyor should be alert to the above conditions and advise the client and architect where necessary.

In addition to the certificate, the contractor is entitled to a 'Notice of Payment' which should be issued within 5 days of the date of issue of an interim certificate, showing the basis of the valuation. Where the employer intends to 'withhold and/or deduct an amount from the payment due', the contractor should be provided with a 'Notice to withhold' which should be issued no later than 5 days from the final date of payment. This should show the amount to be withheld/deducted, stating the grounds for such action. Whilst neither the surveyor nor the architect should exclude amounts from the certificate, when there are grounds for withholding, they should advise the employer of the entitlement to do so, including provision of the required detail.

Accuracy

The valuation for certificates should be made as accurately as is reasonably possible. In preparing or verifying the valuation, the surveyor has two opposing concerns:

- The contractor is entitled under the contract to the value of work done, less a specified retention sum. If the valuation is kept low, the retention sum is in effect increased. To a contractor having a number of contracts in hand, these excessive amounts of 'retention' will mount up and demand additional capital, which may have serious consequences.

- The client must be protected against the possible insolvency of the contractor. When an overpayment resulting from an excessive valuation cannot be recovered from the contractor, as in the case of insolvency, the additional payment will be effectively 'lost' and may become an additional expense to the client. In turn, this additional amount may become the liability of the surveyor.

It is reasonable to assume that to the client's surveyor, the latter consideration will be given more significance than the former since self-preservation is a powerful incentive. It appears that some surveyors translate their understandable caution into the under-valuation of contractors' work. This tendency, which may be greater amongst less experienced surveyors, should be resisted for the reasons outlined above. Unfortunately, in cases where the financial reputation of the contractor becomes in doubt, the reasonable inclination of the surveyor is to become more cautious, which in turn may result in greater financial difficulties.

In determining the need for accuracy, the surveyor should appreciate that an interim valuation is merely a snapshot of the progress of the works, which, depending on the work stage, contractors' programme, deliveries to site, etc., may change significantly within 24 hours of the assessment.

Timing

If, as is usually the case, the contractor is entitled to certificates at regular monthly intervals, (in terms of JCT 98, this should strictly be adhered to), it will be found convenient to arrange the dates at the beginning of the contract: say, the last Thursday in every month. Since the timing of the first interim certificate determines the dates of the remainder, it is important that this is done with some forethought. Sometimes the dates must be fixed to suit the client's convenience, particularly when payment is passed at a board or committee meeting held at fixed intervals. Similarly, where there are monthly site meetings which the surveyor needs to attend, it may be possible to arrange the valuation for the same day. This is particularly beneficial where the site may be some distance from the surveyor's office. In any event all parties should be aware of the implications of failure to certify and pay correctly in accordance with the conditions of contract.

In the past, the client's surveyor found it very helpful if the contractor submitted a statement with supporting invoices, delivery notes, etc. as a basis for the valuation. This approach saved a great deal of time and was also possibly more accurate since the contractor was able to provide more detail than may otherwise have been possible to establish during a site visit. JCT 98 now reflects this previously accepted practice by means of clause 30.1.2.2. This allows the contractor to prepare and submit an application for interim payment, incorporating applications for payment from nominated subcontractors, 'no later than 7 days before the date of an Interim Certificate'. It is important to emphasise that this action does not remove the responsibility for the valuation from the client's surveyor who, in normal circumstances, will be liable for its correctness and in the absence of the contractor's application is still obliged to prepare a valuation in accordance with clause 30.1.2.1. (Although the correctness of the certificate is the responsibility of the architect, reliance on the quantity surveyor's valuation is normal and thus, in practice, transfers liability for its accuracy.) In order to verify the contractor's application, it is sensible for the client's surveyor to arrange a meeting on site with the contractor's surveyor and, where necessary, make any adjustment to the contractor's statement. Where such an adjustment occurs, the client's surveyor is obliged to provide the contractor with a statement showing the revised amount of valuation, together with supporting detail to allow the contractor to identify and understand the changes that have been made.

Nominated subcontractors should be notified by the main contractor of the dates of the valuations and be required to submit statements by those dates. If preferred, the surveyor can make those arrangements, but it should be part of the main contractor's responsibility to do so. Dealings with the contractor's domestic subcontractors should only be through the main contractor with whose rates alone the surveyor is concerned.

Extent of measurement

The extent to which measurement will be necessary in making valuations for certificates will depend on the nature of the job and the stage it has reached. It may very often be possible to take the priced bill, identify the items that have been done, and build up a figure in that way. Some items will, of course, be only partly done, and in that case a proportion will have to be allocated. At a first valuation, for instance, there may be little beyond foundations, and to identify the appropriate items in the bill should not be difficult. If it is agreed that the foundations are two-thirds complete then the amount can be easily calculated. When, however, it comes to the superstructure, it may be necessary to take approximate measurements of such things as brickwork, floors and roofs. The surveyor should always bear in mind the value of the works being measured in determining the most appropriate approach. To avoid excessive labour in the measurement of relatively complex but low cost items for valuation purposes, it may be more reasonable to agree with the contractor's surveyor that 'half the total value of the plumbing works' is a fair assessment of the works carried out. It should be remembered that detailed measurement for valuation purposes will likely have no further bearing beyond the interim valuation in hand and is therefore of passing value only.

Figure 13.1 indicates the apportionment approach to the preparation of an interim valuation, reflecting both a necessary pragmatism and also a reasonable level of accuracy. In this example, concrete work has been collected into work between ground and first floor, first floor and second and second floor to roof. A tour of the site will allow a prompt but reasonable assessment.

Bill Ref	Brief description (Concrete works)	Total £	Previous %	Amount £	Present %	Amount £
	Interim valuation 5;					
	Date on site 20 March 2001					
18/3 B–G	Reinforced Concrete in Cols					
	Say 40% GF–1st	24 000	100	24 000	100	24 000
	Say 30% 1st–2nd	18 000	75	13 500	90	16 200
	Say 30% 2nd–Roof	18 000	Nil	Nil	10	1 800
18/4 A–F	Formwork to Cols					
	Say 40% GF–1st		100		100	
	Say 30% 1st–2nd		100		100	
	Say 30% 2nd–Roof		50		75	
18/5 A–H	Reinforcement in Cols					
	Say 40% GF–1st		100		100	
	Say 30% 1st–2nd		100		100	
	Say 30% 2nd–Roof		50		75	
	Total carried forward					

Fig. 13.1 Apportionment of works for valuation purposes.

The surveyor should consider several approaches within the calculation of the interim valuation. As indicated by the example, the usual method of valuation is to assess the total amount of work performed at each interim stage on a gross basis (*not* as previous payment plus a little more). This approach negates any errors that may have occurred in a previous valuation, although inclusion of columns showing the previous assessment may be a useful guide. There are various further shortcuts that may be taken, for example, the annotation of a copy of the bills of quantities with inserted columns for amounts of work carried out. Information technology, of course, can assist greatly, either by use of an electronic copy of the bills, if available, or by the generation of a spreadsheet that could also be used in the assessment of amounts for fluctuations.

When dealing with housing, or other projects for which there are a large number of similar units, it should be possible from the bill of quantities to arrive at an approximate value of one house at various stages; for example:

• Brickwork up to damp-proof course
• Brickwork to first floor level, with joists on
• Brickwork to eaves
• Roof complete
• Plastering and glazing complete
• Doors hung
• Plumbing and fittings complete
• Decoration complete.

The value for different types of the same size of house will not vary sufficiently to make a difference for certificate purposes. The work done at any time can be valued by taking the number of houses that have reached each stage, and pricing for half and quarter stages. With such projects, if the contractor's surveyor intends to submit a detailed valuation in accordance with JCT 98, details of the approach should be agreed with the client's surveyor at the outset to avoid disagreement and abortive work.

On projects without firm bills of quantities, the value of the work carried out will be assessed through measurement of work on site or, where appropriate, by proportion of the individual items on the tender summary. It may be convenient to invest some time at the commencement of the project to agree the value of particular work stages as a basis for interim valuations.

Towards the completion of the project, it is a good idea to check what is left to complete, as a safeguard against error in a cumulative total. For the last two or three valuations, the contract sum might be taken as a basis, and deduction made of all PC or provisional sums and percentage additions and of work not yet done, the various accounts against the first of these being added together with percentage additions pro rata, adjustment being made for the approximate value of variations and price adjustment. Similarly, once identifiable sections of the works are almost complete, a similar approach can be adopted whereby, for example, with reference to Fig. 13.1 above, concrete on each floor can be calculated as complete less minor amounts of work not yet done.

Preliminaries items

Each valuation will take into account the pricing of the preliminary bill or preliminaries items. There may be a number of items separately priced, or there may be one total for sections or the whole in which case further analysis will be required. In addition, they may show an allocation between fixed and time-related costs in accordance with SMM7.

Each priced item should be considered and a fair proportion of each included. Single payments, time related costs and value related costs should be considered separately. Single payments occur where there is an identifiable item of work, for example a site notice board with a single cost payable on construction at the beginning of the project and a further payment on removal at completion. Time related items relate to items that attract costs on a regular basis during the works, for example, site management, the amount for which that is included in the preliminaries could be divided by the period of the contract to give a suitable monthly sum. Value related items could be valued on the basis of the proportion of the measured items completed by the contractor. Thus, if 25% of the measured works were completed, the same proportion of that element of the preliminaries would be incorporated accordingly. For example, the cost of electricity for the works, part of which will be linked to the amount of work carried out.

Some preliminaries items may be allocated to more than one or all of these categories, for example, the cost of telephones. A proportion of the telephone charges during the construction of the works will depend on works progress and will therefore be value related, part of the cost will be fixed (perhaps relating to connection fees) and some may be time related (standing charges). Similarly, the price for provision of offices, mess facilities and storage units could be split into delivery cost (single payment), weekly rent (time related) and removal cost (single payment), and valuation made accordingly.

If it is anticipated that the contract time will be exceeded, suitable reductions should be made on the time related items to relate payments on account more accurately to the work actually carried out. If an extension of time award has been made, this could affect the amount of the preliminaries allowance also.

A cashflow forecast of preliminaries costs relating to the duration of the works may be prepared for agreement at the first interim valuation. Once this is accepted it may be used for future valuations, not forgetting to monitor the progress of the works and adjust if necessary. A partial example of this is shown in Fig. 13.2; this would reflect the apportionment to single, time, and value related costs.

Prelim item	Months												Total £
	1	2	3	4	5	6	7	8	9	10	11	12	
Site offices													
Electricity													
Water													
Telephones													
Temporary roads													
Insurances													

Fig. 13.2   Indicative example of a pro-forma for preliminaries assessment.

It should be noted that the use of either a time related or a cost related approach for the total preliminaries assessment at interim valuation stage is bound to be flawed and less accurate than the above method.

Nominated subcontractors and suppliers

NB   The position of the nominated subcontractor and nominated supplier should not be confused with that of the contractor's domestic subcontractors (see next section).

The use of prime cost sums in a project allows the architect (and hence the client, via the architect) the opportunity of selecting a particular firm to carry

out certain items of work (i.e. nominated subcontractor) or a firm to manufacture and supply materials (i.e. nominated supplier). This opportunity to
nominate a particular organisation is used where the work is of a specialist
nature and where the architect desires greater control of the subcontractor
choice and thereby quality. It may also be used to overcome a known shortage. For example, the lead-in time for structural steelwork in the late 1980s
was such that if no order was placed for the steel until the contractor was
appointed, delays were very likely. The ordering of the steelwork by the
employer, prior to the appointment of the main contractor and thereafter
nominating the selected subcontractor, resolved this.

This opportunity to interfere with the freedom the contractor generally has
in carrying out the works brings with it certain obligations. The position of the
nominated subcontractor and, to a certain extent, the nominated supplier is a
special one in terms of the contract in which the related procedures and
requirements are precisely stated (clauses 35 and 36 of the JCT 98 form).

With regard to nominated subcontractors, this special position demands a
strict approach in terms of the contract at interim valuation stage. The subcontractor's claims will be taken one by one and examined, and a suitable
figure added for each. The surveyor should have received either direct or
from the architect, a copy of the subcontractor's accepted estimate. This may
or may not be the same as that for arriving at the PC sum when the bill was
prepared. It may give some detail of measurements and rates or may just give
a lump sum. If the latter, and some subdivision is required, it can be asked for
as a guide for valuations and a help at a later stage in measuring variations.

To arrive at an interim valuation of the subcontractor's work is sometimes
very difficult. One may arrive on the site and find stacks of, say, metal windows and curtain walling in sections and pieces, with bags of bolts and fittings, and be presented with a statement 'To materials delivered: £10 000'.
There should be delivery notes indicating the portions of the subcontract for
which materials have been delivered, and even though it may not be practicable to make a complete detailed check, it should be possible to assess the
portion of the relative accepted estimate. When using this approach at
valuation, the surveyor should ensure that the cost of assembling and fixing is
deducted. This should be possible via the costs of material supply where
available but may require some approximation.

It is good practice to notify each nominated subcontractor of the amount
included in the surveyor's recommendation, though the architect is required
by JCT 98, clause 35.13, to notify the subcontractor of the amount included on
the certificate. This should be done by use of the RICS form *Statement of
Retention and of Nominated Sub-Contractors Values* (see Fig. 13.3) The contract
requires the surveyor to be satisfied that payments included have been made,
and this should be done by asking the contractor to produce reasonable proof,
for instance by provision of copies of the relevant receipts, at the next
valuation.

It should be noted that nominated suppliers are in a different position. They
are not entitled to be paid directly by the employer and therefore should be

Statement of Retention and of Nominated Sub-Contractors' Values

Surveyor: Franklin + Andrews
Address:

Works: Shops and Offices
Willow Centre

This Statement relates to:
Valuation No: 6
Date of Issue:
Reference: 123
Date

	Gross Valuation £	Basis of Gross Valuation (See note 1) Clause No.	Amount subject to:				Amount of Retention £	Net Valuation £	Amount Previously Certified £	Balance £
			Full Retention of 3 % £	Half Retention of % £	No Retention £					
Main Contractor	346,280		330,930	–	15,350		9,928	336,352	280,000	56,352
Nominated Sub-Contractors										
G & H Engineering	40,000	4.17	40,000	–	–		1,200	38,800	–	38,800
I & J Electrical	15,000	4.17	15,000	–	–		450	14,550	–	14,550
K & L Windows	10,000	4.17	10,000	–	–		300	9,700	–	9,700
TOTAL	411,280		395,930	–	15,350		11 878	399,402	280,000	119,402

Notes:
(1) The basis of the gross valuation in respect of Nominated Sub-Contractors is:
   for interim payments – clause 4.17 of NSC/C
   for final payments   sub-contracts based on a lump sum – (clause 3.1 of NSC/A) clause 4.23 of NSC/C
                         sub-contracts based on measurement – (clause 3.2 of NSC/A) clause 4.24 of NSC/C
(2) No account has been taken of any discounts for cash which the Contractor may be entitled if discharging the balance within 17 days of the issue of the Architect/Contract Administrator.
(3) The sums stated are exclusive of VAT.

© RICS 2000

Fig. 13.3   Statement of retention and of nominated subcontractors' values.

excluded from the *Statement of Retention and of Nominated Sub-Contractors Values.*

To be consistent with JCT 98, the Standard Conditions of Nominated Sub-contract, 1998 Edition (NSC/C) states that payment by the contractor to nominated subcontractors should be within 17 days of the issue of the interim certificate. This provides an additional 3 days to that allowed for with the client's payment to the contractor, thus accommodating the payment of the contractor before the need to pay the subcontractor. This being said, failure on the part of the employer to pay the contractor within the 14 day time period is not a valid reason for non-payment of the subcontractor within 17 days.

In the event that the contractor fails to pay the subcontractor in accordance with the contract, the subcontractor is entitled to the payment of interest and to suspend the works, similar to the remedies available to the contractor where the employer fails to pay. In addition, the nominated sub-contractor can be paid directly by the client. When there is failure by the main contractor to provide proof of payment of nominated subcontractors (the reason for this should be verified, e.g. it may be due to the sub-contractor's failure to produce a valid receipt), the architect should issue a certificate of non-payment. Following this, at the next issue of an interim certificate, the amount concerned should be deducted by the employer from that due to the contractor and paid directly to the subcontractor. This is outlined in detail in clause 35.13 and the surveyor will be required to advise the architect and client accordingly.

In accordance with the NSC/C contract conditions referred to above, the contractor is entitled to withhold from amounts certified to nominated sub-contractors (i.e. set off) sums that can be attributed to some failing of the subcontractor.

Domestic subcontractors

Apart from the subletting of works to nominated subcontractors, the contractor is allowed to appoint subcontractors to carry out portions of the works, provided written consent is obtained from the architect in accordance with JCT 98, clause 19.2.2. This consent is required to permit the subletting and does not relate to the approval of the subcontractor selected by the contractor, although in practice, consent may be withheld until the details of the proposed subcontractor are known (Ndekugri and Rycroft 2000).

The payment of interim amounts to domestic subcontractors is the responsibility of the contractor's surveyor. Applications for payment from subcontractors often form the basis of the main contractor's own application. Payments will be made to each subcontractor, generally in line with amounts certified to the main contractor. Reconciliation on a monthly basis will be required. The contractor's surveyor will analyse income received through certificate payments against costs of subcontractor payment and direct costs (see section 'Cost control and reporting' later in this chapter).

The client's surveyor should be aware that the interim accounts prepared by domestic subcontractors should be considered as though the main contractor had produced them.

Named subcontractors

Named subcontractors are, as their title suggests, named by the architect and in this respect only are similar to nominated subcontractors. By providing a list of subcontractors and/or suppliers in the contract documents (at least three names must be provided for each portion of the works – as JCT 98, clause 19.3.2.), from whom specified work or materials should be obtained, the architect is able to restrict and therefore control possible sources of supply. Once a subcontractor has been so named (JCT 98, clause 19.3; IFC 98, clause 3.3), when finally selected by the contractor, they become domestic subcontractors in exactly the same way as subcontractors chosen entirely at the discretion of the main contractor. No special requirements therefore arise regarding the client's surveyor's duties at interim valuation or final account stage.

In practice, named subcontractors may pose a problem to the contractor. The rates submitted by the contractor at tender stage for portions of the works covered by the named subcontractor provision are at the risk of the main contractor. It is therefore important that rates for the work, which is to be carried out by one of the named subcontractors, are adequate and that they have been obtained from one of the named subcontractors. Failure to conform in this regard, for example by using rates from an unnamed subcontractor with whom work is regularly sublet, is exposing the contractor to significant additional price risk. Additional names may be added to the list by either party if approval is obtained from the other (clause 19.3.2.1).

Unfixed materials

Besides the value of work done, most forms of contract allow payment to be made to the contractor for unfixed materials. The payment for such materials is an area of additional risk for the employer in that:

- At the time of payment, ownership of the materials may not be vested in the contractor but with subcontractors or suppliers. Therefore, in such situations, payment by the employer does not transfer ownership from the contractor to whom it did not belong in the first place.
- The materials, being unfixed, may be more easily lost, damaged or stolen. This remains the risk of the contractor, in accordance with clause 16.1, unless, of course, insolvency of the contractor occurs.
- In the event of contractor insolvency, unfixed materials, irrespective of true ownership, may be easily removed from site.

The risks associated with unfixed materials are increased where the materials are stored off-site and this aspect is discussed further below.

In an attempt to protect the employer, JCT 98 makes special provision regarding the payment for unfixed materials, both on-site and off-site. In consideration of the contract conditions, the surveyor should only include payment for unfixed materials stored on-site where:

- The materials are correctly stored. Storage on building sites may be less than ideal and wastage rates are generally considered to be too high. Payment for materials, which due to damage cannot be incorporated within the works, should not be allowed.
- The materials are delivered *reasonably, properly and not prematurely.* Materials delivered too far in advance of their incorporation within the works should not be paid for. There are several factors that should be considered in determining the reasonable timing of deliveries, including material availability, ownership of price risk (e.g. will the employer gain benefit from early purchase and delivery thus avoiding an imminent price increase) and works progress.
- The materials are required for the project. For example, materials being stored on a particular site for convenience of the contractor and eventual use on another site should not be allowed.
- Adequate insurance of the unfixed materials is provided by the contractor.

In practice, the surveyor will benefit by requesting a list of materials to be submitted by the valuation date, to be checked during the site visit. Where the contractor submits an application for payment, now in accordance with the new provisions in JCT 98, this should be provided. The surveyor should bear in mind that consideration should be given for changes in material stock occurring between submission of the application and site visit. An item included as unfixed material in an application for payment prepared several days before the valuation date, may be incorporated within the works by the time of site verification. If this occurs, the value of the works will have increased, without any consideration in the payment application, and therefore, if any adjustment is made it should be an increase rather than decrease.

JCT 98 now states that the contractor must also be paid for unfixed materials stored off-site, something that previously was left, rather unsatisfactorily in some situations, to the discretion of the architect. This payment depends on adherence to the following conditions:

- Materials or goods or items pre-fabricated for inclusion, which should be in accordance with the contract, should be identified in a list, provided by the employer, that should be annexed to the contract bills. This provision removes the uncertainty that existed previously; the contractor now knows, in advance, the extent of the materials off-site that will be allowed and may make a tender allowance for costs in connection with any item excluded from the list.
- Proof that the property is vested in the contractor, thereby allowing transfer of ownership upon payment of the certificate, should be provided.

- If stated as a requirement in the appendix to the contract, a surety bond for the value of such materials should be given.
- The materials are to be set apart in the premises in which they are manufactured, assembled or stored and must be correctly labelled showing the name of the employer, the contractor (or subcontractor) and the intended works.
- Proof of adequate insurance cover for the materials must be provided by the contractor, protecting the interests of the employer and the contractor in respect of the specified perils (clause 30.3.5).

The contract differentiates between uniquely identified 'listed items' (e.g. purpose made glazing units) and those that are not uniquely identified (e.g. possibly, sanitary ware). Where an item is not 'uniquely identified', the provision of a surety bond for the value of such materials is not an optional requirement.

Problems have arisen over retention of title of goods when certifying payments for materials on or off-site. In the case of *Dawber Williamson Roofing Ltd v. Humberside County Council* (1979) 14 BLR 70, it was held that title in a quantity of roofing slates had not passed to the main contractor at the time he was paid by the client. The subcontractor was not paid, and the main contractor subsequently went into liquidation. As title had not been passed to the main contractor, the subcontractor (plaintiff) was entitled to be reimbursed the value of the slates by the client. It is important therefore to ensure that such materials are, at the time they are paid for by the client, the lawful property of the contractor. JCT 98 attempts to ensure that the value of any unfixed materials included within an interim certificate become the property of the employer. The contract also provides that any domestic subcontract provisions are consistent with this requirement. Despite the contractual provision in JCT 98, which is intended to achieve greater security for the employer, there may be co-existent supplier agreements that retain the title of the goods with the supplier, until paid for, and thus prevent the contractor from transferring ownership.

Advance payment (JCT 98, clause 30.1.1.6)

JCT 98 makes provision for the employer to make an advance payment to the contractor, to be supported by an advance payment bond provided by the contractor when required. The amount of the advance payment, and the timing of the payment, will be stated in the appendix to the conditions of contract. At interim valuation stage, where a prior advance payment has been made, it will be necessary to take into account the reimbursement provisions. The amounts and timing of these reimbursements will also be stated in the appendix.

Variations and claims

At interim valuation stage, the assessment of the value of some variations, provisional items or sections and claims may cause difficulty. For instance, where the foundations are 'All Provisional' it may not be possible to adequately remeasure the works prior to their completion on site and the contractor may need to be paid in total. In such cases, where the eventual construction varies substantially from the provisional measurement, the risk of under or over-payment is increased. Similarly, a major variation requiring significant re-measurement may be completed on site before such work can be fully remeasured. The surveyor will need to use varying methods of approximate estimating in order to make a fair allowance for such items.

Contractors' claims for loss and expense are discussed in Chapter 14 on Final Accounts. With regard to payment for these at interim stage, the surveyor should note that such amounts should be paid in full to the contractor once ascertained, without the deduction of retention. There may be some pressure on the client's surveyor to include payments on account prior to ascertainment; no such payment should be incorporated without the direction of the architect, although as later stated, in practice the surveyor's advice is usually sought in such matters.

Price adjustment

If the traditional method of adjusting fluctuations is in operation, that is, by the use of clause 39 of JCT 98, it is valuable to start checking the records of price adjustment at an early stage, at any rate the labour portion, when a running total can be kept month by month for inclusion in the certificate valuation. Materials are rather more difficult to keep up to date than labour, owing to the time lag in rendering invoices. In either case, increased costs, whether in respect of labour or materials, should not be included in interim certificates unless supporting details have been made available.

As stated elsewhere, by far the most common method of adjusting fluctuations is by way of the price adjustment formulae. With this method, reimbursement of increased cost is automatic in each interim certificate by the application of the formulae to the current indices relevant to the proportions of the work categories actually carried out. This is more fully discussed in Chapter 14. It is now usual for information technology to be used to assist in this process.

Retention

It is standard in building contracts to incorporate a provision whereby the client is entitled to retain part of the assessed value of the works at interim valuation stage. In JCT 98 a maximum of 5% of the contract sum will be used unless:

- A lower percentage is stated in the appendix to the contract conditions
- The estimated contract sum is in excess of £500 000, in which case the retention should be no more than 3%.

Retention benefits the client by providing a sizeable fund at the end of a contract that acts as an incentive to the contractor to complete the works and to make good defects where they occur. There are no perceived benefits to the contractor; in fact, with the use of insurance bonds, there may be some reasonable argument against their justification.

There are some components of the interim valuation that are not subject to retention and these are listed in clause 30.2.2 of the standard form. With reference to this document, these are outlined below:

- The early final payment of nominated subcontractors
- Reimbursement of fluctuations, unless calculated by the formula method as in clause 40
- Remedial work in connection with damage for which insurance provision had been made under clauses 22B and 22C (i.e. where employer takes out insurance)
- Reimbursement of loss and expense claims in accordance with clause 26 and also clause 34.3 relating to loss and expense concerning the discovery of antiquities
- Payments to nominated subcontractors where the NSC/C conditions state that the amounts are not subject to retention
- Reimbursement of amounts paid by the contractor in connection with: fees and charges relating to local authorities and statutory undertakers; opening up and inspection of the works, provided the works are found to be in accordance with the contract; compliance with architect's instructions which infringe upon royalties and patent rights; taking out insurance in accordance with clause 21.2.1 (insurance against injury to persons or property).

When work is substantially complete, part of the retention sum is released, the balance being held as security for making good of defects that may be found necessary within the defects liability period. In compliance with the standard form, this retention release occurs in the first interim valuation following the issue by the architect of the certificate of practical completion. Hence, this provides a clear incentive for the contractor to reach this stage. In the standard form, half (one moiety) is to be released. The remainder of the retention is released after the expiry of the defects liability period or the issue of the certificate of making good defects, whichever occurs later. Again, this provides a clear incentive for the contractor, on this occasion, to promptly remedy any defects that may have occurred.

The defects liability period, if nothing is stated in the Appendix to the contract, is 6 months. The purpose of the defects liability period is to provide a reasonable period during which defects may become apparent. Therefore, its length should be situation dependent rather than an automatic inclusion or default to 6 months.

JCT 98 makes special allowances for the application of retention to nominated subcontractors' work. Each and every nominated subcontract is treated as a small contract within the main contract with its own start and finish dates and its own certificates of practical completion. This means that nominated subcontractors are entitled to the release of part or all of the retention money held on their subcontract at varying times before releases become due to the main contractor. This is beneficial to nominated subcontractors completing their portion of the works early in a contract, for instance, in month 2 of a project of 24 months duration.

Where part of the works is to be handed to the employer prior to contract completion, the release of retention for that section will be dealt with accordingly. This is incorporated within clause 18 of the standard form.

Clause 30.5 of JCT 98 covers the rules pertaining to the treatment of retention money. The employer's interest in the retention is as a fiduciary trustee, whereby the employer holds the money on behalf of the contractor and/or subcontractors, although 'without obligation to invest'. This is intended to provide some protection to the contractor against default by the client. In the private edition of the contract, both main contractor and nominated subcontractors can direct the employer to place the retention funds in a separately identified bank account. Thereafter, the employer should issue a confirmatory certificate to the architect, copied, where relevant, to the contractor and subcontractors.

In some forms of contract, the percentage retained of the value of unfixed materials may be different from that retained from the value of work done, and the statement must be prepared accordingly.

Liquidated and ascertained damages

To many clients, the completion of a construction contract by a particular date is vitally important and therefore most contracts incorporate a fixed date. Where the contractor fails to achieve this date, it is likely that the employer will suffer a loss. To compensate for such occurrences, most contracts and certainly JCT 98 under clause 24, allow the employer to deduct an amount, i.e. liquidated and ascertained damages, calculated on the basis of a rate stated in the appendix to the contract bills (e.g. £10 000 per week or part thereof) from amounts due to the contractor. The delay may be calculated on the basis of the completion date stated in the appendix, or such extended period if an extension of time has been granted by the architect in accordance with clause 25 of JCT 98.

The pre-ascertainment of the rate of damages is an important aspect of this provision. It must represent a reasonable pre-estimate of the loss that will be incurred by the client in the eventuality of a delay and must thereby provide all parties with a known amount at commencement of the contract. The benefits of this are clear since otherwise, actual damages would need to be calculated on each such occasion, a costly process and carrying with it additional risk to the contractor in that at the time of entering into the contract, the full contractual liability for delay is unknown. Once damages are fairly pre-ascertained, the amount paid to the employer in the event of a delay is that stated in the appendix and is not dependent on actual loss which may be more, less or nil.

Although a delay in completion may have occurred, neither the surveyor nor the architect is entitled to deduct any liquidated and ascertained damages from the amount due to the contractor within either an interim or final certificate. In accordance with the contract, this entitlement falls to the employer. The architect must issue a certificate to the employer, advising of the contractor's failure to complete the works by the completion date, as a prerequisite to any deduction. Although any action may lie with the employer and architect, it is good and pro-active practice for the surveyor to monitor any situation where liquidated and ascertained damages may arise and advise the architect and employer where necessary. This advice should include a calculation of the deduction that may be applied.

The employer is entitled to waive the right to deduct liquidated and ascertained damages or reduce the amount to be applied by notification to the contractor in writing. In practice, this may be done in consideration of: the contractor's withdrawal of a contractual claim thus avoiding a lengthy dispute; or a reduction in the actual loss to the employer relative to the amount pre-ascertained, although as stated above, the employer is under no such obligation.

Predetermined stage payments

Predetermined payments on account, based on stage payments, have been traditionally used on large multiple contracts such as housing; however, to use such a method on a complex building contract is much less feasible. Predetermined payments are not featured within the JCT 98 contract; however, the process involved in stage payments may have some practical application within the preparation of an interim valuation, without any contractual basis.

Where stage payments are used, the contractor is paid an agreed amount when work reaches a certain stage of completion, for example, when the substructure is complete £8500 will be due, and so forth with additional payments upon the completion of each determined progress point such as external walls, upper floors and roof.

Use of stage payments allows both parties, contractors and clients, to know in advance the probable cash flow for the contract and to arrange their finances accordingly, although the completion of each stage is still dependent on contractor's progress. From the client's surveyor's point of view, a great deal of time is saved: the time taken to prepare an interim valuation is, where stage payments are used, a matter of hours not days, which it often is under the traditional system. For contractors the same saving of time is available, although for their requirements it is often necessary to know in more detail the value of work done for their own internal purposes and for paying domestic subcontractors.

Previous certificates

A careful check should be made to ensure that the figure shown as already certified is correct, as a slip here may make a serious error in the valuation. The architect should confirm the amount of the previous payment, or the figure may be referred to as 'previous valuations', the architect being asked to verify before certifying.

Specimen forms

A specimen valuation is set out on the standard RICS valuation form in Fig. 13.4. This form is similar in design to the corresponding RIBA certificate form in Fig. 13.5 and gives all the information necessary to enable the architect to complete the certificate.

Care should be taken not to refer to the valuation as the certificate or to the surveyor as certifying. The surveyor only recommends, and it is for the architect to certify, who may take into account other matters than those within the surveyor's sphere, such as defective work.

Certificate/valuation papers

The surveyor's copy of each statement should be kept together with all the papers relating to one valuation. The attached papers will include such things as subcontractors' applications, lists of unfixed materials and interim statements of price adjustment. Similarly, related computerised records should be retained within a suitable folder or file system with adequate back-up storage.

Valuation on insolvency

In the event of the contractor becoming insolvent it is prudent for the client's surveyor to make a valuation of the work executed, by taking the necessary measurements of the work up to the stage at which work ceases or is continued by another contractor. The valuation will include unfixed materials and plant, which the architect, or the clerk of works on the architect's behalf, will be responsible for seeing are not removed from the site (see JCT 98, clauses 16 and 27). The purpose of such a valuation is that all parties may be aware of the financial position, and some estimate of money outstanding to the insolvent contractor can be made.

Insolvency of the contractor is likely to severely disrupt the works and result in costs to the client. It is a complex area of involvement, which increases risk to the professional advisor. There may be several actions that the surveyor is able to take in such situations and further discussion on this aspect is contained in Chapter 15.

Valuation for JCT Standard Form of Contract (1998 Edition)

Surveyor
Franklin + Andrews
Address

Works
Shops and Offices
Willow Centre

Valuation No: 6
Date of Issue: Date
Reference: 123

To Architect/Contract Administrator
Smith & Jones Architects
Address

As at _____ Date _____   I/We have made, in accordance with the terms of the
Contract, an Interim Valuation, the basis on which the amount shown as due has been calculated is
clauses 30.2 and 30.4 of the Conditions of Contract, and report as follows:

Gross Valuation   £   411,280.00
(excluding any work or material notified to me/us by the Architect/Contract Adminstrator in writing as
not being in accordance with the Contract).

Less total amount of Retention, as attached Statement.   £   11,878.00

Employer
Willow Development Ltd
Address   £   399,402.00

Less total amount of Interim Certificates previously issued by the Architect/Contract Administrator up
to and including Interim Certificate No.   5   and any advance payment due for   £   280,000.00
reimbursement by the date given below for the issue of the next Certificate.

Balance (in words)   One Hundred and Nineteen Thousand
                      Four Hundred and Two Pounds   £   119,402.00

Contractor
ABC Construct Ltd
Address

Signature _____   Surveyor Tech RICS/ARICS/FRICS
                                           (delete as applicable)

Contract sum   £   4,268,750.84

Notes:
(1) All the above amounts are exclusive of VAT.
(2) The balance stated is subject to any statutory deductions which the Employer may be obliged to make under the provisions of the
     Construction Industry Scheme where the Employer is classed as a 'Contractor' for the purposes of the relevant Act.
(3) It is assumed that the Architect/Contract Administrator will:
     (a) satisfy him or herself that there is no further work or material which is not in accordance with the Contract.
     (b) notify Nominated Sub-Contractors of payments directed for them and of Retention held by the Employer in accordance with
          clause 35.13.
     (c) satisfy him or herself that the previous payments directed for Nominated Sub-Contractors have been discharged in
          accordance with clause 35.13.
(4) The Architect/Contract Administrator's Certificate should be issued on _____ (see clause 30.2).

© RICS 2000

Fig. 13.4 RICS Valuation Form.

**Interim
Certificate**

and Direction

Issued by:	Smith and Jones Architects
address:	Address

JCT 98

Employer:	Willow Developments Ltd	Serial no:	G
address:	Address		
		Job reference:	456
Contractor:	ABC Construct Ltd	Certificate no:	6
address:	Address		
		Date of valuation:	Date
Works:	Shops and Offices	Date of issue:	Date
situated at:	Willow Centre		
		Final date for payment:	Date

Contract dated: Date

Original to Employer

This Interim Certificate is issued under the terms of the above-mentioned Contract.

Gross valuation	£	411,280.00
Less Retention as detailed on the Statement of Retention	£	11,878.00
Sub-total	£	399,402.00
Less reimbursement of advance payment	£	
Sub-total	£	399,402.00
Less total amount previously certified	£	280,000.00
Net amount for payment	£	119,402.00

I/We hereby certify that the **amount due** to the Contractor from the Employer is (in words)
One hundred and nineteen thousand four hundred and two pounds

All amounts are exclusive of VAT.

I/We hereby direct the Contractor that this amount includes interim or final payments to Nominated Sub-Contractors as listed in the attached *Statement of Retention and of Nominated Sub-Contractor's Values*, which are to be paid to those named in accordance with the Sub-Contract.

To be signed by or for the issuer named above

Signed _____ J. Smith ._____

[1] Relevant only if clause 1A of the VAT Agreement applies. Delete if not applicable.

[1] The Contractor has given notice that the rate of VAT chargeable on the supply of goods and services to which the Contract relates is 17.5 %

[1] 17.5 % of the amount certified above .... £ 20,895.35

[1] Total of net amount and VAT amount (for information) .... £ 140,297.35

This is not a Tax Invoice.

F801 for JCT 98

© RIBA Publications 1999

Fig. 13.5 RIBA Certificate.

Cost control and reporting

It is vital to the client and, of course, the design team, that costs are effectively managed throughout the construction of a project. Clients generally desire the final cost of a project to be no more than the contract sum; for some clients this may be their most dominant concern throughout the project. It is the role of the client's surveyor to try to manage these costs by a process of monitoring design and site developments and advising the client and members of the design team of their likely impacts and remedies.

The client's surveyor, if working closely with the members of the design team, should be aware at the earliest opportunity of proposed variations to the contract, including drawing amendments. Advance knowledge of proposed changes enables a full evaluation in terms of cost, quality and programming implications to be carried out in advance of their issue.

Although the initial estimate of variations to the contract is likely to be of a budgetary nature based on approximate measurements and notional rates or merely lump sums, it is important that such estimates be progressively updated as more detailed information becomes available in the form of firm measurements, quotations or daywork records. It is also necessary for the surveyor to review all correspondence and meeting minutes issued on the project in order to identify the potential cost implications of the issues contained therein. Similarly, it is also beneficial if the client's surveyor is aware of what is actually happening on site. Occasionally, changes may occur which are undocumented but for which the client may be liable.

Regular financial reports will be required to advise the client of the anticipated outturn costs. These are commonly produced at monthly intervals. As mentioned earlier, the report will be tailored to meet specific client requirements. Certain clients will only require a simple summary statement of the current financial position (see Fig. 13.6), others will require a detailed report identifying the cost implication of each instruction (whether issued or anticipated) and the reason for it. On a complex project, this may result in a lengthy document. In addition to the advice given in the regular financial statement, it may be necessary to provide the client and members of the design team with cost advice more promptly if a major issue arises.

The regular report will identify adjustments to the contract sum in respect of the following:

- Issued instructions
- Adjustment of PC and provisional sums
- Remeasurement of provisional work
- Dayworks
- Increased costs (if applicable)
- Provision for claims and anticipated future changes.

An updated cash flow (see later in this chapter) may also be included with the report to identify for the client the actual current level of expenditure

SHOPS AND OFFICES DEVELOPMENT

WILLOW CENTRE

COST REPORT NO. 6

Date

SUMMARY	£	£
Contract Sum		4,268,751
Less Contingencies		120,000
		4,148,751
Adjustments for:		
Instructions Issued – Section 1	62,138	
PC Sum Expenditure – Section 2	(8,619)	
Provisional sum Expenditure – Section 3	(4,603)	
Anticipated Variations – Section 4	30,190	
Ascertained Claims	-	
	79,106	79,106
Anticipated Final Account	£	4,227,857
Current Approved Sum		4,268,751
Balance of Contingencies	£	40,894

Notes: *Costs exclude VAT, Professional fees and direct client costs*

Fig. 13.6 Financial statement.

relative to that previously anticipated. This will allow the adjustment of the future budgetary provision. Supporting calculations should be filed with each report for future reference when it comes to reviewing and updating the costs.

Where significant cost increases occur, it is good practice to prepare an outline of possible remedies to such budgetary excess, before advising the client. Almost inevitably this information will be required and advance preparation for this request will be helpful.

The contractor's surveyor also submits regular financial reports to his senior managers and directors. These will show a different emphasis to reports prepared for the benefit of the client. The contractor will carry out frequent cost/value reconciliations which are likely to have three broad cost elements:

- *Actual value*   The real value of the works in accordance with the quantity of work performed valued at the rates estimated at the time of tender, contained in the contract documents.
- *Actual cost*   This is the real cost of carrying out the works on site, irrespective of the tender estimate, upon which the contract sum is based. Predominantly, this will be work carried out by domestic subcontractors.
- *External valuation*   This is the valuation that is agreed by the client's surveyor and is included in the interim certificate for payment by the client. In a perfect world, this amount, subject to retention, should be equal to the 'actual value' whenever an interim valuation is carried out. In practice however, the nature of the interim valuation process makes this a difficult objective to achieve.

The relationship of these three elements of cost, value and external valuation is of key importance to both the contractor and the client. Figure 13.7 considers three project situations that may occur at interim valuation and financial report stage:

- *Project A*   The contractor is in a profit making situation since the cost of performing the works is less than the value of the works contained in the contract sum. Also, in the short term relating to the interim stage, the contractor's cash flow is positive. This project is therefore in a relatively harmonious position, albeit that the client is paying in excess of the true value of the works. This additional payment is in effect a 'hidden borrowing' by the contractor.

	Project A	Project B	Project C
Actual value	£15 000	£16 000	£14 000
Actual cost	£14 000	£15 000	£15 000
External valuation	£16 000	£14 000	£16 000

Fig. 13.7   Cost reconciliation.

- *Project B*   As with Project A, the contractor is in a profit-making situation. However, in the short term, due to the shortfall between actual cost incurred and payment received, the contractor's cash flow is negative. This may prove to be a serious situation for the contractor, leading ultimately to liquidity problems.
- *Project C*   The contractor is in an overall loss making situation since the cost of performing the works is more than the value of the works contained in the contract sum. This position may be disguised in the short term due to the excessive external valuation, which, as for Project A, contains some 'hidden borrowing'. Unfortunately, whilst the contractor may be avoiding a short-term cash flow problem, if this cost/value balance continues in the long term, the contractor will suffer a loss on the project. In such a situation, in addition to the obvious problems to the contractor, others may also suffer negative consequences. The contractor will be motivated toward attempting to find legitimate opportunities to retrieve the loss from other parties including the client, the subcontractors and suppliers, the consultants and possibly employees.

Cash Flow

A forecast of cashflow is normally requested by clients and provided by the surveyor. This should be prepared in association with the contractor since it will be greatly influenced by the intended programme of works. Software is available which will assist in the preparation of a cashflow forecast based on criteria specific to the project and the 'S' curve of expenditure shown in Fig. 13.8.

Cashflow forecasts are useful for two reasons; they may be used as a basis upon which to arrange project finance, and they can assist in monitoring the progress of the works. With regard to the latter, it may be found useful to have on file a note of the net amount of the contractor's work (excluding provisional sums), so that an eye can be kept on the proportion of this kept in each

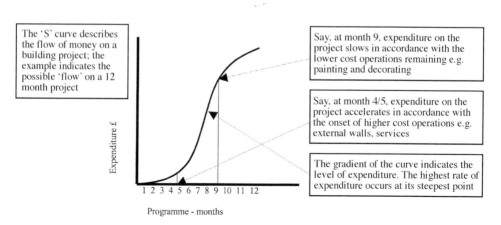

Fig. 13.8   Indicative 'S' curve.

valuation. The value of certificates can be graphically represented to enable comparison with the anticipated cash flow. There may be reasons, such as site conditions or inclement weather, that result in a shortfall against that anticipated, but any serious departure from regularity should be looked into as it may be an early indication of delays and difficulties being experienced by the contractor.

Bibliography

Aqua Group *Contract Administration for the Building Team*, 8th ed. Blackwell Science. 1996.

The Association of Consultant Architects Limited *ACA Standard Form of Contract for Project Partnering*. 2000.

Chappell D. and Powell-Smith V. *The JCT Design and Build Contract*, 2nd ed. Blackwell Science. 1999.

The Joint Contracts Tribunal Limited *Standard Form of Building Contract 1998 Edition, Private with Quantities*. RIBA Publications. 1998.

The Joint Contracts Tribunal Limited *Intermediate Form of Building Contract for works of simple content 1998 Edition incorporating amendments 1:1999; 2:2000*. RIBA Publications. 2000.

Ndekugri I. and Rycroft M. *The JCT 98 Building Contract, Law and Administration*. Butterworth Heinemann. 2000.

14 Final Accounts

Introduction

The majority of construction projects result in a final cost that is different to that agreed by the client and contractor at commencement of the construction works. The calculation and agreement of this final construction cost, the final account, is usually of the utmost importance to both the employer and contractor. Therefore, parties to the contract need to ensure that the final account incorporates a fair valuation of the works carried out. This chapter deals with the principles of measuring for variation accounts and the practical implications of contract conditions covering the calculation and agreement of the final account. Within lump sum contract arrangements the price agreed by the client at commencement will usually require adjustment for several matters, including:

- Variations
- Provisional measurements
- Provisional sums
- Prime cost sums
- Fluctuations
- Claims.

These are considered below. In addition to the contractual provisions, there are other external factors that are likely to influence the project environment, the contract administration and the preparation of the final account. The degree to which this applies may depend on a range of factors including:

- *Status of documentation at formation of the contract*
  The quality of the contract documentation will have a bearing on the proximity of the final project cost with that of the agreed contract sum. For example, a thorough pre-contract design process allied to accurate contract bills is likely to result in fewer post contract changes than projects with incomplete designs and less accurate contract bills.
- *Skills of the contract administration and cost management team*
  An experienced contract administration and cost management team will be more able to maintain construction costs within the client budget.
- *Market forces*
  In times of recession, contractors and subcontractors may be operating

within particularly small profit margins. In such economic conditions, the tendency toward contractual claims may be more acute.

- *Client and contractor attitude*
  An adversarial contract environment, a frequent occurrence in the construction industry, is likely to be both a consequence of and a contributor to cost variations. In recent years, the construction industry has recognised this problem and has encouraged a change of attitude, for example via the promotion of partnering (see Chapter 10 on Procurement).
- *Accuracy of contingency allowance*
  It is accepted practice to provide an allowance for unknown circumstances that may result in an increase to the construction cost established at tender stage. This allowance is known as the contingency and is usually provided as a lump sum addition to the contract. A well considered and realistic contingency allowance will assist in maintaining the final cost within the client's budget.
- *Resources*
  Limited post contract services, sometimes a consequence of clients wishing to reduce fees, is likely to reduce the extent and quality of post contract control resulting in a greater risk of cost variation.

Variations

General procedures

Once a contract has been concluded, its terms cannot be changed unless the contract itself contains provision for variation, or the parties make a further valid agreement for alteration. The standard form contracts contain extensive machinery for variation, but the only variations thereby permitted are those that fall clearly within the contractual terms. If the desired change is not covered by those terms it can only be effected properly by fresh agreement. In this connection care should be exercised to ensure that the new agreement is itself a valid contract and, in particular, that it is supported by consideration given by both parties. When making visits for interim certificate valuations or site meetings, the surveyor should keep an eye on the variations in the contract that have arisen. It is often valuable to have seen the work in course of construction.

The responsibility for issuing instructions is with the architect. The surveyor requires such architect's instructions as an authority to incorporate the value of any resultant variation within the final account. Architects' instructions may be issued for many reasons; however the most common is to amend the design in some way. Although JCT 98, clause 4.3.1 states that 'All instructions issued by the Architect shall be issued in writing', it is not necessary for the architect to issue an instruction using a standard form. It is, however, both usual and good practice, and an example of an architect's instruction using JCT 98 is shown in Fig. 14.1. Under clause 4.3, provision is

Issued by: address:	Smith and Jones Architects Address		**Architect's Instruction**
Employer: address:	Willow Developments Ltd Address	Job reference: Instruction no:	456 10
Contractor: address:	ABC Construct Ltd Address	Issue date: Sheet:	Date 1 of 1
Works: situated at:	Shops and Offices Willow Centre		
Contract dated:	Date		

Under the terms of the above-mentioned Contract, I/we issue the following instructions:

	Office use: Approximate costs
	£ omit | £ add

Construct inspection chamber and
install drainage pipework in
accordance with drawings 456/12B,
13C and 14D

ON ARCHITECT
AND QS COPIES
ONLY

To be signed by or for
the issuer named
above

Signed _____ J. Smit. _____

Amount of Contract Sum	£
± Approximate value of previous Instructions	£
Sub-total	£
± Approximate value of this Instruction	£
Approximate adjusted total	£

Distribution	☐ Contractor	☐ Quantity Surveyor	☐ Clerk of Works	☐
	☐ Employer	☐ Structural Engineer	☐ Planning Supervisor	☐
	☐ Nominated Sub-Contractors	☐ M&E Consultant	☐	☐ File

F809   for JCT 98 / IFC 98 / MW 98   © RIBA Publications 1999

Fig. 14.1   Architect's instruction.

made for dealing with instructions other than in writing and this is discussed later in this chapter.

The contract may also provide (e.g. JCT 98, clause 2.2) that errors in the bill of quantities shall be treated as a variation and adjusted. Although no specific instruction will be required for doing this, the architect who has to certify the final account upon completion, and the employer, should be told of any substantial items, even where fault may lie with the client's surveyor.

Drawing revisions

Many architect's instructions will be accompanied by revised drawings. These should be dated on receipt and used to update a database of drawings which should be carefully maintained, as during the pre-contract stage. It is good practice to indicate that these drawings are post-contract, likewise drawings which are superseded by new drawing issues should be recorded and identified as such. This procedure will reduce the risk of using redundant information in the preparation of the final account.

There is some possibility that drawings will continue to be issued during the tendering period, i.e. once the contract bills have been completed and issued to the tendering contractors. If the changes contained in these revisions are relatively minor, it will be adequate for the client's surveyor to measure and price approximately and advise accordingly. However, if the changes are significant, it may be necessary to prepare addendum contract bills (see Chapter 12) and issue them as a further document to the tendering contractors; thus the cost implications of the revisions will be included in the contractor's tenders.

Surveyors should also note the practice of design consultants to include on their drawings a schedule of revisions, indicating an outline of the changes contained in each updated drawing issue. This may be very helpful in identifying variations to design; however, it should not be relied on solely since some drawing revisions may not be adequately scheduled. Each new drawing issue should be carefully examined to identify any amendment to the design.

A separate file for the architect's instructions should be kept with other variation related correspondence. Such information may be found to be explanatory of the instructions and indicate the designer's intent, so helping when it comes to measurement.

Procedure for measurement and evaluation

As with the process of preparing interim valuations, JCT 98 now recognises and has formalised what had previously become generalised practice, whereby the contractor's surveyor evaluates the cost relating to variations and submits a statement to the client's surveyor for approval. Under clause 13.4.1.2, 'Alternative A: Contractor's Price Statement', the contractor may, upon receipt of an instruction, submit a price for carrying out the work known as the price statement. The process and timescales to which both parties must adhere are detailed in the contract. This contractual provision merely reflects the contractor's primary role in the process; it does not interfere with the valuation rules, which should be followed in any case, nor does it interfere with the contractual standing of the architect's instruction. The contract does identify some situations for which Alternative A should not apply; however, it is generally intended to be the manner in which variations are priced. In brief, the Alternative A process requires that:

- Within 21 days from issue of the instruction, the contractor may submit a price statement to the client's surveyor subject to availability of required information. Details relating to additional loss or expense and extensions of time can also be included.
- Within 21 days of receipt of the contractor's price statement, the client's surveyor, after consultation with the architect, should advise the contractor that the price statement is accepted, accepted in part or not accepted. Where all or part of the price statement is not allowed, the client's surveyor should provide supporting information 'in similar detail' and a new price statement to the contractor. It should be noted that where the client's surveyor makes no response to the submission of the price statement within the 21 days, it is deemed not to be accepted. In such a situation the contractor may refer the situation to adjudication.
- Within 14 days of receipt of the amended price statement the contractor must state whether it is accepted totally or in part.

Failure to arrive at an agreed price may result in adjudication if referred by one of the parties or otherwise. In such situations where no reference to the adjudicator is made, Alternative B will apply.

The contract also provides for the client's surveyor to value the work relating to variations in the manner which previously was the accepted but not generally practised, contractual method. This is described in the contract as Alternative B, whereby the contractor plays a more passive role whilst the client's surveyor carries out the valuation work. In practice, most contractors will take the opportunity to use Alternative A and, provided the client's surveyor thoroughly checks the contractor's price statement, which is an obligation, the process should not be detrimental to the client.

Oral variations

Variations that have yet to be formally authorised by the architect are occasionally contentious and care needs to be taken to ensure that they are valid in terms of the contract. Whilst the contract states that all instructions must be in writing, in practice they are not. There are occasionally situations of convenience or perceived necessity whereby an instruction may be given orally. With regard to instructions other than in writing, the contract (clause 4.3.2) states that:

- The instruction shall be of no immediate effect.
- The instruction must be confirmed in writing by the contractor within seven days of issue and, if not dissented to by the architect following a further seven days from receipt, will take effect. This requirement on the part of the contractor is relaxed where the architect confirms an oral instruction within the seven-day confirmation period.

A contractor wishing to ensure payment for a variation arising from an oral instruction should therefore follow the contract accordingly. Failure to follow the confirmation procedure may result in non-payment, although the architect may confirm any such instruction before issue of the final certificate.

Measurement

The evaluation of variations will usually include two distinct operations: measurement, either from revised drawings or from site, and valuation. The procedures for both measurement and costing are outlined below.

Irrespective of who does the work, it is likely that the measurement of variations would be more easily carried out in the office although there are situations where it may be useful or essential to physically see the work carried out; for example, where provisional quantities form part of the contract and require site measurement, such as replastering in refurbishment projects. There may be several approaches to site measurement, depending upon circumstance. For instance, traditionally site measurements may be taken using a dimension book that will be 'worked up' later in office conditions. Alternative approaches may include the use of schedules of items that can be neatly pre-prepared in the office and used as a site tick sheet, or drawings that can be accurately dimensioned or annotated during a site visit. Site measurement can be a cold, dirty and dangerous task and any initiative that improves the process should be tried! Where measurement occurs on site, it is not essential that the omissions be set down as the additions are measured. It is more pragmatic while on site to measure the additions, leaving the omissions to be evaluated in the office.

As a general principle, adjustment will be made by measuring the item as built and omitting the corresponding measurements from the original dimensions. However, there will be occasions when it may be easier to adjust a contract item by either 'add' or 'omit' only. For example, if all emulsion on walls is amended from two coats to three coats, an 'add' item of the contract quantity at the price for the additional coat would be a more efficient approach.

It is very important to keep omissions and additions distinct, and it is suggested that the words 'omit' or 'add' should always be written at the top of every page and at every change from omission to addition. This advice may sound pedantic, but the scale of error, should inversion between 'omit and 'add' occur, may be very large. When the measurement, calculation and billing process are separated and performed by various staff within an organisation it is easy to see how this type of error could result. Each item of variation should be headed with a brief description and instruction number. In accounts for public authorities, the architect's instruction references may well be required by the auditors.

Grouping of items within the final account

Before any abstracting or bill of remeasurements is started, the surveyor should decide on the suitable subdivision into terms that will be adopted in the account. Since items may or may not correspond with the architect's instructions, they may be arranged in a different order: an instruction may be subdivided or several grouped together, if their subject matter suits. The arrangement of variations within the final account may reflect other objectives, for example, where fluctuations require the categorisation of work or where capital allowances may be sought on some aspects of the completed building.

Quite probably, the adjustment of foundations will be the first variation for which measurements are taken. If there is a large difference between the contract provision for foundations and the as built foundations, there may be some urgency, notwithstanding the provisions of Alternative A and Alternative B, for remeasurement and provisional agreement. In a situation of under-provision, the contractor will require to be paid for the additional amount of work and the employer will need to accommodate the revised cost in the budget provision. Conversely, where the contract allowance is in excess of the as built foundations, the consultant will need to ensure that over-payment does not occur and the only way to do this accurately is to carry out a remeasure. At this stage of the contract it may not be known what other variations there will be; however the foundation adjustment can be regarded as an item with which other variations will not interfere to any great extent. In the event that there is a minor change in plan for which an architect's instruction is issued, any subsequent change to the foundations may be dealt with as a variation within a variation. Unless there is any special reason for distinguishing, the lesser variation will be absorbed in the greater. When it eventually comes to adjusting for the change in plan, this will be done for the superstructure only.

It might, however, happen that the complete value of the change in plan is separately required. For example, in the rebuilding of a fire-damaged building, for which reimbursement from insurers applied, it might be that a change in plan was being made at the client's request and additional expense. In that case the foundation adjustment would have to be subdivided to give the separate costs required. If the variation is a completely additional room, then the foundation measurements for that room can easily be kept separate from those for the foundations generally, which is preferable as it gives more relative values.

As the list of variations develops, the surveyor will be able to decide on how to group them. For instance, there may be one architect's instruction for increasing the size of storage tanks, another for the omission of a drinking water point and a third for the addition of three lavatory basins. Each of these will be measured as a separate item, but the surveyor may, for convenience, decide to group these together as 'variations on plumbing'. But if the client has ordered the three lavatory basins and does not know about the storage tanks or drinking water point (which are changes in the architect's ideas), it may be advisable to have the value of the extra for basins separately available for reporting. It is good practice to highlight the 'reason for variation' in cost reports to ensure that the client is able to appreciate why costs have changed.

It will be convenient to group the very small items under the heading of 'Sundries', preferably in such a way that the value of each can be traced.

The role of the clerk of works

If there is a clerk of works, the client's surveyor should ensure that arrangements are made for records of hidden work to be kept in the form required. This will assist when examining accounts submitted by the contractor or otherwise prepared. Clerks of works vary, of course, in their ability and experience and it would be unwise to assume that the clerk of works knows exactly what is required without any guidance. Also, other duties may prevent the clerk of works from carrying out remeasurement work as and when it is necessary. The depths of foundations, position of steps in foundation bottoms, thickness of hardcore and special fittings in drainage (i.e. items of work which will become hidden) are all examples of items that the clerk of works may be asked to note and record. If these records are carefully kept and agreed at the time with the foreman, the client's and contractor's surveyors should have no difficulties from lack of knowledge.

The clerk of works may also play an important role in verifying materials, labour and plant records which relate to variations for which dayworks are to be utilised in their evaluation (see later in this chapter).

Where employed, a clerk of works may issue instructions on behalf of the architect. Such instructions will not take effect unless the architect confirms them in writing within two working days of issue.

Pricing variations

Pre-costed variations

The preparation and agreement of a final account can be a time consuming and expensive process for both parties, so much so that in many cases it has been found that the measurement period often exceeds the contract period, although an attempt to limit this problem is contained within JCT 98. In addition, where a major and complex variation occurs, there may be considerable cost uncertainty at the time of issuing the required architect's instruction to carry out the works. In an attempt to overcome these problems, the principle of pre-costing variations is incorporated within JCT 98 by way of clause 13A.

Under this condition of contract, the architect has the power, if thought appropriate, to seek a firm price quotation from the contractor for variations before confirming the order. Notification of the intended variation is sent to the contractor, who is then required to price the instruction, breaking the cost down into the cost of the work and the cost of any concomitant prolongation and disruption. The price is then submitted for scrutiny by the quantity surveyor, who passes recommendations to the employer who, if the price is acceptable, provides the contractor with an acceptance in writing. This is followed by the issue of a confirmed acceptance from the architect. This procedure is subject to a strict timetable, and provision is made for adequate information to be supplied by both the architect and the contractor. If an acceptable price cannot be achieved using this procedure, then the traditional methods of agreeing the cost are adopted.

Under the terms of clause 13A of JCT 98, this procedure is subject to the agreement of the contractor who is required, in addition, to provide a method statement.

Pre-costing of variations may save a great deal of time and provide cost certainty with regard to the variation affected. However, there are drawbacks, not least of which is that pre-costed variations would be expected to be more expensive than those arrived at by traditional means:

- The pre-costing of variations lacks the element of competition provided in the traditional approach wherein tendered contract rates form the basis for pricing variations
- The costing of prolongation and disturbance, both totally unknown factors at the time of pricing, has to be something of a gamble, and contractors must err on the pessimistic side in order to safeguard their position
- The time frame is such that the contractor may have inadequate time to prepare (thus encouraging mistakes) and the client little time to consider (thus encouraging oversight)
- In the event that the employer does not accept a clause 13A quotation that has been prepared on a reasonable basis, a fair and reasonable amount will be added to the contract sum for the abortive work in connection with its preparation.

The pricing of measured work

The methods of pricing variations are described in the contract conditions (Clause 13.5, 'Valuation Rules', in JCT 98) and follow a logical and hierarchical sequence in terms of their choice of application:

- Where applicable, the rates in the contract bills (or relevant schedule of rates) should be used. Clearly this will apply to omissions; however, additions may vary in terms of not only specification but also the nature of the work execution. For example, it is reasonable to expect that the rate for paint to soffits 2.5 m above floor level will be less than the same painting specification at a height of 5 m, which will involve additional labour. Likewise, there may be a significant change in the quantity of work resulting in less or greater efficiency.

- Where contract bill rates are not applicable, they may be adjusted to take into account the revisions in working conditions and quantity. In the 'paint to soffits' example above, the new rate for valuation of the variation may be adjusted to reflect the additional labour involved. It may be possible to use other bills of quantities or schedule items of work in this agreement. For example, we may have an alternative painting specification, at both soffit heights, showing a price differential of say, £0.20/m^2 reflecting the additional labour involved at the greater height. It may therefore be reasonable to use this price differential in establishing a revised rate for the new item of work.
- Where variations do not resemble any contract bills item in terms of either specification or work context, a ' fair valuation' should be carried out. This may involve returning to the first principles of estimating whereby the rate for the item of work is considered in terms of material, labour and plant costs incorporating an addition for overheads and profit. This process may be avoided or reduced where the new item of work is relatively common and/or where there is available evidence of similar work, perhaps from a recent similar project.

Dayworks

Certain variations, which it may not be reasonable or possible to value on a measurement basis, may be charged on a prime cost basis. Daywork sheets, 'referred to as vouchers in JCT 98, clause 13.5.4', will be rendered for these by the contractor; they set out the hours of labour of each named operative, a list of materials and details of plant used. It is the duty of the architect to verify these, not later than the end of the week following that in which the work was carried out. If there is a clerk of works, it will usually be one of his/her duties to verify the dayworks voucher on behalf of the architect. The clerk of works' signature is not in any way authority for a variation, nor does it signify that the item is to be valued on a daywork basis instead of by measurement. When there is no clerk of works the architect will be expected to sign the sheets. Neither the architect nor employer's surveyor, without being continuously on site, which is unlikely, can correctly guarantee that the time and material are correct, but, if these appear unreasonable for the work involved, they can make enquiry to satisfy themselves.

JCT 98, clause 13.5.4 provides for pricing daywork as a percentage addition on the prime cost. The definition of prime cost is laid down in *Definition of Prime Cost of Daywork Carried Out Under a Building Contract* (RICS/Building Employers Confederation (now the Construction Confederation)), and the percentages required by the contractor are to be inserted in a space to be provided in the contract documents. These tendered percentage allowances will be used in the calculation of any dayworks arising during the project. (See Fig. 14.2.)

For work within the province of some specialist trades, there may be different definitions of prime cost agreed, and these must be taken into account in the preparation of subcontracts.

The provision made for daywork should be taken into account when considering the amount of any provisional sum for contingencies.

Generally, the attitude of the client's and the contractor's surveyors toward dayworks is very different. As far as the client is concerned, payment for work on the basis of cost reimbursement, which is what dayworks is, brings several disadvantages. With dayworks, the contractor will be reimbursed the full cost of all labour, materials and plant used, plus a percentage addition for overheads and profit. Therefore, the contractor has no incentive to complete the works in an efficient manner; in fact, as the cost of the variation work increases, so does the contractor's overheads and profit. For this reason, from the client's perspective, the use of dayworks will be resisted. However, they are likely to be to the advantage of the contractor. As with cost reimbursement contracts, dayworks can be expected to result in higher costs than with the methods of measurement and valuing previously outlined.

In practice, on most projects, there are likely to be situations for which dayworks are the only fair method of valuation, i.e. where work cannot be properly measured; for example, work to remedy a design error, which has been discovered post-construction, as shown in Fig. 14.2.

With reference to the above example of a completed dayworks voucher (Fig. 14.2), please note that the signatures affirm that the work recorded thus has been carried out, not that the work shall be valued on a dayworks basis, nor if priced, that the rates are correct in accordance with the contract. When calculating the amounts for inclusion into the final account, these should include the tendered allowance for overheads and profit, which may be a different amount for each of the three categories, materials, labour and plant.

Performance specified work

The employer may incorporate within a contract, otherwise designed by his appointed architect, portions of work that will be designed by or on behalf of the contractor. Such work should be considered as a design and build element of a traditional contract and corresponding rules therefore apply. Where the contract incorporates work that is being carried out in accordance with clause 42, Performance Specified Work, several additional factors may need to be considered when dealing with related variations:

- Additional design work carried out by or on behalf of the contractor must be allowed. This may apply to omissions as well as additions.
- If a change is necessary in order for the specified work to 'perform', this will be at the expense and resolution of the contractor.

ABC CONSTRUCT LIMITED	
JOB No. 2436	DAYWORK No. 120
CONTRACT: WILLOW CENTRE	AUTHORISATION
W/E: DATE	AI No.
	CVI No. 102
	OTHER

DESCRIPTION OF WORK

Break out floor adjacent manhole. Insert 2 no. 100D 30 degree bends to form swan-neck. Install 100D

vertical pipe within manhole with r/eye and rest bend. Adapt manhole benching, insert branch bend and

Make good benching, brickwork and floor slab.

LABOUR

Name	Trade	M	T	W	T	F	S	S	Total	Rate	Add %	£
C Rose	B/layer			5					5	8.53	70	72.50
											Total Labour £	72.50

MATERIALS / PLANT / SPECIAL CHARGES

	No	Unit	Rate	Add %	£
Materials					
100D uPVC drain	1.5	m	5.35	10	8.83
...30 degree bends	2	No	10.86	10	23.89
...rest bend	1	No	12.18	10	13.40
...r/eye	1	No	15.34	10	16.87
...coupler	2	No	2.97	10	6.53
Site mixed concrete	1	Item	5.00	10	5.50
Cement and sand	1	Item	2.50	10	2.75
Plant					
Kango	5	Hrs	1.10	10	6.05
Angle grinder	5	Hrs	0.55	10	3.03
Task lighting	5	Hrs	0.20	10	1.10
Transformer and leads	5	Hrs	0.20	10	1.10
			Total materials etc £		89.05
			Total for sheet £		**161.55**

Signed by ABC CONSTRUCT LIMITED	Signed by Client's Representative
Date	Date

Fig. 14.2 Daywork sheet.

- The rates to be used in pricing the variation are likely to be less clearly stated in that they may be contained in a contract analysis that is less detailed than contract bills.

Overtime working

Though there is nothing to prevent a contractor's employee from working overtime, subject to trade union control, this is normally entirely a matter for the contractor's organisation. No extra cost of overtime can be charged without a specific order. Where, therefore, overtime is charged on a daywork sheet, it will be corrected to the standard time rates unless there is some such special order.

It may be that owing to the urgency of the job, a general order is given for overtime to be worked, the extra cost to be charged as an extra to the contract. Or the order may be a limited one with the object of expediting some particular piece of work. When an operative paid, say, £10.00 per hour works an hour per day extra at time-and-a-quarter rate, i.e. £12.50, the quarter hour (£2.50) will be chargeable in such cases. As a matter of convenience, on the pay-sheet, if the normal day is 8 hours @ £10.00 and 1 hour @ £12.50, it will be $9\frac{1}{4}$ hours @ £10.00. The quarter hour is not 'working time' at all, and is therefore sometimes called 'non-productive overtime': the extra cost of payment for overtime work over normal payment. Any charges that are to be based on working time, such as daywork (where overtime is not chargeable as extra), must exclude the quarter hour. Where the extra cost of overtime is chargeable, the data will be collected from the contractor's pay sheets and verified if necessary from the individual operative's time sheets.

Provisional measurements

It often happens that such work as cutting away and making good after engineers is covered by provisional quantities of items such as holes through walls and floors, or making good of plaster and floor finishings. The original bill may have been taken from a schedule supplied by the engineers, and the need for remeasurement on site must not be overlooked. These items should be distinguished in the contract bills by the label of 'provisional' where applicable to single items, or where an entire section is provisional, for example, foundations, the entire section would be marked as 'Substructures; ALL PROVISIONAL'. Such labelling would denote the need for the remeasurement of those items affected. It does sometimes happen that the provisional quantities reasonably represent the work carried out and can therefore be left without adjustment, but this should not be done merely to avoid what is certainly a rather laborious job. Non-technical auditors are apt to frown upon such procedure. One of the few things they can do to check a technical account is to go through the original bill and see that all provisional items have been dealt with. An appendix to the variation account, showing how this has been done, can be of help to an auditor.

The main reason for the incorporation of provisional quantities within the contract bills is:

- To make a reasonable provision for work which will be required but for which exact detail is unavailable
- To obtain contract rates for provisionally measured items, which can be used in subsequent remeasurement.

The amount of work thus included should be a reasonable representation of the work involved and not a wild guess.

The valuation of remeasured approximate quantities may be based on the associated bill rates. However, where the approximate quantity allowance in the bills is not a reasonably accurate forecast, adjustment will be necessary to accommodate the cost differential caused by the revised quantity. (See example in Fig. 14.3.)

It should be noted that 'provisional quantities' are not to be confused with 'provisional sums' which are discussed below. In terms of the contract, which in this matter follows the General Rules of the Standard Method of Measurement (SMM7), provisional quantities shall be used:

'Where work can be described and given in items in accordance with these rules but the quantity of work required cannot be accurately determined, an estimate of the quantity shall be given and identified as an approximate quantity [i.e. being marked 'Provisional' as discussed above].

Provisional sums

Provisional sums are provided at tender stage for items of work for which there is little information or for work to be executed by a statutory body, e.g. electricity supply. Their inclusion provides a tender allowance for known work that cannot be properly measured or valued until later in the project. In terms of the contract, as with provisional quantities discussed above following SMM7, provisional sums are used 'where work cannot be described ... it shall be given as a Provisional Sum and identified as for either "defined" or "undefined" work as appropriate'. Examples of these are provided below:

Defined work

Defined work relates to work that is not completely designed but for which particular information is available, which with reference to the contract/ SMM7 incorporates:

- The nature and construction of the work
- A statement of how and where the work is fixed to the building and what other work will be fixed thereto

Scenario: The refurbishment of 65 houses for a local authority

Treatment of existing plasterwork:

The existing plasterwork is of variable condition throughout the properties and therefore it is not cost effective to remove and replace all plaster throughout the scheme, nor is it possible to prepare a detailed schedule of the location and extent of plaster to be hacked off and replaced. Not only is the latter unfeasible at design stage, it is practically impossible due to access to individual properties, the effects of damage arising from other refurbishment works (e.g. chasing for new wiring) and concealment due to wall coverings, furniture, etc.

Therefore, a sensible approach in pre-contract measurement is to approximate the amount of replastering per house (marking such quantities as '(Provisional)' and to later remeasure the exact amount of work carried out. The approximation may be based on an inspection of say, two to three properties, or previous experience.

Extract from notional final account

BQ Ref		Quantity	Unit	Rate	£	
	House type: C: 23 Giles Street					
	Adjustment of provisional quantities					
	Omit					
18/3 B	Hack off/key/bond/2 ct plaster (Provisional)	28	m²	6.25	175	00
					175	00
	Add					
18/3 B	Hack off/key/bond/2 ct plaster	47	m²	6.25	293	75
					293	75

Fig. 14.3   Example of provisional quantities.

- A quantity or quantities which indicate the scope and extent of the work
- Any specific limitations and the like identified in Section A35 [of SMM7].

For instance, for an ornamental steel canopy at the entrance to a hotel: the nature and construction are given in the description of the work; the type and extent of work are clearly stated; the location of the canopy is given and the method of fixing shall be by 'bolting to steel columns'.

Undefined work

Undefined work is identified as necessary at the time of tender; however, in addition to the lack of full design information upon which to measure, the particular details outlined above for defined work are unavailable. For instance, it may be known that landscaping work for the hotel project is required, however no further detail is available. A provisional sum calculated on the basis of a previous project is included in the contract bills.

The important distinction to be made between defined and undefined provisional sums relates to programming, planning and pricing of related preliminaries. In the case of the steel entrance canopy, the contractor is required to allow for such in the tender submission. Provided no changes to these details occur, no adjustment will be made to the preliminaries, nor will the contractor be able to make reference to programme or planning matters in connection therewith. However, with regard to 'undefined work' due to the 'inferior' information available at tender stage, no such allowance is made. When the design of the related work is finalised and priced, the contractor will be entitled to include costs relating to preliminaries items and will also give consideration to planning and programming matters.

Prime cost sums

As with provisional sums, an item with which they are usually included in the documentation, there is a requirement to omit all prime cost sums provision and adjust in accordance with the actual work carried out.

The surveyor is responsible for the checking of the accounts of nominated subcontractors, and when such accounts contain measurable items, measurements will need to be taken. It may be more satisfactory to meet and measure with the subcontractor than to wait for the account to be rendered. If measurements are agreed and taken together, there should be nothing factually wrong with the account when it comes in.

The client's surveyor should have received from the architect copies of the accepted estimates of nominated subcontractors, and these must be studied to see that the relative accounts are in accordance with them. For some specialist installations, it may be necessary to rely on an engineer or specialist cost advisor for advice. Where this occurs, such information should be clearly identified in the final account.

If any extra items are chargeable on a dayworks basis, the rates should be fixed in the same way as for the main contractor. Under JCT 98, clause 13.5.4, provision is made for the use of the definition of prime cost of a particular trade association, when works of a specialist nature fall within the province of such an association.

As well as adjusting the nominated subcontractor's account against the prime cost sums, it is also necessary to adjust the main contractor's profit and attendance. The profit, being cost related, is usually priced in the contract bills as a percentage of the prime cost sum, and the same percentage is therefore applied to the subcontractor's total in the final account. Occasionally, a contractor will price the profit as a lump sum. Irrespective of this, the amount should be regarded as a percentage addition and adjusted accordingly.

Attendance, whether it be general or other 'special' attendance, is work related. For example, unless there are some very special requirements, the attendance on a carpet-layer laying carpet at £10.00 per square metre is the same even if the carpet costs £40.00 per square metre. Occasionally, a contractor will price attendance as a percentage for convenience, but more often it will be priced as a sum. Consequently, unless the amount of contractor's work that is defined as attendance has changed, then the attendance sum will not be adjusted and the amount included in the bill of quantities will be the same figure as in the final account. The fact that the original pricing was by way of a percentage will make no difference, and the sum will remain the same.

In earlier versions of the contract, consideration was given to discounts in that the contractor was allowed $2\frac{1}{2}\%$ on work carried out by nominated sub-contractors and 5% in respect of nominated suppliers. This frequently resulted in the need to adjust for such allowances in the final account. Under the terms of JCT 98, discounts no longer apply.

Fluctuations

Fluctuations are an allowance for building cost inflation that may or may not be reimbursed to the contractor, subject to the provisions of the contract. The amount of this cost factor depends on levels of inflation existing during the contract period. At times, this may be negligible; however at certain times, for instance in the 1970s, building cost inflation may be at a very high level.

It is important to note that building cost inflation should be considered apart from tender price levels; it is quite possible for both to be moving in opposite directions at the same time. For example, as indicated by Fig. 14.4, between 1990(i) and 1991(i), tender price levels fell by 15%, whilst building cost inflation increased by approximately 8%.

Date	Tender index	General BCI
1990 (i)	137	128
1991 (i)	116	138
% change	(137 − 116)/137 * 100 = −15.33%	(138 − 128)/128 * 100 = +7.81%

Fig. 14.4   BCIS Indices 1990 (i) and 1991 (i).

When such circumstances prevail, it is quite possible for an unfortunate client to suffer a relatively high level of poor value due to an untimely commencement date and, with the benefit of hindsight, misjudged contract option. Considering the tender and building cost indices above, a client that opted for a fluctuating contract commencing in 1990(i) would be considerably worse off than had the project been delayed to 1991(i) and let on a firm price basis.

Fluctuations, also referred to incorrectly as 'increased costs' and 'escalations' (since both terms suggest a single direction of price movement), can be calculated by either a traditional method or by a formula method. JCT 98, clause 37, outlines the choice of method to be used by reference to clauses 38, 39 and 40, which are contained in a separate contract publication. Where neither clause 39 (traditional) or 40 (formula) are selected and stated in the appendix, clause 38 applies.

Clause 38 – firm price contracts

In situations where the client wishes to distribute the risk of building cost inflation to the contractor, clause 38 is used. The choice of this contract option will require consideration of several factors including contract duration, market conditions and levels of present and predicted building cost inflation. Although such a contract choice will transfer the main burden of inflation risk to the contractor, clause 38 does provide for the reimbursement of some inflation costs to the contractor where caused by statutory matters such as changes relating to contributions and taxes on labour. These are identified in JCT 98. In addition, clause 38.7 provides for a percentage to be inserted in the appendix to the contract, by the contractor, to be applied to all fluctuations to allow for cost inflation relating to some preliminaries items, overheads and profit.

Clause 39 – the traditional method

Labour

The traditional way of adjusting fluctuations in the cost of labour and materials, although today rarely encountered in practice, is by way of a price adjustment clause (JCT 98, clause 39). Under such a clause any fluctuation in the officially agreed rates of wages, or variation in the market price of materials, is adjusted. JCT 98, clause 39.8, provides for a percentage to be inserted in the appendix to the contract, by the contractor, to be applied to all fluctuations to allow for cost inflation relating to some preliminaries items, overheads and profit.

The checking of wages adjustment should be fairly straightforward on an examination of the contractor's pay-sheets. The rates of wages are officially published by the National Joint Council for the Building Industry (NJCBI) so there should be no doubt as to the proper amount of increases or decreases, or the dates on which they came into effect. To these increases will be added allowances for increases arising from any incentive scheme and any pro-ductivity agreement and for holiday payments as set out in the contract. These increases will apply to workpeople both on and off-site and to persons employed on-site other than workpeople.

Care must be taken that there is no overlapping with the rates charged for daywork when dealing with price variations. If daywork has been priced at actual rates (as required by JCT 98, clause 13.5), say with labour 10p per hour above basic rates, the number of hours so charged in daywork must be deducted from the total on which price adjustment is being made. In this way the contractor gets, for the hours charged in daywork, a percentage on the difference in cost, whereas adjustments under the price variation clause are strictly net differences. If, of course, the contract provides for daywork to be valued at basic rates, the point does not arise.

Materials

The adjustment of materials prices is more difficult. The contractor will produce invoices for those materials from which the quantities and costs can be abstracted and the value will be set against the value of corresponding quantities at the basic prices. Prices must be strictly comparable. If the basic rate for eaves gutters is for 2 m lengths, an invoice for 1 m lengths cannot be set against that rate. The 1 m length rate corresponding to the 2 m length basic rate must be ascertained. There is also the difficulty of materials bought in small quantities, perhaps by the foreman from the local ironmonger, when again the price paid is not comparable with the basic rate. JCT 98, clause 39, says 'if the market price ... increases or decreases' and these are significant words. When in doubt the applicability of the contract wording must be considered.

As for labour, reference must be made to the rates charged in daywork for materials, and adjustment made, if necessary, on the totals being dealt with for price adjustment. Invoices should be requested for *all* materials appearing on the basic list. Claims for materials not appearing on the basic list are to be excluded from the calculation. The surveyor is responsible for seeing that fluctuations in either direction are adjusted. This is another case where non-technical auditors are apt to worry if all items do not appear in the account.

The surveyor should also see that the quantities of the main materials on which price adjustment is made bear a reasonable relation to the corresponding items in the bill of quantities and variation account. An approximation, for instance, can be made of the amount of cement required for the concrete and brickwork, and any serious discrepancy should be investigated.

Clause 40 – the formula method

The more common method of price adjustment in building contracts is by way of formulae to calculate the adjustment.

Unlike the traditional method, in which a calculation of actual amounts of increases and decreases are made, the formula method uses indices to calculate the amount of reimbursement. As such, on a particular project, this calculation will therefore be technically inaccurate since it is a generalised approach for use across the construction sector. However, the use of the formula method is generally more popular than the traditional method for several reasons:

- The results are likely to be more predictable, particularly in unstable economic conditions

- The protection against price fluctuations is more comprehensive. With the traditional method there is likely to be a considerable shortfall in overall recovery on the contract.
- The formula method greatly simplifies the administration of price fluctuation provisions
- The simplified process facilitates prompt payment of fluctuations in interim valuations
- The scope for dispute is greatly reduced
- Contractors can quote competitively on current prices with the confidence that reimbursement will be in terms of current prices throughout the contract
- The formula method can benefit from the application and use of information technology.

Two documents (*Price Adjustment Formulae for Building Contracts: Guide to Application and Procedure* and *Procedure and Price Adjustment Formulae for Building Contracts: Description of the indices* (The Stationery Office)) have been published that explain the formulae and provide information and assistance to those using them. The formulae are of two kinds, the building formula and specialist engineering installations formulae.

The building formula uses standard composite indices (each covering labour materials and plant) for similar or associated items of work, which have been grouped into work categories. For example, the breakdown of concrete work categories reflects the differing material input and weighting of the index calculations. Despite the general heading of 'concrete' each of the items is subject to different cost influences – e.g. labour balance, cement, aggregates, fuel, timber, steel – and therefore justifies a different category. Rationalisation within the process can be seen by consideration of the work group for 'concrete: in situ'. The weighting of the two main material components, cement and aggregate, will differ for 1:2:4 concrete and 1:3:6 concrete; however no differentiation is made in the calculation of fluctuations by the formula method. In reality, an increase in the cost of cement will have a greater impact on 1:2:4 than 1:3:6 concrete; however this detail is sacrificed for ease of application (i.e. to limit the work categories to a manageable number).

The formula is applied to each valuation, which will need to be separated into the appropriate work categories. In practice this is done at the commencement of the contract by annotating the contract bills. As stated previously, the use of IT can assist in this process.

There are alternative applications of the formula available. Each of the work categories indices may be applied separately. This provides the most sensitive possible application of the formula. Alternatively, the work categories may be grouped together to form work groups. Clearly, as explained above, the fewer work groups used, the less sensitive will be the indices to changes. It must also be practicable to analyse the tender and the value of work carried out in each valuation period into the selected work groups. This entails less work in separating the value of work carried out in every valuation. This application of the formula to the main building contract does not prevent the use of one or more of the work categories to subcontracted work should the parties so desire.

These alternative uses are described in detail in the Guide mentioned above, which also gives notes on the application of the formula at pre-contract, interim valuation and final account stages, with sample forms and worked examples.

The specialist engineering installations formulae cover electrical installations, heating, ventilating and air-conditioning installations. They are applicable whether the work is performed by direct contract or by nominated subcontract. These formulae use separate standard indices for labour and for materials, the respective weightings of which are to be given in the tender documents, except for lift installations where the weightings are standardised. In each case the formula is expressed in algebraic terms and has been devised in conjunction with the appropriate trade association. It is intended that these specialist formulae will normally be applied to valuations at monthly intervals.

Completing the account

In terms of the contract:

- Clause 30.6.1.1:   'not later than 6 months after Practical Completion of the works the Contractor shall provide the ... Quantity Surveyor' with all information necessary for the preparation of the final account
- Clause 30.6.1.2:   'not later than 3 months after receipt ... by the Quantity Surveyor' of the information from the contractor, the client's surveyor should prepare the final account and submit it to the contractor and relevant parts to nominated subcontractors.

These timescales will be affected by the completeness of the information provided by the contractor and the communication process between the parties.

As stated, whilst it is the client's surveyor's role to prepare the final account, the information required to do so will be provided by the contractor. Normally, subject to the considerations relating to variations discussed above, this will effectively include the preparation of the variation account.

In practice, the agreement of the final account will be helped by a good and sensible working relationship between the surveyors involved. The contractor, having examined the account, is fairly certain to have some criticism. Unless the criticisms are of a minor nature, which can be settled by correspondence, an appointment will be arranged for the contractor's surveyor to call at the client's surveyor's office and go through the points. The new contract provisions relating to variations should limit the extent of any dis-agreement at final account stage.

Audit

It is frequently assumed that the main role or function of an audit, whether it is of a company balance sheet, profit and loss account or the final account of a construction project, is to detect errors or more importantly fraud. This is an incorrect assumption and forms only subsidiary objectives. An audit of a final account, or any account, involves the examination of the account and the supporting documentation and more importantly the designated procedures involved. This enables an auditor to report that the account has been prepared to provide a true and fair view of the account. The auditor will:

- Compare the final account with contract bills
- Examine the records available
- Discuss aspects with relevant staff
- Examine the procedures used
- Prepare a report on the findings.

The auditor will use the skill and diligence that is normally expected and the process will involve an examination of all transactions involved. A technical audit, perhaps using the skills and knowledge of a quantity surveyor, may sometimes precede the more usual audit process.

The extent of the examination of the final account will depend on the auditor's experience and assessment of the internal controls that have been adopted. The audit will set objectives and incorporate what is known as the audit plan (Ashworth 1979). The process is not intended to repeat that which has already been carried out by the quantity surveyor. It is chiefly concerned:

- With the processes used
- That the processes have not been departed from without good reason
- That the accounts are free from error
- That the final account is a fair and true record
- That sound accounting principles have been adopted and used throughout.

The following are the essential features of the audit plan:

- Critical examination and review of the system used for the preparation of the final account and the methods of internal control adopted
- Critical examination of the final account in order that a report can be made to the client as to whether the accounts are a true and fair record
- Ensure that the accounts have been prepared on sound accounting principles and in accordance with professionally accepted procedures.

The auditor will give particular attention to those types of transactions that could offer particular facilities for fraud. The amount of checking that will need to take place will depend on the quality and reliability of the system that is used. A good system usually relies on the collusion of two or more individuals and this provides some safeguard on which the auditor can base judgements.

The majority of errors that are discovered will be due to miscalculation, carelessness or ignorance. However, on occasions, what may appear to be nothing more than a simple clerical error, may ultimately be found to be fraudulent manipulation. Errors may be the result of careless arithmetic, although the use of information technology has now greatly reduced these occurring in practice. An auditor can never guarantee the discovery of all fraud, since ingenious schemes to avoid possible detection may have been introduced. There are many examples of these in the business world and they are frequently reported in the technical press (Smith 1992). The auditor must, however, be able to show that reasonable skill and care have been exercised in designing the audit trail. Areas that appear dubious will be checked and spot checks made generally where it is considered necessary.

The culmination of the auditor's work results in a written report being sent to the client indicating the opinion regarding the reliability of the outcomes and processes used. It will also offer suggestions of how these might be improved. The auditor's report will comment on the following.

The tender

The auditor should make sure that any relevant standing orders have been complied with and that the tenders were received and opened in the prescribed manner. Where the lowest price has not been accepted, the auditor will look for careful documentation as to why this was not so. The auditor will need to be satisfied that appropriate arithmetical and technical checks were performed on the contractor's price and that errors were corrected within the agreed rules. Good tendering practices should be in evidence, with some account of modern methods of contractor selection being considered and justified.

Interim payments

It is usual for clients to maintain a contracts payment register to record all of the payments made in respect of a project. It will be closed on the agreement and payment of the final account. The auditor will need to scrutinise the payments made to ensure that they are in accordance with the contract and the architect's or engineer's certificate and that proof of payment has been made to subcontractors. It is becoming more common to ensure that both nominated and domestic subcontractors have been appropriately paid to avoid the possibility of a client having to pay a subcontractor twice.

Variations

The auditor will need to establish that the correct protocols were applied when issuing and authorising variations as described in the contract documents. The various conditions of contract lay down precise rules of instruction and valuation. These should have been followed unless there is good and documented reasons to the contrary.

The final account

The settlement of the final account is a lengthy and complex process and frequently extends beyond the period stated in the contract. The auditor's final task is to ensure that the amount of the final payment added to the sums that have already been paid equals the final account for the project. In order to reduce any possible delays in making the payment to the contractor, the auditor should examine the account as speedily as possible. Contractual claims may remain to be agreed for some time and the auditor may need to include provision for the auditing of these at some later date.

Where the client has been partially responsible for either the purchase of construction materials or the execution of a specialist portion of the works, the auditor will need to be satisfied that these have not been included within the final account.

Liquidated damages

Liquidated damages become due where the contractor fails to complete the works on time, unless there are agreed reasons that are beyond the control of the contractor. It is a rare occasion when an auditor will need to verify such an amount since extensions of time are frequently granted to cover for such a delay. However, the auditor should be satisfied that such a waiver was only granted for adequate and carefully documented reasons.

Fees

An auditor will also be involved in verifying the fees paid to the consultants. These may be within an agreed fee scale or more commonly will be by special agreement between the client and the consultants. They are usually influenced by the tender sum and the additional work involved during the progress of the works.

Timing and resources

It is not intended that final account preparation should commence only upon the completion of the construction of a project. Whilst this may be the case in some situations, it is neither correct nor good practice. If we assume a project duration of 18 months, there will be ample opportunity for final account measurement during the course of the works. For example, at completion of the substructures, say after month 2/3 of the programme, it will be in the interest of all parties to remeasure and if possible finalise the account for this element of the works. At this time, events are fresh in the mind and uncertainties relating to payment and final project cost can be reduced by prompt agreement. Continuation of such action throughout the course of the works will reduce the time required for completion of the final account at the end of the contract period. Again, this is advantageous to all parties. In the case of the client's internal financial arrangements it may be very important to achieve an early completion. A further factor that should be borne in mind relates to the turnover of surveying personnel. In the event that final account measurement is left until the end of the project, it is quite possible that either (or both) the contractor or project consultant no longer employs the surveyors responsible for the earlier stages of a project. In such situations, measurement by surveyors without the benefit of direct involvement during the works will probably result. This is much more difficult, time consuming and therefore inefficient.

In recognition of the factors outlined above, it may be beneficial to maintain a 'running' final account for which measurements and agreements occur throughout the project. Unfortunately, this philosophy may go awry, for example, due to lack of available resources or where disputes arise. This is regrettable and will almost certainly lead to delays in the completion of final accounts, some of which are legendary in their duration, despite the obligations stated in the contract. Clients are entitled to be critical of our practices in these situations; it is often stated that construction is the only sector of business where the client is not aware of the final cost until several months – or years! – after product purchase.

Despite the view above that it is expedient to prepare aspects of the final account throughout the progress of the works, it is important to add a note of caution to this advice. It is not advisable to start too soon on measurement of variations when future developments, which cannot be foreseen, might affect the surveyor's work. One might, for instance, measure a number of adjustments of foundations or drains, only to find later that the whole of one of these sections must be remeasured complete.

Bibliography

Aqua Group *Contract Administration for the Building Team*. Blackwell Science. 1996.

Ashworth A. *The auditing of building contracts*. QS Weekly. December 1979.

The Joint Contracts Tribunal Limited *Standard Form of Building Contract 1998 Edition*. RIBA Publications. 1998.

Ndekugri I. and Rycroft M. *The JCT 98 Building Contract, Law and Administration*. Butterworth Heinemann. 2000.

Smith T. *Accounting for Growth*. Business Books. 1992.

15 Insolvency

Introduction

Insolvency is a generic term that covers both individuals and companies. Bankruptcy applies specifically to individuals and liquidation to companies. The law relating to bankruptcy is governed by the Bankruptcy Act 1914 and that of insolvency is contained in the Insolvency Act 1986 and relevant sections of the Companies Act 1985. Unlike death or illness, the effect of these do not by themselves have the effect of terminating a contract.

The construction industry is responsible for more than its fair share of bankruptcies and liquidations. Limited liability companies become insolvent and then go into liquidation. The annual report from the Department of Trade and Industry (DTI) is often greeted with a mixture of sensationalism and 'as expected' as far as the construction industry is concerned. Builders and contractors always head the list.

A company becomes insolvent when the value of everything that it owns comes to less than the value of its debts. An example of a statement of a contractor's affairs, following liquidation, is illustrated in Fig. 15.1. A company may enter voluntary liquidation or, more commonly, have been forced in this direction by a single creditor. The single creditor is usually a financier, such as a bank, who refuses to extend a loan or chooses to call in a debt. Even a profitable company may suffer in this way because of a shortage of cash to pay its bills. Hence, it suffers a cash-flow crisis.

In times of a recession or slump, the rate of the collapse of companies in the UK exceeds over 1000 per week (1990s recession), many of which are in the construction industry. For companies to weather the business cycle it is essential that they are careful with whom they do business, employ sound financial disciplines and verify and monitor companies. In times of recession, new as well as long-established companies cease to trade and more companies begin to pay their bills late. This causes other firms to fail. A way out of the vicious circle has been to introduce legislation to improve payment performance. During the recession of the early 1990s, insolvencies in the construction industry more than doubled from an already high base. But it is not just in times of recession that insolvency occurs. It is a common feature throughout the business cycle.

The kind of firm that goes into bankruptcy or liquidation ranges from the one-person business, subcontractors, suppliers, general contractors through to, on occasion, the national contractor. Employers and consultants are also

Harry Parker (Builders) Ltd
Statement of Affairs 08-03-98

	Book value		Estimated to realise
Assets			
Land and buildings		330 000	
Less Norwich Union Group	48 000		
Less National Westminster Bank	223 860	−271 860	58 140
Goodwill	5 700		0
Plant and equipment – owned	195 000		45 000
Value subject to HP	40 180		
Less outstanding HP	37 550		2 630
Motor vehicles	36 500		27 250
Stock – Chair frame department	13 250		13 250
– Builder's yard	90 000		35 000
Work in progress	372 000		185 000
Debtors Chair frame dept.	16 500		16 500
Trade contract	274 650		190 000
VAT	3 000		3 000
Cash ABU plc	13 500		
Rogers Plc	4 000		17 500
Available assets			593 270
Liabilities			
Preferential creditors			
PAYE	55 200		
NHI	47 750		
Holiday pay	19 250		122 200
Amount available to unsecured creditors			471 070
Unsecured creditors			
Redundancy pay	23 800		
Trade and expenses	685 550		
Sale contractors	395 500		1 104 850
Deficiency regarding creditors			−633 780
Share capital			
20 000 Ordinary shares of £1.00 each fully paid			20 000
Total deficiency			−653 780

Fig. 15.1 Statement of affairs.

not exempt from these statistics. When this happens a knock-on effect is created and other firms teetering on the edge often go out of business in the same way. The reasons for construction company failures include the following:

- A recognition that the construction industry is a risky business and often the risks involved are not fully evaluated

- Construction projects are used as economic regulators, with price fluctuations depending considerably on the state of the market
- Competitive tendering has been cited to explain the high incidence of contractor and subcontractor failure, although this has not been verified
- The quality of management and financial expertise, which has traditionally relied on the self-made man image without proper training, is frequently lower than in other industries
- Neither the best of British brains nor the aristocracy, not necessarily the same, have involved themselves in the construction industry
- Insolvency has a knock-on effect on other, often smaller, firms.

Avoiding the possibility of contractor insolvency in the first place is the preferred route to be followed, although this can never be completely assured. The Code of Practice for the Selection of Main Contractors identifies the following precautions that should be taken prior to inviting a firm to submit a tender for a construction project:

- Check the firm's financial standing and record
- Identify the firm's general experience and reputation for the type of project being considered
- Evidence recent experience of building over similar contract periods
- Examine the adequacy of management capability
- Establish whether the firm has the capacity to carry out the proposed project.

The general reasons for any company failures are shown in Fig. 15.2, indicating the owner's viewpoint and those of the creditors. The perception of these two different groups regarding the financial failure of a company is markedly different in many respects.

	Owner's opinion %	Creditor's opinion %
Business depression	68	29
Inefficient management	28	59
Insufficient capital	48	33
Domestic or personal factors	35	28
Bad debt losses	30	18
Competition	38	9
Decline in assets values	32	6
Dishonesty and fraud	0	34
Excessive overhead expense	24	9

Fig. 15.2   Reasons for company failures.

The role of the quantity surveyor

It is important, for all concerned, that quantity surveyors carry out their work to the highest professional standards and integrity. In this context they should only work for bona fide employers. They should ensure that procurement practices are fair and reasonable and that risks are allocated to those parties who are best able to control them. Only financially stable construction firms should be recommended and where necessary performance bonds used. Interim payments should always be in accordance with the contract provisions, remembering also that these represent the lifeblood of the industry. Quantity surveyors should, as far as possible, seek to protect employers from undue loss and expense resulting from additional payments and extensions of time. One of the important roles of the quantity surveyor is financial propriety between all parties involved in the construction project.

Prior to a contractor going into liquidation, there are often signs that the firm is in some sort of financial difficulties. These may include:

- Complaints from subcontractors and suppliers about the non-payment of their accounts
- Pressure to maximise interim payments
- A reduction in the progress of the works due to a reduced labour force or a lack of supply of material deliveries
- Changes in members of staff
- Rumours, which may be unfounded, and which may be especially damaging to a firm which has known difficulties.

It may be necessary to make photographic records of the works at the time of the insolvency.

Scenario

Liquidation is rarely a total surprise. For example, a contractor had cash-flow problems in paying subcontractors, especially a national supplier of ready-mixed concrete. Cash would eventually be received from profitable contracts currently being completed by the contractor. But rumours began to emerge about the firm and especially its financial standing. The contractor, at the same time, was restructuring its operations and introduced a new policy, for office-based staff, that company cars would no longer be provided. This appeared to endorse the rumour and the contractor's shares began to slide. Rumours began to spread, both from the supplier and by staff in the firm and eventually by others in the industry. There was a belief that there was no smoke without fire! Contracts, where the firm had submitted the lowest tender, were surprisingly awarded to other firms. This fact then became public knowledge. Suppliers of materials and goods became cautious, exacerbating the cash-flow problem. The lack of new orders meant redundancies, increasing the contractor's problems and credibility. On fixed price contracts, it is arguable that more profit is made at the beginning of the project than towards the end. It is a belief that new contracts tend to subsidise those nearing completion. New contracts would therefore have helped the contractor's position. News eventually broke that the firm had suffered major losses on a project overseas. That was the final straw. The bank called in its loans, which the firm was unable to meet. The firm went into receivership on the basis of rumour and predicted loss. Without the rumour it may have survived. But who knows?

The role of the liquidator

The commonly held view about receivers and their advisors is that of an undertaker employed to perform the last rites for an ailing construction firm. However, the true role adopted by the receiver is to preserve and salvage any or all the parts of the firm. This is based on the fact that where insolvency occurs all those involved are losers; there are no winners. The types and values of assets which can be recovered vary considerably depending on whether the company is a contractor or developer, manufacturer or even a consultant. Contractors have become wise enough to separate the company's activities into groups such as plant hire, house building, general contracting, etc, so that if hard times occur then the whole business might not be lost. When insolvency becomes a possibility then speed becomes of the essence. The whole assets of the contractor must be maintained and not traded against favours elsewhere.

In the construction industry when receivers are appointed a firm of specialist quantity surveyors arrives at the same time. For each contract there are usually three choices available:

- Completion of the project. This is desirable and the more advanced a project is towards completion, the better is the likelihood of this occurring
- Abandon it. This is the least desirable option, because there are usually assets still tied up in it
- Sell the project to a third party.

In each of the above cases, the quantity surveyor calculates the amounts of work done, the materials on site, what is owed to subcontractors, suppliers and other creditors, amounts outstanding in retention, etc. In about 75% of receiverships, projects are either completed or sold to other firms.

For example, a contractor could be 60% of the way through a £10 m project, but of the £6 m work completed, the contractor might only have received £5 m owing to work being completed since the last interim valuation and outstanding retention sums. Coupled with this there is a good possibility that future profits may exist in the remaining work that needs to be carried out. However, life is never down to simple arithmetic and other factors will need to be taken into account, such as the amounts owing to the different creditors, the lowering of site morale and motivation, and the fact that the project might have been financially front-end loaded.

The law

The machinery to wind up a company may be set in motion either by the debtor themselves or by the creditors. The courts make the receiving order and require the debtor to submit to the official receiver or trustee in bankruptcy a statement of affairs showing assets and liabilities (see Fig. 15.1). A creditor's meeting is usually held to decide whether to accept any suggested scheme or whether to declare the firm as insolvent.

The official receiver will eventually, on completion of the liquidation, turn all of the assets into cash and then divide this amongst the creditors, paying them at a rate of so many pence per pound that is owed. Certain creditors may have preference, e.g. those who hold preference shares and the Inland Revenue. Most creditors rank equally. Insolvency is broadly concerned with a firm or company's inability to pay its debts. Within the Insolvency Act 1986 various situations can arise:

- *Voluntary liquidation*   This can be the result of either the share-holders or creditors making a resolution which is then accepted by the company.
- *Compulsory liquidation*   This occurs because a company refuses to cease trading and is the result of a court order for a company to be wound up.

Creditors

Creditors may be secured, i.e. those who hold a mortgage, charge or lien upon the property of the debtor, or they may be unsecured. Unsecured creditors may be ordinary trade creditors, preferential creditors or deferred creditors. Preferential debts include the costs of insolvency proceedings. The proceeds of liquidation are distributed in accordance with the following hierarchy:

- Fixed charge holders
- Liquidators' fees and expenses
- Preferential creditors such as the Inland Revenue, Customs and Excise, National Insurance contributions, pensions and employees' pay
- Floating charge holders
- Unsecured creditors
- Shareholders.

Determination of contract (contractor insolvency)

All of the standard forms of construction contract incorporate provisions aimed at regulating the events of a contractor's insolvency. It usually results in one of two courses of action being taken. Either the contractor's employment is terminated and a new contract probably made with a new contractor, or alternative ways are examined to enable the same contractor to complete the works. On those occasions where the personal skill of the contractor is the essence of the contract, completion may only be acceptable under those terms. This situation is likely to be unusual in the construction industry and will usually only be applicable to specialist firms.

It should be recognised that insolvency does not by itself have the effect of terminating the contract, since the liquidator will normally have the power, after obtaining leave, to carry on the business of the debtor as may be necessary for the beneficial winding up of the company.

A liquidator has the power within twelve months of appointment to disclaim unprofitable contracts which are still uncompleted at the commencement of the insolvency. The liquidator may decide to disclaim, when perhaps most of the more financially fruitful work has been completed, or when some retention, such as for example, sectional completion, has been released.

Where the work is reasonably far advanced, a liquidator is not likely to disclaim it if this can be avoided. Where a relatively small amount of work needs to be completed up to completion, then this will enable outstanding retention monies that are due to be released. When a liquidator does disclaim a contract at this stage, the employer is likely to be in the most favourable position, since the retention sums can be used as a buffer when inviting other firms to tender for the outstanding work that needs to be completed.

Where the construction work is at a relatively early stage on a project when insolvency occurs, it is the employer who will want to ensure that the contractor completes the contract as originally envisaged. The employer, under these circumstances, is likely to have to pay higher prices to have the work completed by another firm, especially where the original contract was awarded through some form of competitive tendering. However, there is much less inducement on the part of the liquidator to want to carry on with such a project, especially if the rates and prices in the contract documents are economically unfavourable.

Where an employer is faced with poor performance from a contractor who is continuing with the project, there is still the right within the contract to determine the contractor's employment; for example, where the progress of the works is not being maintained.

Provision in the forms of contract

Clause 27 of the JCT 98 form of contract and clause 63 of the ICE Conditions of Contract make provisions for insolvency. Similar clauses are found in the other forms of contract. Clause 27.3 (JCT 98) requires the contractor to inform the employer if it is intended to make a composition or arrangement with creditors, or the contractor becomes bankrupt (insolvent). More usually where the contractor is a company, the employer must be informed if one of the following occurs:

- The contractor makes a proposal for a voluntary arrangement for a composition of debts or scheme of arrangement in accordance with the Companies Act 1985 and the Insolvency Act 1986
- A provisional liquidator is appointed
- A winding-up order is made
- A resolution is passed for voluntary winding-up, other than in the case of amalgamation or reconstruction
- Under the Insolvency Act 1986 an administrator or administrative receiver is appointed.

The forms of contract allow the employer in the above situations to:

- Ensure that the site materials, the site and the works are adequately protected, including offsetting any of the costs involved against monies due to the contractor
- Employ and pay others to carry out and complete the works
- Make good defects
- Use all temporary buildings, plant, tools, equipment and site materials
- Purchase materials and goods that are necessary to complete the works
- Have any benefits for the agreement for the supply of materials or goods assigned from the contractor
- Make payments to suppliers or subcontractors for work already executed and deduct these amounts from any monies due to the contractor
- Sell any temporary buildings, plant, tools and equipment (for the benefit of the contractor), if the contractor does not remove these when requested
- Withhold the release of any retention monies
- Calculate the costs involved of the contractor's insolvency and show these as a debt to the contractor.

Where the temporary buildings, plant, tools, equipment and site materials are not owned by the contractor, the consent of the owner will usually be required. The costs for these and the use of the contractor's facilities, described above, must be paid for by the employer. However, such costs will be offset against any payments that are made to complete the works. The legal title to the goods and materials must be clear (*Dawber Williamson Roofing* v. *Humberside County Council* (1979)).

Factors to consider at insolvency

Until the contractor's legal insolvency becomes a fact, the employer is in a rather frustrating position. The employer must continue to honour the contract, otherwise the contractor may pursue a claim for breach of contract. Any interference on the part of the employer may also exacerbate the unfortunate situation.

The following are some of the principal actions that an employer should take immediately following the insolvency of a contractor.

Secure the site

The construction site should be secured as quickly and as expeditiously as possible. This is to prevent unauthorised entry or vandalism. It is also to avoid the possibility of materials or equipment being removed by the contractor or subcontractors. Although this would be in breach of the contract, it is clearly more beneficial to the employer to retain these rather than to have to go through the courts for their return when their whereabouts may have become unknown.

Materials

Materials on site for which the employer has paid belong to the employer unless their title is defective. Furthermore they cannot be removed from site without the employer's written permission (JCT 98, clause 16). Similar conditions exist in all the major forms of contract. Materials on site that have not been paid for can be used by the employer to complete the works. No payment is made directly, since they will help to reduce the total costs of achieving completion. They will therefore reduce the financial indebtedness of the contractor. Materials off site for which the employer has paid are also in the ownership of the employer, providing that the provisions of clause 30 (JCT 98) have been complied with. A list of the materials on site should be quickly made with a note of which of these have been paid for by the employer.

Plant

The contractor's directly owned plant and other temporary structures on site can be used freely to secure completion. Hired plant and that which belongs to subcontractors cannot be used without express permission and payment. However, no plant passes directly to the ownership of the employer. Hired plant that is temporarily supporting the structure will obviously be retained by the employer, but at the usual hire rates.

Retention

Retention by the employer is one of the main buffers the employer has to face any possible loss. Any balance as a result of underpayment to the contractor or for work completed since the last interim payment, will be used for similar effect. Retention that is held on behalf of nominated subcontractors will be retained until its release becomes due.

Subcontractors

A review of the firms claiming that they have not been paid will also be required. There is, however, no legal obligation for the employer to pay any firm, not even nominated subcontractors, whilst there remains provision in JCT 98 to make payments to such firms direct. However, such a firm is unlikely to be willing to complete their part of the works unless some payment for work completed and assurance that future work will be paid for in full is agreed. Only the retention sums accruing before determination must be paid to the nominated firms.

Payments

The quantity surveyor will need to ascertain two factors about payments. It will be wise to check first that such firms have not been overpaid for the work carried out, and secondly, that the main contractor has passed on payments to respective nominated subcontractors. An estimate of the costs involved in completing the works will also be required.

Other matters

It will be prudent to ensure that insurances remain effective at all times. If a bond holder is involved, then these must be kept informed of what is happening and any progress that is being achieved.

Completion of the contract

An early meeting of everyone concerned should be arranged to consider the best ways of completing the works that are outstanding. It is usual for the liquidator to attend this meeting, but where this is not possible, then the liquidator should be kept fully informed of all the decisions that are made.

If the liquidator decides to disclaim the contract there are several different ways that can be used to appoint a replacement contractor. It will be necessary, at a later date, to show the liquidator and the bond holder that due care was taken to complete the project as economically as was originally intended. The bulk of the work involved in drawing up a new contract will be performed by the quantity surveyor.

Where the amount of work carried out from the original contract is small, then the contract bills may be used to invite new contractors to tender for the work. Adjustments for the work completed will, of course, need to be made. If the contract is in its early days, then it is likely that priced documents will be available from the previously unsuccessful firms. Where the work is significantly advanced, then new documents or addendum bills of quantities will need to be prepared. The time delay involved in this may be unacceptable to the employer and alternative methods may need to be adopted. A new contract may, for example, be negotiated with a single contractor, perhaps on the basis of a single percentage addition to the original contract. Again adjustments for the work completed will need to be made. The main advantage here is that the new contractor can start work on site immediately, with a minimum of delay, if this is possible. A third alternative is to pay for the remainder of the work on a cost plus basis, which may not be favourable to the employer. It is likely that the original contract was the most competitive and any new arrangement will therefore be more expensive.

With each of these methods, an allowance in the form of a provisional sum needs to be made to cover any remedial works or making good defects that have been left by the insolvent contractor. Whilst some of these defects may be apparent, others may not show for some time. Where the work is piecemeal and almost at practical completion, it may be better to employ a contractor who is suitably able to carry out such work; for example, if the outstanding work includes macadam hard standings then it may be more appropriate to employ a firm who specialises in this kind of work.

An alternative method of securing completion is to award the new contract to a contractor for a fee. The selected contractor would then complete the works on exactly the same basis as the original contractor, using the contract rates and prices and accepting total responsibility for the project including its defects. The negotiated fee might be based on a percentage or lump sum to cover the higher costs involved in completing the project and the responsibility, for example, for defects.

A further suggestion is to offer the contract to a new firm on exactly the same basis as that for the original contract, using the same rates and prices. This may appear, at first, to be an unattractive option for three reasons, which no contractor will accept. Firstly, the insolvent contractor was probably selected on a lowest price tender that no other firms could match, hence the prices could be uneconomical for other firms. Secondly, costs will need to be expended on rectifying the partially completed works. Thirdly, the new contractor will be responsible for the first contractor's work, including the making good of any defects. However, the attractiveness of this proposal lies in the fact that retention sums are outstanding and these may provide more incentive than the three disadvantages combined.

The employer's loss

The main sources of loss to the employer are the probable delays in completion and the potential additional costs that might be incurred. If the original contractor had not become insolvent then the loss due to delays would normally have been recovered by way of liquidated damages. The employer is still entitled to show this as a loss, using the basis of calculation shown in the appendix to the form of contract. However, in practice, because of the contractor's insolvency, there may be insufficient funds to make this payment.

A second source of loss involves the additional payments that the employer may need to make to complete the project. This will include the temporary protection and extra site security, which might include erecting additional hoardings, fencing, locking sheds and a twenty-four hour guard. Additional insurances are likely to be required, especially to cover the period prior to appointing the new contractor. Additional fees will also be necessary for the services involved in placing and managing the new contract. Also, because of a moral obligation to nominated firms, the employer may be involved in making double payments, especially where the original contractor had defaulted in making payments to these firms (*Dawber Williamson Roofing* v. *Humberside County Council* (1979)).

Expenditure involved

It is necessary to calculate a hypothetical final account, which would have been the amount payable to the original contractor had this firm completed the works. For most of the items involved this entails a translation of the actual final account by using the rates and prices from the original contract. A careful note must be made of dayworks, which may otherwise, in the original contract, have been described as measured works. Claims for loss and expense that might have arisen may be a matter for professional judgement. In the case of fluctuations, had the original contract been on a fixed price basis then no account of these need be considered for the original contractor. The additional fluctuations due to the later completion can be genuinely deducted as some compensation against liquidated damages. Remedial work charged by the new contractor for the unsatisfactory work of the original contractor will be excluded from the hypothetical final account. Examples of typical calculations are shown in Figs 15.3 and 15.4.

Determination of contract (employer insolvency)

Whilst a greater number of contractors become insolvent than employers, nevertheless the insolvency of employers is something that does occur from time to time during the execution of a contract. Clause 28.3 (JCT 98), for example, includes the same provisions as clause 27.3 relating to the contractor. When insolvency of the employer arises, the employer must inform the contractor in writing of its occurrence. The following are the contractual consequences of insolvency of the employer:

- The contractor can remove from the site all temporary buildings, plant, tools, equipment, goods and materials. This must be done reasonably and safely to prevent injury, death or damage occurring.
- Subcontractors should do the same.
- Within 28 days of determination of the employment, the employer must pay the contractor the retention that has already been deducted, prior to determination.

```
Contract 1
Amount of original contract                                                    1356000
Agreed additions for variations, prime cost
   sums, dayworks, fluctuations, claims¹                                         82800
Amount of the final account had the original
   contractor completed the works                                             1438800

Amount of completion contract                       838200
Agreed addition for second contractor only           63050
Amount paid to the original contractor²             495000
Additional professional fees                         12500             1408750
Debt due to the original contractor                                        £30050
```

¹ This includes all variations priced at the original contractor's rates and prices.
² The total amount of the first contractor's certificate, plus work done since then, was estimated to be £570000. The original contractor actually receives in total £525050.

Fig. 15.3 Examples of financial summary.

```
Contract 2
Amount of original contract                                                  2292000
Agreed additions (as above)                                                   111150
Debt due to the original contractor                                         2403150

Amount certified to original contractor           240100
Amount of completion contract                    2163050
Agreed lump sum fee                               225000
Additional professional fees                       36000             2664150
Debt payable by the trustee in bankruptcy¹                              £261000
```

¹ If there was a bond for 10 per cent of the contract sum, then the employer should receive £229200 towards the above debt. If the final dividend of five pence in the pound was paid to creditors at some later date, the employer would receive a further £1590 (£31800 @ 5p). The ultimate employer's loss is therefore £30210.

Fig. 15.4 Examples of financial summary.

- The contractor prepares an account setting out the following, which includes the relevant amounts from nominated subcontractors:
  - The total value of work properly executed up to the date of determination, calculated in accordance with the contract provisions.
  - Any sum in respect of direct loss and expense incurred either before or after determination.
  - The reasonable costs associated with the removal of temporary works, plant and materials.
  - Any direct loss or damage caused to the contractor by the determination.

– The cost of materials or goods properly ordered for the works which the contractor has already paid. These items become the property of the employer.

Construction contracts involve giving credit to the employer by the contractor in respect of work carried out and goods and materials supplied to the site prior to the issue of an interim certificate. The payment of the certificate, which can take place up to 14 days after certification, is not made in full but is subject to retention. Also a contractor has no lien on the finished work and the employer's insolvency may place the contractor in some real difficulty until matters are finally resolved. This difficulty can result in the contractor's own insolvency. A prudent contractor will, prior to signing a contract, wish to establish whether an employer is able to keep their side of the bargain.

Under JCT 98 the employer's interest in retention monies is fiduciary as trustee on behalf of the contractor and for any nominated subcontractor. This is to protect the contractor and nominated subcontractors in the event of an employer's insolvency. It is now strongly recommended that the full provisions of the contract are invoked. A separate bank account should be used, jointly in the names of the employer and the contractor, for the depositing of retention monies.

The employment of the quantity surveyor and architect may not necessarily end at the employer's insolvency. However, if they are to continue with their work they will require some assurances from the liquidator that they will be paid for their services in full.

Determination of contract (nominated subcontractor insolvency)

Under clause 35.24.7 (JCT 98), where a nominated subcontractor becomes insolvent the subcontractor's employment is terminated. The architect must then make such further renomination as necessary. This may include aspects of making good or replacing defective work. The architect must take all reasonable steps to nominate another subcontractor and any delays in respect of this may give the main contractor grounds for an extension of time (clause 25.4.7). In *Bickerton* v. *NW Metropolitan Regional Hospital Board* (1970) AER 1039, important principles were laid down for when a nominated subcontractor became insolvent.

As with all nomination of subcontractors, the main contractor can refuse to accept the new subcontract. Also, the main contractor is not bound to carry out any of this work, unless it is otherwise agreed. This would require the issue of a formal variation order.

Any firm withdrawing from a contract, for any reason, is likely to give rise to disputes and extra costs arising. It is therefore equally important to ensure that any firm involved in the project should be able to fully comply with the contractual provisions that are involved.

Insolvency of the quantity surveyor or architect

Insolvency of architects or quantity surveyors is fortunately an unusual occurrence, but in common with other businesses nevertheless does occur. Where an architect's or surveyor's practice becomes insolvent then the employer must within 21 days nominate a successor (articles 3 and 4, JCT 98). The contractor can raise reasonable objections and if these are upheld then the employer must nominate other firms. Under renomination, the firms appointed cannot over-rule anything that has previously been agreed and accepted. These include matters relating to certificates, opinions, decisions, approvals or instructions. The new firms can make changes, as necessary, but these will always constitute a variation under the terms of the contract.

Performance bonds

A performance bond is a written undertaking by a third party, given on behalf of the contractor to an employer, wherein a surety accepts responsibility to ensure the due completion of the contractual works. Local and central government have frequently requested a contractor to take out a bond for the due completion of the work. This is often in the order of 10% of the contract sum. Main contractors may also require performance bonds to be provided by their own subcontractors as a form of guarantee or insurance.

Bond holders are frequently banks or insurance companies. They are responsible for paying the amounts involved, up to the bond limit, should the contractor default, as in the case of insolvency. However, they have no control over the way in which the work is carried out or the project completed.

When an employer declares that a contractor has failed to perform the works adequately, the surety has normally three courses of action to follow:

- Pay damages up to the full value of the bond
- Engage another contractor to complete the work
- Make such arrangements that the contractor is able to finish the works.

Other bonds may be used which guarantee performance of the contractor. In these instances the surety will satisfy themselves that the bid tendered is responsible, practical and complete. The charge for the bond is included within the contractor's tender and is thus ultimately borne by the employer as a form of insurance.

Wherever possible standard forms of bond should be used where each party is then clearly aware of its implications. The ICE Conditions of Contract provide a standard form of bond. There is no JCT equivalent.

Bibliography

CIB. *Code of Practice for the Selection of Main Contractors*. Thomas Telford. 1997.
Newman P. *Insolvency Explained*. RIBA Publications. 1992.
Rajak S. and Davis P. *Insolvency a Business by Business Guide*. Butterworth Tolley. 2001.

16 Contractual Disputes

Introduction

From time to time quantity surveyors find themselves involved in contractual disputes either in litigation in the courts, in arbitration or in alternative dispute resolution cases (ADR) cases. Their involvement is often as witnesses of fact: that is, someone who was actually there at the time as project surveyor or manager. However, more often they are involved as expert witnesses, adjudicators, arbitrators themselves or as neutrals or mediators in ADR cases. Each of these roles is considered in this chapter, as alternatives to litigation in the courts, under the following headings:

- Litigation
- Arbitration
- Adjudication
- Alternative dispute resolution
- Expert witness
- Lay advocacy.

Disputes are a common feature of the construction industry. They occur daily and fortunately many are solved amicably between the parties involved, without the need to resort to one of the above. The number of reported legal cases confirms the litigious nature of the construction industry. The costs associated with resolving these differences of opinion or interpretation are often high and damage the image of the industry.

Why disputes arise

The construction industry is a risky business. It does not build many prototypes, with each different project being individual in so many respects. Even apparently identical building and civil engineering projects that have been constructed on different sites create their own special circumstances, are subject to the vagaries of different site and weather conditions, use labour that may have different trade practices and result in costs that are different. Even the identical project constructed on an adjacent site by a different contractor will have different problems and their associated different costs of construction. Disputes can therefore arise, even on projects that have the best intentions. Even when every possibility of disagreement has been potentially eliminated, problems can still occur – such is human nature. Some of the main areas for possible disputes occurring are:

General

- Adversarial nature of construction contracts
- Poor communication between the parties concerned
- Proliferation of forms of contract and warranties
- Fragmentation in the industry
- Tendering policies and procedures.

Employers

- Poor briefing
- Changes and variation requirements
- Changes to standard conditions of contract
- Interference in the contractual duties of the contract administrator
- Late payments.

Consultants

- Design inadequacies
- Lack of appropriate competence and experience
- Late and incomplete information
- Lack of coordination
- Unclear delegation of responsibilities.

Contractors

- Inadequate site management
- Poor planning and programming
- Poor standards of workmanship
- Disputes with subcontractors
- Delayed payments to subcontractors
- Co-ordination of subcontractors.

Subcontractors

- Mismatch of subcontract conditions with main contract
- Failure to follow and adopt agreed procedures
- Poor standards of workmanship.

Manufacturers and suppliers

- Failure to define performance or purpose
- Failure of performance.

Litigation

Litigation is a dispute procedure which takes place in the courts. It involves third parties who are trained in the law, usually solicitors and barristers, and a judge who is appointed by the courts. This method of solving disputes is often expensive and can be a very lengthy process before the matter is finally resolved, sometimes taking years to arrive at a decision. The process is also frequently extended to higher courts involving additional expense and time. Also, since a case needs to be properly prepared prior to the trial, a considerable amount of time can elapse between the commencement of the proceedings and the trial.

A typical action is started by the issuing of a writ. This places the matter on the official record. A copy of the writ must be served on the defendant, either by delivering it personally or by other means such as through the offices of a solicitor. The general rule is that the defendants must be made aware of the proceedings against them. The speed of a hearing in most cases depends on the following:

- Availability of competent legal advisers to handle the case, i.e. its preparation and presentation
- Expeditious preparation of the case by the parties concerned
- Availability of courts and judges to hear the case.

The amount of money involved in the case will determine whether it is heard in the County Court or High Court. Where the matter is largely of a technical nature the case may be referred in the first instance to the Technology and Construction Court, formerly the Official Referee's Court. A circuit judge whose court is used to hearing commercial cases usually presides over these cases, and hence handles most of the commercial and construction disputes. Under these circumstances a full hearing does not normally take place, but points of principle are established. The outcome of this hearing will determine whether the case then proceeds towards a full trial.

Under some circumstances, the plaintiff may apply to the court for a judgment on the claim (or the defendant for a judgment on the counterclaim), on the ground that there is no sufficient defence. Provided that the court is satisfied that the defendant (or plaintiff) has no defence that warrants a full trial of the issues involved, judgment will be given, together with the costs involved.

Every fact in a dispute that is necessary to establish a claim must be proved to the judge by admissible evidence whether oral, documentary or of other kind. Oral evidence must normally be given from memory by a person who heard or saw what took place. Hearsay evidence is not normally permissible.

In a civil action the facts in the dispute must be proved on a balance of probabilities. This is unlike a criminal case where proof beyond reasonable doubt is required. The burden of proof usually lies on the party asserting the fact.

Arbitration

Disputes between parties to a contract are traditionally heard in the courts, but in building contracts the chosen method has more often been arbitration. Arbitration to resolve disputes in building contracts comes about following the agreement of the parties, either when the dispute arises, or more often as a term of the original contract. For instance, the JCT forms of contract all provide that if a dispute arises between the parties to the contract then either party can call for arbitration. When such clauses exist in contracts the courts, if asked, will generally rule that arbitration, having been the chosen path of the parties, is the proper forum for the dispute to be heard and will stay any legal action taken in breach of the arbitration agreement under section 9 of the Arbitration Act 1996.

The JCT publish arbitration rules for use with arbitration agreements referred to in the JCT contracts. They set out rules concerning interlocutory (intermediate) matters, conduct of arbitrations and various types of procedures: without hearing (documents only), full procedure with hearing, and short procedure with hearing, each containing strict timetables.

Arbitration and the law relating to it are subjects on their own. The traditional advantages of arbitration over the courts are four-fold:

- Arbitration proceedings are quicker than the courts
- Arbitration is cheaper than litigating in the courts
- The parties get a 'judge' of their choosing, a person knowledgeable about the subject matter in dispute, but with no knowledge of the actual case, rather than a judge imposed on them
- Unlike proceedings in the courts, arbitration proceedings are confidential.

With regard to the first of these traditional advantages, provided the proceedings are kept simple then arbitration can still prove quicker than proceeding through the courts. However, the modern tendency is to involve lawyers at all stages and to complicate disputes. This has eroded this advantage, and there is now often very little difference between the time it takes to get a dispute settled either in arbitration or in the courts. Equally, arbitration is no longer the cheaper option that it used to be. Legal costs, and the fact that the parties have to pay for the 'judge and courtroom' in arbitration proceedings instead of having them provided at the taxpayer's expense, have eroded this traditional advantage as well, although under section 65 of the Arbitration Act 1996 the arbitrator may limit costs to a specified amount unless the parties agree not to let this happen.

However, the third and fourth advantages, choice of judge and confidentiality, still exist and are considered by many to be of overriding importance. Hence the continued popularity of arbitration references, although statutory adjudications under the Housing Grants, Construction and Regeneration Act 1996 appear to have resulted in fewer references.

The duty of arbitrators is to ascertain the substance of the dispute, to give directions as to proceeding, and to hear the parties as quickly as possible and make their decision known by way of an award. Arbitrators hear both sides of an argument, decide which they prefer and award accordingly. They cannot decide that they do not like either argument and substitute their own solution. This would lead to an accusation of misconduct (see below).

An arbitrator may be named in a contract, although this is rare. It is usually thought better to wait until the dispute arises and then choose an appropriate person. The choosing will be by the parties. Each side exchanges suitable names and usually an acceptable choice emerges. If the parties are unable to agree then a presidential appointment will be sought from a body such as the Chartered Institute of Arbitrators, the Royal Institute of British Architects or The Royal Institution of Chartered Surveyors. If a quantity surveyor is thought the most appropriate choice then the President of the RICS would be the most likely to be approached. When appointed, an arbitrator calls the parties together in a preliminary meeting. At this meeting the nature and extent of the dispute are made known to the arbitrator and an order is sought for directions, fixing a timetable for submission of the pleadings (i.e. points of claim, points of defence, etc.) The directions normally end by fixing a date and venue for a hearing.

As the date for the hearing approaches, the parties will keep the arbitrator informed of the progress they are making in working their way through the timetable. If a compromise is achieved and the matter is settled, they will inform the arbitrator immediately. At the hearing each party puts their case and then calls their witnesses, first the witnesses of the facts and then the expert witnesses. All witnesses normally give evidence under oath and are examined and cross-examined by the parties' advocates.

All arbitrators are bound by the terms of the Arbitration Act 1996. Their awards, once made, are final and binding. If an award is not honoured, then the aggrieved party can call on the courts to implement the award. The only exception to this is if the arbitrator is found to be guilty of misconduct, or the arbitrator is wrong at law. If either of these events occurs a party can apply to the courts for leave to have the arbitrator's award referred back for reconsideration or, in extreme cases, to seek the removal of the arbitrator.

Being wrong at law is self-explanatory. The arbitrator may be a lawyer but more likely does not hold that qualification. There is therefore no disgrace in getting the law wrong. If in doubt, an arbitrator has the power under the Act to seek legal assistance and often this is good advice.

Misconduct is more difficult to describe. It is not misconduct in the usual understanding of the word. It can be defined in this context as a failure to conduct the reference in the manner expressly or impliedly prescribed by the submission, or to behave in a way that would be regarded by the court as contrary to public policy. Failure to answer all the questions asked and hearing one party without the other party being present are examples of misconduct that the courts would consider and direct as they thought fit.

Quantity surveyors are well suited to act as arbitrators in construction disputes, as the dispute frequently involves measurement, costs and loss and/or expense and interpretation of documents. These are all matters falling within the expertise of quantity surveyors. When the matters in dispute concern quality of workmanship or design faults then arbitration is best left to architects or engineers. Equally, when matters of law are the prime consideration then the arbitrator should be a lawyer or at least have a law qualification.

Adjudication

Statutory adjudication

Sections 108 to 113 of the Housing Grants, Construction and Regeneration Act 1996 impose statutory adjudication in most written construction contracts (there are some exceptions, e.g. oil and gas contracts and private homes). This scheme has revolutionised dispute resolution for construction contracts (which include contracts between employers and construction professionals) because if one party to the contract wishes a dispute to be heard he can call for adjudication, and the adjudicator, when appointed, has 28 days to make his award. The award will be binding and must be paid forthwith and will stand unless overturned in a later arbitration or court case. Many cases in the Technology and Construction Court now deal with the enforcement of adjudication awards and the judges are determined to uphold them unless it can be shown that there is no contract in fact or some really major breach of natural justice has occurred.

Obviously in the limited time available it is difficult to resist a claim which may have been copiously compiled (usually by the contractor or sub-contractor) before the adjudication is demanded, and quantity surveyors must look sharp to analyse it and prepare a response to be put before the adjudicator. The statutory scheme must either be replicated in the construction contract or it will be imposed. It has therefore largely supplanted other adjudication provisions found in standard forms of contract.

One of the benefits of adjudication is that it can often lead to a settlement without the matter going any further. This is because a party that has lost in an adjudication, will think very carefully before proceeding with very expensive litigation or arbitration. They might well lose again, with the additional penalty of paying the other side's costs. Current statistics suggest that few adjudications lead on to full arbitration or litigation.

Alternative dispute resolution

Alternative dispute resolution, or ADR as it is generally known, originated in the USA and was adopted in the UK in the 1980s. It is now practised worldwide. ADR provides a means of resolving disputes without resorting to arbitration or the courts. In that respect it is nothing new. Quantity surveyors and contractors have over the years traditionally settled disputes by nego-tiation. With ADR the process is somewhat more formal. The advantages of ADR can be summarised as follows:

- Private: confidentiality is retained
- Quick: a matter of days rather than weeks, months or even years
- Economic: legal and other costs resulting from lengthy litigation are avoided.

However, none of these advantages will be achieved unless one vital ingre-dient is present. There must be goodwill on both sides to settle the matter on a commercial rather than a litigious basis. If this goodwill does not exist, then the parties have no option but to resort to arbitration or the courts, without wasting further time and resources.

ADR can take a variety of forms, and of these the first two are the most commonly met:

- Mini-trial
- Mediation
- Mutual fact-finding
- Mutual expert
- Private judging
- Dispute resolution boards.

Mini-trial

Each of the parties is represented, generally but not necessarily by a lawyer. The lawyer makes a short presentation of their client's case to a tribunal. This presentation will have been preceded by limited disclosure of documentation, or discovery as it is known. The purpose of this limited discovery is to ensure that each party is aware of the opposite side's case and is not taken by surprise by the presentation.

The tribunal usually takes the form of a senior managerial representative of each party and an independent advisor referred to as a neutral. It is important to the success of the mini-trial that each of the parties' representatives should not have been directly involved in the project. There will then be less emo-tional involvement than with someone who has lived with the dispute and has difficulty in taking a detached view. It is also essential that both parties' representatives have full authority to settle the matter. There is nothing worse than arriving at what appears to be consensus, for one party then to disclose that they can only agree it subject to authorisation from a chairman, board, council, chief officer or some other third party.

The neutral has to be someone with a knowledge of the industry but no knowledge or interest in the dispute. In this respect the same requirements as that of a good arbitrator are required. However, unlike an arbitrator, whose task it is to hear the arguments and decide which is preferable, a neutral becomes much more involved, listening, suggesting and giving advice on matters of fact and sometimes on law as well.

After the initial presentation, experts and witnesses of fact may be called, following which the managers enter into negotiation with a view to coming to a consensus. The length of these negotiations will depend very much on the complexity of the matters in dispute. They will be assisted by the neutral, who may if the parties remain deadlocked, give a non-binding opinion. This may lead to a settlement after further negotiation.

Once a negotiated settlement is reached, the neutral will there and then draft the heads of a statement of agreement, which the parties will each initial. This will then be followed by a formal agreement ending the matter.

Mediation

This is a less formal method of proceeding than that described for a mini-trial; however it is more commonly used and is becoming more popular than the mini-trial. The parties, with assistance from their experts or lawyers, will select a neutral whose background will reflect the matters in dispute. A preliminary meeting will be arranged by the neutral to discover the substance of the dispute and to decide how best to proceed.

At a subsequent meeting the parties will make formal presentation in a joint session. This is then followed by a series of private meetings, or 'caucuses' as they are termed, between the neutral and each of the parties on their own. The neutral moves from one caucus to the next, reporting, with agreement, the views of each party in turn. This should lead to the neutral's being able to suggest a formula for agreement, which in turn may lead to a settlement. Such agreement is terminated in the same way as in a mini-trial.

Mutual fact-finding

Resolution of a dispute by mutual fact-finding is an informal procedure. The parties, possibly at a different level from those closely involved, take a pragmatic and commercial approach to settling the dispute with or without the assistance of a mutual expert.

Dispute resolution boards

The appointment of dispute resolution boards under specific forms of contract (e.g. dispute adjudication board under the FIDIC conditions of contract) is becoming more common. These boards comprise individuals appointed by the parties to the contract, the boards' role being to adjudicate on disputes referred to them by either party.

Conclusion

To summarise, ADR provides a dispute resolution mechanism that concentrates on resolving disputes by consensual, rather than adjudicative methods. To quote from the Centre for Dispute Resolution's introduction to ADR, 'These techniques are not soft options, but rather involve a change of emphasis and a different challenge. The parties cooperate in the formulation of a procedure and result over which they have control.' The main features are easily captioned under:

- *Consensus* – a joint objective to find the business solution
- *Continuity* – a desire to find a solution in the context of an ongoing business relationship
- *Control* – the ability to tailor a solution that is geared towards a business result rather than a result governed by the rule of law, which may be too restrictive or largely inappropriate
- *Confidentiality* – avoiding harmful washing of dirty linen in public.

Quantity surveyors have a role to play in ADR. They are obvious candidates for the post of neutral in construction disputes, provided they have good negotiating skills and have undergone the necessary training.

Expert witness

Quantity surveyors, particularly those more experienced, may be briefed to give expert witness in a variety of circumstances:

- Litigation in the High Court or in the County Court
- In arbitration
- Before a tribunal.

While proceedings in court tend to be more formal than in arbitration, the same rules apply.

Expert evidence is evidence of opinion to assist with the technical assertions of each party. The expert must be seen at all times to be independent and have no financial interest in the outcome. Expert witnesses are there to assist the court, the arbitrator or the tribunal and must not be seen to be solely advocating their client's case. To emphasise this, two quotations from court judgments are relevant.

In the case of *Whitehouse* v. *Jordan* (1981) 1 WLR 247, Lord Wilberforce warned:

'Whilst some degree of consultation between experts and legal advisers is entirely proper it is necessary that expert evidence presented to the court should be and should be seen to be the independent product of the expert and uninfluenced as to form or content by the exigencies of litigation. To the extent that it is not, the evidence is likely to be not only incorrect but self-defeating.'

The second quotation comes from the judgment of Sir Patrick Garland in the case of *Warwick University* v. *Sir Robert McAlpine and Others* (1988) 42 BLR:

> 'It appeared to me that some (but by no means all) of the experts in this case tended to enter into the arena in order to advocate their client's case. This led to perfectly proper cross-examination on the basis: "You have assembled and advanced explanations which you consider most likely to assist your client's case". It is to be much regretted that this had to be so. In their closing speeches counsel felt it necessary to challenge not only the reliability but the credibility of experts with unadorned attacks on their veracity. This simply should not happen where the court is called upon to decide complex scientific and technical matters.'

An expert opinion must be based on facts, and these facts have to be proved unless they can be agreed. The process of agreement is achieved by meetings of the experts. These are frequently ordered by a judge or arbitrator to agree facts and figures wherever possible, and to narrow the issues in dispute. These meetings are usually described as being 'without prejudice'. That is, nothing discussed can be used in evidence. Such meetings are followed by a joint statement of what has been agreed, and of those matters that are still outstanding. In fact, such meetings can often lead to a settlement of the dispute without troubling the tribunal further.

The Civil Procedure Rules, which now govern procedure in the courts following the far-reaching reforms of Lord Woolf, strictly regulate the procedure relating to expert evidence and should be studied by all involved in the process of adducing such evidence.

Acting as an expert witness is a time-consuming and therefore an expensive exercise. There needs to be careful reading of all relevant matters, some research where appropriate and a studiously prepared proof of evidence. As has been stated above, such proofs of evidence have to be seen as being in the sole authorship of the expert. While they may listen to advice, the final document, on which they stand to be cross-examined, is theirs and theirs alone.

Lay advocacy

Advocacy in the High Court and in the County Courts is restricted to barristers and solicitors. There is no such requirement when it comes to arbitration or appearing before a lay tribunal. Anyone can advocate their own or their client's case.

It sometimes happens that when a matter is strictly technical, such as a dispute on measurement or computation of a final account, an arbitrator may direct that the two quantity surveyors should appear before him or her to present their client's case. When this happens, quantity surveyors are acting as lay advocates and are dealing with matters very much within their own expertise. Occasionally it is suggested that a quantity surveyor might act as lay advocate on the whole case, not just that part of it within his or her own discipline.

Advocacy is a skilled art that is not easily learned. It involves meticulous preparation, the ability to ask the right questions in the right way, and the ability to think on one's feet and respond quickly to answers from witnesses or points made by one's opponent. For this reason quantity surveyors should consider very carefully whether or not to accept an invitation to act as advocate, and unless they are quite confident that they are able to, should politely decline.

Claims

It is evident, from society in general, that as individuals we are becoming more claims conscious. Firms of lawyers are now touting their services, often on a contingency fee basis, although this is still more the exception than the rule in construction cases.

Contractual claims arise where contractors assess that they are entitled to additional payments over and above that paid within the general terms and conditions of the contract for payment of work done. For example, the contractors may seek reimbursement for some alleged loss that has been suffered, for reasons beyond their control. Claims may arise for several different reasons, such as:

- Extensions of time
- Changes to the nature of the project
- Disruption to the regular progress of the works by the client or designer
- Variations to the contract.

Claims arise in respect of additional payments that cannot be recouped in the normal way, through measurement and valuation. They are based on the assumption that the works, or part of the works, are considerably different from or executed under different conditions than those envisaged at the time of tender. The differences may have revised the contractor's intended and preferred method of working, and this in turn may have altered or influenced the costs involved. The rates inserted by the contractor in the contract bills do not now represent fair recompense for the work that has been executed.

Where a standard form of contract is used, attempts may be made by contractors to invoke some of the compensatory provisions of the contract, in order to secure further payment to cover the losses involved. As with many issues in life, contractual claims are rarely the fault of one side only. If the claim cannot be resolved, then one of the methods of dispute resolution referred to earlier may need to be invoked. Special care, therefore, needs to be properly exercised in the conduct of the negotiations since they may have an effect upon the outcome of any subsequent legal proceedings. Claims usually reflect an actual loss and expense to a contractor. Once the contract is made, the contractor is responsible for carrying out and completing the works in the prescribed time and for the agreed sum. Entitlement to additional payments occurs if a breach of contract is committed by the employer or a party for whom the employer is responsible, or if circumstances arise that are dealt with in express terms of the contract providing for additional payment.

Contractual claims

Contractual claims are claims that have a direct reference to conditions of contract. When the contract is signed by the two parties, the contractor and the employer (or promoter), this results in a formal agreement to carry out and complete the works in accordance with the information supplied through the drawings, specification and contract bills. Where the works constructed are of a different character or executed under different conditions, then it is obvious that different costs will be involved. Some of these additional costs may be recouped under the terms of the contract, through, for example, remeasurement and revaluation of the works, using the appropriate rules from the contract or express terms of the contract allowing the recovery of loss and expense or cost. Other additional costs that an experienced contractor had not allowed for within the tender may need to be recovered in a different way. This is usually under the heading of a contractual claim. However, costs incurred by contractors because of their own mistakes in pricing or whilst executing the works cannot form the basis of a successful claim.

Ex-gratia payments

Ex-gratia payments are claims not based on the terms or conditions of contract. The carrying out of the works has nevertheless resulted in some loss and expense to the contractor. The contractor has completed the project on time, to the required standards and conditions and at the price agreed. Perhaps, due to a variety of different reasons, and at no fault of the contractor, a loss has been sustained that cannot relate to the express or implied terms of the contract. On rare occasions, a sympathetic employer may be prepared to make a discretionary payment to the contractor. Such payments are made out of grace and kindness. They may be made because of a long standing relationship and trust between employer and contractor, or because of outstanding service and satisfaction provided by the contractor. Nevertheless such payments are rare.

The quantity surveyor

The details of claims are usually investigated by quantity surveyors, since claims invariably have a financial consequence. A report will subsequently be made to the architect, engineer or other lead consultant. The report should summarise the arguments involved and set out the possible financial effect of each claim. Quantity surveyors frequently end up negotiating with contractors over such issues, in an attempt to solve the financial problems and agree wherever possible an amicable solution. This is preferable to lengthy legal disputes described above.

The quantity surveyor may well be requested to negotiate with the contractor on specific issues relating to a claim before there is resort to adjudication, arbitration or litigation. To guard against commitment, correspondence in the period before action is often marked 'without prejudice'. This will usually preclude reference to such correspondence in subsequent litigation but it is not, as is sometimes mistakenly believed, a safeguard against any form of binding obligation. In fact should an offer made in such correspondence be accepted, a binding agreement will usually result. This may be so even if the matter agreed relates only to a detail and the negotiations as a whole eventually collapse.

The decision on the outcome of a claim usually rests with the architect, or engineer on civil engineering works. This is except in such matters of valuation as the parties to the contract have entrusted to the quantity surveyor. The quantity surveyor, in a preliminary consideration of them, should remember the principles that must guide the architect or engineer in a decision. The following thoughts are suggested as a guide to a decision on claims:

- What did the parties contemplate on the point at the time of signing the contract? If there is specific reference to it, what does it mean?
- Can any wording of the contract, though not specifically mentioning it, be *reasonably* applied to the point? In other words, if the parties had known of the point at the time of signing the contract, would they have reckoned that it was fairly covered by the wording?
- If the parties did not contemplate the particular matter, what would they have agreed if they had?
- If the claim is based on the contract, does it so alter it as to make its scope and nature different from what was contemplated by the parties signing it? Or is it such an extension of the contract as would be beyond the contemplation of the parties at the time of signing it? In either case the question arises whether the matter should not be treated as a separate contract, and a fair valuation made irrespective of any contract conditions.
- The value of the claim in monetary terms should not affect a decision on the principle.
- If the claim is very small, however, whichever party is concerned might be persuaded to waive it, or it may be eliminated by a little 'give and take'.

In particular, any action of the client that may have been a contributory cause should be given due importance. If the claim is based on unanticipated misfortune, consideration of what the parties would have done, if they had anticipated the possibility, will often indicate whether it would be reasonable to ask the client to meet the claim to a greater or lesser extent.

The architect or engineer may make a recommendation to the client. If the contractor does not accept the client's offer then it may be necessary to invoke a third party to help resolve the difficulty, although if the architect or engineer is the certifier under the contract he must make a decision on the validity of the claim and certify accordingly.

Forms of contract

The Standard Form of Building Contract, JCT 98, seeks to clarify the contractual relationship between the employer and the contractor. As far as possible, ambiguities have been eliminated, but some nevertheless remain. If such forms or conditions of contract were not available, then the uncertainty between the two parties would be even greater. This could have the likely effect of increasing tender sums. Under the present conditions of contract, the contractual risks involved are shared between the employer and the contractor. Claims may arise most commonly under clause 26, and these are known as loss and expense claims. They may also arise due to a breach of contract. The contractor must make a written application to the architect, in the first place, stating that a direct loss and expense has occurred or is likely to occur in the execution of the project. The contractor must further state that any reimbursement under the terms of the contract is unlikely to be sufficient (clause 26.1). This information should be given to the architect as soon as possible in order to allow time to plan for other contingencies.

Under clause 52 (4) of the ICE Conditions it is the contractor's responsibility to inform the engineer within 28 days of an event that a claim may arise. The contractor must keep the necessary records in order to reasonably support any claim that may be subsequently made. Without necessarily accepting the employer's liability that a claim may exist, the engineer can instruct the contractor to keep and maintain such records. Where required the engineer is then able to inspect such records and have copies supplied where these are appropriate.

As soon as it is reasonably possible, the contractor should provide a written interim account providing full details of the particular claim and the basis upon which it is made. This should be amended and updated when necessary or when required. If the contractor fails to comply with this procedure, then this might prejudice the further investigation of the claim and any subsequent payments by the employer to the contractor.

Contractors are entitled to have such amounts included in the payment of interim certificates. However, in practice a large majority of claims are often not agreed until the completion of the contract. In these circumstances the contractor is entitled to receive part of the claim included in an interim certificate, if it has been accepted in principle. Additional monies in the form of interest payments may also become due.

Contractors

Many contractors have well organised systems for dealing with claims on construction projects and the recovery of monies that are rightly due under the terms of the contract. They are likely to maintain good records of most events, but particularly those where difficulties have occurred in the execution of the work. However, some of the difficulties may be due to the manner in which the contractor has sought to carry out the work and they thus remain the entire responsibility of the contractor.

Claims that are notified or submitted late will inevitably create problems in their approval. In these circumstances the architect or engineer might not have the opportunity to check the details of the contractor's submission, and suitable records might not have been maintained. Such occurrences will not be looked on favourably by either the architect or engineer and the employer.

The contractor must prepare a report on why a particular aspect of the work has cost more than expected, substantiate this with appropriate calculations and support it with reference to instructions, drawings, details, specifications, letters, etc. The contractor must also be able to show that an experienced contractor could not have foreseen the difficulties that occurred. They will also need to satisfy themselves that the work was carried out in an efficient, effective and economic manner.

Example

The construction of a major new business park on a green-field site requires a large earthmoving contract. The quantities of excavation and its subsequent disposal have been included in contract bills and priced by the contractor. During construction, due to variations to the contract and the unforeseen nature of some of the ground conditions, the quantities of excavated materials increase by 25% by volume, all of which needs to be removed from the site.

The contractor's pre-tender report indicates that a variety of tips at different locations and distances from the site will be used for the disposal of the excavated materials. The contractor's tendering notes indicated that the tips nearer the site would be filled first. In this case they result in lower haulage costs, and, in this example, also have lower tipping charges. The disposal of the excavated material therefore includes two separate elements:

- haul charges to the tip
- tipping charges.

In the contract bills, the rate used by the contractor for disposal of excavated materials represents an average calculated rate. This is based on the average haul distances and average tipping charges using the weighted quantities in each tip (Fig. 16.1). The actual rate for the disposal of the excavated materials can be calculated as shown in Fig. 16.1.

To continue to apply the contract bill rates is unfair. The rates no longer reflect the work to be carried out and the contractor's method of working. Other questions will also need to be asked. Is the type of material being excavated similar to that described in the contract bills? Does this material bulk at the same rate? Is it more difficult to handle? Does it necessitate the same type of mechanical plant?

Contract bills

Excavated materials for disposal in the contract bills $1\,000\,000\,m^3$

Contract bill rate is based on:

Tip A $500\,000\,m^3$	distance 1 km	Tip charge £0.10 per m^3
Tip B $300\,000\,m^3$	distance 2 km	Tip charge £0.20 per m^3
Tip C $200\,000\,m^3$	distance 4 km	Tip charge £0.30 per m^3

$$\text{Average distance} = \frac{500\,000 + 600\,000 + 800\,000}{1\,000\,000} = 1.9\,km \text{ per } m^3$$

$$\text{Average tip charge} = \frac{50\,000 + 60\,000 + 60\,000}{1\,000\,000} = £0.17 \text{ per } m^3$$

Final account

Actual quantities in the final account

Tip A $500\,000\,m^3$	distance 1 km	Tip charge £0.10 per m^3
Tip B $300\,000\,m^3$	distance 2 km	Tip charge £0.20 per m^3
Tip C $300\,000\,m^3$	distance 4 km	Tip charge £0.30 per m^3
Tip D $150\,000\,m^3$	distance 6 km	Tip charge £0.50 per m^3

$$\text{Average distance} = \frac{500\,000 + 600\,000 + 1\,200\,000 + 900\,000}{1\,250\,000} = 2.56\,km \text{ per } m^3$$

$$\text{Average tip charge} = \frac{50\,000 + 60\,000 + 90\,000 + 75\,000}{1\,250\,000} = £0.22 \text{ per } m^3$$

Note: bulking of the soil has been ignored.

Fig. 16.1 Earthmoving claim.

Some other factors that the contractor may also consider include:

- The increase in the amount of excavated materials, on this scale, may also have other repercussions, such as an extension of the contract time.
- The method of carrying out the works might also now be different from that originally envisaged by the contractor.
- Different types of mechanical excavators may have been more efficient than the plant originally selected to do the work.
- The mechanical plant on site may no longer be the most appropriate to do the job. This is especially so where cut and fill excavations are considered, where motorised scrapers may need to be substituted for excavators and lorries.
- The contractor may also be involved in hiring additional plant at higher charges and employing workpeople at overtime rates, in order to keep the project on schedule.

The preparation of the claim includes two aspects:

- A report outlining the reasons why additional payments should be made to the contractor.
- An analysis showing how the additional costs have been calculated.

The client's quantity surveyor

The quantity surveyor will recognise that most building and civil engineering contractors desire to carry out the works to the complete satisfaction of the employer. However, their main reason for being in business is to make a financial profit from the project.

The client's advisors are very much in control of the project and can approve or disapprove of the contractor's methods of working. They can issue instructions to the contractor under the terms of the contract, order additional works, approve or nominate subcontractors, etc. They will also have had some input into appointing the contractor, before the contract was awarded. A contractor may have to request information from the architect or engineer. This may be a positive step on the part of the contractor in alleviating a claim at some later stage. The architect or engineer must respond to such requests within a reasonable time.

After receiving a contractual claim from the contractor the following should be considered:

- Is the contractor's claim reasonable?
- What are the costs involved?
- What clauses in the conditions of contract are relevant?
- What basis is the contractor using to justify a claim?

It is easy to attempt to dismiss a contractor's claim out-of-hand. It is well recognised that claims generally, and contractors' are no exception, are often inflated on the assumption that it will be contested and a reduced amount negotiated. Contractors are also unlikely to be entirely faultless in the matter, and some of the losses are likely to be of their own making. The agreed amount of the claim is therefore always likely to be lower than that originally requested or calculated by the contractor.

The instinct at first may be to reject the claim, since it might appear to reflect badly on those appointed by the client or promoter. It may imply that they have not been carrying out their duties under the contract correctly. Where this is the case, the employer might have some redress against the architect or engineer for professional negligence. Where the matter cannot be resolved, by the parties involved, then other ways of dealing with the problem, as described above, may need to be adopted.

Bibliography

Appleby G. *Contract Law*. Sweet & Maxwell. 2001.
Barrett F.R. *Cost Value Reconciliation*. Chartered Institute of Building. 1992.
Bartlett A. *Emden's Construction Law*. Butterworth. (Annual.)
Brown H. and Marriott A. *ADR Principles and Practice*. Sweet & Maxwell. 1999.
Chappell D. *Powell-Smith & Sims' Building Contract Claims*. Blackwell Science. 1997.
Chappell D. *Parris's Standard Form of Building Contract: JCT 98*. Blackwell Science. 2001.

Chappell D., Marshall D., Powell-Smith V. and Cavender S. *Building Contract Dictionary*. Blackwell Science. 2001.

Darbyshire P. *Eddey and Darbyshire on the English Legal System*. Sweet and Maxwell. 2001.

Elliot R.F. *Building Contract Disputes: Practice and Precedents*. Sweet and Maxwell. (Annual.)

Furmston M.P. *Powell-Smith and Furmston's Building Contract Casebook*. Blackwell Science. 1999.

Furmston M.P. *Cheshire, Fifoot and Furmston's Law of Contract*. Butterworth. 2001.

Harris B., Planterose R. and Tecks J. *The Arbitration Act 1996*. Blackwell Science. 2000.

Hibberd P. and Newman P. *ADR and Adjudication in Construction Contracts*. Blackwell Science. 1999.

Holtham D. and Taylor P. *Berryman's Building Claims Cases*. Butterworths. 1994.

Lewis S. *et al. Tolley's Guide to Construction Contracts*. Tolley. (Annual updates.)

Ndekurgri I. and O'Gorman C. *Construction Law and Contractual Procedures*. Butterworths. 2001.

Povey P.J., Wakefield R. and Danaher K.F. *Walker-Smith on the Standard Form of Building Contract*. Tolley. (Annual.)

Ramsey V. and Furst S. *Keating on Building Contracts*. Sweet and Maxwell. 2000.

Reynolds M.P. *The Expert Witness in Construction Disputes*. Blackwell Science. 2001.

Rutherford L. *Oxborn's Concise Law Dictionary*. Sweet and Maxwell. 2001.

Scriven J., Pritchard N. and Delmon J. *A Contractual Guide to Major Construction Projects*. Sweet and Maxwell. 1999.

Sheridan P. *Construction and Engineering Arbitration*. Sweet and Maxwell. 1999.

Sykes J. *Construction Claims*. Sweet and Maxwell. 1999.

Uff J. *Construction Law*. Sweet and Maxwell. 1999.

Wallace I.D. *Hudson's Building and Engineering Contracts*. Sweet & Maxwell. 1994.

17 Project Management

Introduction

Increasingly, clients are adopting a project culture in all aspects of their business. Project management is not new or specific to construction contracts.

The organisation and management of construction projects has existed in practice since buildings were first constructed. The process long ago was much simpler but, as knowledge increased and societies became more complex, so the principles and procedures in management evolved. In some countries, notably in the USA, the management of construction works began to emerge as a separate and identifiable professional discipline some years ago alongside architecture and engineering. Because of the differences in the way the construction industry is structured in the UK, the professions have not developed in the same way, or to the same extent. It is now, however, being accepted by more and more clients that, to succeed in construction, someone needs to take the responsibility for the overall management of the construction project. Project management is a very different function from either design or construction management and requires other, different qualities which are not necessarily inherent in the more traditional disciplines.

There has in recent years been a considerable interest amongst quantity surveyors in project management of one sort or another. This has been evidenced by the increased number of postgraduate courses, textbooks and other publications on the subject, and of practitioners seeking to specialise in this type of work. Some quantity surveyors anticipating the possible threat to their traditional role have seen project management as a source of work for the future. Others suggest that the financial expertise of quantity surveyors makes them ideally suited to such a role.

To many quantity surveyors, much of the project management service has been provided in the past as part of their extended traditional role, usually without acknowledgement or recognition. The degree to which this occurred was largely dependent on the relative level of skills and experience of the project surveyor, architects and engineers. However, it is important to distinguish between this extended quantity surveying involvement and formal project management. The quantity surveyor must take a substantial step in order to provide the comprehensive project management service required by clients.

As part of their agenda for change initiative, the Royal Institution of Chartered Surveyors has recognised the specialist activity of project management and its importance to the surveying professions by the establishment of a separate Project Management Faculty. In addition to the RICS, professional recognition of the project management function can be obtained via the Association of Project Managers, an organisation which, with regard to qualification, is more interested in professional competence than academic achievement and to which many quantity surveyors belong.

Justifying project management by adding value

The success of the design team in achieving the client's objectives is greatly influenced by their ability to recognise each other's activities and to integrate them to the full. However, it is the nature of most professionals to see the project objectives in terms of their own discipline and to operate, to a large extent, from within their specialist perspective. Project management provides the important management function of bringing the project team together and has been described as:

'The planning, control and coordination of a project from conception to completion (including commissioning) on behalf of a client. It is concerned with the identification of the client's objectives in terms of utility, function, quality, time and cost, and the establishment of relationships between resources. The integration, monitoring and control of the contributors to the project and their output, and the evaluation and selection of alternatives in pursuit of the client's satisfaction with the project outcome, are the fundamental aspects of construction project management.' (Walker 1989)

This definition reveals the essence of project management as that of managing and leading the project team toward the successful completion of the client's project objectives. In execution, the role demands an array of management and technical skills with particular emphasis on the important aspect of human resource management.

Within most projects, there are several key aspects that are of importance to the client, and each will fall within the remit of the project management function. These include the fundamental considerations of time, cost and quality and their interrelationship, and within this framework, the management of procurement, risk and value, each of which is considered in detail elsewhere in this book. To justify the appointment of a project manager, it is important to be able to demonstrate the added value that the function brings to clients in respect to these key considerations.

There is some disagreement within the industry about the value of the service provided by dedicated project management, particularly from those that have previously performed this role, for example:

'It will be seen that in the orthodox process of managing building there is a tendency for middlemen of various sorts to come between the exponents.

They emerge in the first place because they can offer some rationalisation of the cost or of the organisation, but in the end there is a tendency for them merely to take a percentage without particular benefit and sometimes they even obfuscate straightforward solutions.' (Moxley 1993)

This illustrates the potential existence of resistance to the project manager, if project management were seen to fall into this middleman category, being paid without adding benefit, or worse, for making the construction process more difficult.

The traditional method used in the management of construction projects has usually involved the architect, or on occasion an engineer, being both principal designer and manager of the process. This role included coordinating and programming the work of co-consultants such as services engineers, structural engineers and quantity surveyors. Whichever discipline led the team, and normally it was the architect, there was a need to perform both a management role and design role simultaneously. Unfortunately, in practice, it is difficult to achieve this and generally the design aspect was given preeminence. That this situation existed is perhaps no surprise given the apparent lack of attention to management subjects in UK Schools of Architecture.

The traditional relationships that have existed between the client, consultants and contractors have increasingly become strained over the years. This has frequently resulted in the dissatisfaction of the client, a central concern highlighted in both the Latham and Egan reports. The problems are largely due to the increasing complexity of design and construction, the importance of completion on time or early completion if desirable, the need for acceptable levels of building performance, and the increasing concern for financial control in its entirety. It is apparent from these demands that there is an urgent need for a much greater understanding and interpretation of the client's requirements. In addition, there has been a necessity for improved communications, together with a closer coordination of the work of all those involved in the design and construction processes. This is in part due to the changed nature of the construction industry and the different procurement routes adopted. Project management adds value by fulfilling the management role within the context of a modern and increasingly complex construction industry and in recognition of client demand.

Terminology

Whatever name is given to the role of the project manager, and alternatives may include project controller, project administrator, or project coordinator, the general intent is usually the same. The idea is that one person or organisation should take overall control and responsibility for coordinating the activities of the various consultants, contractors, subcontractors, processes and procedures for the full duration of the project. The project duration in this context starts at inception and ends on the completion of the defects liability period. The management process may also extend into the time when the building is in use and thus link with the facilities management role. This whole-life view will be beneficial in bringing the design and development function more closely together with that of occupation and use.

Whilst the general intent of the project management role is understood, irrespective of designation, the title given to this function may denote differing levels of service. For example, the term 'project co-ordinator' is likely to indicate the exclusion of the responsibility for the appointment of the other consultants. In any event, the terminology used will always require precise definition in terms of the service to be provided that is stated in the terms of engagement. Clarification is certainly required to ensure that there is no misunderstanding as to the level of professional indemnity cover required. Figure 17.1 indicates a comprehensive list of project management duties differentiating between the project co-ordinator and project manager designations in regard to both external and in-house situations (CIOB 1996).

When acting in the dedicated role of project manager, there should be no attempt to perform any of the functions normally undertaken by the design team, including the traditional duties of the quantity surveyor. These should always be separate to avoid having to make any compromised decisions that might otherwise occur.

The term project manager may be seen within several contexts and is commonly used throughout industry. Within construction, it is important to distinguish between a contractor's project manager, who will primarily manage the construction process, and the client's project manager to whom this chapter is dedicated.

A further development of the management function may be seen in management-based contracts, for instance, construction management. Such a procurement route necessitates the appointment of a construction manager whose role involves the management of the design, procurement and construction. No main contractor exists; instead, the construction manager manages the trade contractors, and, as reimbursement is by way of a fee, this role can be carried out in a more objective manner with due recognition of the client's and project's interests. Although the duties of the construction manager differ from those of the project manager, with the former having a detailed responsibility for the management of the construction process, there is some commonality in the roles.

Attributes of the project manager

It is difficult to be dogmatic about the attributes of the project manager because there are no real rules. However, there are certain qualities that are both desirable and helpful in staff who have to fulfil the particular processes of management. There is a need, for example, for integrity, and for clarity of

Duties*	Client's requirements			
	In-house project management		Independent project management	
	Project management	Project co-ordination	Project management	Project co-ordination
Be party to the contract	●		○	
Assist in preparing the project brief	●		●	
Develop project manager's brief	●		●	
Advise on budget/funding arrangements	●		○	
Advise on site acquisition, grants and planning	●		○	
Arrange feasibility study and report	●	○	●	○
Develop project strategy	●	○	●	○
Prepare project handbook	●	○	●	○
Develop consultant's briefs	●	○	●	○
Devise project programme	●	○	●	○
Select project team members	●	○	○	○
Establish management structure	●	○	●	○
Co-ordinate design processes	●	○	●	○
Appoint consultants	●	●	●	○
Arrange insurance and warranties	●	●	●	○
Select procurement system	●	●	●	○
Arrange tender documentation	●	●	●	○
Organise contractor pre-qualification	●	●	●	○
Evaluate tenders	●	●	●	○
Participate in contractor selection	●	●	●	○
Participate in contractor appointment	●	●	●	○
Organise control systems	●	●	●	●
Monitor progress	●	●	●	●

(Contd)

Duties*	Client's requirements			
	In-house project management		Independent project management	
	Project management	Project co-ordination	Project management	Project co-ordination
Arrange meetings	●	●	●	●
Authorise payments	●	●	●	○
Organise communication/ reporting systems	●	●	●	○
Provide total coordination	●	●	●	○
Issue safety/health procedures	●	●	●	○
Address environmental aspects	●	●	●	○
Coordinate statutory authorities	●	●	●	○
Monitor budget and variation orders	●	●	●	●
Develop final account	●	●	●	●
Arrange pre- commissioning/ commissioning	●	●	●	●
Organise handover/ occupation	●	●	●	●
Advise on marketing/ disposal	●	○	●	○
Organise maintenance manuals	●	●	●	○
Plan for maintenance period	●	●	●	○
Develop maintenance programme/staff training	●	●	●	○
Plan facilities management	●	●	●	○
Arrange for feedback monitoring	●	●	●	○

*Duties vary by project and relevant responsibility and authority
Symbols ● = suggested duties; ○ = possible additional duties

Fig. 17.1 A comprehensive list of project management duties (*Source:* CIOB 1996).

expression when speaking or writing. Loyalty, fairness and resourcefulness are also necessary. The following are some of the more important attributes that a good project manager should possess.

Personal traits

There are those who will attempt to argue that good managers are born and not made and that particular inherent qualities must already be present in an individual. They will equally argue that no amount of education and training or even experience can produce good managers. However, improvement in performance can always be achieved by encouragement in the right direction, and hence further study.

Self-motivation and the ability to motivate others are very important, as is the relationship with those with whom the manager has to work. Own personal goals and moral values, coupled with own attitude to work and that of others, also need to be considered. The response to the various aspects of the project will vary depending on the project manager's own professional allegiance.

Appropriate knowledge and skills

The project manager is required to have a good balance of technical and managerial skills. Figure 17.2 indicates some of the key areas of knowledge and their interrelationships that contribute to the project management function. Whilst it is not a realistic expectation that the project manager is proficient in each aspect of the construction process, a working knowledge through indirect experience should be requisite.

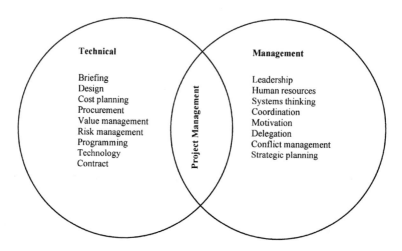

Fig. 17.2   Balance of knowledge and skills.

Technical knowledge

Technical knowledge is an important element of project management. There is something unique about the construction industry, and project management within it is a rather specialised form of management. The techniques derived from manufacturing industry, for instance, often do not work on a construction site, as construction is concerned with one-off projects undertaken on the client's premises. Ideally therefore, the project manager will already be a member of one of the construction professions. An understanding of the process and the product of construction, and a working knowledge of the structure of the industry, will clearly be advantageous if not essential. The importation of managers with no knowledge of the industry or its workings has drawbacks, and their appointment should be approached with caution. Quantity surveyors have a thorough overview of the design and construction process and are technically well positioned for the role of project manager.

Management skills

Management is essentially a human matter, and this fact overshadows all other considerations. No one professional group therefore has a monopoly of the skills required, although the quantity surveyor is well suited to this role and perhaps better suited than many others. Various individuals have, however, chosen to specialise in management, having emerged from backgrounds in architecture, engineering, building and surveying.

In considering the performance of the function of project management, it is important to stress the importance of management skills. This is in the realisation that management is a job in its own right and is not something that other professions are able to do without certain qualities and additional skills. The manner in which managers are selected should also be borne in mind. Business organisations, including those within the construction sector, will generally appoint management personnel on the basis of the achievements of staff performing at a more operational level. Unfortunately, the range of skills and personal qualities necessary for such achievement often differ from those required in a management position. A successful project architect, quantity surveyor or engineer may be less successful in a management role. As previously emphasised, good management skills are an essential attribute of a good project manager.

Leadership qualities

Whenever a group of people work together in a team, the situation demands that one of the members becomes the leader. In many situations, leadership is an outcome of the inherent qualities of each member of the group; however, with the appointment of a project manager, the choice of leader is made. The project manager is the designated leader of the project team, whose duty it is to ensure that the whole work is carried out as efficiently as possible. The responsibility of combining the various human resources and obtaining the best from them is the project manager's, who must seek to complement the attributes of the various members of the team and keep conflict to a minimum.

It is important to recognise the difference between project administration and project management, which includes this essential function of leadership. The ability to lead and motivate others while commanding their respect is an essential characteristic, not required in administration but essential to effective management. Project management incorporates leadership and recognises the need to deal with people; project administration is a bureaucratic function, considerably less complex and often confused with true management.

In aspiring to project management, the responsibility for leadership should be accepted. However, conformity to a particular leadership style is not desired since there is no one perfect approach and various project situations may demand some flexibility. In the extreme, leaders may be autocratic or manage by some means of consensus. Clearly there are advantages and disadvantages to each. This is not to suggest that managers in practice execute a choice between these extremes since they will be governed by their natural tendencies. They should however recognise their own strengths and weaknesses and adjust their approach to meet the circumstances. Figure 17.3, which relates to the project management for a large commercial development, illustrates this need for flexibility.

With regard to construction project management, it should be accepted that the other team members will be experienced and competent, otherwise their appointment should not have occurred. It is therefore probable that in most situations a good project manager will tend toward the consensus approach, relying on the contribution of other team members and recognising their independence.

A good leader rarely needs to act ruthlessly, as this creates conditions of stress, strain and insecurity. The project manager's character and ability will set the tone from the beginning, and from this the loyalty of the other members of the team will be gained. The project manager must of course know when to praise and when to reprove, and must also have the courage to admit a mistake, to make changes or to proceed against opposition.

Clarity of thought

The ability to think clearly is also an important aspect of management. A confused mind creates confusion around it and may result in confused instructions to other members of the project team, which signifies that the manager is not in full control of the project situation. The inability in the first place to think clearly originates from an inadequate understanding of the objectives and priorities associated with the problem.

Effective delegation

The total amount of knowledge required in the management of a project is beyond the scope of a single individual. The manager must therefore be able

Example: A project manager's need for flexibility in management style
Scenario: Development of an inner city commercial residential scheme, part new build, part refurbishment. An in-house project manager was involved from the outset to manage the project.

Objective A
The project team needed to resolve a range of issues at sketch design stage, including design issues, budget, procurement, etc. The management style used by the project manager was very consensus focused and successful in bonding the group. In addition, solutions were found to all of the key problems, including those relating to design, budget and procurement approach. There were positive contributions from all members of the team.

Objective B
During the course of design development, several problems were encountered with the project, largely due to the constraints imposed by the refurbishment element of the scheme. At this stage, programme difficulties were encountered and confrontation had arisen between key members of the design team. Several design team meetings were held in an attempt to resolve key issues and monitor/encourage progress. As with objective A, a consensus approach was adopted; however, this failed to achieve clear direction. The end result was a significant and costly extension to the design period and a less than perfect working atmosphere, which continued throughout the project.

A key reason for this situation was the management style of the project manager at this crucial stage in the project. His democratic approach, successful in earlier stages of the scheme, was inappropriate in the latter phase when a more autocratic and authoritarian approach is likely to have mitigated many of the difficulties.

The management approach should be a function of the situation, not the opposite. Flexibility in approach is preferred to dogmatism.

Fig. 17.3   Example of need for flexibility.

to delegate certain tasks and duties to others involved in the project, and be able to rely on and receive advice from them. The inability to delegate is likely to result in overwork for the project manager, frustration on the part of others and a generally badly run project. Everyone must feel that they are able to make a valid contribution to the overall success of the project.

Decision-making

Decisions need to be made at all levels in the organisation of a construction project. Those made at the top will be concerned more with policy, client objectives and the framework for the project as a whole. At lower levels, they tend to relate more to the solving of particular problems. The aptitude for making decisions is an important quality that distinguishes the manager from the technician. The general level of complexity of construction projects and the number of consultants involved make the decision-making process for the project manager particularly difficult. Making a rapid decision requires a certain amount of courage. Sticking to a decision in the face of criticism, opposition or apparent failure requires a large amount of conviction. It is, of course, vitally important for the project manager to make the right decision, and this can only consistently occur through experience. The ability to sense a situation and exercise correct judgement will always improve with practice.

There has been much behavioural related research carried out over many years incorporating various aspects affecting the decision-making process. Whilst practitioners are unlikely to afford the time to participate in such activities themselves, they should be aware of the complexities surrounding the decision-making process and should understand the significance of this research in the context of their work.

Duties and responsibilities of the project manager

The project manager's terms of engagement, extent of authority and basis of fee reimbursement must be established prior to appointment. The experienced project manager will realise the importance of unambiguous conditions of appointment. Notwithstanding the cautionary comments outlined further below regarding the single system approach, the Project Management Agreement and Conditions of Engagement 1992 and associated guidance note, both issued by the RICS, will be beneficial in this regard.

The duties of a project manager in the construction industry will vary from project to project. Different countries around the world will also expect a different response to the situation, depending on the contractual systems that are in operation. The mistake, and perhaps the reason for the failure, of the traditional system in certain instances is that an attempt is made to use a single system to suit all circumstances. Any contractual arrangement, however good, must be adapted to suit the needs of the client and the project, and not vice versa. The project manager will need to employ a wide variety of skills and options for a whole range of different solutions. The key duties of the project manager identified in the RICS Project Management Agreement and Conditions of Engagement 1992 are to:

- Communicate to the consultants the requirements of the client's brief
- Monitor the progress of design work, and the achievement of function by reference to the client's brief
- Monitor and regulate programme and progress
- Monitor and use reasonable endeavours to coordinate the efforts of all consultants, advisors, contractors and suppliers directly connected with the project
- Monitor the cost and financial rewards of the project by reference to the client's brief.

Although not stated in the above outline of duties, it is implicit that the project manager will also lead the project, and therefore other expectations of the project manager, previously considered, should not be forgotten. The list above is relevant but is a bureaucratic response to the need to formalise the service provided.

The following sections provide more detailed consideration of some, but not necessarily all, of the duties of the project manager. In considering these duties, please note the significance of other sections of this book that are of major importance in project management, for instance, procurement, value management and risk management.

Client's objectives

The starting point of the project manager's commission is to establish the client's objectives in detail. The success of any construction project can be measured by the degree to which it achieves these objectives. The client's need for a building or engineering structure may have arisen for several reasons: to meet the needs of a manufacturing industry, as part of an investment function, or for social or political demands. In an attempt to provide satisfaction for the client, three major areas of concern will need to be considered. The weighting given to these factors will vary depending on the perception of the client's objectives:

- *Performance*
  The performance of the building or structure in use will be of paramount importance to the client. This priority covers the use of space, the correct choice of materials, adequate design and detailing, and the aesthetics of the structure. Attention will also need to be paid to future maintenance requirements once the building is in use. Clients are more likely to be concerned with the functional standards of the project, and to a lesser extent, the aesthetics.
- *Cost*
  All clients will have to consider the cost implications of the desired building's performance. The price that they are prepared to pay will temper, to some extent, the differences between their needs and wants. Clients today are also more likely to evaluate costs not solely in terms of initial capital expenditure, but rather on a basis of life cycle cost management. This is increasingly the case with central government and local government construction activity, as well as projects that are procured via an arrangement within the structure of the Private Finance Initiative.
- *Time*
  Once clients decide to build, they are generally in a hurry for their completed building. Although they may spend a great deal of time deliberating over a scheme, once a decision to build has been reached they often require the project to be completed as quickly as possible. In any event, in order to achieve some measure of satisfaction, and to prevent escalating costs, commissioning must be achieved by the due date.

The project manager's strategy for balancing the above three factors will depend on an interpretation of the client's objectives. It would appear, however, that there is some room for improvement in all three areas. The improvement of the design's completeness, particularly, should reduce the contract time and hence the constructor's costs. The correct application of project management should be able to realise benefits in these areas.

The client's objectives should be used as a goal for the broader issues involved in the design and construction of the project. The discernment of these objectives will assist the project manager to decide which alternative construction strategies to adopt. It is very important that an adequate amount of time is allowed for a proper evaluation of the client's needs and desires. Failure to identify these properly at the outset will make it difficult for the project to reach a successful conclusion upon completion.

Client's brief

This involves the evaluation of the user requirements in terms of space, design, function, performance, time and cost. The whole scheme is likely to be limited one way or another by cost, and this in turn will be affected by the availability of finance or the profits achieved upon some form of sale at completion. It is necessary therefore for the project manager to be able to offer sound professional advice on a large range of questions, or to be able to secure such information from one of the professional consultants who are likely to be involved with the scheme. This will include the coordination of all necessary legal advice required by the client. It is most important that the client's objectives are properly interpreted, as at this stage ideas, however vague, will begin to emerge, and these will often then determine the course of the project in terms of both design and cost. It is the project manager's responsibility to ensure that the client's brief is clearly transmitted to the various members of the design team, and also that they properly understand the client's aims and aspirations.

An increasingly used technique at this stage of a project is value management (see Chapter 8). This will assist in establishing clearly what the client's objectives are and is an excellent approach to the achievement of a consensus view of the brief, incorporating an evaluation of the needs and desires of all key stakeholders. Similarly risk management (see Chapter 9) is also an important consideration at this stage of the project.

Contractor involvement

The client will probably require some initial advice on the methods available for involving the contractor in the project. The necessity for such advice will depend on the familiarity of the client with capital works projects, although the growth and complexity of procurement options is such that some advice will almost certainly be of benefit. The correct evaluation of the client's objectives will enable the project manager to recommend a particular method of contractor selection. It may be desirable, for example, to have the contractor involved at the outset or to use some hybrid system of contractor involvement (see Chapter 10). The project manager will be able to exercise expert judgement in this respect by analysing the potential benefits and disadvantages of the project concerned. This decision will need to be made reasonably quickly, as it can influence the entire design process and the necessity of appointing the various consultants.

Design team selection

The project manager may be responsible for the selection of the design team. If this is the case, the task should be carried out in a professional manner, with the same amount of care as in the selection of the contractor. Although some situations will demand prompt negotiation with a proven team, if circumstances allow, proposals should be sought from three to six consultants. Ideally, the information submitted by the consultants should include matters relating to design and supervision methodology, and, possibly as a separate submission, a fee proposal. It will assist the decision-making process if matters relating to method and level of service provision are considered before and apart from the fee submission. The fee element should only be considered if these key aspects are acceptable or preferred.

If the client has been involved in capital works projects previously, they may already have designated consultants with whom the project manager will need to work. If this is the case, the project manager should make clear, at the outset, relevant concerns relating to any of the client appointed consultants, including past performance, location and resources. Where the consultants are appointed on a regular basis by the client, the project manager may experience problems due to existing relationships and lines of authority. This will be particularly difficult in situations where the client is using project management for the first time.

The project manager is likely to be responsible for agreeing fees and terms of appointment of all consultants on behalf of the client. In certain instances, the project manager may appoint the consultants direct as subconsultants. Under such circumstances, the only contractual link is between the client and the project manager. Where the contractor is to be appointed during the design stage, then the project manager will need to consider the means of selection. Whatever the circumstances, the project manager must control rather than be controlled by either the contractor or any of the consultants. The relationships between the contributions from each consultant must be clear at the outset to avoid any misunderstandings that may occur later.

Feasibility and viability reports

During the early stages of the design process, it will be necessary for the project manager to examine both the feasibility and the viability of the project. Sound professional advice is very important at this stage, as it will determine whether or not the project should proceed. A feasible solution is one that is capable of technical execution and may only be found after some site investigation and discussion with the designers. A feasible solution may, however, prove not to be viable in terms of cost or other financial consideration. Unless the project is viable in every respect, it will probably not proceed. The investigation work should be sufficiently thorough while taking note of the fees involved, particularly if the project should later be abandoned.

At this stage of the project it will be beneficial to carry out a detailed risk analysis of the proposed scheme or various options that are under consideration. Risk is an inherent part of every project and whilst a development may be determined as feasible, such a decision is reliant on assumptions and predictions relating to uncertainties that exist. Project management should incorporate a professional approach to the identification, assessment and management of risk. It should not rely solely on instinct, which may be subject to optimism, pessimism or other elements of bias (see Chapter 9). Opportunity for value management at feasibility stage also exists.

Planning and programming

Once the project has been given the go-ahead it will then become necessary to prepare a programme for the overall project, incorporating both design and construction. The programme should represent a realistic coordinated plan up to the commissioning of the scheme. The project manager must carefully monitor, control and revise where necessary. Several useful techniques exist for programming purposes, and since these can be computer-assisted, rapid updating can easily be achieved. The selection of the appropriate technique will allow the project to be properly controlled in terms of time.

The construction industry has a poor reputation with regard to achieving project completion dates. It is a difficult task to predict the completion date of a proposed development at inception. There are likely to be many unknown factors, not least those relating to site conditions, design solution and construction method. Notwithstanding the difficulties, project management will only be considered a success if project deadlines are met.

With regard to the programming of the construction phase, subject to the method of procurement, additional difficulties exist throughout the project's duration. This is due to the method of construction being largely unknown until tenders are received and, in any event, forecasts are reliant on the contractor's expertise and cooperation.

Design process management

Project information is often uncoordinated, and this leads to inefficiency, a breakdown in communications between the design team, frequent misunderstandings and an unhappy client. For example, the delayed involvement of service engineers often results in changes to the design of the structure both to accommodate the engineering work and also incorporate good engineering ideas. An important task therefore for the project manager is to ensure that the various consultants are appointed at appropriate times and that they easily and frequently liaise with each other while maintaining their own individual goals. There is not much room in the design team for those who wish to go it alone; teamwork is very much underrated, but it is vital for the success of the project. The project manager will therefore need to exercise both tact and firmness in ensuring that the client's objectives remain paramount.

The project manager, although not directly involved in the process of designing in its widest sense, must nevertheless have some understanding of design in order to appreciate the problems and complexities of the procedures involved. Responsibility for the integration and control of the work from various consultants rests with the project manager who, in the first instance, will be directly answerable to the client for all facets of the project. This will include ensuring quality control of all aspects of the design (and construction) process and carrying out regular technical audits on the developed design solutions.

Problems with the design process are more likely to occur when construction market conditions are very active. Although the project manager will endeavour to establish, prior to appointment, that each of the appointed consultants has the resources available to complete the commissioned work, circumstances may quickly change. This may be due to the acceptance by one of the consultants of additional work, perhaps for a larger client with the promise of additional work in the future. The cyclical nature of the construction industry and human nature may make it very difficult for some consultants to decline the opportunity of such commissions, despite concerns they may have about available resources. Although the terms of engagement should clarify time-scales, there may be problems with their enforcement, and delays in the design process can result when consultants become over committed. Project managers are likely to be in a better position to deal with this situation than a client, particularly those clients that are only involved in construction work occasionally. In this respect, it is important for the project manager to properly inform the client about the work of the consultants, something clients often feel is lacking.

The project manager must also be kept informed of the cost implications as the design develops, usually the function of an independent quantity surveyor. The design team must be informed of what can or cannot be spent and promptly advised when problems are envisaged. In this respect the control of the costs should be more effective than when relying on the efforts of the architect alone. The project manager must, of course, have a very clear understanding of the client's intentions and will also need to advise the client in those circumstances where the original requirements cannot be met in terms of design, cost or time. The project manager will always have an eye on the future state of the project and must keep at least one step ahead of the design team.

During this stage, unless the contractor has been appointed earlier, the project manager will need to consider a possible list of firms who are capable of carrying out the work, and to ensure that the proper timely action is taken to obtain all statutory approvals.

Supervision and control during construction

Subject to the selected method of procurement, the project manager should try to make sure that the design of the works is as near complete as possible prior to tendering. This is likely to result in fewer problems on site, a shorter contract period with a consequent reduction in costs, and commissioning at the earliest possible date. During the contract period the project manager will need to have regular meetings with the consultants and contractor and his subcontractors. Progress of the works must be monitored and controlled and any potential delays identified. The effect on the programme and the budget of any variations will also need to be monitored. The project manager must be satisfied that the project is finished to the client's original requirements; although one of the consultants may be responsible for the quality control, the project manager will need to be careful about accepting substandard or unfinished work. Some problems may need to be discussed with the client, but early decisions should be sought to bring the project to a successful conclusion. The project manager might have an ongoing role after the main construction contract to administer fitting-out work for occupiers and tenants.

Evaluation and feedback

This represents the final stage of the project manager's duties. It should be ascertained that all commissioning checks have been carried out satisfactorily, that the accounts have been properly agreed and that the necessary drawings and manuals have been supplied to the client. The project manager will need to advise on the current legislation affecting the running of the project, on grants, taxation changes and allowances. It may also be necessary to 'arbitrate' between consultants and contractors in order to safeguard the client's interests. The client should be issued with a 'close-out' report to identify that responsibilities of all parties have been satisfactorily discharged, and this will also assist in any future capital works that the client might undertake.

Quantity surveying skills and expertise

The skills of the quantity surveyor traditionally included measurement and valuation and to these were later added accounting and negotiation. As the profession evolved, these skills were extended to include forecasting, analysing, planning, controlling and evaluating, budgeting, problem solving and modelling. Knowledge has also been considerably developed both by a better understanding of the design and construction process and by having a broader base. The quantity surveyor of the new millennium continues to increase the expertise base further and a survey of the contents of this book will reveal the extent to which the profession is growing, with the development of a wide range of skills and techniques to meet the varying demands of clients.

This provides the quantity surveyor with an excellent background, which is appropriate for project management. Indeed, a significant number of those already engaged in this work are members of the quantity surveying profession. The traditional role of the quantity surveyor, including that within the contracting organisation, is usually seen as advisory and reactive rather than managerial and proactive. In essence, the difference between the traditional role of the quantity surveyor, one that is diminishing, and that of the project manager, is one of attitude and method of approach. Consideration of the detailed list of duties of the project manager shown in Fig. 17.1 will serve to demonstrate the relative proximity of the two disciplines of quantity surveying and project management. This is certainly true from the perspective of larger firms of consultants that are able to provide a wide spectrum of specialist services.

Fees

In most countries, including the UK, the fees charged for professional services include the management of projects for clients. If the service being offered is enhanced by project management, then some extra charge will be deemed equitable. As the existing poor management organisation in construction is to some extent responsible for the poor quality, time delays and extra costs, then a process that attempts to rectify these problems should be worth paying for. The professional fee involved may in any case show a saving to the client overall. This, to a certain extent, will depend on the 'discount' given by other consultants for the omission of the management element from their service. However, it is clear that the type of management envisaged was never deemed to be included in the existing traditional fee structures.

The project manager will in the first instance need to negotiate a fee with the client. This fee will need to take into account the type of service being offered, the complexity of the project, its volume and its duration. In periods of heavy competition, clients tend to require lump sum fees to be agreed for project management services. It is essential therefore that the basis of the fee in terms of scope and time-scale is clearly stated in the terms of appointment.

Education and training for the project manager

Quantity surveying education is constantly changing to meet the needs of the profession and industry of the future. Subjects that were once seen as being of paramount importance have been demoted as new subjects vie for space in the curriculum. This process is rarely without controversy and debate, partially due to the widening remit of the quantity surveying discipline.

A significant element of this change may be attributed to the development of project management skills within the profession. Quantity surveying undergraduate courses now include a range of subject matter that may once have been considered beyond the traditional role. This material, including topic areas such as risk management, human resource management, procurement management and value management, is provided with the view that many graduates may be practising in these areas in their early careers. This may be either in a project management role or in other management related areas of the construction industry.

Despite the acknowledgement given to the development of project management within undergraduate programmes, as with facilities management, there are many who regard the training and education as a postgraduate issue, supplementing a suitable first degree. There are several of these available, including master's courses, and in addition, for those surveyors who have not had any formal education in management, opportunity exists for attendance at short training courses and seminars.

The Association of Project Management (APM), which was established in 1972, is dedicated to the development of the discipline and provides control of the standards that must be attained to gain certification. The qualification gained from the APM is awarded on the basis of proven competence rather than academic achievement, and is therefore dependent on actual project management experience. The process for application involves submission of a report on a project for which the applicant had 'carried appropriate executive authority' and attendance at an interview. The association is broad in terms of subject matter; however, it has catered for particular specialisms by the establishment of special interest groups. Membership of the association is intended to bring with it advantages similar to those provided by other institutions, including the recognition of competence, opportunity for professional development, the marketing of services, a benchmark to employers and the control of standards of entry.

The RICS have also recognised the significance of project management by the establishment of a separate project management faculty in 2000. This is a significant development in that the discipline may now be developed within a major international organisation and well directed resources and significant membership should enhance the abilities and status of all project managers within the institution.

Bibliography

Bennett J. *International Construction Management*. Butterworth-Heinemann. 1991.
Centre for Strategic Studies in Construction. *Trusting the Team*. University of Reading. 1995.
CIC. *Project Management Skills in the Construction Industry*. Construction Industry Council. 1996.

CIOB. *Code of Practice for Project Management for Construction and Development*. Longman/Chartered Institute of Building. 1996.

Fryer B. *Construction Management: Principles and Practice*. Blackwell Science. 1997.

Langford D., Hancock M.R., Fellows R. and Gale A.W. *Human Resources Management in Construction*. Longman. 1995.

Lavender S. *Management for Building*. Longmans. 1996.

Moxley R. *Building Management by Professionals*. Butterworth-Heinemann. 1993.

RICS. *Conditions of Engagement*. RICS Books. 1992.

RICS. *Project Management Agreement and Conditions of Engagement: Guidance Note*. RICS Books. 1992.

Walker A. *Project Management in Construction*. Blackwell Science. 1989.

Woodward J.F. *Construction Project Management: getting it right first time*. Thomas Telford. 1997.

Website

The Association of Project Management. Certification available on line at http://www.apm.org.uk/ac/cert.htm.

18 Facilities Management

Introduction

The emergence of facilities management is in response to the growing realisation that a company's property assets are of vital importance to business success. This may be considered in two ways:

- In most companies, the costs associated with real estate are a major overhead, often representing the largest cost after wages and salaries. The control of this overhead, via cost management and use optimisation, is therefore likely to make a significant contribution to profitability.
- In addition, the impact that real estate may have upon income generation may be significant, indeed, more significant than the direct costs of provision. For instance, a car factory with an ageing and inefficient layout may be unable to compete with a modern facility that is able to accommodate new techniques, for example, robotics.

Recognition of the importance of facilities management is a vital stage in the development of this relatively new profession. Not that the function of facilities management is new; every company has needed to manage the facilities requirements of their business in some way. For example, consider the facilities management occurring in a typical small office situation, described in Fig. 18.1.

In this situation neither the appointment of a dedicated in-house facilities manager nor the outsourcing (see later in this chapter) of the facilities management (FM) role (much though the senior partner of the practice would probably like it) is practical due to the size and resources of the firm. Nevertheless, the FM function is occurring, and the cost of this to the practice can be evaluated in terms of the time of the senior partner, which, if considered in terms of opportunity cost, may be very significant.

Until recent years, the majority of facilities management, including that relating to larger concerns, would be handled from within a company's own organisation. This continues to be a common situation; however, there is a growing realisation that the outsourcing of this management function offers several benefits to the client including:

- It allows a company to concentrate on its core business activities
- It allows expertise to be developed through specialism

A small firm of accountants operating from a leased, single office location comprising a late Victorian terraced house located on the fringe of a provincial city centre. The decisions relating to the office facility are made by the senior partner and/or the office manager and are likely to include matters relating to:
- The property lease, renewal, rent and rates
- Repairs and maintenance to the building within the terms of the lease
- General furniture and fittings
- Office equipment including IT, copiers, telephones, etc.
- Insurances
- Health and safety aspects
- Security
- Ancillary services including kitchen provision, WC provision
- Car parking arrangements for staff
- Operational expenses relating to utilities, etc.

Fig. 18.1   Facilities management in a typical small office situation.

- It allows smaller organisations, unable to justify the direct full-time employment of specialist FM staff, to access experienced FM personnel
- It may provide economies of scale.

Facilities managers have evolved from the existing professions and those practising include personnel from various surveying disciplines, other construction professionals, contractors, and professions beyond the construction domain, e.g. accountants – such is the size and attractiveness of the market opportunity. Despite the scale and variety of this competition, it is accepted that the quantity surveying profession is well placed to provide a facilities management service. This may be done by adapting and expanding the existing quantity surveying skills and knowledge base, a large part of which is central to the facilities management process.

In a book of this type it is by no means possible to adequately cover the entire subject matter that falls under the umbrella of facilities management. As shown below, the range of activities is potentially diverse and the knowledge and skills necessary for the fulfilment of each requires specialist attention. The purpose of this chapter therefore, is to introduce the reader to the world of facilities management, examine some of the general practice and procedures relating to it and highlight the opportunity it provides to the quantity surveyor.

The work of the facilities manager

There is some confusion as to exactly what facilities management is and there is an array of published definitions, the variety of which displays a range of differing interpretations. These are likely to be influenced by the particular interests of their originating body, reflecting professional strengths and institutional perspectives. One of the simplest and most direct definitions of facilities management is that given by the Royal Institution of Chartered Surveyors, which states that 'FM involves the total management of all services that support the core business of an organisation'. This emphasises the management role and indicates the sphere of activity as that relating to services 'supporting' the core business.

In practice, the scope of a facilities management service may range from the provision of a single service at operational level, for example maintenance management, to that in which a comprehensive range of services is provided including those at a strategic level. Although it is likely that quantity surveyor involvement in facilities management is at present largely restricted to operational matters, typically maintenance management, it is important to recognise the discipline as much more. Failure to do so demeans the role of facilities management and deprives both the client body and consultant of value adding opportunity. The remainder of this section therefore, considers the work of the facilities manager in the wider context and identifies the opportunity that this relatively new discipline provides to the quantity surveying profession.

Space planning

The pace of change in the business environment in recent years has been great and is generally seen to be accelerating. This places a continual demand upon the workplace to adapt. Companies must respond to change; otherwise they will deteriorate in their importance and in the worst situations disappear entirely.

In terms of property, it is essential that this changing demand be reflected in the space provided for the business to operate effectively, which in terms of survival also means competitively. Facilities managers need to research and analyse the space requirements of an organisation, which may include a complete range of working environments, for example, manufacturing, retailing, storage, administration, health and education.

Workspace is an expensive commodity and therefore its provision must be fully justified in terms of need and output. The process of space planning should incorporate the following stages.

Identifying and evaluating demand

As a company grows and develops, its demands on property will change. The nature of property is such that there is a need to plan for future needs since there is invariably a time lag between need and delivery. Unfortunately, it is a common feature within organisations that space provision becomes inadequate and inefficient before action is properly considered. In forecasting future needs, the factors to be considered are wide and include anticipated company growth, changes in working practices (e.g. hot-desking), the impact of technology, changes in function and expected duration of need. In some businesses, much of this changing need can be seen in the concept of the 'virtual office' that to many people is already becoming a reality.

Since the cost of space is a high proportion of a company's outlay, there is likely to be some emphasis on the reduction of space costs to an optimum; perhaps this may be particularly so if managed from a traditional quantity surveying perspective. Whilst this approach may lead to a reduced cost, the effect that such a policy may have on revenue should also be considered. It has already been established (Chapter 8, Value Management) that value is increased by the elimination of unnecessary costs. Therefore, within the context of space planning, it is only unnecessary space costs that should be eliminated. The elimination or downgrading of space necessary to support creative work, marketing, image, and other aspects that may affect productivity or sales, are unlikely to add value. The impact that the correct space configuration may have on efficiency may be considered by comparison of the relative attributes and constraints of cellular and open plan office layouts. For example, the level of privacy achieved in a cellular layout is likely to enhance concentration, however at the same time deprive the workforce of the benefits derived from the close proximity of colleagues, such as support, learning and team working.

In order to identify and evaluate demand, an objective research process should be carried out which will allow the determination of the optimum space allocation and layout for the various working activities within a business organisation. In assessing the needs of staff, there are many factors that will need to be taken into consideration including the need for privacy; access and use of equipment; status; communications; anticipated churn; meeting requirements; storage requirements; functional needs; staff interaction; patterns of working; power supplies; and security provision. The methods used in acquiring the required information will include staff interviews and/or questionnaires, observation of space use, e.g. to assess room or workspace vacancy, and the application of benchmarked data.

Determining supply

Once the accommodation needs of a business are established, the availability of premises may be considered via the consideration of existing properties owned or leased by the company, or by the procurement of additional space. To allow the optimum use of space, an assessment of the attributes and constraints of the available premises is necessary. The considerations will include those of efficiency, quality of environment and aspects relating to aesthetics and image. In addition, factors at a relatively micro level will also need to be considered. For example, in attempting to provide a satisfactory space solution for an office premises, the following factors may impact on the eventual layout:

- Positions of windows limiting the position of partitions in a cellular layout
- Depth of office space

- Points of access and emergency egress
- Lift provision and location
- Position of electricity mains distribution
- Existing serviced amenities
- Building structure
- Position of cables and ducts.

Frequently, the provision of new space will come from existing building stock and therefore involve the refurbishment of existing premises. The decision to refurbish rather than procure new premises is unlikely to be simply that of a straightforward choice depending on the relative merits of the space provided; existing stock must be used or disposed of and capital costs, existing lease arrangements and time factors are likely to have a significant impact. In deciding to refurbish existing premises, the conflicting aspects of continued occupation, construction speed and safety must be considered. Where a building will continue in use during refurbishment works, aspects of comfort and safety should be to the fore and the impact that such provisions will have on speed of construction understood and fully accommodated within the business programme. The problems associated with working in existing buildings are considered in more detail in the next section.

In addition to providing new accommodation, either from the refurbishment of existing stock or the procurement of new, the need to deal with excess space due to obsolescence may also occur.

Maintenance management

One area of facilities management for which the traditional quantity surveyor skills can be successfully applied is that of maintenance management. This is a very large market opportunity with a total expenditure estimated by Building Maintenance Information in 1997 to be approximately £40 bn (Building Maintenance Panel of the RICS 2000). In addition to the size of the market, the workload activity is less vulnerable to market fluctuations in that maintenance is required to existing building stock and is not reliant on investment in new buildings.

An illustration of the areas and distribution of maintenance expenditure relating to a modern air-conditioned building is shown in Fig. 18.2.

There are two broad categories of building maintenance: preventative maintenance and corrective maintenance. In terms of any piece of equipment, there are some items that will be attended to following 'failure'; however, there are distinct advantages in adhering to a policy of preventative maintenance. For example, consider the example of a service to a car. Figure 18.3 highlights typical items of work that may be carried out and shows the category of service provided with reference to preventative and corrective maintenance. The benefits of carrying out the preventative maintenance work are clear. For instance, the timing chain, which may cost say £200 to replace, could lead to a repair bill in excess of £1000 if its failure occurred during road

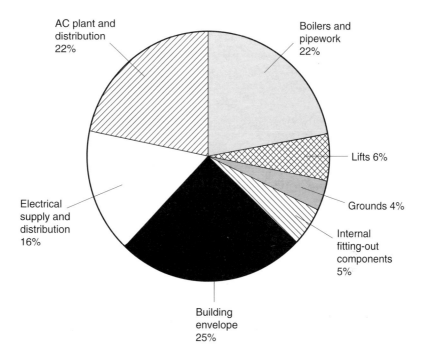

Fig. 18.2 Maintenance expenditure relating to air-conditioning (*Source:* Bernard Williams Associates, 1994).

Preventive maintenance	Corrective maintenance
Replace timing chain	Replace indicator bulb
Oil change	Renew illegal tyre
Replace air filter	Touch up paintwork
Replace oil filter	Replenish screen wash
Replace brake pads	Adjust handbrake

Fig. 18.3   80 000-mile service on a car.

use. Likewise, the oil change, air filter and oil filter are relatively cheap measures that will protect the engine and extend its life. In addition to the long-term benefits, preventative maintenance provides peace of mind and improves reliability.

This philosophy works equally well in buildings; however, the complex nature of buildings and the business organisations that use them may result in a less well-organised approach.

The maintenance of buildings is an important element of facilities management in that it is essential to the efficient use and costs of operation. The production of a maintenance policy, similar in concept to the list of checks at various service intervals during the life of a car, will provide the direction necessary to achieve good standards of maintenance. The policy should consider the various categories of maintenance work, the standards to be attained, health and safety requirements, security factors and building access. In addition, an action plan in regard to each category of work, including response times and lines of communication, needs to be established, as well as methods of budgeting and payment.

Problems in existing buildings

There are unique problems to be overcome when working in existing buildings. The difficulties may be extended to the design, planning, costing and execution of the work and incorporate the following considerations:

- Working conditions: Work in existing buildings is likely to be hindered by continued occupation. Whilst this may not impact on some types of work, the execution of any major repair or maintenance will need to accommodate the needs of existing users. Health and safety provisions (see later in this chapter) must be strictly enforced and general nuisance factors such as noise and dust can cause serious disruption to the main activities of a business. Similarly, the image of a company may be adversely affected due to building operations. To compound the problems, working around occupants can be very time consuming and thus costly. Careful planning of work in existing buildings is essential if disruption and costs are to be minimised.
- Abnormal hours: Some aspects of a business cannot be interrupted during normal business hours; for example, any work to an existing IT installation may necessitate the closure of a networked system preventing internal and external communications, business transactions and the like as well as the general use by all members of staff of the IT facility. This is major disruption that could result in a substantial loss to a business. Therefore, work of this type should be carried out beyond normal working hours where possible. Similarly, power supplies are vital to any organisation and must be maintained to allow continued production. Consider the cost implications of a loss in power in a large manufacturing organisation resulting in standing time of one hour.
- Layout constraints: The installation of new floor layouts, services and specialist installations may be dramatically constrained by the existing floor heights, internal walls and structures. Many older buildings are unsuited to adaptation and this factor may ultimately result in their obsolescence and disposal.
- Legal constraints: Planning restrictions and building regulations may restrict refurbishment potential. In particular, listed buildings, whilst possibly providing a unique atmosphere and enhancing company image, pose particular problems by preventing alteration and generating additional expense for simple repairs and maintenance.

- Unique building structures: Depending on the age and status of a building, repairs and maintenance may be problematic due to external controls, the availability of suitable materials and the inability to accurately assess and plan repairs. Some typical problems encountered are considered in the example in Fig. 18.4.

Premises: Large landmark Victorian building being used as main administration head-quarters

Site problems:
- Repairs to existing façade required following storm damage; availability of matching imperial bricks caused delay and expense
- Outbreak of dry rot on upper floor detected during the works. Extensive access required to check for dry rot throughout the building, causing disruption to the occupiers due to remedial work and adherence to health and safety provisions
- Installation of secondary glazing throughout the west elevation of the building to exclude external noise. Irregularity of the window sizes and types involved much customisation and delay
- Large ornate window requires replacement. Due to listed building status, the replacement window must comply with the requirements of the planning authority and be an exact replica – a very expensive purpose-made unit taking several weeks to manufacture
- All external stonework needs to be cleaned and repaired. The organisation and budgeting of this work is difficult due to the inability to accurately assess the scope of the works. Full details will not be known until scaffolding is erected and cleaning occurs.

Fig. 18.4

Due to the uncertainties that may exist, procurement of work to existing structures needs careful consideration. Without the opportunity to prepare adequate detailed designs, which as outlined above is not always achievable, it is likely that the client will be required to accept more risk than with new works.

Procurement

The approach to the execution of maintenance work will be influenced by the size and type of client. Large client organisations may have a comprehensive in-house team fulfilling the professional, technical and construction roles of building maintenance, whilst smaller businesses will be unable to sustain such an internalised operation and need to outsource all of the maintenance requirements. The issues surrounding the merits and concerns relating to outsourcing are discussed later in this chapter.

With regard to maintenance work, the employer may choose to contract with several contractors to carry out individual projects or maintenance contracts, or appoint a single management contractor responsible for the entire maintenance requirement.

The types of maintenance work required by the employer will vary, and as stated above, broadly include work of a preventative nature or corrective nature. Although there is varying terminology in use, including that defined in BS 3811, the outline shown in Fig. 18.5 provides a clear indication of the range of maintenance work encountered.

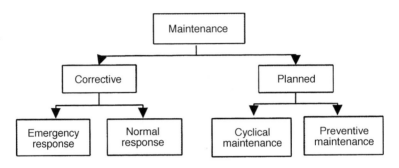

Fig. 18.5   Types of maintenance (adapted from Spedding 1994).

The procurement of maintenance work will depend on the type of work required, as follows.

- *Corrective maintenance*
  Emergency response   Where sudden breakdown or accident occurs, prompt action may be necessary, for example in order to maintain a service or make a building safe, secure or watertight. This may extend to a 24 hour/ 365 day service.
  Normal response   It would be inefficient and costly to categorise all corrective maintenance as 'emergency' work. Some items of work may be deferred until a regular visit occurs, for example the replacement of a light bulb or ceiling tile, or attendance to a dripping tap.

  The organisation for the execution of corrective maintenance work will require the pre-definition of items of emergency work, financial limits, response times and clear lines of action. There may be a desire for local client facilities representatives to pursue emergency action in non-emergency situations. Surveyors involved in the maintenance process may be required to give appropriate direction in accordance with corporate policy and arrangements when a possible emergency situation is referred.
  The most appropriate contractual response for corrective maintenance work is likely to be some sort of term arrangement (see later in this chapter) with a general building contractor and/or specialist contractors.

- *Planned maintenance*
  Cyclical   It is usual to carry out some areas of maintenance work at regular intervals, for example, painting and decorating, irrespective of the actual condition of the building fabric. This type of work may also be influenced

by cash-flow factors, e.g. leaving the repainting work until the following summer when a better financial position is anticipated. To some extent, this approach may defeat the purpose of the planned interval of work, which is the long-term protection of the premises. The choice of procurement for this type of work will be situation dependent. Term contracting may be appropriate but individual contracts are likely to be more suitable.

Preventive   This work is essential to the ongoing safety and reliability of key components, for example a boiler or air conditioning plant. The suppliers of the equipment will usually recommend a programme of maintenance and also offer the maintenance service itself. Some care should be taken to ensure that neither under nor over-maintenance occurs. In some instances, statutory requirements must also be adhered to, for example with lift installations. The most appropriate method of procurement is likely to be via a term contract, probably with the supplier of the equipment or other suitable specialist.

Tendering and contractual arrangements

Methods of selecting the contractor and tendering procedures have been discussed in Chapter 10, Procurement, the contents of which are equally applicable to maintenance work.

With maintenance work, particularly that relating to emergency situations, the location of the contracting organisation, relative to the properties to be included within the maintenance contract, should be carefully considered to ensure that logistics are consistent with an adequate response.

The choice of contract will relate to the nature of the work outlined above. The employer may appoint a contractor on a single project basis or on a term basis whereby the agreement will stand for a given period of time.

Project contracts

Individual project work may be let via one of the many arrangements that are discussed elsewhere in this book, depending on the procurement objectives relating to the specific project. These will include both measurement and cost reimbursement based contracts.

Measured term contracts

A measured term contract may be awarded to cover a number of different buildings. It will usually apply for a specific period of time, say 2 to 3 years, although this may be extended depending on the necessity of maintenance standards and the acceptability of the contractor's performance. The contractor will at the outset be offered the maintenance work for various trades. The work when completed will then be paid for using rates from an agreed schedule. This schedule may have been prepared specifically for the project concerned, or it may be based on a standard document such as the PSA schedule of rates or the NSR (National Schedule of Rates) or BMI (Building Maintenance Information) Price Book. This incorporates labour constants and current prices for major trades in the maintenance field from demolitions and alterations to external works and drainage. Such rates may be updated at monthly intervals, for instance by use of the BMI indices.

Where the client supplies the rates for the work, the contractor is given the opportunity of quoting a percentage addition to or deduction from these rates. The contractor offering the client the most advantageous percentage will usually be awarded the contract. An indication of the amount of work involved over a defined period would therefore seem appropriate for the contractor's assessment of the prices quoted. The JCT publishes a Measured Term Form of Contract (1998) suitable for use with any schedule of rates.

The nature of maintenance work is such that it is likely to be difficult and expensive to cost manage. The surveyor is unlikely to find it practical, or the client to find it cost efficient, to verify every item of maintenance work carried out. A pragmatic approach often used is to check, say, 10% to 20% of the total work, relying on the contractor for the remainder of the account (Building Maintenance Panel of the RICS 2000). This approach is a valid compromise since the measurement sampling process permits an acceptable audit that would reveal any errors requiring an alternative form of cost management.

Managed contracts

A single management contractor may be appointed to manage the entire maintenance requirements of a client. Some clients may prefer this strategy since it reduces their input significantly and allows the benefits of outsourcing to be more fully achieved. With this approach, individual sections of maintenance work will be suitably packaged, procured and managed on behalf of the client by the management contractor.

Facilities management contract

In 1999, the CIOB introduced a Standard Form of Facilities Management contract in partnership with Cameron McKenna. This contract is intended to focus on facilities management issues and may be used for a range of private and public sector facilities management work including maintenance, cleaning, security, etc.

The CIOB contract is compliant with all current legislation and deals with TUPE, the Construction Act and fair payment provisions. The contract allows the parties to agree the services to be provided and the specification to be met. (Copies of the contract may be obtained from Construction Books Direct on 01344 630811, quoting reference no. 2447.)

Budget and cost control

As mentioned earlier, the definition of facilities management from the RICS states that 'FM involves the total management of all services that support the

- Total cost of maintenance work per m^2
- Cost of maintenance work per unit of occupancy (e.g. bed spaces)
- Percentage of emergency responses within the stated response time.

This approach to monitoring value is particularly helpful within large organisations that have sufficiently large portfolios to enable internal benchmarking comparisons to be made. Benchmarking can be applicable to all areas of facilities management.

Health and safety

The need for any business organisation to correctly attend to health and safety matters could hardly be overstated. The extent of legislation, including that derived from the European Commission, and the increasing prevalence of associated litigation are such that most organisations are rightly zealous in their pursuit of high standards of health and safety in the workplace. In addition, the impact that certain health and safety matters may have on the efficiency of the workforce are well recognised, for instance in connection with sick building syndrome or problems relating to VDUs. This latter point may be unheeded in some organisations; the psychological effects of lighting or the impact of incorrect temperature or humidity levels on physical activity may be overlooked whilst the slavish adherence to legislation, necessary though it is, is seen as paramount.

Although the overall management for health and safety matters is likely to lie with a senior member of staff or, in larger organisations, a contingent of staff dedicated to this function, the facilities manager may have a significant responsibility in many related areas. For example, consider the design, or management of the design, of new accommodation. Under the terms of the Construction (Design and Management) Regulations 1994, the client, design team and constructors are obliged to consider health and safety in the use of the completed building as well as during construction. Therefore, the facilities manager, if acting on behalf of the client, will need to ensure that the regulations are fully complied with.

The surveyor acting in the role of facilities manager must be aware of client expectations and legal responsibilities in regard to health and safety matters. A sound understanding of the issues and an appreciation of the ownership of the various risks involved are of great importance. Whilst specialist knowledge may lie with others, the development of the facilities management discipline and its attendant expert status brings with it close involvement with health and safety affairs, particularly when problems may occur.

Outsourcing

In recent years, there has been an increasing trend to contract out or outsource certain support functions, usually regarded as non-core to the main raison d'etre of the business, rather than provide such services via the employment of in-house personnel. This is consistent with the downsizing philosophy that many companies follow and is said to offer an efficient and cost-effective alternative to large, internally staffed empires.

The policy of outsourcing can be applied to many support services including catering, security, fleet management, IT management, maintenance and repairs to buildings and services, waste management, landscape management, travel, recruitment ... the list is extensive. Although outsourcing may be applicable to a wide range of functions, it should not be seen as synonymous with facilities management, merely one approach to be considered in obtaining necessary services. There may be strong reasons for a service to remain under direct staff control, for example, where commercial security is vital and would be endangered by the outsourcing of office cleaning contracts. Some of the issues surrounding the outsourcing philosophy include:

- *Competition*   In-house provision is prone to become less efficient due to the absence of competition. Outsourcing will promote economies of scale, right-sizing, and is generally seen to result in a reduction in costs. Where services are provided internally, benchmarking may assist in identifying inefficiencies and provide a means of comparison when competition is absent.
- *Specialisation*   In contracting out services, companies will have access to experts they would otherwise be unable to adequately justify as full-time personnel on their payroll. For example, a small company will be unable to sustain the employment of a quantity surveyor. In practice, the range of facilities management related skills required are such that some out-sourcing is inevitable.
- *Limited experience*   In-house personnel are generally restricted in exposure to one set of systems and are likely to work in isolation of other organisations and professional associates, thus limiting technical and managerial development. Alternatively, the in-house team are immersed in the business operations of their company which may be advantageous compared to the external organisation that is poorly acquainted with the client organisation.
- *Quality*   An external contractor is motivated toward profit maximisation, albeit via the provision of an adequate service, and can achieve this by providing the minimum acceptable service at the lowest possible cost. It is reasonable to assert that in-house teams are motivated simply to provide a service to the employer and that the quality objective cannot be compromised by the profit motive. Alternatively, in-house staff may be in sheltered employment positions and as a consequence may be poorly motivated generally.
- *Confidentiality/security*   Some aspects of an organisation may be vulnerable to poor security/confidentiality. These would be better served by the provision of in-house services.
- *Community culture*   Personnel employed on a contract basis may be very transient and be uninvolved with anything other than the service they are

contracted to provide. Rapport with other staff and extended knowledge of the organisation will be absent. As a consequence, social benefits enhancing the service provided may be absent.

- *Flexibility*   In-house staff will be more widely involved within an orga-nisation which may result in more flexibility of service, for example, cleaners may be requested to move furniture.
- *Employment law*   In deciding to outsource a particular service, attention should be given to relevant employment law.

Once the decision to outsource particular services has been taken, con-sideration as to how to organise and procure each particular service needs to be made. The organisation of contracted-out services may be dealt with in a variety of ways:

- *Individual contracts*   Each service required to be outsourced may be done on an individual contract basis, for example, to supplement an otherwise comprehensive in-house facilities management provision. This may be managed either centrally or by several appropriate management or cost centres within an organisation. For instance, photocopying costs, furniture costs and cleaning costs may be handled by a sectional office manager whilst IT provision is managed centrally. Centralising the outsourcing of service contracts promotes more efficient administration and performance monitoring.
- *Bundling*   Bundling involves the collection of particular facilities man-agement services that may be grouped on the basis of efficiency or con-venience and placed with a single supplier, for instance, cleaning, security and catering. This approach reduces the points of responsibility and may lead to economies of scale.
- *Total outsourcing*   With this approach, which is an extension to 'bundling', all aspects of facilities management are outsourced to a single facilities management company, including those that are operational as well as managerial..This approach allows a business organisation to benefit from a single point of contact, although the facilities management company appointed will be unable to provide all of the services required by the client and will in turn subcontract some of these out. There are further advantages to the appointment of single contractors. Administration should be reduced, economies of scale are likely to be achieved and, due to the increased commercial significance to the contractor, a larger commit-ment and better service should result.

The quantity surveyor has considerable knowledge and skills that may be applied to the procurement of services and is well placed to manage the outsourcing requirements of a business. An understanding of the principles surrounding effective procurement, including selection procedures and the preparation of relevant documentation, are important aspects and are within the traditional remit of the profession. Matters relating to the specification of particular services are likely to need the support of in-house advisors and other professional consultants.

Facilities management opportunities for the quantity surveyor

Many quantity surveyors are now employed in the sector of facilities management, which relative to the traditional quantity surveyor market offers great opportunity in that it provides the prospect of being involved beyond the initial procurement of a building. The facilities management market has spread from the USA throughout Europe and Japan and therefore on an international scale is immense.

The quantity surveyor has many of the skills required in the provision of a facilities management service, although when considering the discipline in the wider context, there are clear limitations in existing quantity surveying expertise. This position is also true of other construction professionals, as a considered review of the work of the facilities manager may reveal. There are some aspects of the role that will be better served by designers or contractors, electrical engineers and building surveyors. Likewise, management consultants and accountants are well placed with regard to strategic management consultancy and are beginning to enter the FM market. It seems that the facilities management function may naturally divide into operational and managerial affairs. Without investment in extensive additional human resources, which is likely to be unavailable to all but the larger practices, the majority of opportunities for the quantity surveyor will remain at the operational level. Previous research has identified that considerable barriers exist to surveying firms becoming strategic consultants Presently, a capability for a more operational consultancy has been identified (Hinks *et al.* 1999).

When considering the service of facilities management, emphasis should be placed on the term management. There is no assertion that the FM role demands the knowledge and ability to apply all of the required skills, any more than a project manager is able to carry out all of the design aspects of a proposed project. However, knowledge of the range of FM functions is important to the adequate fulfilment of the management role.

Consideration of the management and specialist skills required in facilities management as listed below (Bernard Williams Associates 1994) will demonstrate the impossibility of entire FM knowledge:

- Business management
- Man management
- Building design
- Interior design
- Space management
- House management
- Office services management
- Energy management
- Building maintenance management
- Services maintenance management
- Property management
- Grounds management
- Security management
- Health and safety management

- Catering management
- Purchasing management
- Motor fleet management
- IT management
- Legal advice
- Facilities audit
- Project management
- Financial management
- Tax management
- Risk management
- Documentation
- Construction technology

- Cost planning and management
- Knowledge of procurement options and processes
- Knowledge of tendering
- Value management and risk management
- Contract formation and administration
- Life cycle costing
- Project management

It is important to note that whilst the quantity surveying profession may possess some of the skills necessary to provide the facilities management service, the discipline of facilities management should be seen apart. The skills relating to cost management can be outsourced in the same way as design or engineering requirements may be. In appointing a facilities manager, clients are seeking managers not technicians.

Education and training for the facilities manager

Despite the acknowledgement given to the development of facilities management within undergraduate programmes, as with project management there are many who regard the training and education as a postgraduate issue, supplementing a suitable first degree. There are several of these available, including master's courses, and in addition for those surveyors who have not had any formal education in management, opportunity exists for attendance at short training courses and seminars.

There are several institutions with an interest in facilities management, which not only promote its professional standing but also provide vehicles for formal training and qualification:

- The British Institute of Facilities Management (BIFM) is dedicated to the development of the discipline and provides control of the standards that must be attained to obtain a recognised qualification. The route to qualification with BIFM is quite flexible with opportunity for entry via direct examination, accredited undergraduate or postgraduate higher education programmes or practical experience. Irrespective of entry route, all applicants are expected to complete their training by submission of a portfolio demonstrating practical skills and experience. The qualification offered is nationally recognised.
- The RICS have also recognised the significance of facilities management by the establishment of a separate facilities management faculty in 2000. This is a significant development in that the discipline may now be developed

within a major international organisation, and directed resources and significant membership should enhance the abilities and status of all facilities managers within the institution.

- Within the CIOB, a FM Society has been established which recognises and promotes the role of the facilities manager. The Society also provides opportunity for CPD courses. The CIOB also examines the subject of facilities management via a Facilities Management Professional Option. This is included within the CIOB education framework, leading to a qualification with chartered designation that is widely recognised in the FM industry

Bibliography

Ashworth A. *Cost Studies of Buildings*. Longmans. 1999.

Ashworth A. and Hogg K.I. *Added Value in Design and Construction*. Pearson Education. 2000.

Barrett P. (ed.) *Facilities Management: Towards Best Practice*. Blackwell Science. 1995.

Bernard Williams Associates. *Facilities Economics*. Building Economics Bureau Ltd. 1994.

Building Maintenance Panel of the RICS. *Building Maintenance: Strategy, Planning and Procurement guidance note*. RICS Business Services Ltd. 2000.

Grigg J. and Jordan A. *Are you managing facilities – getting the best out of buildings*. Allied Dunbar Financial Services Limited; Nicholas Brealy Publishing Ltd. 1993.

Hinks J. *et al. Facilities Management and the Chartered Surveyor: an investigation of chartered surveyors' perceptions*. RICS. 1999.

McGregor W. and Then Shiem-Shin D. *Facilities management and the business of space*. Arnold. 1999.

Park A. *Facilities Management: An explanation*. Macmillan. 1998.

RICS Research findings number 33. RICS. 1999.

Spedding A. (ed.) *CIOB Handbook of Facilities Management*. Longmans. 1994.

Website

CIOB Facilities Management online at: http://www.ciob.org.uk/default.htm

Index